SCOTS
MERCANTILE
LAW

SCOTS MERCANTILE LAW

Enid A. Marshall
M.A., LL.B., Ph.D.

*Solicitor, Reader in Business Law
at the University of Stirling*

EDINBURGH
W. GREEN & SON LTD.
Law Publishers
1983

First Published in 1983

©
1983
W. Green & Son Ltd.

ISBN   Hardback 0 414 00720 4
Paperback 0 414 00712 3

Printed in Great Britain
by
McQueen Printers Ltd.
Galashiels, Scotland

PREFACE

The author's aim has been to produce a readable students' textbook on the major topics of mercantile, commercial or business law as studied at Scottish universities and colleges.

Despite the apparent length of the book, beginners need have no fears: the statutory language, if complex, has been explained in words of few syllables (without, it is hoped, too much sacrifice of accuracy), the text has been illustrated with brief accounts of, and quotations from, decided cases, there are virtually no footnotes, and all the Latin maxims have been provided with translations.

Each chapter ends with a short list of "Further Reading." In these lists the letter "E." has been prefixed as a warning to those works which deal with English law and only incidentally (or not at all expressly) with Scots law. References to "Gloag and Henderson" are to the eighth edition by A.B. Wilkinson and W.A. Wilson and assistant editors (1980, W. Green & Son Ltd.) and references to David M. Walker's *Principles of Scottish Private Law* are to the third edition (1982-83, Clarendon Press, Oxford). J.J. Gow's *The Mercantile and Industrial Law of Scotland* was published in 1964 by W. Green & Son Ltd. The author gratefully acknowledges the debt owed to all items mentioned in the "Further Reading" lists: without them this book could not have been written.

The author wishes to record her thanks for assistance willingly given by John Birds (Chapter 11), Lilian Carmichael (Chapter 3), Professor J. Milnes Holden (Chapter 7), Robert Howie (Chapter 12), Geoffrey Morse (Chapter 3), J.C. Mullin (Chapter 11), William A.R. Mutch (Chapter 7), H.R.M. Macdonald (Chapters 4 and 6), and especially by A.J. Sim and Professor W.A. Wilson, both of whom have somehow found the time in the midst of many other commitments to read and offer valuable comments on several chapters. The author is also indebted to Robert Buick, D.B. White and T. Erskine Wright for guidance on specific passages in the book. Finally, the author is most grateful to the publishers for the opportunity to write this book—to Robert Shaw who first suggested it, to Douglas Purdom who encouraged and to Iris Stewart who assisted at every stage—and to the printers whose careful workmanship has been a pleasure to handle.

The law is intended to be stated as at January 1, 1983, though it has been possible to add some material which became available not later than May 10, 1983.

May 27, 1983   Enid A. Marshall

CONTENTS

TABLE OF CASES

ix

TABLE OF STATUTES

CHAPTER 1

AGENCY

INTRODUCTION

THE law of agency is that part of the law of contract which is specially concerned with the situation where a person, instead of acting personally, engages another person to act on his behalf. The first person is the "principal," and the person who acts for him is the "agent," but these are general terms and it should be recognised that the principles of the law of agency extend to cases where the parties, though they stand in the legal position of principal and agent towards one another, are not commonly referred to as "principal" and "agent"; for example, a partner is an agent

1

for his firm, a director is an agent for his company, and a wife, in ordering goods for the household, is an agent for her husband.

1–02 There is no statutory definition of the term "agency." It may be used to denote the *relationship* between principal and agent. Agency may therefore be described as the relationship which exists where one party, the principal, authorises another party, the agent, to act on his behalf in a transaction with a third party. Alternatively, the term "agency" may be used to denote the *contract* out of which such a relationship arises. Agency is then regarded as one of the particular contracts (just as the contract of carriage or the contract of insurance is a particular contract), and may be described as a contract by which one party, the principal, authorises another party, the agent, to act on his behalf in a transaction with a third party.

1–03 Agency involves three parties and two contracts. The three parties are the principal (on whose behalf the transaction is being entered into), the agent (who acts for the principal in the transaction), and the third party (the person with whom the agent transacts on his principal's behalf). The two contracts involved are the contract between the principal and the agent (by which their relationship to one another is governed) and the contract between the agent and the third party (entered into on the principal's behalf by his agent). The purpose of agency is to bring the principal into a contractual relationship with the third party.

1–04 The law of agency in Scotland, as in England, is for the most part, common law, to be found in decided cases and in authoritative writings. Statutory inroads on the common law have been relatively minor: examples are the Prevention of Corruption Acts of 1906 and 1916, equally applicable to both legal systems, the Powers of Attorney Act 1971, only one section of which is applicable to Scotland, and the Estate Agents Act 1979 (see 1–50 *et seq.*, below).

1–05 The influence of English law in this branch of Scots law is strong. English cases are often relied on where no Scottish cases are available. A typical instance of this approach is:

"In the absence of Scottish decisions the pursuers rely upon . . . cases in English law. . . . Those decisions no doubt are not binding upon us, but on a mercantile question like the present it is desirable that as far as possible the same rule should be applied in both countries" (*per* Lord Moncreiff in *Rederi Aktiebolaget Nordstjernan* v. *Salvesen & Co.* (1903) 6 F. 64, at p. 76).

The English influence is particularly strong where there is "a whole series of English cases" (as on the question of warranty of authority in *Anderson* v. *Croall & Sons Ltd.* (1903) 6 F. 153, *per* Lord Stormonth-Darling (Ordinary) at p. 156), and where the relationship of the parties concerned is seen as being the same in the two countries and the English law is already "completely settled" (*e.g.* the relationship at a public auction among seller, buyer and auctioneer in *Mackenzie* v. *Cormack,* 1950 S.C. 183, *per* Lord Mackay at p. 191).

1–06 On the other hand, English authorities have been occasionally rejected (as in *Copland* v. *Brogan,* 1916 S.C. 277 (see 1–10, below), in which the standard of care required of an agent who was acting gratuitously was held to be that supported by a statement in Bell's *Principles*, in preference to that supported by English authorities.

The subject-matter of this chapter is dealt with below under these headings:

     I. Capacity;
    II. Constitution of the relationship;
   III. Categories of agent;
   IV. Agent's authority;
    V. Duties of agent to principal;
   VI. Rights of agent against principal;
  VII. Third party's rights and liabilities; and
 VIII. Termination of the relationship.

As a preliminary, it is appropriate to note the distinction between:

(a) agency and mandate; and between
(b) agency and sub-contract.

(a) Agency and Mandate

The distinction between agency and mandate now is that agency is onerous (*i.e.* the agent receives a commission or other reward for his services), whereas mandate is gratuitous.

The following definitions of the two terms bring out the distinction:

"Agency is a bilateral onerous consensual contract whereby one party, the principal, authorizes another, the agent, to execute business on his behalf for reward" (David M. Walker, *Principles of Scottish Private Law* (3rd ed.), Vol. II, p. 212).

"Mandate is a bilateral gratuitous consensual contract by which one empowers another to act in some respect on his behalf" (*ibid.*, p. 210).

In mandate, the terms "mandant" and "mandatary" correspond to "principal" and "agent" respectively.

The term "mandate" points to the derivation of our law of agency from the *mandatum* ("agency") of Roman law.

In early writings (*e.g.* in Bell's *Commentaries*), as in early reported cases, the term "mandate" was used in a wider sense—denoting the onerous as well as the gratuitous relationship.

Mandatary's Duty to Exercise Reasonable Care

Although acting gratuitously, a mandatary is under a duty to exercise reasonable care. This duty was considered in *Copland* v. *Brogan*, 1916 S.C. 277:

B., a carriage-hirer, had been in the habit of acting gratuitously as a messenger for C., a schoolmaster.

On one occasion C. asked B. to cash three cheques for him at a bank in a neighbouring town and bring back the cash to him.

B. received the cash at the bank, but failed to pay it over to C. There was no evidence as to how the loss had occurred.

Held that B. was liable to pay C., since B. had failed to exercise reasonable care, which was taken, in accordance with a statement in Bell's *Principles*, to mean "such care as a man of common prudence generally exercises about his own property of like description."

Lord Justice-Clerk Scott Dickson said (at p. 282): "Now, the packet having gone astray while it was in the defender's custody, the *onus*,[1] in my opinion, rests on him to explain how this happened or at least to show that he exercised the necessary reasonable care. . . . There is enough to shew that the defender, in executing his commission, did not exercise the care which a prudent man would have taken with regard to a valuable packet of this kind."

(b) Agency and Sub-Contract

1–11 An agent may be an employee or he may be an independent contractor; *e.g.* a manager or purchasing officer, engaged full-time in his company's business, is most likely to be both an agent and an employee, whereas an estate agent, working in his own premises and for several different clients, is most likely to be an independent contractor. In some situations it is difficult to ascertain whether the agent is an employee or an independent contractor. The importance of the distinction lies in the different legal consequences which flow from the different relationships. An illustration is *Smith* v. *Scott & Best* (1881) 18 S.L.R. 355:

S. & B., contractors for certain waterworks including the construction of a bridge over the Esk, were approached by Cameron who agreed to do that part of the work for £40 less than the schedule price.

Cameron obtained stones from Smith, but later deserted the work and disappeared, leaving Smith unpaid.

S. & B. declined to pay Smith, on the ground that they had already paid Cameron for all the work done and material supplied by him.

Held that as S. & B. had taken no steps to prevent Cameron from being considered their foreman and as a belief to that effect had become current in the district, there was no sub-contract, and so S. & B. were liable to pay Smith for the stones supplied by Smith to Cameron.

If there had been a sub-contract, Cameron would have been an independent contractor, not an employee, and Smith could then have looked only to Cameron for payment.

The question of whether an agent is an employee or an independent contractor is decided by a consideration of all the circumstances.

1–12 A case which may be contrasted with *Smith* v. *Scott & Best* is *Trojan Plant Hire Co. Ltd.* v. *Durafencing (Northern) Ltd.*, 1974 S.L.T. (Sh. Ct.) 3:

McAlpine Ltd., the principal building contractor on a site at Dundee, engaged D. Ltd. for certain fencing work. D. Ltd. instructed Arkle, a contractor who had a work force at his disposal, to carry out the fencing work.

Arkle, using one of D. Ltd.'s vans, hired plant for the fencing work from T. Ltd., and the question arose of whether D. Ltd. was liable to T. Ltd. for the hire charges.

Held that D. Ltd. was not liable to T. Ltd. because there was not sufficient evidence that D. Ltd. had authorised Arkle to hire the plant.

The effect of the decision was to place Arkle in the position of an independent contractor, to whom alone T. Ltd. could look for payment.

---

[1] "burden" (of proof).

I CAPACITY

Both principal and agent must have the legal capacity necessary for their respective roles; a principal can in general authorise another person to do anything which the principal himself could do, but cannot enlarge his own capacity by appointing an agent (*e.g.* if the principal is a minor and is therefore subject to some limitations as regards his contractual capacity, he cannot free himself of these limitations merely by authorising an agent of full age to carry out the transaction on his behalf).

Similarly, a principal who has no legal capacity at all or who is in the eyes of the law non-existent cannot even appoint an agent. A limited company which has not yet been registered is an instance of a non-existent principal:

Tinnevelly Sugar Refining Co. Ltd. v. *Mirrlees, Watson & Yaryan Co. Ltd.* (1894) 21 R. 1009: On July 11, 1890, Darley & Butler, purporting to act on behalf of T. Ltd., which was registered on July 29, 1890, entered into a contract with M. Ltd. for the supply by M. Ltd. of machinery to the new company.

T. Ltd. brought an action of damages against M. Ltd. on the ground that the machinery supplied was defective and had caused great loss to T. Ltd.

Held that T. Ltd. had no title to sue M. Ltd., since Darley & Butler could not have acted as agents for T. Ltd. before it was in existence.

Lord President J.P.B. Robertson said (at p. 1014): "Where there is no principal there can be no agent; there having been no Tinnevelly Company at the date of this contract, Darley & Butler were not agents of that company in entering into the contract."

II CONSTITUTION OF THE RELATIONSHIP

The relationship of principal and agent may be constituted by:
  (a) express appointment;
  (b) implied appointment;
  (c) holding out;
  (d) ratification; or
  (e) necessity.

(a) Express Appointment

The express appointment of an agent may take any form. There may be a formal writing, *e.g.* a power of attorney (in common use where a person is out of the country) or a factory and commission (a deed by which a landed proprietor who is leaving the country commits the charge of his estate to another person such as his solicitor). Alternatively, the writing appointing the agent may be informal, *e.g.* letters of mandate. An express appointment may also be merely oral, and there is no restriction on the method by which such an oral appointment may be proved. Evidence which would not be admissible to prove a contract of employment for more than a year may therefore be brought forward to prove the existence of an agency relationship for any duration:

Pickin v. *Hawkes* (1878) 5 R. 676: P. claimed that in November 1876 he entered into an oral contract with H., whereby he was to act as sole agent for H. in Scotland from January 1, 1877, for three years.

In June 1877, H. intimated that P. was no longer in H.'s employment, and P. brought an action of damages for breach of contract.

H. argued that the contract, being a contract of service for a period of more than a year, could not be proved by parole evidence.

Proof at large was allowed.

The Lord Ordinary (Craighill) said (at p. 677): "Service, undoubtedly, in a certain sense is involved, but agency is the fundamental characteristic," and he was of the opinion that the limitations in proof which affected certain types of contract such as the contract of service for a period of more than one year ought not to be further extended.

(b) Implied Appointment

1–17   The relationship of principal and agent is often created by implication. For example, by section 5 of the Partnership Act 1890, every partner is an agent of the firm and his other partners for the purpose of the business of the partnership, and it is equally clear that by the common law relating to companies a director is impliedly an agent of the company. Other instances of implied appointment occur where a person is made manager of a business or is in some other way placed in a supervisory or responsible position. The master of a ship is impliedly the agent of the owners, as may be illustrated by *Barnetson* v. *Petersen Brothers* (1902) 5 F. 86:

A steamship owned by P. Brothers had been chartered to G., who appointed B. as shipbroker at Methil.

B., having made disbursements and rendered services in accordance with G.'s instructions, brought an action against P. Brothers for outlays and commission.

P. Brothers pleaded that they were not liable because B. had been employed by G.

Held that, as the master of the ship had accepted B.'s services as shipbroker and as P. Brothers had got the benefit of these services, P. Brothers were directly liable to B. for his disbursements and services.

1–18   An implied agency may be terminated by lapse of time and material change of circumstances; actual notice is not necessary to terminate the relationship. An instance is *Ferguson and Lillie* v. *Stephen* (1864) 2 M. 804:

F. & L., tailors in Glasgow, supplied clothes to S. for himself and his two sons, from 1853 to 1857 when the family lived in Glasgow. Accounts were rendered to and paid by S.

In 1861, when S. had been residing for some years in Dundee and his sons, then 27 and 17 years of age respectively, were resident in Edinburgh, the sons placed an extravagant order for a large quantity of clothes with F. & L., and these goods were delivered to the sons' Edinburgh address.

Held that S. was not liable to pay for these goods.

Lord Justice-Clerk Inglis said (at p. 807): "It is not possible to give effect to the plea of implied agency or mandate, or to say that the supplying of these things was authorised by the father; the dealings which he had authorised had been long before, were different in kind, and the goods were sent to his own house, not to a different place."

(c) Holding Out

Agency may be inferred where one party has held out another as his agent and so justified a third party in believing that the second party is in fact the appointed agent of the first party. The principle operating in such a situation is personal bar by holding out. (In English law agency constituted in this way is termed "agency by estoppel.") Any private arrangement between the first and second parties does not defeat the right of the third party to rely on the existence of the agency relationship:

Hayman v. *American Cotton Oil Co.* (1907) 45 S.L.R. 207: A. & Co., an American firm of oil merchants, in newspaper advertisements and in letters to prospective customers, represented McN. & Co., a Glasgow firm, as their exclusive agents for the sale of their cotton-seed oils in Scotland.

F. & Co., also of Glasgow, bought oil from McN. & Co. and paid for it before delivery.

McN. & Co. became bankrupt, and there were competing claims to the oil which had been shipped from America to Glasgow. A. & Co. contended that McN. & Co. had been merely buyers and distributors of their products, while F. & Co. contended that McN. & Co. had been acting as A. & Co.'s agents.

Held that A. & Co., having held out McN. & Co. as their ordinary agents, were barred from maintaining that McN. & Co. had been their agents only in the special and limited sense of being distributing agents.

Lord Justice-Clerk J.H.A. Macdonald said (at p. 212): "McNairn & Company were held out as being the American Company's agents in quite distinct terms, and without any qualification whatever. . . . It is unnecessary to consider any question as to whether as between themselves the company and McNairn & Company had some special arrangements whereby, although the latter were held out as agents, and only as agents, the position of McNairn & Company to the Oil Company was of a special nature, and did not put McNairn & Company in a position of ordinary agents. Of that the customers could know nothing."

(d) Ratification

Where a person has acted on behalf of another without having authority to do so, the party for whom the act was done may later ratify the act. The effect of the ratification is retrospective, *i.e.* the act becomes as valid and binding as it would have been if the person who did the act had then had the proper authority.

Ratification may be express, or it may be implied by conduct of the principal.

For agency to be created by ratification, the following conditions must be fulfilled:

(i) The principal must have been in existence, not merely at the time of the ratification, but also at the time when the unauthorised act was done. Thus contracts made on behalf of a company before its incorporation cannot be ratified by the company once it has come into existence; a new contract (which may be on the same terms) is required. In the case of *Tinnevelly Sugar Refining Co. Ltd.* v. *Mirrlees, Watson & Yaryan Co. Ltd.* (see 1–14, above), there was no attempt by the new company to ratify the contract made by Darley & Butler, but any such attempt would have been futile.

1–24   (ii) The act being ratified must be one which the principal was originally capable of authorising. Thus in company law the general principle of the common law (now modified to some extent by section 9 of the European Communities Act 1972) is that a contract which is *ultra vires* ("beyond the powers") of the directors but *intra vires* ("within the powers") of the company itself can be ratified by the company, whereas a contract which is *ultra vires* of the company cannot be ratified; even unanimous consent of the shareholders would not suffice (*Ashbury Railway Carriage and Iron Co. Ltd.* v. *Riche* (1875) L.R. 7 H.L. 653 (see 3–225, below)).

1–25   (iii) Ratification must be timeous: if the validity of an act depends upon its being done within a certain time, ratification must follow within that time. For example, an unauthorised stoppage *in transitu* ("in transit") of goods on behalf of an unpaid seller could be ratified by the unpaid seller only so long as the goods were in transit: it would be too late to ratify once the goods had been delivered to the buyer at their destination, and if the buyer were bankrupt the goods would form part of the sequestrated estate (*Bird* v. *Brown* (1850) 4 Ex. 786; 154 E.R. 1433). Another instance is *Goodall* v. *Bilsland,* 1909 S.C. 1152:

G., a wine and spirit merchant, applied to a licensing court for renewal of his public-house certificate.

A solicitor, duly authorised by clients, lodged objections to the granting of the renewal at the licensing court. The renewal was granted.

The solicitor then, without consulting his clients, lodged an appeal to the licensing appeal court, and was successful in this appeal.

Held that G. was entitled to have the licensing appeal court's decision set aside because (1) the solicitor had had no authority to appeal to the licensing appeal court, (2) the solicitor's actings could not be ratified after the lapse of the 10 days allowed for appeal, and (3) the proceedings in the licensing appeal court had therefore been null and void.

1–26   (iv) The agent must have professed to be acting on behalf of an identifiable principal who later ratifies the agent's act; the agent must not have been contracting in his own name with the mere expectation that his action would be ratified, nor must he have been acting for a person other than the principal who ratifies the act. This condition may be expressed as the rule that an undisclosed principal cannot ratify.

The authority for this point is the English case *Keighley, Maxsted & Co.* v. *Durant* [1901] A.C. 240:

Roberts, a corn merchant at Wakefield, was authorised by K. & Co. to buy wheat on a joint account for himself and them at a certain price.

Having failed to buy at the authorised price, Roberts, without authority from K. & Co., made a contract with D., a corn merchant in London, to buy wheat from him at a higher price. Roberts made this contract in his own name, but intended it to be on a joint account for himself and K. & Co. That intention was not disclosed to D.

The next day, K. & Co.'s manager agreed with Roberts to take the wheat on a joint account.

Roberts and K. & Co. failed to take delivery of the wheat. D. resold it at a loss and sued for damages.

Held that as Roberts had not professed at the time of making the contract to be acting for K. & Co., D. was not entitled to sue K. & Co. on the contract.

(v) The principal must at the time of ratification be aware of all the material facts, unless his words or conduct can be interpreted as an unqualified adoption of the agent's acts, whatever they were.

(e) Necessity

"Agency of necessity" exists where in an emergency one person without authority takes action on behalf of another whose interests are at stake and with whom it is impossible to communicate. Such an agency is a form of *negotiorum gestio* ("management of affairs"), a branch of quasi-contract.

The courts do not readily extend the principle of agency of necessity to new situations, and the improvement in communications in modern times also restricts the instances of this type of agency.

Well-recognised examples of agents of necessity are the carrier of perishable goods who finds it necessary to sell or otherwise dispose of the goods without having obtained the owner's authority, and the master of a ship who, in order to raise sufficient money to complete his voyage, grants security over the ship or cargo by a bond of bottomry or a bond of respondentia respectively (see 8–34 *et seq.*, below).

III CATEGORIES OF AGENT

Agents are appointed in many different circumstances, and their authority often depends, not only on the instructions actually given (which may have been very brief), but also on the category to which the agent belongs.

General Agents and Special Agents

The major classification of agents is into general agents and special agents.

A general agent is one who has authority to act for his principal in all the principal's affairs or in all his affairs of a particular kind, *e.g.* the master of a ship or a solicitor. A special agent has authority to act for his principal in a particular transaction only.

Third parties dealing with a general agent are entitled to assume that the agent has all the authority which an agent of that type normally has by trade or professional usage, whereas third parties dealing with a special agent must satisfy themselves as to the exact extent of the agent's authority, since anything done by the special agent beyond his actual instructions will not be binding on the principal.

The distinction between general and special agents was considered in *Morrison* v. *Statter &c.* (1885) 12 R. 1152:

Calder, head shepherd on S.'s farm, on one occasion bought sheep from M. without instructions from S.

Held that as Calder had had no particular authority and as there had been no general course of conduct by S. from which authority could have been inferred, S. was not liable to M.

Lord Young said (at p. 1154): "Where you have a particular agent employed by a principal, to perform a particular piece of business for him, he must act within the instructions given for the particular occasion, and does not bind his principal if he acts otherwise. If you have a general agent, employed generally in his master's or his principal's affairs, or in a particular department, he is assumed to have all the authority which is necessary to enable him to serve his master as such general agent, or general agent in a particular department."

Mercantile Agents

1–36   Mercantile agents may be factors or brokers. Both are employed to buy and sell goods, and have authority to act in accordance with the custom of the particular market on which they deal.

1–37   A factor differs from a broker in that he has possession of his principal's goods and in that he has authority to sell in his own name. A factor, on account of his possession of the goods, has a lien on them for what is due to him by his principal, whereas a broker, having no possession, has no lien.

1–38   There are special classes of both factors and brokers: auctioneers are a special class of factors, and special classes of brokers are stockbrokers, shipbrokers ("middlemen" between shipowners and persons who wish to have goods shipped, and between sellers and buyers of ships), and insurance brokers (who are intermediaries between insurance companies and persons wishing to take out insurance).

1–39   In order to decide whether a mercantile agent is a factor or broker, one must look to the substance of the transaction being undertaken, not solely at the agent's designation. For example, in *Glendinning* v. *Hope & Co.*, 1911 S.C. (H.L.) 73, a stockbroker was held to have had the legal position of a factor and so to be entitled to a factor's lien:

On August 19, G. instructed H. & Co., stockbrokers, to purchase for him 100 shares in a certain mining company. The shares were duly purchased, and G., on August 26, paid the price for them to H. & Co.

On September 1, G. instructed H. & Co. to purchase a further 200 shares for him in the same company. G. then became dissatisfied with H. & Co.'s services and arranged for another firm of stockbrokers to act for him in this second transaction.

H. & Co. claimed that G. was indebted to them in respect of the second purchase, and declined to deliver to G. the transfer of the 100 shares already paid for.

G. brought an action for delivery of the transfer.

Held that H. & Co. were entitled to retain the transfer until payment for the second transaction had been made.

Lord Kinnear said (at p. 79): "For the balance which may arise on his general account the factor has a right of retention or lien over all the goods and effects of the principal which, coming into his hands in his character of factor, may be in his actual or civil possession at the time when the demand against him is made. . . . The conditions upon which the right depends in the case of a mercantile factor are exactly those which govern the relation of a stockbroker and his client. The factor's general right to retention depends upon two considerations—first, that he is required to make payments or undertake liabilities for his principal; and secondly, that the goods and effects belonging to his principal come into his possession and control in the ordinary course of his employment. But that is exactly the position of the stockbroker who buys with a liability to pay the vendor and receives a transfer for delivery to his client."

A similar explanation of the distinction between factor and broker was given by Lord President Inglis in *Cunningham* v. *Lee* (1874) 2 R. 83 (1–118, below), a case in which a law-agent who had bought shares in his own name for a client was held not to have been entitled to appropriate the shares to himself when the client failed to pay for them. Lord President Inglis said (at p. 87):

"I should be inclined to say that Lee occupied the position of a factor rather than of a broker. Certain distinctions between the offices of broker and factor lead me to this conclusion. Thus a broker buys and sells, not in his own name, but in the name of his principal, whereas a factor buys in his own name. Again, a broker has no possession of the subject, no control over it, no power of disposal. The factor has such powers and a consequent lien over the subjects. In these respects Lee was rather a factor than a broker."

A factor who is a mercantile agent is distinct from a factor who manages an estate (see *Macrae* v. *Leith*, 1913 S.C. 901, 1–61, below).

Auctioneers

Auctioneers are agents who sell other persons' heritable or moveable property by public auction. The auction need not take place in the auctioneer's saleroom; thus, in *Mackenzie* v. *Cormack*, 1950 S.C. 183, the circumstance that the auction of the furniture of a castle took place in the castle was held not to affect the legal principle involved.

On many occasions an auctioneer will be selling on behalf of an exposer whose name he does not disclose, but where the exposer is named, the auctioneer incurs no liability to a person who, claiming to be a purchaser, brings an action for implement or damages (*Fenwick* v. *Macdonald, Fraser & Co. Ltd.* (1904) 6 F. 850, *per* Lord Kyllachy (Ordinary)).

Where the exposer's name has not been disclosed at the sale, but is made known to the purchaser at a later date, the purchaser, if he returns the subject purchased as faulty to the exposer, is regarded as having elected to sue the exposer and is no longer entitled to sue the auctioneer (*Ferrier* v. *Dods &c.* (1865) 3 M. 561 (1–154, below)).

English cases on auction sales are taken as authoritative in Scotland: this is supported by *dicta* ("remarks") in *Anderson* v. *Croall & Sons Ltd.* (1903) 6 F. 153, in which an auctioneer, like any other agent, was held to be liable in damages for breach of warranty of authority (see 1–160, below), and *Mackenzie* v. *Cormack*, 1950 S.C. 183, in which an auctioneer, like any other mercantile factor, was held to have a lien over the price for his charges and commission and so to have a title to sue the successful bidder for the price.

Del Credere Agents

1–46   A *del credere* agent is a mercantile agent who for an extra commission undertakes to indemnify the principal if the third party with whom the agent deals fails to pay what is due. The phrase "*del credere*" is Italian. A *del credere* agent guarantees the solvency of the third party; an ordinary agent undertakes no such liability. (The function of *del credere* agents has been largely taken over in modern practice by "confirming houses," which guarantee the transactions of parties who pay them a commission.)

Property Agents

1–47   Agents whose work relates to heritable property include estate agents and house and estate factors.

Estate Agents

1–48   Estate agents, whose main function is to find purchasers for houses and other heritable property which their clients wish to sell, are less prominent in Scotland than in England: much of the work which would in England be done by estate agents is in Scotland done by solicitors.

1–49   Estate agency work is to some extent regulated by the Estate Agents Act 1979.

Estate Agents Act 1979[2]

1–50   This Act is the culmination of many attempts in Parliament to produce legislation which would protect members of the public from the activities of dishonest persons who, without any qualifications, could set up in business as "estate agents." Most of these attempts at legislation sought to introduce a system of registration for estate agents. The system which finally found sufficient support to enable the Act of 1979 to be passed, however, is not a system requiring registration of estate agents, but a licensing system operated by the Director General of Fair Trading and designed to guarantee certain minimum standards. Any person remains free to adopt the title of "estate agent," and set up in business as such.

1–51   The Act is basically within the field of consumer-protection legislation, though, by amendments made to the Bill at a late stage in its passage through Parliament, the Act extends to dealings with commercial as well as residential property and so protects many persons other than consumers.

1–52   The Act does not define "estate agent"; the central definition is that of "estate agency work," *i.e.* things done by any person in the course of a business (including a business in which he is an employee) on instructions received from another person ("the client") who wishes to dispose of or acquire an interest in land—

(a) in order to introduce to the client a third person who wishes to acquire or dispose of such an interest; and

---

2 The main provisions of this Act came into force on May 3, 1982 (Estate Agents Act 1979 (Commencement No. 1) Order 1981 (S.I. 1981 No. 1517)).

(b) in order, after the introduction, to secure the disposal or acquisition of that interest.

The Act expressly provides that it does not apply to things done by a practising solicitor in the course of his profession (s. 1).

The leading provisions of the Act are as follows:

(a) *Orders by Director General of Fair Trading*

Power is conferred on the Director General of Fair Trading to make an order prohibiting a person from doing any estate agency work at all or from doing estate agency work of a specified description. Before making any such order the Director must be satisfied that the person is unfit on one or other of several grounds which include convictions for fraud, dishonesty or violence, discrimination in the course of estate agency work and failure to comply with certain provisions of the Act (s. 3).

The Director has also power to give a warning order where a person has failed to comply with certain provisions of the Act; the person concerned is then not considered as unfit to practise unless he fails to comply with the warning order (s. 4).

There are provisions dealing with revocation and variation of orders and with appeals (ss. 6 and 7).

Particulars of all orders, including warning orders, are entered on a register kept by the Director and open to public inspection on payment of a prescribed fee (s. 8).

(b) *Information, entry and inspection*

The Director in discharging his functions under the Act may compel persons to furnish information to him (s. 9), but he is prohibited from disclosing such information without the consent of the person to whom it relates (s. 10).

Where there is reasonable cause to suspect that an offence has been committed, a duly authorised officer has power to enter premises and require documents to be produced to him (s. 11).

(c) *Clients' money and accounts*

The Act declares that clients' money received by any person engaged in estate agency work in Scotland is held by him as agent for the person who is entitled to call for it (s. 13).

Clients' money must be kept in a "client account" (s. 14).

Accounts regulations may require an estate agent to account for the interest on any clients' money (s. 15).

Clients' money must be protected by indemnity insurance, so that in the event of the estate agent failing to account for it a claim may be made against the insurance company (s. 16). Application may be made to the Director for exemption from this provision (s. 17).

(d) *Regulation of other aspects of estate agency work*

Details must be disclosed to the client of his prospective liabilities, including the remuneration which will become payable to the estate agent; failure to comply could result in the estate agent being unable to enforce the contract (s. 18).

Pre-contract deposits (which in England may, within prescribed limits, be required from prospective purchasers (s. 19)) are prohibited in Scotland (s. 20).

Any personal interest which the estate agent has in the property must be disclosed to the client (s. 21).

Regulations may be made by statutory instrument to ensure minimum standards of competence for persons engaged in estate agency work; by this means there might come to be a prescribed degree of practical experience and a prescribed professional or academic qualification for persons engaged in such work (s. 22).

An undischarged bankrupt must not engage in estate agency work except as an employee (s. 23).

(e) Supervision and enforcement

1–58 The Director and his staff count as a "tribunal," and so come under the supervision of the Council on Tribunals (s. 24).

The working and enforcement of the Act are under the general superintendence of the Director (s. 25).

The enforcement authorities, other than the Director, are the local weights and measures authorities (s. 26).

House and Estate Factors

1–59 House and estate factors are appointed by the owner of houses or an estate to manage the property on the owner's behalf.

1–60 Usually the houses which the house factor manages will have been let by the owner to different tenants. The house factor does not himself have implied authority to grant new leases, but he has implied authority to receive notice from tenants as to defects in the property:

McMartin v. *Hannay* (1872) 10 M. 411: H. was the owner of a Glasgow tenement of 12 houses access to which was by one common stair. H. managed the property through a factor.

McM. claimed damages from H. for the death of his seven-year-old daughter, Tiny, who had fallen through a gap in the railing on the common stair when visiting the premises.

Notice of the gap in the railing had been given at the factor's office many months before the accident.

Held that H. was liable in damages though he had had no personal knowledge of the defect.

1–61 A factor managing property has no lien on leases or other documents which he holds for the owner of the property, as was decided in *Macrae* v. *Leith*, 1913 S.C. 901, in which M., the heritable creditor in possession of an estate, was held entitled to a court order against L., who claimed to be the factor of the estate, for delivery of the leases and other estate documents in L.'s possession. An estate factor was distinguished from a mercantile factor:

"There is a common enough use of the expression 'factor's lien,' but the use is, I think, confined to cases of mercantile agency, and has not been extended beyond that. It was because in mercantile agency goods are often bought and sold, shipped and received, advances made thereon, and responsibilities undertaken thereanent that the lien was given to mercantile agents over what could be turned into money, such as goods, claims, bills, and so on, and I do not think it has ever in practice been held that this factor's lien could or should extend to an estate manager, who is called in Scotland a factor, but who in England would be called a land-agent" (*per* Lord Johnston at p. 906).

Shipmasters

The master of a ship is the agent of the shipowner or the charterer in the navigation and management of the ship.

Where a master has, to the benefit of the shipowner, accepted the services of a shipbroker, the shipowner is liable to pay the shipbroker (see *Barnetson* v. *Petersen Brothers* (1902) 5 F. 86 (1–17, above)).

As agent of necessity a master may grant security over the ship or cargo by a bond of bottomry or a bond of respondentia respectively (see 1–30, above).

The master does not have authority to make unnecessary alterations in the charterparty entered into by the shipowner:

Strickland and Others v. *Neilson and MacIntosh* (1869) 7 M. 400: The ship "Tornado," owned by N. & M., had been chartered to carry passengers and cargo from Liverpool to two ports in New Zealand—Auckland and Wellington.

On the arrival of the ship at Auckland, the master, because of difficulties with the crew, arranged with S. & Co., the charterers' agents at Auckland, that the passengers and cargo would be taken on to Wellington in other vessels. The master drew bills of exchange on N. & M. to meet the expense of this operation which was undertaken by S. & Co.

N. & M. refused to accept the bills.

Held that as the deviation from the charterparty had not been necessary for the safety of the ship, it had not been within the master's authority, and that N. & M. were therefore not liable for the expenses incurred by S. & Co.

Solicitors

Solicitors, formerly called "law-agents," are agents employed by their clients for the conduct of legal business. The extent of their authority depends on the nature of the work which is entrusted to them, and is considered in the next part of this chapter (1–83, below).

IV AGENT'S AUTHORITY

Questions as to the scope of an agent's authority may arise in two situations:

(a) as between the principal and the agent; and
(b) as between the principal and the third party.

(a) As between Principal and Agent

1–68   In this situation, questions as to the scope of the agent's authority are resolved by interpretation of the contract, whether express or implied, which established the agency relationship between the parties.

1–69   If the agent has acted beyond the scope of the agency, he is liable in damages for breach of contract (*cf. Gilmour* v. *Clark* (1853) 15 D. 478 (1–99, below)), and he will not be entitled to the commission agreed on for the period during which he has been in breach of his contract (*cf. Graham & Co.* v. *United Turkey Red Co. Ltd.*, 1922 S.C. 533 (1–101, below)).

(b) As between Principal and Third Party

1–70   In this situation the scope of the agent's authority is of central importance in the attainment of the object of agency—the creation of a legal relationship between the principal and the third party—and questions are not resolved solely by a consideration of the terms of the contract between principal and agent.

1–71   The agent's authority emanates from his principal in one or other of two ways—by contract or by operation of law.

1–72   The following terms are used to describe the nature of the agent's authority in different circumstances:

    (i)   express authority;
    (ii) implied authority;
    (iii) ostensible or apparent authority; and
    (iv) presumed authority.

The term "actual authority" is used to cover both (i) and (ii); the authority in both these cases arises out of contract. In (iii) and (iv), on the other hand, the law is not concerned with whether or not there was actual authority; the circumstances are such that authority is deemed to exist, *i.e.* the authority arises by operation of law.

1–73   It is not always easy to identify in a reported case which category of authority is in question. In particular, the dividing line between implied authority (authority which actually exists) and ostensible (or apparent) authority (authority which does not exist) is not clearly drawn in Scottish cases or in pre-twentieth century English cases. For the end result (though not as regards the evidence which must be brought before the court) the distinction is insignificant: the actions in question are generally brought by the third party against the principal with the object of establishing that the principal is bound by the agent's actings and so is liable to the third party; in such an action the third party is equally satisfied with the court's decision whether the court has held that the principal is bound because the agent was acting within his implied authority or within his ostensible (or apparent) authority.

(i) *Express Authority*

1–74   The contract between the principal and the agent may expressly define the scope of the agent's authority. This is essential where the agent appointed is a special agent, as distinct from a general agent. The third party may not, at the time of negotiating with the agent, know the agent's express authority, but he is entitled to found on the express authority, when he comes to know of it, as establishing the contractual relationship between himself and the principal.

(ii) *Implied Authority*

It is common for the agent's authority not to be expressed in detail in his appointment, but to be left to be implied from the mere fact of the appointment coupled with the surrounding circumstances.

An agent has implied authority to do whatever is incidental to, or ordinarily necessary for, the completion of the transaction committed to him. If he belongs to a recognised profession, he impliedly has the authority usually conferred on members of that profession. Similarly, implied authority may be defined by custom and usage of trade.

The nature of implied authority and the circumstances in which it exists may be illustrated as follows:

1. A general agent has no implied authority to borrow money:

Sinclair, Moorhead & Co. v. *Wallace & Co.* (1880) 7 R. 874: S. & Co., produce merchants in Glasgow, had an important branch in Dundee. Low was general manager of the Dundee branch, but was not a partner in the firm.

Low borrowed money, saying that it was required by S. & Co. for their business.

Later Low absconded, leaving large deficiencies.

Held that the firm of S. & Co. was not liable for the loan.

Lord Young (at p. 877) referred to Low as having had "all the general powers which an agent managing a mercantile business can have. He had power to buy and sell, accept bills, and open a bank account,—in short, general powers such as a general manager in his position is in use to have."

However, of the power to borrow money in name of the principals, Lord Young said: "That is a very important power, and when it is intended to be given it would be well that it should be given expressly, and within certain limits. I apprehend that such is the practice. No prudent money-lender would be likely to lend money to an agent without seeing his authority to borrow, and satisfying himself that the demand is within the prescribed limits. Here we have nothing of that sort."

2. An agent who has authority to open a bank account for his principal does not have implied authority to create an overdraft on the account:

Royal Bank of Scotland v. *Skinner,* 1931 S.L.T. 382 (O.H.): S., a solicitor, opened a bank account for his client Mrs Cameron, who had a drapery business. The account was headed with the solicitor's name followed by the words "for Mrs Duncan Cameron."

After a few years the account fell gradually into debit, Mrs Cameron became bankrupt, and the bank raised an action against S. for payment of the outstanding principal sum and interest.

Held that S. was not liable.

This was not a case in which the agent could be made liable for breach of warranty of authority (see 1–157, below).

Lord Mackay (Ordinary) said (at p. 387): "The fact that a principal permits his agent to open an account with a credit does not involve that he is willing to let him draw upon it under his general agency so as to create indefinite debits. . . . A person who purports to contract as agent on behalf of an alleged principal is liable on an implied warranty of his authority *only* if the other party relied on the existence of the authority. . . . Now the bank do not, and could not, say that they so relied."

1–80   3. A salesman has implied authority to take orders on behalf of his principal:
   Barry, Ostlere & Shepherd Ltd. v. *Edinburgh Cork Importing Co.*, 1909 S.C. 1113: B. Ltd., manufacturers of floorcloth and linoleum, negotiated with Lawrie, the manager or salesman of cork merchants, for the supply of cork shavings to B. Ltd.
   Delivery was not made, the price of cork shavings had risen, and B. Ltd. brought an action of damages for breach of contract against the cork merchants.
   The cork merchants claimed that they had not intended Lawrie to make a final bargain.
   Held that a contract had been formed, since the pursuers were entitled to assume that a person in Lawrie's position had authority to conclude the bargain.
   Reference was made to the earlier case of *Milne* v. *Harris, James & Company* (1803) Mor. 8493, in which an order for a quantity of tea given in Edinburgh to a travelling agent of a London firm was binding on the London firm, with the result that that firm was liable in damages for failure to deliver the tea. This case was the authority for the statement in Bell's *Commentaries* (vol. II, p. 515): "In general, it appears that a riding or travelling agent has not only authority to receive payment for his principal of the moneys due to him, but to take orders by which the principal shall be bound as much as if he himself had accepted and bound the contract."

1–81   4. The master of a ship has implied authority to accept the services of a shipbroker (*Barnetson* v. *Petersen Brothers* (1902) 5 F. 86 (1–17, above)), but not to deviate unnecessarily from the charterparty (*Strickland and Others* v. *Neilson and MacIntosh* (1869) 7 M. 400 (1–65, above)).

1–82   5. An architect has in certain circumstances implied authority to employ a surveyor. Two contrasting cases illustrate the circumstances in which such an implied authority exists:
   (a) *Black* v. *Cornelius* (1879) 6 R. 581: C. engaged Deas as his architect in connection with certain houses and shops which C. was about to erect on a site in Edinburgh.
   Deas had the plans measured by B., a surveyor.
   The buildings were not proceeded with, and B. claimed fees from C.
   C. resisted payment on the ground that he had not employed B., and further, that he had made an express agreement with Deas, by which Deas's fee was to include the surveyor's work.
   Held that C. was liable to pay B.
   "An architect employed in the ordinary way has authority to employ a surveyor, and . . . the surveyor, if not otherwise paid, has a good claim

against the person who employs the architect" (*per* Lord Ormidale at p. 582).

(b) *Knox & Robb* v. *Scottish Garden Suburb Co. Ltd.*, 1913 S.C. 872: K. & R., alleging that they had done surveying work on the instructions of the architect of a building company, claimed payment for their work from the building company.

Held that, as the building plans were in this case only proposals which had not been finally approved, the architect had had no implied authority to employ surveyors.

6. A solicitor's implied authority depends on the character of the work entrusted to him.

If the solicitor is instructed to bring an action in court, he has implied authority to take any incidental step in procedure, but not to appeal to a higher court (see *Goodall* v. *Bilsland,* 1909 S.C. 1152 (1–25, above)), or to defend proceedings if an appeal is made by the other party:

Stephen v. *Skinner* (1873) 2 M. 287: Stephen claimed to be ranked as a creditor in the sequestration of a Stornoway merchant, but the trustee in the sequestration rejected his claim.

Stephen instructed a Stornoway firm of solicitors to appeal to the sheriff against this rejection. The action was successful.

The trustee then appealed to the Court of Session, and the Stornoway solicitors instructed Skinner, an Edinburgh solicitor, to protect Stephen's interests in the appeal. The Court of Session decided the appeal in the trustee's favour, and found Stephen liable in expenses.

Held that Stephen was not liable to pay the Stornoway solicitors the expenses incurred in the Court of Session proceedings, since he had not authorised these proceedings.

Similarly, a solicitor instructed to bring an action on behalf of his client has no implied authority to abandon the action or settle it out of court (*Thoms* v. *Bain* (1888) 15 R. 613[3]), or to submit the question to arbitration (*Black* v. *Laidlaw* (1844) 6 D. 1254).

A solicitor has no implied authority to receive repayment of money lent by his client:

Peden v. *Graham* (1907) 15 S.L.T. 143 (O.H.): P. obtained a loan of £100 through a solicitor, Aitken. P. paid interest on the loan, and also two repayments of £20 each of the capital, to Aitken.

Aitken embezzled the £40, and subsequently became bankrupt and mentally deranged.

Held that the loss fell on P., since Aitken had had no authority to receive repayment of the capital on behalf of his client.

7. An agent may have implied authority to employ a solicitor, but this will depend on circumstances such as the nature of the work and the category of agent appointed. For instance, in *J.M. & J.H. Robertson* v. *Beatson, McLeod & Co. Ltd.*, 1908 S.C. 921, a chartered accountant appointed to carry through an amalgamation of two limited companies was held not to have had implied authority to employ a solicitor to prepare a certain deed; the result was that the solicitor was not entitled to claim payment of his account from the principal.

---

[3] Contrast the English case *Waugh* v. *H.B. Clifford & Sons Ltd.* [1982] Ch. 374 (C.A.).

(iii) *Ostensible or Apparent Authority*

1–85   This is authority which the agent has not actually had conferred on him either expressly or impliedly, but which is deemed to exist on the principle of personal bar by holding out. There is a binding relationship between the principal and the third party because the principal has held out the agent as having the necessary authority.

1–86   Such authority can arise where the principal has withdrawn an agent's actual authority without giving proper notice to third parties of the withdrawal. It may also arise where the principal has made some private arrangement with his agent, limiting the agent's usual authority and has not notified third parties of these special limitations: a third party is justified in believing that the agent has the ordinary powers of an agent of the category to which he belongs.

1–87   The following two cases illustrate ostensible authority:

(1) *Hayman* v. *American Cotton Oil Co.* (1907) 45 S.L.R. 207: See 1–19, above.

(2) *International Sponge Importers Ltd.* v. *Watt & Sons*, 1911 S.C. (H.L.) 57: Cohen, a commercial traveller for a sponge importing company, was in the habit of selling to saddlers parcels of sponges which he was allowed to carry with him and hand over to purchasers. He had no authority to receive payment except by crossed cheques in favour of the company.

Occasionally W. & Sons, saddlers in Edinburgh, had paid for sponges by cheque in favour of Cohen, and the company knew of this but did not object. On one occasion W. & Sons paid £120 in cash to Cohen.

Cohen was shown to have been acting dishonestly, and the company sought to recover the irregular payments from W. & Sons.

Held that W. & Sons were not liable, since, in the circumstances, they had had no reason to believe that Cohen was not entitled to receive payment by those methods.

Contrast *British Bata Shoe Company Ltd.* v. *Double M. Shah Ltd.,* 1981 S.L.T. (Notes) 14 (O.H.): S. Ltd. obtained several consignments of goods from B. Ltd. Kreager, B. Ltd.'s cashier, without actual authority, regularly received payment for the goods from S. Ltd. by cheques on which, at Kreager's request, the payee's name was left blank.

Kreager embezzled the money, was convicted, and became bankrupt.

B. Ltd. sued S. Ltd. for the price of the goods. S. Ltd., relying on *International Sponge Importers Ltd.* v. *Watt & Sons*, argued that Kreager had had ostensible authority to receive the cheques.

Held that B. Ltd. was entitled to succeed: there was no evidence that B. Ltd. had known of the payments made to Kreager, and so B. Ltd. had not represented to S. Ltd. that Kreager had been acting on B. Ltd.'s behalf in receiving payment.

This case is a good illustration of the point that the representation which gives rise to ostensible authority must be a representation made by the principal to the third party: a representation made by the agent alone is not enough.

Moreover, the circumstances in this case, especially Kreager's odd request for cheques with the payee's name left blank, were sufficiently suspicious to cast upon S. Ltd. a duty of inquiry.

(iv) *Presumed Authority*

Presumed authority is authority which the law presumes the principal would have granted if he had been consulted in advance.

In agency of necessity (see 1–28, above) the agent's authority is presumed authority.

Such authority also arises out of a *praepositura* ("superintendence") in a household or a business.

In a household a wife is presumed to be *praeposita negotiis domesticis* ("placed in charge of domestic affairs") and so to have authority to order necessaries for which her husband will be liable to pay.

The question whether items are necessaries or luxuries is decided according to all the family circumstances. For example, in *Buie* v. *Lady Gordon &c.* (1827) 5 S. 464; (1831) 9 S. 923, a list including expensive food and drink and charges for chaises supplied to Lady Gordon had to be revised because, while the Lord Ordinary had taken account of the husband's rank and fortune, he had failed to take account also of the husband's embarrassed circumstances.

There is no presumed authority, and so no liability on the husband, where the third party has been relying solely on the wife's own credit. An instance is *Arnot* v. *Stevenson* (1698) Mor. 6017:

S.'s wife bound her son as apprentice to A., an apothecary, and paid part of the fee for the apprenticeship.

A. brought an action against S. for 100 merks, the balance of the fee not paid, and for damages on the ground that the son had run away from his apprenticeship after two years.

Held that S. was not liable, since S.'s wife had not been acting as agent of her husband in relation to the apprenticeship.

A wife's presumed authority may be terminated by the husband. Express notice to the individual supplier or the recording of letters of inhibition in the Register of Inhibitions and Adjudications in Edinburgh terminates the authority, but a newspaper advertisement has no legal effect unless the supplier is proved to have been aware of it.

The person who is *praeposita negotiis domesticis* is not necessarily the wife of the householder; for instance, in *Hamilton* v. *Forrester* (1825) 3 S. 572, the eldest daughter of the householder, who was a widower, was in that position and so not personally liable for the necessaries ordered for the family.

In a business the person who is *praepositus negotiis* ("placed in charge of affairs") has presumed authority to conduct the business on behalf of the owner of the business. An instance is:

Gemmell v. *Annandale & Son Ltd.* (1899) 36 S.L.R. 658: G., a rag-merchant, brought an action against A. Ltd. for the price of rags supplied to A. Ltd.

A. Ltd. claimed that, when G. had been in prison, the price had been paid to, and a receipt granted by, G.'s father as *praepositus negotiis*.

Held that payment to G.'s father in that capacity was good payment in a question between G. and A. Ltd.

V DUTIES OF AGENT TO PRINCIPAL

The duties of an agent to his principal may be considered under the following headings:

      (a) instructions;
      (b) delegation;
      (c) skill and care;
      (d) accounting;
      (e) relief; and
      (f) fiduciary duty.

(a) Instructions

1–98 The agent must perform what he has been instructed to do, and in doing so must act in accordance with the authority conferred on him, or with the customs and usages of the trade, business or profession. If the instructions are express, they must be complied with. Where there are no instructions, express or implied by custom or usage of trade, the agent must act to the best of his judgment.

1–99 There is an instance of an agent's failure to comply with express instructions in *Gilmour* v. *Clark* (1853) 15 D. 478: G., a merchant in Edinburgh, instructed C., a carter there, to cart a bale of goods to Leith to be put on board "The Earl of Zetland" bound for Orkney.

C.'s servant put the goods on board "The Magnet" instead, and that ship was lost.

Held that C. was liable to G. for the value of the goods.

1–100 Express instructions are not necessarily detailed instructions; for example, a solicitor instructed to make up a purchaser's title to heritable property or to prepare a conveyance is in breach of his duty to his client if he fails, without first obtaining the client's dispensation, to make a search for incumbrances (*Fearn* v. *Gordon & Craig* (1893) 20 R. 352).

1–101 An agent who fails to comply with the stipulations in his contract of appointment loses his right to claim the agreed commission for the period during which he is in breach:

Graham & Co. v. *United Turkey Red Co. Ltd.*, 1922 S.C. 533: A contract entered into in February 1914 between G. & Co. as agents and U. Ltd. as principal prohibited G. & Co. from selling cotton goods supplied by parties other than U. Ltd.

From July 10, 1916, G. & Co. regularly sold goods in contravention of that term.

In November 1917, G. & Co. brought an action of accounting against U. Ltd. for the whole period of the agency.

Held that G. & Co. were entitled to an accounting only for the period prior to July 10, 1916.

Lord Ormidale said (at p. 550): "Having ceased to perform the stipulated services in terms of their contract they forfeited the right to call for commissions—the reward stipulated in the contract for these services—the one being the direct counterpart of the other."

(b) Delegation

1–102 The general presumption in agency is that the agent must act personally. The maxim applicable is *delegatus non potest delegare* ("an agent cannot delegate").

Delegation, may, however, be expressly permitted, or may be impliedly authorised by custom or usage of trade. It may also be later ratified by the principal, or may be justified by necessity.

Where there is permissible delegation, the principal is liable to pay for the sub-agent's services.

Black v. *Cornelius* (1879) 6 R. 581 (1–82, above) is authority for the architect's right to delegate to a surveyor.

(c) Skill and Care

An agent must exercise due skill and care. If a professional man, he must show the degree of knowledge, skill and care expected of a reasonably competent and careful member of the profession.

A case in which an agent, acting as a mutual friend and not as a member of any particular profession, was held not to have exercised reasonable care is *Stiven* v. *Watson* (1874) 1 R. 412:

S., a merchant in Dundee, purchased a quantity of yarn from Annan & Co., Pitscottie Mills, Fife. Annan & Co. failed to deliver all the quantity purchased, and S. threatened to take legal proceedings to compel delivery.

W. proposed an arrangement, which was agreed to, by which Annan & Co. were to forward a quantity of tow belonging to them and then lying at Dundee to Dairsie station and to grant a delivery-order for it in favour of W.

W. received the delivery-order, but failed to intimate it to the station-master at Dairsie. The result was that when the tow arrived at the station, it was removed by Annan & Co.

A few days later Annan & Co. became bankrupt.

S. never received the balance of the yarn, and he brought an action against W. for damages.

Held that (i) W. was liable for the damage caused by his failure to intimate the delivery-order; and (ii) W.'s plea that no damage had been suffered because the transaction would have been reducible under the Bankruptcy Act 1696 could not be sustained because there was no certainty that the retention of the tow would not have persuaded Annan & Co. to deliver the yarn.

Similarly, in *Copland* v. *Brogan*, 1916 S.C. 277 (1–10, above), an agent, though acting gratuitously, was held liable for failure to exercise reasonable care.

Professional persons, provided they show reasonable knowledge and skill and act with reasonable care, are not liable for errors of judgment. Solicitors have thus been held liable to clients for having founded on the wrong section of a statute (*Hart* v. *Frame* (1839) McL. & R. 595; (1836) 14 S. 914), and for having delayed bringing an action against a local authority until the action was barred by the Public Authorities Protection Act 1893 (*Simpson* v. *Kidstons, Watson, Turnbull & Co.*, 1913 1 S.L.T. 74 (O.H.)), but not for failure to reclaim income tax on behalf of a religious body through ignorance of English practice and of an English House of Lords decision in which an earlier Scottish case had been disapproved (*Free Church of Scotland* v. *MacKnight's Trustees*, 1916 S.C. 349).

(d) Accounting

1–110   An agent must keep accounts and make good any deficiency which he cannot explain, even although no dishonesty on his part is proved.

Tyler v. *Logan* (1904) 7 F. 123: T. owned a number of branch establishments for the sale of boots. He appointed L. as manager of his branch in Dundee.

At a stock-taking conducted by T., there was a deficiency of about £62 at the Dundee branch, and T. brought an action against L. for payment of that amount.

There was no evidence of dishonesty or negligence on L.'s part, but no explanation of the deficiency.

Held that T. was entitled to payment.

(e) Relief

1–111   If a principal is held liable on a transaction entered into by an agent exceeding his authority, or for a default by an agent, he is entitled to relief from the agent.

Milne v. *Ritchie &c.* (1882) 10 R. 365: A house was being built for D. M., who was D.'s architect, had authority, limited to £1,465 to enter into a contract for the mason-work.

M. accepted an offer from R. to execute the mason-work for £1,646.

R. raised an action against D. for payment of £1,646, and was successful.

D. then raised an action of relief against M., and was successful.

(Subsequently M. brought an action against R. for reduction of the acceptance of the offer, alleging that he had been induced to sign it by fraudulent misrepresentations of R.

Held that M. had a title to sue.)

(f) Fiduciary Duty

1–112   The relationship of agency is of a fiduciary character: the principal ought to be able to rely on the agent's giving him full benefit of his services in accordance with the contract of agency.

1–113   The agent's fiduciary duty is restricted to what he does in the course of the agency: in outside matters the agent is entitled to further his own interests or those of other principals; restraints would require to be expressly provided for in the contract of agency or to arise by necessary implication from it. The comparatively recent case of *Lothian* v. *Jenolite Ltd.*, 1969 S.C. 111, is a warning against stating the agent's fiduciary duty in over-wide terms:

J. Ltd., an English company, entered into an agreement with L., by which L. was to sell certain of J. Ltd.'s products in Scotland and receive a commission on sales. The contract was to last for four years from July 1964, but in November 1965 J. Ltd. terminated it.

L. claimed damages for breach of contract. J. Ltd. alleged in defence that L. had without their consent bought and resold products supplied by a competitor of theirs and had instructed his staff to sell these products in place of J. Ltd.'s products, and was therefore in material breach of contract.

Held that it was not an implied condition of L.'s contract with J. Ltd. and that L. should not, without J. Ltd.'s consent, sell a competitor's products.

Lord Walker said (at p. 124): "The defenders had not stipulated that the pursuer should be their full-time agent, or that he should sell their goods exclusively, or that his freedom to carry on his own business should be restricted in their interests. . . .

". . . The rule that the agent must act with a single eye to the interests of his principal . . . is, I think, limited to what the agent does in the course of his agency. Here what he did as agent and what he did as an individual were quite separate from one another. . . . If the defenders intended to impose a restriction on the pursuer's freedom to trade, they should have contracted with him to that effect."

For an agency in which there was a restriction prohibiting the agent from selling goods supplied by parties other than the principal, see *Graham & Co.* v. *United Turkey Red Co. Ltd.*, 1922 S.C. 533 (1–101, above).

Three important aspects of the agent's fiduciary duty relate to situations where:

  (i) the agent transacts with his principal;
 (ii) the agent receives a benefit from the third party; and
(iii) the agent is in possession of confidential information.

(i) *Agent Transacting with Principal*

Where an agent, instead of fulfilling the essential purpose of the agency, *i.e.* the establishment of a legal relationship between the principal and a third party, transacts with himself in his individual capacity, a conflict is likely to arise between the personal interest of the agent and his duties to his principal. In such a situation, the agent should disclose the circumstances to the principal.

Thus, if the agent is instructed to sell property for his principal, he must not secretly purchase it himself:

McPherson's Trustees v. *Watt* (1877) 5 R. (H.L.) 9: W., an advocate in Aberdeen, bought for his brother, Dr W. of Darlington, four houses in Aberdeen from McP.'s trustees.

W. was also the law-agent for the trustees.

Before the contract had been made, W. had arranged with his brother, without the knowledge of the trustees, to take over two of the houses himself on paying one-half of the price.

Held that, because W. had not disclosed to the trustees the fact that he was purchasing partly for himself, the transaction was invalid on account of W.'s confidential relationship to the trustees.

Lord Blackburn said (at p. 20): "The writer or attorney must stand towards his client in a position in which there has been, or rather in which there is, confidence more or less reposed in the attorney by his client. . . .

". . . I think the law both in England and Scotland is that in such cases we do not inquire whether it was a good bargain or a bad bargain before we set it aside. The mere fact that the agent was in circumstances which made it his duty to give his client advice puts him in such a position that, being the purchaser himself, he cannot give disinterested advice—his own interests coming in contact with his client's, that mere fact authorises the client to set aside the contract, if he chooses so to do."

1–118   A further illustration is *Cunningham* v. *Lee* (1874) 2 R. 83:

L., a solicitor, had been instructed to buy certain shares for his client, Kirk. L. did so, but Kirk failed to pay the price on the settling day. Instead of then selling the shares, which had fallen considerably in value, L. retained them and some weeks later, when they had risen again, sold them without loss.

Held, on Kirk's sequestration, that L. was not entitled to claim the difference between the price at which the shares had been bought and the market price on the settling day.

Lord President Inglis said (at p. 87): "No agent can buy the property of his principal in any case, except when he is specially authorised to do so. But here there was no authority or consent. Lee obviously took the course which he did in the belief he was entitled to do so. . . . But . . . his actings were quite against the settled rule of law."

1–119   Similarly, an agent whose instructions are to buy goods for his principal must , not, without the principal's knowledge, buy from himself; the principal is entitled to repudiate any such offer.

(ii) *Agent Receiving Benefit from Third Party*

1–120 An agent must not take a secret profit for himself beyond the commission or other remuneration allowed him by his principal. With the principal's consent, express or implied by usage of trade (*e.g.* tips or shared commission in some situations), the agent may receive benefits additional to the remuneration stipulated for in the contract of agency itself.

1–121   An agent who receives a discount or donation from the third party must credit the principal with the amount:

Ronaldson &c. v. *Drummond & Reid* (1881) 8 R. 956: Hill, a solicitor acting for Gray's trustees, engaged Dowell, an auctioneer, to sell furniture.

Dowell paid to Hill a portion of the commission charged by him, describing the sum as a "donation" directly out of his own pocket.

Held that Hill was bound to credit Gray's trustees with that amount.

1–122   The consequences of an agent's receiving a secret profit are that the agent must surrender the secret profit to the principal, loses his right to his lawful remuneration on the transaction, and is liable to be dismissed, and that the principal may recover damages from the third party for bribing the agent and may refuse to implement the contract with the third party. There are also penalties imposed on the offer and receipt of secret commissions under the Prevention of Corruption Acts of 1906 and 1916.

(iii) *Agent in Possession of Confidential Information*

1–123 An agent must treat as confidential all information relating to his principal's business which comes to his knowledge as a result of the agency. An obvious instance is the solicitor's duty of confidentiality concerning his client's affairs. Another instance is *Liverpool Victoria Legal Friendly Society* v. *Houston* (1900) 3 F. 42:

H. had been an agent of a friendly society for about four years, during which time he had had the opportunity of seeing lists of persons insured with the society.

After having been dismissed by the society, H. offered lists of such persons to officials of a rival society.

Held that the lists contained confidential information acquired by H. in the course of his agency and that he was not entitled to make use of them to the detriment of his former principal. H. was also held liable in damages for the loss of business which the society had sustained as a result of having its members canvassed by the agents of the rival society.

VI RIGHTS OF AGENT AGAINST PRINCIPAL

The rights of an agent against his principal are considered below under these headings:
(a) remuneration;
(b) reimbursement of expenses;
(c) relief; and
(d) lien.

(a) **Remuneration**

The principal is bound to pay the agreed commission or other remuneration. If there is no express provision, then the remuneration will be the amount which is customary in the particular branch of agency: there may be a scale of fees, as for solicitors. If there is neither an express provision as to the amount nor a professional custom, the amount will be *quantum meruit* ("as much as he has earned"):

Kennedy v. *Glass* (1890) 17 R. 1085: G. was a dealer in old building material and old machinery.

K., an architect, had on several occasions introduced G. to persons who had old material for sale, and for this K. had been paid a commission by G.

In 1883 K. introduced G. to a sugar refining company with a view to a proposed sale of machinery and plant by the company.

Negotiations were protracted, but in 1888 G. finally entered into a contract with the company for the purchase of the machinery and plant at the price of £7,250.

G. subsequently failed to carry out the contract. K. claimed that there had been an oral arrangement between himself and G. by which he was to receive £250 as commission. G. contended that he had only arranged to give K. £50 if anything came of the transaction.

There was evidence to show that throughout the negotiations K. had acted as G.'s representative and had taken a great deal of trouble in promoting the transaction.

Held that although K. was not a professional broker he was entitled to £50 commission, *i.e.* to commission on a *quantum meruit* basis.

Difficulty can arise in deciding whether the agent has earned his commission. Has he done what the contract of agency required him to do in order to earn the commission? Is the result obtained by the principal fairly attributable to the agent's activities? An illustration is *Walker, Fraser & Steele* v. *Fraser's Trustees*, 1910 S.C. 222:

F., the owner of the estate of Balfunning, employed W. & Co., estate agents, to sell it at a minimum price of £38,000.

In 1903 Scott applied to W. & Co. for information regarding the estate of Dalnair, and in reply W. & Co. sent particulars also of a few other estates including Balfunning. Negotiations were then broken off for a time.

In 1906 Scott applied to W. & Co. for particulars of Balfunning, and was urged by them to make an offer for it, but did not do so.

In October 1907 Scott advertised in the *Glasgow Herald* for property of the general description which he desired, and the following month received from F. a letter about Balfunning. Negotiations followed which resulted in a sale of that property to Scott at £31,000.

W. & Co. sued F. for £310 commission.

Held that, as W. & Co.'s exertions had to a material degree contributed to the sale to Scott, W. & Co. were entitled to the commission.

Lord Dundas said (at p. 229): "Actual introduction of the purchaser to the seller is not a necessary element in a case of this sort; it is enough if the agents introduce the purchaser to the estate, and by their efforts contribute in a substantial degree to the sale. A careful consideration of the evidence leads me to hold that the pursuers have sufficiently complied with the test indicated."

(b) **Reimbursement of Expenses**

1–127   The agent has a right to be reimbursed by the principal for all expenses properly incurred in the performance of the agency.

Drummond v. *Cairns* (1852) 14 D. 611: D. instructed C., a stockbroker, to purchase 100 shares of the East India Railway Company. The price was 20/6d per share, and the settling day was May 28.

C. duly intimated the transaction to D., but when the settling day arrived D. was not prepared to pay the price.

On June 10, C. sold the shares at 9/4d each.

Held that D. was liable to reimburse C. for the difference between the two prices.

1–128   The agent has no right of reimbursement if the expenses have not been properly incurred:

Tomlinson v. *Liquidators of Scottish Amalgamated Silks Ltd.*, 1935 S.C. (H.L.) 1; 1934 S.C. 85: The articles of association of S. Ltd. provided for the indemnification of any director against all costs, losses and expenses which he might incur by reason of any act done by him as director.

S. Ltd. went into voluntary liquidation, and T., who had been a promoter and director, was tried for alleged fraud, the charges being that he had issued a fraudulent prospectus and had fraudulently misapplied funds of the company.

T. was acquitted, and then lodged a claim in the liquidation for the expenses, amounting to over £11,000, incurred by him in his defence. The liquidators rejected the claim.

Held that T. was not entitled to his expenses either under the indemnity clause in the articles or at common law, since expenses incurred in defending himself against an allegation that he did something which he did not in fact do and which it was not his duty to do, were not expenses incurred by him as a director or as an agent of the company in the discharge of his duties.

(c) **Relief**

The principal must relieve the agent of all liabilities incurred by the agent and arising out of the proper performance of the agent's duties.

Stevenson v. *Duncan* (1842) 5 D. 167: D. instructed stockbrokers to sell 20 shares of the London, Leith, Edinburgh and Glasgow Shipping Company on his behalf. D. did not in fact hold such shares.

The stockbrokers purported to sell the shares to Cullen.

In an action brought by Cullen against the stockbrokers, Cullen was found entitled to £83 damages. The stockbrokers raised an action of relief against D.

Held that D. was bound to relieve them.

An agent who had not acted properly in the execution of the agency was held not entitled to relief in *Robinson &c.* v. *Middleton* (1859) 21 D. 1089:

M., a wood-merchant in Strathmiglo, engaged R., an agent in London, to effect a sale of wood.

R. sold the wood to Perry who was acting for a firm in Melbourne, Australia. Perry arranged with R. that he (Perry) should incur no liability, but this arrangement was not communicated to M.

The price took the form of a bill of exchange drawn by Perry on the Melbourne firm, which, by the time the cargo arrived in Melbourne, was insolvent.

A bank which had discounted the bill sold the cargo but the price obtained fell short of the amount of the bill by about £1,000. R. paid the deficiency to the bank, and then claimed relief from M.

Held that as R. had, without M.'s knowledge or consent, transacted with Perry so as to release him from his liability as drawer of the bill, R. was not entitled to recover from M.

(d) **Lien**

A mercantile agent has a general lien over any of the principal's property in his possession, *i.e.* he has a right in security over that property until he is paid his commission or other remuneration and has been relieved of debts incurred by him in the execution of the agency.

An illustration of a factor's general lien is *Sibbald* v. *Gibson* (1852) 15 D. 217:

S., corn factor in Leith, employed G. & Co., corn merchants in Glasgow, for several transactions during the years 1850-51.

In December 1850, S. had instructed G. & Co. to purchase for him a large quantity of oats, which were placed in G. & Co.'s store and later distributed from there in small parcels to S.'s customers.

S. and G. & Co. disagreed as to the rate of commission which was due to G. & Co. on these transactions.

In September 1851, S. sent a quantity of beans to G. & Co. for sale, and in remitting the proceeds of the sale G. & Co. deducted an amount for the higher rate of commission which G. & Co. claimed on the oats transactions.

Held that G. & Co. were entitled to retain their commission on the earlier transactions from the proceeds of the sale of the later transaction.

See also *Mackenzie* v. *Cormack*, 1950 S.C. 183 (1–145, below), as to an auctioneer's lien over the goods being sold and over the price paid to him by the successful bidder.

1–133   A solicitor also has a general lien (see 8–157, below).

1–134   Agents other than mercantile agents and members of some professions, have only a special lien: for example, accountants have probably only a special lien (see 8–140, below).

VII THIRD PARTY'S RIGHTS AND LIABILITIES

1–135   As the essential function of agency is to establish a legal relationship between the principal and a third party, the rights and liabilities of the third party are of central importance in the topic of agency.

1–136   These rights and liabilities are affected by the way in which the agent contracts with the third party. A concise statement of the main rules applied is to be found in the opinion of Lord Anderson in *A.F. Craig & Co. Ltd.* v. *Blackater,* 1923 S.C. 472, at p. 486:

"If A contracts as agent for a disclosed principal, A cannot competently sue or be sued with reference to the contract. Again, if A contracts for an undisclosed principal, A may sue and is liable to be sued as a principal, the third party having no knowledge that he is anything but a principal. If, however, A contracts for an undisclosed principal who is subsequently disclosed to the third party, the latter may sue either agent or principal. He cannot, however, sue both. If an action is raised against the third party he may insist that it be at the instance of the disclosed principal."

1–137   Four situations are given further consideration below; these are:

(a)   where the agent names his principal;

(b)   where the agent states that he is an agent but does not give the name of his principal;

(c)   where the agent does not disclose the agency at all, with the result that the third party believes that the agent is himself a principal; and

(d)   where the agent has no authority, with the result that no binding relationship is established between principal and third party and the agent incurs liability to the third party for breach of warranty of authority.

(a) **Agent Naming his Principal**

1–138   The general rule is that where the principal is named, the contract takes legal effect as if the two parties to it had been the principal and the third party; the agent is regarded as having dropped out of the situation: he cannot sue on the contract nor is he liable to be sued. An illustration is *Stone & Rolfe Ltd.* v. *Kimber Coal Co. Ltd.,* 1926 S.C. (H.L.) 45:

A ship owned by S. Ltd. was chartered to the Atlantic Baltic Co., Copenhagen, to carry a cargo of coal from Grangemouth to Denmark.

The charterparty had been negotiated in Glasgow by G. & Co. for the owner and by K. Ltd. for the charterers. The document, a printed form with blanks filled in before signature, had an additional manuscript clause: "Freight and demurrage (if any in loading) to be paid in Glasgow by K. Ltd." The signature on behalf of the charterers was:

"For the Atlantic Baltic Co., Copenhagen,
              J.B. Jamieson of K. Ltd."

S. Ltd. brought an action against K. Ltd. for demurrage incurred at Grangemouth.

Held that K. Ltd. was not liable because (i) the form of signature showed that K. Ltd. had signed as agent only and (ii) the manuscript clause was not sufficient to rebut the inference drawn from the form of the signature.

The same general rule applies where the principal's name is not actually given but can be ascertained by the third party:

Armour v. *Duff & Co.*, 1912 S.C. 120: A. received from D. & Co., who carried on business as "steamship owners and brokers," the following order: "Please supply the s.s. 'Silvia' with the following stores to be put on board at Port-Glasgow. . . ."

A. delivered the goods, and rendered an account to D. & Co., whom he believed to be the owners of the vessel. D. & Co. were not, and had never been, the owners, and they refused to pay the account.

Held that, as A. could, by examining the Register of Shipping, have discovered who the owners of the "Silvia" were, D. & Co. were not liable since they had been acting as agents for a disclosed principal.

The same general rule applies even where the principal is a foreign principal. This point was unsettled in England until the decision of the Court of Appeal in *Teheran-Europe Co. Ltd.* v. *S.T. Belton (Tractors) Ltd.* [1968] 2 Q.B. 545, but in Scotland was established more than a century earlier by *Millar* v. *Mitchell &c.* (1860) 22 D. 833, a decision of the whole Court of Session:

Mitchell & Co. of Leith, acting as agents for C. of Hamburg, entered into a contract with Millar of Mussleburgh for the supply of a quantity of bones to be shipped from Denmark in March and April 1854.

The bones were not shipped in accordance with these terms, and Millar brought an action for damages against Mitchell & Co. for the loss sustained as a result.

Held (by a majority of the whole Court) that (i) there was no *praesumptio juris* ("presumption of law") that an agent acting for a named foreign principal incurred personal liability, and (ii) the evidence in this case did not establish that Mitchell & Co. had undertaken personal liability.

There are four main exceptions to the general rule:

(i) The agent may voluntarily undertake personal liability. An illustration is *Stewart* v. *Shannessy* (1900) 2 F. 1288:

Shannessy was appointed sales manager for a cycle company and also for a tyre company, with authority to appoint travellers at the expense of the respective companies.

Shannessy wrote a letter, on paper headed with the name of the cycle company, to Stewart, appointing Stewart as representative for the two companies on stated terms as to salary and commission. The letter was signed "J.J. Shannessy."

Stewart raised an action against Shannessy for payment of commission. Shannessy maintained that Stewart's only claim lay against the two companies.

Held that Shannessy was personally liable, since he had signed the letter in his own name without qualification and without indicating that he did not intend to bind himself as principal.

1–143   Similarly, in *Brebner* v. *Henderson*, 1925 S.C. 643, a director and the secretary of a limited company were held to have undertaken personal liability by signing a promissory note which read:

". . . we promise to pay . . ." The signatures took the form:

> "JAS. R. GORDON, Director
> ALEX. HENDERSON, Secretary
> The Fraserburgh Empire Limited."

The reasoning was that the word "we" referred *prima facie* ("until the contrary was proved") to the individuals who signed the note, and that the words which followed the signatures were merely descriptive of the positions held by the signatories and did not have the effect of exempting them from personal liability.

1–144   (ii) The agent may incur personal liability by custom of trade.

The case of *Livesey* v. *Purdom & Sons* (1894) 21 R. 911 was an unsuccessful attempt by an English solicitor, L., to make Scottish solicitors, P. & Sons, liable to pay for an action raised in the English courts, on P. & Sons' instructions, for a named client of P. & Sons. L. relied on the custom in England by which a solicitor employing another solicitor on behalf of a client was liable for the costs of an action, unless he expressly stipulated to the contrary. The court held that L. had failed to prove that that custom extended to the situation where the solicitor conducting the action was employed by a Scots law-agent.

(Since the Solicitors (Scotland) Act 1976 (s. 20) a solicitor employing another solicitor on the business of a client, *whether or not he discloses the client,* has been liable to that other for fees and outlays unless he disclaims liability when the employment takes place. See now the consolidating Solicitors (Scotland) Act 1980 (s. 30).)

1–145   (iii) An agent who can show that he has some interest of his own in the transaction entered into on his principal's behalf with the third party has a title to sue the third party; an instance is *Mackenzie* v. *Cormack*, 1950 S.C. 183:

M., an auctioneer, acting on the instructions of Knight, the owner of Keiss castle, conducted a sale of the furnishings of the castle in the castle.

C. was the successful bidder for a carpet, but, alleging that the carpet had not been delivered to him, refused to pay the price at which it had been knocked down to him.

M. brought an action against C. for the price, and C. pleaded that M., being an agent for a disclosed principal, had no title to sue.

Held that as M. was a mercantile agent with a lien over the price for his charges and commission he had a title to sue C. for the price.

(iv) If the principal is not a legal person, the agent is personally liable to the third party.

A familiar example is the contract made by persons acting on behalf of a company not yet registered: the "agents" remain personally liable (European Communities Act 1972, s. 9(2)) and the company, once registered, has no title to sue the third party (*Tinnevelly Sugar Refining Co. Ltd.* v. *Mirrlees, Watson & Yaryan Co. Ltd.* (1894) 21 R. 1009 (1–14, above)).

The legal position is the same where the principal is a church congregation (*McMeekin* v. *Easton* (1889) 16 R. 363, in which a minister and two other persons who had signed a promissory note on behalf of a church were held personally liable for payment of the note), or where the principal is a club (*Thomson & Gillespie* v. *Victoria Eighty Club* (1905) 43 S.L.R. 628 (O.H.), in which the members of the committee, but not the club itself or its ordinary members, were held liable to pay for liquor supplied to the club).

(b) Agent Contracting "as Agent" for Unnamed Principal

Where the agent contracts "as agent" without naming his principal, the same general rule applies as to the situation under (a), above: the third party is made aware that the person with whom he is dealing is only acting on behalf of another person, and so the third party cannot be regarded as having relied on the agent's credit.

A consequence of the general rule is that if the principal sues the third party on the contract, the third party cannot plead compensation of a debt due to him by the agent:

Matthews v. *Auld & Guild* (1873) 1 R. 1224: M. instructed Henderson, a stockbroker in Dundee, to sell certain securities and purchase other securities for him.

Henderson employed A. & G., stockbrokers in Glasgow, to carry out the transaction. He did not disclose M.'s name to A. & G., but represented throughout that he was acting for a client.

On completion of the transaction, a balance of about £83 remained in the hands of A. & G.

Shortly afterwards, Henderson absconded, leaving a large balance due by him to A. & G.

A. & G. sought to retain the £83 in their hands against the much larger debt due by Henderson to them.

Held that A. & G. were not entitled to plead compensation, since they had known that Henderson was acting for a client, although the client's name had not been disclosed.

An agent who has contracted as agent without naming his principal incurs personal liability if he declines to name his principal when requested to do so by the third party:

Gibb v. *Cunningham & Robertson*, 1925 S.L.T. 608 (O.H.): G. entered into negotiations with C. & R., a firm of solicitors, for the sale to them of 1,000 shares in G.'s family company and of G.'s house. The correspondence showed that C. & R. were acting for others (in fact for the other directors in respect of the shares and for the company itself in respect of the house), but the missives in which the price of £5,000 was agreed did not name any principals.

C. & R. failed to pay the full price, and they were asked to state to G. the names of the principals for whom they had been acting. C. & R. made no answer to the inquiry.

Held that G. was entitled to sue C. & R. for implement of the bargain or, failing implement, for damages.

(c) **Agent Contracting Ostensibly as Principal**

1–151 In this third situation, the third party is unaware of the existence of any principal behind the agent, and looks only to the agent for performance of the contract.

1–152 The principal may disclose himself, and he has then a title to sue the third party.

Bennett v. *Inveresk Paper Co.* (1891) 18 R. 975: B., a newspaper proprietor in Sydney, Australia, through Poulter & Sons, his London agents, entered into a contract with the I. Co. for the supply of paper which was to be shipped to him in Australia. At the time of the making of the contract, the I. Co. did not know of B.

The paper was duly paid for, but on arrival at Sydney was found, owing to bad packing, to be damaged and spoiled.

B. brought an action of damages for breach of contract against the I. Co.

Held that B. had a sufficient title to sue the action.

1–153 When the third party discovers the identity of the principal, he must elect whether to sue the principal or to sue the agent: he cannot sue both. Election, once made, is final.

1–154 The best known case on the third party's right of election is *Ferrier* v. *Dods &c.* (1865) 3 M. 561. In this case the third party was held to have elected to sue the principal.

D., an auctioneer, advertised a sale by auction of certain horses, all warranted good workers. At the sale F. bought a mare for £27.

A few days later, F. informed D. that the mare was utterly unsound and unfit for work. D. admitted F.'s right to return the mare if unsound, but he requested F. to return her direct to her former owner, Bathgate, whose name had not been disclosed at the auction.

F., having returned the mare to Bathgate, brought an action both against D. and against Bathgate.

Held that F., by returning the mare to Bathgate, had elected to sue Bathgate, the principal, and the action as against D., the agent, was dismissed.

1–155 A case in which the third party was held to have elected to sue the agent was *A.F. Craig & Co. Ltd.* v. *Blackater,* 1923 S.C. 472:

C. Ltd. supplied two marine boilers to B., shipowners, at a price of £5,900. The full price was not paid, and C. Ltd. brought an action against B. for the unpaid balance.

B., averring that the boilers had been disconform to contract, brought a counter-action for over £9,000 as damages for breach of contract.

The two actions were conjoined, and in the course of the proof it transpired that B. were not the registered owners, but only the managing owners, of the ship in question, and that the registered owners were the Cadeby Steamship Co. Ltd.

C. Ltd., as defenders in the counter-action, then pleaded that B. had no title to sue, and had sustained no loss through any breach of contract on C. Ltd.'s part.

Held that, by prosecuting their own action to decree, C. Ltd. had elected to treat B. as their debtors in the contract, and, therefore, that B. were entitled to counter-claim for damages.

Lord Anderson, explaining the third party's right of election, said (at p. 486): "When the two actions were raised the principals were undisclosed. It was only during the course of the proof in the conjoined actions that it was casually divulged that the Cadeby Steamship Co. were the principals in the contract. When this fact became known to Messrs Craig they were, in my opinion, put to their election. They had to determine whether or not they would proceed to decree against Messrs Blackater or against their true debtors the Cadeby Co. . . . . There would have been no difficulty, by our procedure, in substituting the one party for the other in both actions. . . . But no proposal to this effect was made by Messrs Craig. They elected to continue the action in which they were pursuers against the agents, but in the counter-action they declined to submit themselves to a decree for damages in respect of their breach of contract. . . . This is plainly inequitable; it is, moreover, a result which is against all legal principle and which is supported by no decided case."

This case was followed in *James Laidlaw and Sons Ltd.* v. *Griffin*, 1968 S.L.T. 278:

L. Ltd., building contractors, entered into a contract with G. for certain structural work at the G. Hotel, which was owned by G. Ltd. In making the contract G. was acting as agent for G. Ltd., of which he was a director, but the agency was not then made known to L. Ltd.

The contract provided that L. Ltd. was to be responsible for all damage to "property of employer," and that "employer" denoted G.

L. Ltd. came to know that G. had been acting on behalf of G. Ltd.

L. Ltd. raised an action against G. for payment of sums certified as due for works executed under the contract, and G. counter-claimed on the ground that L. Ltd. had caused serious damage to the hotel. L. Ltd. argued that the only damage claimable under the contract was damage to G.'s property and the hotel did not belong to G., but to G. Ltd.

Held that, as L. Ltd. had elected to sue G. as agent for G. Ltd., G., in his capacity as agent for G. Ltd., was entitled to counter-claim for the damage to the hotel.

(d) Breach of Warranty of Authority

Where an agent, contracting as agent, exceeds both his actual and his ostensible authority, no binding relationship arises between the principal and the third party unless the principal chooses to ratify the agent's unauthorised actings.

The third party is not entitled to sue the unauthorised agent *on the contract* which the agent purported to make between the principal and the third party, but has the right to sue the agent on the basis of a collateral contract incorporating an implied undertaking on the agent's part that he had the necessary authority to form a binding relationship between the third party and the principal.

1–159   If the agent's misrepresentation of his authority was fraudulent, the agent is liable to the third party in damages for fraud. If the agent's misrepresentation was innocent (*i.e.* if he himself really believed that he did have the necessary authority), he is liable to the third party in damages for breach of warranty of authority, since the law regards him as having impliedly "warranted" (*i.e.* guaranteed) to the third party that he did have the necessary authority. The measure of damages for breach of warranty of authority is the loss sustained by the third party as a result of his not having a binding relationship with the principal.

1–160   The best-known Scottish case on this topic is *Anderson* v. *Croall & Sons Ltd.* (1903) 6 F. 153:

At the Musselburgh Race Meeting held in October 1902, a mare which had come second in a race was, by an innocent mistake, auctioned by C. Ltd. The successful bidder was A., and the price £36.15s.

A. paid the price and received a delivery-order, but the owner refused to give delivery of the mare, on the ground that the sale had been wholly unauthorised by him.

In May 1903, the mare was sold by auction at York for 70 guineas.

Held that, since an auctioneer, in common with other agents, warrants his authority, A. was entitled to damages from C. Ltd., the sum awarded (£26.5s.) being based on the difference between the two auction prices with a deduction for cost of keep and transit. In addition, A. was entitled to the return of the purchase-price which he had paid to C. Ltd.

1–161   In that case A. had been deprived, through the auctioneer's breach of warranty of authority, of a bargain with the principal which would have given A. possession of a mare worth more than he was paying for her. If, however, it is shown that the third party claiming damages for breach of warranty of authority would have been in no better position even if the contract had been enforceable against the principal, then no damages are awarded other than possibly nominal damages such as can be claimed for the infringement of any legal right. An illustration is *Irving* v. *Burns*, 1915 S.C. 260:

B., the secretary of the Langside Picture House Ltd., falsely professing that he had the authority of the directors, accepted an offer made by I. for the execution of certain plumber-work in connection with a hall or theatre which the company was about to erect.

After the work had been executed and I. had ascertained that the contract was in fact not binding on the company, I. brought an action against B. for damages for breach of warranty of authority. In this action I. averred that the company had no assets.

Held that since it appeared from this averment that I. would have been in no better position if the contract had bound the company, he had suffered no loss from (and so could recover no damages for) B.'s breach of warranty.

"The defender, no doubt, warranted his authority to contract on behalf of the company. If he had in fact had authority the company would have been bound; but as it has no assets the damage arising from a breach of the warranty is nil" (*per* Lord Salvesen at p. 269).

VIII TERMINATION OF THE RELATIONSHIP

Agency may be terminated in the following ways:
- (a) by completion of the transaction or expiry of time;
- (b) by mutual agreement;
- (c) by revocation by the principal;
- (d) by renunciation by the agent; and
- (e) by frustration.

(a) Completion of Transaction or Expiry of Time

Agency is brought to an end by completion of the transaction or expiry of the time for which it was created.

There is an instance of termination by expiry of time in *Brenan* v. *Campbell's Trustees* (1898) 25 R. 423:

B., a civil engineer and architect with a practice in Oban, was engaged by C. to be factor on C.'s estate for four years from Martinmas 1890 on the express condition that B. should take C.'s stepson as an apprentice for four years from that date.

In October 1894, B. was informed that his services as factor would not be required on C.'s estate after Martinmas 1894.

B., claiming that he was entitled to six months' notice of termination of his factory, raised an action against C. for six months' pay in lieu of notice.

Held that, as B. was not a servant but a professional man employed by a number of clients, he was not entitled to notice of termination of his employment, and further that the special contract limited the period of his factory to four years.

For an implied agency terminated by lapse of time and material change in circumstances see *Ferguson and Lillie* v. *Stephen* (1864) 2 M. 804 (1–18, above).

(b) Mutual Agreement

Principal and agent may agree that the agency is to be at an end.

In some situations, however, this does not take effect until third parties are properly notified, because, though the agent's actual authority is at an end, he may have ostensible authority; *e.g.* in partnership a retiring partner's authority is not terminated effectively unless notice of the retirement is given in the *Edinburgh Gazette* and to individual customers of the firm (Partnership Act 1890, s. 36(1) and (2)).

(c) Revocation by Principal

Some agencies are irrevocable by the principal without the agent's consent. This is so where the authority has been given to enable the agent to do something in his own interest. The agent is then said to have "a procuratory *in rem suam* ('for his own benefit')" (corresponding to "an authority coupled with an interest" in English law). The two cases usually given as illustrations of a procuratory *in rem suam* are:

1–169 (i) *British Linen Co. Bank* v. *Carruthers and Ferguson* (1883) 10 R. 923: The holder of a cheque for £161, which had been granted to him in payment of the price of sheep, was refused payment by the drawer's bank because the drawer had no more than £136 in his current account. However, the presentation of the cheque to the bank was held to have operated as an assignation in favour of the holder of the cheque of the funds actually in the account, with the result that the holder of the cheque was entitled to about £136 in the drawer's sequestration.

The case was decided under the common law, but the rule is now section 53(2) of the Bills of Exchange Act 1882, a provision applicable only to Scotland (see also 7–97 *et seq.*, below).

The holder of the cheque was regarded as having a procuratory *in rem suam* in this case, as was explained by Lord President Inglis (at p. 926):

"A cheque is nothing more than a mandate to the mandatary to go to the bank and get the money. The mandate may be granted for various causes, and the mandatary may be merely the hand of the mandant, to do for him what he might have done for himself. But when a cheque is granted for value then the case is very different. It is a bare procuratory (to use the language of the older law), when it is granted gratuitously, but when it is granted for value it is a procuratory *in rem suam*, which is just one of the definitions of an assignation. Therefore I cannot doubt that this cheque, being granted for onerous causes, was an assignation, and if that is so undoubtedly the demand for payment was a good intimation of it."

1–170 (ii) *Premier Briquette Co. Ltd.* v. *Gray*, 1922 S.C. 329: The case concerned an underwriting contract and a sub-underwriting contract relating to shares in a new company, P. Ltd. The purpose of the sub-underwriting contract was to lessen the burden of the shares which might require to be taken up by the underwriter.

G., the sub-underwriter, sent his application for shares, which was addressed to P. Ltd., to the underwriter, M. Ltd., along with a letter stating that the contract and application were irrevocable. M. Ltd. passed on G.'s application to P. Ltd. and shares were allotted by P. Ltd. to G. as a result.

Held that the allotment to G. was valid, since neither the sub-underwriting contract nor the application could have been revoked by G.

The effect of the transaction was that G. as principal had conferred on M. Ltd. as agent an irrevocable authority, which was for the benefit of M. Ltd., to apply to P. Ltd. for the shares allotted.

1–171 Where it is open to a principal to revoke an agent's authority, the principal must give proper notice to third parties if he wishes to avoid the possibility that they may hold him liable on the ground of the agent's ostensible authority.

1–172 Moreover, the principal may be liable in damages to the agent if the revocation amounts to a breach of a term, express or implied, of the contract of agency between principal and agent. An instance is *Galbraith & Moorhead* v. *Arethusa Ship Co. Ltd.* (1896) 23 R. 1011:

G. & Co., shipbrokers, offered to take £500 in shares in the "A." Ship Co. Ltd., provided that they were appointed sole chartering brokers for the "A." The offer was accepted.

G. & Co. took the shares, and the agreement was acted on for several years. There was then a change in the management, and G. & Co., averring that the "A." Ship Co. Ltd. was no longer employing them as sole chartering brokers, raised an action against the company for £500 damages.

Held that the agreement was not terminable at the pleasure of the company.

The underlying reason for the decision, as expressed by Lord Adam (at p. 1015) was as follows: "This case depends solely upon the construction of the agreement . . . by which the pursuers were appointed sole chartering brokers for the 'Arethusa,' and the question is, whether that agreement could be determined by the defenders on reasonable notice, or on reasonable cause only. Now, it will be observed that the pursuers paid for the appointment of sole charterer's brokers, and the consideration was their taking £500 in shares of the company, which it is not disputed they did. I have great difficulty in holding that an agreement for which consideration had been thus given could be terminated at will by the other contracting party."

By way of contrast, there were in *Walker* v. *Somerville* (1837) 16 S. 217 circumstances in which authority was held to be revocable at pleasure provided the principal indemnified the agent for his trouble and expenses:

W. by letter promised to S. 15 per cent of any sums which S. might recover by means of an action against W.'s father.

A summons was raised against W.'s father, but within two months of the date of the letter, W. and his father made an agreement by which an annuity was settled on W., and his claims against his father were discharged.

S. claimed that W. had had no power to settle the action to the prejudice of the stipulations in S.'s favour in the letter.

Held that the nature of the agreement between W. and S. was such that W. had been entitled to recall it at pleasure, subject to any claims for disbursement and remuneration for trouble which S. could prove.

(d) Renunciation by Agent

The agent may renounce his agency.

The renunciation will in some situations be a breach of the contract of agency between principal and agent, making the agent liable in damages to the principal.

(e) Frustration

Frustration operates in agency as in the general law of contract; *e.g.* if property which the agent is employed to sell is accidentally destroyed, that amounts to *rei interitus* ("destruction of the subject-matter"), which brings the contract of agency to an end.

1–177   Special mention may be made of:
    (i)   death of principal or agent;
    (ii) bankruptcy of principal or agent;
    (iii) insanity of principal or agent; and
    (iv) discontinuance of the principal's business.

(i) Death of Principal or Agent

1–178   The death of the principal normally terminates the agency.

1–179   Even the death of one of several principals was held to have terminated the agent's authority in *Life Association of Scotland* v. *Douglas* (1886) 13 R. 910:

A bond and disposition in security had been granted to the Life Association of Scotland by the Athole Hydropathic Co. Ltd. and the directors of that company. The deed had been signed by the several granters of it on different dates, between May 11 and July 23. One of the directors, D., who had signed on May 11, died on July 4. The secretary of the company continued to hold the deed until, after it had been signed by all the granters, it was delivered to the Life Association on July 24 in exchange for the sum advanced.

There was failure to pay the full sum in the bond, and the Life Association raised an action against certain of the co-obligants, including D.'s executor.

Held that the executor was not liable, because the implied authority given by D. for delivery of the deed once all the signatures had been obtained had fallen by D.'s death.

1–180   On the other hand, *Campbell* v. *Anderson* (1829) 3 W. & S. 384 is a departure from the normal rule: a factor on a landed estate who had contracted in the *bona fide* belief that his principal, who had died abroad, was still alive was held to have bound his principal and not to be personally liable on a bill of exchange which he had drawn expressly as agent. The authority of this House of Lords decision may, however, have diminished somewhat owing to the passage of time and the improvement in communications; in addition, the case appears to be contrary to the generally accepted rule that death is a public fact of which no notice need be given.

1–181   The death of the agent likewise normally brings the agency to an end. The general rule that an agent must act in person and not delegate prevents the agent's representatives from taking the deceased's place in the agency.

(ii) Bankruptcy of Principal or Agent

1–182   Agency is terminated by the bankruptcy of the principal. An instance is *McKenzie* v. *Campbell* (1894) 21 R. 904:

Fraser, a corn-factor, had been arrested on various charges of forgery. From prison he wrote to C., a law-agent, asking him to act in his defence. He also delivered to C. about £285, authorising him to use the money for the defence proceedings and for paying out sums as directed by Fraser himself.

A few days later, on October 25, Fraser's estates were sequestrated, and McK., the trustee, called on C. to account for his transactions with Fraser's money.

On December 27, Fraser pleaded guilty and was sentenced.

According to C.'s account, the sum which he had received from Fraser had been more than exhausted by the cost of the defence proceedings coupled with payments made on Fraser's directions.

Held that C.'s agency had fallen by Fraser's sequestration, and that C. was therefore bound to account to McK. for all sums belonging to Fraser in his hands as at October 25.

Similarly, in *Dickson* v. *Nicholson* (1855) 17 D. 1011, the authority of a commercial traveller was held to have terminated when his firm stopped payment, and so the traveller was not entitled, in the knowledge of the firm's insolvency, to collect the firm's money from customers and retain it in payment of the remuneration due to himself by the firm.

The bankruptcy of the agent also terminates the agency. Because of the *delectus personae* ("choice of person") involved in the contract of agency between principal and agent, the trustee in bankruptcy is not entitled to adopt the agency. A new agreement to which the principal, the agent and the trustee would be parties could enable the bankrupt agent to continue his work as agent.

Bankruptcy, like death, is regarded as a public fact of which no notice need be given.

(iii) *Insanity of Principal or Agent*

The effect of a principal's prolonged insanity was fully considered in the early case of *Pollok* v. *Paterson*, 10 Dec. 1811, F.C., though the question actually before the court for decision was whether or not a sequestration of an insane person should be recalled.

David Paterson had carried on business in Edinburgh for many years as a banker and insurance broker. In 1805, on going to London, he granted a procuration in favour of his son, John Paterson, empowering John to manage his affairs in his absence.

When in London, David became insane, and returned to reside at home in Scotland. Visitors of the family knew of his insanity, but no public notice was taken of it until 1811.

Meantime John carried on business on his father's account, making use of the procuration.

In 1809 John enlarged the sphere of his operations and entered into several speculations with a merchant Kerr, but in 1810 the concern with Kerr became bankrupt.

Pollok, the holder of a bill of exchange which had been accepted by John per procuration of David, claimed payment from David.

A petition was presented and granted for David's sequestration, and it was with the recall of this sequestration that the case was directly concerned.

The argument put forward for David's family was that the agency of John had been terminated at the commencement of David's insanity. The argument on the other side was that insanity did not of itself terminate an agency: publication of the insanity was required for that, and here there had been no publication.

The views expressed by the judges were to the general effect that the principal's insanity did not of itself terminate an agency, and that a third party who was *in bona fide* ("in good faith," *i.e.* unaware of the principal's insanity) was entitled to regard the agent as still having authority until notification of the insanity had been given.

1–187   In the slightly later case of *Wink* v. *Mortimer* (1849) 11 D. 995 the court held that a principal's temporary insanity had not terminated the agency. The agent had continued to act as agent during a period when the principal was confined to a lunatic asylum, and later, after the principal had regained his sanity and had had his estates sequestrated, the agent was held to be entitled to claim in the sequestration for the amount of his business account, part of which related to the few weeks of the principal's temporary insanity.

1–188   Insanity of the agent terminates the agency.

,(iv) *Discontinuance of Principal's Business*

1–189   If the principal discontinues the business in which the agent is engaged, the agency is terminated and the agent is not entitled to damages for breach of contract unless he can show that it was an express or implied term of the agency that the principal should continue the business for a specified period. Illustrative cases include the three following:

1–190   (1) *Patmore & Co.* v. *B. Cannon & Co. Ltd.* (1892) 19 R. 1004: C. & Co., warehousemen, agents and merchants of Glasgow and Leith, agreed with C. Ltd., of Lincoln, to act as C. Ltd.'s agents in Scotland for the sale of goods manufactured by C. Ltd., consisting of leather goods, dip and glue, for a period of five years from October 1891.

In January 1892 C. Ltd. intimated to P. & Co. its intention to give up its fancy leather trade.

Held that P. & Co. were not entitled to damages for breach of contract, because C. Ltd. had not in the agreement bound itself to carry on its business, or any part of it, for five years, or for any other period, simply for the benefit of P. & Co.

1–191   Reference was made in the opinions in this case to the decision of the House of Lords in the English case *Rhodes* v. *Forwood* (1876) 1 App. Cas. 256, in which a colliery owner, who had appointed an agent on a commission basis for seven years for the sale of coal from the colliery, was entitled, when four years later he sold the colliery, to refuse to pay further commission to the agent, the reason being that no term could be implied into the contract that the owner would not sell the colliery and so disable himself from supplying the agent with the coal for sale.

1–192   (2) *London, Leith, Edinburgh and Glasgow Shipping Co.* v. *Ferguson* (1850) 13 D. 51: In 1827 F. had been appointed agent at Greenock for the L. Shipping Co., and was paid by a commission on his transactions. He continued to hold the appointment until April 1847, when the L. Shipping Co. resolved to discontinue its trade at Greenock.

F. claimed commission up to April 1848 on the ground that it had been understood between the parties that his engagement was a yearly one and that there was a custom of trade to that effect.

Held that F., being an agent, had not been engaged from year to year as a servant would have been, and that the L. Shipping Co. was entitled to discontinue its trade whenever it saw fit, without giving prior notice or paying compensation to F.

(3) *S.S. "State of California" Co. Ltd.* v. *Moore* (1895) 22 R. 562: The State Steamship Co. Ltd. had for many years carried on a regular series of sailings between Glasgow and New York.

In 1889 certain of the shareholders agreed to form a new company, C. Ltd., for the purpose of acquiring a new steamer of modern type, and the two companies entered into an agreement by which the State Steamship Co. Ltd. would for ten years from the launching of the new steamer give that steamer her regular turn in the transatlantic service along with other steamers.

About a month after the launching of the new steamer in 1891, the State Steamship Co. Ltd. passed a resolution for winding up.

C. Ltd. claimed damages from the liquidator.

Held that the agreement between the two companies had to be interpreted as being subject to an implied condition that it was to last only so long as the State Steamship Co. Ltd. carried on its business, and that C. Ltd. was therefore not entitled to damages for breach of contract.

Further Reading

Gloag and Henderson, *Introduction to the Law of Scotland*, Chapter XXIII

David M. Walker, *Principles of Scottish Private Law*, Chapters 4.7 (part) and 4.14

David M. Walker, *The law of Contracts and related obligations in Scotland* (1979, Butterworths), Chapter 6

J.J. Gow, *The Mercantile and Industrial Law of Scotland*, Chapter 9

B.S. Markesinis and R.J.C. Munday, *An Outline of the Law of Agency* (1979, Butterworths)

G.H.L. Fridman, *Law of Agency* (5th ed., 1983, Butterworths)

Bowstead on Agency, 14th ed. by F.M.B. Reynolds and B.J. Davenport (1976, Sweet & Maxwell)

Enid A. Marshall, *Scottish Cases on Agency* (1980, W. Green & Son)

Chapter 2

PARTNERSHIP

INTRODUCTION

2–01 THE main principles of the law of partnership are to be found in the Partnership Act 1890, an Act which, for the most part, applies equally to England and Scotland. Though sometimes described as a codifying Act, it is not a complete code of partnership law (*e.g.* it does not deal with goodwill or bankruptcy). Of the aspects of partnership law which are to

44

be found in other statutes, specially noteworthy are the Limited Partnerships Act 1907 and the provisions in Part II of the Companies Act 1981 on business names.

In this chapter references to "the Act" are to the Partnership Act 1890 except where the context indicates otherwise.

The Act did not substantially alter the common law. Therefore, cases decided before 1890 may be used to illustrate the principles embodied in the Act.

Further, the Act is itself a comparatively short and simple one, and, to cover situations for which no express provision has been made, it provides that the rules of the common law applicable to partnership continue in force except so far as they are inconsistent with the express provisions of the Act (s. 46).

A partnership (or "firm") governed by the Partnership Act 1890 must be distinguished from that other important form of business organisation—the limited company registered under the Companies Acts. For legal purposes, the latter is not a "firm"—a term which, despite its colloquial use, should be reserved for a partnership. Company law is dealt with in Chapter 3, below.

The most striking practical difference between a partnership and a limited company is that the members of a partnership (with the partial exception of a limited partnership) are liable personally without any limitation of liability for the firm's debts, whereas the members of a limited company are liable only for the amount, if any, which is unpaid on their shares.

Further, the liability of the individual partners is "joint and several," so that a creditor of the firm whose debt has not been satisfied by the firm may exact full payment of the debt from any one partner, who will then be left to reimburse himself, as best he may, by claiming a *pro rata* ("proportionate") amount from his copartners. Creditors of a limited company, on the other hand, have no right to claim payment from individual shareholders.

The law of partnership draws major principles from the law of agency (the partners being agents for their firm) and from the law of cautionry (the partners guaranteeing, *i.e.* being in the position of cautioners for, the firm's debts).

Other prominent features are the fiduciary nature of the relationship between the partners (evident in the rules against secret competition with the firm's business) and the element of *delectus personae* ("choice of person"), which prevents a person from being introduced as a partner without the consent of all existing partners and enables the firm to be dissolved by notice in certain circumstances under section 32 or by the court as provided for by section 35.

Following the arrangement of the Act, the subject-matter of this chapter comes under these headings:

    I. Definition of partnership;
   II. Constitution of partnership;
  III. Separate *persona* ("personality") of the firm;
  IV. Relations of partners to persons dealing with them;
   V. Relations of partners to one another; and

VI. Termination of partnership.

2–11   There then follow three additional sections:
VII. Limited Partnerships Act 1907;
VIII. Business names; and
IX. Goodwill.

I DEFINITION OF PARTNERSHIP

2–12   "Partnership" is defined in section 1(1) of the Act as "the relation which subsists between persons carrying on a business in common with a view of profit." By section 45 of the Act the expression "business" includes every trade, occupation or profession.

2–13   If left unqualified, this definition in section 1(1) would be too wide: in particular, it would be wide enough to cover the many limited companies in which persons carry on business in common with a view of profit. Section 1(2) therefore restricts the definition quoted above by providing that the relation between members of any company or association which is:

(a) registered as a company under one of the Companies Acts; or

(b) formed or incorporated by or under any other Act of Parliament or letters patent or royal charter; or

(c) a company engaged in working mines in the Stannaries (a reference to a special jurisdiction applicable to tin mines in Devon and Cornwall) is not a partnership for the purposes of the Act.

2–14   From the definition it is apparent that there must be at least two persons before there can be a partnership. A sole trader, therefore, even though he may be trading under a name which suggests that he has business associates (*e.g.* "Andrew Brown & Sons"), is not a partnership.

2–15   An upper limit on the number of partners in a partnership is imposed by the Companies Act 1948 (s. 434), as amended by the Companies Act 1967 (s. 120): the maximum number of partners is 20, but partnerships of solicitors, of accountants and of members of a recognised stock exchange are exempt from this restriction, and the Department of Trade has power to extend the exemption to partnerships formed for other specified purposes. Where the number of persons carrying on the business exceeds 20 and no exemption applies, a company must be formed, the usual procedure being registration under the Companies Acts.

Joint Adventure

2–16   The term "joint adventure" is not defined in the Act. A joint adventure may be described as a partnership of a transient nature. It is entered into for a single "adventure" or undertaking, and is dissolved by the termination of that adventure or undertaking (s. 32).

2–17   An instance of a joint adventure occurs in *Mair* v. *Wood*, 1948 S.C. 83 (see 2–40, below): of the five partners in that joint adventure one contributed the fishing boat and its gear, while the other four contributed their services as crew.

Lord President Cooper said (at p. 86): "A joint adventure is simply a species of the genus partnership, differentiated by its limited purpose and duration (which necessarily affect the extent of the rights and liabilities flowing from the relationship), but in all other essential respects indistinguishable from any other partnership."

II CONSTITUTION OF PARTNERSHIP

The contract out of which partnership arises is a "consensual" contract, *i.e.* a contract which may be formed by mere agreement, without writing. Partnership may, therefore, be constituted by a written document ("a contract of copartnery"), or by an oral agreement, or by facts and circumstances (*e.g.* from the fact that X, Y and Z are found to be carrying on a business together and sharing its profits and losses).

The question as to whether or not a partnership exists may arise either between the alleged partners or between the alleged partners and a "third party" (an outsider). In the first of these situations, the question is decided by discovering what the intention of the alleged partners was. Where, on the other hand, there is a third party involved, he will usually be attempting to establish that there was a partnership so that he can obtain payment of a debt; in that event the question is decided by considering whether the alleged partners held themselves out to be in partnership, and the court may decide that, even where the alleged partners expressly agreed with one another that they were not to be held to be partners, a partnership was nevertheless constituted. Such a situation came before the court in *Stewart* v. *Buchanan* (1903) 6 F. 15:

Buchanan let business premises to Saunders, and supplied fittings for the premises and capital for the carrying on of the business. An agreement between Buchanan and Saunders provided that Buchanan was not to "be or be held to be a partner in the said business, or liable for its debts and obligations."

Stewart, a wine merchant, brought an action against the alleged partnership and against Saunders and Buchanan for payment of a sum for goods supplied to the business.

Held that Buchanan was liable, the agreement being regarded as merely a device to enable him to carry on the business without incurring liability for its debts.

Rules for Determining Existence of Partnership

By section 2 of the Act, in determining whether a partnership does or does not exist regard must be had to certain rules. These rules substantially re-enact an Act of 1865 on the law of partnership, known as "Bovill's Act," and are as follows:

(a) *Joint or Common Property or Tenancy, or Part Ownership*

Joint tenancy, tenancy in common, joint property, common property, or part ownership does not of itself create a partnership, whether the tenants or owners do or do not share any profits made by the use of the property.

2-22   *Sharpe* v. *Carswell*, 1910 S.C. 391: S. owned ten sixty-fourth shares of the schooner "Dolphin," and was employed as its master at a fixed remuneration.

S. died as a result of injuries sustained on board while he was in the course of his employment, and his widow claimed compensation under the Workmen's Compensation Act 1906 on the ground that he had been a "workman" in the sense of that Act.

Held that S. had been a "workman," and that the fact that he had been a part owner of the schooner had not made him a partner in its trading.

(b) *Gross Returns*

2-23   The sharing of gross returns does not of itself create a partnership, whether the persons sharing the returns have or have not a joint or common right or interest in any property from which the returns are derived.

2-24   *Clark* v. *G.R. & W. Jamieson*, 1909 S.C. 132: C. was one of two men engaged to work a small cargo boat in Shetland. His remuneration was a share of the gross earnings of the boat.

C. was drowned by an accident arising out of and in the course of his employment, and when his mother and sister claimed compensation under the Workmen's Compensation Act 1906, the question which the court had to decide was: "Had C. been a 'workman' within the meaning of the Act?"

Held that C. had been a "workman," and not a partner in a joint adventure.

(c) *Profits*

2-25   In this rule the word "profits" means net profits, *i.e.* the amount remaining after the expenses of the business have been deducted from the gross returns.

2-26   The rule is that the receipt by a person of a share of the profits of a business is *prima facie* evidence that he is a partner in the business, *i.e.* the sharing of net profits is not conclusive evidence of the existence of a partnership but is evidence of its existence unless and until the contrary is proved.

2-27   Formerly at common law the sharing of profits was regarded as conclusive evidence of partnership, but the decision of the House of Lords in the English case of *Cox* v. *Hickman* (1860) 8 H.L. Cas. 268; 11 E.R. 431, established the rule of the common law as being that parties may share profits without necessarily being partners. In that case creditors who were carrying on their bankrupt debtors' business and dividing the net profits amongst themselves in payment of the debts due to them were held not to be partners.

2-28   In accordance with the decision in *Cox* v. *Hickman*, the Act provides that the receipt of a share of the profits, or of a payment contingent on (*i.e.* dependent on) or varying with the profits of a business, does not of itself make the recipient a partner in the business. Five situations are then specified illustrating this point:

(i) Receipt by a person of a debt by instalments out of the accruing profits of a business does not of itself make him a partner in the business or liable as such.

(ii) A contract for the remuneration of a servant or agent of a person engaged in a business by a share of the profits of the business does not of itself make the servant or agent a partner in the business or liable as such.

(iii) A deceased partner's widow or child who receives as an annuity a portion of the profits made in the business in which the deceased person was a partner is not, merely because of the annuity, a partner in the business or liable as such.

(iv) Where money is lent to a person engaged in a business on a contract that the lender is to receive a rate of interest varying with the profits or is to receive a share of the profits, the lender is not, merely on that account, a partner in the business or liable as such, but so close is the relationship to partnership in this instance that the contract must be in writing and signed by or on behalf of all the parties to it; otherwise the lender would be held to be a partner.

(v) A person who has sold the goodwill of a business and receives as payment a portion of the profits is not, merely on that account, a partner in the business or liable as such.

With reference to situations (iv) and (v), above, if the person engaged in the business or the person who has purchased the goodwill becomes bankrupt, the lender or the seller of the goodwill respectively is treated as a postponed creditor, *i.e.* he will not receive any of his loan or any part of the price for the goodwill until the ordinary creditors of the bankrupt have been paid in full (which is unlikely to be the case) (s. 3).

III SEPARATE *PERSONA* OF THE FIRM

Section 4(1) of the Act provides that persons who have entered into partnership with one another are called collectively a firm, and the name under which their business is carried on is called the firm-name.

Section 4(2), which applies to Scotland only, preserves a fundamental principle of the common law of partnership in Scotland dating from the seventeenth century: "In Scotland a firm is a legal person distinct from the partners of whom it is composed." It is this provision which is the source of most of the distinctive rules in the Scots law of partnership.

A firm is not, however, a full corporation, as a limited company is. A firm has no royal charter, nor has it been incorporated by special Act of Parliament or registered under the Companies Acts. It may be formed and dissolved by mere agreement of its members, and, unless there is agreement to the contrary, is dissolved by the death or bankruptcy of any partner (s. 33). "It is a quasi corporation, possessing many, but not all the privileges which law confers upon a duly constituted corporation" (*per* Lord Medwyn in *Forsyth* v. *Hare and Co.* (1834) 13 S. 42, at p. 47).

Some consequences of the doctrine of the separate *persona* ("personality") of the firm, as well as some of the limitations on that personality are indicated in the following paragraphs. For a fuller description reference may be made to the opinion of Lord Medwyn in *Forsyth* v. *Hare and Co.* (1834) 13 S. 42, at p. 46, and to that of Lord President Cooper in *Mair* v. *Wood,* 1948 S.C. 83, at p. 86.

(a) **Firm as Debtor or Creditor to Partners**

2–34   A firm may stand in the relation of debtor or creditor to any of its partners, and may sue a partner or be sued by a partner.

(b) **Contracts**

2–35   A firm may enter into contracts with third parties, the individual partners acting as agents and the firm being in the position of principal.

2–36   In accordance with the usual principle of agency, the firm as principal is entitled to sue the third party and is liable to be sued by the third party, while the individual partner who acted as the firm's agent is neither entitled to sue nor liable to be sued.

2–37   However, since the individual partners are in the last resort liable jointly and severally for the firm's debts (s. 9), any one partner may be held liable by the third party after, but only after, the debt has been constituted against the firm and has not been paid by the firm. The individual partners are liable only *subsidiarie* ("subsidiarily"), and not primarily. They stand in the position of cautioners for the firm, liable to pay only where the firm as principal debtor has itself failed to do so. The Act provides that an individual partner may be charged on a decree or diligence directed against the firm, and on payment of the debts is entitled to relief *pro rata* ("proportionately") from the firm and its other members (s. 4(2)).

(c) **Delicts**

2–38   A firm may be the victim of a delict (civil wrong) or may itself commit a delict. A claim for damages may then be made in an action by or against the firm.

2–39   In *Gordon* v. *British and Foreign Metaline Co. &c.* (1886) 14 R. 75, an action for damages for judicial slander, the court held that a firm, despite the fact that its personality is artificial, could be guilty of malice.

2–40   A firm is, however, not liable to one of its partners who has suffered an injury as a result of a delict committed by another partner:

Mair v. *Wood*, 1948 S.C. 83: M. was one of five partners in a share-fishing joint adventure.

When the boat was at sea, the propeller was fouled, and, to clear the obstruction, the skipper, who was one of the five partners, removed the engine-room floor boards. Before the boards were replaced, M., on descending to the engine-room, put his foot through the opening and was seriously injured.

Held that the firm was not liable to M. for the skipper's negligence.

(d) **Property**

2–41   A firm may own heritable and moveable property. Partnership property must be held and applied exclusively for partnership purposes (s. 20(1)), and not treated by the partners as their own personal property.

2–42   Partners do not own even a share of partnership property: their interest in the property is an indirect one—to a share of the surplus of assets over liabilities when the affairs of the partnership are wound up. This share is moveable property, even although the firm's property is partly or wholly heritable (s. 22)—a point of practical importance in the law of succession on death and in the law of diligence: a deceased partner's share of the firm property will be subject to the legal rights of *jus relictae, jus relicti* and legitim which can be claimed by widow, widower and children respectively out of the deceased's moveable (but not heritable) estate, and the appropriate diligence for a creditor who wishes to attach a partner's share of the partnership property for debt is arrestment in the hands of the firm, *i.e.* the diligence used where moveable property is not in the debtor's own possession but in that of a third party.

Exceptionally, the formal legal title to heritable property held on feudal tenure cannot be taken in the firm-name: it is taken by the partners, or some of them, as trustees for the firm. The formal title to all other property, including leases, may be either in the firm-name or in the name of partners as trustees for the firm.

(e) **Compensation**

Where a question arises as to whether one debt may be wholly or partly set off against another so that the first debt is wholly or partly extinguished, effect is given to the separate personality of a firm by the rule that a partner is not a creditor in a debt due to the firm. Therefore, for instance, if X owes the firm A, B & Co. £5,000, and A, one of the partners in A, B & Co., owes X £1,000, and X brings an action against A for £1,000, A cannot plead compensation of the debt which X owes to the firm. Similarly, if in the same circumstances an action were to be brought by the firm against X for £5,000, X could not plead compensation of the debt of £1,000 due to him by A.

On the other hand, because of the ultimate liability of an individual partner for the debts of the firm, a partner is, for the purposes of compensation, treated as a debtor in a debt due by his firm. If, therefore, the firm A, B & Co. owes X £5,000 and X owes the individual partner A £1,000, and A brings an action against X for £1,000, X can plead compensation of the debt which the firm owes to him.

(f) **Bankruptcy**

A firm may become bankrupt without any of the partners becoming bankrupt, and conversely individual partners may become bankrupt while the firm remains solvent.

However, because individual partners are ultimately liable without any limitation of liability for the debts of the firm, concurrent bankruptcies of firm and individual partners are common. In such a situation, a creditor of the firm who obtains a dividend of so much in the £ from the firm's bankrupt estate can obtain a dividend on the balance from the individual partner's bankrupt estate. The rule against double ranking prevents the creditor from obtaining a dividend on the full amount from both estates.

IV RELATIONS OF PARTNERS TO PERSONS DEALING WITH THEM

The relations of partners to persons dealing with them are described below under two headings:

(a) liability for a firm's debts; and

(b) effect of change in a firm on contracts.

2–49   Partners may, in their contract of copartnery, make provision for the conduct of the firm's external relations. Any such provisions will be binding as amongst the partners themselves, but are not allowed to override the provisions of the Act which are designed to protect third parties (the outsiders).

(a) **Liability for a Firm's Debts**

2–50   Principles of the law of agency and of the law of cautionry operate here.

2–51   The first question which presents itself is whether the firm itself is liable for a debt incurred or obligation undertaken by a partner. In answering this question the principles of the law of agency are applied, the partner being the agent of the firm and the firm being the principal. The partner is said to be *praepositus negotiis societatis* ("placed in charge of the affairs of the partnership"). Further consideration is given to this question under the heading "Authority of Partners and Others to Bind the Firm," below.

2–52   The second question arising is whether the person dealing with the firm is entitled to hold individual partners or other persons liable for the firm's debts. In answering this question principles of the law of cautionry are applied, individual partners being in the position of cautioners for the firm's debts, liable to pay if the firm itself fails to do so. The leading provision is in section 9: all partners are liable jointly and severally for all the firm's debts and obligations incurred during the partnership. This enables a third party to hold any individual partner liable for the firm's debts and obligations once there has been failure on the firm's part. That partner will then have a right of relief against the other partners, but, if they are bankrupt, that right may be of little value.

2–53   The liability of incoming and outgoing partners requires special consideration, and in certain circumstances a person who is not a partner may be liable on the principle of "holding out."

Authority of Partners and Others to Bind the Firm

Implied mandate of partners

2–54   Section 5 of the Act provides that every partner is an agent of the firm and of his other partners for the purposes of the business of the partnership, and then sets out the rule to be applied where the partners have agreed among themselves to limit a partner's authority to some extent: the acts of every partner who does any act for carrying on in the usual way business of the kind carried on by the firm bind the firm and his partners, *unless*:

(i)   the partner so acting has in fact no authority to act for the firm in the particular matter; *and*

(ii) the person with whom he is dealing *either* knows that he has no authority, *or* does not know or believe him to be a partner.

This gives the third party protection against any secret limitations on a partner's authority.

2–55   The implied mandate or authority conferred on each partner by section 5 is restricted to acts "for carrying on in the usual way business of the kind carried on by the firm." For acts beyond that scope the firm will not be bound unless the partner had express authority.

In applying section 5 one must take into account not only the nature of the firm's business but also the way in which the partner has been acting.

For instance, if the firm is a mercantile or trading firm, each of the partners has an implied mandate to borrow money on behalf of the firm, with the result that the firm will be liable to repay the loan to the lender. Thus, in *Bryan* v. *Butters Brothers & Co.* (1892) 19 R. 490, where a firm of contractors, engineers and machinery merchants in Glasgow was sued by the wife of one of its partners for repayment of a loan which she had made through her husband to the firm, the firm was held liable.

Again, in *Ciceri* v. *Hunter & Co.* (1904) 12 S.L.T. 293 (O.H.), the circumstances were that S. and H. had entered into a copartnery to carry on a business of hotelkeepers in Edinburgh under the name of "H. & Co.," H. having the sole control of the business and S. not being bound to give personal attention, though he had the right to be consulted on all matters of importance.

H. instructed C. to make a revaluation of the furnishings for the purposes of the firm's balance-sheet. Before C.'s fee had been paid, H. and H. & Co. became bankrupt.

Held that C. was entitled to recover his fee from S., the solvent partner, because in instructing the revaluation H. had acted within the scope of his mandate as managing partner and so the firm, and not merely H., was bound.

The Act has further provisions relating to a partner's implied mandate in sections 15 and 16: an admission or representation made by any partner concerning the partnership affairs, and in the ordinary course of its business, is evidence against the firm (s. 15); and notice to any partner who habitually acts in the partnership business of any matter relating to partnership affairs operates as notice to the firm, except in the case of a fraud on the firm committed by or with the consent of that partner (s. 16).

Cases decided before the Act may also be used to illustrate a partner's implied mandate: *e.g.* in *Nisbet* v. *Neil's Trustee* (1869) 7 M. 1097, a letter which was holograph of (*i.e.* written wholly in the handwriting of) a partner was held to be holograph of the firm, because the partner was entitled to bind the firm.

Acts on firm's behalf

Persons other than partners may also have authority to deal with third parties on behalf of the firm, but such persons have no implied mandate: the third party must be on his guard to see that they have in fact authority. Section 6 provides that an act or document relating to the business of the firm done or signed in the firm-name, or in any other way which shows an intention to bind the firm, by any person authorised to do so, whether a partner or not, is binding on the firm and all the partners. This provision does not affect the general rules of law as to the execution of deeds (formal legal documents) or negotiable instruments (*e.g.* cheques and other bills of exchange).

2–62   A partner may have been given special authority by the other partners
to act on the firm's behalf in some way which would not be covered by the
implied authority with which section 5 is concerned. It is for the third
party to satisfy himself that the partner does in fact have that special
authority: otherwise the third party will have to rely on the personal
liability of the partner. Section 7 provides that where one partner pledges
the credit of the firm for a purpose apparently not connected with the
firm's ordinary course of business, the firm is not bound, unless he is in
fact specially authorised by the other partners.

Agreed restriction on partner's authority

2–63   Where partners agree that some restriction be placed on the power
of any one or more of them to bind the firm, the agreement is binding on
the partners *inter se* ("amongst themselves"), and also on third parties
who have notice of (*i.e.* know of) it (s. 8), but it does not affect other third
parties.

2–64   Where the circumstances are such that the third party ought to suspect
that the partner is contravening some restriction on his authority, the firm
is not bound:

Paterson Brothers v. *Gladstone* (1891) 18 R. 403: The firm of P.
Brothers, builders and joiners in Edinburgh, had three partners, Robert,
William and John. The contract of copartnery provided that William
should have full charge of the financial affairs of the firm and be the only
partner to sign the firm's name on financial documents.

Robert signed the firm's name on certain promissory notes in favour of
G., a moneylender, discounted them with G. at the rate of 40 per cent.
and fraudulently applied the proceeds to his own use.

Held that the firm was not liable to pay the promissory notes: G. ought
to have suspected that a partner in such a firm would not have authority to
raise money in this way for the firm.

Liability of the Firm for Wrongs

2–65   The main rule relating to liability of a firm for wrongs is in section 10:
where, by any wrongful act or omission of any partner acting in the
ordinary course of the business of the firm, or with the authority of his
copartners, loss or injury is caused to any person who is not a partner, or
any penalty is incurred, the firm is liable to the same extent as the partner
who has been guilty of the act or omission.

2–66   All the partners are jointly and severally liable to third parties for the
firm's wrongs (s. 12), though as between the partners themselves an
innocent partner is entitled to be relieved by the guilty partner.

2–67   *Kirkintilloch Equitable Co-operative Society Ltd.* v. *Livingstone and
Others*, 1972 S.C. 111, gives an illustration of the application of sections
10 and 12 in a case of alleged professional negligence:

A partner in a firm of chartered accountants had acted as auditor of an
industrial and provident society from 1952 to 1967, his audit fee being
paid to the firm.

After the dissolution of the firm in 1967, the society brought an action
of damages for professional negligence based on alleged errors in the
audited accounts.

Held that the society was entitled to sue not only the auditor but also his copartners.

Where the wrong for which a firm is being sued is fraud, the names of the partners who are alleged to have committed the fraud must be specified, because fraud is regarded as always personal (*Thomson & Co.* v. *Pattison, Elder & Co.* (1895) 22 R. 432).

It is, however, no objection to an action against a firm for a wrong that malice must be proved (*Gordon* v. *British and Foreign Metaline Co. &c.* (1886) 14 R. 75 (2–39, above)).

A firm cannot be made liable to one partner for the fault of another partner (*Mair* v. *Wood*, 1948 S.C. 83 (2–40, above)): section 10 is concerned only with wrongs done to a person who is not a partner.

Misapplication by partner of third party's money or property

Section 11 makes specific provision for two cases where a partner has misapplied money or property belonging to a third party: the firm is liable to make good the loss to the third party where either:

(i) a partner acting within the scope of his apparent authority receives the third party's money or property and misapplies it; or

(ii) the firm in the course of its business receives the third party's money or property and it is misapplied by one or more of the partners while it is in the custody of the firm.

Improper employment of trust property for partnership purposes

Section 13 provides that if a partner who is a trustee in a trust improperly employs trust-property in the business or on the account of the partnership, no other partner is liable for the trust-property to the beneficiaries in the trust. This provision does not, however, affect any liability incurred by another partner who has notice of (*i.e.* knows of) the breach of trust, and it does not prevent trust-money from being followed and recovered from the firm if it is still in the firm's possession or under the firm's control.

Liability of Incoming Partner

A person who is admitted as a partner into an existing firm does not thereby become liable to the creditors of the firm for anything done before he became a partner (s. 17(1)).

An incoming partner may, however, incur liability for pre-existing debts, either through an agreement made between the new firm and the creditor (amounting to delegation—the substitution, with the creditor's consent, of a new debtor for the original debtor) or because the circumstances show that the new firm has taken over the liabilities of the former firm (involving *jus quaesitum tertio* ("right conferred on a third party"), arising from the express or implied agreement between the partners of the new firm).

Circumstances which made an incoming partner liable for pre-existing debts are exemplified in the three following cases:

(i) *Miller* v. *Thorburn* (1861) 23 D. 359: D., a jeweller in Dumfries, obtained a cash credit from a bank to pay for stock-in-trade and to carry on his business.

Some years later he took his son, John, into partnership. John brought no capital to the business.

The following year D. died, and the firm's estate was sequestrated.

T., a cautioner under the cash credit bond, paid to the bank the balance of £225 due on the cash account, and then claimed to be ranked as a creditor for that amount in the firm's sequestration.

Held that he was entitled to be so ranked.

Lord Cowan said (at p. 362): "In the general case where the whole estate of a company is given over to and taken possession of by a new concern or partnership, the business being continued on the same footing, the estate goes to the new company *suo onere* [literally, 'with its own burden']—that is, the liabilities go along with the effects. . . . This is the general presumption, although there may be special circumstances in particular cases not admitting of its application."

2–77   (ii) *Heddle's Executrix* v. *Marwick & Hourston's Trustee* (1888) 15 R. 698: M., the owner of a long-established general merchant's business in Kirkwall, took H., the manager of it, into partnership. There was no written contract of copartnery, H. contributed no capital, and the business was carried on as before.

Held that the firm was liable for a pre-existing trade debt which had been contracted by M.

Lord Shand said (at p. 709): "It must always be a question of circumstances whether a new firm becomes responsible for the obligations of the old. On the one hand, if an old-established firm, consisting of one or two partners, arranges to take in a clerk and give him a future share of the profits, or if one of the partners has a son who has just come of age and is taken into the business, and they arrange to give him a share of the profits of the new firm thereby constituted, it appears to me that, if the new firm takes over the stock in trade and the book debts and whole business of the old firm and the goodwill of that business, equity requires that they shall take over its obligations. . . . On the other hand, if a partner comes into a business, paying in a large sum of capital, and the other partners merely put in their shares of a going business as their shares of the capital, a different question might arise. In such a case as that, probably some special circumstances would require to be proved in order to impose liability on the new partner for transactions entered into prior to the date when he became a partner. Then, again, intermediate cases will occur between these two classes. In all of them I think it must be a question of circumstances, to be determined by the Court upon the facts, whether there has been liability undertaken, or adoption of the debt of the old firm."

2–78   (iii) *Miller* v. *MacLeod*, 1973 S.C. 172: In 1955 MacL., a solicitor practising on his own account, undertook the winding up of a large and involved executry estate. Owing to ill health he was unable to attend to his business regularly and his books and accounts got into a state of disorder.

In April 1958 MacL. entered into partnership with Parker, who knew that the financial state of the business was precarious. No agreement was made as to how much, if any, capital Parker would contribute, and the partnership took over and continued MacL.'s business without fresh instructions from clients.

In June 1958 MacL. died, and in 1959 Parker entered into partnership with Piacentini, and the new partnership continued to carry on the business including the winding up of the executry.

In 1962 the executrix, claiming that £10,000 was due to her, raised an action against (1) the firm, (2) Parker, (3) Piacentini and (4) MacL.'s executrix. She sued for (first) an accounting against all four defenders jointly and severally for the period from 1955 to MacL.'s death in June 1958 and (second) an accounting against the first, second and third defenders jointly and severally for the period from MacL.'s death to 1962.

The firm and the partners denied that they were liable to make an accounting for any period before April 1958.

Held that the proper inference from the circumstances was that the firm and its members had accepted the liabilities attaching to the business including liability to account for the period before April 1958.

A contrasting case is *Thomson & Balfour* v. *Boag & Son,* 1936 S.C. 2:

B., a joiner, assumed his foreman as a partner. The foreman contributed £340 as capital, and there was an agreement between the partners that B. should realise debts due to him and pay debts due by him in connection with his own business.

Held that neither the partnership nor the foreman was liable for debts incurred when B. had been in business on his own account.

Lord President Normand, referring to the earlier cases, said (at p. 10): 'It is a settled principle of law that, when the whole assets of a going concern are handed over to a new partnership and the business is continued on the same footing as before, the presumption is that the liabilities are taken over with the stock. . . . The principle is that it would be inequitable to allow a trader to injure his trade creditors by assuming a partner and handing over his whole trading assets to the new partnership without liability to pay the trade debts. But this presumption must not be extended beyond the circumstances to which it properly applies.''

Liability of Retired Partner

A distinction must be made between:
  (i) debts incurred before retirement; and
  (ii) debts incurred after retirement.

i) Debts incurred before retirement

A partner who retires from a firm does not thereby cease to be liable for partnership debts or obligations incurred before his retirement (s. 17(2)).

A retiring partner may be discharged from any existing liability by an agreement to that effect between himself and the members of the firm as newly constituted and the creditors; this agreement may be either express or inferred from the course of dealing between the creditors and the firm as newly constituted (s. 17(3)).

An agreement amongst the partners themselves does not affect the right of creditors to hold the retiring partner liable. This is in accordance with the general rule of the law of contract that delegation (the substitution of a new debtor) requires the consent of the creditor.

(ii) Debts incurred after retirement

2–83   The liability of a retired partner for debts of the firm incurred after his retirement rests on the principle of "holding out," a form of personal bar. So far as the rights of creditors are concerned, the question is not what the partners themselves have agreed on, but whether the creditors have been properly notified of the retirement.

2–84   Section 36(1) provides that where a person deals with a firm after a change in its constitution he is entitled to treat all apparent members of the old firm as still being members of the firm until he has notice of the change. The effect of this is that customers of the business must be individually notified of the retirement of a partner; otherwise they may hold the retired partner liable for future transactions with the new firm; an advertisement will not be sufficient unless the customer can be proved to have read it.

2–85   As regards persons who have not had dealings with the firm, an advertisement in the Gazette (*i.e.* the *Edinburgh Gazette* if the principal place of business is in Scotland, or the *London Gazette* if the principal place of business is in England or Wales) is sufficient (s. 36(2)).

2–86   As these rules are based on the principle of holding out, a retired partner who has not been known to the person dealing with the firm to be a partner, is not liable for debts contracted after his retirement whether proper notice has been given or not (s. 36(3)).

2–87   The estate of a partner who dies, or who becomes bankrupt, is also not liable for partnership debts contracted after the death or bankruptcy, these being regarded as public or notorious events (s. 36(3)).

2–88   A well-known English case involving section 36(3) as well as other provisions of the Act is *Tower Cabinet Co. Ltd.* v. *Ingram* [1949] 2 K.B. 397:

In 1946 Ingram and Christmas began to carry on business in partnership as household furnishers under the name of Merry's. By agreement the partnership was dissolved in April 1947. Ingram gave notice of the dissolution to the firm's bankers and arranged with Christmas to notify those dealing with Merry's that Ingram had ceased to be connected with it. No advertisement was put in the *London Gazette*.

In January 1948 T. Ltd., which had not had previous dealings with Merry's, received an order for furniture from it. Without Ingram's knowledge that order was confirmed by Christmas on old headed notepaper bearing Ingram's name.

T. Ltd. sought to hold Ingram liable.

Held that (1) Ingram had not knowingly suffered himself to be represented as a partner in Merry's, and so was not liable on the ground of "holding out" (s. 14(1)) (see 2–89, below); (2) he was not liable as an "apparent" member under section 36(1) because the phrase "apparent members" in that provision meant members who were apparently members to the person who was dealing with the firm; and (3) he was protected from liability by section 36(3) because he had not been known to T. Ltd. as a partner before the dissolution of the firm.

Liability by "Holding Out"

A person who is not in fact a partner may be liable for the firm's debts on the principle of "holding out," which is one of the forms of personal bar. The person holding himself out as a partner, or allowing others to do so, may be, for instance, an employee in the business, or a retired partner of whose retirement proper notification has not been given. Section 14(1) provides that every one who by words, spoken or written, or by conduct, represents himself or knowingly suffers himself to be represented as a partner in a particular firm is liable as a partner to any one who has on the faith of that representation given credit to the firm.

An illustration of holding out occurs in *Hosie* v. *Waddell* (1866) 3 S.L.R. 16:

H., when suing W. for a debt, was met by the defence that W. had paid the debt to C., whom he believed to be H.'s partner.

H. maintained that C. had never been his partner, but only manager of the business.

Held that, in the circumstances of the case, C. had been held out as a partner, that W. had made payment of the debt to C. in the *bona fide* belief that C. was a partner, and that therefore payment to C. was good payment.

Where after a partner's death the partnership business is continued in the old firm-name, the continued use of that name or of the deceased partner's name as part of it does not of itself make the deceased's estate liable for partnership debts contracted after the death (s. 14(2)).

(b) Effect of Change in a Firm on Contracts

The Act does not contain any general provision as to the effect which a change in the membership of a firm has on existing and continuing contracts of the firm. The rule of the common law, therefore, remains applicable, that only contracts involving *delectus personae* ("choice of person") will be terminated.

Where, however, there is not merely a change in the membership of the firm, but the conversion of the firm into a registered company, the company is not a party to the contracts of the firm whose business it has taken over (*Grierson, Oldham & Co. Ltd.* v. *Forbes, Maxwell & Co. Ltd.* (1895) 22 R. 812, in which the company G., O. & Co. Ltd., which was continuing the wine business of the firm G., O. & Co., was held to have no title to sue for implement of a contract by which F. Ltd. had undertaken to pay a rent to the firm for a space in the firm's advertising wine-list for a period of three years).

The Act makes express provision for only one type of contract—cautionary obligations (guarantees). Section 18 provides that a continuing cautionary obligation is, in the absence of agreement to the contrary, revoked as to future transactions by a change in a firm where either:

(i) the cautionary obligation has been given to the firm, *i.e.* the firm is the creditor; or

(ii) the cautionary obligation has been given in respect of the firm's transactions, *i.e.* the firm is the principal debtor.

V RELATIONS OF PARTNERS TO ONE ANOTHER

2–95   Two general principles operate in the relations of partners *inter se* ("amongst themselves"). The first of these is that the contract out of which partnership arises is a contract involving *delectus personae* ("choice of person"): the personal qualities of a partner are important to his copartners. The second general principle is the fiduciary character of the relationship: the partners must act in good faith towards each other, making full disclosure of all matters affecting the partnership to their copartners and not seeking to obtain a personal gain in contravention of the partnership agreement.

2–96   These two general principles can be seen to underlie the specific provisions of the Act regulating the relations of partners to one another.

2–97   Another general point is that partners are free to make such agreement as they choose concerning their relations to one another. The agreement may be a written contract of copartnery, or an oral agreement, or an agreement implied by conduct. The partners are also free to agree on variation of their relations from time to time. The provisions of the Act governing relations between the partners themselves apply only where no different provisions have been made by the partners' own agreement. This is in contrast to the provisions of the Act governing relations of partners to persons dealing with them, considered above. Section 19 provides that the mutual rights and duties of partners, whether ascertained by agreement or defined by the Act, may be varied by the consent of all the partners, and such consent may be either express or inferred from a course of dealing.

Partnership Property

2–98   The term "partnership property" is defined in section 20(1) as meaning "all property and rights and interests in property originally brought into the partnership stock or acquired, whether by purchase or otherwise, on account of the firm, or for the purposes and in the course of the partnership business."

2–99   Partnership property belongs to the firm as a separate legal person from the partners, but, since the personality of the firm is artificial, partnership property is in the actual hands of and is managed by the partners, who must not, however, treat it, or even a share of it, as their own personal property. Section 20(1) provides that partnership property must be held and applied by the partners exclusively for the purposes of the partnership, and in accordance with the partnership agreement.

2–100   The formal legal title to partnership property may be either in the name of the firm or in the name of individual partners, with the one exception of the formal legal title to heritable property held on feudal tenure: this cannot be taken in the firm-name; usually it will be in the name of two or more of the partners as trustees for the firm.

2–101   One of the rules for determining the existence of partnership is, as was mentioned above (2–21), that joint property, common property, or part ownership does not of itself create a partnership, whether the owners do or do not share any profits made by the use of the property (s. 2). It is also possible, however, that persons may be co-owners of heritable property and be partners as to the profits made by the use of that property without the property being partnership property. For such a situation section 20(3) provides that if the co-owners purchase other heritable property out of the profits for the purpose of using that other property in the same way, then, in the absence of agreement to the contrary, that other property belongs to them, not as partners, but as co-owners.

Disputes may arise as to whether property in the possession or in the name of an individual partner is partnership property or his own personal property. There is an instance of such a dispute in *Munro* v. *Stein*, 1961 S.C. 362 (O.H.), in which Lord Wheatley (Ordinary) held that (i) it was competent to prove by parole evidence that a dance hall was partnership property, and (ii) on the evidence the dance hall had been proved to be such. Section 21 provides that, unless the contrary intention appears, property bought with money belonging to the firm is deemed to have been bought on account of the firm.

It follows from the firm's separate personality that where heritable property has become partnership property, it must, unless the contrary intention appears, be treated as between the partners (including the representatives of a deceased partner) as moveable and not as heritable property (s. 22).

Rights of Partners

Section 24 sets out nine rules as to the interests of partners in the partnership property and as to their rights and duties in relation to the partnership. These rules are all "subject to any agreement express or implied between the partners."

(1) All the partners are entitled to share equally in the capital and profits of the business, and must contribute equally towards the losses, whether of capital or otherwise, sustained by the firm.

(2) The firm must indemnify every partner for payments made and personal liabilities incurred by him:

    (a) in the ordinary and proper business of the firm; or

    (b) in or about anything necessarily done for preservation of the business or property of the firm.

(3) A partner making, for the purpose of the partnership, any actual payment or advance beyond the amount of capital which he has agreed to subscribe, is entitled to interest at five per cent. from the date of the payment or advance.

(4) A partner is not entitled, before the ascertainment of profits, to interest on the capital subscribed by him.

(5) Every partner may take part in the management of the partnership business.

(6) No partner is entitled to remuneration for acting in the partnership business.

(7) No person may be introduced as a partner without the consent of all existing partners.

(8) Any difference arising as to ordinary matters connected with the partnership business may be decided by a majority of the partners, but no change may be made in the nature of the partnership business without the consent of all existing partners.

(9) The partnership books must be kept at the principal place of business of the partnership, and every partner may, when he thinks fit, have access to and inspect and copy any of them.

2–105   Partners may have a right to expel one of their number, but such a right requires an express provision in the contract of copartnery. Section 25 provides: "No majority of the partners can expel any partner unless a power to do so has been conferred by express agreement between the partners."

Partnership at Will

2–106   A partnership at will exists in either of two situations: (a) where there never has been any time fixed for the duration of the partnership, and (b) where the partnership was originally for a fixed period and has been continued after the expiry of that period without any express new agreement. In the second situation there is said to be "tacit relocation" ("silent renewal").

2–107   It is of the essence of a partnership at will that it may be brought to an end by notice given by any partner. This follows from the *delectus personae* inherent in partnership.

2–108   With reference to situation (a), the Act provides that where no fixed term has been agreed upon for the duration of a partnership, any partner may terminate the partnership at any time on giving notice of his intention to do so to all the other partners (s. 26(1)). If the partnership has originally been constituted by deed (a formal legal document such as a contract of copartnery signed by the partners in the presence of witnesses), a notice in writing, signed by the partner giving it, is sufficient to terminate the partnership (s. 26(2)). The firm will be dissolved as from the date mentioned in the notice as the date of dissolution, or, if no date is mentioned, as from the date of the communication of the notice (s. 32).

2–109   With reference to situation (b), the Act provides that where a partnership entered into for a fixed term is continued after the term has expired, and without any express new agreement, the rights and duties of the partners remain the same as they were at the expiration of the term, so far as is consistent with the incidents of a partnership at will (s. 27(1)). A continuance of the business by the partners, or by those partners who have been habitually acting in the business during the original term, without any settlement or liquidation of the partnership affairs, is presumed to be a continuance of the partnership (s. 27(2)).

2–110   Difficulties can arise as to whether or not a particular clause in the original agreement is "consistent with the incidents of a partnership at will," so that it is carried over into the partnership at will under section 27(1). Two contrasting cases may be referred to by way of illustration:

2–111   *Neilson* v. *Mossend Iron Co. &c.* (1886) 13 R. (H.L.) 50: A contract of copartnery for a period of seven years contained a clause stipulating that any partner was to have the option of being bought out by his copartners on condition that he gave notice of his desire to exercise that option "three months before the termination of this contract."

Held that this clause had not been carried forward into the partnership at will which had commenced at the end of the seven-year period.

Lord Watson said (at p. 56): "The condition and the rights and obligations arising out of it are totally inapplicable to a contract-at-will. They have plain reference to a fixed *punctum temporis* ['point of time'], the termination of the original contract; but how are they to be applied to a contract which has no definite currency? Time is of the essence of the condition, but a contract-at-will affords no terminus from which it can be measured or computed."

McGown v. *Henderson,* 1914 S.C. 839: H., M. and C. entered into a contract of copartnery to carry on a business as wine and spirit merchants for a period of five years. The contract contained a pre-emption clause giving to H., as holder of the licence, the option, at the expiry of the five years, to pay out to M. and C. the amount due to them.

After the expiry of the five years, the partnership continued for several years as a partnership at will. H. then terminated the partnership by notice and claimed the right to exercise the option conferred by the pre-emption clause.

Held that H. was entitled to do so, there being nothing to prevent the pre-emption clause from being carried forward into the partnership at will.

Fiduciary Character of Partnership

The fiduciary character of partnership underlies the duties of partners to one another set out in sections 28, 29 and 30 of the Act:

(a) *Duty to Render Accounts and Information (s. 28)*

Partners are bound to render true accounts and full information of all things affecting the partnership to any partner or his legal representatives.

(b) *Accountability for Private Profits (s. 29)*

Every partner must account to the firm for any benefit derived by him without the consent of the other partners from any transaction concerning the partnership, or from any use by him of the partnership property, name, or business connection.

This section applies also to transactions undertaken after a partnership has been dissolved by the death of a partner, and before its affairs have been completely wound up, either by any surviving partner or by the representatives of the deceased partner.

(c) *Duty not to Compete with Firm (s. 30)*

If a partner, without the consent of the other partners, carries on any business of the same nature as and competing with that of the firm, he must account for and pay over to the firm all profits made by him in that business.

The following three cases illustrate these fiduciary duties:

(i) *McNiven* v. *Peffers* (1868) 7 M. 181: M. and P. were partners in a wine and spirit business which was carried on in leased premises. P. was sole manager of the business, and the lease was in his name.

Shortly before the lease was due to expire, P. entered into negotiations with the landlord which resulted in P.'s obtaining a renewal of the lease for himself. M. was not informed of these proceedings.

Held that P. was bound to share with M. the profits of the business carried on under the new lease.

Lord Justice-Clerk Patton said (at p. 186): "It appears to me perfectly plain that a partner, and especially a managing partner, who goes to the landlord, and, behind the back of his partner, obtains from the landlord a new lease of the partnership premises, is not entitled to retain the profits of that lease for himself. . . .

". . . It follows, as the natural result of the plainest principles of equity applied to such a case, that a partner so acting must communicate the benefit of the lease so obtained to the copartnery, the interests of which he was bound to have attended to. The effect of refusing the remedy would be that a valuable interest in the copartnery, that of goodwill, would be destroyed, and a private benefit secured by an act grossly wrong in itself."

2–120   (ii) *Stewart* v. *North* (1893) 20 R. 260: In 1876 North obtained from a municipal council in Peru a concession of the exclusive right to supply the town with piped drinking water, and in 1877 he entered into a contract of joint adventure with Speedie and Cockburn for the purpose of carrying out the work.

In 1878, after the work had begun, North, partly by means of the concession, obtained for himself a lease of property belonging to the T. Water Company, which was then supplying stored fresh water to the town. North then stopped the work of the joint adventure, and, in partnership with Speedie, continued the business of the T. Water Company. Cockburn knew of these proceedings, but took no action.

In 1885 Cockburn became bankrupt, and in 1887 his interest in the joint adventure was assigned by his trustee to Stewart.

Stewart brought an action of accounting against North, claiming that the profits derived from the lease of the T. Water Company's property belonged to the joint adventure.

Held that (1) Cockburn would have been entitled to a share of these profits because (a) the business being carried on covered the same ground as that of the joint adventure and (b) North had used the joint adventure's property (the concession) to obtain the lease, but (2) the claim was barred by lapse of time.

Lord Adam said (at p. 270): "I think that where a partner is not bound by a contract entered into by a copartner, but is entitled and desires to have the benefit of it, he must make his claim without delay. He is not entitled to lie by in order to see whether the contract turns out a profitable one or not. If he is to have the benefit he must be prepared to run the risk of loss."

2–121   (iii) *Pillans Brothers and Others* v. *Pillans* (1908) 16 S.L.T. 611 (O.H.): In 1905 three brothers, Alexander, John and Richard, arranged to become partners in carrying on business as rivet, bolt and nut manufacturers in Motherwell and elsewhere.

The following year, Richard purchased a rivet, bolt and nut manufacturing business at Greenfield, about four miles from Motherwell.

Held that (1) there was a subsisting partnership when the Greenfield works were acquired; (2) that business had to be regarded as having been acquired for the firm; and (3) Richard was therefore bound to account to the firm and his brothers for the profits made at Greenfield.

Assignation of Share in Partnership

Because of the *delectus personae* inherent in partnership, no partner may, without the consent of his copartners, assign his interest in the partnership with the effect of making the assignee a partner in the firm.

A partner may assign his share in the partnership, either absolutely or by way of security, but this does not of itself change the constitution of the partnership: the assigning partner (the cedent) remains a partner, and the assignee does not become a partner.

During the continuance of the partnership, the assignee is not entitled, as against the other partners, to interfere in the management of the business, or to require any accounts of the partnership transactions, or to inspect the partnership books; he is entitled only to receive the share of profits to which the cedent would otherwise be entitled, and the assignee must accept the account of profits agreed to by the partners (including the cedent) (s. 31(1)). On the dissolution of the partnership, the assignee is entitled to receive the share of the partnership assets to which the cedent is entitled as between himself and the other partners, and, for the purpose of ascertaining that share, the assignee is entitled to an account as from the date of the dissolution (s. 31(2)).

VI TERMINATION OF PARTNERSHIP

The relationship of partnership may be brought to an end by:
  (a) rescission; or
  (b) dissolution.

Rescission involves the reduction (setting aside) of the contract out of which the partnership has arisen, and *restitutio in integrum* ("restoration to the original position"). It is governed mainly by the rules of the common law relating to the invalidity of contracts.

Dissolution is the ending of a relationship which is regarded as having validly subsisted for some time. It results in a winding up of the partnership affairs, including apportionment of the final balance amongst the individual partners according to their rights and obligations in the contract of copartnery. The main rules relating to dissolution and its consequences are set out in the Act.

A point of contrast between the law of partnership and company law is that, whereas in the former dissolution (the termination of the relationship) is followed by winding up, in the latter winding up precedes dissolution (*i.e.* the company continues in existence as a legal person until the winding-up (or liquidation) procedure has been completed).

(a) Rescission

As in the general law of contract, the rescission may be on the ground of fraudulent misrepresentation (or fraud) or on the ground of innocent misrepresentation; in the former case, the partner rescinding has also a claim for damages. It may also be that partnership is one of the contracts *uberrimae fidei* ("of the utmost good faith"), and if so, mere failure to disclose material facts will confer on the other party or parties the right of rescission.

2–130   The case of *Ferguson* v. *Wilson* (1904) 6 F. 779 is an instance of rescission on the ground of innocent misrepresentation:

W., an engineer in Aberdeen, advertised for a partner. F. replied to the advertisement, and negotiations took place in the course of which W., without fraudulent intent, misrepresented the trading results of his business.

W. and F. agreed to enter into partnership.

Held that F. was entitled to rescind the agreement on the ground that he had entered into it under an essential error induced by W.'s innocent misrepresentation.

2–131   The Act confers certain additional rights on a partner who is entitled to rescind on the ground of fraud or misrepresentation: by section 41 he is entitled:

(i)   to a lien on, or right of retention of, the surplus of the partnership assets, after satisfying the partnership liabilities, for any sum of money paid by him for the purchase of a share in the partnership and for any capital contributed by him;

(ii)   to stand in the place of the creditors of the firm for any payments made by him in respect of partnership liabilities; and

(iii)   to be indemnified by the person guilty of the fraud or making the representation against all the debts and liabilities of the firm.

(b) Dissolution

2–132   The grounds of dissolution are considered first, and then, under the heading "Winding Up," the consequences of dissolution.

Grounds of Dissolution

2–133   The circumstances which bring about a dissolution of the relationship of partnership are set out in sections 32 to 35 of the Act:

(i)   expiration or notice (s. 32);
(ii)   death or bankruptcy (s. 33);
(iii)   illegality (s. 34); and
(iv)   order of the court (s. 35).

(i) Expiration or notice (s. 32)

2–134   Subject to any agreement between the partners, a partnership is dissolved:

(a) if entered into for a fixed term, by the expiration of that term;

(b) if entered into for a single adventure or undertaking, by the termination of that adventure or undertaking;

(c) if entered into for an undefined time, by any partner giving notice to the other or others of his intention to dissolve the partnership.

On (b), see "Joint Adventure," 2–16, above.

In situation (c) the partnership is dissolved as from the date mentioned in the notice as the date of dissolution, or, if no date is mentioned, as from the date of the communication of the notice.

(ii) Death or bankruptcy (s. 33)

Subject to any agreement between the partners, every partnership is dissolved as regards all the partners by the death or bankruptcy of any partner.

An instance of agreement to the contrary may be seen in *Hill* v. *Wylie* (1865) 3 M. 541:

H. and W. were in partnership as coalmasters. The contract of co-partnery, which was for a term of 19 years, provided that "in the event of the death of either of the parties during the currency of this contract, the copartnership shall not come to an end, but the surviving partner shall continue to carry on the business along with the representatives of the deceasing partner."

W. died during the 19-year period.

Held that the partnership had not been dissolved by his death.

However, the mere bequest of estate which includes the deceased's share in a partnership does not make the legatee a partner:

Thomson v. *Thomson*, 1962 S.C. (H.L.) 28; 1961 S.C. 255: Two brothers, Hector and Andrew, carried on a bakery business in partnership. The deed of copartnery provided that "either partner may by will nominate his widow to his share in the partnership."

Hector died leaving a will in which he bequeathed all his estate to his widow, but did not expressly nominate her as a partner.

Held that the widow was entitled to Hector's share in the partnership assets, but was not nominated as a partner in the business.

(iii) Illegality (s. 34)

A partnership is in every case dissolved by the happening of any event which makes it unlawful for the business of the firm to be carried on or for the members of the firm to carry it on in partnership.

An instance of dissolution by illegality occurs in *Hugh Stevenson and Sons Ltd.* v. *Aktiengesellschaft für Cartonnagen-Industrie* [1918] A.C. 239 (see 2–158, below): the admitted effect of the outbreak of war between Britain and Germany was to dissolve the partnership between the English company and the German company.

(iv) Order of the court (s. 35)

Section 35 sets out six cases in which a partner may apply to the court for the court to decree a dissolution of the partnership. The applicant will not necessarily succeed: the court has a discretion in the matter. The six cases are:

(*a*) when a partner is found lunatic by cognition, or is shown to the satisfaction of the court to be of permanently unsound mind;
(In this case the application may be made either by the insane partner's *curator bonis* (his guardian) or by another partner.)

(*b*) when a partner, other than the partner suing, becomes in any other way permanently incapable of performing his part of the partnership contract;
(In this case much depends on what the partner who has become incapable had necessarily to do himself in the partnership business; an illustration is provided by *Eadie &c.* v. *MacBean's Curator Bonis* (1885) 12 R. 660:

M., the owner of a long-established manufacturing business in Glasgow, assumed three younger men as partners in the business. The contract of copartnery provided that M. alone was to be entitled to sign cheques and indorse bills of exchange and promissory notes, but that in the event of his indisposition or of his being unable to attend to business from other causes, any of the other partners should be entitled to do so. The three junior partners were to devote their whole time and attention to the business.

M., by a stroke of paralysis, became permanently incapable of taking any further active part in the business, and the other partners petitioned the court to appoint a judicial factor to wind up the partnership affairs.

Petition *refused*, on the ground that it was not an essential part of the contract of copartnery that M. should give his personal services, and that therefore the other partners were not entitled to dissolve the partnership.)

(*c*) when a partner, other than the partner suing, has been guilty of such conduct as, in the opinion of the court, is calculated to prejudicially affect the carrying on of the business;
(Regard must be had to the nature of the business.)

(*d*) when a partner, other than the partner suing, wilfully or persistently commits a breach of the partnership agreement, or otherwise so conducts himself in matters relating to the partnership business that it is not reasonably practicable for the other partner or partners to carry on the business in partnership with him;
(This provision was applied in *Thomson, Petr.* (1893) 1 S.L.T. 59:

A partner, after drawing a cheque in the firm's name, disappeared, taking the money with him.

On the ground that this was a breach of the express terms of the contract of copartnery the other partner petitioned the court to dissolve the partnership.

The court *granted* the order for dissolution.)

(*e*) when the business of the partnership can only be carried on at a loss;

(*f*) whenever in any case circumstances have arisen which, in the opinion of the court, render it just and equitable that the partnership be dissolved.
(The court's jurisdiction is not ousted by a general arbitration clause in the partnership contract providing for all disputes to be settled by arbitration (*Roxburgh* v. *Dinardo*, 1981 S.L.T. 291 (O.H.)).)

Winding Up

2–141   In relation to winding up, the Act includes provision for the following matters:

(i)   right of partners to notify dissolution (s. 37);

(ii) continuing authority of partners for purposes of winding up (s. 38);

(iii) rights of partners as to application of partnership property (s. 39);

(iv) apportionment of premium where partnership prematurely dissolved (s. 40);

(v) right of outgoing partner in certain cases to share profits made after dissolution (s. 42); and

(vi) distribution of assets on final settlement of accounts (s. 44).

Primarily the right and duty to wind up the affairs of a partnership rest on the partners themselves, but, in cases of difficulty, the court has power to appoint a judicial factor whose function it is to wind up the firm's affairs under the eyes of the court. This power existed at common law, and is preserved by the provision in section 39 of the Act that any partner or his representatives may, on the termination of the partnership, apply to the court to wind up the business and affairs of the firm.

The following two cases illustrate circumstances which have been held to justify appointment of a judicial factor:

(1) *Allan* v. *Gronmeyer* (1891) 18 R. 784: A, B and C were partners in a wine and spirit business. The capital of about £22,000 had been contributed entirely by A and B. An article in the contract of copartnery provided that at the termination of the partnership the duty of winding up its affairs was to lie with C.

In 1888 the partners agreed that the partnership should be dissolved and that C should wind up its affairs in accordance with that article.

C took no steps towards winding up but carried on the business as a going concern, with its capital undiminished.

In 1890 A and B presented a petition for the appointment of a judicial factor, and the court *appointed* an accountant to that office.

Lord Adam said (at p. 787): "The petitioners . . . have a very clear interest to see that that capital is safe."

(2) *Carabine* v. *Carabine*, 1949 S.C. 521: A husband and wife were partners in a hotel business, to which both had contributed capital. There was no written contract of copartnery.

The partnership terminated when the wife left her husband. All efforts on the wife's part to have the business realised failed, the husband carrying it on against her wishes. There was an imminent risk that a building society to which interest was due would force a sale of the premises in circumstances disadvantageous to both partners.

The court *appointed* a judicial factor in order that the wife might obtain her rights under section 39 of the Act.

Lord Justice-Clerk Thomson said (at p. 527): "Here there is no harmony, and the impression I take from what I have been told is that the respondent has just been staying on running the hotel and that he has not the slightest intention of settling up the partnership affairs unless he is subjected to pressure, and this puts the petitioner in a very awkward position and prevents her from enjoying her rights under the Act. That is just the sort of situation which seems to me to make it necessary or expedient that we should intervene. This is not just a dispute between the winding-up partner and the late partner on some matter of detail

or accounting arising out of the winding-up; it is something much
more fundamental which attacks the propriety of the course adopted
altogether."

2–146   On the other hand in *Thomson, Petr.* (1893) 1 S.L.T. 59 (2–140, above)
the court, while granting the order for dissolution, refused to authorise
winding up by the petitioner or to appoint a judicial factor, on the ground
that at common law a partner had on dissolution full power to wind up.

2–147   In *Dickie* v. *Mitchell* (1874) 1 R. 1030 (a case in which a judicial factor
was appointed where the two partners in a joint farming adventure were
both incapable of managing the farm), Lord President Inglis (at p. 1033)
formulated three general principles:

> (1) When all the partners are dead, the court will appoint a judicial
> factor.
> (2) If there are surviving partners without fault or incapacity, the
> court will not interfere but will leave them to extricate their affairs in their
> own way.
> (3) Where there is a surviving partner who is unfitted for winding up
> the affairs, the court can, and, if satisfied of the necessity, will appoint a
> factor. All such cases are, in their nature, cases of circumstances.

2–148   The specific provisions of the Act may now be looked at:

(i) Right of partners to notify dissolution (s. 37)

2–149   On the dissolution of a partnership or retirement of a partner any
partner may publicly notify the fact, and may require the other partner or
partners to concur for that purpose in all necessary or proper acts which
cannot be done without his or their concurrence.

2–150   The importance of this section in practice is linked to the provisions
in section 36, already noticed (2–83–86, above) in connection with the
possible liability of retired partners for the future debts of the firm.

(ii) Continuing authority of partners for purposes of winding up (s. 38)

2–151   After the dissolution the authority of each partner to bind the firm,
and the other rights and obligations of the partners, continue so far as is
necessary to wind up the affairs of the partnership, and to complete
transactions begun but unfinished at the time of the dissolution, but not
otherwise.

2–152   However, it is specially provided that the firm is in no case bound by
the acts of a partner who has become bankrupt, though this will not affect
the liability of any person who has after the bankruptcy represented
himself or knowingly allowed himself to be represented as a partner of the
bankrupt.

2–153   Section 38 was applied in *Dickson* v. *National Bank of Scotland Ltd.*,
1917 S.C. (H.L.) 50; 1916 S.C. 589:

> A sum of money forming part of a trust-estate was deposited with a
> bank. The deposit-receipt stated that the sum was to be repayable on the
> signature of a legal firm, A, B & C, the law-agents to the trust.
> The firm A, B & C was subsequently dissolved, and eight years after
> the dissolution B, one of the former partners, by signing the firm-name on
> the deposit receipt, uplifted the money and embezzled it.

The beneficiaries in the trust brought an action against the bank for payment of the sum deposited.

Held that as the uplifting of the deposit was necessary for one or other of the purposes mentioned in section 38, B had authority to sign the firm-name, and the bank was justified in paying over the money to him; and action *dismissed* as irrelevant.

(iii) **Rights of partners as to application of partnership property (s. 39)**

On the dissolution of a partnership every partner is entitled to have the partnership property applied in payment of the debts and liabilities of the firm, and to have the surplus assets applied in payment of what may be due to the partners respectively after deducting what may be due from them as partners to the firm.

(iv) **Apportionment of premium where partnership prematurely dissolved (s. 40)**

Section 40 relates to the situation where one partner has paid a premium to another on entering into a partnership for a fixed term, and the partnership is dissolved before that term has expired. The court may then order the repayment of the premium, or of such part of it as the court thinks just, considering the terms of the partnership contract and the length of time during which the partnership has continued, unless:

(1) the dissolution has been caused by the death of a partner; or

(2) the dissolution is, in the court's judgment, wholly or chiefly due to the misconduct of the partner who paid the premium; or

(3) the partnership has been dissolved by an agreement containing no provision for a return of any part of the premium.

(v) **Right of outgoing partner in certain cases to share profits made after dissolution (s. 42)**

It may be that where a member of a firm has died or otherwise ceased to be a partner, the surviving or continuing partners carry on the business of the firm with its capital or assets without any final settlement of accounts as between the firm and the outgoing partner or his estate. For that situation the Act provides that, in the absence of any agreement to the contrary, the outgoing partner or his estate is entitled to an option, *viz.* either:

(1) such share of the profits made since the dissolution as the court may find to be attributable to the use of his share of the partnership assets; or

(2) interest at five per cent. on the amount of his share of the partnership assets (s. 42(1)).

Where, however, by the partnership contract an option is given to surviving or continuing partners to purchase the interest of a deceased or outgoing partner, and that option is duly exercised, then the estate of the deceased partner, or the outgoing partner or his estate, as the case may be, is not entitled to any further or other share of profits (s. 42(2)).

Section 42 applies even where the dissolution is caused by illegality: *Hugh Stevenson and Sons Ltd.* v. *Aktiengesellschaft für Cartonnagen-Industrie* [1918] A.C. 239: An English company and a German company had carried on business as a clamp factory in England until the partnership was dissolved by the outbreak of war between Britain and Germany.

During the war the English company continued to carry on the business and to use the partnership plant.

Held that, at the end of the war, the German company was entitled to a share of the profits made by the carrying on of the business during the war.

(vi) Distribution of assets on final settlement of accounts (s. 44)

2–159　In settling accounts between the partners after a dissolution, the following rules must, subject to any agreement, be observed:

(a) Losses, including losses and deficiencies of capital, must be paid first out of profits, next out of capital, and lastly, if necessary, by the partners individually in the proportion in which they were entitled to share profits.

(b) The assets of the firm, including any sums contributed by the partners to make up losses or deficiencies of capital, must be applied as follows:

(1) in paying the debts and liabilities of the firm to persons who are not partners;

(2) in paying to each partner rateably what is due to him for advances as distinct from capital;

(3) in paying to each partner rateably what is due from the firm to him in respect of capital.

The ultimate residue, if any, must then:

(4) be divided among the partners in the proportion in which profits are divisible.

VII LIMITED PARTNERSHIPS ACT 1907

2–160　The Limited Partnerships Act 1907 was passed to enable partnerships to be formed in which one or more (but not all) of the partners are not liable beyond a fixed limit for the firm's debts. Section references here are to sections of the Act of 1907.

2–161　The Act provides that a limited partnership must consist of one or more persons, called "general partners," who are liable in the usual way for all the firm's debts and obligations, and of one or more persons, called "limited partners," who at the time of entering into the partnership contribute a sum as capital, or contribute property valued at a stated amount, and who are not liable for the firm's debts or obligations beyond the amount contributed. A limited partner must not, during the continuance of the partnership, draw out any part of his contribution: if he does so, he remains liable for the firm's debts and obligations up to the amount drawn out (s. 4(2) and (3)).

2–162　Limited partnerships, unlike ordinary partnerships, must be registered with the Registrar of Companies (s. 5). For a limited partnership whose principal place of business is situated or proposed to be situated in Scotland the appropriate registration office is that in Edinburgh (ss. 8 and 15).

The particulars which must be registered are:

(*a*) the firm name;

(*b*) the general nature of the business;

(*c*) the principal place of business;

(*d*) the full names of each of the partners;

(*e*) the term, if any, for which the partnership is entered into, and the date of its commencement;

(*f*) a statement that the partnership is limited, and of who are the limited partners; and

(*g*) the sum contributed by each limited partner, and whether paid in cash or how otherwise (s. 8).

Changes in these particulars must also be registered (s. 9(1)).

These provisions for registration are intended to give protection to members of the public who deal with a limited partnership. Any person is entitled, on paying the appropriate fee, to inspect, or require copies of or extracts from, the documents filed with the Registrar (s. 16(1)). Hence, on account of this publicity, members of the public are deemed to have notice of the fact that at least one of the partners has only a limited liability for the firm's debts. A further provision of the Act designed to secure publicity is the provision that any arrangement by which a general partner becomes a limited partner or by which a limited partner's share is assigned must be immediately advertised in the Gazette (*i.e.* the *Edinburgh Gazette* in the case of a limited partnership registered in Scotland): until that is done, the arrangement is deemed to be of no effect (s. 10).

Limited partnerships are governed by the Partnership Act 1890 and by the common law to the same extent as ordinary partnerships except in so far as the Limited Partnerships Act 1907 expressly provides otherwise (s. 7). The following are the main modifications made by the Act of 1907:

(a) Management

A limited partner must not take part in the management of the partnership business, and has no power to bind the firm. He may, however, either personally or through an agent, at any time inspect the books of the firm and examine into the state and prospects of the partnership business, and may advise with his copartners on these matters.

If a limited partner takes part in the management of the partnership business, he becomes liable as if he were a general partner for all the debts and obligations of the firm incurred while he takes part in the management (s. 6(1)).

(b) Dissolution

A limited partnership is not dissolved by the death or bankruptcy of a limited partner, and the lunacy of a limited partner is not a ground for dissolution of the partnership by the court unless the lunatic's share cannot be otherwise ascertained and realised (s. 6(2)).

(c) Winding Up

On the dissolution of a limited partnership its affairs are wound up by the general partners unless the court orders otherwise (s. 6(3)).

2–171   A limited partnership registered in Scotland[1] and consisting of eight or more partners may be wound up as an "unregistered company" under Part IX of the Companies Act 1948 in the following circumstances:

(i)   if the partnership is dissolved, or has ceased to carry on business, or is carrying on business only for the purposes of winding up its affairs;

(ii)   if the partnership is unable to pay its debts; or

(iii)   if the court is of opinion that it is just and equitable that the partnership should be wound up (Companies Act 1948, ss. 398 and 399(5)).

In general the procedure followed is the same as that for the winding up of registered companies by the court.

2–172   The historical background to these provisions of the Companies Act 1948 is complex: originally the Act of 1907 (s. 6(4)) *required* the winding up of limited partnerships to be by the court under the Companies Acts then in force; the Companies (Consolidation) Act 1908 repealed that provision and *permitted* the winding up of limited partnerships to be by that mode. The case of *Muirhead* v. *Borland*, 1925 S.C. 474, was decided under the Act of 1908:

A limited partnership consisted of one general partner and one limited partner. The general partner presented a petition for a winding up by the court, and the limited partner objected that the better course would be a winding up by a judicial factor.

The circumstances seemed to make it inevitable that serious questions regarding the limited partner's liability would be raised, and the court therefore took the view that winding up by the court was the preferable procedure and *granted* the prayer of the petition.

Under the provisions of the Act of 1948 the procedure of winding up by the court is no longer available unless the limited partnership consists of eight or more partners.

(d) Rules Applicable between the Partners

2–173   Subject to any agreement, expressed or implied, between the partners:

(i)   any difference arising as to ordinary matters connected with the partnership business may be decided by a majority of the general partners;

(ii)   a limited partner may, with the consent of the general partners, assign his share in the partnership, and the assignee then becomes a limited partner with all the rights of the cedent;

(iv)   a person may be introduced as a partner without the consent of the existing limited partners;

(v)   a limited partner is not entitled to dissolve the partnership by notice (s. 6(5)).

2–174   The limited partnership has not been a popular form of business organisation, principally because the private limited company, with a minimum membership of two, was introduced in the same year, and enabled two persons, with only a little more formality, to carry on business as a limited company, each securing for himself a limit on his personal liability for the company's debts and at the same time, if

---

[1] Limited partnerships registered in England and Northern Ireland are expressly excluded.

appointed as a director, being entitled to take part in the management of the company's business.

VIII BUSINESS NAMES

Part II of the Companies Act 1981 (headed "Company Names and Business Names") includes two main sections on business names, whether the name is that of a partnership, an individual or a company; these relate to:

(a) control of business names (s. 28); and
(b) disclosure of names of persons using business names (s. 29).

Provisions formerly requiring the registration and publication of business names, contained in the Registration of Business Names Act 1916 and the Companies Act 1947, were repealed by the Companies Act 1981.

(a) Control of Business Names

Section 28 applies to any person who has a place of business in Great Britain and who carries on business in Great Britain under a name which—

(a) in the case of a partnership, does not consist of the surnames of all partners who are individuals and the corporate names of all partners who are bodies corporate (e.g. companies) without any addition other than a permitted addition;

(b) in the case of an individual, does not consist of his surname without any addition other than a permitted addition;

(c) in the case of a company capable of being wound up under the Companies Act 1948, does not consist of its corporate name without any addition other than a permitted addition.

The following are permitted additions—

(a) in the case of a partnership, the forenames of individual partners or the initials of their forenames, or, where two or more individual partners have the same surname, the addition of "s" at the end of that surname; or

(b) in the case of an individual, his forename or the initials of his forename;

(c) in any case, any addition merely indicating that the business is carried on in succession to a former owner of the business.

A person to whom section 28 applies must not, without the written approval of the Secretary of State, carry on business in Great Britain under a name which—

(a) would be likely to give the impression that the business is connected with the Government or with any local authority; or

(b) includes any word or expression specified in regulations made under section 31 of the Act.

The first Regulations to be made under section 31 were the Company and Business Names Regulations 1981 (S.I. 1981 No. 1685), which came into operation on February 26, 1982. They list 87 words or expressions for the use of which in a business name the Secretary of State's approval is required (e.g. "Chamber of Commerce," "Institute," "Scottish" and

"Trade Union"). In the case of many of the words and expressions listed there is a "relevant body" which must first be approached, with a written request that it should indicate whether (and if so why) it has any objections to the proposed use, and a copy of any response received must then be submitted to the Secretary of State (*e.g.* for the expression "Contact Lens" the relevant body is the General Optical Council, for the words "Dental" and "Dentistry" the relevant body is the General Dental Council and for the expression "Nursing Home" the relevant body is the Department of Health and Social Security).

2–181   A person contravening section 28 is guilty of an offence and liable to be fined.

(b) Disclosure of Names of Persons Using Business Names

2–182   Section 29 provides that any person to whom section 28 applies must state in legible characters on all business letters, written orders for goods or services, invoices and receipts and written demands for payment of debts—

    (i) in the case of a partnership, the name of each partner;

    (ii) in the case of an individual, his name;

    (iii) in the case of a company, its corporate name; and

    (iv) in relation to each person so named, an address within Great Britain at which service of any document will be effective.

These requirements are modified in the case of a partnership of more than 20 persons provided the document states the address of the principal place of business and that a list of the partners' names is open to inspection at that place.

2–183   A second requirement of section 29 is that any person to whom section 28 applies must display a notice containing all names and addresses in a prominent position so that it may be easily read in any premises where the business is carried on and to which the customers of the business or suppliers of goods or services have access.

2–184   A third requirement is that any person to whom section 28 applies must, on request, give a written notice of all names and addresses to any person with whom anything is done or discussed in the course of the business.

2–185   A person contravening any of these three requirements of section 29 is guilty of an offence and liable to be fined. In addition there is the following civil remedy: where legal proceedings are brought to enforce any right arising out of a contract entered into at a time when the pursuer was in breach of section 29, they will be dismissed if the defender shows that, because of the breach, he has been unable to pursue a claim against the pursuer or has suffered some financial loss; however, to this there is the exception that the court may permit the proceedings to continue if it is satisfied that it is just and equitable to do so (Companies Act 1981, s. 30).

IX GOODWILL

2–186   One of the assets of a business, whether the business is carried on by a partnership, or by an individual or by a company, is likely to be goodwill, a matter governed by the common law.

It has been said that "goodwill is an elastic term of which it is not easy, if it is possible, to give an exhaustive definition" (*per* Lord Wellwood in *Hughes* v. *Assessor for Stirling* (1892) 19 R. 840, at p. 842).

The best-known attempted definition is that of Lord Chancellor Eldon in the English case *Cruttwell* v. *Lye* (1810) 17 Ves. Jun. 335; 34 E.R. 129:

L., who had a long-established trade as a common carrier, became bankrupt and his business was sold by auction in lots. Lot 1 was L.'s carrying trade from Bristol and Bath to London with premises and goodwill, and it was purchased by C. Lot 2 was L.'s carrying trade from Bristol and Bath to Warminster and Salisbury with stock on the premises, and it was purchased in trust for L., who commenced trade again to London by that different route.

C. sought but was refused an injunction to prevent L.'s trade: L. had set up a similar trade, but not the same trade as that which had been sold to C.

Lord Eldon said (at 17 Ves. Jun. p. 346; 34 E.R. p. 134) that the goodwill which had been sold to C. was "nothing more than the probability, that the old customers will resort to the old place."

That definition was criticised by Lord Herschell in *Trego* v. *Hunt* [1896] A.C. 7, at p. 17, as being "far too narrow" if it had been intended as an exhaustive definition.

The facts in *Trego* v. *Hunt* were that T., a varnish and japan manufacturer, had taken H. into partnership under an agreement which provided that the goodwill of the business should remain the sole property of T.

H. acquired a list of the firm's customers with a view to obtaining their custom for himself at the termination of the partnership.

The House of Lords held that T. was entitled to an injunction restraining H. from asking any customer of the firm to deal with him after the firm's dissolution.

Lord Herschell said (at p. 17): "It is the connection . . . formed [*with customers*], together with the circumstances, whether of habit or otherwise, which tend to make it permanent, that constitutes the goodwill of a business. It is this which constitutes the difference between a business just started, which has no goodwill attached to it, and one which has acquired a goodwill. The former trader has to seek out his customers from among the community as best he can. The latter has a custom ready made."

Goodwill is an incorporeal asset. It may be heritable or moveable or partly heritable and partly moveable. If and in so far as it is associated with premises in which the business has been carried on, it is heritable, and if and in so far as it is associated with the reputation of the trader, it is moveable. Decided cases relating to the valuation of premises, especially licensed premises, and to the law of succession illustrate the importance of the distinction, *e.g.*:

(a) *Hughes* v. *Assessor for Stirling* (1892) 19 R. 840 was a case in which for valuation purposes the goodwill of a publican's business at the Commercial Inn, Denny, was held to be partly heritable and partly moveable.

(b) In *Assessor for Edinburgh* v. *Caira and Crolla*, 1928 S.C. 398, the same decision was reached in relation to a fish restaurant business.

2–193   (c) *Graham* v. *Graham's Trustees* (1904) 6 F. 1015 concerned a point in the law of succession. G. had been the occupier of public-houses in Glasgow. On his death the question arose of whether the goodwill formed part of his moveable estate, out of which his son was entitled to claim legitim. The circumstances in the case were such that the court held that the goodwill was heritable (and so was not estate out of which legitim could be claimed).

2–194   A person selling the goodwill of his business is barred from representing that he is continuing the business himself. He therefore cannot solicit the customers of his former business to transfer their custom to him, nor can he use the firm name to which the goodwill attaches. These two consequences are illustrated in the following cases:

2–195   (a) *Dumbarton Steamboat Co. Ltd.* v. *MacFarlane* (1899) 1 F. 993: The firm of MacFarlane, Lang & Co., whose partners were MacF. and L., had conducted business as carriers at Dumbarton. The firm sold its business and its assets including goodwill to the promoters of D. Ltd., a company which was afterwards formed. MacF. and L. became employees of D. Ltd., but after about three years MacF. was dismissed. He began business on his own account, soliciting orders from the customers of the former firm, and D. Ltd. raised a process of interdict against him.

Held that it was against the good faith of the contract of sale for MacF. to solicit the custom of his former firm, the goodwill of which had been transferred to D. Ltd., and interdict *granted*.

2–196   (b) *Smith* v. *McBride & Smith* (1888) 16 R. 36: James Smith and Joseph McBride had carried on business in partnership as aerated water manufacturers in Greenock under the name "Smith & McBride." In 1884 their partnership terminated, and they agreed that Smith should pay £300 to McBride for the latter's share in the business and that Smith should acquire the business with goodwill, machinery and stock in trade and carry it on in his own name.

McBride entered into partnership with William Smith, a brother of James Smith, and traded under the name "Smith & McBride."

Held that James Smith was entitled to an interdict restraining McBride and William Smith from trading under that name.

Further Reading

> *Scots Mercantile Law Statutes* (annual reprint from *The Parliament House Book*) (W. Green & Son) for Partnership Act 1890 and Companies Acts
>
> Gloag and Henderson, *Introduction to the Law of Scotland*, Chapters XXIV and XXXVII (part)
>
> David M. Walker, *Principles of Scottish Private Law*, Chapters 3.10, 5.19 (part) and 5.39 (part)
>
> Robert Burgess and Geoffrey Morse, *Partnership Law and Practice in England and Scotland* (1980, Sweet & Maxwell)
>
> James Bennett Miller, *The Law of Partnership in Scotland* (1973, W. Green & Son)

J. J. Gow, *The Mercantile and Industrial Law of Scotland*, Chapter 10
Charles D. Drake, *Law of Partnership* (2nd ed., 1977, Sweet & Maxwell)
Enid A. Marshall, *Scottish Cases on Partnerships and Companies*, Part I (1980, W. Green & Son)

COMPANIES

INTRODUCTION

The aim of this chapter is to give an elementary account of the most prominent aspects of company law, a branch of mercantile law of ever-increasing complexity. More than any other topic included in this book, company law is justifiably regarded as a subject in its own right, the principles and practical details of which must be sought in more specialist works.

The companies with which this chapter is concerned are *registered* companies, *i.e.* companies incorporated by registration under the Companies Acts. Most, but not all, registered companies are *limited* companies, *i.e.* companies in which the members are liable only up to a fixed amount for the company's debts.

The registration system was introduced to Scotland by the Joint Stock Companies Act 1856. This branch of the law is therefore, by legal standards, a modern one, largely consisting of statute law, enacted, amended and re-enacted with amendment in a long succession of Companies Acts since that year. The Acts now applicable to all existing and new registered companies are *the Companies Acts 1948 to 1981*.

The principal Act is the Companies Act 1948, and in this chapter references to sections of a statute are, except where the context requires otherwise, references to sections of that Act.

The precise meaning of the collective title "the Companies Acts 1948 to 1981" is:

the Companies Act 1948,
Parts I and III of the Companies Act 1967,
the Companies (Floating Charges and Receivers) (Scotland) Act 1972,
section 9 of the European Communities Act 1972,
sections 1 to 4 of the Stock Exchange (Completion of Bargains) Act 1976,
section 9 of the Insolvency Act 1976,

the Companies Act 1976,
the Companies Act 1980, and
the Companies Act 1981 (except sections 28 and 29).
This definition is to be found in the final section (s. 119) of the Companies
Act 1981. In this chapter references to the "1967 Act," the "1976 Act,"
the "1980 Act" and the "1981 Act" are, unless the context requires
otherwise, references to the Companies Act 1967, the Companies Act
1976, the Companies Act 1980 and the Companies Act 1981, respectively.

3–06   Despite the great volume of legislation applying to companies,
company law has never been codified. There have been several consolidating Companies Acts, each lasting for a span of years as the principal
Companies Act until it reached the state of having been so much amended
by later Acts that a new consolidating Act was passed to gather together
once more into a single Act all the then existing statute law on companies.
The Companies Act 1948 is the latest consolidating Act, and the Acts
which have been passed since 1948 are amending Acts.

3–07   A fresh consolidating Act is now overdue: there has been no comprehensive enactment of the recommendations made by the Jenkins
Committee in the last systematic review of company law (*Report of the
Company Law Committee* (1962) Cmnd. 1749). The Act of 1981 has
introduced the possibility that, in connection with the next consolidation
of the Companies Acts, amendments may be made by an Order in
Council on the joint recommendation of the Law Commission and the
Scottish Law Commission (1981 Act, s. 116). This procedure would
dispense with the need for an amending Act to be passed shortly before
the new consolidating Act as has hitherto been the pattern (*e.g.* the
Companies Act 1947, most of which never came into force until it was
incorporated in the consolidating Act of 1948).

3–08   The following are prominent features of company law:

(i) *Increasing statutory control*—The legislation relating to companies
has vastly increased in volume and complexity since its introduction in the
middle of the nineteenth century. At no time has the increase been more
rapid and extensive than in recent years, and there is no sign of abatement
in the near future.

(ii) *Case-law*—Since company law is consolidating and not codifying,
it is superimposed on the common law, and this basis of common law is to
be found expressed in decided cases. In addition there are the very
numerous cases in which the courts have been called on to interpret and
apply the statutory provisions. Where statutory provisions have been
carried forward unaltered into new consolidating Acts, cases decided on
the earlier enactment retain their authority. On the other hand, there
have been several cases which have prompted the legislature to make
statutory changes; *e.g.* the case of *Derry* v. *Peek* (1889) 14 App. Cas. 337
showed the inadequacy of the law relating to mis-statements in a prospectus and led to the passing of the Directors' Liability Act 1890 (now
represented by section 43 of the Act of 1948).

(iii) *E.E.C. influence*—An important feature in the development of
company law at the present day is the need to comply with E.E.C.
Directives on Harmonisation of Company Law. For example, section 9 of
the European Communities Act 1972 was necessary in order to give effect

in the United Kingdom to the First Directive; the changes concerned protection for persons dealing with a company or its directors and new publicity for certain information concerning a company. Similarly, the Acts of 1980 and 1981 had as their primary objectives the implementation of the Second and Fourth Directives respectively, though both Acts include further measures of reform; the Second Directive related to the formation and capital of public companies, and the Fourth was concerned with company accounts.

(iv) *A company's wider responsibilities*—A new trend emerging in company legislation is the recognition of a company as an institution with social and economic responsibilities to groups other than its share-holders; *e.g.* the Act of 1980 made a start on the recognition of a company's responsibilities to its employees.

Scots company law is for the most part the same as English company law, but for the following two reasons there are some distinctions:

(i) There are some statutory provisions which make a distinction between Scotland and England. An obvious instance is the Companies (Floating Charges and Receivers) (Scotland) Act 1972, which applies only to Scotland, and in the winding-up provisions in the Companies Act 1948 there are numerous instances of separate provisions for the two legal systems.

(ii) Since company legislation is consolidating, and not codifying, it is superimposed on the common law of the two different legal systems, and that common law is not necessarily the same in Scotland as in England; this point is important because most of the statutory provisions are confined to matters of detail, leaving many of the broad principles to rest still on the common law.

The selected aspects of company law considered in this chapter are all of an introductory nature. It is appropriate to look first at:

I. The classification of registered companies.

The topic dealt with next is the most important principle of all in company law:

II. The separate personality of a registered company.

The stage has then been reached for appreciating:

III. A comparison of registered companies with partnerships.

The remainder of the chapter is devoted to the two documents which comprise the constitution of a registered company:

IV. The memorandum of association; and

V. The articles of association.

At this preliminary stage it may be useful for the reader to have a brief explanation of some of the terms commonly met with in any study of company law:

(a) registration;
(b) promoters;
(c) members, shareholders and stockholders;
(d) directors;
(e) share capital;
(f) debentures and debenture stock; and
(g) meetings and resolutions.

(a) **Registration**

3–12 Frequent mention is made throughout company law of the need to register documents. Registration means delivery of the documents in question to the appropriate registrar of companies. If the company's registered office is in Scotland, the appropriate registrar is the Registrar of Companies for Scotland, Companies Registration Office, 102 George Street, Edinburgh EH2 3DJ.

3–13 The purpose of the registration requirements is to secure publicity: any member of the public has the right to inspect a company's file kept by the registrar of companies. An inspection will yield information about the company's constitution (contained in the company's memorandum of association and articles of association), and about important matters arising during the company's operation (including special resolutions and, if the company is a limited company, its annual accounts).

(b) **Promoters**

3–14 Promoters are the persons who take the necessary steps to set the company going. They give instructions to solicitors or other professional persons for the preparation and registration of documents such as the memorandum and articles and they may procure capital for the new company. Professional persons employed by the promoters are not, merely because of their employment, promoters themselves.

3–15 Promoters are not agents for the company which they bring into existence, because until incorporated the company is not a legal person and so can have no agents. Contracts which promoters purport to make on behalf of a company before its formation are binding on the promoters personally (*Kelner* v. *Baxter* (1866) L.R. 2 C.P. 174 and European Communities Act 1972, s. 9(2)). Similarly, a new company once formed cannot sue for damages for breach of a pre-incorporation contract entered into on its behalf by its promoters (*Tinnevelly Sugar Refining Co. Ltd.* v. *Mirrlees, Watson & Yaryan Co. Ltd.* (1894) 21 R. 1009).

3–16 Promoters stand in a fiduciary relationship to the company which they are forming, and must disclose any profit which they make out of the promotion either to an independent board of directors or to the existing and intended shareholders. In a small private company it is quite usual for the promoters to be themselves the first shareholders and directors, and in that case there is unlikely to be any difficulty over the duty of disclosure.

(c) **Members, Shareholders and Stockholders**

3–17 The members of a company are the persons who together own the company. They are often called "shareholders" because, in the commonest type of company (the company limited by shares), each member holds a number of shares in the capital of the company.

3–18 "Members" is, however, a wider term than "shareholders." This is because companies limited by guarantee and unlimited companies need not have a share capital: some companies, therefore, have no shareholders, but they do have members.

3–19 A member is not necessarily a natural person (*i.e.* an individual): artificial legal persons (such as partnerships and companies) may be members of a company.

A company may convert its shares, provided they are fully paid up, into *stock* (s. 61(1)). If it has done so, it will have "stockholders" instead of "shareholders." Shares are at the present day usually fully paid up in any case, and so the distinction between shareholders and stockholders is seldom of any practical importance.

(d) **Directors**

Directors are the persons who manage the company. They may or may not be members. Their powers depend on the provisions of the company's articles of association, and are often wide; *e.g.*:

"The business of the company shall be managed by the directors, who . . . may exercise all such powers of the company as are not, by the Companies Acts 1948 to 1981 or by these regulations [i.e. *these articles*], required to be exercised by the company in general meeting. . . ." (Sched. 1, Table A, reg. 80, as amended by the 1981 Act, s. 119 and Sched. 3).

An important topic in company law is the extent to which members may exercise control over directors.

Directors, as such, are not employees of the company: they are its officers or agents. It is, however, possible for a director to be also an employee; *e.g.* a managing director is both a director and an employee of the company.

Directors occupy a fiduciary position (*i.e.* a position of trust) towards the company as a legal person distinct from the individual members.

In performing their functions directors must have regard to the interests of the company's employees in general as well as the interests of its members (1980 Act, s. 46(1)). This statutory duty is owed by the directors to the company (and to the company alone) and is enforceable in the same way as any other fiduciary duty owed to the company by its directors (1980 Act, s. 46(2)).

(e) **Share Capital**

Most companies have a share capital, and this will be divided into a number of shares of a certain amount each; *e.g.* a company may have a share capital of £100,000, divided into 400,000 shares of 25p each.

A distinction is made between *nominal* (also referred to as *authorised*) capital, allotted capital, *called-up* capital, and *paid-up* capital. The meaning of the term *"the authorised minimum,"* introduced by the Companies Act 1980, should also be noted.

The *nominal* (or *authorised*) capital is the amount stated in the company's memorandum of association as being the capital of the company. The allotted, called-up, or paid-up capital can never exceed the amount of the nominal capital.

The *allotted* capital is the amount of capital held by the shareholders; *e.g.* if a company has a nominal capital of £100,000, divided into 400,000 shares of 25p each, it may be that only £75,000 has been allotted; there will then be 300,000 shares of 25p each held by shareholders.

Called-up capital is the amount of capital which the company has actually called up from its shareholders. It is usual now for companies to call up all the allotted capital in full very soon after it has been allotted. Usually, therefore, if a company has allotted 300,000 shares of 25p each, its called-up capital will be £75,000 because each shareholder will have been asked to pay the full 25p on each share held. Where a company's allotted capital has not been fully called up, each shareholder remains liable to pay to the company, when a call is made, the amount unpaid on his shares.

3–31 *Paid-up* capital is the amount which has actually been paid by the shareholders to the company. Normally it will be the same as the called-up capital, but there is the possibility that some shareholders will have fallen into arrears in the payment of calls.

3–32 The term *"the authorised minimum"* means £50,000, or such other sum as the Department of Trade may, by statutory instrument, specify instead (1980 Act, s. 85(1)). The Act of 1980 provides that the nominal capital of a *public* company must be not less than the authorised minimum (s. 3(2)), and that before such a company can do business the registrar of companies must be satisfied that the company's allotted share capital is not less than the authorised minimum (s. 4(2)). The capital of a private company may be of any amount.

3–33 The shares forming the share capital are often of two or more different classes, *e.g.* preference shares, entitling their holders to a preference dividend of, say, 7 per cent, and ordinary shares, whose holders will not be entitled to any dividend unless there is a surplus of profits after the preference dividend has been paid. *Prima facie* ("Unless the contrary is proved") a preference dividend is cumulative, *i.e.* if the profits of one year are insufficient to pay it, the arrears will require to be paid in a subsequent year before any ordinary dividend is paid in that year.

(f) Debentures and Debenture Stock

3–34 In investment circles debentures and debenture stock are bought and sold in much the same way as shares and stock. In law, however, debentures and debenture stock are quite different in nature from shares and stock.

3–35 A debenture is a document in which the company acknowledges that it is liable to pay a specified amount, say, £100. The person holding the debenture (the "debenture holder") is, in law, a *creditor* of the company, entitled to be paid his £100 out of the company's assets before any distribution is made to shareholders. Like other creditors, the debenture holder may or may not have a right in security over property belonging to the company, *i.e.* his debenture may be a secured debenture or an unsecured debenture. The security may be a fixed security (*e.g.* a standard security over the company's heritable property) or a floating charge over all or any of the company's property and undertaking for the time being.

3–36 Debentures differ from debenture stock in that debentures are each for a fixed amount such as £100, whereas debenture stock consists of a mass of indebtedness which may be divided into parcels of any amount desired, so that one debenture stockholder may hold £25 of the debenture stock, another £100 and so on.

3–37 The interest which falls due on debentures and debenture stock at fixed intervals is, like the debentures and debenture stock themselves, a *debt* due by the company: there can be no question of paying dividends to shareholders unless and until the interest due to debenture holders and debenture stockholders has been fully paid.

(g) Meetings and Resolutions

There are three kinds of meetings of the *members* of a company:

(i) annual general meetings, which must be held each calendar year;

(ii) extraordinary general meetings (*i.e.* all general meetings other than the annual general meetings); and

(iii) if the share capital of the company is divided into different classes, class meetings (*e.g.* a meeting of preference shareholders).

Normally these meetings are convened by the directors, but section 132 of the Act of 1948, one of several minority rights' sections in the Acts, enables a general meeting to be requisitioned (*i.e.* demanded) by the holders of not less than one-tenth of the paid-up capital carrying the right to vote at general meetings (or if the company does not have a share capital, members representing not less than one-tenth of the total voting rights of all the members with a right to vote at general meetings). If the directors do not within 21 days from the date of the deposit of the requisition at the company's registered office proceed duly to convene a meeting, the requisitionists or the majority of them may themselves convene a meeting.

Business is transacted at company meetings by the passing of resolutions, which may be *ordinary* resolutions (requiring only a simple majority of votes), *special* resolutions (requiring a three-fourths majority and 21 days' prior notice) or *extraordinary* resolutions (also requiring a three-fourths majority but only 14 days' prior notice).

The type of resolution required depends on the nature of the business, *e.g.*:

ordinary resolution—appointment or removal of a director;

special resolution—alteration of the company's articles of association (s. 10(1));

extraordinary resolution—voluntary winding up on the ground of inability to pay debts (s. 278(1)(c)).

Where neither the Acts nor the company's articles of association require a special or an extraordinary resolution, then an ordinary resolution is sufficient.

Special resolutions are distinct from *those ordinary resolutions which require special notice*: *e.g.* an ordinary resolution for the removal of a director under section 184 requires special notice (s. 184(2)). The procedure for special notice is laid down in section 142; it involves giving notice *to* the company *28 days* before the meeting at which the resolution is to be passed.

Meetings of the *directors* of a company are referred to as *"board meetings."* Proceedings at these meetings are regulated by provisions in the company's articles of association (see, *e.g.*, Sched. 1, Table A, regs. 98 to 109, which, amongst other things, enable the board to delegate its powers to committees and to appoint and fix the remuneration of a managing director).

I CLASSIFICATION OF REGISTERED COMPANIES

3–43   The classifications of registered companies to be considered here are:
   (a) companies limited by shares, companies limited by guarantee and unlimited companies;
   (b) public companies and private companies; and
   (c) holding companies and subsidiaries.

(a) Companies Limited by Shares, Companies Limited by Guarantee and Unlimited Companies

3–44   All registered companies are embraced within this classification, *i.e.* every registered company must take one of the three forms:
   (i)   company limited by shares;
   (ii) company limited by guarantee; and
   (iii) unlimited company.

Brief mention will also be made of:
   (iv) conversion from limited to unlimited and *vice versa*.

(i) *Company Limited by Shares*

3–45   This is by far the commonest type of registered company. It may be public or private. Its name will always include the word "limited."

3–46   A company limited by shares is defined as "a company having the liability of its members limited by the memorandum to the amount, if any, unpaid on the shares respectively held by them" (s. 1(2)(*a*)). The amount unpaid may be called up by the company at any time. It is, however, now usual for all the shares which a company has issued to be fully paid up from a date early in the company's life, and so a member usually has no liability to pay anything at all to the company.

3–47   When the company is wound up, the member will be entitled to receive back from the company the amount which he (or a former member from whom he has obtained a transfer) has paid to the company on each share, but this repayment of capital to the member is made only where all the company's creditors have been paid in full.

3–48   The *nominal* value (also referred to as "the par value") of a share (*e.g.* £1 if the company's capital is divided into shares of £1 each) is in law the measure of the member's stake in the company: he may lose his £1 per share, but he cannot be held liable for more, however great the company's own liabilities to its creditors may be.

3–49   In reality, of course, the member will regard his stake in the company as being the amount which he has paid to the company (if he is one of the original shareholders) or to the former member from whom he has himself obtained the shares by transfer. This purchase price is seldom the same as the nominal or par value of the shares. A company may, for instance, allot its £1 shares at a "premium" of 25p; this means that the applicant will be required to pay £1·25p to the company for each share, that the company will hold the £1 as paid-up capital and transfer the 25p to a special capital account called the "share premium account," and that the shares will be fully paid shares with £1 operating as the measure of the member's entitlement to dividends and, if the company is wound up and all creditors are fully paid, to first the return of nominal capital (*i.e.* £1 per share) and secondly the division of surplus assets.

The memorandum of association of a company limited by shares must be in the form (as nearly as circumstances admit) set out in:

(1) Table B of Schedule 1 to the Act of 1948, if the company is a private company (s. 11); or

(2) Part I of Schedule 1 to the Act of 1980, if the company is a public company (1980 Act, s. 2(4)).

A company limited by shares need not register articles of association. If it chooses to register articles, these may adopt all or any of the regulations contained in Table A of Schedule 1 to the Act (s. 8(1)). If it does not register articles, the regulations contained in Table A are treated as the company's articles. Further, if the company registers articles, Table A is still treated as containing the company's articles except in so far as the registered articles exclude or modify the regulations contained in Table A (s. 8(2)).

(ii) *Company Limited by Guarantee*

A company limited by guarantee is defined as "a company having the liability of its members limited by the memorandum to such amount as the members may respectively thereby undertake to contribute to the assets of the company in the event of its being wound up" (s. 1(2)(*b*)).

The distinctive clause in the memorandum of a guarantee company is the clause by which "every member of the company undertakes to contribute to the assets of the company in the event of its being wound up while he is a member . . . such amount as may be required, not exceeding £10" (or £20, *etc.*). This liability can arise only when the company is being wound up: it is available as a protection for creditors who would otherwise be left not fully paid at the end of the company's life.

Just as the company cannot during its active existence call up the guarantee fund, so it cannot give any particular creditor security over the fund. An attempt to do this was held to be of no effect in *Robertson* v. *British Linen Co.* (1890) 18 R. 1225 (O.H.), a case to be contrasted with *Lloyds Bank Ltd.* v. *Morrison & Son*, 1927 S.C. 571, in which a guarantee company was held entitled to assign to its bank a guarantee obtained from M. (who was not a member), quite distinct from the company's statutory guarantee fund.

There are two forms of guarantee company—commonly described as the "pure" form and the "hybrid" form. The pure form has no share capital: the creditors can look only to the statutory guarantee fund for protection and that will not exist until the company is being wound up. The hybrid form has a share capital (available for the protection of creditors during the company's active existence) as well as a guarantee fund. This hybrid form has been rarely used and the Act of 1980 prohibited the creation of any *further* companies of this kind (1980 Act, s. 1(2)).

By definition a public company must be either a company limited by shares or a company limited by guarantee and having a share capital (1980 Act, s. 1(1)). It follows that all pure forms of guarantee company are private companies.

3–57   The memorandum of association of a company limited by guarantee must be in the form (as nearly as circumstances admit) set out in:

(1) Table C of Schedule 1 to the Act of 1948, if the company has no share capital (the pure form of guarantee company and necessarily private) (s. 11); or

(2) Table D of Schedule 1 to the Act of 1948, if the company has a share capital and is a private company (the hybrid form, which will in time die out) (s. 11 and 1980 Act, s. 2(4)); or

(3) Part II of Schedule 1 to the Act of 1980, if the company has a share capital and is a public company (again the hybrid form, which will in time die out) (1980 Act, s. 2(4)).

3–58   A company limited by guarantee must always register articles of association (s. 6). A model form of articles for the pure form of guarantee company is set out in Table C of Schedule 1 to the Act of 1948 and a model form of articles for the hybrid form of guarantee company is set out in Table D of that Schedule (s. 11).

3–59   The articles of every guarantee company must state the number of members with which the company proposes to be registered (s. 7(2)). The purpose of this provision is to enable persons dealing with the company to find out the amount of the guarantee fund. Where the number of members is increased beyond the registered number, the company must give notice of the increase to the registrar of companies within 15 days (s. 7(3)).

3–60   A private guarantee company is on certain conditions exempt from the requirement that the word "limited" should be part of its name. The conditions which must be fulfilled are:

(1) the company's objects are the promotion of commerce, art, science, education, religion, charity or any profession and anything incidental or conducive to any of those objects; and

(2) the company's memorandum or articles:

(i) require its profits or other income to be applied in promoting its objects;

(ii) prohibit the payment of dividends to its members; and

(iii) require all the assets which would otherwise be available to its members generally to be transferred on its winding up either to another body with objects similar to its own or to another body whose objects are the promotion of charity and anything incidental or conducive to charity (1981 Act, s. 25).

(iii) *Unlimited Company*

3–61   An unlimited company is defined as "a company not having any limit on the liability of its members" (s. 1(2)(c)).

3–62   This type of registered company was becoming virtually obsolete by 1967, when the Companies Act of that year somewhat revived it, because it was by that Act made the only type of registered company which could keep its balance-sheet secret.

3–63   Since by definition a public company must be either a company limited by shares or a company limited by guarantee (and having a share capital (1980 Act, s. 1(1)), it follows that all unlimited companies are private companies.

An unlimited company may, but need not, have a share capital. A model form of memorandum and articles for an unlimited company with a share capital is set out in Table E of Schedule 1 to the Act of 1948 (s. 11).

An unlimited company must always register articles (s. 6).

Much of the common law of Scotland relating to companies came to light as a result of cases involving unlimited companies, especially the Western Bank of Scotland and the City of Glasgow Bank, in the nineteenth century.

(iv) *Conversion from Limited to Unlimited and* Vice Versa

Procedures for conversion of a limited company into an unlimited company and *vice versa* are contained in sections 43 and 44 respectively of the Act of 1967, as amended by the Act of 1980. Each involves re-registration and the issue by the registrar of companies of a new certificate of incorporation.

The first-mentioned type of conversion might be desired to enable the company to obtain the privilege of keeping its financial affairs secret —a privilege available only to unlimited companies. The whole procedure hinges on a prescribed form of assent to the company's being re-registered as unlimited; the form must be subscribed by or on behalf of *all* the members: nothing short of unanimity will do. This is in accordance with the dominant principle of company law that no member of a limited company can ever be required, without his written agreement, to undertake a liability which exceeds the fixed limit of his liability (see 1948 Act, s. 22).

Conversion from an unlimited company to a limited company can be achieved by a special resolution, but in this case it is vital that creditors be given adequate protection since they will no longer be able to rely on the members being liable without limit for the company's debts: if the company goes into liquidation within three years after the conversion those who were members at the time of the conversion are still liable without limit for debts and liabilities contracted before the conversion.

Each of the procedures is available only once: re-conversion is not permitted.

(b) **Public Companies and Private Companies**

The matters considered here are:
  (i)   the definitions of "public company" and "private company";
  (ii) the differences between public companies and private companies; and
  (iii) conversion from private to public and *vice versa*.

Radical changes in this part of company law were made by the Act of 1980; this resulted in complicated transitional provisions, but these are not dealt with here.

(i) *Definitions of "Public Company" and "Private Company"*

The Act of 1980 (s. 1(1)) gives a definition of "public company," and then provides: " 'private company,' unless the context otherwise requires, means a company that is not a public company."

3–73   "Public company" is defined as meaning "a company limited by shares or limited by guarantee and having a share capital, being a company—

   (*a*)   the memorandum of which states that the company is to be a public company; and

   (*b*)   in relation to which the provisions of the Companies Acts as to the registration or re-registration of a company as a public company have been complied with."

3–74   "The provisions of the Companies Acts as to the registration or re-registration of a company" referred to in that definition are to be found in the Act of 1948, as amended by Part I of the Act of 1980.

3–75   The main provisions as to *registration* are as follows:

The memorandum delivered to the registrar of companies (under section 12 of the Act of 1948) must state: "The company is to be a public company" (1980 Act, s. 2(4)). The amount of the share capital stated in the memorandum as that with which the company proposes to be registered must not be less than "the authorised minimum" (1980 Act, s. 3(2)). "The authorised minimum" means £50,000 or such other sum as is specified in a statutory instrument made under section 85 of the Act of 1980.

The certificate of incorporation given by the registrar (under section 13 of the Act of 1948) must contain a statement that the company is a public company; that statement is conclusive (1980 Act, s. 3(3), (4)).

3–76   The provisions as to *re-registration* apply in two possible situations:

   (1)   where the company is a private company with a share capital and wishes to convert itself into a public company (1980 Act, ss. 5, 6); and

   (2)   where the company is an "old public company," *i.e.* a company which was a public company within the meaning of the pre-1980 Companies Acts *and* which is either a company limited by shares or a company limited by guarantee and having a share capital (1980 Act, s. 8).

The re-registration provisions relating to the first situation will be indicated under heading (iii), below; those relating to the second situation are of a transitional character and are not further considered.

(ii)   *Differences between Public Companies and Private Companies*

3–77   The prominent difference between a public company and a private company originally was that the minimum number of members in a public company was seven whereas in a private company it was two. The Act of 1980 (s. 2(1)) removed that difference: the minimum membership for either type of company is now two. In other respects, however, the Act of 1980 greatly accentuated the differences between public and private companies, and the advantages enjoyed by the latter over the former.

3–78   The pre-1980 definition of a private company required the company's articles to include restrictions on the transfer of the company's shares and a limitation on the company's membership to 50 (excluding employees and former employees who had continued to hold shares). Though these distinctive requirements are no longer of statutory force, private companies commonly in practice have restrictions on the transfer of their shares and have a comparatively small membership.

The following are now the main statutory differences between public and private companies:

(1) Form of memorandum

The memorandum of a public company must be in one of the forms set out in Schedule 1 to the Act of 1980, or as near thereto as circumstances admit (1980 Act, s. 2(4)). The Schedule referred to has two Parts— Part I consisting of a form of memorandum for a public company limited by shares, and Part II consisting of a form of memorandum for a public company limited by guarantee and having a share capital. The latter type of company is rare and will eventually disappear completely because of the provision in the Act of 1980 that in future no company may be formed as, or become, a company limited by guarantee with a share capital (1980 Act, s. 1(2)).

The memorandum of a private company takes one of the forms set out in Tables B to E of Schedule 1 to the Act of 1948 or comes as near to one of these forms as circumstances admit (s. 11).

(2) The company's name

The name of a public company must end with the words "public limited company." Permitted alternatives are the abbreviation "p.l.c." and the Welsh equivalent "cwmni cyfyngedig cyhoeddus," which may be abbreviated as "c.c.c." The alternatives in Welsh are permissible only if the memorandum states that the company's registered office is to be situated in Wales (1980 Act, ss. 2(2), 78).

A private company may be either limited or unlimited. If it is a limited company, the last word of its name will be "limited" (or the abbreviation "ltd.") or (but only if the company is a Welsh company) "cyfyngedig" (or its abbreviation "cyf.") (1948 Act, s. 2(1)(a), 1976 Act, s. 30(3), 1980 Act, s. 78). An unlimited company must not use "limited" or "cyfyngedig" or any contraction or imitation of either of these words as the last word of its name; penalties are imposed for the improper use of these terms (1948 Act, s. 439, as amended by 1976 Act, Sched. 2). A private guarantee company is on certain conditions exempt from the requirement that the word "limited" (or any of its alternatives) should be part of the company's name (1981 Act, s. 25—see 3–60, above).

(3) Commencing business

A private company may commence business on the issue of its certificate of incorporation.

A public company is prohibited from doing business or exercising any borrowing powers until the registrar of companies has issued to it a certificate entitling it to do so. Before issuing such a certificate the registrar must be satisfied that the nominal value of the company's allotted share capital is not less than "the authorised minimum," and there must be delivered to the registrar a statutory declaration (in a prescribed form and signed by a director or secretary of the company) stating the amount paid up on the allotted share capital, preliminary expenses and the benefits paid to promoters (1980 Act, s. 4).

(4) **Directors and secretary**

3–86   A private company need have only one director, whereas a public company must have at least two (s. 176).

3–87   In a public company two or more directors cannot be appointed by a single resolution, unless a resolution has first been passed approving of that procedure without any vote being given against it. In a private company there is no rule requiring the appointment of directors to be voted on individually (s. 183).

3–88   The directors of a private company, unlike the directors of a public company, are not required to retire at the age of 70 years, unless the company is a subsidiary of a public company (s. 185).

3–89   As regards loans by a company to its directors and similar transactions, a private company, unless it is in a group of companies which includes a public company, is in a favourable position. The detailed provisions are in Part IV of the Act of 1980 as amended by the Act of 1981. The provisions start with the basic rule that a company must not make a loan to any of its directors or to any of the directors of its holding company and must not enter into any guarantee or provide any security in connection with a loan made by any person to such a director. Additional prohibitions are then made applicable to "relevant companies" (*i.e.* companies which either are public companies themselves or are private companies within a group which includes a public company); these wider prohibitions extend to "quasi-loans," to persons "connected with" directors, and to "credit transactions"; each of these special terms has a detailed statutory definition. There are important exceptions both to the basic rule and to the wider prohibitions (1980 Act, ss. 49-53, 64, 65).

3–90   A person appointed to the office of secretary of a public company must hold certain qualifications (*e.g.* membership of specified professional bodies) (1980 Act, s. 79). There is no such requirement in the case of a private company.

(5) **Capital**

3–91   Two differences arise out of the definition of "public company" (3–73 *et seq.*, above):

(a) A public company must have a share capital, whereas a private company need not.

(b) The share capital of a public company must not be less than "the authorised minimum" (at present £50,000), whereas the share capital of a private company may be of any amount, however small.

3–92   In addition, Part II of the Act of 1980 (headed "The Capital of a Company") has a number of groups of provisions involving differences between public and private companies:

(a) *The issue of share capital*

3–93   A private limited company must not offer any of its shares to the public. For contravention of this provision the company and its officers may be fined, but the validity of the allotment is not affected nor does the company lose the status of private company (1980 Act, s. 15).

3–94   Where a public company offers its shares to the public as it may do by a prospectus, no allotment can be made of the capital offered for subscription unless either the capital is subscribed for in full or the other conditions specified in the offer are satisfied (s. 16). (The Act of 1948 also restricts allotment following a prospectus: the "minimum subscription" (defined in Schedule 4 to that Act) must first be subscribed (s. 47), and no allotment can be made until the "time of the opening of the subscription lists" (s. 50).)

(b) *Pre-emption rights*

A company proposing to issue "equity" shares (*i.e.* broadly, ordinary, as opposed to preference, shares) for cash must first offer them to existing equity shareholders in proportion to their existing holdings, but in the case of a private company this rule may be excluded by a provision in the company's memorandum or articles (1980 Act, s. 17).

(c) *Payment for share capital*

In a public company payment for shares or for any premium on shares must not take the form of an undertaking given by any person to do work or perform services, whereas in a private company it may do so (1980 Act, s. 20(2)).

On an allotment of a share by a public company at least one-quarter of the nominal value of the share and the whole of any premium must be paid up; this is not required in the case of a private company (1980 Act, s. 22).

Where a share is allotted as fully or partly paid up otherwise than in cash, the non-cash consideration must not in the case of a public company include an undertaking which is to be performed more than five years after the allotment; there is no such restriction in the case of a private company (1980 Act, s. 23).

A public company must not as a general rule allot shares for a non-cash consideration unless that consideration has been valued by an "independent person," *i.e.* a person qualified to be the auditor of the company; no such valuation is required in the case of a private company (1980 Act, s. 24, as amended by 1981 Act, Sched. 3).

Where a public company is being formed and enters into an agreement with a subscriber to the memorandum for the transfer by him during the company's first two years of one or more non-cash assets, and the consideration to be given by the company is one-tenth or more of the nominal value of the company's issued share capital, the non-cash assets must be valued by an "independent person," and the terms of the agreement must be approved by an ordinary resolution of the company; these provisions do not apply to a private company (1980 Act, s. 26).

In a public company the shares for which a subscriber to the memorandum has undertaken, in the memorandum, to subscribe must be paid up in cash; in a private company such shares may be paid for in some other way (*e.g.* by the transfer of property to the company) (1980 Act, s. 29). The normal practice, however, is for the minimum number of subscribers (now two) to subscribe the memorandum for only one share each; the provision mentioned has therefore only a limited effect.)

(d) *Maintenance of capital*

3–102 Where the net assets of a public company fall to half or less of the amount of the company's called-up share capital, the directors must call an extraordinary general meeting to consider what measures should be taken to deal with the situation; in a private company directors are under no such obligation (1980 Act, s. 34).

3–103 There are strict rules as to the treatment of shares in a public company which come to be held by the company itself as a result of various circumstances including forfeiture and surrender; these rules do not apply to private companies (1980 Act, s. 37).

3–104 As a general rule a public company cannot have a lien or other charge on its own shares; there is no similar prohibition applying to a private company (1980 Act, s. 38).

3–105 Two sets of provisions in the Act of 1981 should be added under this heading:

(i) As a general rule it is not lawful for any company to give financial assistance to enable a person to acquire its own shares, but with certain safeguards relaxation of that rule is allowed in the case of private companies (1981 Act, ss. 42-44).

(ii) Any company, if authorised by its articles, may purchase its own shares (including any redeemable shares) out of distributable profits or out of the proceeds of a fresh issue, but only private companies are permitted to redeem or purchase their own shares out of capital (1981 Act, ss. 45-58).

(6) **Restriction on distribution of assets**

3–106 A public company must not make any distribution of its assets, in cash or otherwise, to its members if the company's net assets are less, or by the distribution would become less, than the total of the company's called-up share capital and "undistributable reserves" (*e.g.* the share premium account and the capital redemption reserve fund); there is no such restriction on a private company (1980 Act, ss. 40-45).

(7) **Proxies**

3–107 In any company with a share capital a member who is entitled to attend and vote at a meeting of the company is entitled to appoint another person (whether a member or not) as his proxy to attend and vote instead of him. In a private company the proxy appointed to attend and vote has the same right to speak at the meeting as the member would have had; in a public company a proxy does not have this statutory right (s. 136).

(8) **Conversion from limited to unlimited**

3–108 A private limited company may convert itself into a private unlimited company under section 43 of the Act of 1967. Such conversion is not available to a public company, since by definition a public company is always a limited company (1980 Act, s. 88 and Sched. 3).

(iii) *Conversion from Private to Public and* Vice Versa

3–109 The rules relating to conversion of a private company into a public company and *vice versa* are in Part I of the Act of 1980.

(1) Conversion from private to public

The procedure is open only to a company which has a share capital (1980 Act, s. 5). Moreover, before the procedure can start, the company must satisfy certain requirements as to its share capital. These correspond to the statutory requirements as to a public company's share capital (see 3–91 *et seq.*, above): the nominal value of the allotted share capital must be not less than "the authorised minimum," each allotted share must be paid up at least as to one-quarter of its nominal value and the whole of any premium, *etc.* (1980 Act, s. 6).

The company must pass a special resolution altering its memorandum so that it states that the company is to be a public company and making any other necessary alterations in its memorandum and articles.

An application for re-registration, in a prescribed form and signed by a director or secretary of the company, is then delivered to the registrar of companies, along with various documents including a printed copy of the memorandum and articles as altered and a copy of a written statement by the company's auditors that in their opinion the balance-sheet shows that the amount of the company's net assets was not less than the total of its called-up share capital and undistributable reserves.

The registrar retains the application and the other documents and issues a certificate of incorporation stating that the company is a public company. The certificate is conclusive evidence that the statutory requirements for re-registration have been complied with and that the company is a public company (1980 Act, s. 5).

(2) Conversion from public to private

The first step here is for the company to pass a special resolution altering its memorandum so that it no longer states that the company is to be a public company and making any other necessary alterations in its memorandum and articles.

An application for re-registration, in a prescribed form and signed by a director or secretary of the company, is then delivered to the registrar, along with a printed copy of the memorandum and articles as altered (1980 Act, s. 10).

During the 28 days after the passing of the special resolution dissenting members may apply to the court for cancellation of the special resolution. The minimum number of members for such an application is—

(a) holders of at least five per cent in nominal value of the company's issued share capital or of any class of the company's issued share capital; or

(b) if the company is not limited by shares, at least five per cent of the company's members; or

(c) at least 50 of the company's members.

The court must then make an order either cancelling or confirming the special resolution. The order may be a conditional one; *e.g.* it may provide for the purchase by the company of the shares of certain members or restrict the company's power to alter its memorandum or articles (1980 Act, s. 11).

Where no application is made to the court or where an application is withdrawn or where the court confirms the special resolution, the registrar issues a certificate of incorporation which is conclusive evidence that the requirements for re-registration have been complied with and that the company is a private company (1980 Act, s. 10).

(c) Holding Companies and Subsidiaries

3–118 Groups of companies are a common feature of modern business organisation. The Companies Acts give recognition to this feature by defining, and making special provisions for, "holding companies" and "subsidiaries."

3–119 A company ("S Ltd.") is deemed to be a subsidiary of another company ("H Ltd.") if, but only if—

(*a*) H. Ltd. *either*—

(i) is a member of S Ltd. *and* controls the composition of S Ltd.'s board of directors; or

(ii) holds more than half in nominal value of S Ltd.'s "equity share capital"; *or*

(*b*) S Ltd. is a subsidiary of any company which is a subsidiary of H Ltd.

3–120 The composition of S Ltd.'s board of directors is deemed to be controlled by H Ltd. if, but only if, H Ltd., without anyone else's consent or concurrence, can appoint or remove all or the majority of S Ltd.'s directors.

3–121 "Equity share capital" is defined as "issued share capital excluding any part thereof which, neither as respects dividends nor as respect capital, carries any right to participate beyond a specified amount in a distribution." The effect of this is that preference shares are normally not "equity share capital" because they normally carry a dividend of only a fixed percentage. "Equity share capital" therefore often means the issued ordinary shares.

3–122 The definition of "holding company" is the converse of the definition of "subsidiary": a company ("H Ltd.") is deemed to be the holding company of another ("S Ltd.") if, but only if, S Ltd. is H Ltd.'s subsidiary (s. 154).

3–123 The relationship of holding company and subsidiary may be—

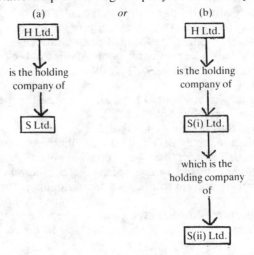

In (b), S(ii) Ltd., as well as being the subsidiary of S(i) Ltd., is the sub-sidiary of H Ltd., and H Ltd. is the holding company of both S(i) Ltd. and S(ii) Ltd. The chain of subsidiaries may extend much further—to S(iii) Ltd., S(iv) Ltd., and so on; in theory it is of infinite length.

There are two sets of provisions for which the relationship of holding company and subsidiary is particularly important:

(i) *Membership of Holding Company*

The general rule is that a company cannot be a member of its holding company, and any allotment or transfer of shares in a company to its subsidiary is void. Exceptions are permitted where the subsidiary holds the shares in a representative capacity as executor or trustee (s. 27).

(ii) *Group Accounts*

Where a company has subsidiaries the general rule is that the annual accounts must include "group accounts," *i.e.* accounts or statements dealing with the state of affairs and profit or loss of the company and the subsidiaries.

Exceptionally, group accounts are not required where the company is itself the wholly owned subsidiary of another British company or where the directors so decide on a limited number of specified grounds; Depart-ment of Trade approval is necessary in respect of some of these grounds (s. 150).

II THE SEPARATE PERSONALITY OF A REGISTERED COMPANY

This most important principle of company law, like several other major principles, is not to be found expressly stated in the Companies Acts; rather it has been developed by the courts professing to interpret the statutory provisions. The relevant provisions are those relating to registra-tion and it is therefore appropriate to look briefly at those provisions before passing to the doctrine of separate personality as illustrated by the cases. By far the most famous of the cases is *Salomon's* case [1897] A.C. 22; it has been applied and also distinguished in many subsequent cases, and the picturesque phrase "lifting the veil" has commonly been used to describe those cases where it has been distinguished. The doctrine of a registered company's separate personality may therefore be considered under these headings:

(a) the registration provisions;
(b) *Salomon's* case;
(c) application of the principle in *Salomon's* case; and
(d) lifting the veil.

(a) **The Registration Provisions**

For the formation of a registered company certain documents must be delivered to the appropriate registrar of companies and certain fees and stamp duties must be paid. If the registered office of the company is to be in Scotland the appropriate registrar is the Registrar of Companies for

Scotland, Companies Registration Office, 102 George Street, Edinburgh EH2 3DJ (s. 12).

3–130   The documents which must be delivered to the registrar are listed below. The first two—the memorandum of association and the articles of association—are the most important: together they comprise the constitution of the company, the memorandum being the dominant document and intended to govern relations between the company and outsiders, and the articles being the regulations for the internal management of the company. These two documents must be "subscribed" (*i.e.* signed) by at least two persons in the presence of at least one witness (ss. 1(1), 9(*d*); 1980 Act, s. 88 and Sched. 3).

3–131   The documents to be delivered to the registrar are:

(i) the memorandum of association, which states amongst other things the objects of the company and the nominal capital with which it is to be registered (s. 12);

(ii) the articles of association, providing for such matters as the holding of meetings of the members, the transfer of shares, and the directors' powers of management (s. 12); it is not compulsory for the commonest type of company—the company limited by shares—to register articles: if it does not do so, the regulations contained in Table A in Schedule 1 to the Act of 1948 will be the regulations of the company just as if they had been contained in duly registered articles (s. 8(2));

(iii) a statement signed by or on behalf of the subscribers of the memorandum:

(1) containing the names and particulars of the first directors and first secretary and a consent signed by each of them to act in the respective capacity (1976 Act, s. 21); and

(2) specifying the intended situation of the company's registered office (1976 Act, s. 23(2));

(iv) a statutory declaration by a solicitor engaged in the formation of the company, or by a person named as director or secretary in the statement mentioned in (iii), above, that the requirements of the Companies Acts have been complied with (1980 Act, s. 3(5)); and

(v) a statement of capital, unless the company is to have no share capital; this is for stamp duty purposes (Finance Act 1973, s. 47(3)).

3–132   On receiving these documents, the registrar must be satisfied that all the requirements of the Companies Acts have been complied with; he may accept the declaration mentioned in (iv), above, as sufficient evidence of compliance (1980 Act, s. 3(1) and (5)).

3–133   If the company is being formed for an unlawful object, the registrar will be justified in declining to register it (*R.* v. *Registrar of Joint Stock Companies, ex parte More* [1931] 2 K.B. 197 (C.A.), concerning the formation in England of a company for the sale there of tickets and chances in the Irish lottery authorised by the Parliament of the Irish Free State).

3–134   On registering the company the registrar issues a certificate of incorporation (the company's birth certificate), and from the date of incorporation mentioned in that certificate the subscribers of the memorandum, together with all the other persons who may from time to time become members of the company, are "a body corporate by the name contained in the memorandum, capable forthwith of exercising all the functions of an incorporated company" (s. 13).

The registrar must publish in the *Edinburgh Gazette* a notice of the issue of any certificate of incorporation to a company registered in Scotland (European Communities Act 1972, s. 9(3)).

A certificate of incorporation is conclusive evidence that the requirements of the Companies Acts have been complied with and that the association is a company authorised to be registered and is duly registered (1980 Act, s. 3(4)(*a*)).

The certificate is not conclusive as to the legality of the company: if a company were registered for an illegal object, proceedings could be brought to have the registration cancelled (*per* Lord Parker of Waddington in *Bowman* v. *Secular Society Ltd.* [1917] A.C. 406, at p. 439).

(b) Salomon's Case

The doctrine of a registered company's separate personality is always associated with the English case of *Salomon* v. *A. Salomon & Co. Ltd.* [1897] A.C. 22, in which the House of Lords reversed the judgment of the Court of Appeal.

Aron Salomon had for many years carried on business on his own account as a leather merchant and wholesale boot manufacturer. He transferred his business to a company consisting of himself and members of his own family. The minimum membership was at that time (under the Companies Act 1862) seven, and so Salomon, his wife, a daughter and four sons each subscribed the memorandum for one share each.

Since Salomon was selling his own business to the new company he received 20,000 shares and £10,000 debentures from the company as payment of the purchase-price. Salomon then held 20,001 shares and no other shares were ever issued. The debentures were secured by a floating charge over the company's property.

Before the transfer the business had been prosperous, but the company soon fell upon bad days owing to a depression in the boot trade and strikes of workmen. As a result the company was wound up. The position then was that if the debentures (representing a debt due by the company to Salomon) were paid, there would be nothing left for payment of the unsecured creditors.

It was argued that the six shareholders other than Salomon were mere dummies, his nominees, and held their shares in trust for Salomon, and that the company was really still a one-man business, it making no difference that all the requirements of the Act of 1862 had been duly observed.

Held that the company had been duly formed and was not the mere "alias" or agent of or trustee for Salomon; that he was not liable to indemnify the company against its creditors' claims; that there was no fraud upon creditors or shareholders; and that the company (or its liquidator) was not entitled to rescission of the contract of purchase.

Lord Macnaghten said (at p. 51): "When the memorandum is duly signed and registered, though there be only seven shares taken, the subscribers are a body corporate 'capable forthwith,' to use the words of the enactment, 'of exercising all the functions of an incorporated company.' Those are strong words. The company attains maturity on its birth. There is no period of minority—no interval of incapacity. I cannot understand how a body corporate thus made 'capable' by statute can lose its individuality by issuing the bulk of its capital to one person, whether he be a subscriber to the memorandum or not. **The company is at law a different person altogether from the subscribers to the memorandum; and, though it may be that after incorporation the business is precisely the same as it was before, and the same persons are managers, and the same hands receive the profits, the company is not in law the agent of the subscribers or trustee for them. Nor are the subscribers as members liable, in any shape or form, except to the extent and in the manner provided by the Act.**"

The words in bold type are the most famous passage in company law.

3–139   By the time when *Salomon's* case was decided the Scottish courts had already worked out the same doctrine independently; two instances are:

3–140   (i) *Grierson, Oldham & Co. Ltd.* v. *Forbes, Maxwell & Co. Ltd.* (1895) 22 R. 812: F. Ltd. entered into an agreement with G. & Co., a firm of wine-merchants, for a space in G. & Co.'s advertising wine-list for a period of three years at a rent of £200 per annum. Shortly after the agreement was entered into, G. & Co.'s business was transferred to a newly-formed registered company, G. & Co. Ltd.

Held that G. & Co. Ltd. had no title to sue F. Ltd. for non-payment of the rent.

Lord Justice-Clerk J.H.A. Macdonald said (at p. 817): "I am of opinion that the new limited company cannot be held to be the same contracting party as the old firm, and that Messrs Forbes, Maxwell, & Company are not under their contract with Messrs Grierson, Oldham, & Company bound to pay for an advertisement in the wine-list of the limited company, with which company they have no contract."

3–141   (ii) *John Wilson & Son Ltd.* v. *Inland Revenue* (1895) 23 R. 18: A partnership, W. & Son, was converted into a registered company, W. & Son Ltd., each partner receiving shares in the new company equal to the value of his holding in the former partnership.

The question arose of whether the conveyance of the assets of the partnership to the new company was a conveyance on sale within the meaning of the Stamp Act 1891.

Held that it was such a conveyance.

Lord McLaren said (at p. 24): "When a number of persons are constituted a company under the Companies Act, the new company is by statute a corporation, having an identity distinct from that of its constituent members or those to whom shares may be allotted."

(c) Application of the Principle in Salomon's Case

3–142   As a general rule the court will not go behind the separate personality of a registered company to find out who the members of the company are. *Salomon's* case is authority for not "lifting the veil of incorporation." The application of this general rule has the following consequences:

3–143   (i) The property of the company belongs to the company itself and not to the individual members, however many shares they may hold. Therefore neither shareholders nor creditors have any insurable interest in the company's assets, as may be illustrated by *Macaura* v. *Northern Assurance Co. Ltd.* [1925] A.C. 619, which reached the House of Lords from Northern Ireland:

M., the owner of Killymoon timber estate in county Tyrone, sold the whole of the timber to the Irish Canadian Saw Mills Ltd. for £27,000 to be paid in fully-paid shares. M. insured the timber against fire by policies in his own name. M. was also a creditor of the company for £19,000.

The greater part of the timber was destroyed by fire, and M. sued the insurance companies.

M.'s action was unsuccessful because he had no insurable interest, though he was virtually the sole shareholder and sole creditor; the fact that the timber was the company's only asset made no difference.

(ii) A company may be the occupier of, and carry on business in, heritable property. If the property is compulsorily acquired, the individual who is the major shareholder and sole director and who devotes his whole time to the business is not entitled to compensation as occupier. This point arose, in connection with a group of companies, in *Woolfson* v. *Strathclyde Regional Council,* 1978 S.C. (H.L.) 90; 1977 S.C. 84:

M. & L. Campbell (Glasgow) Ltd. ("C. Ltd.") was the occupier of a retail shop and carried on business there. The issued share capital of C. Ltd. was 1,000 shares, of which 999 were held by W. and one by W.'s wife. W. was the sole director of C. Ltd., managed the business and was paid a salary which was taxed under Schedule E.

The premises were owned partly by W. and partly by Solfred Holdings Ltd. ("S. Ltd."), the shares in which were held as to two-thirds by W. and as to the remaining one-third by W.'s wife.

Glasgow Corporation as highway authority made a compulsory purchase order in respect of the shop.

W. claimed compensation on the basis that he, C. Ltd. and S. Ltd. should all be treated as a single entity embodied in W. himself.

Held, applying the principle of *Salomon's* case, that W., C. Ltd. and S. Ltd. were each a separate legal *persona* ("person").

A comparable English case, *DHN Food Distributors Ltd.* v. *Tower Hamlets London Borough Council* [1976] 1 W.L.R. 852 had been differently decided by the Court of Appeal, but was explained both in the Court of Session and in the House of Lords as being clearly distinguishable on its facts from *Woolfson's* case. (The question may be raised of whether the real difference was not as to the facts but as to the approach taken.)

(iii) Where there are two or more companies, each has a separate legal *persona*, though the companies may in reality be related or form part of the same group; thus in *Taylor, Petitioner,* 1976 S.L.T. (Sh. Ct.) 82, two related companies were held to be separate entities; see also *Woolfson* v. *Strathclyde Regional Council* (3–144, above).

(d) Lifting the Veil

The exceptional cases in which the veil of incorporation is lifted (or, as is sometimes said, "pierced") fall into two groups:

(i) statutory instances; and
(ii) common law instances.

(i) *Statutory Instances*

3–147 Statutory instances of lifting the veil are to be found not only in the Companies Acts but also in other legislation. Of the instances given below, the first two are from such other legislation:

(1) Trading with the enemy

3–148 The common law recognised that in time of war a company registered in the United Kingdom was an alien enemy if its agents or the persons *de facto* ("in fact") in control of its affairs were alien enemies, and that the enemy character of individual shareholders and their conduct might be material on the question of control.

3–149 During the two World Wars the common law was strengthened by the Trading with the Enemy Act 1914 and the Trading with the Enemy Act 1939.

3–150 A well-known case on this area of the law is *Daimler Co. Ltd.* v. *Continental Tyre and Rubber Co. (Great Britain) Ltd.* [1916] 2 A.C. 307:

C. Ltd. was an English company most of whose shares were held by a German company. The holders of the remaining shares (except one) and all the directors were Germans resident in Germany. The one exceptional share was registered in the name of the secretary who had been born in Germany but who had become a naturalised British subject and resided in England.

An action was commenced in the name of C. Ltd. for a sum of money alleged to be due to it by D. Ltd. The summons was opposed on the grounds that the plaintiff and its officers were alien enemies (with the consequence that it could not bring proceedings) and that D. Ltd. in paying the amount claimed would be contravening the Trading with the Enemy Act 1914.

The House of Lords held that C. Ltd. was an enemy company for the purposes of the Act of 1914 because the effective control was in enemy hands.

(2) Taxation

3–151 In the law of taxation the test of residence is applied, and a company is not necessarily resident in the country where it has its registered office and where it has been incorporated. A company is ordinarily resident where the actual management of the company is carried on, and so it is necessary to lift the veil of incorporation.

3–152 Another aspect of the law of taxation which requires the veil to be lifted is the set of complex rules relating to "close companies"; the rules are designed to ensure that shareholders in small companies cannot avoid paying income tax by deciding that the company is not to pay out its profits as dividends to shareholders but retain them in the business to achieve capital growth.

(3) Membership below minimum

3–153 If a company carries on business without having at least two members for more than six months, then a person who, after these six months, is a member of the company *and* knows that it is carrying on business with only one member is liable (jointly and severally with the company) for payment of the company's debts contracted after the expiry of the six months. This is an exception to the general rule that the company's debts cannot be enforced against its members (s. 31, as substituted by 1980 Act, s. 88 and Sched. 3).

(4) Holding company and subsidiaries

In order to find out whether the relationship of holding company and subsidiary exists, the veil of incorporation is lifted because the membership of the subsidiary company must be looked at (s. 154—see 3–119, above).

The requirement to have group accounts where the relationship of holding company and subsidiary exists is a further illustration of lifting the veil (s. 150—see 3–126, above).

(5) Department of Trade investigations

An inspector appointed to investigate a company's *affairs* may, if he thinks it necessary, investigate also the affairs of related companies (*e.g.* the holding company and subsidiary companies) (s. 166).

Department of Trade investigations into a company's *membership* are a still more obvious instance of lifting the veil (s. 172).

(6) Sole director not to be secretary

Every company must have a secretary, and a sole director must not also be the secretary (s. 177(1)). It is possible for a director or secretary to be not an individual but a corporation (*e.g.* another company), and so, to prevent the provision mentioned being avoided by the device of incorporation, there is the additional provision that it is not permissible for a company—

(a) to have as secretary a corporation whose sole director is also the sole director of the company in question; or

(b) to have as sole director a corporation whose sole director is also the secretary of the company in question (s. 178).

This additional provision amounts to a lifting of the veil for the purpose of ensuring that the two offices of secretary and sole director are in reality, and not merely in theory, held by two different persons.

(7) Disclosure of directors' interests

A director is under an obligation to notify the company of his interests in shares in and debentures of the company (1967 Act, s. 27), and one of the rules designed to give effect to that obligation is the provision that a person ("X") is to be taken to be interested in shares or debentures if a body corporate is interested in them *and*—

(a) that body corporate is accustomed to act in accordance with X's directions or instructions; or

(b) X is entitled to exercise, or control the exercise of, one-third or more of the voting power at general meetings of that body corporate (1967 Act, s. 28(4A), as substituted by 1981 Act, s. 119(4) and Sched. 3). The veil is here being lifted to see how the body corporate is controlled.

(ii) *Common Law Instances*

3–160 The following are some of the instances in which the courts, in the exercise of their discretion and in the interests of justice and equity as seen by them, have lifted the veil of incorporation:

(1) **Company formed to enable valid contract in restraint of trade to be broken**

3–161 *Gilford Motor Co. Ltd.* v. *Horne* [1933] Ch. 935 (C.A.): H. was managing director of G. Ltd. His contract of employment included a valid covenant in restraint of trade, by which he undertook that after the termination of his employment he would not solicit G. Ltd.'s customers.

Shortly after the termination of his employment H. formed a company, J.M.H. & Co. Ltd., for the sale of spare parts of G. Ltd.'s vehicles, and sent out circulars to G. Ltd.'s customers. The business of J.M.H. & Co. Ltd. was carried on wholly by H.

Held that J.M.H. & Co. Ltd. was a mere channel, a mere cloak or sham for the purpose of enabling H. to commit a breach of his covenant, and an injunction[1] was granted against both H. and J.M.H. & Co. Ltd. to restrain further breach of the covenant.

(2) **Transfer of land in breach of contract of sale**

3–162 *Jones* v. *Lipman* [1962] 1 W.L.R. 832: L. agreed to sell freehold land to J. Before the land was transferred, L., for a lesser price, sold and transferred the land to Alamed Ltd., in which L. and his clerk were the only shareholders and directors.

J. brought an action for specific performance[2] against L. and Alamed Ltd.

Held that J. was entitled to the decree of specific performance sought because Alamed Ltd. was the creature of, and a mask for, L., who was in a position, through his control of Alamed Ltd., to cause the contract with J. to be completed.

(3) **Subsidiary company as agent of holding company**

3–163 *Smith, Stone & Knight Ltd.* v. *Birmingham Corporation* [1939] 4 All E.R. 116: The case arose out of the compulsory purchase of S. Ltd.'s factory by Birmingham Corporation for the purpose of building a technical college. The premises had been let by S. Ltd. to its subsidiary, Birmingham Waste Co. Ltd., and the question was whether S. Ltd. could claim compensation for disturbance of the business carried on by its subsidiary.

Atkinson J. asked six questions and gave an affirmative answer to each:

 (a) Were the profits treated as the profits of S. Ltd.?

 (b) Were the persons conducting the business appointed by S. Ltd.?

 (c) Was S. Ltd. the head and the brain of the trading venture?

 (d) Did S. Ltd. govern the adventure, decide what should be done and what capital should be embarked on the venture?

---

[1] The Scots law equivalent is "interdict."
[2] The Scots law equivalent is "specific implement."

(e) Did S. Ltd. make the profits by its skill and direction?

(f) Was S. Ltd. in effectual and constant control?

The judge concluded that he had no doubt that the business was S. Ltd.'s business and was being carried on under S. Ltd.'s direction. S. Ltd. was therefore entitled to claim compensation for disturbance of the business.

The judge emphasised that the question is one of fact in each case, depending on the arrangements made between the holding company and the subsidiaries.

The question raised may be the converse one—whether the holding company is the agent of its subsidiary.

Compare the two contrasting cases *Woolfson* v. *Strathclyde Regional Council* and *DHN Food Distributors Ltd.* v. *Tower Hamlets London Borough Council* (3–144, above).

(4) Court's discretion in relation to "take-over bid" (s. 209)

Section 209 of the Act of 1948 enables a company (referred to as "the transferee company") which has made an offer for the shares of another company ("the transferor company") and which has had its offer accepted by the holders of nine-tenths of the shares of the transferor company to acquire compulsorily the remaining one-tenth held by the "dissenting shareholders" (*i.e.* shareholders who have resisted the "take-over" by declining the transferee company's offer). A dissenting shareholder, however, has the right to apply to court, and the court, if it "thinks fit" may "order otherwise," *i.e.* order that the transferee company is not entitled to acquire the dissentient's shares compulsorily.

An instance of the exercise of this discretion by the court occurred in *Re Bugle Press Ltd.* [1961] Ch. 270 (C.A.):

B. Ltd., a publishing company, had three shareholders and an issued capital of 10,000 £1 shares, of which Shaw held 4,500, Jackson 4,500 and Treby 1,000.

A new company, Jackson & Shaw (Holdings) Ltd. ("J. & S. Ltd."), was formed with only Jackson and Shaw as shareholders and directors. J. & S. Ltd. made a "take-over bid" for all the shares of B. Ltd. Treby did not accept the offer, and J. & S. Ltd., as transferee company, gave notice of its intention to exercise its right of compulsory acquisition under section 209.

Treby applied to court for a declaration that J. & S. Ltd. was not entitled to acquire his shares compulsorily.

Held that Treby was entitled to the declaration sought because section 209 was being abused for the purpose of enabling the majority shareholders to expropriate or evict the minority.

The court was here lifting the veil for the purpose of revealing that the transferee company was in reality the same in identity as the majority shareholders of B. Ltd. Treby won his case by showing that "the transferee company was nothing but a little hut built round his two co-shareholders, and that the so-called scheme was made by themselves as directors of that company with themselves as shareholders and the whole thing, therefore, is seen to be a hollow sham" (*per* Harman L.J. at p. 288).

(5) Decision of all the members taking effect as decision of the company

3–166   Where all the members of a company agree to dispense with formalities such as the holding of meetings and the passing of resolutions, their own actings are regarded as the actings of the company, *e.g. Re Express Engineering Works Ltd.* [1920] 1 Ch. 466 (C.A.):

Five persons formed a private company in which they were the only shareholders. Having bought a property for £7,000, they sold it to the company for £15,000, the price to be paid by debentures issued by the company. The transaction was carried out at a "board meeting" for the purpose of which the five persons appointed themselves directors. A provision in the articles prohibiting a director from voting on a contract in which he was interested was disregarded.

Held that no fraud was involved, that the company was bound by the unanimous agreement of its members and that consequently the debentures were valid.

III COMPARISON OF REGISTERED COMPANIES WITH PARTNERSHIPS

3–167 In Scots law both registered companies and partnerships are artificial legal persons, distinct from the members of whom they are composed.

3–168   The personality of the two types of body, however, arises from different sources: the personality of a registered company comes from the incorporation effected by the issue of the certificate of incorporation (s. 13), whereas the personality of a partnership depends on the provision in the Partnership Act 1890 (s. 4(2)), reproducing the common law of Scotland, that a firm is a legal person distinct from the partners of whom it is composed; a partnership is an unincorporated body.

3–169   There are some principles of law which credit a partnership with a personality which is less full than the personality of a registered company. In particular:[3]

3–170   (i) In the case of a firm, it is permissible, if the firm itself does not meet its debts and obligations, for a creditor to go behind the firm and hold the individual partners liable jointly and severally for these debts and obligations; this does not happen in the case of a registered company: even when the company is being wound up, and even though it may be hopelessly insolvent, a creditor has no direct access to any individual member; any liability attaching to a member (*e.g.* if the shares which he holds are not fully paid shares) is a liability to pay *to the company* (or its liquidator as representing it in a winding up) and not to the company's creditors.

3–171   (ii) A firm, like a registered company, has rights of ownership in property, both heritable and moveable, but the formal legal title to heritable property held on feudal tenure must be taken in the names of the individual partners or of other individuals in trust for the firm. In the case of a registered company, on the other hand, there is no such obstacle.

3–172   Separate personality is the most striking feature which is common to registered companies and partnerships in Scotland. In considering the

---

3 See also 2–30 *et seq.*, above.

differences between the two types of body it is convenient to make a division between:

(a) those respects in which a registered company has advantages over a partnership; and

(b) those respects in which a partnership has advantages over a registered company.

(a) **Advantages of Registered Company**

Because the personality of a partnership is less full than that of a registered company, there are some respects in which the registered company is at an advantage (see, *e.g.*, 3–170 and 3–171, above).

The following advantages, however, are of greater practical importance:

(i) *Limited Liability*

In a registered company (unless the company is an unlimited company) all members enjoy limited liability for the company's debts, whereas in a partnership the general rule is that all the partners are jointly and severally liable for the firm's debts if the firm itself fails to pay. If the partnership is a limited partnership, as is allowed by the Limited Partnerships Act 1907, one or more of the partners may enjoy limited liability, but there must always be one or more general partners who incur the usual joint and several liability; further, in a limited partnership a limited partner must not take part in the management: if he does so, he becomes liable as a general partner; in a registered company, on the other hand, all the members may, by having themselves appointed directors, take part in the management without losing their limited liability.

(ii) *Transferability of Shares*

The basic rule in company law is that shares are freely transferable, though it is usual in private companies for the articles to contain some restriction on the transfer of shares (*e.g.* there may be the restriction that a shareholder wishing to transfer his shares must first offer them to other shareholders—a "pre-emption" clause). In public companies shares are always freely transferable.

In a partnership, on the other hand, owing to the element of *delectus personae* ("choice of person"), a new partner cannot be introduced without the consent of all existing partners unless the existing partners have made some agreement to the contrary (Partnership Act 1890, s. 24(7)).

(iii) *Management by Directors*

In a registered company management is in the hands of directors: they are the agents of the company, and members, as members, have no powers of management. This opens up a great range of possibilities for the business organisation: at one end of the scale there is opportunity for an investor on the stock exchange to purchase shares in a large public company purely as a financial venture, without even contemplating that he would be expected to attend to the day-to-day management of the concern, while at the other end of the scale there is the small private company where all the members of a particular family may so arrange matters that they are all directors as well as shareholders, and so manage the family business in much the same way to outward appearances as if they were in fact partners.

3–179   In partnership, on the other hand, the principle is that every partner is an agent of the firm and his other partners for the purpose of the business of the partnership (Partnership Act 1890, s. 5). As regards the relations between the partners themselves, every partner may take part in the management of the partnership business unless there is agreement to the contrary (Partnership Act 1890, s. 24(5)). The special disability of the limited partner in a limited partnership is mentioned above (3–175). Partnership as a form of business organisation is designed rather for a small concern where all the members are envisaged as taking part in the running of the business; it does not offer anything like the range of possibilities available in registered companies.

(iv) *No Limit in Number of Members*

3–180   The minimum membership for both registered companies and partnerships is two. In a registered company there is no maximum, whereas in a partnership there is a general limit of 20 (Companies Act 1948, s. 434), exceptions being allowed for partnerships of solicitors, accountants, stockbrokers and other categories specified in regulations (Companies Act 1967, s. 120).

3–181   A consequence of the limit in the number of partners is that it is generally impossible for a partnership to raise such a large capital as may be raised by a registered company.

(v) *Changes in Membership*

3–182   Changes in the membership of a registered company do not disturb the continuing existence and operation of the company, whereas changes in the membership of a partnership may result in the discontinuance of the partnership; *e.g.* finding a replacement for a retiring partner requires, unless there is agreement to the contrary, consent of all the continuing partners (Partnership Act 1890, s. 24(7)), questions of liability of retiring and new partners to creditors of the firm may arise, and a partnership is, unless there is agreement to the contrary between the partners, dissolved as regards all the partners by the death or bankruptcy of any partner (Partnership Act 1890, s. 33(1)).

(vi) *Borrowing and Granting Security*

3–183   A registered company may borrow by issuing debentures and debenture stock, and it may grant security to lenders by creating floating charges over the whole of its undertaking (Companies (Floating Charges and Receivers) (Scotland) Act 1972); it may, for instance, grant a floating charge over its moveable stock-in-trade. However, in the case of a small private company, it can often happen that a creditor such as a bank will require a personal guarantee from the person who is in actual control of the company, the effect being that that person will not have the protection of limited liability in respect of the debt due to that creditor.

Partnerships do not issue debentures or debenture stock, and they are subject to the ordinary principles relating to rights in security, *i.e.* delivery is essential for the creation of a valid right in security and any attempt to create a floating charge is of no legal effect.

(vii) *Taxation*
In some cases (but not always) a registered company will have advantages over a partnership in relation to taxation.

(b) **Advantages of Partnership**
The advantages of a partnership—normally outweighed by the advantages of a registered company—include the following:

(i) *No Formalities in Formation*
A partnership may be formed by simple agreement: there is no need for formal writing (though a contract of co-partnery is advisable), and the relationship may even be inferred from conduct without any words being spoken. No publicity is necessary. There need be no legal costs.

A registered company can be formed only by compliance with a registration procedure. A memorandum of association and articles of association together with other documents in proper legal form, delivered to the registrar of companies, involve publicity and expense.

(ii) *No Formalities in Carrying on Business*
A partnership is not required to deliver to any public office information relating to the carrying on of its business. This again means less publicity and less expense.

A registered company is required to file an annual return, copies of various resolutions and other documents. These must all be prepared in an acceptable form and are kept open to public inspection at the office of the registrar of companies.

(iii) *No Disclosure of Financial Affairs*
A partnership is not required to file at a public office any copy of the business accounts: its financial affairs are therefore not made public. This can be a highly prized advantage.

A registered company, on the other hand, (unless it is an unlimited company) must file with the registrar of companies, and so give publicity to, its annual accounts. Modified accounts, however, are permitted under the Act of 1981 for small and medium-sized companies.

(iv) *Absence of* Ultra Vires *Doctrine*
A partnership is not subject to the *ultra vires* ("beyond the powers") doctrine: the partners may do anything lawful which they agree to do; *e.g.* they may branch out into a completely different line of business.

A registered company, on the other hand, must keep within the objects stated in its memorandum of association. (In practice, however, the memorandum is usually so widely drawn that there will be virtually no activity which will be *ultra vires*.)

(v) *No Restrictions on Share Capital*

3–195 A partnership is free to alter its capital in any way agreed on by the partners.

3–196 A registered company, on the other hand, is subject to various restrictions in relation to its share capital; *e.g.* limited companies are subject to the principle of maintenance of capital as modified by the Act of 1981, there are statutory procedures for variation of capital, and the Act of 1980 introduced additional statutory restrictions on the issue of and payment for share capital.

(vi) *Arrangements with Creditors*

3–197 A partnership is free to make any arrangement with its creditors that is agreed on, whereas a registered company can make only such arrangements as are authorised by the Companies Acts (1948 Act, ss. 206, 245, 303, 306).

(vii) *Taxation*

3–198 There are some situations in which a partnership will have advantages over a registered company in relation to taxation.

IV MEMORANDUM OF ASSOCIATION

3–199 The two documents which contain the constitution of any company (its "constitutional" documents) are the memorandum of association and the articles of association. This part of the chapter will deal first with (a) the relationship between the two documents and then with (b) the contents of the memorandum.

(a) **Relationship between Memorandum and Articles**

3–200 The memorandum governs the external transactions of the company: it is the public document from which persons dealing with the company may ascertain the company's name, whether the company is public or private, the country of its registration, its objects, whether it is limited or unlimited, and, in the case of a limited company with a share capital, the amount of that share capital; it ends with an association clause which shows, and is signed by, the two or more persons who will be the company's first members.

3–201 The articles, on the other hand, govern the company's internal affairs: they deal with such matters as the transfer of shares from one person to another, company meetings, directors and dividends.

3–202 Originally the memorandum was unalterable, whereas the articles were alterable by the members. Although there are now many statutory provisions which permit the several contents of the memorandum to be altered, the original rule is still reflected in the statutory wording:

"A company may not alter the conditions contained in its memorandum except in the cases, in the mode and to the extent for which express provision is made in the Companies Acts 1948 to 1981" (s. 4, as amended by 1981 Act, Sched. 3); and

"Subject to the provisions of the Companies Acts 1948 to 1981 and to the conditions contained in its memorandum, a company may by special resolution alter its articles" (s. 10(1), as amended by 1980 Act, Sched. 4, and 1981 Act, Sched. 3).

The memorandum is the dominant of the two documents. If, however, there is an ambiguity in its provisions, the articles, being a "contemporaneous" document, may be looked at for assistance in interpretation. Such difficulties can arise where matters which might have been set out in the articles have been included in the memorandum instead, *e.g.*:

Marshall, Fleming & Co. Ltd., Petitioners, 1938 S.C. 873 (O.H.): The memorandum of M. Ltd. divided the shares into preference shares and ordinary shares, with certain rights attached to each class. The articles contained a clause enabling special rights to be altered.

Held that M. Ltd. could, by following the procedure prescribed in the articles, alter the rights of the different classes of shareholders as set out in the memorandum.

(b) Contents of Memorandum

The Companies Acts provide model forms of memoranda for the different types of registered companies. These have been indicated under "Classification of Registered Companies" (3–43 *et seq.,* above). The contents of a memorandum, together with some of the law associated with them, are considered here under the headings:

   (i) name;
  (ii) statement that company is to be a public company;
 (iii) registered office;
 (iv) objects;
  (v) statement that liability is limited;
 (vi) share capital;
 (vii) additional clauses; and
(viii) association clause.

(i) *Name*

The main rules are that the name of a private company limited by shares or by guarantee must have "limited" as the last word of its name (s. 2(1)) and that the name of a public company must end with the words "public limited company" (1980 Act, s. 2(2)). For the permitted abbreviations and the Welsh equivalents, see 3–82 *et seq.,* above, and for the exemption from the use of the word "limited," which on certain conditions is open to private companies limited by guarantee, see 3–60, above.

Examples of name clauses in the model memoranda are:

"The name of the company is 'The Eastern Steam Packet Company, Limited' " (1948 Act, Sched. 1, Table B);

"The name of the company is, 'The Western Steam Packet, public limited company' " (1980 Act, Sched. 1, Part I); and

"The name of the company is 'The Patent Stereotype Company' " (1948 Act, Sched. 1, Table E).

(1) Choice of name

3–207   There are statutory provisions relating to the choice of name in Part II of the Act of 1981:

A company must not be registered by a name which is the same as a name appearing in the index of names (which includes the names of limited partnerships) kept by the registrar of companies or by a name the use of which would in the opinion of the Department of Trade constitute a criminal offence or by a name which in the opinion of the Department of Trade is offensive.

In addition certain names require prior approval of the Department of Trade; these are:

(a) names likely to give the impression that the company is connected in any way with the Government or with any local authority; and

(b) names including a word or expression specified in regulations (1981 Act, ss. 22, 23, 31).

As regards (b), the regulations at present in force are the Company and Business Names Regulations 1981 (S.I. 1981 No. 1685). Examples of words and expressions specified are "Chamber of Commerce," "Giro," "Stock Exchange" and "Trust." In respect of some words and expressions the Regulations also specify a Government department or other body as the "relevant body," *i.e.* as the body which must first be asked whether (and if so why) it has any objections to the proposed name; *e.g.* for the expression "Health Centre" the relevant body is the Department of Health and Social Security.

3–208   In addition to these statutory provisions there is a principle of the common law which enables a person to obtain an interdict from the court prohibiting the adoption of a name likely to cause confusion between his own existing business and the new concern. An English illustration is *Ewing* v. *Buttercup Margarine Co. Ltd.* [1917] 2 Ch. 1 (C.A.), in which E., who had a chain of shops trading under the name "Buttercup Dairy Company," was held entitled to an injunction restraining a new company from carrying on business under the name "Buttercup Margarine Co. Ltd." Two Scottish cases in which interdicts were refused because the new name was not calculated to deceive the public are:

Dunlop Pneumatic Tyre Co. Ltd. v. *Dunlop Motor Co. Ltd.*, 1907 S.C. (H.L.) 15; (1906) 8 F. 1146: The name "Dunlop Motor Co. Ltd." adopted by a small new motor repairing company in Kilmarnock was held not calculated to deceive the public into purchasing that company's goods in the belief that they were goods of a large English company, Dunlop Pneumatic Tyre Co. Ltd., manufacturers of motoring accessories.

Scottish Union and National Insurance Co. v. *Scottish National Insurance Co. Ltd.*, 1909 S.C. 318: The similarity of names in this case was held not likely to deceive the public because the first-mentioned company carried on general insurance business excluding marine insurance, whereas the newly registered company was to confine its business to marine insurance.

(2) Change of name

3–209   A company may change its name by special resolution (1981 Act, s. 24(1)).

There are statutory provisions under which a company may be required to change its name in certain circumstances: where a company has been registered by a name which is the same as or, in the opinion of the Department of Trade, too like a name already in the index of names kept by the registrar, the Department of Trade may within 12 months of the registration direct the company to change its name within a specified period (1981 Act, s. 24(2)); if, in the opinion of the Department of Trade, the name by which a company is registered gives so misleading an indication of the nature of its activities as to be likely to cause harm to the public, the Department may direct it to change its name, but the company receiving such a direction has a right to apply to the court to set the direction aside (1967 Act, s. 46).

(3) Publication of name (1948 Act, section 108)

Every company must:

(a) paint or affix its name on the outside of every office or place in which its business is carried on, in a conspicuous position, in letters easily legible;

(b) have its name engraven in legible characters on its seal; and

(c) have its name mentioned in legible characters in all business letters of the company and in all notices and other official publications of the company, and in all bills of exchange, promissory notes, indorsements, cheques and orders for money or goods signed by or on behalf of the company, and in all bills of parcels, invoices, receipts and letters of credit of the company.

There are penalties imposed on a company and officers of a company for failure to observe these provisions.

In addition, an officer or other person acting on behalf of the company may become personally liable to the holder of a bill of exchange, promissory note, cheque or order for money or goods if the company's name is not mentioned in the document in question and the company itself fails to make due payment. This provision was applied in *Scottish and Newcastle Breweries Ltd.* v. *Blair and Others*, 1967 S.L.T. 72 (O.H.):

S. Ltd. drew a bill of exchange for £7,500 on Anderson & Blair (Property Development) Ltd., but misnamed the drawee as "Messrs. Anderson & Blair." The bill was accepted on behalf of the company by two directors and the company secretaries.

On presentation for payment, the bill was dishonoured, and later the company went into liquidation.

Held that the signatories were liable to S. Ltd. for the amount of the bill.

(4) Business names

Where a registered company carries on business under a name other than its corporate name, it is subject to the provisions in the Act of 1981 relating to business names, *i.e.* section 28 ("control of business names"), section 29 ("disclosure of names of persons using business names") and section 30 ("civil remedies for breach of section 29") (see 2–175 *et seq.*, above).

(ii) *Statement that Company is to be a Public Company*

3–215 The second clause in the memorandum of a public company is "The company is to be a public company" (1980 Act, Sched. 1, Parts I and II). It is part of the definition of "public company" that the memorandum contains this statement (1980 Act, s. 1(1); see 3–73, above).

(iii) *Registered Office*

3–216 The second clause in the memorandum of a private company and the third clause in the memorandum of a public company must state whether the registered office of the company is to be situated in England or in Wales or in Scotland (1948 Act, s. 2(1); 1976 Act, s. 30(1)). The actual address of the registered office need not be, and in practice never is, stated in this clause, which is an unalterable part of the memorandum. The clause fixes the company's nationality and domicile.

3–217 Every company must at all times have a registered office to which all communications and notices may be addressed. Before the incorporation of the company, the intended address of the registered office must be specified in a statement delivered to the registrar of companies and if the company later changes its registered office to a new address (necessarily within the country of its domicile) notice of the change must be given to the registrar within 14 days (1976 Act, s. 23) and the registrar must cause notice of the change to be published in the Gazette (*i.e.* the *Edinburgh Gazette* in the case of a company registered in Scotland) (European Communities Act 1972, s. 9(3), as amended by 1976 Act, s. 23; 1948 Act, s. 455(1)).

3–218 The Acts do not require any resolution of the company to be passed for a change in the address of the registered office. The change may be decided on by the board of directors. It will not, however, take effect until intimated to the registrar (*Ross* v. *Invergordon Distillers Ltd.*, 1961 S.C. 286).

3–219 The address of the company's registered office as well as the place of registration and the registered number must be mentioned in legible characters in all business letters and order forms of the company (European Communities Act 1972, s. 9(7)).

3–220 Several books and documents are required to be kept at the registered office and to be open to inspection there by members during business hours (a minimum of two hours a day), *e.g.* the register of members (unless it is made up at another office) (s. 110(2)), the minutes of proceedings at general meetings (s. 146(1)) and copies of instruments creating charges registered under Part IIIA of the Act of 1948 (s. 106H, added by the Companies (Floating Charges and Receivers) (Scotland) Act 1972, s. 2 and Sched.).

(iv) *Objects*

3–221 The memorandum of every company must state the objects of the company (s. 2(1)). In the case of a private company the objects clause will be the third clause of the memorandum and in the case of a public company it will be the fourth. The statutory example given for a public company limited by shares is:

"The objects for which the company is established are, 'the conveyance of passengers and goods in ships or boats between such places as the company may from time to time determine, and the doing of all such things as are incidental or conducive to the attainment of the above object' " (1980 Act, Sched. 1, Part I).

The model for a private company limited by shares is substantially the same (1948 Act, Sched. 1, Table B).

In practice the objects clause will be the longest clause in a company's memorandum; it commonly extends to several pages. This departure from the short statutory model clauses is aimed at avoidance of the *ultra vires* ("beyond the powers") doctrine. This important doctrine is further considered below and a brief account is also given of the statutory provisions for alteration of objects.

(1) Ultra vires doctrine

The *ultra vires* doctrine is to the effect that an artificial legal person, such as a company, incorporated by or under an Act of Parliament has capacity to pursue only those objects which Parliament has authorised it to pursue. The doctrine was applied to statutory companies such as railway companies in the nineteenth century: the special Act of Parliament incorporating each company was the measure of its capacity. When the doctrine came to be applied to registered companies, the measure of a company's capacity was to be found in the objects as expressed in the company's memorandum—a document open to public inspection: any transaction which the company purported to enter into beyond the scope of its expressed objects was void and could not be ratified even by all its members.

(a) *Purpose of the doctrine*

The doctrine was intended to have a two-fold purpose: first, it would protect investors in the company: they would know the objects to which their money was to be devoted; secondly, it would protect creditors of the company: they would know that the company's funds were not to be dissipated in unauthorised activities. In fact company law and practice developed in such a way that the doctrine served neither of these purposes: investors came to have no protection because company promoters framed the objects clauses in memoranda in the widest possible terms, while creditors, being unlikely in practice to consult a company's memorandum before transacting with the company, could find themselves without any valid claim against the company if the transaction was in fact beyond the scope of the memorandum.

(b) *Illustrative cases*

The leading case was *Ashbury Railway Carriage and Iron Co. Ltd.* v. *Riche* (1875) L.R. 7 H.L. 653: A. Ltd.'s objects were: (1) to make, and sell, or lend on hire, railway carriages and wagons; (2) to carry on the business of mechanical engineers and general contractors; (3) to purchase, lease, work and sell mines, minerals, land and buildings, *etc.*

The directors entered into a contract to purchase a concession for making a railway in Belgium.

Held that the contract was *ultra vires* of the company and void and that therefore even the whole body of shareholders could not subsequently ratify it.

The words "general contractors" were to be taken along with the immediately preceding words and so indicated the making generally of contracts connected with the business of mechanical engineers.

Lord Chancellor Cairns' speech in this case includes one of the most famous passages in company law: he said (at p. 672):

"Now, I am clearly of opinion that this contract was entirely, as I have said, beyond the objects of the memorandum of association. If so, it was thereby placed beyond the powers of the company to make the contract. If so, my Lords, it is not a question whether the contract ever was ratified or was not ratified. If it was a contract void at its beginning, it was void because the company could not make the contract. If every shareholder of the company had been in the room, and every shareholder of the company had said, 'That is a contract which we desire to make, which we authorise the directors to make, to which we sanction the placing of the seal of the company,' the case would not have stood in any different position from that in which it stands now. The shareholders would thereby, by unanimous consent, have been attempting to do the very thing which, by the Act of Parliament, they were prohibited from doing."

3–226   A Scottish illustration of the operation of the doctrine is *Life Association of Scotland* v. *Caledonian Heritable Security Co. Ltd. in Liquidation* (1886) 13 R. 750: C. Ltd. had power to lend money on heritable security and to do all things incidental or conducive to the attainment of that object. It lent £10,500 on a postponed heritable bond over property which was already subject to a prior bond of £14,000.

Later, in order to prevent an immediate sale by the prior bondholder, C. Ltd. entered into an agreement with the prior bondholder by which C. Ltd. became bound to pay interest on the prior bond.

Held that the agreement was *ultra vires* of C. Ltd. on the ground that the memorandum did not confer express power to enter into such an agreement and that the agreement could not be regarded as "incidental or conducive to the attainment" of C. Ltd.'s objects.

3–227   Of the many other decided cases illustrating the doctrine the three following are amongst the best-known twentieth century cases:

3–228   (1) *Re Jon Beauforte (London) Ltd.* [1953] Ch. 131: A company, authorised by its memorandum to carry on business as costumiers and gown-makers, started the business of making veneered panels, which was *ultra vires*.

Builders engaged to erect a factory, persons who had supplied veneers and coke merchants who had sold coke for the factory were all held to have no valid claims as creditors in the company's liquidation.

3–229   (2) *Parke* v. *Daily News Ltd.* [1962] Ch. 927: D. Ltd. had agreed to sell the major part of its business to Associated Newspapers Ltd., but was to continue trading. The board of directors, with the approval of the general meeting, proposed to distribute the proceeds of the sale among former employees.

P., a minority shareholder, was held entitled to veto the proposed distribution, on the ground that it was *ultra vires* of D. Ltd. to make a distribution which could not be shown to be for the purpose of promoting its prospects.

(3) *Introductions Ltd.* v. *National Provincial Bank Ltd.* [1970] Ch. 199 (C.A.): The main object of I. Ltd. was to provide entertainments and services for overseas visitors. The objects clause included a power to borrow money and provided that each of the stated objects was to be an independent object.

I. Ltd. undertook pig-breeding, which was *ultra vires,* and a bank, which had been supplied with a copy of the company's memorandum, made a loan for the purpose of that business and received debentures as security.

Held that as borrowing money was not an end in itself but had to be for some purpose, and as the loan made by the bank had been for an *ultra vires* purpose, the debentures were void.

(c) *Statutory modification of the doctrine*

As part of its implementation of the First E.E.C. Directive, section 9(1) of the European Communities Act 1972 modified the *ultra vires* doctrine by the following provision:

"In favour of a person dealing with a company in good faith, any transaction decided on by the directors shall be deemed to be one which it is within the capacity of the company to enter into . . .; and a party to a transaction so decided on shall not be bound to enquire as to the capacity of the company to enter into it . . ., and shall be presumed to have acted in good faith unless the contrary is proved."

That provision has not abolished the *ultra vires* doctrine. It has merely limited its operation to some extent in favour of persons dealing with the company in good faith; for example, it would appear that the provision would have been of benefit to Riche in *Ashbury Railway Carriage and Iron Co. Ltd.* v. *Riche* and to the creditors in *Re Jon Beauforte (London) Ltd.* The doctrine still applies if the person dealing with the company knows of the limits on the company's capacity and it still operates as between the company and its shareholders (with the result that a shareholder could obtain an interdict to prevent the company from acting *ultra vires*).

The provision in section 9(1) raises some doubts as to its interpretation, in particular as to what is meant by "decided on by the directors" and as to whether a person who has been supplied with the company's memorandum (but who has not in fact consulted it) would be held to be dealing "in good faith" (*cf. Introductions Ltd.* v. *National Provincial Bank Ltd.,* above).

(d) *Limitations on the scope of the doctrine*

The *ultra vires* doctrine is limited in scope by the following considerations:

(i) The doctrine is to be reasonably applied: the company will be held to have capacity to undertake whatever is incidental to its stated objects. Lord Chancellor Selborne said in *Att.-Gen.* v. *Great Eastern Railway Co.* (1880) 5 App. Cas. 473 (at p. 478) that the doctrine "ought to be reasonably, and not unreasonably, understood and applied, and . . . whatever may fairly be regarded as incidental to, or consequential upon, those things which the Legislature has authorised, ought not (unless expressly prohibited) to be held, by judicial construction, to be *ultra vires*." The contract in question in that case was held not to be *ultra vires* because it was within the company's special Act of Parliament as being incidental to what was expressly authorised.

3–236   (ii) The practice developed of including in a company's objects clause virtually every possible object, even although the promoters had not the remotest intention of pursuing the object.

3–237   In order to counter this means of avoiding the operation of the *ultra vires* doctrine, the courts applied the "main objects" rule of construction, namely: "where a memorandum of association expresses the objects of the company in a series of paragraphs, and one paragraph, or the first two or three paragraphs, appear to embody the 'main object' of the company, all the other paragraphs are treated as merely ancillary to this 'main object,' and as limited or controlled thereby" (*per* Salmon J. in *Anglo-Overseas Agencies Ltd.* v. *Green* [1961] 1 Q.B. 1, at p. 8).

3–238   In turn promoters adopted the device of the "independent objects" clause, *i.e.* they would incorporate in an objects clause which specified the leading object and perhaps some 20 other objects a provision such as: "the various businesses or objects specified shall be regarded as independent objects, and in nowise restricted . . . by reference to the name of the Company, or to the businesses or objects contained in any other paragraph" (*London and Edinburgh Shipping Co. Ltd., Petitioners*, 1909 S.C. 1). The courts expressed disapproval of the device, but nevertheless held it to be an effective means of excluding the *ultra vires* doctrine (*e.g. Cotman* v. *Brougham* [1918] A.C. 514, in which a rubber company was held to have acted *intra vires* ("within its powers") in underwriting shares in an oil company).

3–239   (iii) Another practice which has been resorted to is the specification of a long list of powers in the objects clause. Such specification is an unnecessary precaution because a company impliedly has all the powers required to pursue its stated objects. The failure to distinguish between objects and powers has been criticised by the courts (*e.g.* in *John Walker & Sons Ltd., Petitioners*, 1914 S.C. 280), and a mere express power in the memorandum such as borrowing money, granting security, drawing bills of exchange *etc.* does not prevent the court from looking into the reality of a transaction and deciding that despite the exercise of one of its express powers the company has acted *ultra vires* (*e.g. Thompson* v. *J. Barke & Co. (Caterers) Ltd.*, 1975 S.L.T. 67 (O.H.), in which repayment by a company cheque of a loan made to one of the company's directors was held to be an *ultra vires* transaction in spite of the express power which the company had to issue cheques).

3–240   (iv) The objects may be so expressed in the memorandum as to give the directors a wide discretion in deciding what activities will be *intra vires;* an instance is *Bell Houses Ltd.* v. *City Wall Properties Ltd.* [1966] 2 Q.B. 656 (C.A.): B. Ltd.'s principal object was the erection of housing estates, but the objects clause also authorised the company "to carry on any other trade or business whatsoever which can, in the opinion of the board of directors, be advantageously carried on by the company in connection with . . . the general business of the company"; a transaction which would otherwise have been *ultra vires* was held to be *intra vires* because the directors *bona fide* believed that the activity was advantageous to the general business of the company.

(v) The *ultra vires* doctrine is concerned with the *company's* lack of capacity, and has no application in the situation where a transaction is within the company's capacity but is beyond the authority of the directors or other agents of the company who are acting on its behalf. Such a transaction may be ratified by the company, even although the party transacting with the company could have discovered the agent's lack of authority by consulting the public documents of the company (such as its memorandum and articles, its special resolutions and other documents filed with the registrar of companies).

Further, section 9(1) of the European Communities Act 1972 provides that in favour of a person dealing with a company in good faith, the power of the directors to bind the company is to be deemed to be free of any limitation under the memorandum or articles, and a party to a transaction decided on by the directors is not to be bound to inquire as to any such limitation on the powers of the directors.

(vi) The *ultra vires* doctrine does not apply where the irregularity of a transaction cannot be discovered by consulting the company's public documents. Even before the modification of the doctrine by section 9(1) of the European Communities Act 1972 (see 3–231, above), outsiders dealing with a company were not required to go beyond the public documents but were entitled to assume that the "indoor management" of the company was in order; as regards internal irregularities such as the failure to pass an ordinary resolution (which need not be filed with the registrar and so is not a public document), the maxim applied is *omnia praesumuntur rite esse acta* ("all things are presumed to have been done correctly"). This rule, referred to as "the rule in *Turquand's* case," was settled early in the history of company law in *Royal British Bank* v. *Turquand* (1856) 6 El. & Bl. 327; 119 E.R. 886:

The case concerned an English company which had registered its "deed of settlement" under pre-1856 legislation (which did not apply to Scotland). The deed of settlement authorised the directors to borrow on bond such sums as should from time to time by a general resolution of the company be authorised to be borrowed. The directors borrowed £2,000 without having the authority of such a resolution, and the lender was held entitled to presume that there had been a resolution duly authorising the loan.

A Scottish instance of the application of *Turquand's* rule in relation to a registered company is *Gillies* v. *Craigton Garage Co. Ltd.*, 1935 S.C. 423: Under the articles of association of C. Ltd. the sanction of an ordinary resolution of the company was required for a loan made by G. to the directors for the purposes of the company; the loan was made without such sanction, and G. was held to have been entitled to assume that the sanction had been duly obtained.

(2) Alteration of objects

3–246   Successive Companies Acts have progressively increased the extent to which a company may alter its objects. As a result, there is unlikely to be a situation where the risk of having an intended activity held *ultra vires* could not be avoided by the company's passing a special resolution for alteration of its objects under section 5 of the Act of 1948.

3–247   The section provides that a company may alter the provisions of its memorandum with respect to the objects of the company, so far as may be required to enable the company:

(a)   to carry on its business more economically or more efficiently; or

(b)   to attain its main purpose by new or improved means; or

(c)   to enlarge or change the local area of its operations; or

(d)   to carry on some business which under existing circumstances may conveniently or advantageously be combined with the business of the company; or

(e)   to restrict or abandon any of the objects specified in the memorandum; or

(f)   to sell or dispose of the whole or any part of the undertaking of the company; or

(g)   to amalgamate with any other company or body of persons.

3–248   The holders of not less than 15 per cent in nominal value of the company's issued share capital or any class of the issued share capital (or, if the company is not limited by shares, not less than 15 per cent of the company's members) may apply to court within 21 days from the passing of the resolution, and the court may make such order as it sees fit.

3–249   In *Incorporated Glasgow Dental Hospital* v. *Lord Advocate*, 1927 S.C. 400, and *Scottish Special Housing Association Ltd., Petitioners,* 1947 S.C. 17, the statutory provisions for alteration of objects were held not to be restricted to alteration of the objects *clause* but to extend to alteration of objects which happened to be stated in other clauses of the memorandum.

(v) *Statement that Liability is Limited*

3–250   The memorandum of every limited company must state that the liability of its members is limited (s. 2(2)). The statement always in practice is simply "The liability of the members is limited," and does not reveal whether the company is a company limited by shares or a company limited by guarantee; that information is derived from the clause which immediately follows the limited liability clause. If the company is a company limited by guarantee that succeeding clause will contain the member's guarantee, *e.g.*:

"Every member of the company undertakes to contribute to the assets of the company in the event of its being wound up while he is a member, or within one year afterwards, for payment of the debts and liabilities of the company contracted before he ceases to be a member, and the costs, charges and expenses of winding up, and for the adjustment of the rights of the contributories among themselves, such amount as may be required not exceeding ten pounds" (Sched. 1, Table C).

3–251   No alteration in a company's memorandum or articles can bind a member, without his written agreement, to take more shares or in any way increase his liability to the company (s. 22).

(vi) *Share Capital*

In the case of a company having a share capital, the memorandum must state, unless the company is an unlimited company, the amount of the share capital with which the company proposes to be registered and the division of the capital into shares of a fixed amount (s. 2(4)). If the company is an unlimited company with a share capital the *articles* must state the amount of the share capital (s. 7).

The statutory model share capital clause for a private company limited by shares is: "The share capital of the company is two hundred thousand pounds divided into one thousand shares of two hundred pounds each" (Sched. 1, Table B). In practice it is unusual for a private company's share capital to be as large as £200,000; it is quite likely to be only £100 or less. There is no statutory minimum or maximum capital for a private company. Shares are now unlikely to be of as large a denomination as £200: they will seldom be larger than £1 each, and are more likely to be of 25p each.

The statutory model clause for a public company limited by shares is: "The share capital of the company is £50,000 divided into 50,000 shares of £1 each" (1980 Act, Sched. 1, Part I). The share capital with which a public company proposes to be registered must not be less than the "authorised minimum" (1980 Act, s. 3(2)), a figure which at present is £50,000 but may be altered by statutory instrument (1980 Act, s. 85(1)).

The share capital stated in the memorandum is the nominal (also referred to as the authorised) capital. For the distinction between this and the allotted, called-up and paid-up capital, see 3–27 *et seq.*, above.

A company with a share capital may, by section 61 of the Act of 1948, alter the nominal capital stated in its memorandum in any of the following ways:

(a) by increasing the share capital by new shares of such amount as it thinks expedient;

(b) by consolidating and dividing all or any of its share capital into shares of larger amount than its existing shares;

(c) by converting all or any of its paid-up shares into stock, and reconverting that stock into paid-up shares of any denomination;

(d) by subdividing its shares, or any of them, into shares of smaller amount than is fixed by the memorandum (retaining, however, the same proportion between what is paid up and what is unpaid (if any) on each share);

(e) by cancelling shares which have not been taken or agreed to be taken by any person, and diminishing the share capital by the amount cancelled.

The conditions which must be fulfilled for an alteration under section 61 are:

(1) Authority to alter must be contained in the articles; otherwise the articles would require first to be altered by special resolution.

(2) The power to alter must be exercised by the company in general meeting; the type of resolution required will be that specified in the articles—usually an ordinary resolution.

As regards (a) (increase of capital), a company which is expanding and allotting further shares will usually wish about the same time to increase its nominal share capital, so as to maintain a suitable margin between its nominal capital and its allotted capital.

3–259 Mode (b) (consolidation into shares of larger amount) is seldom resorted to.

3–260 Likewise, mode (c) (conversion of paid-up shares into stock and reconversion) has now little practical significance. Shares are distinguishable from stock in that:

(1) Shares cannot be bought or sold or transferred in fractions, whereas stock is a mass of capital which can be divided into fractions of any amount. However, this point of distinction is lessened by the fact that the articles usually provide for stock to be divided into stock units (*e.g.* stock units of 25p each) which cannot be sub-divided.

(2) Only shares may be allotted in the first instance by the company; if the company wishes to have stock it must exercise the power of conversion under section 61.

(3) Shares may be partly paid (though in practice now they are usually fully paid); stock must always be fully paid.

(4) Formerly each share in a company had to be distinguished by its appropriate number and the main advantage of converting shares into stock was the avoidance of the work involved in the numbering of shares. However, it is now permissible to dispense with distinguishing numbers on shares provided all the allotted shares, or all the allotted shares of a particular class, are fully paid up and rank *pari passu* ("rateably," "equally") for all purposes—which will usually be the case.

3–261 Mode (e) (diminution) is distinct from reduction of capital. Diminution relates only to the nominal capital and to shares in that capital which have not yet been allotted. Reduction, on the other hand, relates to the allotted capital and involves, for example, extinction of liability on shares which are not fully paid up or cancellation of paid-up share capital which is lost or unrepresented by available assets or which is in excess of the wants of the company. Reduction is permitted under section 66 of the Act of 1948 but only on the conditions that:

(1) authority for reduction is contained in the articles;

(2) the company passes a special resolution for the reduction; and

(3) the court confirms the reduction.

3–262 The shares which comprise the share capital may be divided into different classes (preference, ordinary, deferred, *etc.*). Such division need not be mentioned in the memorandum. Usually the articles will confer power to divide shares into different classes and specify how the special rights attaching to each class may be altered. For example, the statutory model articles for a company limited by shares provide that "any share in the company may be issued with such preferred, deferred or other special rights or such restrictions, whether in regard to dividend, voting, return of capital or otherwise as the company may from time to time by ordinary resolution determine" (Sched. 1, Table A, reg. 2), and "if at any time the share capital is divided into different classes of shares, the rights attached to any class may . . . be varied with the consent in writing of the holders of three-fourths of the issued shares of that class, or with the sanction of an extraordinary resolution passed at a separate general meeting of the holders of the shares of the class" (Sched. 1, Table A, reg. 4, as amended by 1980 Act, Sched. 4).

If a company's share capital is divided into different classes of shares and a provision in the memorandum or articles authorises variation of the special rights subject to the consent of a specified proportion of the holders of the shares of the class or subject to the sanction of a resolution passed at a separate class meeting, then, by section 72 of the Act of 1948, after the variation procedure has been followed, holders of not less than 15 per cent of the allotted shares of the class, provided they are persons who did not consent to the resolution for variation, have the right to apply to the court to have the variation cancelled. The application must be made within 21 days after the giving of the consent or the passing of the resolution. If the court is satisfied, having regard to all the circumstances of the case, that the variation would unfairly prejudice the applicants, it will disallow the variation; otherwise it will confirm it.

(vii) *Additional Clauses*

The memorandum may include other clauses which are not required by the Acts to be included in it. The commonest instance is an additional clause dealing with the special rights attached to a particular class of shares.

Section 23 of the Act of 1948 enables any condition which is contained in a company's memorandum but which could lawfully have been contained in its articles instead to be altered by special resolution in much the same way as the objects of the company may be altered under section 5 of the Act. Section 23, however, does not apply where the memorandum itself provides for or prohibits alteration of the condition, nor does the section authorise any variation or abrogation of the special rights of any class of members. This latter exception makes section 23 of little importance in practice because it is unlikely that an additional clause will relate to anything other than special rights.

(viii) *Association Clause*

The association clause is the clause by which the subscribers to the memorandum declare that they desire to form a company and by which they agree to take shares. The clause is followed by a list of the names, addresses and descriptions of the subscribers, each subscriber stating opposite his name the number of shares which he is taking (s. 2(4)). The memorandum must then be signed by each subscriber in the presence of at least one witness who must also sign (s. 3).

However large a company may be contemplated and however many shares in it the subscribers to the memorandum may be intending to take, the memorandum will in practice be subscribed by two persons only, of whom each will take only one share.

Thus the final part of the model memorandum for a public company limited by shares is in the following form (1980 Act, Sched. 1, Part I):

"We, the several persons whose names and addresses are subscribed are desirous of being formed into a company, in pursuance of this memorandum of association, and we respectively agree to take the number of shares in the capital of the company set opposite our respective names.

Names, Addresses and Descriptions of Subscribers			Number of shares taken by each Subscriber
'1. Thomas Jones	in the county of	merchant	1
2. Andrew Smith	in the county of	merchant	1
Total shares taken	. . . . . .		2'

Dated   day of   19

Witness to the above
signatures
A.B., 13, Hute Street,
Clerkenwell, London."

3–269   The subscribers of the memorandum are deemed to have agreed to become members of the company, and on its registration must be entered as members in the company's register of members (s. 26(1)). Subscribers of the memorandum therefore become members even before their names are entered in the register of members. Persons other than subscribers do not become members until (1) they have agreed to become members and (2) their names have been entered in the register of members (s. 26(2)).

V ARTICLES OF ASSOCIATION

3–270   This part of the chapter is devoted to:
       (a) the form and contents of articles;
       (b) alteration of articles; and
       (c) the effect of the memorandum and articles.

(a) **Form and Contents of Articles**

3–271   The Act of 1948 provides that articles must:
       (i) be printed;
       (ii) be divided into paragraphs numbered consecutively; and
       (iii) be signed by each subscriber of the memorandum in the presence of at least one witness, who must also sign (s. 9).

3–272   Table A in the First Schedule to the Act of 1948 consists of a model set of articles (or, as they are called in the Act, "regulations") for a company limited by shares. Table A is particularly important because of the provisions of sections 6 and 8 of the Act. The effect of these sections is that a company limited by shares need not register articles along with its memorandum and that if it does not do so, the regulations in Table A will be the articles of the company just as if they had been contained in duly registered articles. A further provision is that if articles are registered a company limited by shares is governed by the regulations in Table A in so far as its own articles do not exclude or modify the contents of Table A. A company limited by guarantee and an unlimited company must always register articles of their own. The promoters of such companies may adopt in whole or in part the model articles in Tables C and E respectively of the First Schedule to the Act of 1948, but there is no statutory provision for the automatic application of these Tables to any company.

The regulations which comprise Table A are grouped under these headings:

"Interpretation" (a short list of definitions);

"Share Capital and Variation of Rights" (see 3–262, above);

"Lien" (the company has a "first and paramount" lien on non-fully-paid shares for money called up or payable at a fixed time in respect of such shares; it may also sell such shares by following a stated procedure);

"Calls on Shares" (seven regulations specify the conditions on which any amount unpaid on shares may be called up by the directors from the shareholders);

"Transfer of Shares" (seven further regulations specify the procedure for transferring shares and deal with the directors' possible right to refuse to register a transfer);

"Transmission of Shares" (transmission occurs when a member dies or becomes bankrupt; regulations specify the rights of other persons who become entitled to the shares on the occurrence of these events);

"Forfeiture of Shares" (a procedure is laid down which enables the directors to forfeit shares of a member who has failed to pay a call on his shares);

"Conversion of Shares into Stock" (this requires an ordinary resolution of the company; see 3–260, above);

"Alteration of Capital" (the company is given power to alter its capital under section 61 of the Act by an ordinary resolution and to reduce its capital under section 66; see 3–256 et seq., above);

"General Meetings" (provisions for the convening of annual and extraordinary meetings of the company); there then follow separate groups of regulations as to notice of and proceedings at general meetings (including the demand for a poll) and as to votes (including proxies); a corporation (such as another company) may appoint a representative to act at company meetings;

"Directors" (here again there are many regulations, covering such matters as appointment, remuneration, borrowing powers, other powers and duties, disqualification, rotation (by which, say, one-third retire each year), proceedings (including meetings and delegation to committees), and appointment of a managing director);

"Secretary" (his appointment and remuneration are decided on by the directors);

"The Seal" (provisions as to the custody and use of the company's seal);

"Dividends and Reserve" (the company in general meeting may declare dividends but not of a greater amount than is recommended by the directors; interim dividends may be paid by the directors; regard must be had to Part III of the Act of 1980 ("Restrictions on Distribution of Profits and Assets"); the directors may set aside reserves before recommending any dividend);

"Accounts" (in deciding what accounting records to keep the directors must comply with the Act of 1976);

"Capitalisation of Profits" (the company in general meeting upon the recommendation of the directors has power to capitalise profits and reserves, with the result that the shareholders receive what are popularly referred to as "bonus" shares);

"Audit" (the regulation simply refers to the statutory provisions in the Acts of 1967, 1976 and 1981);

"Notices" (provisions as to the giving of notices where there are joint holders of shares, where the shareholder has died or become bankrupt or has no registered address in the United Kingdom, *etc.*);

"Winding up" (the liquidator, with the sanction of an extraordinary resolution of the company, would have power to divide the company's assets in kind amongst the members); and

"Indemnity" (any director or other officer may be indemnified by the company against liability incurred in civil or criminal proceedings if judgment is given in his favour or if he is acquitted or if the court considers that he ought fairly to be excused for some negligence, default, breach of duty or breach of trust for which he may be liable).

3–274   ·Because articles are habitually based closely on the statutory model in Table A, questions as to the validity of an article seldom reach the courts. An exception is the case of *St Johnstone Football Club Ltd.* v. *Scottish Football Association*, 1965 S.L.T. 171 (O.H.):

A football club brought an action against an association of football clubs, of which it was itself a member. The association sought to rely on one of its articles which, it maintained, prohibited any member from taking legal proceedings except with the prior consent of the Council of the association.

Held by Lord Kilbrandon (Ordinary) that the article in question was not wide enough to debar the club's action, and that, if it were, it was contrary to public policy and therefore not binding.

(b) Alteration of Articles

3–275   By section 10 of the Act of 1948, as amended by the Acts of 1980 (Sched. 4) and 1981 (Sched. 3), a company may, subject to the provisions of the Companies Acts 1948 to 1981 and to the conditions contained in its memorandum, alter its articles by special resolution, and any alteration is, subject to the provisions of the Acts, as valid as if originally contained in the articles and is subject in like manner to alteration by special resolution.

3–276   A company's power to alter its articles under section 10 is wide: the only limitations on it are:

3–277   (i) It is subject to the provisions of the Companies Acts 1948 to 1981; *e.g.* no alteration in the articles could require a member, without his written consent, to take more shares or in any way increase his liability to the company (1948 Act, s. 22); nor could any alteration deprive minorities of their various statutory rights (such as the right of a 15 per cent minority to apply to court where special rights have been varied under section 72 of the Act of 1948 (see 3–263, above)).

3–278   (ii) The power to alter is also subject to the conditions contained in the company's memorandum. Since the memorandum is the ruling document, any alteration of the articles which would conflict with conditions in the memorandum would be of no effect.

3–279   (iii) The power to alter must be exercised *bona fide* for the benefit of the company as a whole. There have been many cases illustrating this common law restriction on the power of alteration, *e.g.*:

(1) *Allen* v. *Gold Reefs of West Africa Ltd.* [1900] 1 Ch. 656 (C.A.): Articles gave the company a lien on partly-paid shares for all debts due by the member to the company. Zuccani had sold property to the company, and was the only holder of fully-paid shares; he also held partly-paid shares.

At his death Zuccani was in debt to the company for arrears of calls on his partly-paid shares, and the articles were altered so as to give the company a lien on fully-paid shares.

Held that the alteration was valid because it had been made in good faith for the benefit of the company as a whole.

The alteration was there aimed at only one person and it was in a sense retrospective in that it enabled the company to exercise a lien on Zuccani's fully-paid shares for debts contracted before the date of the alteration.

Lord Lindley M.R. said (at p. 671) that the power conferred on companies to alter articles "must, like all other powers, be exercised subject to those general principles of law and equity which are applicable to all powers conferred on majorities and enabling them to bind minorities. It must be exercised, not only in the manner required by law, but also bona fide for the benefit of the company as a whole, and it must not be exceeded. These conditions are always implied, and are seldom, if ever, expressed."

In a somewhat similar Scottish case, however, the court refused to allow an alteration to have retrospective effect:

Liquidator of W. & A. McArthur Ltd. v. *Gulf Line Ltd.*, 1909 S.C. 732: G. Ltd.'s articles gave the company a lien on all shares which were not fully paid.

M. (South Africa) Ltd., which held both fully-paid shares and partly-paid shares in G. Ltd., transferred the fully-paid shares to M. Ltd. at a time when a call was due on the partly-paid shares.

G. Ltd. then altered its articles so as to give it a lien on all shares registered in the name of a member for all calls due on any shares registered in the member's name.

Held that M. Ltd. was not affected by that alteration but was entitled to have its name placed on the register of members in accordance with the articles in force at the time when it had presented the transfer for registration.

The alteration came into force only at its own date; further, it had been made not so much because the directors considered it to be required in the general interests of the company as simply to meet the case of one particular transfer.

(2) An alteration may still be *bona fide* for the benefit of the company as a whole although it has the effect of prejudicing a particular shareholder or class of shareholders:

Crookston v. *Lindsay, Crookston & Co. Ltd.*, 1922 S.L.T. 62 (O.H.): L. Ltd. was a private company in which C. and three other directors held amongst them the whole of the issued shares.

L. Ltd. altered its articles so as to include a provision that any member desiring to sell his shares had first to offer them to the directors at par (*i.e.* at their nominal value).

C., alleging that the alteration had been devised to enable the other three directors ultimately to acquire C.'s shares at a price far below their fair value, sought to interdict the alteration.

Held that the alteration was valid, even although it might have the effect of prejudicing C.'s rights under the original articles.

3–283   (3) An alteration of the articles which amounts to a breach of a contract entered into by the company is nevertheless valid, but the other party is entitled to damages from the company:

Southern Foundries (1926) Ltd. v. *Shirlaw* [1940] A.C. 701: S., a director of S. Ltd., had been appointed managing director for 10 years by a contract outside the articles.

The articles provided that the managing director, *subject to his contract with the company,* could be removed in the same way as the other directors and that if he ceased to be a director he would automatically cease to be managing director.

Later, Federated Foundries Ltd. ("F. Ltd.") acquired the shares of S. Ltd., and the articles were altered so as to empower F. Ltd. to remove any director of S. Ltd.

Before the expiry of the 10 years of S.'s contract, F. Ltd. removed S. from his office of director, and treated S. as having ceased to be managing director.

Held that S. was entitled to damages from S. Ltd. for breach of the implied term in S.'s contract of employment that S. Ltd. would not remove S. from his position as director during the 10 years for which he had been appointed managing director.

(c) **Effect of Memorandum and Articles**

3–284   Section 20(1) of the Act of 1948 provides that, subject to the provisions of the Act, the memorandum and articles when registered bind the company and its members to the same extent as if they had been signed and sealed by each member and contained covenants on the part of each member to observe all the provisions of the memorandum and articles.

3–285   The effect of section 20(1) is open to some doubt. The following are amongst the points raised by the provision:

3–286   (i) Members in their capacity as members are bound to the company as if each member had himself signed and sealed the memorandum and articles. An illustration is *Hickman* v. *Kent or Romney Marsh Sheep-Breeders' Association* [1915] 1 Ch. 881:

Articles provided that differences between the company and any of its members should be referred to arbitration.

H., a member, brought an action against the company in connection with a dispute as to his expulsion from the company.

Held that the company was entitled to have the action stayed, since the articles constituted a contract between the company and its members in respect of their ordinary rights as members.

3–287   (ii) The provision does not expressly state that the company is bound to its members as if the company had signed and sealed the memorandum and articles, but this has been held to be so:

Wood v. *Odessa Waterworks Co.* (1889) 42 Ch. D. 636: Articles empowered the company to declare a dividend "to be paid" to the shareholders.

The company, instead of paying a dividend, passed a resolution to issue to the shareholders debenture bonds bearing interest and redeemable over 30 years.

Held that the words "to be paid" meant paid in cash and that a shareholder could therefore restrain the company from acting on the resolution, on the ground that it contravened the articles.

(iii) The memorandum and articles do not constitute a contract between the company and its members in some capacity other than as members (*e.g.* as promoters, solicitors or directors):

Eley v. *Positive Government Security Life Assurance Co. Ltd.* (1876) 1 Ex. D. 88 (C.A.): Articles provided that E. should be the solicitor to the company for the usual fees and charges and should not be removed from office except for misconduct.

E. was employed for a time, but later the company ceased to employ him and employed other solicitors.

Held that E. was not entitled to damages for breach of contract, because the articles did not create a contract between the company and E. in his capacity as solicitor to the company.

(iv) It is, however, possible for the articles to be used as the basis for a contract outside the articles between the company and a member in some capacity other than that of member:

Re New British Iron Co., ex parte Beckwith [1898] 1 Ch. 324: An article provided that the remuneration of the directors should be the annual sum of £1,000. The directors, who were also members, accepted office on the footing of that article.

For some time prior to the liquidation of the company the directors acted as such but were not paid.

Held that they were entitled to rank as ordinary creditors for the arrears of remuneration, since the provision in the articles had been embodied in the contract between them (as directors) and the company; the remuneration was not due to the directors in their character of members.

(v) The memorandum and articles constitute a contract between individual members, and if a member thus obtains a personal right, he may enforce the contract directly against another member without the aid of the company:

Rayfield v. *Hands* [1960] Ch. 1: Articles of a private company required a member who was intending to transfer his shares to inform the directors and provided that the directors should take the shares equally between them at a fair value.

Held that the directors (who were also members) were bound by the articles to take the plaintiff's shares because of the contractual relationship between the plaintiff as a member and the directors as members, and that it was not necessary for the company to be a party to the action.

Further Reading
    Scots Mercantile Law Statutes (annual reprint from *The Parliament House Book*) (W. Green & Son) for Companies Acts 1948 to 1981

Gloag and Henderson, *Introduction to the Law of Scotland*, Chapter XXV

David M. Walker, *Principles of Scottish Private Law*, Chapter 3.13

Charlesworth & Cain Company Law, 12th ed. by Geoffrey Morse (Scottish Editor: Enid A. Marshall) (1983, Stevens)

Topham and Ivamy: Company Law, 16th ed. by E.R. Hardy Ivamy (Scottish Supplement by David M. Walker) (1978, Butterworths)

J. J. Gow, *The Mercantile and Industrial Law of Scotland*, Chapter 11

Palmer's Company Law, 23rd ed. by Clive M. Schmitthoff, Maurice Kay and Geoffrey K. Morse (Specialist Editor for Scottish Law: David A. Bennett) (1982, Stevens & Sons, W. Green & Son)

Enid A. Marshall, *Scottish Cases on Partnerships and Companies*, Part II (1980, W. Green & Son)

E. *Gower's Principles of Modern Company Law*, 4th ed. by L.C.B. Gower, J.B. Cronin, A.J. Easson and Lord Wedderburn of Charlton, with Supplement by L.C.B. Gower (1979 (Supplement 1981), Stevens)

SALE OF GOODS

INTRODUCTION

THE law on the sale of goods was first codified by the Sale of Goods Act 1893. That Act was subsequently amended, notably by the Supply of Goods (Implied Terms) Act 1973, and the Sale of Goods Act 1979 was passed to consolidate the law on the subject. The Act of 1979, which came into force on January 1, 1980, repealed the Act of 1893 and its amendments, but, being a consolidating Act, did not alter the substance of the law.

4-02   The code of law on the sale of goods is therefore now to be found in the Sale of Goods Act 1979, and in this chapter references to sections are, unless the context indicates otherwise, references to sections of that Act of 1979. A remarkable, but convenient, feature of the Act of 1979 is that the numbering of its sections has for the most part been made to correspond with the numbering of the sections of the Act of 1893.

4-03   Most of the statutory provisions dealt with in this chapter apply equally throughout the United Kingdom.

4-04   The codification which took place in 1893 was based mainly on the common law of England, and was a continuation of the process of assimilation of Scots and English law which had begun with the Mercantile Law Amendment Act Scotland 1856. The effect was to alter substantially the Scots law on sale of goods, since the common law of Scotland had closely followed the Roman law of sale.

4-05   Especially important was the statutory change made by the introduction of the English theory and principles affecting the time at which the ownership of the goods passed from seller to buyer. By the common law of Scotland, delivery had been essential: a contract for the sale of goods was no more than a contract giving rise to personal rights between seller and buyer: up to the time of delivery the buyer had a *jus ad rem* ("right with regard to the thing") and not a *jus in re* ("right in the thing"), *i.e.* he had not a right of ownership (a "real" as opposed to a "personal" right). By the common law of England, on the other hand, ownership passed to the buyer independently of delivery: the sale was not only a contract but also a conveyance (*i.e.* a transfer of ownership). Founded on this basic difference in theory between Scots and English law were the different principles applicable, at common law, in the two legal systems: in Scots law the ownership of the goods did not pass to the buyer until the goods were delivered, whereas in English law the ownership passed at the time when the contract was entered into, or, if the goods were not then in existence or were for some other reason not then ready for delivery, it passed as soon as the goods were ready for delivery. The principles of English law, now applicable to Scotland also, are set out in sections 16 to 20 of the Act of 1979 under the heading "Transfer of property as between seller and buyer."

4-06   The Act of 1979, like its predecessor of 1893, is a comparatively short Act, and does not cover all aspects of the law as to sale of goods: the rules of the common law are expressly preserved in so far as they are consistent with the express provisions of the Act. In particular, the rules relating to agency, and to fraud, misrepresentation and other grounds of invalidity, continue to apply to contracts for the sale of goods (s. 62(2)). The common law of Scotland, therefore, still governs many aspects of the law as to sale of goods.

4-07   In recent years there has been a considerable growth in "consumer-protection" legislation. For the purposes of this chapter such legislation may be regarded as falling into two categories:

4-08   First, there have been the statutes amending the Act of 1893 where the specific provisions of that Act were thought to operate unfairly. The most important provisions within this category were contained in the Supply of Goods (Implied Terms) Act 1973, the Consumer Credit Act

1974, and the Unfair Contract Terms Act 1977. These provisions are now all consolidated in the Act of 1979.

Secondly, a number of statutes have been passed to regulate matters which were not dealt with at all by the Act of 1893. Statutes in this second category are the Trading Stamps Act 1964, the Trade Descriptions Act 1968, and the Consumer Safety Act 1978, and, on auction sales, the Auctions (Bidding Agreements) Acts 1927 and 1969 and the Mock Auctions Act 1961. These statutes have introduced civil and criminal provisions designed to restrict practices considered to be undesirable. They form distinct bodies of legislation, supplementary to, but outwith, the Sale of Goods Act 1979. Though important in practice, they will receive only incidental mention in this chapter, which is confined to an account of "the law relating to the sale of goods" in the narrower, traditional sense of that phrase.

Where a foreign element is involved, it may also be necessary to take into account the provisions of the Uniform Laws on International Sales Act 1967. That Act represents an attempt to establish agreed rules which would apply to overseas sales, *i.e.* to sales where the parties are in different States: it has no application to cross-Border transactions within the United Kingdom. It came into force in 1972. The Uniform Laws, however, apply only where the parties expressly adopt them, and this is rarely done in practice. (See also 4–339 *et seq.*, below.)

Following the arrangement of the first six Parts of the Act of 1979, the subject-matter of this chapter comes under these headings:

   I. Contracts to which the Act applies;
  II. Formation of the contract;
 III. Effects of the contract;
 IV. Performance of the contract;
  V. Rights of unpaid seller against the goods; and
 VI. Actions for breach of the contract.

Part VII of the Act ("Supplementary") includes, as well as miscellaneous provisions, a section on:

 VII. Auction sales.

At the end of the chapter a brief indication is given of:

VIII. Other statutory provisions on sale of goods.

I CONTRACTS TO WHICH THE ACT APPLIES

Part I of the 1979 Act consists of only one section.

The section declares that the Act applies to contracts of sale of goods made on or after (but not to those made before) January 1, 1894 (the date when the Act of 1893 came into force) (s. 1(1)).

The section then goes on to state what is in effect a transitional provision: in relation to contracts made on certain dates, the Act applies *subject to the modification of certain of its sections*, as mentioned in Schedule 1 to the Act (s. 1(2)). The contracts which are within the transitional provisions are mainly those which have been made on or after May 18, 1973 (when the amendments to the 1893 Act made by the Supply of Goods (Implied Terms) Act 1973 came into force) and before January 1,

1980 (the date on which the 1979 Act came into force). Although the 1979 Act is a consolidating Act, the wording of its sections is not precisely the same as the wording of the sections which it consolidated. For example, the effect of the transitional provisions is that, in relation to contracts made between May 18, 1973 and January 1, 1980, section 14 (the well-known section concerning implied terms about quality or fitness) is to be applied as set out in the Act of 1973 instead of as set out in the Act of 1979. There is no need to look back to the Act of 1973 for the precise wording: it is given in Schedule 1 to the Act of 1979. Similarly, in relation to contracts made before May 18, 1973, the section 14 which is to be applied is that of the 1893 Act, and it also is now to be found in Schedule 1 to the Act of 1979.

II FORMATION OF THE CONTRACT

4–15   The provisions in Part II of the Act are dealt with below under the following headings:
   (a)   definition and nature of the contract;
   (b)   formalities of the contract;
   (c)   subject-matter of the contract;
   (d)   the price; and
   (e)   terms of the contract.

(a) Definition and Nature of the Contract
"Sale" and "Agreement to Sell"

4–16   The statutory definition of "a contract of sale of goods" is such that it covers both (i) a "sale" and (ii) an "agreement to sell."

4–17   "A contract of sale of goods is a contract by which the seller transfers or agrees to transfer the property in goods to the buyer for a money consideration, called the price" (s. 2(1)). Where under a contract of sale the property in (*i.e.* the ownership of) the goods is transferred from the seller to the buyer, the contract is called a "sale," but where the transfer of the property in the goods is to take place at a future time or subject to some condition which has still to be fulfilled, the contract is called an "agreement to sell" (s. 2(4), (5)). An agreement to sell becomes a sale when the time elapses or the conditions are fulfilled (s. 2(6)).

4–18   A contract of sale may be absolute or conditional (s. 2(3)). There are two types of condition to which a contract may be subject—suspensive and resolutive.

4–19   If the condition is a suspensive one, the contract will be held in suspense until the condition is fulfilled. The property in the goods will therefore not be transferred to the buyer, and the contract will necessarily be in the meantime only an "agreement to sell," and not a "sale." There are several instances of suspensive conditions in section 18 of the Act; *e.g.* when goods are delivered to the buyer on approval, the property in the goods passes to the buyer when he indicates his approval to the seller.

4–20   A resolutive condition, on the other hand, does not suspend the completion of the contract, but makes the contract liable to be "resolved" (dissolved) if the condition is fulfilled. Such a condition therefore allows the property in the goods to pass to the buyer, though, if the condition is fulfilled, the property may later require to be restored to the seller. Because the passing of the property to the buyer is not delayed by the presence of a resolutive condition, the contract will be a "sale," and not merely an "agreement to sell," for the purposes of the Act. An instance of a resolutive condition can be seen in *Gavin's Trustee* v. *Fraser*, 1920 S.C. 674 (see also 4–27, below): a haulage contractor who had sold his plant to a timber merchant was, by the terms of the agreement between them, entitled to buy back the plant within a year for £1,200 with interest at 6 per cent.

Sale and Barter

The words "for a money consideration, called the price" included in the definition serve to differentiate a contract of sale from a contract of barter by which moveable property is exchanged for other moveable property without any money being paid.

Barter continues to be governed by the common law, its principles being in line with the principles formerly applicable also to a contract for the sale of goods. An illustration is *Widenmeyer* v. *Burn, Stewart & Co. Ltd.*, 1967 S.C. 85, in which the common law rules as to the passing of the risk were applied to an exchange of a specified quantity of 1962 whisky for a specified quantity of 1964 whisky.

Though barter is now seldom of commercial importance in purely home transactions, it can be of considerable utility in some international commerce (*e.g.* to avoid problems of establishing exchange rates).

Sale and Security

It is important in certain circumstances to distinguish between a contract of sale and a contract which is in the form of a sale but is really intended to create security over moveables (which remain in the apparent seller's possession) in favour of a creditor who is the apparent buyer. The Act of 1979 does not apply to such fictitious sales: by section 62(4) "the provisions of this Act about contracts of sale do not apply to a transaction in the form of a contract of sale which is intended to operate by way of mortgage, pledge, charge, or other security."

The importance and the operation of section 62(4) are most easily understood by an example selected from the many decided cases in which the court has been called upon to apply the corresponding provision (s. 61(4)) of the Act of 1893:

Robertson v. *Hall's Trustee* (1896) 24 R. 120: H. purchased a crane-making business with its machinery, plant and stock of materials. He had, however, no capital, and borrowed £400 from R., a moneylender, to pay the first instalment of the price.

H. and R. agreed that H. "sold" the machinery *etc.* to R., that H. was to remain in possession of it, using it for the purposes of the business, and to pay a "hire" of 20 per cent on the "purchase" price of £400, and that, after the £400 had been repaid (which was to be by half-yearly instalments), R. would "resell" the articles to H.

About a year after this agreement had been entered into, H. became bankrupt, and there was competition for the machinery *etc.* between the trustee in H.'s sequestration and R.

Held that the circumstances showed that the parties had intended a security and not a sale; R.'s claim was therefore repelled because H. had in reality remained the owner.

Section 61(4) of the Act of 1893 was there said to be "in effect a statutory declaration that a pledge of or security over moveables cannot be created merely by completion of what professes to be a contract of sale. If the transaction is truly a sale, the property will pass without delivery. But the form of the contract is not conclusive. The reality of the transaction must be inquired into; and if, contrary to the form of the contract, and even the declaration of the parties, it appears from the whole circumstances that a true sale was not intended, it will be held that the property has not passed and that no effectual security has been acquired" (*per* Lord Moncreiff at p. 134).

4-26 Other cases in which the court came to the same conclusion include *Jones & Co.'s Trustee* v. *Allan* (1901) 4 F. 374 (J., a bicycle dealer, obtaining a loan from A. and giving A. a receipted invoice stating fictitiously that A. had paid £72 for certain specified bicycles which remained in J.'s possession), *Rennet* v. *Mathieson* (1903) 5 F. 591 (a landlord "purchasing" his tenant's wood-turning plant and then "hiring" it to the tenant), *Hepburn* v. *Law*, 1914 S.C. 918 (a creditor obtaining from his debtor a "receipt" for £130 stated to be the price of specified articles of furniture which remained in the debtor's house), and *Scottish Transit Trust Ltd.* v. *Scottish Land Cultivators Ltd.*, 1955 S.C. 254 (public works contractors "selling" their tractors and other vehicles to dealers in such vehicles who then advanced a lump sum to the contractors and entered into an apparently ordinary hire-purchase agreement with them).

4-27 The narrowness of the distinction can be seen by contrasting with these cases the case of *Gavin's Trustee* v. *Fraser*, 1920 S.C. 674, in which the court held that there had truly been a contract of sale where a haulage contractor had sold his plant to a timber merchant for £1,200, had continued to use the plant for the performance of a contract previously entered into with the timber merchant, and was to be entitled to buy back the plant within a year for £1,200 with interest at 6 per cent.

Capacity to Buy and Sell

4-28 Capacity to buy and sell is regulated by the general law concerning capacity to contract, except for the special rule that where necessaries are sold and delivered to a minor or to a person who by reason of mental incapacity or drunkenness is incompetent to contract, he must pay a reasonable price for the goods. The word "necessaries" means goods suitable to the condition in life of the minor or other person, and to his actual requirements at the time of the sale and delivery (s. 3).

4-29 Since the rule requires only a "reasonable" price, and not the contract price, to be paid, it is part of the law of quasi-contract rather than of contract.

4-30 Food and clothing would often be held to be "necessaries," but this would not always be so, as may be illustrated by the well-known English case *Nash* v. *Inman* [1908] 2 K.B. 1 (C.A.):

A Savile Row tailor brought an action for £145 10s.3d., the price of clothing "of an extravagant and ridiculous style" (including 11 fancy waistcoats) supplied to an undergraduate at Cambridge University. He met with the defence of "infancy," the defendant having been under the age of majority (21 years at that time).

Held that the onus was on the plaintiff to prove not only that the goods were suitable to the condition in life of the infant but that he was not sufficiently supplied with goods of that class at the time of the sale and delivery.

(b) Formalities of the Contract

Except where there is some provision to the contrary in any statute (as there is, for instance, in the case of the sale of a ship), there are no special formalities, either for constitution of the contract or for proof of it. The contract may be made in writing, or by word of mouth, or partly in writing and partly by word of mouth, or may be implied from the conduct of the parties (s. 4(1)). It may be proved *prout de jure* ("by any competent evidence, including parole evidence"):

Allan v. *Millar,* 1932 S.C. 620: A tenant was selling to his successor in the tenancy his "whole stock, crop, buildings, implements *etc.*" Some items of heritable property—growing raspberry bushes and a shed—were included in the tenant's stock.

Held that since the contract was for the sale of an *universitas* (a "totality") which was preponderatingly moveable it could competently be proved *prout de jure*.

(c) Subject-Matter of the Contract

The subject-matter of the contract is "goods," defined, in section 61(1), as including "all corporeal moveables except money." Incorporeal moveables, such as stocks and shares, are not "goods." Money is a corporeal moveable, but is necessarily excluded in the definition because in a sale of goods the goods and the price (which must be in money) are contrasted.

The term "goods" includes industrial growing crops (*e.g.* a growing crop of potatoes at a specified price per acre, as in *Paton's Trustee* v. *Finlayson,* 1923 S.C. 872 (4–212, below)), and things attached to or forming part of the land which are agreed to be severed before sale or under the contract of sale (*e.g.* a quantity of growing timber, as in *Munro* v. *Liquidator of Balnagown Estates Co. Ltd.,* 1949 S.C. 49 (4–118, below)) (s. 61(1)).

Existing or Future Goods

The goods may be either (i) existing goods, owned or possessed by the seller, or (ii) "future goods," defined as goods to be manufactured or acquired by the seller after the making of the contract of sale. It is possible to have a contract for the sale of goods, the acquisition of which by the seller depends upon a contingency which may or may not happen. There cannot be a present sale of future goods: the contract must, in the case of future goods, operate as an agreement to sell (with the result that the ownership of the goods does not pass to the buyer at the time of the making of the contract) (s. 5):

Stark's Trustees v. *Stark*, 1948 S.C. 41: S., by will dated July 10, 1946, bequeathed to his nephew "any motor car which I may possess at the date of my death." At that date, S. had a car on order.

S. died on August 23, 1946, before the car had been supplied.

Held that since at the date of S.'s death the car was still "future goods," it did not form part of S.'s estate, and that therefore the legacy failed.

Specific or Generic Goods

4–35   "Specific goods" are defined as meaning "goods identified and agreed on at the time a contract of sale is made" (s. 61(1)).

4–36   The Act has two provisions concerned with the possibility of the destruction of specific goods:

4–37   (i) Where there is a contract for the sale of specific goods, and the goods without the knowledge of the seller have perished at the time when the contract is made, the contract is void (s. 6).

4–38   (ii) Where there is an agreement to sell specific goods, and subsequently the goods, without any fault on the part of the seller or buyer, perish before the risk passes to the buyer, the agreement is avoided (s. 7). The passing of the risk is regulated by section 20 (see 4–106, below): the general rule is that *prima facie* ("unless the contrary is proved") the risk passes from seller to buyer at the same time as the ownership of the goods passes from seller to buyer.

4–39   In contrast to specific goods are generic goods (*e.g.* a specified quantity of a commodity such as flour). There are no provisions in the Act to make a contract for the sale of generic goods void should the goods be destroyed: the theory is *genus nunquam perit* ("the class never perishes"). The effect is that the loss will fall on the seller.

(d) **The Price**

4–40   The price must always be in money (s. 2(1)). Otherwise the contract would be one of barter.

4–41   The price may be fixed by the contract, or may be left to be fixed in a manner agreed by the contract, or may be determined by the course of dealing between the parties. Where the price is not determined in any of these ways, the buyer must pay a reasonable price, and what is a reasonable price is a question of fact dependent on the circumstances of each particular case (s. 8). A reasonable price is not necessarily, though it often will be, the market price.

4–42   An illustration of the application of the corresponding provisions in section 8 of the Act of 1893 is *Glynwed Distribution Ltd.* v. *S. Koronka & Co.*, 1977 S.C. 1:

G. Ltd. delivered to K. & Co., manufacturers of agricultural implements, a quantity of hot rolled steel. K. & Co. accepted the steel, thinking that they had bought "British steel" at a price of £103·50 per tonne; G. Ltd. thought that they had sold "foreign steel" at a price of £149 per tonne.

G. Ltd. raised an action in the sheriff court at Cupar for the unpaid balance of the price, representing the difference between the two prices.

The sheriff fixed £135 as a reasonable price.

On an appeal to the sheriff principal, the decision of the sheriff was reversed on the ground that G. Ltd. had not proved that there was a contract to sell at £149 per tonne, and that in any event there was no *consensus in idem* ("mutual agreement").

Held, on an appeal to the Court of Session, that (i) there was an agreement as to the subject-matter, namely, hot rolled steel, and therefore there was *consensus in idem;* and (ii) "reasonable price" meant something different from the market price, and there was a basis in fact upon which the sheriff could reach a decision as to what was a reasonable price in this case.

One of the ways in which the price may be left to be fixed "in a manner agreed by the contract" is where a valuation is to be made by a third party. The question may then arise of whether the valuator has adopted the correct basis for his valuation:

Macdonald v. *Clark,* 1927 S.N. 6 (O.H.): M., the owner of a hotel at Dalmellington, was selling the hotel property and business to C. The parties agreed that the price for the furniture and plant was to be fixed by valuators.

Held that the valuators were justified in valuing the articles, not at their market value, but as parts of a going concern, *i.e.* at a value greater than the sum of the values of the separate articles.

The Act provides that where there is an agreement to sell goods at a price to be fixed by the valuation of a third party, and the third party cannot or does not make the valuation, the agreement is avoided (*i.e.* cancelled), but if the goods or any part of them have been delivered to and appropriated by the buyer he must pay a reasonable price for them. Where the third party is prevented from making the valuation by the fault of the seller or buyer, the party not at fault may bring an action for damages against the party at fault (s. 9).

The parties may agree that part of the price is to be paid as a "deposit" at the time when the contract is entered into, the stipulation being that the deposit will be forfeited if the buyer does not duly pay the full price at the later date when it becomes due. The deposit is regarded as a guarantee for the due performance of the contract:

Roberts & Cooper Ltd. v. *Christian Salvesen & Co. Ltd.*, 1918 S.C. 794: An agreement was entered into for the sale of the vessel "Giralda" by S. Ltd. to R. Ltd. for £30,000, payable as to £3,000 on the signing of the agreement and as to the balance within five days after the vessel was ready for delivery. The agreement stipulated that failing due payment by the buyers, the sellers were to be at liberty to resell the vessel, the deposit would be forfeited, and any deficiency between the amount realised and the amount due would be borne by the buyers.

R. Ltd. failed to obtain the necessary Government permit for their intended trade with the "Giralda," and they repudiated the contract. S. Ltd. resold the vessel.

R. Ltd. brought an action to recover the deposit on the ground that it was a penalty and that in fact S. Ltd. had suffered no loss through R. Ltd.'s failure to implement the contract.

Held that the £3,000 had been deposited as a guarantee for the performance of the contract, and that R. Ltd. were not entitled to recover it.

Lord President Strathclyde said (at p. 806): "It is well-settled law that where, in a contract of sale, the intending buyer deposits part of the price, he cannot, if he repudiates the contract without justification, claim repayment of the deposit. That is upon the ground either that a man who repudiates a contract is not entitled to rescind that contract, or that a man who is in default cannot take advantage of his own default, or that a man who has paid down money as a security for performance of a contract cannot have that money back if he deliberately elects to throw up the contract."

(e) Terms of the Contract

4–46   Sections 10 to 15 of the Act relate to the terms of the contract. Some important changes have been made in these sections by recent legislation: in particular, the Supply of Goods (Implied Terms) Act 1973 and the Consumer Credit Act 1974 have substituted new provisions for some of the original provisions, and the Unfair Contract Terms Act 1977 has further affected some of the provisions.

4–47   The terms of the contract depend primarily on the agreement made between the parties. There are also terms implied by law. The general effect of the recent legislation is to restrict the freedom of contract allowed by the original provisions: parties are no longer as free as they were to choose their own terms and reject the terms implied by statute. The general position is stated in section 55(1) (a new provision substituted for the original provision of the 1893 Act by the Supply of Goods (Implied Terms) Act 1973 and itself amended by the Unfair Contract Terms Act 1977): where a right, duty or liability would arise under a contract of sale by implication of law, it may be negatived or varied by express agreement, or by the course of dealing between the parties, or by usage if the usage be such as to bind both of the parties, but this provision is subject to the provisions of the Unfair Contract Terms Act 1977.

4–48   The terms of the contract must be distinguished from collateral representations, such as statements contained in advertisements and expressions of opinion. Such representations may have induced the buyer to make the purchase, but they are not themselves terms of the contract.

4–49   *Flynn* v. *Scott*, 1949 S.C. 442 (O.H.): S. and F. entered into an oral contract for the purchase by F. of S.'s motor van. In the course of the negotiations F. had informed S. that he wanted the van for the general purposes of a haulage contractor and S. had said that the van was in good running order.

Seven days after the sale, the van, loaded with bedding from an aerodrome, broke down at the beginning of a journey, and 21 days after that breakdown F. intimated to S. his rejection of the van, and claimed repayment of the purchase price.

Held that S.'s statement that the van was in good running order was a mere expression of opinion and not a misrepresentation entitling F. to reject the van. (The Lord Ordinary also held that in any event the rejection had not been timeous.)

4–50   As well as using the phrase "terms of the contract" the Act uses the words "stipulations" (*e.g.* "stipulations as to time" in section 10), "conditions" (*e.g.* in sections 12 to 15), and "warranties" (*e.g.* in section

12). The word "stipulation" has no technical meaning: it simply denotes any term of the contract. The words "condition" and "warranty," however, do have technical meanings, and, in addition, these meanings differ as between Scots and English law.

In English law a "condition" is a fundamental term of the contract. Breach of a condition gives rise to a right to treat the contract as repudiated (s. 11(3)). A "warranty" means an agreement relating to the goods but collateral to the main purpose of the contract, and breach of a warranty gives rise to a claim for damages, but not to a right to reject the goods and treat the contract as repudiated (s. 61(1)). The question whether a term in a particular contract is a condition or a warranty is decided by the interpretation of the contract, and the word chosen by the parties is not conclusive (s. 11(3)). The Act provides that where a seller is in breach of a condition, the buyer may choose to treat that breach as a breach of warranty instead of as a ground for treating the contract as repudiated (s. 11(2)).

Scots law draws a distinction between material and non-material parts of a contract, and this distinction corresponds generally to the English distinction between conditions and warranties. Hence section 11(5) provides:

"In Scotland, failure by the seller to perform any material part of a contract of sale is a breach of contract, which entitles the buyer either within a reasonable time after delivery to reject the goods and treat the contract as repudiated, or to retain the goods and treat the failure to perform such material part as a breach which may give rise to a claim for compensation or damages."

The meaning of the word "warranty" in Scots law approaches to the meaning of "condition" in English law, and this accounts for the provision in section 61(2) that as regards Scotland a breach of warranty shall be deemed to be a failure to perform a material part of the contract.

This divergence in terminology between Scots and English law has led to uncertainty in the application to Scotland of sections 12 to 15 of the Act when read along with sections 11(5) and 61(2). The original Act of 1893 was first drafted (by Sir Mackenzie Chalmers) with the intention that it should codify the then existing law of England, and it was only after the Bill had been before Parliament for some four years (1889 to 1892) that the question of extending its provisions to Scotland was settled. Sections 12 to 15 have retained the language of the common law of England in so far as they reflect the clear dividing line in that system between a "condition" and a "warranty." As regards Scotland, the Scots common law distinction between material and non-material parts of a contract has been introduced by section 11(5), but it has not been made clear that in the application of sections 12 to 15 to Scotland the word "condition" is to be read as a material part and the word "warranty" as a non-material part; further, the provision in section 61(2) whereby a breach of warranty is to be deemed to be a failure to perform a material part of the contract suggests that sections 12 to 15 in so far as they deal with warranties have a different application in the two legal systems. (See also 4–88 and 4–182 et seq., below.)

4–54   An express condition or warranty does not negative one implied by
the Act unless they are inconsistent (s. 55(2)).

Stipulations as to Time

4–55   Unless a different intention appears from the terms of the contract,
stipulations as to time of payment are not of the essence of the contract (s.
10(1)). Whether any other stipulation as to time (*e.g.* as to the time of
delivery) is or is not of the essence of the contract depends on the terms of
the contract (s. 10(2)).

4–56   Where one party is in breach of a stipulation as to time which is of the
essence of the contract, the other is entitled to rescind the contract. Two
contrasting cases may serve as illustrations:

4–57   (i) *Shaw, Macfarlane & Co.* v. *Waddell & Son* (1900) 2 F. 1070: A
contract for the sale of a cargo of coal at a fixed price per ton included a
stipulation that the coal should be delivered at Grangemouth for shipment by the "L'Avenir" between April 12 and 16. At the time when the
contract was made a strike of miners in Wales was imminent and the price
of Scotch coal was rising rapidly.

The "L'Avenir" did not sail from Antwerp for Grangemouth until
April 19, and would not have been ready to load until April 23. Meantime
the sellers' railway sidings had become completely blocked by the
waggons containing the coal intended for the "L'Avenir," and the sellers
rescinded the contract.

Held that as in the circumstances the time of taking delivery was of the
essence of the contract the sellers were justified in rescinding the contract, and so the buyers were not entitled to damages for the sellers'
failure to implement the contract.

4–58   (ii) *Paton & Sons* v. *David Payne & Co. Ltd.* (1897) 35 S.L.R. 112
(H.L.): In March engineers undertook to supply a new printing machine
to be delivered in six weeks. The machine was not supplied until July.

Held, on an interpretation of the correspondence between the parties,
that time was not an essential element and that therefore the buyers,
though entitled to damages, were not entitled to reject the machine. (The
ground on which the House of Lords decided the case was that in any
event the rejection of the machine by the buyers had not been timeous.)

Implied Terms about Title, etc.

4–59   Section 12 of the Act of 1893 was altered by the Supply of Goods (Implied
Terms) Act 1973, and section 12 of the Act of 1979 consists of substantially the same provisions as those of the Act of 1973, although a new
arrangement has been adopted.

4–60   Section 12 now has six subsections. The last of these contains the
transitional provisions (see 4–14, above) that in relation to a contract
made before May 18, 1973, the provisions in paragraph 3 of Schedule 1 to
the Act are to apply instead (*i.e.* the provisions of section 12 of the Act of
1893 are preserved to that extent).

4–61   Subsections (1) to (5) fall into two groups: the first two subsections
are those which are of general application, while the remaining three
subsections apply to the exceptional situation where there is a limitation
on the title which is to be transferred by seller to buyer.

(i) Subsections (1) and (2) provide that in a contract of sale, other than one to which subsection (3) applies, there is:

(1) an implied condition on the part of the seller that in the case of a sale he has a right to sell the goods, and in the case of an agreement to sell he will have such a right at the time when the property is to pass; and

(2) an implied warranty that—

(*a*) the goods are free, and will remain free until the time when the property is to pass, from any charge or encumbrance not disclosed or known to the buyer before the contract is made; and

(*b*) the buyer will enjoy quiet possession of the goods except so far as it may be disturbed by the owner or other person entitled to the benefit of any charge or encumbrance which was disclosed or known.

In *McDonald* v. *Provan (of Scotland Street) Ltd.*, 1960 S.L.T. 231 (O.H.), there were circumstances where (if the facts were proved to be as the pursuer alleged) there had been a breach of both the implied condition in subsection (1) and legs (*a*) and (*b*) of the implied warranty in subsection (2):

The front part of a stolen Ford car had been welded to the rear portion of another Ford, and the composite vehicle had then been sold to P. Ltd. who acquired it in good faith.

P. Ltd. resold the vehicle to M. Three months later, the police took possession of it from M., and M. brought an action of damages against P. Ltd. for breach of the three undertakings as to title *etc.* (as provided for in section 12(1) to (3) of the Act of 1893).

P. Ltd. attempted to escape liability by the doctrine of *specificatio* ("manufacture of a new object"), arguing that the composite vehicle was a new entity belonging to the person who had constructed it.

Held that *specificatio* required good faith on the part of the manufacturer, and that therefore there might have been a breach of section 12. (There was, however, wide disagreement as to the facts, and proof before answer was allowed.)

(ii) Subsections (3) to (5) apply to the situation where the contract or the circumstances show that the seller intends to transfer only such title as he or a third person may have. In that situation there is:

(1) an implied warranty that all charges or encumbrances known to the seller and not known to the buyer have been disclosed to the buyer before the contract is made; and

(2) an implied warranty that none of the following will disturb the buyer's quiet possession of the goods, namely—

(*a*) the seller;

(*b*) the third person (in a case where the parties intend that the seller should transfer only such title as a third person may have);

(*c*) anyone claiming through or under the seller or the third person otherwise than under a charge or encumbrance disclosed or known to the buyer before the contract is made.

The obligations arising from section 12 cannot be excluded or restricted by agreement (Unfair Contract Terms Act 1977, s. 20(1)(*a*), as amended by 1979 Act, s. 63(1) and Sched. 2, para. 21).

Sale by Description

4–66   Section 13 as originally enacted in the Act of 1893 was amended by the Supply of Goods (Implied Terms) Act 1973 so as to clarify the meaning of sale by description. Before the Act of 1973 it was clear that there would be a sale by description if the buyer did not see the goods, and it was equally clear that a sale of a specific article as such, without any reference (express or implied) to a description, would not be a sale by description. The point which the Act of 1973 put beyond doubt was that a sale might still be a sale by description where the goods were exposed for sale and were selected by the buyer (*e.g.* in a self-service shop) (s. 13(3)).

4–67   However, not all difficulties about the meaning of sale by description have yet been eliminated. In particular there is the question whether the word "description" extends to the qualitative character of the goods or is restricted to the identification of the goods.

4–68   Earlier cases tend to support the former, wider meaning of "description." For example, in *Varley* v. *Whipp* [1900] 1 Q.B. 513 a seller agreed to sell for £21 a second-hand self-binder reaping machine which the buyer had never seen and which the seller stated had been new the previous year and had been used to cut only 50 or 60 acres. The buyer was held entitled to return the machine on the ground that since it did not correspond with the seller's statements there had been a breach of section 13.

4–69   Some recent English cases have included criticisms of this approach, *e.g.*:

4–70   *Ashington Piggeries Ltd.* v. *Christopher Hill Ltd.* [1972] A.C. 441: H. Ltd., well-known animal feeding stuff compounders, contracted to sell to A. Ltd. a mink food to be manufactured according to a formula prepared by A. Ltd. and including as one of its ingredients herring meal.

Unknown to either party, some quantities of the food supplied contained in the herring meal a substance dimethylnitrosamine (DMNA), which was highly toxic to mink.

A. Ltd. claimed damages for losses sustained by the death of and injury to the mink, alleging breaches of the conditions implied by sections 13 (description), 14(1) (fitness for purpose) and 14(2) (merchantable quality) of the Act of 1893.

Held that there had been breaches of section 14(1) and (2), but not of section 13.

The "key" to section 13 was held to be identification (*per* Lord Diplock at p. 504).

"A term ought not to be regarded as part of the description unless it identifies the goods sold" (*per* Lord Hodson at p. 470).

"Herring meal is still herring meal notwithstanding that it may have been contaminated by DMNA" (*per* Lord Guest at p. 472).

"The proposition is . . . that the herring meal ingredient did not correspond with the description because it contained DMNA. . . .

". . . I do not believe that the Sale of Goods Act was designed to provoke metaphysical discussions as to the nature of what is delivered, in comparison with what is sold. The test of description, at least where commodities are concerned, is intended to be a broader, more common sense, test of a mercantile character. The question whether that is what the buyer bargained for has to be answered according to such tests as men in the market would apply, leaving more delicate questions of condition, or quality, to be determined under other clauses of the contract or sections of the Act. . . . The defect in the meal was a matter of quality or condition rather than of description. I think that buyers and sellers and arbitrators in the market, asked what this was, could only have said that the relevant ingredient was herring meal, and, therefore, that there was no failure to correspond with description. In my opinion, the appellants do not succeed under section 13" (*per* Lord Wilberforce at p. 489).

Another recent House of Lords case, *Reardon Smith Line Ltd.* v. *Hansen-Tangen* [1976] 1 W.L.R. 989, includes an interesting *obiter dictum* from the same Law Lord. The case concerned the identification of a vessel which had been given two different yard numbers—one by the builders and the other by the sub-contract builders. The authorities as to description in sale of goods cases were held not to extend to the contract in question, but Lord Wilberforce expressed the view (at p. 998) that he found some of the cases on sale of goods by description to be "excessively technical and due for fresh examination in this House. Even if a strict and technical view must be taken as regards the description of unascertained future goods (*e.g.* commodities) as to which each detail of the description must be assumed to be vital, it may be, and in my opinion is, right to treat other contracts of sale of goods in a similar manner to other contracts generally so as to ask whether a particular item in a description constitutes a substantial ingredient of the 'identity' of the thing sold, and only if it does to treat it as a condition."

Section 13(1) provides that in a sale by description there is an implied condition that the goods shall correspond with the description. If the sale is by sample as well as by description, the bulk of the goods must correspond both with the sample and with the description (s. 13(2)).

A typical example of a sale by description would be a sale of a quantity of fertiliser described as having added to it a certain proportion of magnesium sulphate intended to correct a deficiency of magnesium in the soil. If the fertiliser supplied had had added to it the weedkiller sodium chlorate instead of magnesium sulphate, the seller would be in breach of section 13 (see *McCallum* v. *Mason*, 1956 S.C. 50 (4–95, below)).

An instance of a specific article sold by description occurred in *Roberts & Co.* v. *Yule* (1896) 23 R. 855:

Machinery merchants sold a second-hand four-horse power nominal gas-engine, described as in "excellent order," to Y. for £47.10s. Y. found that the engine required an expenditure of £8.10s. on it to put it right.

Held that Y. was entitled to reject the engine as disconform to description.

Contracting out of section 13 is allowed only to a strictly limited extent. No exclusion or restriction at all is allowed as against the consumer in a consumer contract (*i.e.* a contract in which one party is dealing in the course of a business and the other party ("the consumer") is not dealing in the course of a business and the goods are of a type ordinarily supplied for private use or consumption). In any other type of contract any exclusion or restriction is of no effect unless it was fair and reasonable as at the time when the contract was made. The onus of proving that a contract is not a consumer contract lies on the party who claims that it is not, and the onus of proving that an exclusion or restriction was fair and reasonable lies on the party who so contends (Unfair Contract Terms Act 1977, ss. 20(2), 24 and 25, as amended by the 1979 Act, s. 63(1) and Sched. 2, paras. 21 and 22). Guidelines for the application of the reasonableness test are set out in Schedule 2 to the Act of 1977: for example, regard should be had to the relative strength of the bargaining positions of the parties, including alternative means by which the customer's requirements could have been met.

4–76   The provisions of section 13 as to sale by description are concerned only with civil law, and are not affected by the Trade Descriptions Act 1968 which makes the use of false "trade descriptions" a criminal offence (see 4–308 *et seq.*, below).

Implied Terms about Quality or Fitness

4–77   Section 14 of the Act of 1979 is derived from section 14 of the Act of 1893 as substituted by the Supply of Goods (Implied Terms) Act 1973 (and also in part by the Consumer Credit Act 1974). The section first sets out the general rule of *caveat emptor* ("let the buyer beware"), and then provides for the exceptions to that general rule—the situations in which there are implied undertakings as to quality or fitness.

4–78   The rule of *caveat emptor* is derived from the English common law. Under the common law of Scotland sale was a contract *bonae fidei* ("of good faith"), with the result that the seller was bound to supply priceworthy goods.

4–79   The general rule now applicable in both legal systems is that, with the exceptions provided for in sections 14 and 15 of the Act and subject to the provisions of any other Act, there is no implied condition or warranty about the quality or fitness for any particular purpose of goods supplied under a contract of sale (s. 14(1)). As a general rule, therefore, it is for the buyer to satisfy himself that the goods which he is buying are of the quality which he desires and are fit for the purpose for which he requires them.

4–80   The exceptions provided for in section 14 are considered below under the headings:

    (i)   merchantable quality;
   (ii) fitness for particular purpose; and
  (iii) usage.

4–81   Contracting out of these implied undertakings is strictly limited in the same way as contracting out of section 13 is limited (see 4–75, above).

4–82   As regards (i) and (ii) the undertakings apply where the seller is selling the goods "in the course of a business." Non-business sales are therefore excluded, but in other respects the phrase has a wide meaning. The goods are not necessarily goods in which the seller ordinarily deals; for example, if a trader were to sell the delivery vans which he had been using to transport his merchandise, that would seem to be a sale "in the course of a business," and in *Buchanan-Jardine* v. *Hamilink*, 1983 S.L.T. 149, the seller of the whole stock of a farm business which was itself being sold or wound up was held to be selling "in the course of a business." The statutory definition of "business" also has the effect of making these provisions wide-ranging. "Business" includes a profession and the activities of any government department, or local or public authority (s. 61(1)).

Another point affecting both (i) and (ii) is the provision added by the Supply of Goods (Implied Terms) Act 1973 and now constituting section 14(5) of the Act of 1979. This deals with the situation where the person who is selling in the course of a business is acting as agent for another person (his principal). The agent may, for instance, be an auctioneer. He will be selling "in the course of a business," but his principal may or may not be selling "in the course of a business." The statutory provision is designed to protect the buyer: the principal, even though he is a private seller, will be liable in respect of the implied undertakings unless he is in fact not selling in the course of a business *and* either the buyer knows that fact or reasonable steps are taken to bring it to the notice of the buyer before the contract is made.

(i) Merchantable quality

Where the seller sells goods in the course of a business, there is an implied condition that the goods supplied under the contract are of merchantable quality, except that there is no such condition—

(*a*) as regards defects specifically drawn to the buyer's attention before the contract is made; or

(*b*) if the buyer examines the goods before the contract is made, as regards defects which that examination ought to reveal (s. 14(2)).

The term "merchantable quality" had been used in the Act of 1893, but had not been defined in that Act, and its interpretation featured in many decided cases. The Supply of Goods (Implied Terms) Act 1973 added a definition, which now comprises section 14(6) of the Act of 1979. The definition appears to be an attempt to codify the definitions supplied by the decided cases: goods are of "merchantable quality" "if they are as fit for the purpose or purposes for which goods of that kind are commonly bought as it is reasonable to expect having regard to any description applied to them, the price (if relevant) and all the other relevant circumstances."

Goods may be of "merchantable quality" without being fit for the purpose for which the buyer requires them. This may be illustrated by *B.S. Brown & Son Ltd.* v. *Craiks Ltd.*, 1970 S.C. (H.L.) 51, a case decided on section 14(1) and (2) in their original form:

B. Ltd., cloth merchants in Manchester, purchased a quantity of rayon cloth from C. Ltd., manufacturers in Forfar, intending to re-sell it for dress material. The cloth supplied was not suitable for dress material, and B. Ltd. sued C. Ltd. for breach of section 14(1) (fitness for particular purpose) and section 14(2) (merchantable quality) of the Act of 1893.

The claim based on section 14(1) failed because B. Ltd. could not prove that they had told C. Ltd. of the particular purpose for which they required the cloth.

The claim based on section 14(2) also failed because the cloth was held to be of "merchantable quality," since it was reasonably capable of being used and was saleable for a number of industrial purposes (*e.g.* for making bags), although there was no evidence that it had in fact been used for industrial purposes.

4-87   Reference was made to a leading English case arising out of the supply of feeding stuffs to the Hardwick Game Farm—*Henry Kendall & Sons* v. *William Lillico & Sons Ltd.* [1969] 2 A.C. 31, in which Lord Reid had said (at p. 75): "Merchantable can only mean commercially saleable."

4-88   A Scottish case decided after the passing of the Act of 1973 involving the interpretation of "merchantable quality" is *Millars of Falkirk Ltd.* v. *Turpie*, 1976 S.L.T. (Notes) 66:

In July 1973, T., a solicitor, took delivery of a new Ford Granada. His Zodiac was taken in part payment and the balance of the price was to be paid by cheque.

The new car had a leak of oil from its steering box and a loose bonnet catch. The dealers made adjustments to correct these faults, but, on finding that there was still a leak of oil, T. intimated his rejection of the car on the ground that it was not of "merchantable quality."

The dealers refused to accept T.'s rejection, and brought an action for the balance of the price. T. counterclaimed for return of the Zodiac or its agreed value of £542·42 and for damages.

Held that as the fault was a comparatively minor matter which could readily have been cured at a cost of no more than £25, the new car was of "merchantable quality," and that T. was therefore not entitled to reject it.

On the definition of "merchantable quality" Lord President Emslie said (at p. 68): "I am of opinion that this definition is the best that has yet been devised, and that in any particular case in which the question of merchantable quality arises it is to be answered as a commercial man would be likely to answer it having regard to the various matters mentioned in the statutory definition."

On this case, however, see also 4–183, below.

(ii) Fitness for particular purpose

4-89   The provision in section 14(3) differs according to whether the sale is an ordinary sale or a sale on credit terms.

4-90   In the case of an ordinary sale, where the seller sells goods in the course of a business and the buyer, expressly or by implication, makes known to the seller any particular purpose for which the goods are being bought, there is an implied condition that the goods supplied under the contract are reasonably fit for that purpose, whether or not that is a purpose for which such goods are commonly supplied, except where the circumstances show that the buyer does not rely, or that it is unreasonable for him to rely, on the skill or judgment of the seller.

4-91   The provision relating to a sale on credit terms covers the situation where a "credit-broker" (*e.g.* the retailer) sells goods to a finance house which then sells them to the retailer's customer (the buyer) on credit. The buyer has the benefit of the same implied undertaking as to fitness for a particular purpose, provided he makes that purpose known to the credit-broker, except where the circumstances show that the buyer does not rely, or that it is unreasonable for him to rely, on the skill or judgment of the credit-broker. The term "credit-broker" means "a person acting in the course of a business of credit brokerage carried on by him, that is a

business of effecting introductions of individuals desiring to obtain
credit—

(*a*) to persons carrying on any business so far as it relates to the
provision of credit, or

(*b*) to other persons engaged in credit brokerage" (s. 61(1)).

The following three cases illustrate the implied undertaking as to
fitness for a particular purpose:

(1) *Jacobs* v. *Scott & Co.* (1899) 2 F. (H.L.) 70: J., a horse-dealer in
Canada, entered into a contract with the Glasgow Tramway and Omnibus
Co. Ltd. to supply to the company 2,100 tons of "best Canadian Timothy
hay."

To carry out this contract J. contracted with S. & Co., hay-dealers in
Canada, for the supply of 900 tons of "No. 1 export hay." It was proved
that S. & Co. knew that the hay to be supplied by them was to be used by
J. to implement in part his contract with the Glasgow company, and it was
also proved that "No. 1 export hay" was a hay composed partly of
Timothy and partly of other grasses and was not of a sufficiently high
quality to satisfy the Glasgow market.

The Glasgow company rejected the hay supplied as disconform to the
contract between them and J., and J. brought an action against S. & Co.
for damages for breach of their contract with him.

Held that in the contract between J. and S. & Co. there had been an
implied condition that the "No. 1 export hay" supplied should be of the
standard required for the Glasgow market.

(The case also illustrates the point that an express "condition or
warranty" does not negative a "condition or warranty" implied by the
Act unless it is inconsistent with the implied one (s. 55(2)).)

(2) *Buchanan & Carswell* v. *Eugene Ltd.*, 1936 S.C. 160: B. & Co.,
hairdressers, bought an electric hair-drying machine from E. Ltd.,
manufacturers and suppliers of hairdressing appliances.

Mrs Pollock, a customer of B. & Co., was injured by the machine when
it was in use in B. & Co.'s premises and in an action against B. & Co.
received an award of damages for her injuries.

B. & Co. sued E. Ltd. to recover these damages on the ground that E.
Ltd. had supplied a machine which was not reasonably fit for the purpose
for which it was required.

Held that this action based on what was then section 14(1) of the Act of
1893 was relevant and that B. & Co. would therefore, if they succeeded in
proving that there had been a breach of the implied condition, be entitled
to an award of damages.

(3) *McCallum* v. *Mason*, 1956 S.C. 50: In 1952 McC., a nurseryman,
whose tomato plants were showing a slightly yellowish tinge, was advised
by M., a dealer in fertilisers, to apply to them M.'s "N.P." fertiliser to
which M. was to add a quantity of magnesium sulphate to correct a
deficiency of magnesium in the soil. McC. purchased two bags supposed
to contain these ingredients from M., and applied the contents of one bag
to his tomato plants. The plants, however, deteriorated and died, and
McC.'s whole tomato crop was lost as a result.

The following year McC. applied the contents of the second bag to
healthy new tomato plants and to chrysanthemum plants. All the plants
deteriorated and died.

Analysis of the mixture showed that it contained no magnesium sulphate but 10 per cent of the weedkiller sodium chlorate.

McC. brought an action of damages against M. for breach of what was then section 14(1) of the Act of 1893 averring that M. had failed to supply goods which were reasonably fit for the purpose for which they were required.

Held that McC.'s case was relevant as far as the first tomato crop was concerned but not as far as the second tomato crop or the chrysanthemums were concerned, since the particular purpose of the purchase as disclosed to M. was limited to the first tomato crop.

4–96   Where goods are commonly used for only one purpose, the purpose is sufficiently made known to the seller by the buyer's merely asking for the goods. For example, actions have been successfully brought against the seller where the plaintiff's wife was scalded by the bursting of a hot water bottle bought from a chemist (*Preist* v. *Last* [1903] 2 K.B. 148 (C.A.)), where the plaintiff's wife died from consuming milk containing germs of typhoid fever (*Frost* v. *Aylesbury Dairy Co. Ltd.* [1905] 1 K.B. 608 (C.A.)), and where the pursuer, having purchased boots for himself, suffered periostitis of a foot as a result of the insole having crumpled up and become knotted and nodular (*Thomson* v. *J. Sears & Co. (Trueform Boot Co.) Ltd.*, 1926 S.L.T. 221 (O.H.)).

(iii) Usage

4–97   An implied condition or warranty as to quality or fitness for a particular purpose may be annexed to a contract of sale by usage (s. 14(4)).

Sale by Sample

4–98   A sale is a sale by sample where there is an express or implied term to that effect in the contract (s. 15(1)). A sale is not a sale by sample merely because a sample has been exhibited and has induced the sale.

4–99   In a sale by sample there are three implied conditions:

(i) that the bulk will correspond with the sample in quality;

(ii) that the buyer will have a reasonable opportunity of comparing the bulk with the sample; and

(iii) that the goods will be free from any defect, making them unmerchantable, which would not be apparent on reasonable examination of the sample (s. 15(2)).

In (iii) the word "unmerchantable" is to be construed in accordance with section 14(6)—the section which defines "merchantable quality" (see 4–85, above) (s. 15(3)).

4–100   Contracting out is limited to the same extent as contracting out of sections 13 and 14 is limited (see 4–75, above).

4–101   A well-known case involving sales by sample is *Godley* v. *Perry* [1960] 1 W.L.R. 9, decided by Edmund Davies J. under the Act of 1893:

G., a boy of six, was injured when firing a stone from a toy plastic catapult which he had bought from P.'s shop: one of G.'s eyes was ruptured and had to be removed.

The catapult had been manufactured in Hong Kong and was one of a quantity bought by P.'s wife from a wholesaler, who had bought from the importer. Both P.'s wife and the wholesaler had tested one of the catapults at the time when they made their respective purchases.

G. brought an action against P. for breach of the implied conditions in section 14(1) and (2) of the Act of 1893 (fitness for purpose and merchantable quality). P. brought in the wholesaler, who in turn brought in the importer, the claims against the wholesaler and the importer being based on breach of the implied condition in section 15 that the goods should be free from any defect, rendering them unmerchantable, which had not been apparent on reasonable examination of the sample.

All the claims succeeded.

III EFFECTS OF THE CONTRACT

Two questions are dealt with in this third Part of the Act:

(a) When does the ownership of the goods (referred to in the Act as "the property in the goods") pass from seller to buyer? The provisions of the Act on this question come under the heading "Transfer of Property as between Seller and Buyer."

(b) Where the seller is not the true owner of the goods, what is the buyer's right in (or "title to") the goods? The provisions of the Act on this question come under the heading "Transfer of Title."

(a) Transfer of Property as between Seller and Buyer

By the common law of Scotland, the property did not pass until the goods were delivered to the buyer. Under the Act, the property may pass independently of delivery: in many cases it will pass when the contract is made, though the goods are still in the possession of the seller.

The rules which govern the passing of the property from seller to buyer are especially important in connection with:

(i) *bankruptcy:* where one of the parties to the contract becomes bankrupt, his property (in the sense of the items which he owns), whether or not it is in his possession, passes to the trustee in his sequestration; many of the decided cases have involved competing claims asserted on bankruptcy;

(ii) *passing of risk:* the general rule is expressed in the maxim *res perit domino* (literally, "a thing perishes to the disadvantage of its owner," *i.e.* it is on the owner that a loss falls); the Act provides that unless otherwise agreed, the goods remain at the seller's risk until the property in them passes to the buyer and that thereafter they are at the buyer's risk whether delivery has been made or not (s. 20(1)); two exceptions are made to this general rule:

(1) Where delivery has been delayed through the fault of either buyer or seller, the goods are at the risk of the party at fault as regards any loss which might not have occurred but for such fault (s. 20(2)). (For instance, the seller may have failed to meet a delivery date and the goods may have been destroyed by a subsequent fire in the seller's warehouse.)

(2) The duties or liabilities of either seller or buyer as custodier of the goods are not affected by the statutory provision (s. 20(3)). (For instance, the seller may be storing the goods until the buyer gets entry to a new house.)

Unascertained Goods

4–107 The first provision of the Act as to the transfer of property from seller to buyer is that the goods must be ascertained: where there is a contract for the sale of unascertained goods, no property in the goods passes to the buyer unless and until the goods are ascertained (s. 16).

4–108 An illustration of section 16 occurs in *Hayman & Son* v. *McLintock*, 1907 S.C. 936:

McNairn & Co., flour-merchants, had a large number of sacks of flour in H.'s store. They sold 250 sacks to X and 100 sacks to Y, and in implement of these sales handed to X and Y delivery-orders addressed to H. The delivery-orders were intimated to H., who acknowledged to X and Y that he held the 250 sacks and 100 sacks respectively subject to their instructions. However, the individual sacks were not marked or separated from the other sacks in the store.

McNairn & Co.'s estates were sequestrated.

Held that the trustee in the sequestration was entitled to all the sacks of flour in H.'s store, because the goods sold to X and Y were unascertained and so no property in the goods had passed to X and Y.

Specific or Ascertained Goods

4–109 Where the goods are specific or ascertained, the property in them passes to the buyer at such time as the parties intend it to pass, and for the purpose of ascertaining the intention of the parties regard must be had to the terms of the contract, the conduct of the parties and the circumstances of the case (s. 17).

4–110 The Act sets out in section 18 five rules for ascertaining the intention of the parties as to the time at which the property is to pass, but these rules apply only where no different intention appears. The following three cases give instances of situations where the rules of section 18 were held not applicable because the intention of the parties was to a different effect:

4–111 (i) *Peebles & Co.* v. *John L. Kerr Ltd.* (1902) 9 S.L.T. 372 (O.H.): A contract for the sale of a motor by P. & Co. to K. Ltd. provided that the price was to be paid by a bill of exchange payable in three months' time. The contract was silent as to the passing of the property.

When delivered, the machine had riveted upon it a brass plate bearing the words: "the property of P. & Co."

Before the price had become payable, K. Ltd. went into liquidation, and P. & Co. brought an action for redelivery of the machine on the ground that the property had not passed to K. Ltd.

Held that the sale had been made under a suspensive condition to that effect, and decree of delivery *granted*.

4–112 (ii) *Sir James Laing & Sons Ltd.* v. *Barclay, Curle & Co. Ltd.*, 1908 S.C. (H.L.) 1; 1908 S.C. 82: B. Ltd., shipbuilders, contracted to build a ship for an Italian company. The price was to be paid by instalments at certain stages of construction. The contract provided that the ship should not be considered as delivered until it had passed a certain trial trip.

After the ship had been built and the greater part of the price had been paid but before the trial trip, L. Ltd. arrested the ship for a debt alleged to be due by the Italian company to L. Ltd.

Held that B. Ltd. were entitled to have the arrestment recalled because the contract showed that the parties had not intended the property to pass to the Italian company until the trial trip had taken place.

Lord Robertson said (at p. 2): "The statute supplies certain rules; but these may or may not come into operation, according as the contract requires it. In the present case I find the contract to require no aid or supplement from the statutory rules, for it seems to me to provide from beginning to completion of this ship for the building of it by the shipbuilders with their materials, and transfers it to the purchasers only as a finished ship and at a stage not in fact yet reached."

(iii) *Woodburn* v. *Andrew Motherwell Ltd.*, 1917 S.C. 533: W., a farmer, sold to M. Ltd. six ricks of hay at an agreed price per ton. The contract provided that the hay was to be placed at the disposal of M. Ltd. in W.'s stackyard so that M. Ltd. could pack it in bales, that W. should then cart it to the railway, and that the weight ascertained there for carriage purposes would also be taken as the weight for fixing the total purchase price.

Some bales of hay were destroyed by fire before they had been removed from W.'s stackyard.

Held that the terms of the contract clearly indicated that the parties intended the property in the hay to pass when the hay was placed at M. Ltd.'s disposal, that the risk of loss by fire therefore lay with M. Ltd., and that W. was entitled to recover from M. Ltd. the price of the bales which had been destroyed.

Lord President Strathclyde said (at p. 538): "The rules in section 18 are merely intended to be a guide in ascertaining the intention of the parties. But, if the intention of the parties is quite plain—as I think it is in this case—that the property should pass at the time when the goods were placed at the disposal of the buyer that he might convert them into bales, then the rules of section 18 do not come into play at all."

Rules for ascertaining intention

Where no different intention appears, the rules which, by section 18, are to be applied for ascertaining the intention of the parties as to the time at which the property in the goods is to pass to the buyer are as follows:

Rule 1

"Where there is an unconditional contract for the sale of specific goods in a deliverable state the property in the goods passes to the buyer when the contract is made, and it is immaterial whether the time of payment or the time of delivery, or both, be postponed."

For the purposes of the Act goods are in a "deliverable state" when they are in such a state that the buyer would under the contract be bound to take delivery of them (s. 61(5)).

4–117 Thus, in *Gowans (Cockburn's Trustee)* v. *Bowe & Sons*, 1910 2 S.L.T. 17 (O.H.), where B. & Sons, potato merchants, had in August bought farmer C.'s whole growing potato crop (specific or ascertained goods), the property in the potatoes passed to B. & Sons once C. had lifted and pitted the potatoes on his farm, with the result that, in C.'s subsequent sequestration, the potatoes did not form part of his estate, and B. & Sons were entitled to remove them.

4–118 Similarly, where there is a contract for the sale of growing trees, the goods are put into a deliverable state when the trees are felled. The property, therefore, passes under rule 1 to the buyer although the timber may not actually have been removed from the estate on which it was grown (*Munro* v. *Balnagown Estates Co. Ltd.*, 1949 S.C. 49).

Rule 2

4–119 "Where there is a contract for the sale of specific goods and the seller is bound to do something to the goods for the purpose of putting them into a deliverable state, the property does not pass until the thing is done and the buyer has notice that it has been done."

4–120 *Brown Brothers* v. *Carron Co.* (1898) 6 S.L.T. 231 (O.H.): Under a contract for the sale of a steam crane by B. to C. it was arranged that B. should keep the crane in his yard until it was required for erection on C.'s vessel and that B. should make some slight alterations on the crane in the course of erecting it.

C., no longer requiring the crane, refused to take delivery.

Held that the property in the crane had not passed to C., and that B. was therefore not entitled to succeed in an action for the price (see s. 49(1)); his only remedy was damages.

Rule 3

4–121 "Where there is a contract for the sale of specific goods in a deliverable state but the seller is bound to weigh, measure, test, or do some other act or thing with reference to the goods for the purpose of ascertaining the price, the property does not pass until the act or thing is done and the buyer has notice that it has been done."

4–122 In *Woodburn* v. *Andrew Motherwell Ltd.*, 1917 S.C. 533 (4–113, above), M. Ltd. made an unsuccessful attempt to have this third rule applied.

Rule 4

4–123 "When goods are delivered to the buyer on approval or on sale or return or other similar terms the property in the goods passes to the buyer:—

(a) when he signifies his approval or acceptance to the seller or does any other act adopting the transaction; [*or*]

(b) if he does not signify his approval or acceptance to the seller but retains the goods without giving notice of rejection, then, if a time has been fixed for the return of the goods, on the expiration of that time, and, if no time has been fixed, on the expiration of a reasonable time."

A contract of "sale or return" can be seen in *Ross & Co.* v. *Plano Manufacturing Co. and Ors.* (1903) 11 S.L.T. 7 (O.H.): Robertson was a commission agent who had obtained 20 binders from the company which manufactured them. At the time of Robertson's bankruptcy the binders were stored with Ross & Co., and competing claims to them were made by the manufacturing company and by Robertson's trustee.

Held that as there had been no absolute sale of the binders to Robertson but only a "sale or return" the property in the binders had remained with the manufacturing company.

A transaction of a similar nature was considered by the court in *Bryce* v. *Ehrmann* (1904) 7 F. 5: E., a wholesale jeweller, sent goods to A., a retail jeweller, on terms that A. was to have power to sell the goods and should then become liable to pay the wholesale price to E. An "approbation note" issued by E. stated that the goods were to remain the property of E. until invoiced by him to A.

A., without E.'s knowledge, pledged a diamond necklace, part of the goods, to B., a pawnbroker.

A. subsequently became bankrupt.

Held that, as A.'s trustee did not insist in his claim to the necklace, E. was entitled to delivery of it, but only after satisfying B.'s claim.

Rule 5

"(1) Where there is a contract for the sale of unascertained or future goods by description, and goods of that description and in a deliverable state are unconditionally appropriated to the contract, either by the seller with the assent of the buyer or by the buyer with the assent of the seller, the property in the goods then passes to the buyer; and the assent may be express or implied, and may be given either before or after the appropriation is made.

"(2) Where, in pursuance of the contract, the seller delivers the goods to the buyer or to a carrier or other . . . custodier (whether named by the buyer or not) for the purpose of transmission to the buyer, and does not reserve the right of disposal, he is to be taken to have unconditionally appropriated the goods to the contract."

Section 19 explains how the seller may "reserve the right of disposal." He may do so by stipulating that the property in the goods is not to pass to the buyer until certain conditions are fulfilled (s. 19(1)) (*e.g.* until the price is paid). Where goods are shipped, and by the bill of lading are deliverable to the order of the seller or his agent, the seller is *prima facie* ("until the contrary is proved") to be taken to reserve the right of disposal (s. 19(2)). Where the seller draws a bill of exchange on the buyer for the price, and sends the bill of exchange and the bill of lading to the buyer together in order that the buyer may accept or pay the bill of exchange, the buyer is bound to return the bill of lading if he does not honour the bill of exchange, and if he wrongfully retains the bill of lading the property in the goods does not pass to him.

A contract of sale may include a "Romalpa" clause—so-called after the decision of the Court of Appeal in *Aluminium Industrie Vaassen B.V.* v. *Romalpa Aluminium Ltd.* [1976] 1 W.L.R. 676:

A Dutch company sold to an English company aluminium foil, some of which was then sold by the English company to sub-purchasers. The Dutch company's standard conditions of sale included a clause providing that the ownership of the foil was to be transferred to the English company only when they had met all that was owing to the Dutch company, that until the date of payment the English company were, if the Dutch company so desired, to store the foil in such a way that it was clearly the property of the Dutch company, that articles manufactured from the foil were to be kept for the Dutch company as a guarantee for full payment of the sums owed by the English company to the Dutch company, and that if the English company sold the articles to third parties, the English company were, if the Dutch company so required, to hand over to the Dutch company the claims which they might have against the third parties.

The English company got into financial difficulty, and a receiver was appointed under powers contained in a debenture.

Held that because of the "Romalpa" clause, the English company had to be regarded, so far as the Dutch company were concerned, as having sold the foil to the third parties as agents and bailees (custodiers), and so the Dutch company were entitled not only to recover the foil still in the possession of the English company but also to trace and claim the proceeds of sub-sales (held by the receiver in a separate account) in priority to the general body of the English company's other creditors including the debenture holders who had appointed the receiver.

The *Romalpa* case was distinguished in two later English cases—*Re Bond Worth Ltd.* [1980] Ch. 228 and *Borden (U.K.) Ltd.* v. *Scottish Timber Products Ltd. and Another* [1981] Ch. 25 (C.A.), while in Scotland there have been two cases in which "Romalpa" clauses have been held to be ineffectual—*Clark Taylor & Co.* v. *Quality Site Development (Edinburgh) Ltd.*, 1981 S.L.T. 308 and *Emerald Stainless Steel Ltd.* v. *South Side Distribution Ltd.*, 1983 S.L.T. 162 (O.H.). For comments on Scottish cases see K.G.C. Reid and G.L. Gretton, C.N. McEachran, T.B. Smith and W.A. Wilson, 1983 S.L.T. (News) 77, 102, 105 and 106.

(b) Transfer of Title

4–130   The basic rule is expressed in the maxim *nemo dat quod non habet* ("no one gives what he does not have"). Therefore, as a general rule, where goods are sold by a person who is not their owner, and who does not have the owner's authority or consent to sell them, the buyer acquires no better title to the goods than the seller had (s. 21(1)). The general rule applies to sales by a person who has merely found goods or has stolen them or has obtained them under a void contract, such as a contract void on account of error in the substantials (*e.g. Morrisson* v. *Robertson*, 1908 S.C. 332 (4–136, below)). The goods are regarded as having a *vitium reale* ("inherent fault"), which prevents even a bona fide purchaser who has given value for them from obtaining a good title to them: the true owner is entitled to recover them.

4–131   There are some exceptions to the general rule, both at common law (*e.g.* in agency of necessity and in *negotiorum gestio* ("management of affairs," a branch of quasi-contract)) and by statutory provisions outside the Sale of Goods Act 1979 (*e.g.* the Factors Act 1889, extended to Scotland by the Factors (Scotland) Act 1890, and the Innkeepers Act 1878). Such exceptions are expressly preserved by the Act of 1979 (s. 21 (2)).

The Act itself provides for exceptions which are explained below under these headings:

    (i) personal bar;
    (ii) sale under voidable title; and
    (iii) seller or buyer in possession after sale.

In England[1] there is the additional exception of "market overt": where goods are sold in "market overt" (*i.e.* shops within the City of London and public, legally constituted, markets outside it), according to the usage of the market, the buyer acquires a good title to the goods, provided he buys them in good faith and without notice of any defect or want of title on the part of the seller (s. 22).

(i) *Personal Bar*

By the operation of the principle of personal bar, the owner of the goods may be precluded from denying the seller's authority to sell (s. 21(1)). This could occur, for instance, where the seller is an agent or employee of the owner and has been placed in such a position by the owner that the buyer is justified in believing that he has the necessary authority to sell.

(ii) *Sale under Voidable Title*

When the seller has a voidable title to the goods, but his title has not been "avoided" (*i.e.* set aside) at the time of the sale, the buyer acquires a good title to the goods, provided he buys them in good faith and without notice of the seller's defect of title (s. 23).

The seller's title may, for instance, be voidable on account of fraud, as in *MacLeod* v. *Kerr,* 1965 S.C. 253:

A rogue, Galloway, giving his name as "L. Craig," persuaded Kerr to sell a car to him, in return for a cheque from a stolen cheque book.

Galloway then, giving his name as "Kerr," sold the car to Gibson, who in good faith paid £200 for it.

Held that, as the first sale had conferred on Galloway a voidable title which had not been avoided by the time of the second sale, Gibson had obtained a good title to the car.

The legal position is different where the first sale is not merely voidable, but void, *e.g.* where there has been error in the substantials, as in *Morrisson* v. *Robertson,* 1908 S.C. 332:

A rogue, Telford, falsely representing that he was the son of Wilson, obtained two cows on credit from Morrisson, who knew Wilson, and relied on Telford's representation.

Telford then sold the cows to Robertson, who purchased them in good faith.

Held that Morrisson was entitled to recover the cows from Robertson, since Telford had, by the first transaction, obtained no title at all to them.

---

[1] but not in Wales—apparently the only surviving distinction between the private law applicable to Wales and that applicable to England (W.A. Wilson: *Introductory Essays on Scots Law,* p. 36).

(iii) *Seller or Buyer in Possession after Sale*

4–137   Two possible situations are provided for by sections 24 and 25. In both situations a sale by the owner has taken place, and following on that sale the person (who may be the seller or may be the buyer) who is then in possession treats the goods as if he were the owner of them in a second transaction, possibly another sale. Such a person is sometimes referred to as the "reputed owner," and the general effect of sections 24 and 25 is to protect the person who deals with a reputed owner from claims by the true owner.

4–138   The terms "mercantile agent" and "document of title" are used in both sections.

4–139   "Mercantile agent" means "a mercantile agent having in the customary course of his business as such agent authority either—

(*a*)   to sell goods, or
(*b*)   to consign goods for the purpose of sale, or
(*c*)   to buy goods, or
(*d*)   to raise money on the security of goods" (s. 26).

4–140   By section 61(1) of the Act of 1979 "document of title to goods" has the same meaning as it has in the Factors Acts. The effect is that the term "document of title" includes "any bill of lading, dock warrant, warehouse-keeper's certificate, and warrant or order for the delivery of goods, and any other document used in the ordinary course of business as proof of the possession or control of goods, or authorising or purporting to authorise, either by indorsement or by delivery, the possessor of the document to transfer or receive goods thereby represented" (Factors Act 1889, s. 1(4), extended to Scotland by the Factors (Scotland) Act 1890, s. 1).

4–141   The provisions of sections 24 and 25 are as follows:

4–142   *Section 24:* Where a person has sold goods and continues or is in possession of the goods, or of the documents of title to the goods, the delivery or transfer by that person, or by a mercantile agent acting for him, of the goods or documents of title under any sale, pledge, or other disposition of them, to any person receiving them in good faith and without notice of the previous sale, has the same effect as if the person making the delivery or transfer were expressly authorised by the owner of the goods.

4–143   *Section 25:* Where a person who has bought or agreed to buy goods obtains, with the seller's consent, possession of the goods or the documents of title to the goods, the delivery or transfer by that person, or by a mercantile agent acting for him, of the goods or documents of title, under any sale, pledge, or other disposition of them, to any person receiving them in good faith and without notice of any lien or other right of the original seller over the goods, has the same effect as if the person making the delivery or transfer were a mercantile agent in possession of the goods or documents of title with the consent of the owner (s. 25(1)).

4–144   For the purposes of the provision in section 25(1) the buyer under a conditional sale agreement is to be taken not to be a person who has "bought or agreed to buy goods," and "conditional sale agreement" means "an agreement for the sale of goods which is a consumer credit agreement within the meaning of the Consumer Credit Act 1974 under which the purchase price or part of it is payable by instalments, and the property in the goods is to remain in the seller (notwithstanding that the buyer is to be in possession of the goods) until such conditions as to the payment of instalments or otherwise as may be specified in the agreement are fulfilled" (s. 25(2)). The coming into force of section 25(2) depends on the appropriate Commencement Order being made under the Consumer Credit Act (s. 25(3) and (4) of the 1979 Act), but in the meantime there is a corresponding provision in the Hire-Purchase (Scotland) Act 1965 (s. 50) excluding conditional sale agreements from the provisions of section 25(1) (1979 Act, Sched. 2, para. 9).

The significance of the concluding words of section 25(1) ("as if the person making the delivery or transfer were a mercantile agent in possession of the goods or documents of title with the consent of the owner") is to be found in the Factors Act 1889 (ss. 2 and 5) as applied to Scotland by the Factors (Scotland) Act 1890 (s. 1): under these statutory provisions, where a mercantile agent is, with the consent of the owner, in possession of goods or of the documents of title to them, any sale, pledge, or other disposition made in the ordinary course of his business is as valid as if he were expressly authorised by the owner of the goods, provided the person who receives the goods acts in good faith without notice of the mercantile agent's lack of authority and provided the sale, pledge, or other disposition is made for valuable consideration.

The provision in the Act of 1893 (s. 25(2)) corresponding to section 25(1) of the Act of 1979 was considered in *Thomas Graham & Sons Ltd. v. Glenrothes Development Corporation,* 1967 S.C. 284:

G. Ltd. supplied building materials to builders who were engaged on building a housing scheme for the development corporation of the new town of Glenrothes. The builders went into liquidation, and a question arose as to the ownership of the materials which were on the site.

G. Ltd.'s claim was based on the term in their contract with the builders that the property in the materials was not to pass to the builders until the full price had been paid, and, G. Ltd. alleged, the full price had not been paid.

The development corporation founded on section 25(2) of the Sale of Goods Act 1893, averring that the builders had been in possession with the consent of the owners, and that the corporation had acted in good faith without notice of the terms of the builders' contract with G. Ltd. and had paid to the builders 80 per cent of the value of all materials placed on the site, having retained the balance until the amount of a counterclaim which the corporation had against the builders should be ascertained.

Held that the corporation's averments were sufficient to entitle them to an inquiry, and a proof before answer was allowed.

IV PERFORMANCE OF THE CONTRACT

Section 27, which is the first section in Part IV of the Act, sets out the central principle that it is the duty of the seller to deliver the goods, and of the buyer to accept and pay for them, in accordance with the terms of the contract. By section 28, unless otherwise agreed, delivery of the goods and payment of the price are concurrent conditions, *i.e.* the seller must be ready and willing to give possession of the goods to the buyer in exchange for the price, and the buyer must be ready and willing to pay the price in exchange for possession of the goods.

4–148   The more detailed provisions of Part IV may therefore be conveniently dealt with under two headings:

(a)   seller's duty to deliver; and

(b)   buyer's duty to accept.

(a) Seller's Duty to Deliver

4–149   "Delivery" means the voluntary transfer of possession of the goods from one person to another (s. 61(1)). It does not refer to the transfer of ownership of the goods, the rules for which come within Part III of the Act.

4–150   Section 29 consists of some rules about delivery which are of general application. Later sections cover special matters—delivery of the wrong quantity, instalment deliveries, delivery to a carrier, and delivery at a distant place.

General Rules about Delivery

4–151   Whether it is for the buyer to take possession of the goods or for the seller to send them to the buyer is a question depending in each case on the contract, express or implied, between the parties (s. 29(1)).

4–152   Apart from any such contract, express or implied, the place of delivery is the seller's place of business if he has one, and if he has not, then his residence, except that if the contract is for the sale of specific goods, which to the knowledge of the parties when the contract is made are in some other place, then that place is the place of delivery (s. 29(2)).

4–153   Where, under the contract of sale, the seller is bound to send the goods to the buyer, but no time for sending them is fixed, the seller is bound to send them within a reasonable time (s. 29(3)).

4–154   Where the goods at the time of sale are in the possession of a third person, there is no delivery by seller to buyer unless and until the third person acknowledges to the buyer that he holds the goods on his behalf, but this does not affect the issue or transfer of any document of title to the goods (s. 29(4)).

4–155   Demand or tender of delivery may be treated as of no effect unless made at a reasonable hour. What is a reasonable hour is a question of fact (s. 29(5)).

4–156   Unless otherwise agreed, the expenses of and incidental to putting the goods into a deliverable state must be borne by the seller (s. 29(6)).

Delivery of Wrong Quantity

4–157   Section 30 sets out rules to cover three situations concerned with delivery of the wrong quantity. All the rules are subject to any usage of trade, special agreement, or course of dealing between the parties (s. 30(5)). Further, the rules will not apply where the margin of error is very slight, since *de minimis non curat lex* ("the law does not concern itself with trifles"), and the terms of the contract may expressly provide that the quantity specified in the contract is an estimated or approximate quantity only.

The provisions of section 30 are as follows:

(i) Where the seller delivers to the buyer a quantity of goods less than he contracted to sell, the buyer may reject them, but if the buyer accepts them he must pay for them at the contract rate (s. 30(1)).

An instance of a rejection under this provision occurred in *Robertson* v. *Stewart,* 1928 S.N. 31 (O.H.):

Shipbreakers sold to S. the wreck S.S. "Shiela" and all the property which had been salved from her by them.

S. claimed that he was entitled to rescind the contract on the ground that the shipbreakers had not tendered all the subjects sold but had disposed of some of the property salved by sale or donation to others.

The shipbreakers offered to return the salved property which had been removed, or to credit S. with its value. They brought an action against S. for the price.

Held that S. had been entitled to rescind and was not bound to accept the shipbreakers' offer of a deduction from the price.

Where the buyer chooses to accept the lesser quantity at the contract rate, he may still have a claim for damages:

Beck & Co. v. *Szymanowski & Co.* [1924] A.C. 43: S. & Co. ordered from B. & Co. 2,000 gross of "200 yards reels" of six-cord sewing cotton. The contract contained a condition that the goods were to be deemed to be in accordance with the contract unless the sellers received notice from the buyers to the contrary within 14 days after delivery.

Eighteen months after delivery, S. & Co. discovered that the length per reel was only about 188 yards, and they brought an action for damages for breach of contract against B. & Co.

B. & Co. pleaded that the condition was a bar to the action.

Held that the condition applied to quality only and not to quantity, and that S. & Co. were therefore entitled to damages.

(ii) Where the seller delivers to the buyer a quantity of goods larger than he contracted to sell, the buyer may accept the goods included in the contract and reject the rest, or he may reject the whole (s. 30(2)). If the buyer accepts the whole of the goods delivered he must pay for them at the contract rate (s. 30(3)).

(iii) Where the seller delivers to the buyer the goods which he contracted to sell mixed with goods of a different description, the buyer may accept the goods which are in accordance with the contract and reject the rest, or he may reject the whole (s. 30(4)).

The word "description" in this provision must be distinguished from "quality," as was made clear in *Aitken, Campbell & Co. Ltd.* v. *Boullen & Gatenby,* 1908 S.C. 490:

In a sale by sample B. & G. contracted to sell 133 pieces of "maroon twills" to A. Ltd. Having discovered that 64 of the 133 pieces delivered were not conform to the sample in quality, A. Ltd. intimated rejection of those pieces and returned them to B. & G.

B. & G. refused to take them back, and sent them again to A. Ltd.

A. Ltd. brought an action against B. & G. to recover the proportionate part of the price which had been paid and for damages.

Held that the defective goods were not goods "of a different description" in the sense of what was then section 30(3) of the Act of 1893, and that A. Ltd. had therefore not been entitled to reject the defective part of the goods and retain the rest. (A. Ltd.'s claim for damages was, however, still open.)

"The word 'description' is there plainly used to denote the kind of goods contracted for, and . . . the right of partial rejection conferred upon the buyer applies only to cases where goods of the kind contracted for are mixed with goods of a different kind, and not to cases where all the goods are of the kind contracted for, but part of them is not of such good quality as the seller was bound to supply. Here the goods contracted for were 'maroon twills,' and the goods delivered were 'maroon twills,' but 64 out of 133 pieces were not of such good quality as the samples which formed the basis of the contract. . . . The pursuers were not entitled to reject the 64 pieces and to retain the remaining 69" (*per* Lord Low at p. 494).

This case is, however, unlikely to be regarded as satisfactory in commercial circles: the rejection by the buyer of the 64 defective pieces was, from the layman's point of view, a reasonable step to take in the circumstances. A reform of the law seems called for.

Instalment Deliveries

4–165   Unless otherwise agreed, the buyer is not bound to accept delivery by instalments (s. 31(1)).

4–166   Where, however, there is a contract for the sale of goods to be delivered by stated instalments, which are to be separately paid for, and the seller makes defective deliveries in respect of one or more instalments, or the buyer neglects or refuses to take delivery of or pay for one or more instalments, it is a question in each case depending on the terms of the contract and the circumstances of the case whether the breach of contract is a repudiation of the whole contract or whether it is a severable breach giving rise to a claim for compensation but not to a right to treat the whole contract as repudiated (s. 31(2)).

Delivery to Carrier

4–167   Where, "in pursuance of" (*i.e.* following on) a contract of sale, the seller is authorised or required to send the goods to the buyer, delivery of the goods to a carrier, whether named by the buyer or not, is *prima facie* ("until the contrary is proved") deemed to be a delivery to the buyer (s. 32(1)), *i.e.* the carrier is treated as the buyer's agent for the purposes of delivery (but not for the purposes of acceptance of the goods as being in conformity with the contract).

4–168   Unless otherwise authorised by the buyer, the seller must make such a contract with the carrier on the buyer's behalf as is reasonable considering the nature of the goods and the other circumstances of the case. If the seller omits to do so, and the goods are lost or damaged in transit, the buyer may decline to treat the delivery to the carrier as delivery to himself, or may hold the seller responsible in damages (s. 32(2)).

Unless otherwise agreed, where goods are sent by the seller to the buyer by a route involving sea transit, under circumstances in which it is usual to insure, the seller must give sufficient notice to the buyer to enable him to insure the goods during their sea transit, and, if the seller fails to do so, the goods are at the seller's risk during the sea transit (s. 32(3)).

Contracts involving sea transit take different forms, including c.i.f., f.o.b., f.a.s. and ex-ship contracts.

In a c.i.f. ("cost, insurance, freight") contract, the seller's obligation is to ship the goods, insure them and pay the freight. Section 32(3) does not apply to such a situation. "In the usual course a contract of sale c.i.f. contemplates delivery of the cargo at the port of discharge, not the port of shipment" (*per* Lord Trayner in *McDowall & Neilson's Trustee* v. *J.B. Snowball Co. Ltd.* (1904) 7 F. 35, at p. 45). This does not mean, however, that delivery is postponed until the ship actually arrives at its port of destination, for the bill of lading is treated as a symbol of the goods while they are at sea, and so the goods can be delivered to the buyer if the seller (or his agent in the foreign port) transfers the bill of lading with the other shipping documents (the insurance policy and the invoice) to the buyer in exchange for the price. The fact that the buyer has taken up the shipping documents does not prevent him from exercising his right to reject the goods if, when they are actually landed, they are found to be not in conformity with the contract.

In an f.o.b. ("free on board") contract it is the duty of the buyer to arrange the shipping, insure the goods and pay the freight. The seller's duty is to deliver the goods on board ship at the agreed port of shipment. Section 32(3) does apply to this situation. An instance of an f.o.b. contract can be seen in *Glengarnock Iron and Steel Co. Ltd.* v. *Cooper & Co.* (1895) 22 R. 672. The seller must pay all the charges incurred up to the delivery of the goods over the ship's rail, but he is not liable for the costs subsequently incurred, such as the cost of stowage on board: these fall on the buyer as owner or charterer of the ship.

An f.a.s. ("free alongside ship") contract is similar to an f.o.b. one: the seller's duty is to deliver the goods alongside the ship, ready for loading. An instance occurs in *Pini & Co.* v. *Smith & Co.* (1895) 22 R. 699. The actual loading of the goods over the ship's rail is the buyer's responsibility.

The distinction between an f.o.b. contract and an f.a.s. contract was commented on by Lord Trayner in *Glengarnock Iron and Steel Co. Ltd.* v. *Cooper & Co.*, at p. 676: "The point of delivery under the two contracts is different, and the consequent risks and the necessary insurance to cover these risks may be very different—the duty of insurance or the risk in the one case lying upon one party, and in the other upon the other party; but as regards the question which is to be at the expense of putting the cargo on board, there is not any difference which I have ever heard between the one contract and the other. In either contract . . . the universal practice is that the ship undertakes the duty and the expense of putting the cargo from the quay or alongside into the hold of the vessel."

In an ex-ship contract, delivery is made by the seller to the buyer from a ship at the port of destination. In this case the shipping, insurance and freight are all the responsibility of the seller. The price becomes payable when the goods are delivered over the ship's rail at the port of destination. An ex-ship contract was considered by the Privy Council in *Yangtsze Insurance Association Ltd.* v. *Lukmanjee* [1918] A.C. 585, an appeal from the Supreme Court of Ceylon:

A quantity of teak logs had been shipped from Bangkok to Colombo on an ex-ship contract. While the buyer, having paid the price, was taking delivery at Colombo, many of the logs, afloat in the form of rafts, were driven out to sea by a gale and lost.

The buyer sued the insurance company under the insurance policy.

Held that, as the insurance had not been effected on his behalf or to cover his interest, he was not entitled to maintain the suit.

Delivery at Distant Place

4–176 Where the seller agrees to deliver the goods at his own risk at a place other than that where they are when sold, the buyer must, nevertheless, unless otherwise agreed, take any risk of deterioration in the goods necessarily incident to the course of transit (s. 33).

(b) Buyer's Duty to Accept

4–177 The Act includes provisions relating to the buyer's right of examining the goods, the buyer's right to reject the goods, and the buyer's liability for not taking delivery of the goods.

Buyer's Right of Examination

4–178 Where goods are delivered to the buyer, and he has not previously examined them, he is not deemed to have accepted them until he has had a reasonable opportunity of examining them for the purpose of ascertaining whether they are in conformity with the contract (s. 34(1)).

4–179 Unless otherwise agreed, when the seller tenders delivery of goods to the buyer, he is bound, on request, to afford the buyer a reasonable opportunity of examining the goods for the purpose of ascertaining whether they are in conformity with the contract (s. 34(2)).

4–180 The application of these rules can have the effect of postponing the buyer's acceptance of the goods, thus keeping open his right to reject them.

Buyer's Right of Rejection

4–181 The buyer's right of rejection is declared in section 11(5): failure by the seller to perform any material part of the contract is a breach of contract which entitles the buyer within a reasonable time after delivery to reject the goods and treat the contract as repudiated.

4–182 There is difficulty in reconciling this provision with section 14 (implied terms about quality or fitness—see 4–77 *et seq.*, above). From section 11(5) taken by itself one might infer that a minor breach would not give the buyer the right of rejection: that would be in accordance with the general principle of the law of contract that to justify rescission a breach must be material and that for minor breaches the remedy is damages. When, however, section 11(5) is taken along with section 14(2) and (3), the interesting question is whether a breach of section 14(2) or (3) (merchantable quality or fitness for particular purpose), however minor, would constitute failure to perform a "material part" of the contract within the meaning of section 11(5).

The question was commented on, but did not require to be decided, in *Millars of Falkirk Ltd.* v. *Turpie,* 1976 S.L.T. (Notes) 66 (see 4–88, above). In that case the new car was held to be of "merchantable quality" and so there was no breach of what is now section 14(2) of the Act of 1979.

Lord President Emslie said (at p. 68): "The defender has failed to establish the breach of either of the implied conditions which formed the starting point of his claim of rejection and for damages. . . . In the result we do not reach the interesting and difficult question of whether mere breach of the implied conditions prescribed by s. 14(2) and (3), however minor or readily remediable the defect which led to the finding of breach, constitutes a failure to perform a material part of the contract within the meaning of s. [*11(5)*]. For the pursuers the argument was that s. [*11(5)*] . . ., so far as a purchaser's right to reject was concerned, merely preserved the former law of Scotland with the result that the materiality of the breach of an implied condition, i.e. the degree of failure in performance, was an essential prerequisite to the existence of the right. . . . The submission has considerable attractions but I am loath to express any opinion upon the matter since we did not have the benefit of any counter argument from the defender upon this important question of construction of s. [*11(5)*], and of principle. In these circumstances I content myself by questioning whether the application of s. [*11(5)*] has ever been properly considered in circumstances in which breach of an implied condition may be an entirely proper finding, and yet the defect in the article which leads to that finding being made is both minor and readily remediable by a willing seller. In England the problem does not arise for the law is not the same and because, in particular, in terms of s. [*11(3)*], the breach of any 'condition' affords, subject only to the de minimis[2] rule, the right to reject. Whether the same result should follow, standing the language of s. [*11(5)*] which applies only to Scotland, is another matter, and it could only follow if it were to be held that failure to fulfil one of the statutory implied conditions amounts, irrespective of the degree of failure, to failure to perform a material part of the contract which would entitle the buyer to reject."

Section 35 regulates the time at which the buyer is deemed to have accepted the goods, and so given up his right to reject them: the buyer is deemed to have accepted the goods:

(i) when he intimates to the seller that he has accepted them; or

(ii) the goods have been delivered to him, and he has been allowed his right of examination in accordance with section 34, and he then *either* does any act in relation to the goods which is inconsistent with the ownership of the seller *or* after the lapse of a reasonable time retains the goods without intimating to the seller that he has rejected them.

Unless otherwise agreed, where the goods which have been delivered to the buyer are goods which he is entitled to refuse to accept, he is not bound to return them to the seller: it is sufficient if he intimates to the seller that he refuses to accept them (s. 36).

---

[2] *De minimis non curat lex* ("the law does not concern itself with trifles").

4–186   As regards (i), above, where there has been an express acceptance on the buyer's part he is no longer entitled to reject the goods. An illustration occurs in *Mechans Ltd.* v. *Highland Marine Charters Ltd.*, 1964 S.C. 48:

H. Ltd. contracted to buy two steel water buses, the "Lomond Lass" and the "Lomond Princess," from M. Ltd. The buses were delivered and, after inspection by Ministry of Transport inspectors as provided for in the contract, acceptance certificates were signed by H. Ltd.

After the buses had been used for a few weeks, H. Ltd. sought to reject them on the ground of major defects.

Held that, on account of the express acceptance, H. Ltd. was no longer entitled to reject the buses.

4–187   In this case the court was following *Morrison & Mason Ltd.* v. *Clarkson Brothers* (1898) 25 R. 427, in which a steam-pump supplied by engineers for pumping water out of a tunnel from a depth of 320 feet was deemed to have been accepted by the buyers because they had successfully tried it for 10 days at a depth of 120 feet and had then kept it out of use for some months until they were ready to place it at the lower level of 320 feet, where it proved unsatisfactory.

4–188   As regards (ii), above, the buyer loses his right of rejection if he does not exercise his right to examine the goods at the proper time and place for that examination. For example, in *Pini & Co.* v. *Smith & Co.* (1895) 22 R. 699, buyers of soil-pipes did not avail themselves of the opportunity to examine the pipes at Glasgow or Liverpool before having them shipped to Buenos Aires, and were held no longer to be entitled to reject the pipes when their customer in Buenos Aires intimated that the pipes were disconform to contract. Similar failure to examine occurred in *W. M. Strachan & Co. Ltd.* v. *John Marshall & Co.*, 1910 2 S.L.T. 108 (O.H.) (boiler delivered at Glasgow, shipped to Japan and there found to require repairs costing more than the full purchase price), and in *Dick* v. *Cochrane & Fleming*, 1935 S.L.T. 432 (O.H.) (earthenware shipped from Glasgow to sub-purchasers in South America).

4–189   The "act in relation to [*the goods*] which is inconsistent with the ownership of the seller" may be a subsale. For instance, in *Hunt* v. *Barry* (1905) 13 S.L.T. 34 (O.H.) there had been a contract for sale by sample between two rag-merchants, and the buyer, having examined the goods on the day of their delivery and having found them not conform to sample, offered them in a second sale by sample to a firm with whom he had had dealings, and delayed intimating rejection to the seller until 10 days after delivery. He was held to have done an act inconsistent with the ownership of the seller, and so lost his right of rejection.

4–190   In the case of machinery the act which is inconsistent with the ownership of the seller may be the fitting up of the machinery (as in *Mechan & Sons Ltd.* v. *Bow, McLachlan & Co. Ltd.*, 1910 S.C. 758, where two steel feed-tanks supplied by engineers to shipbuilders were fitted by the shipbuilders into a tug which they were building for the Admiralty) or the act may be the continued use of the machinery.

4–191   The fitting up and use of machinery, however, does not always deprive the buyer of his right of rejection. For example, in *Aird & Coghill* v. *Pullan & Adams* (1904) 7 F. 258, buyers were held entitled to reject a printing machine which had been fitted in their works and had been used for about a year and a half before rejection, and in *Munro & Co.* v. *Bennet & Son,* 1911 S.C. 337, the buyer of a deep-well pump from artesian well engineers was held entitled to reject the pump after a similar period. In both cases complaints had been made in the time intervening between fitting up and rejection and in response to these complaints the sellers had been attempting to remedy the defects without success.

The right to reject the goods must be exercised within a reasonable time. In *Hunt* v. *Barry* (4–189, above) Lord Pearson (Ordinary) said, at 13 S.L.T. p. 36: "The 'reasonable time' referred to in Sect. 35 means a reasonable time for examining and testing the goods in order to see whether they conform to the contract." A general comment was made with reference to latent defects by Lord Justice-Clerk Grant in *Mechans Ltd.* v. *Highland Marine Charters Ltd.* (4–186, above), at 1964 S.C. p. 63: "I think that in the case of goods which are not expressly accepted and which may be subject to latent defects the Courts will be generous in fixing the 'reasonable time' which must elapse before acceptance is deemed or implied."

The nature of the goods is also an important factor in the decision of what is a reasonable time. For instance, in *Flynn* v. *Scott*, 1949 S.C. 442 (O.H.) (4–49, above), Lord Mackintosh (Ordinary), holding that the rejection of a motor-van three weeks after it had broken down was not timeous, said (at p. 446) that intimation of rejection ought to have been made "within a very few days." A longer time could be reasonable in the case of goods such as works of art, but in *Hyslop* v. *Shirlaw* (1905) 7 F. 875, a buyer was held not entitled to reject four paintings as not being genuine a year and a half after their delivery to him. "*Prima facie* a delay of eighteen months is unreasonable. . . . The *onus* is on the pursuer to shew that he could not, by any examination reasonably possible, have discovered earlier the disconformity on which his rejection proceeded" (*per* Lord Kyllachy at p. 882). Mere length of time, however, is not *per se* ("of itself") conclusive, as was recognised in *Burrell* v. *Harding's Executrix*, 1931 S.L.T. 76 (O.H.), in which Lord Moncrieff (Ordinary) allowed a proof before answer in the case of a sale by an art dealer of a supposedly fifteenth-century English reredos, which the buyer sought to reject after a lapse of more than two years on the ground that an expert examination had shown that it was partly modern. The question of what is reasonable is as in other contexts a question of fact depending on all the circumstances of the case, *e.g.* on the circumstances that in *Hyslop's* case the pictures had been hanging in the buyer's house for the year and a half, whereas in *Burrell's* case the reredos had been in store.

Buyer's Liability for not Taking Delivery

When the seller is ready and willing to deliver, and requests the buyer to take delivery, and the buyer does not within a reasonable time after that request take delivery, he is liable to the seller for any loss caused by his neglect or refusal to take delivery, and also for a reasonable charge for the care and custody of the goods (s. 37(1)). This provision does not affect the rights of the seller where the neglect or refusal of the buyer to take delivery amounts to a repudiation of the contract (s. 37(2)).

4–195   In *Shaw, Macfarlane & Co.* v. *Waddell & Son* (1900) 2 F. 1070 (4–57, above), there were circumstances in which the buyers' failure to take delivery of coal timeously amounted to a repudiation of the contract which justified the sellers in rescinding the contract.

V RIGHTS OF UNPAID SELLER AGAINST THE GOODS

4–196   Under Part V of the Act a seller has certain rights against the goods themselves, as distinct from his remedies against the buyer (which come into Part VI of the Act).

4–197   The three main rights in Part V belong only to an "unpaid seller," and a seller is an "unpaid seller" for the purposes of the Act—

  (a) when the whole of the price has not been paid or tendered; or

  (b) when a bill of exchange or other negotiable instrument has been received as conditional payment, and the condition on which it was received has not been fulfilled by reason of the dishonour of the instrument or otherwise (s. 38(1)).

4–198   The term "seller" in Part V includes any person who is in the position of a seller, *e.g.* an agent of the seller to whom the bill of lading has been indorsed, or a consignor or agent who has himself paid (or is directly responsible for) the price (s. 38(2)).

4–199   The unpaid seller's rights against the goods are:

  (a) a lien on the goods or right to retain them for the price while he is in possession of them;

  (b) in the case of the insolvency of the buyer, a right of stopping the goods in transit[3] after he has parted with them; and

  (c) a right of re-sale as limited by the Act (s. 39(1)).

Also included in Part V of the Act there is:

  (d) in Scotland a seller's right of attachment by arrestment or poinding (s. 40).

4–200   The rights of lien and stoppage in transit are appropriate only if the goods are no longer owned by the seller, *i.e.* only if the property has passed to the buyer. The Act, however, in effect extends these rights to the situation where the seller is still the owner, by providing that where the property in goods has not passed to the buyer, the unpaid seller has, in addition to his other remedies, a "right of withholding delivery similar to and co-extensive with his rights of lien or retention and stoppage in transit where the property has passed to the buyer" (s. 39(2)).

4–201   Further provisions of the Act which relate to both lien and stoppage in transit may be appropriately noted here before these rights are separately considered:

4–202   (1) These rights are not as a general rule affected by any sale or other disposition of the goods which the buyer may have made, unless the seller has assented to it (s. 47(1)).

4–203   However, where a document of title to goods has been lawfully transferred to any person as buyer or owner of the goods, and that person

---

[3] The Latin phrase *"in transitu"* used in the Act of 1893 was replaced by its English translation in the Act of 1979.

transfers the document to a person who takes it in good faith and for valuable consideration, then—

(*a*) if that transfer was by way of sale, the unpaid seller's right of lien or retention or stoppage in transit is defeated; and

(*b*) if the transfer was by way of pledge or other disposition for value, the unpaid seller's right of lien or retention or stoppage in transit can only be exercised subject to the rights of the transferee (s. 47(2)).

Further, since the general rule stated in section 47(1) is made "subject to this Act," the provisions in sections 21 to 26 as to transfer of title (see 4–130 *et seq.*, above) must be kept in mind.

(2) The contract of sale is not as a general rule rescinded by the mere exercise by an unpaid seller of his right of lien or retention or stoppage in transit (s. 48(1)), but where an unpaid seller who has exercised his right of lien or retention or stoppage in transit re-sells the goods, the buyer acquires a good title to them as against the original buyer (s. 48(2)).

(a) Lien

The unpaid seller who is in possession of the goods is entitled to retain possession of them until payment or tender of the price in the following cases:

(i) where the goods have been sold without any stipulation as to credit; or

(ii) where the goods have been sold on credit but the term of credit has expired; or

(iii) where the buyer becomes insolvent (s. 41(1)).

A person is deemed to be insolvent for the purposes of the Act if he either has ceased to pay his debts in the ordinary course of business or cannot pay his debts as they become due (s. 61(4)). He need not have had his estates sequestrated, nor need he be notour bankrupt: practical, as distinct from absolute, insolvency is all that is required.

The fact that the seller is in possession of the goods as agent or custodier for the buyer does not prevent him from exercising his lien or right of retention (s. 41(2)).

Where the seller has made part delivery, he may exercise his lien or right of retention on the remainder, unless the part delivery has been made under such circumstances as to show an agreement to waive the lien or right of retention (s. 42).

The seller's lien or right of retention is terminated:

(i) when the seller delivers the goods to a carrier or other custodier for transmission to the buyer without reserving the right of disposal of the goods (which he could do by the terms of the contract or by making the goods deliverable to his own agent in a foreign port); or

(ii) when the buyer or his agent lawfully obtains possession of the goods; or

(iii) by waiver of the lien or right of retention (s. 43(1)).

The seller does not lose his lien or right of retention merely because he has obtained a decree from the court against the buyer for the price (s. 43(2)).

A case which illustrates this right of the unpaid seller is *Paton's Trustee* v. *Finlayson*, 1923 S.C. 872:

P., a potato merchant, had bought a farmer's growing crop of potatoes at a specified price per acre. P. supplied the labour to lift the potatoes and pit them on the farm, but by the terms of the contract the farmer undertook to cart the potatoes to the pits and later to the railway. While the potatoes were in the pits and before the full price had been paid, P.'s estates were sequestrated.

Held that the farmer was still in possession of the potatoes, and was therefore entitled to exercise a lien over them. (It was not disputed that the property in the potatoes, as distinct from possession of them, had passed to P. at the time when they were removed from the soil: see *Gowans (Cockburn's Trustee)* v. *Bowe & Sons*, 1910 2 S.L.T. 17 (O.H.), (4–117, above)).

4–213   The Act does not expressly provide for the revival of the unpaid seller's lien in the situation where the unpaid seller, having once parted with possession of the goods, regains possession of them. There is a sheriff court case which is authority for the proposition that the lien does not revive:

4–214   *London Scottish Transport Ltd.* v. *Tyres (Scotland) Ltd.*, 1957 S.L.T. (Sh. Ct.) 48: T. Ltd. had sold and delivered to L. Ltd. tyres and allied accessories which were not paid for.

T. Ltd., suspecting that L. Ltd. was on the verge of insolvency, instructed one of its agents to retake possession of as much of the goods supplied as could be found at L. Ltd.'s depot at Alva. Goods to the value of £548 9s. thus came again into the possession of T. Ltd.

L. Ltd. went into liquidation, and an action was brought by that company and its liquidator against T. Ltd. for redelivery of the goods or alternatively for payment of their value.

T. Ltd. claimed that its lien had revived.

Held that in the circumstances of the case T. Ltd.'s lien, having been lost on delivery of the goods, had not been revived.

Sheriff-Substitute (W.J. Bryden) said (at p. 49): "Before it could be argued that a lost lien had revived it would be necessary, in my opinion, to show that the goods had been handed back to the sellers by the purchasers with the particular intention that the sellers' lien should revive."

4–215   It is possible that the legal position would be different if the goods were repossessed by the seller in circumstances from which it could be inferred that the buyer had accepted that all the original conditions attaching to the contract continued to exist; the argument for revival would then be based on the broad principle of mutuality of obligations. This possibility was left open in *Hostess Mobile Catering* v. *Archibald Scott Ltd.*, 1981 S.L.T. (Notes) 125 (O.H.):

S. Ltd. had sold and delivered to H. a piece of equipment called a Paragon refreshment trailer unit. A few months later the unit had, by agreement, been taken back to S. Ltd.'s premises so that S. Ltd. might repair it under a guarantee contained in the original contract. When the repairs had been completed, S. Ltd. refused to redeliver the unit to H. until a balance of the original purchase price, which S. Ltd. claimed was still due, was paid.

The Lord Ordinary (McDonald) rejected the argument that the right of lien "ran" with the goods (with the effect that it could be exercised by the unpaid seller, whatever the means by which he had regained possession), but as regards the argument based on the principle of mutuality of obligations the Lord Ordinary was not prepared to decide the case without further knowledge of the circumstances under which repossession had been obtained and he allowed the parties a proof before answer.

(b) Stoppage in Transit

The unpaid seller who has parted with possession of the goods has the right to stop them in transit in one case only, *viz:* when the buyer becomes "insolvent" in the sense explained above. This right enables the seller to resume possession of the goods as long as they are in course of transit to the buyer, and then retain them until payment or tender of the price (s. 44).

The right appears to have been first recognised as being part of Scots law in the case of *Jaffrey and Others, Partners of the Stirling Banking Company (Stein's Creditors)* v. *Allan, Stewart & Co.* (1790) 3 Pat. 191:

S. had been carrying on an extensive distilling trade under great financial difficulties until he finally stopped payment in February 1788. Between October 1787 and February 1788, while S. was "verging towards and on the eve of bankruptcy," A. & Co. had supplied him with 20 or 30 cargoes of grain. At the time of S.'s bankruptcy in February 1788 four of the cargoes were not landed but were lying in the ships at the port of delivery.

Held that A. & Co. were entitled to take possession of these four cargoes.

Lord Chancellor Thurlow said (at p. 196): "Within the last hundred years, a rule has been introduced, from the customs of foreign nations, that in the case of the vendee's bankruptcy, the vendor might stop and take back the goods *in transitu*[4], or before they came into the hands of the vendee; and this is certainly now a part of the law of England, and I understand it to be the law likewise of Scotland."

The common law on the subject as worked out in cases decided before the Act of 1893 is now represented by the rules set out in sections 45 and 46 of the Act of 1979 as to:
  (i) duration of transit; and
  (ii) how stoppage in transit is effected.

(i) *Duration of Transit*

The rules in section 45 as to duration of transit are:
  (1) Goods are deemed to be in course of transit from the time when they are delivered to a carrier or other custodier for the purpose of transmission to the buyer, until the buyer or his agent takes delivery of them from the carrier or other custodier.
  (2) If the buyer or his agent obtains delivery of the goods before their arrival at the appointed destination, the transit is at an end.
  (3) If, after the arrival of the goods at the appointed destination, the carrier or other custodier acknowledges to the buyer or to the buyer's agent that he holds the goods on his behalf and continues in possession of

---

[4] "in transit."

them as custodier for the buyer or the buyer's agent, the transit is at an end, and it does not matter that a further destination for the goods may have been indicated by the buyer.

4–223   This third rule was considered in *Muir* v. *Rankin* (1905) 13 S.L.T. 60 (O.H.):

M., a farmer, had sold oats to R. and had consigned them in 100 sacks to Buchanan Street goods station, Glasgow. No part of the price was ever paid, and M. on being informed of R.'s insolvency intimated to the railway company that delivery to R. was stopped.

In the meantime, however, R. had obtained possession of three of the sacks, had received an "advice note" and had also signed the "advice note delivery book"—formalities which, according to the railway company's practice, signified that it was holding the grain on behalf of the consignee.

(The ground of the decision was that M. was entitled to rescind the contract because of R.'s fraudulent representation as to his financial standing.)

4–224   (4) If the goods are rejected by the buyer, and the carrier or other custodier continues in possession of them, the transit is not deemed to be at an end, even if the seller has refused to receive them back.

4–225   (5) When goods are delivered to a ship chartered by the buyer it is a question depending on the circumstances of the particular case whether they are in the possession of the master as a carrier or as agent of the buyer.

4–226   Illustrations are to be found in *McDowall & Neilson's Trustee* v. *J.B. Snowball Co. Ltd.* (1904) 7 F. 35, in which the New Brunswick seller of timber which by the bill of lading was to be delivered at Glasgow to the seller's order was held entitled to stop the timber on the ship's arrival at Glasgow, and in *Cowdenbeath Coal Co. Ltd.* v. *Clydesdale Bank Ltd.* (1895) 22 R. 682, in which opinions were expressed that the coal company had no right of stoppage in transit over a cargo of coal shipped for export to a sub-purchaser in a vessel chartered by the buyer, the bill of lading being in the buyer's name.

4–227   (6) Where the carrier or other custodier wrongfully refuses to deliver the goods to the buyer or to the buyer's agent, the transit is deemed to be at an end.

4–228   (7) Where part delivery of the goods has been made to the buyer or his agent, the remainder of the goods may be stopped in transit, unless the part delivery has been made under such circumstances as to show an agreement to give up possession of the whole of the goods.

4–229   In *Mechan & Sons Ltd.* v. *North-Eastern Railway Co.*, 1911 S.C. 1348, where there had been a contract for the sale of two lifeboats, which were dispatched to the purchaser by rail, the railway company, after it had given up possession of one of the boats to a carter, received notification of stoppage in transit from the sellers. It nevertheless delivered the second boat to the liquidator on the buyer's estate.

Held that the railway company was liable in damages to the sellers. The court found no evidence that the delivery of the first boat had been made under such circumstances as to show an agreement to give up possession of the other boat.

(ii) *How Stoppage in Transit is Effected*

The unpaid seller may exercise his right of stoppage in transit either by taking actual possession of the goods, or by giving notice of his claim to the carrier or other custodier in whose possession the goods are (s. 46(1)). That notice may be given either to the person in actual possession of the goods or to his principal (s. 46(2)), but in the latter case the notice must be given at such a time and under such circumstances that the principal, by the exercise of reasonable diligence, will be able to communicate it to his servant or agent in time to prevent delivery to the buyer (s. 46(3)).

The carrier or other custodier who receives notice of stoppage in transit must re-deliver the goods to, or according to the directions of, the seller, and the expenses of the re-delivery must be borne by the seller (s. 46(4)).

As the case of *Mechan & Sons Ltd.* v. *North-Eastern Railway Co.* (4–229, above) shows, a carrier who disregards a notice of stoppage in transit (with the result that the goods pass into the hands of the trustee or liquidator who is administering the bankrupt buyer's estate instead of being returned to the seller) is liable to the seller in damages for the loss caused to the seller by disregard of the notice.

(c) **Re-Sale**

An unpaid seller has no general right to re-sell the goods: he has only a right of re-sale "as limited by" the Act (s. 39(1)).

In some circumstances the seller who is unpaid will be justified in treating the buyer's failure to pay as a repudiation of the contract and be entitled to rescind the contract, thus placing himself in a position to enter into another contract of sale. However, as was noticed above (4–205), the Act provides that a contract of sale is not rescinded by the mere exercise by an unpaid seller of his right of lien or retention or stoppage in transit (s. 48(1)). If, therefore, the contract has not been rescinded, the seller may retain the goods and at some later date, when he is confident that he will be paid, deliver them or send them for delivery to the buyer.

It has also been already noticed (4–205, above) that if a seller who has exercised his right of lien or retention or stoppage in transit re-sells the goods, the buyer acquires a good title to the goods as against the original buyer (s. 48(2)). This is not to say, however, that in all cases the seller who has exercised one of these rights has necessarily then a right to re-sell to a second buyer: the provision is intended to protect the second buyer, and does not affect the legal relationship between the seller and the original buyer. Therefore, if the first sale has not been rescinded, the seller, by thus putting it out of his power to implement that contract, will be liable to the original buyer in damages for breach of contract.

The limited right of re-sale which is provided for by the Act is as follows:

(i) Where the goods are of a perishable nature, or where the unpaid seller gives notice to the buyer of his intention to re-sell, and the buyer does not within a reasonable time pay or tender the price, the unpaid seller may re-sell the goods and recover from the original buyer damages for any loss caused by his breach of contract (s. 48(3)).

(ii) Where the seller expressly reserves a right of re-sale in case the buyer should make default, he may then, on the buyer's default, re-sell the goods. The original contract is rescinded, but without prejudice to any claim which the seller may have for damages (s. 48(4)).

4–238   The fact that rescission of the original contract is specifically provided for in section 48(4) and not in section 48(3) caused some controversy, the question being whether, in the situation covered by section 48(3), the original contract must be treated as still in existence at the time of the re-sale. The point has a practical importance where the seller makes a profit out of the re-sale: if the contract has not been rescinded, the seller will be selling as holder of the goods in security and will be bound to account to the original buyer for the profit, whereas if the contract has been rescinded, he will be selling as owner and be entitled to retain the profit. The former view was supported by *Gallagher* v. *Shilcock* [1949] 2 K.B. 765, in which a seller who had re-sold a motor-boat for a higher price than the original contract price was held to be bound to account to the original buyer for part of the deposit which that buyer had already paid. This decision, however, was overruled by the Court of Appeal in *R.V. Ward Ltd.* v. *Bignall* [1967] 1 Q.B. 534:

B. contracted to buy a Ford Zodiac and a Vanguard estate car from W, Ltd. for £850 and paid a deposit of £25, leaving the cars in W. Ltd.'s possession pending payment of the balance.

Later, alleging misrepresentation as to the age of the Vanguard, B. suggested that either the price should be reduced to £800 or he should purchase only the Zodiac for £500. W. Ltd., rejecting both suggestions, gave notice that, if the full price was not paid, they would sell both cars elsewhere and claim damages from B.

W. Ltd. resold the Vanguard for £350, and sued B. for damages of £497 10s., being the balance of the purchase price (£825), less £350, plus £22 10s. advertising costs.

The Court of Appeal found W. Ltd. entitled to only £47 10s. damages, *i.e.* £497 10s. less the agreed value of the Zodiac (£450), holding that the re-sale had not left the original contract intact as *Gallagher* v. *Shilcock* suggested but had necessarily rescinded the original contract and caused the property in the cars, if it had passed to B., to revert to W. Ltd.

(d) Attachment by Arrestment or Poinding

4–239   Section 40 provides that in Scotland a seller may attach the goods while they are in his own hands or possession by arrestment or poinding,[5] and that such arrestment or poinding is to have the same operation and effect in a competition or otherwise as an arrestment or poinding by a third party.

4–240   It should be noted that this right differs from the other rights in Part V of the Act in that it belongs to "a seller," not merely to "the unpaid seller." Another peculiarity is that the terms "arrestment" and "poinding" normally refer to moveables which are in the hands of a third party or the debtor, respectively, whereas in the present context they refer to goods which are in the creditor's hands.

4–241   This "bizarre"[6] provision originated as section 3 of the Mercantile Law Amendment Act Scotland 1856. The right is superfluous where the

---

[5] pronounced "pinding."
[6] J.J. Gow, *The Mercantile and Industrial Law of Scotland*, p. 627.

seller is an "unpaid seller" seeking to retain the goods in his own hands as security for the price: the seller in that situation has the protection of the provisions as to lien (see 4–206 *et seq.*, above).

Some light is thrown on the situation where a seller might derive benefit from section 40 by considering:

(i) the fuller version of the right as expressed in section 3 of the Act of 1856; and

(ii) the case of *Wyper* v. *Harveys* (1861) 23 D. 606, a decision of the whole Court of Session on provisions of the Act of 1856 including section 3.

(i) Section 3 of the Act of 1856 provided that "any seller of goods may attach the same while in his own hands or possession by arrestment or poinding, at any time prior to the date when the sale of such goods to a subsequent purchaser shall have been intimated to such seller, and such arrestment or poinding shall have the same operation and effect in a competition or otherwise as an arrestment or poinding by a third party."

(ii) *Wyper* v. *Harveys*: H. & Co. sold to Risk five puncheons of whisky which were left lying in H. & Co.'s warehouse. Risk re-sold the whisky to W. W. paid the price to Risk, and Risk paid the price due by him to H. & Co.

Risk then became bankrupt. H. & Co. raised an action against Risk for £1,113 11s.6d., the alleged amount of a general balance on account due by Risk to H. & Co., and on the same day they caused an arrestment to be executed in their own hands of all goods in their hands belonging to Risk.

W. then gave notice to H. & Co. of the sub-sale by Risk to him, and demanded delivery of the whisky.

Held that W. was not entitled to demand delivery, since H. & Co.'s arrestment in their own hands was prior in date and therefore preferable to W.'s intimation.

It would therefore appear that section 40 would enable a seller to retain goods (the price of which he has received) as security for debts due to him by the buyer on other transactions.

VI ACTIONS FOR BREACH OF THE CONTRACT

Part VI of the Act is divided into two Parts:

(a) seller's remedies; and

(b) buyer's remedies.

The provisions of the Act do not, however, amount to a comprehensive codification of the remedies available to the parties, and much is left to rest on the general principles of the common law of contract.

Partly this is achieved by express saving of particular rights—*e.g.* the seller's right to interest on the price (s. 49(3)), the buyer's right of specific implement (s. 52(4)) and the right of the buyer or the seller at common law to recover interest or special damages or to recover money paid where the consideration for the payment of it has failed (s. 54).

Special damages become payable at common law where, because of special circumstances known to both parties at the time of the formation of the contract, a breach of contract results in losses greater than those which would normally be foreseeable. The distinction between ordinary damages and special damages is always associated with the English case of *Hadley* v. *Baxendale* (1854) 9 Ex. 341. The Act gives guidance as to the measure of ordinary damages, but has no provisions as to special damages beyond the saving in section 54 of the common law right to such damages in appropriate circumstances.

4–250 The right to recover money paid where the consideration for the payment of it has failed arises out of quasi-contract in accordance with the principle *condictio causa data causa non secuta* ("the action applicable where consideration has been given and where consideration for it has not followed"). An illustration is *Cantiere San Rocco S.A.* v. *Clyde Shipbuilding and Engineering Co. Ltd.*, 1923 S.C. (H.L.) 105, in which a buyer of marine engines was held entitled to recover an instalment of the price when fulfilment of the contract became impossible owing to an outbreak of war.

4–251 In addition to the express saving of particular rights, there is the general saving of the common law in section 62(2): the rules of the common law, except in so far as they are inconsistent with the provisions of the Act (and in particular the rules relating to principal and agent and to the effect of fraud, misrepresentation, duress or coercion, or other invalidating cause) are made to continue to apply to contracts for the sale of goods.

4–252 This general saving would apply to the common law right which a buyer has to damages for wrongful detention of the goods by the seller (and in certain situations by a third party) where the property in the goods has passed to the buyer and he does not obtain delivery of them; the damages are measured by the value of the goods.

4–253 Another matter which illustrates the general saving of the common law is the court's common law discretion to order consignation of the whole or part of the price where the buyer is being sued for the price and claims (under section 53(1)(*a*) of the Act) to set up a breach of contract by the seller in diminution or extinction of the price. This common law discretion was exercised by the court in *George Cohen, Sons & Co. Ltd.* v. *Jamieson & Paterson*, 1963 S.C. 289 (O.H.):

C. Ltd. had supplied to J. & P., scrap merchants, a hydraulic scrap metal press. J. & P. refused to pay the contract price, though they continued to use the machine.

C. Ltd. brought an action against J. & P. for the price, and in this action J. & P. pleaded that the machine was neither fit for its purpose nor of merchantable quality, that C. Ltd. were in breach of the contract and that the price had to be reduced on that account.

C. Ltd. asked the court to require J. & P. to consign the sum sued for, either under section 59 of the Act of 1893 (now section 58 of the Act of 1979—"Payment into court in Scotland"), or at common law.

Held that section 59 applied to the situation where a buyer was making a "claim for damages" and not to the situation where the buyer was, under section 53(1)(*a*), setting up the breach of contract in diminution or extinction of the price, but that at common law the court had a discretion to order consignation in such latter circumstances; and J. & P. *ordained* to consign half of the sum sued for.

What follows here is restricted to a consideration of the statutory remedies.

(a) Seller's Remedies

The seller has two remedies against the buyer personally (as distinct from the rights which he has against the goods themselves under Part V):

(i) He may bring an action against the buyer for the price.

(ii) He may claim damages for non-acceptance.

(i) *Action for Price*

The seller may bring an action against the buyer for the price in the following cases:

(1) where, under the contract, the property in the goods has passed to the buyer, and the buyer wrongfully neglects or refuses to pay for the goods according to the terms of the contract (s. 49(1)); or

(2) where, under the contract, the price is payable on a certain day irrespective of delivery, and the buyer wrongfully neglects or refuses to pay on that day.

In case (2), the action for the price may be brought even although the property in the goods has not passed and even although the goods have not been appropriated to the contract (s. 49(2)).

When sued for the price, the buyer may put forward the defence that he has a claim for damages against the seller in respect of a breach of the contract by the seller. This is not expressly provided for in the Act, but is in accordance with the general principle that in mutual contracts even an illiquid claim may be used as a defence so as to extinguish or diminish a liquid claim of the other party. The point was established with reference to a contract for the sale of goods by *British Motor Body Co. Ltd.* v. *Thomas Shaw (Dundee) Ltd.*, 1914 S.C. 922:

B. Ltd. sued S. Ltd. for £135 10s., the agreed price of a car-body which B. Ltd. had built and supplied to S. Ltd. The order had been given in February, 1912, and the body was delivered in October, 1912. No specific time for delivery was specified in the contract.

S. Ltd. put forward the defence that the body had not been delivered within a reasonable time, and that they were entitled to set off £75 as damages against the price.

Held that this was a competent defence.

The seller's common law right to recover interest on the price from the date of tender of the goods, or from the date on which the price was payable, as the case may be, is expressly preserved by the Act (s. 49(3)).

(ii) *Damages for Non-Acceptance*

Where the buyer wrongfully neglects or refuses to accept and pay for the goods, the seller may sue him for damages for non-acceptance (s. 50(1)).

The measure of damages is the estimated loss directly and naturally resulting, in the ordinary course of events, from the buyer's breach of contract (s. 50(2)).

Where there is an available market for the goods in question, the measure of damages is *prima facie* ("unless the contrary is proved") to be ascertained by the difference between the contract price and the market or current price at the time when the goods ought to have been accepted, or, if no time was fixed for acceptance, then at the time of the refusal to accept (s. 50(3)).

4–262 An instance of an action for damages for non-acceptance is *Govan Rope and Sail Co. Ltd.* v. *Weir & Co.* (1897) 24 R. 368:

A rope-manufacturing company contracted to supply 20 tons of a specified quality of rope to W. & Co., shipowners, in quantities to be ordered by W. & Co., the whole of the rope to be taken by the end of 1894.

By that date, however, W. & Co. had ordered and obtained delivery of only about five and a half tons of rope, and the manufacturers sued for damages for non-acceptance in respect of the balance.

W. & Co. put forward the defence that the rope supplied had been of inferior quality to that specified in the contract, but failed to prove this.

Held that, as there was no "market or current" price for the kind of rope contracted for, the measure of damages to which the manufacturers were entitled was the "loss directly and naturally resulting in the ordinary course of events" from W. & Co.'s breach of contract, *i.e.* in this case the difference between the contract price of the 14½ or so tons and the cost of the raw material required for its manufacture plus the cost of manufacture.

(b) Buyer's Remedies

4–263 Part VI sets out provisions relating to the following three remedies of the buyer:

    (i) damages for non-delivery;

    (ii) specific performance; and

    (iii) remedy for breach of "warranty."

In addition, under section 11(5) in Part II of the Act, there is the remedy for breach of a material part of the contract, *viz*:

    (iv) rejection, or retention and damages.

(i) *Damages for Non-Delivery*

4–264 Where the seller wrongfully neglects or refuses to deliver the goods to the buyer, the buyer may sue the seller for damages for non-delivery (s. 51(1)).

4–265 The measure of damages is the estimated loss directly and naturally resulting, in the ordinary course of events, from the seller's breach of contract (s. 51(2)).

4–266 Where there is an available market for the goods in question, the measure of damages is *prima facie* ("unless the contrary is proved") to be ascertained by the difference between the contract price and the market or current price of the goods at the time when they ought to have been delivered, or, if no time was fixed, then at the time of the refusal to deliver (s. 51(3)).

(ii) *Specific Performance*

4–267 If the goods are specific or ascertained, the court may, if it thinks fit (on an application being made to it by the buyer), direct that the contract be performed specifically, *i.e.* the court will not give the seller the option of retaining the goods and merely paying damages (s. 52(1)). The decree of the court may be unconditional, or on such terms and conditions as to damages, payment of the price, and otherwise, as seem just to the court (s. 52(3)). This remedy of specific performance is supplementary to, and does not derogate from, the common law right of specific implement in Scotland (s. 52(4)).

The term "specific performance" is derived from English law, and section 52(1) enacted the English principle that specific performance would be granted only at the court's discretion. In contrast, the remedy of specific implement in Scots law is regarded as the primary remedy where a seller has failed to deliver a specific article, the court being bound to grant specific implement except in a limited number of situations (such as where implement would be impossible or inequitable).

(iii) *Remedy for Breach of "Warranty"*

In section 53 which deals with this remedy the term "warranty" is used in the English law sense of "non-material term." It is unsatisfactory that section 61(2), which provides that "as regards Scotland a breach of warranty shall be deemed to be a failure to perform a material part of the contract," has not been qualified by a phrase such as "unless the context or subject matter otherwise requires" (contrast section 61(1)). See also 4–51 *et seq.*, above. On the other hand, there is in section 53 the express provision that nothing in the section prejudices or affects the buyer's right of rejection in Scotland as declared by the Act (s. 53(5)).

By section 53(1), where there is a breach of "warranty" by the seller, the buyer is not by reason only of that breach entitled to reject the goods, but he may either—

(*a*) set it up against the seller in diminution or extinction of the price (as in *British Motor Body Co. Ltd.* v. *Thomas Shaw (Dundee) Ltd.*, 1914 S.C. 922 (4–257, above); or

(*b*) sue the seller for damages for the breach of "warranty."

The measure of damages is the estimated loss directly and naturally resulting, in the ordinary course of events, from the breach of "warranty" (s. 53(2)). In the case of breach of "warranty" of quality, that loss is *prima facie* ("unless the contrary is proved") the difference between the value of the goods at the time of delivery to the buyer and the value they would have had if they had fulfilled the "warranty" (s. 53(3)).

The fact that the buyer has availed himself of the first alternative (setting up the breach of "warranty" to diminish or extinguish the price) does not prevent him from suing for the same breach of "warranty" if he has suffered further damage (s. 53(4)).

Amongst the situations in which section 53 would provide a remedy would be failure on the seller's part to deliver the goods by a stipulated date: unless the time of delivery was of the essence of the contract, the seller's failure would not entitle the buyer to reject the goods, but would give him, under section 53, a defence if he were sued by the seller for the price and a right to bring an action for damages. In *Paton & Sons* v. *David Payne & Co. Ltd.* (1897) 35 S.L.R. 112 (H.L.) (4–58, above), for instance, the time of the delivery of the printing machine was held not to have been of the essence of the contract and so on the seller's failure to deliver by the agreed date the buyers, while not entitled to reject the machine, were entitled to damages.

(iv) *Rejection, or Retention and Damages*

4–274   The alternative remedies of rejection on the one hand and retention and damages on the other hand are provided for in section 11(5), a subsection applicable only to Scotland.

4–275   Failure by the seller to perform any material part of the contract entitles the buyer either—
(1) within a reasonable time after delivery to reject the goods and treat the contract as repudiated; or
(2) to retain the goods and treat the failure to perform the material part as a breach which may give rise to a claim for compensation or damages.

4–276   These alternatives correspond to the *actio redhibitoria* ("right to reject") and the *actio quanti minoris* ("right to deduct") of the Civil Law. Under the common law of Scotland there was an *actio redhibitoria* which entitled the buyer to reject goods which were not conform to the contract, but there was no *actio quanti minoris, i.e.* the buyer was not entitled (unless there was a special agreement to that effect) to retain the goods which were disconform to contract and claim a reduction in the price on account of the disconformity.

4–277   Section 11(5) gives the buyer an option: he may choose one remedy or the other, but he is not entitled to exercise both at the same time:
Lupton & Co. v. *Schulze & Co.* (1900) 2 F. 1118: L. & Co. entered into a contract for the sale of cloth to S. & Co. Part of the cloth being disconform to contract, S. & Co. intimated that they rejected it, but insisted on retaining it as security for their claim of damages.
L. & Co. brought an action against S. & Co. for the unpaid contract price, and S. & Co. brought an action against L. & Co. for damages. The two actions were conjoined.
Held that S. & Co., having rejected the goods, had taken up a wrong position in retaining them, and were liable to pay the full price to L. & Co., and that S. & Co.'s claim for damages was barred by their election to reject the goods.
"The appellants had open to them an alternative course. They could reject the goods and place them at the disposal of the respondents, or they could keep the goods at the contract price, and claim damages on the ground that the sellers had failed to perform a material part of their contract. Between these alternatives the appellants had to choose; they could adopt either, but they must adopt one of them" (*per* Lord Trayner, at p. 1121).

4–278   Where, however, the buyer's purported rejection is invalid, he may have recourse to the alternative remedy of retention and damages. Accordingly, in *Aitken, Campbell & Co. Ltd.* v. *Boullen & Gatenby,* 1908 S.C. 490 (4–164, above), the attempt by the buyers to reject the part of the goods which was not conform to sample in quality was held not to bar them from adopting the alternative remedy by retaining the whole of the goods and claiming damages. This point of law—that the buyer's election of the right of rejection is not necessarily a final election having the effect of barring him from recourse to the alternative of retention and damages—has the support of an *obiter dictum* ("remark which is not an essential part of the decision") of Lord Dunedin (with whom the other four Law Lords concurred) in *Pollock & Co. v. Macrae*, 1922 S.C. (H.L.) 192, at p. 201. Lord Dunedin there expressed the opinion that *Electric Construction Co. Ltd. v. Hurry & Young* (1897) 24 R. 312 (in which the First Division of the Court of Session had, by a majority, held that a buyer who had, invalidly, rejected a dynamo was not entitled to fall back on the alternative of retention and damages) had been "wrongly decided."

(1) Rejection

The buyer who chooses the first leg of section 11(5) as his remedy is, on rescinding the contract on account of the seller's repudiation of it, entitled to recover the price if that has been paid and also damages for loss which he may have suffered as a result of the seller's breach. It is uncertain whether this remedy is available for a minor breach (see 4–182 *et seq.*, above).

The right of rejection must be exercised timeously. In particular, it is no longer open if the buyer has accepted the goods. On this, see "Buyer's Right of Rejection" (4–181 *et seq.*, above), where some illustrative cases have been included.

The right of rejection may still be open although the property in the goods has passed to the buyer:

Nelson v. William Chalmers & Co. Ltd., 1913 S.C. 441: C. Ltd. entered into a contract to build a motor yacht for N. A clause in the contract provided that the property in the yacht was to pass to N. on payment of the first of the four instalments of the price.

The first instalment was paid. When completed the yacht was disconform to contract, and N. rejected it and brought an action against C. Ltd. for repayment of the instalment paid and for damages. C. Ltd. maintained that N. was barred from rejecting the yacht because, under the terms of the contract, it had become his own property.

Held that as N. had never accepted the yacht as conform to contract, he was not barred from rejecting it.

(2) Retention and damages

In choosing the alternative *actio quanti minoris* under the second leg of section 11(5), the buyer is deemed to have accepted the goods. The measure of damages does not differ from that applicable under section 53(2) to breach of a non-material term (4–271, above).

A buyer who has chosen this remedy may, if sued by the seller for the price, be required, at the court's discretion, to consign or pay into court the price of the goods or part of the price, or to give other reasonable security for the due payment of the price (s. 58). This provision is "intended to guard against the abuse of the alternative remedy given to the buyer by section 11(2) [*of the Act of 1893*]" (Brown on *Sale of Goods* (2nd ed.), p. 405, quoted by Lord Kilbrandon (Ordinary) in *George Cohen, Sons & Co. Ltd. v. Jamieson & Paterson*, 1963 S.C. 289 (O.H.), at p. 291 (see 4–253, above)).

VII AUCTION SALES

4–284   The Act in some respects altered the common law of Scotland as to sales by auction. As a result, the rules applicable to auction sales of goods differ to some extent from the rules applicable to auction sales of heritable property and incorporeal moveables.

4–285   Section 57 sets out the following rules as to auction sales:

4–286   (a) Where goods are put up for sale by auction in lots, each lot is *prima facie* ("unless the contrary is proved") deemed to be the subject of a separate contract of sale (s. 57(1)).

4–287   The rule of the common law was to the same effect, as is clear from *Couston, Thomson & Co.* v. *Chapman* (1872) 10 M. (H.L.) 74; (1871) 9 M. 675, in which the buyer of several lots of wine by sample at an auction was held not to have timeously rejected three of the lots which were disconform to sample, and so was liable to pay the price of all the lots.

"There can be no question whatever that the purchase of each lot was a separate and distinct contract, and that it was perfectly competent to the defenders to object to the completion of the purchase with respect to the three lots they object to, if they had good grounds for so doing, irrespective wholly of the view which they might take of the other purchases which they made, and with which they are content" (*per* Lord Chancellor Hatherley at p. 76).

4–288   (b) A sale by auction is complete when the auctioneer announces its completion by the fall of the hammer, or in other customary manner; until that announcement is made any bidder may retract his bid (s. 57(2)).

4–289   From this provision the court deduced in *Fenwick* v. *Macdonald, Fraser & Co. Ltd.* (1904) 6 F. 850 that until the fall of the hammer the exposer is free to withdraw the goods from sale. "There is no sale until the fall of the hammer, and . . . until then any competitor is entitled to withdraw his bid. Of course, it follows that any proprietor is entitled to withdraw the article he is selling. One party is not bound while the other is free" (*per* Lord Young at p. 853).

4–290   As was explained by Lord Trayner in that case (at pp. 853-854), the common law rule was different: a bidder could not withdraw his bid, and the seller, even if only one bid had been made, could not withdraw the article from sale.

4–291   (c) A sale by auction may be notified to be subject to a reserve or upset price, and a right to bid may also be reserved expressly by or on behalf of the seller (s. 57(3)).

4–292   Where a right to bid is expressly reserved (but not otherwise) the seller or any one person on his behalf may bid (s. 57(6)).

4–293   The distinction in practice between a reserve and an upset price is that the former is in writing, sealed up and only made known after the fall of the hammer, whereas an upset price is made known to prospective bidders before the sale has begun. Reserve prices have been commoner in England, and upset prices in Scotland.

4–294   (d) Where a sale by auction is not notified to be subject to a right to bid by or on behalf of the seller, it is not lawful for the seller to bid himself or to employ any person to bid at the sale, or for the auctioneer knowingly to take any bid from the seller or from that other person (s. 57(4)).

A sale which contravenes that rule may be treated as fraudulent by the buyer (s. 57(5)).

A person employed by the seller to bid with a view to raising the price is commonly referred to as a "white-bonnet."

These statutory rules operate within a framework provided by the common law of agency: the auctioneer is a mercantile or commercial agent, selling on behalf of a disclosed or undisclosed principal; he has a lien on the price for the charges and commission due to him by the seller (*Mackenzie* v. *Cormack*, 1950 S.C. 183), he is freed from liability to the buyer if the buyer, having discovered the identity of the previously undisclosed seller, elects to return the goods to the seller (*Ferrier* v. *Dods &c.* (1865) 3 M. 561), and if the auctioneer sells without having the seller's authority to sell, with the result that the buyer loses a bargain, he is liable to the buyer in damages for "breach of warranty of authority" (*Anderson* v. *Croall & Sons Ltd.* (1903) 6 F. 153) (see also 1–42 *et seq.*, above).

Auction sales are also governed by other statutes (see 4–299 *et seq.*, below).

VIII OTHER STATUTORY PROVISIONS ON SALE OF GOODS

There are numerous other statutory provisions besides the Act of 1979 which affect particular aspects of contracts for the sale of goods. The legislation of the 1960s and the 1970s, with its accompanying subordinate legislation, is voluminous, and must be looked for in more specialised works. What follows here is no more than an indication of the existence of the main statutes and their subject-matter.

Auctions (Bidding Agreements) Acts 1927 and 1969

The Act of 1927 made it a criminal offence for any dealer to give any gift or consideration to any other person to induce that other person to abstain from bidding at an auction sale, and also for any person to accept or to attempt to obtain from a dealer any gift or consideration for such purpose (s. 1(1)). A "dealer" for the purposes of the Act is "a person who in the normal course of his business attends sales by auction for the purpose of purchasing goods with a view to reselling them" (s. 1(2)).

The amending Act of 1969 introduced increased penalties for offences under the Act of 1927 (s. 1(1)), empowered the court to prohibit convicted persons from attending auctions for up to three years (s. 2(1)), and provided the civil remedy by which the seller may avoid the contract (s. 3(1)) and if the goods are not restored to him may recover any loss sustained by him not only from the buyer but from any of the parties to the prohibited bidding agreement (s. 3(2)).

Copies of both Acts must be exhibited at the auction (1927 Act, s. 3; 1969 Act, s. 4).

Mock Auctions Act 1961

4–303 This Act made it a criminal offence to promote a "mock auction" at which lots of, or including, "prescribed" articles are offered for sale (s. 1(1)).

4–304 A "mock auction" is a sale of goods by competitive bidding at which:
(a) a lot is sold to a person for less than the amount of his highest bid, or part of the price is repaid or credited to him; or
(b) the right to bid is restricted or stated to be restricted to persons who have bought or agreed to buy one or more articles; or
(c) any articles are given away or offered as gifts (s. 1(3)).

4–305 The "prescribed" articles are any plate, plated articles, linen, china, glass, books, pictures, prints, furniture, jewellery, articles of household or personal use or ornament, or any musical or scientific instrument or apparatus (s. 3(2)).

Trading Stamps Act 1964

4–306 This Act was passed to regulate the issue and redeeming of trading stamps.

4–307 It requires the promoter of the trading stamp scheme to redeem the stamps for their cash value if their holder so chooses (s. 3(1)). Each stamp must bear on its face a value expressed in the current coin of the realm (*e.g.* "·033p") and the promoter's name (s. 2(1) and (2)).

Trade Descriptions Acts 1968 and 1972

4–308 These Acts replace, but are of much wider scope than, the Merchandise Marks Acts 1887 to 1953. They are aimed against false or misleading trade descriptions, and are part of the criminal law: contravention of these Acts does not of itself affect the validity or enforceability of a contract (1968 Act, s. 35).

4–309 The leading provision of the Act of 1968 is that any person who, in the course of a trade or business—
(a) applies a "false trade description" to any goods; or
(b) supplies or offers to supply any goods to which a "false trade description" is applied is guilty of an offence (s. 1(1)).

4–310 "Trade description" is any indication, direct or indirect, and by whatever means given, of a wide variety of matters relating to goods, *e.g.* quantity, size, method of manufacture, fitness for purpose, approval by any person, history (s. 2(1)) (*e.g.* a false mileometer reading on a second-hand car as in *MacNab* v. *Alexanders of Greenock Ltd. and Another*, 1971 S.L.T. 121).

4–311 "False trade description" means a trade description which is false "to a material degree" (s. 3(1)), but the Act also provides that if a trade description is misleading, though not false, it is deemed to be a false trade description (s. 3(2)) (*e.g.* "where whisky which is not made in Scotland is placed in a bottle bearing a label pictorially suggestive of Scottish origin but also disclosing in small print the actual place of manufacture" (G.H. Treitel in his annotation to this provision in *Current Law Statutes Annotated*)).

4–312 False indications as to the price of goods (s. 11(1)) (*e.g.* false statements such as "less than the recommended price" or "reduced"), and false indications concerning services (s. 13) (*e.g.* a false statement that goods are repaired "free of charge" during a guarantee period when in fact there is a labour charge for such a repair) are also offences under the Act.

A person charged with an offence will be acquitted if he proves that:

(a) the commission of the offence was due to a mistake or to reliance on information supplied to him, or to the act or default of "another person," an accident or some other cause beyond his control; *and*

(b) he took all reasonable precautions and exercised all due diligence to avoid the commission of the offence by himself or any person under his control (s. 24(1)).

The best-known case on the Act of 1968 was concerned with the interpretation of this statutory defence:

Tesco Supermarkets Ltd. v. *Nattrass* [1972] A.C. 153: T. Ltd., at one of its branch supermarkets, was advertising a "special offer" of "Radiant" washing powder at 2s. 11d. instead of the normal price of 3s. 11d. Some packets marked at 3s. 11d. were in fact on the shelves, and a customer who selected one of these was charged 3s. 11d.

T. Ltd. was successful in its defence to a charge under the Act, since the commission of the offence had been due to the default of "another person," namely, the store manager whose duty it was to see that the correct goods were on the shelves, and since T. Ltd. also satisfied part (b) of the defence by having devised a proper system for the store and having done all it could do to see that the system was implemented.

The decision has led to some criticism of the defence as making it too easy for parties in the position of T. Ltd. to obtain immunity.

The short amending Act of 1972 requires certain names and marks applied to imported goods to be accompanied by an indication of the country of origin of the goods.

Unsolicited Goods and Services Acts 1971 and 1975

These Acts are aimed at protecting persons who receive "unsolicited" goods, *i.e.* goods sent to them without any prior request having been made for the goods by or on behalf of the recipients (1971 Act, s. 6).

The Acts enable the recipient of unsolicited goods, provided certain conditions are satisfied, to use, deal with or dispose of them as if they were an unconditional gift to him, all the rights of the sender to the goods being extinguished (1971 Act, s. 1(1)). The recipient must have no reasonable cause to believe that the goods were sent with a view to their being acquired for the purposes of a trade or business. He must not have agreed to acquire them, nor must he have agreed to return them. He must not have unreasonably refused to permit the sender to take possession of them, and he must either have held the goods for six months or have given the sender 30 days' notice (1971 Act, s. 1(2)).

A person who makes demands for payment for unsolicited goods is guilty of an offence (1971 Act, s. 2(1)).

The amending Act of 1975 added to the Act of 1971 a new section enabling regulations to be made as to the contents and form of notes of agreement, invoices and similar documents (1971 Act, s. 3A).

Fair Trading Act 1973

4–320   This long Act, consisting of 140 sections and 13 Schedules, established the office of Director General of Fair Trading (s. 1(1)), whose duty it is to keep under review commercial activities relating to goods or services supplied to consumers in order to make himself aware of practices which might adversely affect the economic interests of consumers (s. 2(1)). The Director has further functions both under this Act and under the Consumer Credit Act 1974.

4–321   The Act empowers the Secretary of State for Trade to make orders, in the form of statutory instruments, to control certain "consumer trade practices" (s. 22). Failure to comply with an order is an offence (s. 23).

4–322   A "consumer trade practice" is any practice which is carried on in connection with the supply of goods (whether by sale or otherwise) to consumers or in connection with the supply of services for consumers and which relates to a variety of matters (*e.g.* the terms or conditions on which goods or services are supplied, methods of salesmanship employed in dealing with consumers, the way in which goods are packed, or methods of demanding payment) (s. 13).

4–323   A recommendation for the exercise of the Secretary of State's powers to make orders may be made by the Director where it appears to the Director that a consumer trade practice has the effect, or is likely to have the effect,—

(a) of misleading consumers as to, or withholding from them adequate information as to, or an adequate record of, their rights and obligations under consumer transactions, or

(b) of otherwise misleading or confusing consumers with respect to any matter in connection with consumer transactions, or

(c) of subjecting consumers to undue pressure to enter into consumer transactions, or

(d) of causing the terms or conditions on which consumers enter into consumer transactions to be so adverse to them as to be inequitable (s. 17(1) and (2)).

4–324   The Act includes provisions enabling the Director to take action against persons who in carrying on business persist in a course of conduct which is unfair to consumers by involving the commission of offences (*e.g.* under the Trade Descriptions Acts) or breach of contract or breach of duty. The Director must "use his best endeavours" to obtain from the person concerned a satisfactory written assurance that he will refrain from continuing his course of conduct (s. 34). If the Director fails to obtain such an assurance or if the assurance is given but not observed, the Director may bring proceedings against the person concerned before the Restrictive Practices Court (s. 35).

4–325   Another notable provision of the Act is the duty imposed on the Director to encourage associations to prepare and distribute to their members codes of practice for guidance in safeguarding and promoting the interests of consumers (s. 124 (3)). The existence of such codes of practice in many trades has the effect of reducing consumers' complaints.

4–326   The Director must make an annual report to the Secretary of State (s. 125(1)). He may also publish information and advice for consumers

(s. 124(1), and there are now numerous booklets and leaflets available free of charge in accordance with this provision.

Unfair Contract Terms Act 1977

The main provisions of this Act are directed against exclusion-of-liability clauses which one party to a contract may seek, by the exercise of superior bargaining strength, to impose on the other party. Amongst the contracts to which these provisions apply are contracts relating to the transfer of the ownership of goods.

In general, any clause excluding or restricting liability for death or personal injury is void, and of clauses excluding or restricting liability for other matters, some are void (*e.g.* in consumer contracts) while the others are of no effect unless they satisfy a "reasonableness" test.

The provisions of the Act which affected sections 12 to 15 of the Sale of Goods Act 1893 have been incorporated in the Sale of Goods Act 1979 and have been considered earlier in this chapter (see 4–59 *et seq.,* above).

Consumer Safety Act 1978

This Act was passed to remedy certain deficiencies in the Consumer Protection Acts 1961-71, which it wholly repealed.

Under the Act the Secretary of State for Trade has a wide power to make regulations "for the purpose of securing that goods are safe or that appropriate information is provided and inappropriate information is not provided in respect of goods" (s. 1(1)). Such regulations are referred to in the Act as "safety regulations" (s. 9(4)).

Safety regulations may relate to composition, design, packing, *etc.* of goods, standards for goods, the marking of warnings and instructions on goods, the prohibiting of persons from supplying goods which the Secretary of State considers are not safe and many other matters listed in the Act (s. 1(2)).

The Act also enables the Secretary of State to make "prohibition orders" and to serve "prohibition notices" and "notices to warn" (s. 3(1)).

A "prohibition order" prohibits persons from supplying any goods which the Secretary of State considers are not safe and which are described in the order (s. 3(1)(*a*)). The making of a prohibition order must be in accordance with Part I of Schedule 1 to the Act (s. 3(2)), which requires the Secretary of State to publish his proposal to make an order and consider representations made to him. An order cannot last longer than 12 months (Sched. 1, Pt. I). A prohibition order may be regarded as an "instant" safety regulation: it resembles a regulation in that it is of general applicability and takes the form of a statutory instrument; it differs from a regulation in that it is limited in duration and does not require to be approved by a resolution of each House of Parliament (s. 7(6) and (7)).

A "prohibition notice" prohibits the person on whom it is served from supplying, except with the consent of the Secretary of State, any goods which the Secretary of State considers are not safe and which are described in the notice (s. 3(1)(*b*)). The procedure for serving a prohibition notice is specified in Part II of Schedule 1 (s. 3(2)): the trader must first be given an opportunity to make representations before the notice is actually served, unless the Secretary of State considers that the risk of danger connected with the goods is such that the notice must come into force without delay.

4–336   A "notice to warn" is a notice requiring the person on whom it is served to publish, in a form and manner and on occasions specified in the notice and at his own expense, a warning about any goods which the Secretary of State considers are not safe and which the person concerned is supplying or has supplied (s. 3(1)(c)). The procedure to be followed is specified in Part III of Schedule 1 (s. 3(2)): advance notification of the proposal to serve a notice to warn must be given to the person concerned.

4–337   Failure to observe a safety regulation, a prohibition order, a prohibition notice or a notice to warn is an offence (ss. 2(1) and 3(3)). In addition, any obligation imposed on a person by safety regulations or a prohibition order or a prohibition notice is a duty owed by him to any other person who may be affected by a failure to perform the obligation, and a breach of that duty gives rise to civil liability (s. 6(1)).

4–338   The Secretary of State has wide powers to obtain information for the purpose of deciding whether to make, vary or revoke safety regulations or prohibition orders or to serve, vary or revoke prohibition notices or to serve or revoke notices to warn (s. 4(1)).

Uniform Laws on International Sales Act 1967

4–339   This Act is aimed at securing some uniformity in international sales of goods. As from 1972 it has given effect to two Conventions signed at a conference at The Hague in 1964. The Conventions are printed as Schedules to the Act: Schedule 1 sets out the Uniform Law on the International Sale of Goods ("the Uniform Law on Sales"), and Schedule 2 sets out the Uniform Law on the Formation of Contracts for the International Sale of Goods ("the Uniform Law on Formation"). The first governs such matters as the seller's obligations as to the time and place of delivery, the conformity of the goods with the contract, and the giving of a good title. The second relates to offer and acceptance.

4–340   The Uniform Law in Schedule 1 applies only if the parties have their places of business or their residences in different "contracting" States (*i.e.* each of the States concerned must have ratified or acceded to the Conventions) (Article 1 of the Uniform Law on Sales). A further limitation on the application of the Uniform Law in Schedule 1 is that the parties to the contract must have chosen it as the law of the contract (1967 Act, s. 1(3)).

4–341   The Uniform Law in Schedule 2 is of an ancillary character and applies only to contracts which, if they were concluded, would be governed by the Uniform Law in Schedule 1 (1967 Act, Sched. 2, Art. 1).

4–342   In some other countries which are parties to the Conventions the Uniform Laws apply automatically unless excluded by the parties to the contract. The preliminary question of private international law which arises is whether the proper law of the contract is that of the United Kingdom or of the foreign country. If the proper law is that of the United Kingdom, the Uniform Laws apply only if adopted by the parties to the contract, whereas if the proper law is that of the foreign country, the Uniform Laws may be applicable without express adoption.

———————

Further Reading

Scots Mercantile Law Statutes (annual reprint from *The Parliament House Book*) (W. Green & Son) for Sale of Goods Act 1979

Gloag and Henderson, *Introduction to the Law of Scotland*, Chapters XVII and XVIII

David M. Walker, *Principles of Scottish Private Law*, Chapter 5.33

J.J. Gow, *The Mercantile and Industrial Law of Scotland*, Chapter 2

Chalmers' Sale of Goods Act 1979, 18th ed. by Michael Mark (1981, Butterworths)

Benjamin's Sale of Goods, 2nd ed. by A.G. Guest (General Editor) (1981, Sweet & Maxwell)

T.B. Smith, *Property Problems in Sale* (1979, Sweet & Maxwell)

M.G. Clarke, "The Buyer's Right of Rejection," 1978 S.L.T. (News) 1, and contributed reply, 1978 S.L.T. (News) 61

CHAPTER 5

CONSUMER CREDIT

INTRODUCTION

THE most important Act on the subject of "consumer credit" is the Consumer Credit Act 1974, and this chapter is mainly concerned with giving an outline account of that Act. It must, however, be noted at the outset that the law on this subject is at present in a transitional state: the Act of 1974 is not yet fully in force, and older legislation (including the Hire-Purchase (Scotland) Act 1965) which will ultimately be repealed under the provisions of the Act of 1974 is in part still applicable.

References in this chapter are, unless the context otherwise requires, references to provisions of the Consumer Credit Act 1974.

The Act applies to the whole of the United Kingdom. Many of its provisions, phrased initially in the terminology of English law, are followed by adaptations for Scotland and Northern Ireland; two examples are:

(a) in section 1 and elsewhere in the Act there is the expression "bailment or (in Scotland) hiring of goods";

(b) section 37 refers to the possibility that the holder of a licence may be "adjudged bankrupt," and section 38 provides that in the application of section 37 to Scotland the phrase "has his estate sequestrated" is to be substituted.

The Act is a long one, consisting of 193 sections and five Schedules, but it is by no means complete in itself. It is in wide terms and is intended as a framework of legal principles. Practical and specific details are to be looked for in regulations which are first issued when the corresponding set of provisions in the Act is about to be brought into force; *e.g.* the Consumer Credit (Advertisements) Regulations 1980 were laid before Parliament on January 29, 1980, along with the Consumer Credit Act 1974 (Commencement No. 6) Order 1980. the effect being to bring into operation on October 6, 1980, the provisions on advertising in Part IV of the Act, supplemented by the Regulations.

5–05   Only a few of the provisions of the Act came into operation on the date of its passing (July 31, 1974). For the remainder there have been or will be "appointed days," fixed by the several commencement orders, which, like the regulations, are statutory instruments. An unusual and useful feature of the Act of 1974 is the provision in section 192(2) that each commencement order must include a provision amending Schedule 3 to the Act. This Schedule, entitled "Transitional and Commencement Provisions," lists those provisions of the Act which did *not* come into operation on July 31, 1974, and states the date on which they will come into operation; *e.g.* the Schedule in its original form provided under the heading "Advertisements" within Part IV of the Act: "Part IV does not apply to any advertisement published before the day appointed for the purposes of this paragraph" (of the Schedule). The Commencement Order No. 6, mentioned above, amends this paragraph of Schedule 3 by the insertion of the date October 6, 1980. If, therefore, the commencement orders are carefully watched and the amendments which they make to Schedule 3 are duly inserted, the Schedule provides immediate information as to whether a particular group of provisions in the Act is or is not in force, and if it is, the date on which it came into force.

The stage of implementation of the Act reached by the beginning of 1983 was that the Department of Trade had circulated in draft for comment all the main regulations necessary to implement the Act, but had decided that regulations to implement certain other provisions of the Act should not meantime be made, because they could be a burden on industry and were not at present necessary. These other provisions are[1]:

Section 53: Display of information on premises of persons carrying on consumer credit or hire businesses

Section 26/54: Conduct of business regulations governing seeking business

Section 55: Disclosure of information to the debtor or hirer before an agreement regulated by the Act is made

Section 64(3): Provision of a copy of a cancellable agreement in addition to that provided when the agreement is signed

Section 112: Realisation of property over which the right has been provided by way of security

Section 156: Power to make regulations in relation to credit brokerage, debt-adjusting or debt-counselling agreements, corresponding to those relating to consumer credit or hire agreements

Section 179: Form and content of secondary documents; for example, credit cards and trading checks.

5–06   As a preliminary to the outline of the Act, it is appropriate to look briefly at:

    (a) the general meaning of the term "consumer credit";

---

[1] *Hansard* (H.C.), July 20, 1982, Written Answers.

(b) the general aim of the Act;
(c) the Crowther Report; and
(d) the structure of the Act.

(a) General Meaning of Term "Consumer Credit"

The phrase "consumer credit" is a comparatively recent addition to the language of the law. Its exact meaning depends on several definitions (especially the definition of "regulated agreement") in Part II of the Act (see 5–49, below). For the present it is sufficient to appreciate that the word "consumer" denotes the ordinary citizen, the "man in the street," who immediately requires something of material value for his own use, while the word "credit" indicates that that same party, being typically without sufficient capital resources of his own, obtains the necessary finance, by way of loan or some similar transaction, from another party who is in business for that very purpose.

The Act is therefore not concerned with finance for industry, but with the various forms of borrowing to which the "small man" resorts when it is impossible or inconvenient for him to pay the full cash price immediately.

Two points of practical importance are:

(i) The consumer may be an individual or may be a partnership, but the Act does not treat a registered company (however small) as a consumer.

(ii) Most of the provisions of the Act do not apply if the amount of the credit exceeds £5,000, and some of the provisions do not apply where only £30 or less is involved. However, these and other monetary limits in the Act may be increased or reduced by statutory instrument. The following increases are proposed to be made during the course of 1983[1]:

Section	Present limit £	Proposed limit £
*8(2) Upper limit for regulated consumer credit agreement	5,000	15,000
*15(1)(c) Upper limit for regulated consumer hire agreement	5,000	15,000
*17(1) Small agreement	30	50
*43(3)(a) Upper exemption limit for advertisement	5,000	15,000
70(6) Maximum fee or commission to credit-broker on cancelled agreement	1	3
*75(3)(b) Cash price limits on joint liability of creditor and supplier	10,000	30,000
7(1), 78(1), 79(1) Fee for copy of agreement	15p	50p
84(1) Maximum liability following misuse of credit token	30	50

[1] *Hansard* (H.C.), July 20, 1982, Written Answers.

Section	Present limit £	Proposed limit £
101(7)(a) Maximum annual hire payments for right of termination of hire agreement after 18 months to apply	300	900
107(1), 108(1), 109(1) Fee for information to surety	15p	50p
110(1) Fee for copy of security instrument	15p	50p
118(1)(b) Upper limit for use of unsworn statement in place of lost pawn-receipt	15	15
120(1)(a) Upper limit of pawned property which passes to pawnee if unredeemed at end of six months	†15	15
155(1) Maximum fee or commission to credit-broker for work not leading to an agreement	1	3
158(1) Fee to credit reference agency for copy of file on individual	25p	1

* Changes in these limits require an affirmative resolution of both Houses of Parliament.

† Until the Pawnbrokers Act 1872 is repealed the limit of £2 in that Act will continue to apply.

(b) General Aim of the Act

5–10 In a consumer credit transaction the consumer is likely to be the weaker party, and is therefore in danger of being required to pay an excessive amount to the other party. The general aim of the Act of 1974 is to embrace within a single Act all the major principles to be applied in the protection of a consumer who enters into a consumer credit transaction.

5–11 The Act is part of a wider movement which has gained momentum in recent years: Parliament has increasingly considered it desirable to protect the consumer by legislation which restricts the freedom which the stronger party would otherwise have at common law to impose his own terms on the consumer. This legislation has not been confined to consumer *credit* transactions; the Act of 1974 is only one of several "consumer protection" measures; other examples are the Trade Descriptions Act 1968, the Unfair Contract Terms Act 1977 and the Consumer Safety Act 1978.

5–12 The principles of the Act of 1974 are, however, not solely of recent origin. Even in the nineteenth century Parliament had regarded the consumer *who was obtaining credit* as being in a particularly vulnerable position. Several statutes had been passed long before 1974 to curb the various abuses as they became apparent, but these statutes were restricted in their scope to particular types of consumer credit transactions; examples are the Pawnbrokers Acts 1872 and 1960, the Moneylenders Acts 1900 to 1927, and hire-purchase legislation consolidated by the Hire-Purchase (Scotland) Act 1965. The general terms "consumer" and "credit" were not in common use, and the legislation was piecemeal and not capable of being extended to new forms of providing credit as these came to be devised.

Since about 1950 there has been a rapid growth in the demand for consumer credit. As is stated in the opening paragraph of the White Paper *Reform of the Law on Consumer Credit* of 1973 (Cmnd. 5427):

"Without the use of credit, the standard of living of many, particularly those in the process of setting up home and starting a family, would be lower."

Legislation was seen as not having kept pace with the changed needs of society.

What the circumstances of modern life required was wide-ranging legislation which would catch all existing forms of consumer credit arrangements and also new arrangements as they came to be devised, and this is what the Act of 1974 is intended to be. It applies comprehensively to the whole field of consumer credit: whether the transaction takes the form of an agreement with a pawnbroker, or a loan by a moneylender, or a hire-purchase agreement, or any other form, it will be subject to the Act provided it falls within the general description of being a consumer credit transaction covered by the Act.

(c) The Crowther Report

The historical background to the passing of the Act of 1974 centres on the Crowther Report *Consumer Credit,* published in 1971 (Cmnd. 4596).

The Committee on Consumer Credit had been appointed by the Government in 1968 under the chairmanship of Lord Crowther to review the then existing law and practice governing the provision of consumer credit and to make recommendations.

The Committee found it impracticable to examine the law of *consumer* credit in isolation, particularly because existing legislation, such as the Moneylenders Acts, was not confined to *consumer* transactions. The Committee therefore extended its study to cover the general legal framework within which the granting of credit and the taking of security were required to operate.

The most serious defects which the Committee found in the then existing law were:

(i) regulation of transactions according to their form instead of according to their substance (*e.g.* if one obtained a loan of money in order to purchase goods, the transaction would be governed by the Moneylenders Acts, whereas if substantially the same result was achieved by means of a hire-purchase transaction, the Hire-Purchase Acts would be applicable;

(ii) failure to distinguish consumer from commercial transactions (*e.g.* the Moneylenders Acts, though intended as a protection for consumers, were equally applicable to loans to companies for business purposes);

(iii) artificial separation of the law relating to lending from the law relating to the security for loans;

(iv) absence of any rational policy in relation to third party rights (*e.g.* the rights of a third party differed according to whether the party from whom he received the goods held them under a conditional sale agreement or under a hire-purchase agreement);

(v) excessive technicality (*e.g.* the slightest contravention of the Moneylenders Acts could deprive the lender of his right to recover the loan, however large); and

(vi) inadequate protection for the consumer in credit transactions, including:

1. absence of statutory control, other than the Moneylenders Acts, on the cost of credit;

2. absence of any requirement that the consumer be informed of the true cost of borrowing;

3. absence of any requirement that the consumer be given a rebate for early settlement;

4. the use of negotiable instruments to defeat defences which the consumer could otherwise have put forward;

5. the total freedom of rental transactions from statutory control;

6. inadequate protection for those entering into guarantees in connection with consumer credit transactions;

7. absence of any effective machinery for enforcing compliance with the legislation.

5–18 The Committee recommended the repeal of all the then existing legislation affecting credit and security (the Moneylenders Acts, the Hire-Purchase Acts, the English Bills of Sale Acts, *etc.*), and its replacement by two new Acts which would clearly distinguish between rules of general application and rules for *consumer* credit transactions; the two Acts would be:

(i) a Lending and Security Act, which would be of general application and which would establish a security register; and

(ii) a Consumer Sale and Loan Act, which would apply a uniform code to consumer sale and consumer loan credit agreements, strengthen the protection of the consumer and provide for proper enforcement through a licensing system operated by a Consumer Credit Commissioner.

5–19 In September 1973, the Government in its White Paper *Reform of the Law on Consumer Credit* (Cmnd. 5427) intimated its intention to give effect to almost all of the recommendations of the Crowther Committee on *consumer* credit, but to postpone any attempt at the fundamental restructuring of the general law of credit and security until consultations with those closely concerned could take place in the light of the situation which would exist after the passing of the Consumer Credit Bill.

5–20 The Bill, introduced to Parliament in November 1973, was lost on the dissolution of Parliament in February 1974. A new Bill, in substantially the same terms, was introduced by the new Government and was passed on July 31, 1974.

(d) **Structure of the Act**

The Act is intended to give effect to three main principles laid down by the Crowther Committee for the protection of consumers:
  (i) the redress of bargaining inequality;
  (ii) the control of trading malpractices; and
  (iii) the regulation of remedies for default.
The Act is divided into 12 Parts:
  I. Director General of Fair Trading;
  II. Credit Agreements, Hire Agreements and Linked Transactions;
  III. Licensing of Credit and Hire Businesses;
  IV. Seeking Business;
  V. Entry into Credit or Hire Agreements;
  VI. Matters Arising During Currency of Credit or Hire Agreements;
  VII. Default and Termination;
VIII. Security;
  IX. Judicial Control;
  X. Ancillary Credit Businesses;
  XI. Enforcement of Act; and
  XII. Supplemental.
Part I is preliminary, dealing with the system of administering the Act. The system is under the control of the Director General of Fair Trading.

Part II is also preliminary. It defines the basic concepts: a new terminology was required for the new system of control being introduced.

Parts III and IV are concerned with the methods by which the business activities of those who provide credit are to be regulated. The methods are a licensing system (Part III of the Act) and control of advertisements and other ways in which those providing credit seek customers (Part IV of the Act). These two Parts together may be regarded as dealing with "trading control," because they control the conduct of the trader's business.

Then come five Parts which deal with what may be called "agreement control," because they regulate individual credit or hire agreements. Part V is concerned with the making of the agreement, Part VI with matters arising during the currency of the agreement, Part VII with default by the consumer and with the termination of the agreement generally, Part VIII with security granted by the consumer or by someone else on his behalf, and Part IX with control exercised by the courts over the agreement.

The remaining three Parts of the Act extend or supplement the earlier Parts. Part X extends Parts III and IV to "ancillary credit businesses" (*e.g.* "credit brokerage" and "debt-collecting"). Part XI deals with enforcement of the Act, and Part XII consists of supplementary provisions (including the comprehensive definition section—section 189—which sets out or refers to the 117 definitions occurring in the Act).

The Act also has five Schedules. Of these Schedule 2 is particularly interesting: it sets out examples of the use of the new terminology, and so is of considerable assistance in bridging the gap between the theoretical language used in the Act and the types of agreement which are commonly met with in practice. For instance, if one is still puzzled by the terms "credit-broker" and "credit brokerage" after reading the definitions of these terms in sections 189 and 145 respectively, a reference to Schedule 2 can be illuminating: example 2 in that Schedule explains that a shopkeeper who introduces one of his customers to a finance company with whom the shopkeeper has a business relationship is a credit-broker.

5–29   The usefulness of Schedule 3 ("Transitional and Commencement Provisions") has already been noted (5–05, above).

5–30   Schedule 5 is also useful for quick reference; it consists of a table of statutory provisions repealed (or to be repealed) by the Act of 1974, *e.g.*:

Short Title	*Extent of Repeal*
Pawnbrokers Act 1872.	The whole Act.
Moneylenders Act 1900.	The whole Act.
Hire-Purchase Act 1964.	The whole Act, except Part III and section 37.
Hire-Purchase (Scotland) Act 1965.	The whole Act.

5–31   In the light of the structure of the Act as outlined above, this chapter may be conveniently divided into:

    I. Administration (Part I of the Act);
    II. Definitions (Part II of the Act);
    III. Trading control (Parts III and IV of the Act);
    IV. Agreement control (Parts V to IX of the Act);
    V. Ancillary credit businesses (Part X of the Act); and
    VI. Enforcement of the Act (Part XI of the Act).

The main provisions of Part XII of the Act ("Supplemental") are incorporated into one or more of these divisions.

5–32   In addition, since the Hire-Purchase Act 1964 is not wholly repealed by the Act of 1974, a brief account is given of its provisions on:

    VII. Motor vehicles on hire-purchase or conditional sale.

5–33   The chapter does not extend to legislation which is still in force but which will be repealed once the Act of 1974 is fully in force: in particular, the Hire-Purchase (Scotland) Act 1965 is excluded from consideration.

I ADMINISTRATION

5–34   Administration of the Act is dealt with mainly by Part I of the Act, which is headed "Director General of Fair Trading."

5–35   All the provisions of Part I of the Act came into force on the date when the Act was passed (July 31, 1974).

5–36   The office of Director General of Fair Trading was already in existence when the Act was passed. It had been established by the Fair Trading Act 1973 to exercise functions in three main fields—monopolies and mergers, restrictive trade practices and consumer protection. The holder of the office is appointed by the Secretary of State for Trade for a period of not more than five years at a time.

5–37   The general functions of the Director General of Fair Trading under the Act of 1974 fall into three groups:

    (a) to administer the licensing system set up by the Act, including the issue, renewal, variation, suspension and revocation of licences;

(b) to superintend the working and enforcement of the Act and the regulations made under it; and

(c) to keep under review and from time to time advise the Secretary of State about social and commercial developments in the United Kingdom and elsewhere relating to the provision of credit or hiring of goods to individuals (s. 1).

Additional functions may be conferred on the Director by the Secretary of State (s. 2).

The Director's functions are partly executive, partly administrative and partly judicial. In the exercise of his judicial functions the Director is regarded as a "Schedule 1 tribunal" for the purposes of the Tribunals and Inquiries Act 1971 (s. 3); he therefore comes under the supervision of the Council on Tribunals, and he must give reasons for his decisions.

The Director must arrange for the dissemination of information and advice to the public about the operation of the Act (s. 4). In accordance with this provision the Office of Fair Trading has published many booklets and leaflets for guidance of laymen and professional bodies on different aspects of the Act.

The Director makes an annual report to the Secretary of State on all his activities, including directions given to him by the Secretary of State under the Act of 1974. The report is laid before Parliament and published in such manner as the Secretary of State may consider appropriate (Fair Trading Act 1973, s. 125 and 1974 Act, s. 5).

Applications to the Director (*e.g.* for the issue of a licence) must be in writing, and in such form, and accompanied by such particulars, as the Director may specify by general notice, and must be accompanied by the specified fee. The Director may require the applicant to publish details of his application (s. 6).

It is an offence for persons knowingly or recklessly to give to the Director information which, in a material particular, is false or misleading (s. 7). Further details on this aspect of the Act are set out in Schedule 1.

II DEFINITIONS

The terms for which definitions have been included in the Act fall into two categories: first, there are terms which would be virtually meaningless unless they were defined, *e.g.* the term "debtor-creditor-supplier agreement"; they are part of the new language adopted, if not actually invented, for the purposes of the Act; secondly, there are terms which are part of normal English, but for which the Act supplies a precise definition not always coinciding with ordinary usage, *e.g.* the terms "business," "credit," and "individual."

The scheme followed in the Act in relation to definitions is that (a) *all* terms defined in the Act are listed in the definition section—section 189 in Part XII ("Supplemental")—from which one may either immediately obtain the definition or be referred to another section of the Act where the definition is to be found, and (b) terms in the first category—the special language of the Act—are also defined at the point in the Act where they are first used; *e.g.* the term "ancillary credit business" is defined in section 145, the first section in Part X ("Ancillary Credit Businesses").

5–46 Before the Act was passed, there was no terminology in ordinary English which suitably described all the various forms of credit which the Act seeks to cover: a completely new set of terms had to be found and given precise definitions before any statutory provisions could be proceeded with. Therefore most of the new terminology is set out as a preliminary to the operative parts of the Act and depends on definitions in sections 8 to 20 which comprise Part II of the Act. These are the definitions which fix the scope of the Act.

5–47 Statutory definitions are not always easily understood, and this is especially so where the statutory provision is defining a term which has itself no recognisable meaning in ordinary usage. Schedule 2 to the Act, however, gives some assistance by setting out 24 "examples" illustrating the use of the Act's terminology. The examples are not exhaustive, and in the case of conflict between the Schedule and any other provision of the Act, the other provision prevails. The Secretary of State may by subordinate legislation amend the Schedule by adding further examples or in any other way (s. 188).

5–48 A further complication is that the definitions about to be considered are not self-explanatory but include terms which themselves require to be defined and the meaning of which will be found set out in another provision of the Act. To overcome this difficulty, one must proceed step by step through each definition, exploring each term used in it, before passing on to the next definition in the list.

(a) **"Regulated Agreement"**

5–49 The definition which is, as it were, the peg on which the provisions of the Act are made to hang is that of "regulated agreement." The answer to the question "What is the scope of the Act?" is: "The Act applies to regulated agreements." The next question is obvious: "What is a regulated agreement?"

5–50 A "regulated agreement" means "a consumer credit agreement, or consumer hire agreement, other than an exempt agreement" (s. 189(1)). There are three terms in this definition which themselves require to be defined:

    (i) "consumer credit agreement";
    (ii) "consumer hire agreement"; and
    (iii) "exempt agreement."

A more detailed account of these terms than is attempted here would reveal some circularity: in section 16 the term "exempt agreement" is explained as including certain "debtor-creditor-supplier" agreements and certain "debtor-creditor" agreements, and these two latter terms are defined in sections 12 and 13 respectively as being "*regulated* consumer credit agreements" with certain characteristics.

(i) *"Consumer Credit Agreement"*

5–51 A "consumer credit agreement" is "a personal credit agreement by which the creditor provides the debtor with credit not exceeding £5,000" (s. 8(2)). In common with other monetary limits in the Act the figure of

£5,000 may be increased or reduced by statutory instrument (s. 181).[2] One must now explore the terms "personal credit agreement" and "credit."

A "personal credit agreement" is "an agreement between an individual ('the debtor') and any other person ('the creditor') by which the creditor provides the debtor with credit of any amount" (s. 8(1)). "Individual" is defined as including "a partnership or other unincorporated body of persons not consisting entirely of bodies corporate" (s. 189(1)).

"Credit" includes "a cash loan, and any other form of financial accommodation" (s. 9(1)), but an item entering into the "total charge for credit" is not treated as credit even though time is allowed for its payment (s. 9(4)).

"Total charge for credit" means "a sum calculated in accordance with regulations under section 20(1)" (s. 189 (1)). The regulations in force are the Consumer Credit (Total Charge for Credit) Regulations 1980 (S.I. 1980 No. 51). The Regulations prescribe what items (interest charges and other charges affecting the cost of borrowing) are to be treated as entering into the total charge for credit, and the method of calculating the rate of the total charge for credit, *i.e.* the true annual percentage rate ("APR"), which enables consumers to compare the cost of borrowing from one lender with the cost of borrowing from another. The simplest way of finding the APR is to use the "Consumer Credit Tables," specially prepared mathematical tables sold in 15 parts by H.M.S.O.

A simple example may now be taken from Schedule 2:

"*Facts.* E agrees to sell to F (an individual) an item of furniture in return for 24 monthly instalments of £10 payable in arrear. The property in the goods [*i.e.* the ownership of them] passes to F immediately.

"*Analysis.* This is a credit-sale agreement. . . . The credit provided amounts to £240 less the amount which, according to regulations made under section 20(1), constitutes the total charge for credit. . . . Accordingly the agreement falls within section 8(2) and is a consumer credit agreement" (Example 5).

(ii) *"Consumer Hire Agreement"*

A "consumer hire agreement" is "an agreement made by a person with an individual (the 'hirer') for the hiring of goods to the hirer, being an agreement which—

    (*a*) is not a hire-purchase agreement, and
    (*b*) is capable of subsisting for more than three months, and
    (*c*) does not require the hirer to make payments exceeding £5,000" (s. 15(1)).

The provision of the Act relating to the monetary limit of £5,000 and the definition of the term "individual" for the purposes of the Act have already been noted.[2] What requires to be explored is the distinction between a "consumer hire agreement" and a "hire-purchase agreement" implied in condition (*a*). What, then, is the Act's definition of "hire-purchase agreement?"

---

[2] For proposed increase in this monetary limit, see 5-09, above.

5–58 A "hire-purchase agreement" means "an agreement, other than a conditional sale agreement, under which—

(*a*) goods are hired in return for periodical payments by the person to whom they are hired, and

(*b*) the property in the goods will pass to that person if the terms of the agreement are complied with and one or more of the following occurs—

   (i) the exercise of an option to purchase by that person,

   (ii) the doing of any other specified act by any party to the agreement,

   (iii) the happening of any other specified event" (s. 189(1)).

Put shortly (and with some sacrifice of accuracy) a hire-purchase agreement is an agreement for the hire of goods with an option (but no obligation) to purchase them.

5–59 A "conditional sale agreement," on the other hand, commits the buyer to buying as well as the seller to selling: there is to be a sale but the ownership of the goods is to remain with the seller until some condition is fulfilled. The Act's definition of a "conditional sale agreement" is "an agreement for the sale of goods or land under which the purchase price or part of it is payable by instalments, and the property in the goods or land is to remain in the seller (notwithstanding that the buyer is to be in possession of the goods or land) until such conditions as to the payment of instalments or otherwise as may be specified in the agreement are fulfilled" (s. 189(1)).

5–60 Both hire-purchase agreements and conditional sale agreements are, of course, within the scope of the Act, but they form part of the first leg of the definition of "regulated agreement" (*i.e.* they are consumer *credit* agreements, not consumer *hire* agreements). Typical of the consumer hire agreements forming the second leg of the definition of "regulated agreement" are machinery or equipment leases.

5–61 An illustration based on Example 20 in Schedule 2 is:

Facts. K agrees with L (an individual) to let out goods on hire to L for three years at £2,000 a year, payable quarterly. The agreement contains no provision for the passing of the property in the goods to L.

Analysis. This is not a hire-purchase agreement, because it does not satisfy paragraph (*b*) in the definition of "hire-purchase agreement," and it is capable of lasting for more than three months. Paragraphs (*a*) and (*b*) in the definition of "consumer hire agreement" are therefore satisfied. Paragraph (*c*), however, is not satisfied, because the payments will exceed £5,000.[2] So the agreement is not a consumer hire agreement, though it would have been such if the hire charge had been, say, £1,500.

(iii) *"Exempt Agreement"*

5–62 "Exempt agreement" means "an agreement specified in or under section 16" (s. 189(1)). The terms "regulated agreement" and "exempt agreement" are opposites of one another. Exempt agreements are not within the scope of the Act at all except that sections 137 to 140 ("extortionate credit bargains") are applicable to them as well as to regulated agreements (s. 140).

---

[2] For proposed increase in this monetary limit, see 5–09, above.

The statutory instruments now in force under section 16 are the Consumer Credit (Exempt Agreements) Order 1980 (S.I. 1980 No. 52), which revoked several earlier Orders, and the Consumer Credit (Exempt Agreements) (Amendment) Orders 1981 and 1982 (S.I. 1981 No. 964 and S.I. 1982 No. 1029).

There are five categories of exemption provided for by section 16 when taken along with these Orders:

1. consumer credit agreements where the creditor is a local authority or building society and the agreement is secured by a heritable security;

2. consumer credit agreements where the creditor is a *specified* insurance company, friendly society, organisation of employers or organisation of workers, charity, land improvement company, or body corporate named in a public general Act, and the agreement is secured by a heritable security; the list of specified bodies is to be found in a schedule to the principal Order, as amended;

3. as 2, except that the body would not itself be specified by being named, but would be an insurance company, friendly society, *etc., of a specified description*; no exemption has so far been provided for in this category;

4. consumer credit agreements where—

(a) the number of payments to be made by the debtor does not exceed the number specified in an order (at present four), or

(b) the rate of the total charge for credit does not exceed the specified rate (at present the higher of 13 per cent and 1 per cent above the highest of the London and Scottish Clearing Banks' base rates 28 days before the making of the agreement), or

(c) the agreement has a connection with a country outside the United Kingdom; and

5. consumer hire agreements of a description specified in an order where either the owner is an electricity, gas or water authority and the subject of the agreement is a meter or metering equipment or the owner is the Post Office or the Kingston upon Hull City Council; in the latter case, according to the Order, the subject of the agreement is telecommunications apparatus of certain types.

It may be useful to list the essentials of a "regulated agreement" which have been gathered from the definitions so far considered. The agreement will be:

(i) a consumer credit agreement or a consumer hire agreement;

(ii) between two parties, of whom one (the creditor in a consumer credit agreement or the owner in a consumer hire agreement) may be a person of any status (individual, partnership or company) and the other (the debtor in a consumer credit agreement or the hirer in a consumer hire agreement) must be an "individual" (a term so defined as to include a partnership, but not a company, however small);

(iii) for credit or for hire charges not exceeding £5,000;[2] and

(iv) not an exempt agreement.

---

[2] For proposed increase in this monetary limit, see 5–09, above.

5–66   An additional essential concerns the date of the making of the agreement. Most of the provisions of Part II came into force on the date of the passing of the Act, but section 8(3) and section 15(2) were postponed until the making of the Consumer Credit Act 1974 (Commencement No. 2) Order 1977 (S.I. 1977 No. 325). Section 8(3) provides that a consumer credit agreement is a regulated agreement if it is not an exempt agreement, and section 15(2) similarly provides that a consumer hire agreement is a regulated agreement if it is not an exempt agreement. As long as these two provisions were not in force there could be no regulated agreements at all. The Commencement Order referred to brought these two provisions into operation on April 1, 1977. Therefore the final essential of a "regulated agreement" is that it has been:

(v) made on or after April 1, 1977.

(b) The Subdivisions of Regulated Consumer Credit Agreements

5–67   The first leg of the definition of "regulated agreement" requires further consideration, because the Act makes three subdivisions of consumer credit agreements. There is only one form of consumer *hire* agreement, but a consumer *credit* agreement may take one of a great variety of forms. The classification is based on the Crowther Report.

5–68   The three subdivisions referred to hinge on the distinction between each of the following pairs:

(i) "running-account credit" and "fixed-sum credit";

(ii) "restricted-use credit" and "unrestricted-use credit"; and

(iii) "debtor-creditor-supplier agreements" and "debtor-creditor agreements."

(i) *"Running-Account Credit" and "Fixed-Sum Credit"*

5–69   It is easiest to approach the statutory definitions of these two terms with a few simple instances in mind. Examples of running-account credit are bank overdrafts and shop budget accounts. Examples of fixed-sum credit are personal and bank loans, pawnbrokers' loans, and hire-purchase, credit sale and conditional sale agreements.

5–70   The distinction between the two types of credit is made by defining running-account credit; the definition of fixed-sum credit is then relatively easy, because fixed-sum credit is in effect any credit other than running-account credit.

5–71   "Running-account credit" is defined as "a facility under a personal credit agreement whereby the debtor is enabled to receive from time to time (whether in his own person, or by another person) from the creditor or a third party cash, goods and services (or any of them) to an amount or value such that, taking into account payments made by or to the credit of the debtor, the credit limit (if any) is not at any time exceeded" (s. 10(1)(*a*)).

5–72   "Fixed-sum credit" is defined as "any other facility under a personal credit agreement whereby the debtor is enabled to receive credit (whether in one amount or by instalments)" (s. 10(1)(*b*)).

5–73   Some further points require to be noted concerning the definition of "running-account credit."

The term "credit limit" used in that definition means the maximum debit balance which, under the agreement, is allowed to stand on the account; any term of the agreement allowing the maximum to be exceeded merely temporarily is disregarded for this purpose (s. 10(2)). From the definition of "regulated agreement" it follows that if the credit limit in a running-account credit is fixed above £5,000,[2] the agreement will not be within the scope of the Act. A credit limit fixed at £5,000[2] or any lower figure brings the agreement within the scope of the Act.

There is an obvious need for some anti-avoidance provisions; otherwise a creditor could place himself beyond the reach of the Act by simply having no fixed credit limit expressed in the credit agreement or by fixing an artificially high credit limit of, say, £10,000[2] in the knowledge that the credit would not be likely to extend beyond, say, £2,000. Therefore the Act provides that a credit facility which is without limit or which has a limit in excess of £5,000[2] will nevertheless be governed by the Act—

    (i) if the debtor is not enabled to draw more than £5,000[2] credit at any one time; or

    (ii) if the rate of the total charge for credit increases, or any other condition favouring the creditor comes into operation, on a rise of the debit balance above a given amount of £5,000[2] or less; or

    (iii) at the time of the making of the agreement it is probable, having regard to the terms of the agreement and any other relevant considerations, that the debit balance will not at any time rise above £5,000[2] (s. 10(3)(b)).

In connection with the distinction between running-account credit and fixed-sum credit a specific provision of the Act concerning a hire-purchase agreement should be noted: the person by whom the goods are hired out to an individual under a hire-purchase agreement is to be taken as providing the individual with fixed-sum credit to finance the transaction of an amount equal to the full price of the goods less the total of the deposit (if any) and the total charge for credit (s. 9(3)). An item entering into the total charge for credit is not treated as credit even though time is allowed for its payment (s. 9(4)).

Some examples may now be looked at as illustrations of the distinction; all are based on the Examples in Schedule 2:

    1. *Facts:* A agrees to make a cash loan to B of £4,500 in nine monthly instalments of £500.

Analysis: This falls within section 10(1)(b) and is fixed-sum credit amounting to £4,500 (Example 9).

    2. *Facts:* A issues to B a credit-card for use in obtaining cash on credit from A. The credit limit is £30. On one occasion B uses the credit-card in a way which increases his debit balance with A to £40. A writes to B agreeing to allow the excess on that occasion only, but stating that it must be paid off within one month.

Analysis: In exceeding his credit limit B, by implication, requests A to allow him a temporary excess, and A grants this implied request. The agreement to allow the excess varies the original agreement by adding a

---

[2] For proposed increase in this monetary limit, see 5–09, above.

new term, but under section 10(2) the new term is disregarded in arriving at the credit limit (Example 22).

5–80   3. *Facts:* The G Bank grants H an unlimited overdraft, with an increased rate of interest on so much of any debit balance as exceeds £2,000.

Analysis: Although the overdraft purports to be unlimited, the stipulation for increased interest above £2,000 brings the agreement within section 10(3)(*b*) (ii) and it is a consumer credit agreement (Example 6).

5–81   4. *Facts:* J is an individual who owns a small shop which usually carries a stock worth about £1,000. K makes a stocking agreement under which he undertakes to provide on short-term credit the stock needed from time to time by J without any specified limit.

Analysis: Although the agreement appears to provide unlimited credit, it is probable, having regard to the stock usually carried by J, that his indebtedness to K will not at any time rise above £5,000.[2] Accordingly the agreement falls within section 10(3)(*b*)(iii) and is a consumer credit agreement (Example 7).

5–82   5. *Facts:* C agrees to hire goods to D in return for periodical payments. The agreement provides for the property in the goods to pass to D on payment of a total of £7,500 and the exercise by D of an option to purchase. The sum of £7,500 includes a down-payment of £1,000. It also includes an amount which, according to the Consumer Credit (Total Charge for Credit) Regulations 1980, constitutes a total charge for credit of £1,500.

Analysis: This is a hire-purchase agreement with a deposit of £1,000 and a total price of £7,500. By section 9(3), it is taken to provide credit amounting to £7,500–(£1,500+£1,000), which equals £5,000. Under section 8(2), the agreement is therefore a consumer credit agreement, and under section 9(3) it is a credit agreement for fixed-sum credit (Example 10).

5–83   6. *Facts:* H agrees with J to open a loan account in J's name on which the debit balance is not to exceed £7,000. Interest is to be payable in advance on this sum, with provision for yearly adjustments. H is entitled to debit the account with interest, a "setting-up" charge, and other charges. Before J has an opportunity to draw on the account it is initially debited with £2,250 for advance interest and other charges.

Analysis: This is a running-account credit agreement with a credit limit of £7,000. By section 9(4), however, the initial debit of £2,250 is not to be treated as credit even though time is allowed for its payment. Although the credit limit of £7,000 exceeds the amount (£5,000[2]) specified in section 8(2) as the maximum for a consumer credit agreement, the agreement is caught by section 10(3)(*b*)(i), because at the beginning J can effectively draw as credit no more than £4,750. The agreement is therefore a consumer credit agreement (Example 19).

(ii) *"Restricted-Use Credit" and "Unrestricted-Use Credit"*

5–84   Easily recognisable instances to have in mind here are—for restricted-use credit, hire-purchase, credit sale and conditional sale agreements and

---

[2] For proposed increase in this monetary limit, see 5–09, above.

shop budget accounts, and for unrestricted-use credit, overdraft facilities, cheque cards and loans of money the use of which is at the free disposal of the borrower.

With this pair of terms again only the first is specifically defined, and the second—"unrestricted-use credit"—is then in effect declared to be the opposite of "restricted-use credit."

A "restricted-use credit agreement" is defined as "a regulated consumer credit agreement—

(a) to finance a transaction between the debtor and the creditor, whether forming part of that agreement or not, or

(b) to finance a transaction between the debtor and a person (the 'supplier') other than the creditor, or

(c) to refinance any existing indebtedness of the debtor's, whether to the creditor or another person" (s. 11(1)).

An "unrestricted-use credit agreement" is defined as "a regulated consumer credit agreement not falling within section 11(1)" (s. 11(2)).

An agreement is not considered as a "restricted-use credit agreement" if the credit is in fact provided in such a way as to leave the debtor free to use it as he chooses (even though certain uses would be contrary to agreement) (s. 11(3)).

The following are illustrative examples based on the Examples in Schedule 2:

1. *Facts:* The N Bank agrees to lend O £2,000 to buy a car from P. To make sure the loan is used as intended, the N Bank stipulates that the money must be paid by it direct to P.

Analysis: The agreement is a consumer credit agreement because of section 8(2). Since it falls within section 11(1)(b), it is a restricted-use credit agreement, P being the supplier. If the N bank had not stipulated for direct payment to the supplier, section 11(3) would have operated and made the agreement into one for unrestricted-use credit (Example 12).

2. *Facts:* Q, a debt-adjuster, agrees to pay off debts owed by R to various moneylenders. For this purpose the agreement provides for the making of a loan by Q to R in return for R's agreeing to repay the loan by instalments with interest. The loan money is not paid over to R but retained by Q and used to pay off the moneylenders.

Analysis: This is an agreement to refinance existing indebtedness of the debtor's, and if the loan by Q does not exceed £5,000 is a restricted-use credit agreement falling within section 11(1)(c) (Example 13).

3. *Facts:* The P Bank decides to issue cheque cards to its customers under a scheme whereby the Bank undertakes to honour cheques of up to £50 in every case where the payee has taken the cheque in reliance on the cheque card, whether the customer has funds in his account or not. The Bank issues a cheque card to Q, who uses it to pay by cheque for goods costing £20 bought by Q from R, a major retailer. At the time, Q has £500 in his account at the P Bank.

Analysis: The agreement under which the cheque card is issued to Q is a consumer credit agreement even though at all times Q has more than £30 in his account. This is because Q is free to draw out his whole balance and then use the cheque card, in which case the Bank has bound itself to honour the cheque. In other words the cheque card agreement provides Q with credit, whether he avails himself of it or not. It is an unrestricted-use credit agreement (Example 21).

Example 21 has been criticised by A.P. Dobson in an article "The Cheque Card as a Consumer Credit Agreement" [1977] J.B.L. 126. He submits that the giving of a cheque card does not of itself amount to an *agreement* that the customer may overdraw, yet an agreement is required by the definition in section 8(1) and that requirement is satisfied in all the other statutory examples in Schedule 2. He suggests that the Secretary of State should exercise his power under section 188(4) to amend this Example.

(iii) *"Debtor-Creditor-Supplier Agreements" and "Debtor-Creditor Agreements"*

5–93   The distinction between the two members of this third pair of terms may be more easily grasped if the terms used by the Crowther Committee are substituted, namely "connected loans" and "unconnected loans," a con-nected loan being one made by the supplier himself or by some other person with whom he has some arrangement, and an unconnected loan being one made by an independent lender who is not himself involved in the transaction for which the debtor needs the money. Where there is a connected loan, the lender and the seller are the same person or are engaged in a joint venture to their mutual advantage, and the two transactions of loan and sale cannot be treated in isolation as they may be in the case of an unconnected loan.

5–94   The term used in the Act for a connected loan—"debtor-creditor-supplier agreement"—suggests at first sight that three parties are involved. It is clear from the last paragraph that this is not necessarily so: the creditor and the supplier may very well be the same person; they will at least have some arrangements with one another.

5–95   A "debtor-creditor-supplier agreement" is defined as "a regulated consumer credit agreement being—

(*a*) a restricted-use credit agreement which falls within section 11(1)(*a*), or

(*b*) a restricted-use credit agreement which falls within section 11(1)(*b*) and is made by the creditor under pre-existing arrangements, or in contemplation of future arrangements, between himself and the supplier, or

(*c*) an unrestricted-use credit agreement which is made by the creditor under pre-existing arrangements between himself and a person (the 'supplier') other than the debtor in the knowledge that the credit is to be used to finance a transaction between the debtor and the supplier" (s. 12).

5–96   Section 13 has a definition of similar length for a "debtor-creditor agreement," the effect of which simply is that a debtor-creditor agree-ment is any regulated consumer credit agreement other than a debtor-creditor-supplier agreement. (Typical instances of debtor-creditor agree-ments are normal bank loans and overdrafts, loans by moneylenders, and personal loans where there is no actual or contemplated arrangement between lender and supplier.)

It is appropriate, therefore, to concentrate on the definition of "debtor-creditor-supplier agreement" set out in section 12.

The use of the word "supplier" is liable to cause confusion, because it is defined in two different ways: " 'supplier' has the meaning given by section 11(1)(b) or 12(c) . . . or, in relation to an agreement falling within section 11(1)(a), means the creditor . . ." (s. 189(1)). Looking back to section 11(1)(b) and 12(c), one finds the word "supplier" appearing in brackets: in section 11(1)(b) "supplier" denotes a person other than the creditor; in section 12(c) "supplier" denotes a person other than the debtor. The result is that in relation to both these provisions three parties are involved—the creditor, the debtor and the supplier; the situation is truly a tripartite one. Looking now to section 11(1)(a), one finds that that provision relates to a restricted-use credit agreement financing a transaction between the debtor and the creditor (whether forming part of that agreement or not); here are only two parties—the debtor and the creditor—and by definition in this situation the "supplier" is the creditor. This emphasises the point already mentioned that in a "debtor-creditor-supplier agreement" there are not necessarily three parties: there may be only two—the debtor and the creditor (also called the "supplier").

It is now possible to proceed to a clearer understanding of the definition of "debtor-creditor-supplier agreement" in section 12. The definition has three limbs.

Limb (a) is "a restricted-use credit agreement which falls within section 11(1)(a)." This covers those agreements in which creditor and supplier are the same person: simple examples are the sale of goods or the supply of services by creditor to debtor on credit. Limb (a) also covers the common form of hire-purchase, in which the finance house buys the goods from a dealer and then lets them on hire-purchase to the customer, because the finance house (not the dealer) is the "supplier" in this situation, and so creditor and supplier are the same person.

Limb (b) is "a restricted-use credit agreement which falls within section 11(1)(b) and is made by the creditor under pre-existing arrangements, or in contemplation of future arrangements, between himself and the supplier." A three-party agreement is involved here, the "supplier" being, as specially defined in section 11(1)(b), a person other than the creditor. The credit will necessarily take the form of a loan, e.g. a loan paid by a finance house (the creditor) to a motor-dealer (the supplier) at the request of the person buying a car (the debtor). The agreement must have been made "under pre-existing arrangements" or "in contemplation of future arrangements" between the creditor and the supplier. Guidance on the interpretation of these two phrases is given in section 187 of the Act; e.g. an agreement is to be treated as entered into under pre-existing arrangements if it is entered into "in accordance with, or in furtherance of, arrangements previously made" between creditor and supplier or their associates (s. 187(1)), and where the creditor is an associate of the supplier's, the agreement is treated, unless the contrary is proved, as entered into under pre-existing arrangements between creditor and supplier (s. 187(5)).

Limb (c) is "an unrestricted-use credit agreement which is made by the creditor under pre-existing arrangements between himself and a person (the 'supplier') other than the debtor in the knowledge that the credit is to be used to finance a transaction between the debtor and the supplier." As in limb (*b*), there are three parties. An instance would be where, as the result of an arrangement previously made between a finance house and a dealer, a customer of the dealer's is directed to the finance house by the dealer and obtains a loan which theoretically is at his free disposal but which, to the knowledge of the finance house, is to be used by him to purchase goods from the dealer. The arrangement must be a pre-existing one: mere "contemplation of future arrangements" is not sufficient to bring an *unrestricted-use* credit agreement within the definition of debtor-creditor-supplier agreement: this is the point of distinction between limb (*b*) and limb (*c*).

5–103   Finally, Example 8 in Schedule 2 may be referred to as illustrating the key position held by the phrase "pre-existing arrangements" in the distinction between "debtor-creditor-supplier agreements" and "debtor-creditor agreements":

Facts: U, a moneylender, lends £500 to V knowing that V intends to use it to buy office equipment from W. W introduced V to U, it being his practice to introduce customers needing finance to him. Sometimes U gives W a commission for this and sometimes not. U pays £500 direct to V.

Analysis: At first sight this falls under section 11(1)(*b*) (a restricted-use credit agreement to finance a transaction between the debtor (V) and a supplier (W, a person other than the creditor)). However, section 11(3) prevents this from being so by providing that if the credit is in fact provided in such a way as to leave the debtor free to use it as he chooses, the agreement will not be a restricted-use agreement. Here U pays the £500 direct to V, and so V would be free to use the credit as he chose. The agreement is therefore an unrestricted-use credit agreement and so, if it is to be a debtor-creditor-supplier agreement, it must satisfy section 12(*c*), *i.e.* it must have been made by the creditor (U) under pre-existing arrangements between himself and the supplier (W) in the knowledge that the credit was to be used to finance the transactions between V and W. The question then arises under section 187(1) of whether the agreement can be taken to have been entered into "in accordance with, or in furtherance of arrangements previously made" between U and W. If it cannot be so treated it will be a debtor-creditor agreement.

(c) "Credit-Token Agreement"

5–104   A "credit-token agreement" is "a regulated agreement for the provision of credit in connection with the use of a credit-token" (s. 14(2)). The term "credit-token" was invented for the purposes of the Act, and is defined in section 14(1). Some examples help to make the definition more readily understood. Examples of credit-tokens are: a credit card issued by a shop authorising the holder to purchase goods from the shop and have his account debited with the price on credit terms; a bank credit card enabling the holder to draw cash from a bank or to buy goods from a third party such as a shop having an arrangement with the bank to accept the card; and a card enabling the holder to draw cash from a machine.

Section 14(1) provides that a credit-token is "a card, check, voucher, coupon, stamp, form, booklet or other document or thing given to an individual by a person carrying on a consumer credit business, who undertakes—

(*a*) that on the production of it (whether or not some other action is also required) he will supply cash, goods and services (or any of them) on credit, or

(*b*) that where, on the production of it to a third party (whether or not any other action is also required), the third party supplies cash, goods and services (or any of them), he will pay the third party for them (whether or not deducting any discount or commission), in return for payment to him by the individual."

For the purposes of that definition, use of an object to operate a machine provided by the person giving the object or a third party is to be treated as the production of the object to him (s. 14(4)). Thus a bank card issued by a bank to enable a customer to obtain cash from an automatic teller is a credit-token if (but only if) the bank has agreed to grant overdraft facilities to the customer.

The definition of "credit-token" was considered by the court in *Elliott* v. *Director General of Fair Trading* [1980] 1 W.L.R. 977 (D.C.):

E. had been convicted of contravening section 51 of the Act which provides that it is an offence to give a person a credit-token if he has not asked for it.

The document which E. had sent to selected members of the public had the appearance of a plastic card like a bank credit card. On its face it had the words "The E. Account" and a series of computer figures, and on the reverse there was a box marked "Signature," along with the statements: "1. This credit card is valid for immediate use. 2. The sole requirement is your signature and means of identification. 3. Credit is immediately available if you have a bank account." In fact these statements were untrue since the production of the card did not entitle the customer to a supply of goods on credit but only to apply for a credit card when he had signed an agreement.

The argument for E. was that the word "undertakes" in the definition was not satisfied in this case because other matters had to be carried out before credit could be obtained.

The court, however, held that the word "undertakes" did not mean that a contractual agreement had to exist; by the wording on the card E. did "undertake" that, on the production of the card, cash or goods would be supplied; the fact that none of the statements was true did not prevent the card from being what it purported to be—a credit-token. In any event the words "whether or not some other action is also required" in section 14(1) brought the card within the definition.

E.'s appeal against conviction therefore failed.

It should be noted that a cheque card is *not* a credit-token. A cheque card is an undertaking by a bank to suppliers generally to whom the card is produced that it will honour cheques drawn by its customer up to the limit stated on the card; the bank, in paying the supplier, is not paying for the goods, but is honouring its guarantee of payment of the cheque.

(d) "Small Agreement"

5–109 It is not a principle of the Act that small agreements should be exempt. The principle is that the provisions of the Act apply to *all* regulated agreements, however small. There are, however, certain provisions of the Act which do not apply to small agreements; in particular, it was felt that it would be burdensome for a creditor to be required to comply with the documentation and cancellation provisions where only a small transaction was involved, so certain categories of small agreement are made exempt from the provisions of Part V of the Act ("Entry into Credit or Hire Agreements") other than the disclosure provisions (s. 74(2)).

5–110   Obviously the Act had to include a precise definition of "small agreement." By section 17(1) a "small agreement" is:

"(*a*) a regulated consumer credit agreement for credit not exceeding £30,[2] other than a hire-purchase or conditional sale agreement; or

(*b*) a regulated consumer hire agreement which does not require the hirer to make payments exceeding £30,[2]

being an agreement which is either unsecured or secured by a guarantee or indemnity only (whether or not the guarantee or indemnity is itself secured)."

5–111   This definition is supported by anti-avoidance provisions to prevent some of the provisions of the Act from being avoided by the splitting up of what is really not a small agreement into two or more small agreements, whether made between the same parties or between associates of these parties (s. 17(3) and (4)).

5–112   The figure £30[2] may be altered by statutory instrument (s. 181).

(e) "Multiple Agreement"

5–113 There are various types of agreement which fall into more than one category; the cause of this may be *either* that the agreement is made up of different parts which belong to different categories *or* that the agreement, though indivisible, includes terms which place it in two or more categories.

"Multiple agreement" is defined as an agreement whose "terms are such as:

(*a*) to place a part of it within one category of agreement mentioned in this Act, and another part of it within a different category of agreement so mentioned, or within a category of agreement not so mentioned, or

(*b*) to place it, or a part of it, within two or more categories of agreement so mentioned" (s. 18(1)).

5–114   As an instance of an agreement falling within (*a*) one may think of an agreement part of which is for fixed-sum credit and another part of which is for running-account credit, or an agreement part of which is a consumer credit agreement and part of which is concerned with the provision of credit to a company (a category of agreement not mentioned in, and so not within the scope of, the Act).

5–115   As an instance of an agreement falling within (*b*) one may think of a credit-card agreement in which the credit card may be used to obtain cash (a debtor-creditor agreement for unrestricted-use credit) or to obtain goods (a debtor-creditor-supplier agreement for restricted-use credit).

---

[2] For proposed increase in this monetary limit, see 5–09, above.

The Act has two separate provisions for the two different types of multiple agreement.

For multiple agreements within (*a*) the provision is that each part must be treated as a separate agreement (s. 18(2)). As a result of this provision it may happen that a multiple agreement providing credit of more than £5,000[2] will be brought within the scope of the Act because it will require to be treated as two or more separate agreements, each below the £5,000[2] ceiling.

For multiple agreements within (*b*) the provision is that the agreement must be treated as an agreement in each of the categories in question (s. 18(3)).

The following is an example of the (*a*) type of multiple agreement:

Facts: F has a current account with the G Bank. Though usually in credit, the account has recently been allowed by the G Bank to become overdrawn.

Analysis: Part of the agreement, *i.e.* the part not dealing with the overdraft, falls within a category of agreement not mentioned in the Act. It is to be treated as a separate agreement from the part of the agreement relating to the overdraft—which is a debtor-creditor agreement for unrestricted-use running-account credit (Schedule 2, Example 18).

The following is an example of the (*b*) type of multiple agreement:

Facts: Under an unsecured agreement, A (Credit), an associate of the A Bank, issues to B (an individual) a credit card for use in obtaining cash on credit from A (Credit), to be paid by branches of the A Bank, or goods from suppliers who have agreed to honour credit cards issued by A (Credit). The credit limit is £30.

Analysis: This is a credit-token agreement. It is a regulated consumer credit agreement for running-account credit. Since the credit limit does not exceed £30[2], the agreement is a small agreement. So far as the agreement relates to goods it is a debtor-creditor-supplier agreement providing restricted-use credit, and in so far as it relates to cash it is a debtor-creditor agreement providing unrestricted-use credit. Since the whole agreement falls within several of the categories of agreement mentioned in the Act, it is to be treated as an agreement in each of those categories (Schedule 2, Example 16).

(f) "Linked Transaction"

The Act recognises that where a debtor has entered into a regulated agreement there are quite likely to be other transactions linked to that regulated agreement, and that such linked transactions also should be to some extent governed by statutory provisions for the better protection of the weaker party. The definition of "linked transaction" is such as to enable the Act to cast its net far and wide. However, the definition is long and complex, and what follows here is no more than an introduction to the definition.

Preliminary points about the definition, which is in section 19, are:

---

[2] For proposed increase in this monetary limit, see 5–09, above.

(i) The transaction need not be one entered into by the debtor or hirer himself: it may be entered into by a "relative" of his, and "relative" has a wide definition: it means an "associate" (s. 189(1)).

(ii) The other party to the transaction need not be the creditor: all that is necessary is that the other party should be a person other than the first party.

(iii) A transaction for the provision of security is *not* a "linked transaction."

(iv) The regulated agreement to which the "linked transaction" is connected is referred to as the "principal agreement."

5–123   The definition embraces three main categories: a transaction is a "linked transaction" if:

(*a*) the transaction is entered into in compliance with a term of the principal agreement; or

(*b*) the principal agreement is a debtor-creditor-supplier agreement and the transaction is financed by the principal agreement; or

(*c*) the creditor or owner (or some other person associated with or representing him) initiated the transaction by suggesting it to the debtor or hirer or his relative, and the latter party enters into the transaction for a purpose connected with the principal agreement (*e.g.* to induce the creditor or owner to enter into the principal agreement).

5–124   Instances of each of (*a*), (*b*) and (*c*) will help to clarify this skeleton of the definition.

(*a*): The regulated agreement may include a term requiring the debtor or hirer to maintain or insure the goods; the contract for maintenance or of insurance will then be a "linked transaction" because it is entered into "in compliance with" a term in the principal agreement.

(*b*): The regulated agreement may be a loan to purchase goods made by a finance house under pre-existing arrangements with the supplier; the contract for the purchase of the goods will be a "linked transaction."

(*c*): The finance house may have suggested to the debtor that he should take out a life insurance policy. If the debtor then does so (either to induce the finance house to enter into the regulated agreement or because he wishes to cover his repayments in the event of his death), the contract of life insurance will be a "linked transaction."

5–125   Finally, Example 11 in Schedule 2 may be referred to:

Facts: X (an individual) borrows £500 from Y (Finance). As a condition of the granting of the loan X is required—

(*a*) to grant a standard security on his house in favour of Y (Finance), and

(*b*) to take out a policy of insurance on his life with Y (Insurances), an associate of Y (Finance).

It is a term of the loan agreement that the policy should be assigned in security to Y (Finance).

Analysis: The standard security on X's house does not count as a "linked transaction" because it is a transaction for the provision of security. The taking out of the insurance policy is a linked transaction because it is taken out in compliance with a term in the principal agreement. The assignation of the policy in security is again a security transaction expressly excluded by the definition. The only "linked transaction" is therefore the taking out of the insurance policy. If X had not been *required* by the loan agreement to take out the policy, but it had been done at the suggestion of Y (Finance) to induce them to enter into the loan agreement, it would have been a "linked transaction."

III TRADING CONTROL

The provisions on trading control are divided into two parts:

(a) licensing of credit and hire businesses (corresponding to Part III of the Act); and

(b) seeking business (corresponding to Part IV of the Act).

(a) Licensing of Credit and Hire Businesses

The enforcement machinery of the Act centres on the licensing system operated by the Director. The provisions of Part III of the Act are in force: in particular the requirement that consumer credit businesses and consumer hire businesses must be licensed was brought into force on October 1, 1977 (Consumer Credit Act 1974 (Commencement No. 2) Order 1977 (S.I. 1977 No. 325)). The following is an outline of the statutory provisions on licensing:

Licensing Principles

The general principle is that a licence is required to carry on a consumer credit business or consumer hire business, but the following do not require a licence to do so—a local authority (*i.e.*, by section 189(1), a regional, islands or district council) and a body corporate empowered by a public general Act naming it to carry on the business (*e.g.* gas and electricity boards) (s. 21). It should be noted that what is being referred to here is an exemption from the *licensing* provisions: these bodies are required to comply with the other provisions of the Act; the only *general* exemption from the provisions of the Act is that arising from "exempt agreements" as defined in section 16 (see 5–62, above).

A licence may be either a "standard" licence, or a "group" licence (s. 22).

For a standard licence the person seeking the licence applies to the Director; the licence names the applicant and covers the activities described in the licence; the licence lasts for the "prescribed" period, which was at first three years but was extended to ten years by the Consumer Credit (Period of Standard Licence) (Amendment) Regulations 1979 (S.I. 1979 No. 796).

A group licence may be issued by the Director on an application being made to him or it may be issued by him of his own motion; it covers the persons and activities described in the licence; it lasts for such period as the Director thinks fit, which may be indefinitely. The Director may issue a group licence only if it appears to him that the public interest is better served by doing so than by requiring each person in the group concerned to apply separately for a standard licence. A group licence may exclude named persons if the Director thinks fit. Group licences so far issued include one to the Law Society of Scotland in relation to solicitors holding current practising certificates.

5–132   A licence may cover all lawful activities done in the course of the business, or it may be limited to certain types of agreement only or in any other way. A licence covers the canvassing off trade premises of debtor-creditor-supplier agreements or regulated consumer hire agreements only if the licence specifically so provides, and such a provision must not be included in a group licence (s. 23).

5–133   A standard licence authorises the licensee to carry on the business under the name or names specified in the licence, but not under any other name (s. 24), and a licence is not assignable (s. 22(2)).

5–134   To obtain a standard licence the applicant must satisfy the Director that—

(*a*) he is a fit person to engage in activities covered by the licence, and

(*b*) the name under which he applies to be licensed is not misleading or otherwise undesirable.

In deciding point (*a*) the Director must have regard to any circumstances appearing to him to be relevant, and in particular any evidence tending to show that the applicant (or any of his employees, agents or associates, past or present) (or, if the applicant is a body corporate, any controller of it) has—

(i) committed any offence involving fraud or other dishonesty, or violence,

(ii) contravened any statutory provision regulating the provision of credit to individuals or other transactions with individuals,

(iii) practised discrimination on grounds of sex, colour, race or ethnic or national origins in carrying on any business, or

(iv) engaged in business practices appearing to the Director to be deceitful or oppressive, or otherwise unfair or improper (s. 25).

These provisions give the Director a wide discretion: he is not bound by strict rules of evidence: he is entitled to base his decision on "evidence tending to show."

5–135   An English case illustrative of section 25 is *North Wales Motor Auctions Ltd.* v. *Secretary of State for Trade* [1981] C.C.L.R. 1, a decision of Sheen J. in the High Court:

In 1977 Thomas applied for a consumer credit licence on behalf of N. Ltd. and two other limited companies, of which he appeared to the Director to be the "controller."

In 1974 Thomas had been convicted of six offences of fraud on the Inland Revenue committed between 1965 and 1970. These had resulted in his being sentenced to two and a half years' imprisonment and a fine of £9,000 and ordered to pay costs of £3,000.

The Director refused the licence applied for, and N. Ltd. appealed from the Director's decision to the Secretary of State for Trade, who upheld the Director's decision.

N. Ltd. then appealed to the court on the ground that the Secretary of State was wrong in law in holding that the frauds were sufficient to justify the refusal of the licence; N. Ltd. contended that it was wrong in law and a denial of natural justice and disproportionate for further punishment to be inflicted by the refusal of the licence in the absence of evidence of improper practices in relation to consumers and customers.

Held that there was evidence on which the Director could reach the conclusion, having regard to all the circumstances which appeared to him to be relevant, that N. Ltd. was not a fit person to be granted a licence.

Sheen J. said (at p. 2): "I do not regard the refusal of a licence as being a punishment. The granting of a licence is a privilege and it is a privilege which is to be granted only to those who are thought by the Director General of Fair Trading, on proper evidence, to be fit persons."

Regulations may be made as to the conduct of a licensee's business, specifying in particular—

(*a*) the books and other records to be kept by the licensee, and

(*b*) the information to be furnished by him to persons with whom he does business or seeks to do business, and the way it is to be furnished (s. 26).[3]

Issue of Licences

Unless the Director decides to issue a licence which has been applied for, he must, before deciding the application—

(*a*) notify the applicant, giving his reasons, that he is minded to refuse the application, or to grant it in terms different from those applied for, and

(*b*) invite the applicant to submit to him representations in support of the application (s. 27).

Where the Director is minded to issue a group licence (whether on the application of any person or of his own motion), and in doing so to exclude any person from the group by name, he must, before deciding the matter,—

(*a*) give notice of that fact to the person proposed to be excluded, giving his reasons, and

(*b*) invite that person to submit representations against his exclusion (s. 28).

Renewal, Variation, Suspension and Revocation of Licences

If the licensee under a standard licence, or the original applicant for, or any licensee under, a group licence of limited duration, wishes the Director to renew the licence, he must apply to the Director for its renewal. The Director may of his own motion renew any group licence (s. 29).

Variation of a licence may be by request (s. 30) or compulsory (s. 31).

Variation by request takes place where the Director varies a standard or group licence in response to an application made to him by the licensee who originally applied for the licence. Variation by request may also take place where a person originally excluded from a group licence applies to the Director to vary the terms of the licence so as to remove the exclusion. Unless the Director decides to vary a licence in accordance with the request being made, he must, before deciding the application—

---

[3] Regulations are not expected to be made for the time being (see 5–05, above).

(*a*) notify the applicant, giving his reasons, that he is minded to refuse the application, and

(*b*) invite the applicant to submit to him representations in support of the application.

5–142 During the currency of a licence the Director may come to be of the opinion that, if the licence had expired at that time, he would have been minded to renew it on different terms. If so, he may compulsorily vary the licence during its currency, but in the case of a standard licence he must first inform the licensee and invite him to submit representations and in the case of a group licence he must first give a general notice of the proposed variations and in that general notice invite any licensee to submit representations; in the case of a group licence originally issued on application the Director must also give individual notice to the applicant and invite him to submit representations; where the variation of a group licence is for the purpose of excluding a named person, individual notice and an invitation to submit representations must likewise be given to that named person.

5–143 The procedure for suspension and revocation of a licence by the Director is similar to that for compulsory variation. Suspension may be for a specified period or may be indefinite; in the latter case the suspension may be ended by a notice given by the Director to the licensee or, if the licence is a group one, by general notice. On revoking or suspending a licence the Director may give directions authorising a licensee to carry into effect agreements made by him before the revocation or suspension (s. 32).

5–144 A licensee may apply to the Director to end a suspension (whether the suspension was for a fixed or for an indefinite period) (s. 33).

Miscellaneous

Representations to Director

5–145 A person who has been invited to submit representations to the Director in connection with the issue *etc.* of a licence has 21 days (or longer if the Director so allows) in which to submit written representations or to give notice that he wishes to make oral representations. Both types of representations must be taken into account by the Director in reaching his decision (s. 34). Further details are contained in the Consumer Credit Licensing (Representations) Order 1976 (S.I. 1976 No. 191).

The register

5–146 The Director is required to maintain a register containing particulars relating to licences and applications for licences and such other matters as he thinks fit. Members of the public are entitled on payment of specified fees to inspect the register, take copies of any entry and obtain certified copies of any entry from the Director (s. 35).

5–147 The register, which is kept in London, is arranged alphabetically under the names of the applicants for licences and existing licences. The particulars take the form of photocopies of documents (or parts of documents) which are required to be registered under the Act.

Duty to notify changes

The holder of a standard licence has a duty to notify the Director of certain changes within 21 working days after their occurrence. The changes include changes in the officers of a company or of its controller and changes in the members of a partnership. Where a change in a partnership has the result that the business ceases to be carried on under the name specified in the standard licence, the licence ceases to have effect (s. 36).

Death, bankruptcy etc. of licensee

A licence held by one individual terminates if he dies or has his estate sequestrated or becomes incapable of managing his own affairs (ss. 37 and 38).

However, the provisions of the Act on these subjects are supplemented by the Consumer Credit (Termination of Licences) Regulations 1976 (S.I. 1976 No. 1002). These Regulations list other events which terminate licences, whether held by an individual, an unincorporated body such as a partnership or a body corporate such as a company. It is to be noted that the events listed do not include the liquidation of a company; this is because the separate *persona* ("personality") of a company continues during the winding-up process and if the liquidator continues the business he does so in the company's name and not in his own; if the statutory provision were that the licence automatically terminated at the commencement of the liquidation, the liquidator would be unable to continue the business without incurring personal liability. The Regulations also provide a period of deferment (limited to 12 months, with no mention of further extension) during which a licence continues in force despite the occurrence of a terminating event; *e.g.* on a licensee's death the licence continues in force for 12 months thereafter, to the obvious convenience of his personal representatives. The effect of this provision as to deferment can be to prolong (but by not more than 12 months) the life of a licence which was about to expire.

A licence can also be voluntarily relinquished by the giving by the licensee of written notice to the Director. The period of deferment is in this case one month after receipt of the notice (Consumer Credit (Termination of Licences) (Amendment) Regulations 1981 (S.I. 1981 No. 614)).

Criminal and civil consequences of contravention of licensing provisions

The Act makes it an offence to engage in activities covered by the Act without having a licence. It is also an offence for the holder of a standard licence to carry on business under a name not specified in the licence and for a person to fail to notify changes as required by section 36 (s. 39).

In addition to these criminal consequences, there is the important civil consequence that a regulated agreement, other than a non-commercial agreement, if made when the creditor or owner was unlicensed, is enforceable against the debtor or hirer only where the Director has made an order under section 40. The effect of obtaining such an order is that the regulated agreements made by the "trader" (*i.e.* the unlicensed person) are treated as if he had been licensed. Application for such an order is made by the trader to the Director. There are the usual safeguards to ensure that the Director will act judicially: before deciding the application adversely to the applicant he must—

(*a*) notify the applicant, giving his reasons, that he is minded to refuse the application, or to grant it in terms different from those applied for, and

(*b*) invite the applicant to submit representations in support of the application.

In deciding whether or not to make an order under section 40 the Director must consider, in addition to any other relevant factors—

(*a*) how far debtors or hirers were prejudiced by the trader's conduct,

(*b*) whether or not the Director would have been likely to grant a licence to the trader for that period if it had been applied for, and

(*c*) the degree of culpability for the failure to obtain a licence.

The Director may limit the order to specified agreements or make the order conditional on the doing of specified acts by the applicant.

Appeals

5–154   A person aggrieved by a determination of the Director (*e.g.* a refusal to issue or renew a licence, an exclusion from a group licence or a refusal to make an order under section 40) may appeal to the Secretary of State (s. 41).

5–155   Details of how appeals are conducted are in the Consumer Credit Licensing (Appeals) Regulations 1976 (S.I. 1976 No. 837). Appeals may be dealt with in certain cases by the Secretary of State without a hearing. In other cases there will be a hearing before an "appointed person" or "appointed persons" drawn from a panel maintained by the Secretary of State. The recommendation made by the appointed person or persons is not binding on the Secretary of State, but is usually accepted by him.

5–156   A further appeal is available on a point of law: the aggrieved person may require the Secretary of State to state a case for the opinion of the Court of Session on any question of law (s. 42).

(b) Seeking Business

5–157   The main purpose of Part IV of the Act ("Seeking Business") is to give effect to the "truth-in-lending" principle which is at the heart of the Act: the aim is that information given to the public should fairly and in sufficient detail indicate the nature and true cost of the credit terms being offered.

5–158   Since October 6, 1980, all the provisions in this Part have been in force, the latest (sections 43 to 47 on advertising) having been brought into operation by the Consumer Credit Act 1974 (Commencement No. 6) Order 1980 (S.I. 1980 No. 50).

5–159   The controls on seeking business are imposed on three main activities:

(i) advertising (ss. 43 to 47);

(ii) canvassing *etc.* (ss. 48 to 51); and

(iii) quotations *etc.* (ss. 52 to 54).

(i) *Advertising*

Advertisements to which Part IV applies

The advertisements to which Part IV of the Act applies are defined in wide terms in section 43: Part IV applies to "any advertisement, published for the purposes of a business carried on by the advertiser, indicating that he is willing—

(*a*) to provide credit, or

(*b*) to enter into an agreement for the hiring of goods by him" (s. 43(1)).

"Advertisement" includes "every form of advertising, whether in a publication, by television or radio, by display of notices, signs, labels, showcards or goods, by distribution of samples, circulars, catalogues, price lists or other material, by exhibition of pictures, models or films, or in any other way" (s. 189(1)).

From the provision quoted from section 43(1) it is clear that Part IV applies to a wider range of transactions than "regulated agreements." There are, however, certain limitations on the provision in section 43(1): Part IV does not apply unless the advertiser carries on a consumer credit business or consumer hire business or a business in the course of which he provides credit to individuals secured on land; nor does Part IV apply to an advertisement which indicates that—

(1) (in relation to the provision of credit) the credit must exceed £5,000,[2] and that no security is required, or the security is to consist of property other than land; or

(2) (in relation to the provision of credit) the credit is available only to a body corporate; or

(3) (in relation to hiring of goods) the advertiser is not willing to enter into a consumer hire agreement (s. 43(2)-(4)).

Although the general effect of these limitations is to restrict Part IV to the consumer field, nevertheless Part IV applies more widely than other provisions of the Act.

Further, an advertiser who carries on business consisting of *unregulated* agreements governed by the law of a foreign country is subject to Part IV of the Act in relation to advertisements published in this country if the agreements would have been regulated agreements under United Kingdom law (s. 43(2)(*c*)).

The Secretary of State may by order provide that Part IV is not to apply to advertisements of a description specified in the order (s. 43(5)). This power has been exercised by the Consumer Credit (Exempt Advertisements) Order 1980 (S.I. 1980 No. 53), which excludes—

(1) certain advertisements for credit where the number of payments does not exceed a certain number or the rate of the total charge for credit does not exceed a specified rate;

(2) certain advertisements for consumer credit connected with foreign trade; and

(3) certain advertisements relating to consumer hire agreements offered by certain public bodies.

---

[2] For proposed increase in this monetary limit, see 5–09, above.

Form and content of advertisements

5–165   By section 44 the Secretary of State must make regulations as to the form and content of advertisements, and the regulations must contain provisions appropriate for ensuring that an advertisement conveys a fair and reasonably comprehensive indication of the nature of the credit or hire facilities offered by the advertiser and of their true cost to persons using them.

5–166   The regulations which have been made are the Consumer Credit (Advertisements) Regulations 1980 (S.I. 1980 No. 54). These divide advertisements into three categories—simple, intermediate and full.

5–167   Simple advertisements are those whose purpose is to keep the name of the advertiser in the public eye, *e.g.* brief messages appearing at a sponsored sporting event or printed on business cards. The Regulations limit the information which may be included in a simple advertisement to the advertiser's name and occupation. An example is:

"A. CREDITOR LTD.

MONEYLENDER."

5–168   Intermediate advertisements allow the advertiser some choice as to what is to be included. Facts which *must* always be given are the creditor's name, his address or telephone number, and an indication that his terms of business may be obtained on application to that address or number. An example is:

"A. CREDITOR LTD.

PHONE 123-4567

FOR WRITTEN DETAILS OF

CREDIT TERMS."

There are other facts which *must* be given if they apply to the credit being offered; these include any need for security or to take out a life insurance policy, and where the credit is for a fixed sum (*e.g.* hire-purchase) and is advertised as being available for the purchase of particular goods, the cash price and also the APR.[4] Further information *may* be given, *e.g.* a statement that the credit is limited to, say, £500, or is available only to persons over a specified age.

5–169   Full advertisements must contain the full range of relevant information specified in the Regulations. There are different levels of disclosure for different types of agreements. Full advertisements must always include, in addition to the information compulsorily included in intermediate advertisements, an indication that the credit is restricted to a particular class of persons (if such is the case), the extent to which credit purchasers are treated differently from persons paying cash (if such is the case), and the APR (which must be given greater prominence than any other statement relating to any other rate of charge).

5–170   The Regulations do not apply to loans made by building societies and local authorities on the security of heritable property.

Offences

5–171   It is an offence—

(1) to contravene the regulations made under section 44 (s. 167(2));

---

[4] the total cost of the credit, expressed as an annual percentage rate of charge.

(2) to advertise restricted-use credit facilities relating to goods or services unless the goods or services are available for cash (s. 45); and

(3) to publish an advertisement which conveys information which in a material respect is false or misleading (even though the advertisement may comply with the regulations) (s. 46).

This criminal liability extends to the publisher of the advertisement, to any person who, in the course of a business carried on by him, devised the advertisement and to any person who procured the publication of the advertisement (s. 47(1)). A defence open to the publisher is that he had no reason to suspect that the publication would be an offence (s. 47(2)).

(ii) *Canvassing* etc.

Canvassing off trade premises

A definition is given in section 48 of "canvassing off trade premises." The definition is based on a contrast between business premises (whether of the creditor or of the debtor) and other premises (*e.g.* the doorstep of the debtor's home).

To canvass a regulated agreement off trade premises means to solicit the consumer to enter into the agreement by making oral representations during a visit carried out by the canvasser for the purpose of making these oral representations and not carried out in response to a request made on a previous occasion, provided the place of the visit is not a place where a business is carried on (whether on a permanent or temporary basis) by—

(*a*)   the creditor or owner, or

(*b*)   a supplier, or

(*c*)   the canvasser, or the person whose employee or agent the canvasser is, or

(*d*)   the consumer (s. 48).

The representations need not be made to the consumer himself: they may be made to any person who is at the place where the unsolicited visit is carried out (*e.g.* representations made to a wife for the purpose of inducing her to persuade her husband to enter into the agreement).

It is an offence to canvass debtor-creditor agreements off trade premises. Criminal liability can be avoided only where the visit has been carried out in response to a *written* request made on a previous occasion (s. 49(1) and (2)). Current accounts of a banking character have been excluded from these provisions by a determination made by the Director General of Fair Trading in the exercise of a power conferred on him (s. 49(3)).

It is not an offence to canvass debtor-creditor-supplier agreements off trade premises. The provisions are aimed against what the Crowther Committee called "unconnected loans" (*e.g.* personal loans), not against transactions such as hire-purchase, conditional sale, credit sale and rental facilities ("connected loans").

Circulars to minors

A person commits an offence if, with a view to financial gain, he sends to a minor (a term defined in relation to Scotland as including a pupil—s. 189(1)) any document inviting him to—

(1) borrow money, or

(2) obtain goods on credit or hire, or

(3) obtain services on credit, or

(4) apply for information or advice on borrowing money or otherwise obtaining credit, or hiring goods.

It is a defence for the person charged with the offence to prove that he did not know, and had no reasonable cause to suspect, that he was a minor. Where a document is received by a minor at any school or other educational establishment for minors, the person sending it to him at that establishment knowing or suspecting it to be such an establishment is deemed to have "reasonable cause to suspect" that he is a minor (s. 50).

5–178 It is *sending* which is made an offence by this section: handing over a document to the minor in person is not covered by the provision, and an offence would be committed even where the document which had been sent never arrived.

Prohibition of unsolicited credit-tokens

5–179 It is an offence to give a person a credit-token if he has not asked for it. To avoid this criminal liability the request must have been a written request except that in the case of a small debtor-creditor-supplier agreement it may have been oral. The prohibition does not apply to the giving of a credit-token for use under a credit-token agreement already made or in renewal or replacement of a credit-token under an existing credit-token agreement (s. 51).

"Give" means "deliver or send by post to" (s. 189(1)).

(iii) *Quotations* etc.

Quotations

5–180 Section 52 authorises the making of regulations—

(1) as to the form and content of any document (a "quotation") by which a person who carries on a consumer credit business or consumer hire business, or a business in the course of which he provides credit to individuals secured on land, gives prospective customers information about the terms on which he is prepared to do business;

(2) requiring a person carrying on such a business to provide quotations to such persons and in such circumstances as are prescribed.

5–181 The section extends to *persons who carry on the types of business mentioned*: the particular agreement which is the subject-matter of the quotation need not be a regulated agreement.

5–182 The regulations which have been made are the Consumer Credit (Quotations) Regulations 1980 (S.I. 1980 No. 55). The aim is to ensure that the consumer is provided with all the relevant details of a prospective transaction.

5–183 The Regulations do not apply to loans made by building societies and local authorities on the security of heritable property.

Display of information

5–184 Section 53 enables regulations to be made requiring a person who carries on a consumer credit business or consumer hire business, or a business in the course of which he provides credit to individuals secured on land, to display prescribed information at any premises where the business is carried on and to which the public have access.[3]

Conduct of business regulations

The regulations made under section 26 as to the conduct by a licensee of his business may include provisions regulating the seeking of business by the licensee (s. 54) (5–136, above).[3]

IV AGREEMENT CONTROL

The five Parts of the Act which are concerned with the control of individual credit or hire agreements are:

(a) Part V ("Entry into Credit or Hire Agreements");
(b) Part VI ("Matters Arising During Currency of Credit or Hire Agreements");
(c) Part VII ("Default and Termination");
(d) Part VIII ("Security"); and
(e) Part IX ("Judicial Control").

Most of the provisions in these Parts of the Act are not yet in force.

(a) Entry into Credit or Hire Agreements

The provisions of Part V of the Act fall under four headings:

(i) preliminary matters;
(ii) making the agreement;
(iii) cancellation of certain agreements within cooling-off period; and
(iv) exclusion of certain agreements from Part V.

(i) Preliminary Matters

Disclosure of information

Regulations may require specified information to be disclosed in the prescribed manner to the debtor or hirer before a regulated agreement is made (s. 55).[3]

Antecedent negotiations

The phrase "antecedent negotiations" has an elaborate definition. It means any "negotiations with the debtor or hirer–

(*a*) conducted by the creditor or owner in relation to the making of any regulated agreement, or

(*b*) conducted by a credit-broker in relation to goods sold or proposed to be sold by the credit-broker before forming the subject-matter of a debtor-creditor-supplier agreement within section 12(*a*), or

(*c*) conducted by the supplier in relation to a transaction financed or proposed to be financed by a debtor-creditor-supplier agreement within section 12(*b*) or (*c*)" (s. 56(1)).

---

[3] Regulations are not expected to be made for the time being (see 5–05, above).

5–190   Typical examples of creditors in each of the three categories may assist—

(*a*): a finance company supplying goods under a hire-purchase agreement;

(*b*): a dealer selling goods to a finance house to be let out on hire-purchase to a person introduced by the dealer to the finance house;

(*c*): a supplier selling goods against a credit card, and a motor dealer selling a car for cash advanced to the buyer by a finance house to whom the buyer was introduced by the dealer.

5–191   In (*b*) and (*c*) the negotiations are deemed to be conducted by the negotiator in the capacity of agent of the creditor as well as in his actual capacity (s. 56(2)). The effect is that the creditor will be liable to the debtor for any misrepresentations made by the negotiator since these will be deemed to have been made by the negotiator as his agent.

5–192   Antecedent negotiations are taken to begin when the negotiator and the debtor or hirer first enter into communication (including communication by advertisement) (s. 56(4)). They may therefore begin before the creditor is aware of the existence of his debtor.

(ii) *Making the Agreement*

Form and content of agreements

5–193   Section 60 requires the Secretary of State to make regulations as to the form and content of documents embodying regulated agreements. The purpose of the regulations is to ensure that the debtor or hirer is made aware of—

(*a*) the rights and duties conferred or imposed on him by the agreement,

(*b*) the amount and rate of the total charge for credit (in the case of a consumer credit agreement),

(*c*) the protection and remedies available to him under the Act, and

(*d*) any other matters which, in the opinion of the Secretary of State, it is desirable for him to know about in connection with the agreement.

5–194   The Director General of Fair Trading has power to direct that an applicant need not comply with some particular requirement of the regulations if compliance would be impracticable, but the Director must be satisfied that the exemption will not prejudice the interests of debtors or hirers.

5–195   No regulations have yet been made under section 60, but an indication of the possible content is given in Appendix II to the White Paper *Reform of the Law on Consumer Credit* ((1973) Cmnd. 5427).

Proper and improper execution

5–196   By section 65 a regulated agreement which is improperly executed cannot be enforced against the debtor or hirer except on an order of the court.

5–197   A regulated agreement is not properly executed unless—

(*a*) a document in the prescribed form itself containing all the prescribed terms and conforming to the regulations to be made under section 60 is signed in the prescribed manner both by the debtor or hirer and by or on behalf of the creditor or owner, and (*b*) the document embodies all the terms of the agreement, other than implied terms, and

(*c*) the document is, when presented or sent to the debtor or hirer for signature, in such a state that all its terms are readily legible (s. 61(1)).

Sections 62 and 63 provide for copies to be supplied to the debtor or hirer. The provisions vary according to the circumstances in which the document is executed (*i.e.* signed by the parties):

(1) If the document is *presented personally* to the debtor or hirer for his signature, and, *on the occasion* when he signs it, the document becomes an executed agreement, a copy of the executed agreement must be there and then delivered to him (s. 63(1)); no further copy is required.

(2) If the document is *presented personally* to the debtor or hirer for his signature, but the creditor or owner does not immediately execute the agreement, then—

(a) a copy of the unexecuted agreement must there and then be delivered to the debtor or hirer (s. 62(1)), and

(b) a further copy of the agreement must be given to him within seven days of its execution (s. 63(2)).

(3) If the document is *sent* to the debtor or hirer for his signature, a copy of it must be sent to him at the same time (s. 62(2)). A further copy of the agreement must be given to him within seven days of its execution, except where the unexecuted agreement became an executed agreement upon the debtor or hirer signing it (which would be so where the document was already signed by the creditor or owner before being sent to the debtor or hirer) (s. 63(2)).

The copies supplied under these provisions must be accompanied by any other document referred to in them.

An exception applies to a credit-token agreement: the seven-days' time limit need not be complied with provided the copy is given before or at the time when the credit-token is given to the debtor (s. 63(4)).

A regulated agreement is not properly executed if the requirements of sections 62 and 63 are not observed (ss. 62(3) and 63(5)).

By section 64, in the case of a cancellable agreement (see (iii), below) notice must be given to the debtor or hirer of his right to cancel, how and when that right is exercisable, and the name and address of a person to whom notice of cancellation may be given. The form of notice is to be prescribed in regulations which have not yet been made.[3] A cancellable agreement is not properly executed if the statutory requirements as to notice of the cancellation right are not observed.

(iii) *Cancellation of Certain Agreements within Cooling-off Period*

The provisions under this heading had their origin in the hire-purchase legislation aimed at discouraging certain forms of doorstep selling: a "cooling-off" period was introduced in respect of hire-purchase agreements not signed at "appropriate trade premises." The provisions of the Act of 1974 are more sophisticated.

By section 67 a regulated agreement may be cancelled by the debtor or hirer if the antecedent negotiations included oral representations

---

[3] Regulations are not expected to be made for the time being (see 5–05, above).

made when in the presence of the debtor or hirer by an individual acting as, or on behalf of, the negotiator, *unless*—

(*a*) the agreement is secured on land, or is a restricted-use credit agreement to finance the purchase of land or is an agreement for a bridging loan in connection with the purchase of land, or

(*b*) the unexecuted agreement is signed by the debtor or hirer at premises at which any of the following is carrying on any business (whether on a permanent or temporary basis)—

(i) the creditor or owner;

(ii) any party to a linked transaction (other than the debtor or hirer or a relative of his);

(iii) the negotiator in any antecedent negotiations.

5–205   The length of the cooling-off period is dealt with in section 68: the debtor or hirer may serve notice of cancellation between his signing of the unexecuted agreement and the end of the fifth day following the day on which he received his second copy (if such is required) or (in other cases) the notice required to be given by him of the cancellation right under section 64.

5–206   By section 69 the notice of cancellation may be served on—

(*a*) the creditor or owner, or

(*b*) the person specified in the notice given under section 64, or

(*c*) the agent of the creditor or owner.

As regards (*c*), the section provides that the following are to be deemed to be the agent of the creditor or owner for the purpose of receiving a notice of cancellation—

(i) a credit-broker or supplier who is the negotiator in antecedent negotiations, and

(ii) any person who, in the course of a business carried on by him, acts on behalf of *the debtor or hirer* in any negotiations for the agreement.

5–207   The notice need not be expressed in any particular words: provided it indicates the intention of the debtor or hirer to withdraw from the agreement, the notice has the effect of cancelling the agreement and any linked transaction and of withdrawing any offer by the debtor or hirer, or his relative, to enter into a linked transaction.

5–208   A notice of cancellation sent by post is deemed to be served at the time of posting, even though it is not actually received.

5–209   The remaining sections under this heading are concerned with the rights and duties which arise on the cancellation of an agreement. Section 70 deals with the recovery of money paid by the debtor or hirer, section 71 with repayment of the credit (if the debtor has already received it), section 72 with return of goods already in the possession of the debtor or hirer, and section 73 with goods delivered by the debtor or hirer in part-exchange during antecedent negotiations.

(iv) *Exclusion of Certain Agreements from Part V*

5–210   Section 74 provides that Part V (except section 56 ("antecedent negotiations")) does not apply to—

(*a*) a non-commercial agreement (defined in section 189(1) as a consumer credit agreement or a consumer hire agreement not made by the creditor or owner in the course of a business carried on by him), or (*b*) a debtor-creditor agreement enabling the debtor to overdraw on a current account (*e.g.* an ordinary bank overdraft), or

(*c*) a debtor-creditor agreement to finance the making of certain prescribed payments connected with a person's death.

The exclusions in (*b*) and (*c*) apply only where the Director so decides and he must be of the opinion that the exclusion is not against the interests of debtors. An addition was made here in relation to (*b*) by the Banking Act 1979 (s. 38(1)): if the creditor is a bank the Director *must* now decide that the exclusion applies unless he considers that it would be against the public interest to do so; the underlying aim of the amendment is to allow flexibility in bank overdraft systems.

Further, none of Part V except sections 55 (disclosure of information prior to the agreement being made) and 56 ("antecedent negotiations") applies to a small debtor-creditor-supplier agreement for restricted-use credit (*e.g.* a credit-sale agreement where the amount of the credit does not exceed £30[2]).

The effect is that the agreements mentioned in section 74 are exempt from the statutory provisions relating to the form, content and execution of agreements and the cancellation of agreements.

(b) Matters Arising During Currency of Credit or Hire Agreements

Part VI has provisions relating to the following matters which may arise during the currency of a credit or hire agreement:

Liability of Creditor for Breaches by Supplier

Section 75 makes the creditor in a debtor-creditor-supplier agreement jointly and severally liable with the supplier for misrepresentation and breach of contract. A creditor who is held liable to the debtor under this provision is entitled to be indemnified by the supplier.

The section applies even though the debtor, in entering into the transaction, may have exceeded the credit limit in his agreement or may have otherwise contravened a term in the agreement.

The section does not apply to a claim—

(*a*)   under a non-commercial agreement, or

(*b*)   relating to a single item to which the supplier has attached a cash price not exceeding £30[2] or more than £10,000.[2]

Section 75 was applied in *United Dominions Trust* v. *Taylor,* 1980 S.L.T. (Sh. Ct.) 28:

U.D.T., a finance company, made a loan to T. for the purchase of a used car from Parkway Cars (the "supplier").

T., alleging that the supplier had misrepresented the condition of the car and had refused to remedy its faults, returned it to the supplier and refused to pay the monthly instalments of the loan repayment as they fell due.

U.D.T. sued T. for the balance of the loan and interest.

T. put forward the defence that as the contract of sale had been rescinded on the ground of the supplier's misrepresentation and breach of

---

[2] For proposed increase in this monetary limit, see 5–09, above.

contract, the rescission, by section 75 of the Act, affected also the contract of loan.

U.D.T.'s reply was that there were two contracts and that the grounds of rescission of the contract with the supplier (namely, misrepresentation and breach of contract) could only apply to that contract.

The sheriff principal, reversing the decision of the sheriff, held that the effect of the Act was that where two contracts were economically part of one credit transaction, the fate of each contract depended on the other, even where the parties to the contracts were different; the rescission of the contract of sale therefore operated as rescission of the credit agreement linked to it, since both contracts formed part of a debtor-creditor-supplier agreement.

Duty to Give Notice before Taking Certain Action

5–218 Section 76 deals with the situation where a regulated agreement is for a specified period and before that period has ended, the creditor or owner wishes to enforce a term of the agreement by—

(a) demanding earlier payment of any sum, or

(b) recovering possession of any goods or land, or

(c) treating any right conferred on the debtor or hirer by the agreement as terminated, restricted or deferred.

5–219 The creditor or owner must give the debtor or hirer no less than seven days' notice of his intention to take any of these steps. The form of notice is to be prescribed in regulations.

5–220 This section does not apply to a right of enforcement arising from a breach by the debtor or hirer—a situation governed by the default notice provisions in Part VII of the Act.

Duty to Give Information

5–221 Sections 77 to 80 are concerned with circumstances in which one of the parties to a regulated agreement has a duty to give information to the other. None of these provisions apply to a non-commercial agreement (*i.e.* a consumer credit agreement or a consumer hire agreement not made by the creditor or owner in the course of a business carried on by him—s. 189(1)).

5–222 (i) The creditor under a regulated agreement for *fixed-sum credit* must, on a written request from the debtor, give the debtor a copy of the executed agreement and of any other document referred to in it, together with a signed statement showing—

(1) the total sum paid under the agreement by the debtor;

(2) the amounts which have become payable under the agreement by the debtor but remain unpaid, with dates; and

(3) the amounts which are to become payable under the agreement by the debtor, with dates.

The creditor need not comply with a request made less than one month after complying with a previous request (s. 77).

5–223 (ii) The creditor under a regulated agreement for *running-account credit* is under a similar duty, but the information to be shown is necessarily different—

(1) the state of the account;

(2) the amount currently payable under the agreement by the debtor to the creditor; and

(3) the amounts (with dates) of any payments which, if the debtor does not draw further on the account, will later become payable under the agreement by the debtor to the creditor.

In addition, the creditor in a running-account credit agreement is under a duty to give the debtor, without any request being made, statements at regular intervals of not more than 12 months showing the state of the account. This latter provision does not apply to a small agreement (s. 78).

(iii) The owner under a regulated consumer *hire* agreement must, on a written request from the hirer, give the hirer a copy of the executed agreement and of any other document referred to in it, together with a signed statement showing the amounts (with dates) which have become payable under the agreement by the hirer but remain unpaid (s. 79).

(iv) Where a regulated agreement requires the debtor or hirer to keep goods to which the agreement relates in his possession or control, he must, within seven working days after receiving a written request from the creditor or owner, tell the creditor or owner where the goods are (s. 80).

Appropriation of Payments

The normal rule in contract is that where several separate debts are due, the debtor may, when making payment, appropriate the money to a particular debt, but that if he makes no appropriation, the creditor may appropriate the money as he chooses. This normal rule is modified in relation to regulated agreements by section 81.

The debtor or hirer is entitled to appropriate the payment in any way he sees fit, but if he does not do so and one or more of the agreements is a hire-purchase or conditional sale agreement, or a consumer hire agreement, or an agreement for which any security is provided, then the payment must be appropriated towards the satisfaction of the sums due under the several agreements in the proportions which those sums bear to one another.

Variation of Agreements

There may be a power in a regulated agreement enabling the creditor or owner to vary the agreement (*e.g.* to alter the rate of interest payable). In exercising such a power the creditor or owner must first give notice in the prescribed manner. This provision does not apply to a non-commercial agreement (s. 82).

The regulations which prescribe the manner of giving notice are the Consumer Credit (Notice of Variation of Agreements) Regulations 1977 (S.I. 1977 No. 328, as amended by S.I. 1979 Nos. 661 and 667).

Misuse of Credit-Tokens and other Credit Facilities

There is a general provision in section 83 that a debtor under a regulated consumer credit agreement is not to be liable to the creditor for any loss arising from use of the credit facility by another person (who is not the debtor's agent). This provision does not apply to a non-commercial agreement or to any loss arising from the misuse of cheques and other documents grouped with cheques by the Cheques Act 1957.

5–232   Section 84 modifies that general provision, but deals only with credit-tokens (*e.g.* a credit-card). The section provides that a debtor can be made liable in certain situations and within certain limits for loss to the creditor arising from misuse of a credit-token:

(i) The debtor may be made liable to any extent for the creditor's loss if the person misusing the credit-token acquired possession of it with the debtor's consent.

(ii) The debtor may be made liable to the extent of £30[2] (or the credit limit if less) if the person misusing the credit-token does so when the credit-token is not in the possession of an "authorised person" (defined as the debtor, the creditor or any person authorised by the debtor to use the credit-token).

(iii) Once oral or written notice has been received by the creditor that the credit-token has been lost or stolen or is for any other reason liable to misuse, the debtor ceases to incur any further liability.

(iv) The credit-token agreement must contain particulars of the name, address and telephone number for the giving of notice of loss *etc.*; if it does not do so, the debtor is free from liability for the creditor's loss.

Duty on Issue of New Credit-Tokens

5–233   When a credit-token (other than the first) is given by the creditor to the debtor, the creditor must give the debtor a copy of the executed agreement and of any other document referred to in it. This provision does not apply to small agreements (s. 85).

Death of Debtor or Hirer

5–234   Section 86 deals with the situation where the debtor or hirer dies before the expiry of the period for which a regulated agreement is specified to last. The section is intended to discourage the creditor or owner from taking such steps as terminating the agreement, demanding earlier payment of any sum, recovering possession or enforcing any security.

5–235   The main provisions are:

(i) If at the death the agreement is fully secured, the creditor or owner is not entitled to take any such step.

(ii) If at the death the agreement is only partly secured or is unsecured, the creditor or owner is entitled to take such a step but only on an order of the court.

5–236   The section does not prevent termination *etc.* of the agreement on death if no period for its duration was specified in the agreement, nor does it prevent the creditor from treating the right to draw on any credit as restricted or deferred (*e.g.* he may refuse to allow further withdrawals).

(c) **Default and Termination**

5–237   The provisions of Part VII of the Act fall under four headings:

(i) default notices;

---

[2] For proposed increase in this monetary limit. see 5–09. above.

(ii) further restriction of remedies for default;

(iii) early payment by debtor; and

(iv) termination of agreements.

(i) *Default Notices*

Where there is a breach by the debtor or hirer of a regulated agreement, service of a "default notice" is necessary before the creditor or owner can become entitled, by reason of the breach,—

(*a*) to terminate the agreement, or

(*b*) to demand earlier payment of any sum, or

(*c*) to recover possession of any goods or land, or

(*d*) to treat any right conferred on the debtor or hirer by the agreement as terminated, restricted or deferred, or

(*e*) to enforce any security.

This provision does not prevent the creditor from treating the right to draw upon any credit as restricted or deferred; for instance, he may refuse to allow further withdrawals, even without serving a default notice.

Regulations may provide that default notices are not to be necessary in the case of certain agreements (s. 87).

A default notice must be in a form to be prescribed by regulations and must specify—

(*a*) the nature of the alleged breach;

(*b*) if the breach is capable of remedy, what action is required to remedy it and the date before which that action is to be taken;

(*c*) if the breach is not capable of remedy, the sum (if any) required to be paid as compensation for the breach, and the date before which it is to be paid.

The date specified in (*b*) or (*c*) must not be less than seven days after the date of service of the default notice.

The notice must contain information in terms to be prescribed about the consequences of failure to comply with the notice (s. 88).

If before the specified date the debtor or hirer takes the required action (in the case of (*b*)) or pays the required compensation (in the case of (*c*)), the breach must be treated as not having occurred (s. 89).

(ii) *Further Restriction of Remedies for Default*

Retaking of protected goods

Sections 90 and 91 enact a restriction which is additional to the need for a default notice. The sections are derived from similar provisions in the hire-purchase legislation, and relate to "protected goods" in hire-purchase and conditional sale agreements.

The restriction is that at any time when—

(*a*) the debtor is in breach of a regulated hire-purchase or a regulated conditional sale agreement relating to goods, and

(*b*) the debtor has paid to the creditor one-third or more of the total price of the goods, and

(*c*) the property in (*i.e.* ownership of) the goods remains in the creditor,

the creditor is not entitled to recover possession of the goods from the debtor except on an order of the court.

5–245   The provision does not apply where the debtor voluntarily terminates the agreement (s. 90).

5–246   If goods are recovered by the creditor in contravention of section 90, then—

    (*a*) the regulated agreement terminates, and

    (*b*) the debtor is released from all liability under the agreement and is entitled to recover from the creditor all sums paid by the debtor under the agreement (s. 91).

Recovery of possession of goods or land

5–247   Section 92 prohibits the creditor or owner in a regulated hire-purchase, conditional sale or consumer hire agreement relating to goods from entering, without an order of the court, any premises to take possession of the goods, and similarly prohibits the creditor in a regulated conditional sale agreement relating to land from recovering possession of the land without an order of the court when the debtor is in breach of the agreement.

Interest not to be increased on default

5–248   By section 93, where the debtor under a regulated consumer credit agreement is in breach of the agreement he cannot be required to pay interest on the outstanding sums at a rate which exceeds the rate of interest provided for in the agreement.

(iii) *Early Payment by Debtor*

5–249   The debtor under a regulated consumer credit agreement is entitled at any time, by notice to the creditor and the payment to the creditor of all amounts payable by the debtor to him under the agreement (less any rebate), to discharge the debtor's indebtedness under the agreement (s. 94).

5–250   One of the important recommendations of the Crowther Committee was that the debtor should be entitled to a rebate of charges where there was an early settlement, and so section 95 enables regulations to be made providing for such a rebate. The regulations may extend to other cases of early settlement besides the case where the debtor exercises his right under section 94, above: for instance, they may cover the case where the debtor's indebtedness becomes payable before the time fixed by the agreement because the debtor is in breach of the agreement. Calculation of rebates is to be as prescribed by the regulations.

5–251   The early settlement of a regulated consumer credit agreement automatically discharges the liability of the debtor, and any "relative" (associate) of his, under a linked transaction, except as regards a debt which has already become payable. This provision does not apply to a linked transaction which is itself an agreement providing the debtor or his relative with credit, and regulations may make further exceptions for linked transactions of a prescribed description (s. 96).

5–252   By section 97 the creditor under a regulated consumer credit agreement must, on the written request of the debtor, give the debtor a statement, in a form to be prescribed by regulations, indicating the amount required to discharge the debtor's indebtedness under the agreement.

(iv) *Termination of Agreements*

Termination on the debtor's or hirer's default was dealt with in (i), above. The provisions under the present heading relate to other modes of termination.

Notice of termination in non-default cases

Where there is no breach of the agreement by the debtor or hirer, the creditor or owner is not entitled to terminate a regulated agreement without giving the debtor or hirer not less than seven days' notice of the termination, but this applies only where a period for the duration of the agreement is specified in the agreement, and it does not prevent a creditor from treating the right to obtain *further* credit as restricted or deferred. Regulations are to prescribe the form of the notice and they may also exempt certain agreements from this requirement for notice (s. 98).

Termination of hire-purchase and conditional sale agreements

By section 99, at any time before the final payment by the debtor under a regulated hire-purchase or regulated conditional sale agreement falls due, the debtor is entitled to terminate the agreement by giving notice to any person entitled or authorised to receive the sums payable under the agreement. This does not affect any liability which has already accrued, and it does not apply to a conditional sale agreement relating to land after the title to the land has passed to the debtor or to a conditional sale agreement relating to goods which have become vested in the debtor and which the debtor has then transferred to a third party.

On termination under section 99, the debtor is liable (unless the agreement provides for a smaller payment, or does not provide for any payment) to pay to the creditor the amount (if any) by which one-half of the total price exceeds the total of sums already paid and sums due immediately before the termination. If the court is satisfied that the loss sustained by the creditor as a result of the termination is in fact less than that amount, then the court may order that only the amount of the loss is to be paid. If the debtor has failed to take reasonable care of the goods or land, the amount payable is increased so as to recompense the creditor for the debtor's failure (s. 100).

Termination of hire agreement

By section 101 the hirer under a regulated consumer hire agreement is entitled to terminate the agreement by giving notice to any person entitled or authorised to receive the sums payable under the agreement. This does not affect any liability which has already accrued.

There are two provisions as to the length of notice:

(1) The notice must not expire earlier than 18 months after the making of the agreement.

(2) The minimum period of notice is three months except where the agreement itself specifies a shorter period or the agreement provides for

the making of payments by the hirer to the owner at intervals which are shorter than three months (in which cases the shorter period is treated as the minimum period of notice).

This right to terminate a hire agreement after only 18 months was likely to cause undue difficulty in equipment leases where the period of hire was usually envisaged by the equipment leasing company as being for a four or five year term. There are therefore several exceptions in section 101 (*e.g.* the section does not apply to agreements in which the payments exceed £300[2] in any year), and in addition the Director General of Fair Trading may grant an exemption to a particular applicant if he thinks that would be in the interest of hirers.

Termination statements

5–259   Section 103 gives the debtor or hirer under a regulated agreement the right to obtain, on request, from the creditor or owner a termination statement to the effect that the indebtedness is discharged and that the agreement is at an end. If it were not for this statutory provision a debtor or hirer might have difficulty in obtaining from the creditor or owner written evidence of termination. The provision does not apply to non-commercial agreements.

Landlord's hypothec

5–260   In a hire-purchase or conditional sale agreement goods which have not become vested in (*i.e.* have not yet come into the ownership of) the debtor are not to be treated as subject to the landlord's hypothec (see 8–44, below) during the following periods:

(1) during the period between the service of a default notice and the date on which the notice is complied with (or, if the notice is not complied with, the date on which it expires); and

(2) (in the case of an agreement which can be enforced only on an order of the court) during the period between the commencement and termination of an action by the creditor to enforce the agreement (s. 104).

(d) Security

5–261   The provisions on security comprise Part VIII of the Act.

The term "security" is widely defined: it means "a mortgage, charge, pledge, bond, debenture, indemnity, guarantee, bill, note or other right provided by the debtor or hirer, or at his request (express or implied), to secure the carrying out of the obligations of the debtor or hirer under the agreement" (s. 189(1)).

5–262   The person by whom any security is provided is referred to in the Act as the "surety" (s. 189(1)).

5–263   The provisions in Part VIII are grouped under four headings:

(i)   general;
(ii) pledges;
(iii) negotiable instruments; and
(iv) heritable securities.

---

[2] For proposed increase in this monetary limit, see 5–09, above.

(i) *General*

Form and content of securities

The security provided must be expressed in writing. The document is referred to as a "security instrument," and must comply in form and content with regulations which are to be made. A copy of the security instrument and a copy of the regulated agreement, and also of any other document referred to in the latter, must be given to the surety. If these provisions are not complied with, the security can be enforced against the surety on an order of the court only (s. 105). If the court dismissed an application, the security would be an "ineffective security," to be treated as never having had effect, and any property lodged with the creditor or owner solely for the purposes of the security would require to be returned immediately, the creditor or owner would require to have entries in any register removed or cancelled, and any amount received by the creditor or owner on a sale of the security would require to be repaid to the surety (s. 106).

Duty to give information to surety

Sections 107, 108 and 109 impose on the creditor or owner a duty to give certain information to the surety under a fixed-sum credit agreement, a running-account credit agreement and a consumer hire agreement, respectively. For instance, in the case of a fixed-sum credit agreement the information to be supplied on the surety's written request is:

(1) a copy of the executed agreement and of any other document referred to in it;

(2) a copy of the security instrument; and

(3) a signed statement showing the total sum paid by the debtor, the amounts payable by him and remaining unpaid (with dates), and the amounts to become payable (with dates).

A request for information need not be complied with if made less than a month after compliance with a previous request. None of the provisions apply to non-commercial agreements.

By section 111, when a default notice or a notice of termination is served on a debtor or hirer, a copy of the notice must be served by the creditor or owner on the surety; otherwise the security can be enforced against the surety on an order of the court only.

Duty to give information to debtor or hirer

Section 110 places the creditor or owner under the duty, on the written request of the debtor or hirer, to give the debtor or hirer a copy of a security instrument. A request made less than one month after compliance with a previous request need not be complied with, and the section does not apply to non-commercial agreements.

Realisation of securities

Regulations may provide for any matters relating to the sale or other realisation, by the creditor or owner, of property provided by way of security. The regulations will not extend to non-commercial agreements, and the provision is subject to section 121 which has specific provisions as to the realisation of a pawn (s. 112).[3]

Act not to be evaded by use of security

5–269   Section 113 contains a number of provisions designed to ensure that the protection given by the Act is not evaded by the use of security. The general provision of the section is that where a security is provided in relation to an actual or prospective regulated agreement, the security is not to be enforced so as to benefit the creditor or owner, directly or indirectly, to a greater extent than would be the case if the security were not provided. Therefore, for example, where a regulated agreement can be enforced only on an order of the court or of the Director, any security can be enforced where such an order has been made, but not otherwise.

(ii) *Pledges*

5–270   Sections 114 to 122 are to replace the Pawnbrokers Acts 1872 and 1960. They do not apply to non-commercial agreements (s. 114(3)).

5–271   "Pawn" is defined as "any article subject to a pledge" (s. 189(1)). The person who pledges the article is referred to as the "pawnor" and the person who receives it is referred to as the "pawnee."

Pawn-receipts

5–272   The pawnee must at the time when he takes the article in pawn under a regulated agreement give the pawnor a "pawn-receipt" in a form to be prescribed.

5–273   A person who takes any article in pawn from an individual whom he knows to be, or who appears to be and is, under the age of majority commits an offence (s. 114).

Redemption period

5–274   A pawn is redeemable at any time within six months after it was taken, but, subject to that limitation, the redemption period is the period fixed by the parties for the duration of the credit secured by the pledge or such longer period as the parties may agree.

5–275   If the pawn is not redeemed by the end of the redemption period, it still remains redeemable until it is realised by a sale or (in the case of credit not exceeding £15) until the ownership passes automatically to the pawnee.

5–276   No special charge can be made for redemption of a pawn after the end of the redemption period, and charges for the safe keeping of the pawn must not be at a higher rate after the end of the redemption period than before (s. 116).

Redemption of pawn

5–277   On surrender of the pawn-receipt, and payment of the amount owing, the pawnee must (so long as the pawn is redeemable) deliver the pawn to the bearer of the pawn-receipt unless the pawnee knows or has reasonable cause to suspect that the bearer of the pawn-receipt is neither the

---

[3] Regulations are not expected to be made for the time being (see 5–05, above).

owner of the pawn nor authorised by the owner to redeem it. A pawnee who acts in accordance with that provision is not liable in delict to any person for delivering the pawn or refusing to deliver it (s. 117).

On the loss of a pawn-receipt the person entitled to redeem the pawn may do so by tendering to the pawnee a prescribed form of statutory declaration or (in the case of credit not exceeding £15) a prescribed form of written statement (s. 118).

If the pawnee without reasonable cause refuses to allow the pawn to be redeemed, he commits an offence (s. 119).

If at the end of the redemption period the pawn has not been redeemed, then—

(1) if the redemption period is six months and the credit does not exceed £15,[5] the property in (*i.e.* ownership of) the pawn passes to the pawnee; or

(2) in any other case, the pawn becomes realisable by the pawnee (s. 120).

Realisation of pawn

Details of the procedure for realisation of a pawn are to be prescribed by regulations. The pawnor must give the pawnee notice prior to selling and information as to proceeds and expenses after the sale has taken place. The result of the sale may be to discharge the debt (in which case any surplus must be paid by the pawnee to the pawnor) or merely to diminish its amount.

If the pawnor alleges that the true market value has not been obtained for the pawn, it is for the pawnee to prove that he and any agents employed by him in the sale used reasonable care to ensure that the true market value was obtained, and similarly if the pawnor alleges that the expenses of the sale were unreasonably high, it is for the pawnee to prove that they were reasonable (s. 121).

Order to deliver pawn

Where a pawn is either an article which has been stolen or an article which has been obtained by fraud, and a person is convicted of the theft or fraud, the court by which the person is convicted may order delivery of the pawn to the owner or other person entitled to it, and may make such an order subject to such conditions as to payment of the debt secured by the pawn as it thinks fit (s. 122).

(iii) *Negotiable Instruments*

Restrictions are placed by the Act on the taking and negotiation of negotiable instruments in connection with consumer credit and consumer hire transactions. The restrictions do not apply to non-commercial agreements. The provisions are aimed at situations where a consumer wishing, for instance, to have central heating installed in his home would give the supplier a bill of exchange or a promissory note which the consumer would be required to pay at a future date to a holder in due course (often a

---

[5] On this monetary limit, see 5–09, above.

finance house to which the supplier negotiated the instrument), even though the installation was defective.

5–285 Section 123 has three leading provisions designed to protect the consumer from such practices:

(1) A creditor or owner must not take a negotiable instrument, other than a bank note or cheque, in discharge of any sum payable—

(a) by the debtor or hirer under a regulated agreement, or

(b) by any person as surety in relation to the agreement.

(2) The creditor or owner who has taken a cheque as payment must not negotiate the cheque except to a bank; this prevents any person other than a bank from becoming a holder in due course.

(3) The creditor or owner must not take any negotiable instrument as security.

5–286 The Secretary of State may by order provide that section 123 is not to apply where the regulated agreement has a connection with a country outside the United Kingdom.

5–287 Failure to comply with section 123 makes the agreement or the security, as the case may be, unenforceable except on an order of the court (s. 124).

5–288 A creditor or owner who takes a negotiable instrument in contravention of section 123 is not a holder in due course, and is not entitled to enforce the instrument, and where a creditor or owner negotiates a cheque in contravention of section 123, his doing so constitutes a defect in his title for the purposes of the Bills of Exchange Act 1882. These provisions do not, however, affect the rights of a holder in due course of any negotiable instrument or prevent a negotiable instrument which has been taken or negotiated in contravention of section 123 from coming into the hands of a holder in due course: the instrument may have been negotiated by the creditor or owner to a person who took it in good faith and without notice of the contravention of section 123. The debtor, hirer or surety ("the protected person") may, therefore, find himself liable to a holder in due course; the Act provides that in such a situation the creditor or owner must indemnify the protected person (s. 125).

(iv) *Heritable Securities*

5–289 A heritable security securing a regulated agreement can be enforced only on an order of the court (s. 126).

(e) **Judicial Control**

5–290 Part IX of the Act is concerned with the powers which the court may exercise in connection with regulated and other agreements.

5–291 The powers fall into two broad groups:

(i) the power to make enforcement orders in actions by creditors or owners; and

(ii) the power to reopen "extortionate credit bargains."

5–292 The term "court" in relation to Scotland in (i) means the sheriff court (s. 189(1)), and in (ii) means either the sheriff court or the Court of Session (ss. 139 and 189 (1)).

5–293 The particular sheriff court which has jurisdiction to enforce regulated agreements, securities relating to them and linked transactions is in general the court for the place where the debtor or hirer is domiciled or carries on business or for the place where any moveable property in question is situated (s. 141, as amended by Civil Jurisdiction and Judgments Act 1982, Sched. 12).

An application to have a credit bargain reopened on the ground that it is extortionate may be made to the Court of Session or to the sheriff court for the district in which the debtor or surety resides or carries on business (s. 139).

(i) Enforcement and Other Orders

The provisions under this heading apply only to regulated agreements.

In making an order the court has a general power to—

(1) make the order conditional on the doing of specified acts by any party to the proceedings; and

(2) to suspend the operation of the order for a time or until the occurrence of a specified act or omission (s. 135).

The court has also power to include in an order such provision as it considers just for amending any agreement or security so as to give proper effect to an order which it is making (s. 136).

Enforcement orders in cases of infringement

As has been mentioned above, there are cases where the creditor or owner must obtain an enforcement order from the court before he can enforce the agreement. This is so where—

(1) the agreement has been improperly executed (s. 65);

(2) a security is not in writing or is improperly executed (s. 105);

(3) a surety has not had a default notice or a notice of termination served on him (s. 111); or

(4) a negotiable instrument has been taken or negotiated in contravention of section 123 (s. 124).

In an application for an enforcement order the court must have regard to prejudice caused to any person by the contravention in question, and the degree of culpability for it. If it appears to the court just to do so, the court may in an enforcement order reduce or discharge any sum payable by the debtor or hirer, or any surety, so as to compensate him for prejudice suffered as a result of the contravention in question.

There are some cases of infringement where the court has no power to make an enforcement order. A prominent instance is infringement of section 64 which requires the debtor or hirer in a cancellable agreement to be given a notice of his right to cancel (s. 127).

Enforcement orders on death of debtor or hirer

It was noted above that by section 86 on the death of a debtor or hirer the creditor or owner is entitled, where the agreement is not fully secured or is unsecured, to take certain steps, such as terminating the agreement, but only if he obtains an order from the court.

By section 128 the court must make an order under section 86 if, but only if, the creditor or owner proves that he has been unable to satisfy himself that the present and future obligations of the debtor or hirer under the agreement are likely to be discharged.

Time orders

5–302   A "time order" is an order of the court providing for one or both of the following, as the court considers just—

(a) the payment by the debtor or hirer or any surety of any sum owed under a regulated agreement or a security by such instalments, payable at such times, as the court, having regard to the means of the debtor or hirer and any surety, considers reasonable;

(b) the remedying by the debtor or hirer of any breach of a regulated agreement (other than non-payment of money) within such period as the court may specify (s. 129).

In the case of a hire-purchase or conditional sale agreement only, a time order of type (a), above, may deal with sums which are not yet due but which are to become payable if the agreement continues in force.

5–303   Where, following the making of a time order in relation to a regulated hire-purchase or conditional sale agreement or a regulated consumer hire agreement, the debtor or hirer is in possession of the goods, he must be treated (except in the case of a debtor to whom the creditor's title has passed) as a custodier of the goods under the terms of the agreement, notwithstanding that the agreement has been terminated. The effect of this provision is that, subject to the time order, the obligations of the debtor or hirer under the terminated agreement are notionally revived: payments again become due under the agreement (as controlled by the time order), and other obligations (e.g. as to insurance and maintenance) are restored.

5–304   While a time order of type (b), above, is in force, the creditor or owner cannot take certain steps, such as terminating the agreement, until the specified period has elapsed.

5–305   The court has power to vary or revoke a time order on an application being made to the court by any person affected by the order (i.e. by either creditor or owner or debtor or hirer) (s. 130).

Protection orders

5–306   Section 131 gives the court power, on the application of the creditor or owner under a regulated agreement, to make such orders as it thinks just for protecting any property of the creditor or owner, or property subject to any security, from damage or depreciation pending the determination of legal proceedings under the Act. The orders which may be made include orders restricting or prohibiting use of the property or giving directions as to its custody.

Financial relief in hire agreements

5–307   The provisions mentioned in (ii), below, on extortionate credit bargains do not apply to hire agreements, but the hirer in a regulated consumer hire agreement is protected from oppression by section 132, which provides that where the owner recovers possession of the goods the court may order that the whole or part of any sum paid by the hirer to the owner be repaid, and that the obligation to pay the whole or part of any sum owed by the hirer to the owner is to cease. In considering whether it is just to make such an order, the court must have regard to the extent of the enjoyment of the goods by the hirer.

Special powers of court in hire-purchase and conditional sale agreements

Section 133 enables the court, if it considers it just, to make "return orders" and "transfer orders" in relation to regulated hire-purchase or conditional sale agreements. A "return order" is an order for the return of the goods to the creditor. A "transfer order" is an order for the transfer to the debtor of the creditor's title to certain goods ("the transferred goods") and the return to the creditor of the remainder of the goods.

A transfer order can be made only where the paid-up sum exceeds that part of the total price which attaches to the transferred goods by at least one-third of the unpaid balance of the total price. The part of the total price which attaches to any goods may be specified in the agreement, but usually there will be no such express provision and in that case it will be for the court to fix an amount which it considers reasonable.

Even though a return order or a transfer order has been made, the debtor can still, before the goods actually enter the possession of the creditor, claim the goods by paying off the balance of the total price and fulfilling any other necessary conditions.

If goods are not returned to the creditor as required by a return order or a transfer order, the court may order the debtor to pay the creditor the unpaid portion of that part of the total price which attaches to the goods in question.

(ii) *Extortionate Credit Bargains*

The provisions of the Act concerning extortionate credit bargains were brought into force on May 16, 1977 (Consumer Credit Act 1974 (Commencement No. 2) Order 1977 (S.I. 1977 No. 325)). They have retrospective effect, *i.e.* they apply to transactions before May 16, 1977, and even before the passing of the Act itself; this follows from the provision in Schedule 3 to the Act that sections 137 to 140 "come into operation on the day appointed for the purposes of this paragraph, and apply to agreements and transactions whenever made" (para. 42).

The provisions are similar to, but more extensive than, provisions previously applicable under the Moneylenders Acts of 1900 and 1927. Moreover, the wording of the Act of 1974 is different: "grossly exorbitant" has replaced "excessive"; the test is thus a stricter one.

The leading provision is in section 137:

"If the court finds a credit bargain extortionate it may reopen the credit agreement so as to do justice between the parties."

The term "credit agreement" as used in this sentence means "any agreement between an individual (the 'debtor') and any other person (the 'creditor') by which the creditor provides the debtor with credit of any amount." "Individual," as elsewhere in the Act, includes a partnership or other unincorporated body of persons not consisting entirely of bodies corporate (s. 189(1)). Sections 137 to 140 are therefore not confined to regulated agreements: they extend to all credit agreements other than those in which the debtor is a body corporate or a partnership of bodies corporate. The credit may be of an amount well beyond the £5,000[2] ceiling generally applicable under the Act, and there is no exemption for

---

[2] For proposed increase in this monetary limit, see 5–09, above.

"exempt agreements," "small agreements" or "non-commercial agreements."

5–316　　The scope of the provisions in sections 137 to 140 is further widened by the use of the term "credit bargain," which means the credit agreement together with any other transaction taken into account in computing the total charge for credit: the power of the court is therefore not confined to an examination of the terms of the credit agreement itself unless no other transaction is to be taken into account in computing the total charge for credit.

When bargains are extortionate

5–317　　Section 138 provides that a credit bargain is extortionate if it—

(1) requires the debtor or an associate of his to make payments (whether unconditionally, or on certain contingencies only) which are grossly exorbitant, or

(2) otherwise grossly contravenes ordinary principles of fair dealing.

5–318　　In deciding whether a credit bargain is extortionate the court must look at evidence on—

(*a*) interest rates prevailing at the time when it was made,

(*b*) factors in relation to the debtor including—

(i) his age, experience, business capacity and state of health, and

(ii) the degree to which, at the time of making the credit bargain, he was under financial pressure, and the nature of that pressure,

(*c*) factors in relation to the creditor including—

(i) the degree of risk accepted by him, having regard to the value of any security provided,

(ii) his relationship to the debtor, and

(iii) whether or not a colourable cash price was quoted for any goods or services included in the credit bargain (the reason for this inclusion being that if the cash price is inflated, the stated rate of charge for credit will be misleading),

(*d*) factors in relation to a linked transaction including the question how far the transaction was reasonably required for the protection of debtor or creditor, or was in the interest of the debtor, and

(*e*) any other relevant considerations.

5–319　　There is an illustration of how the court applies these provisions in the English High Court case *A. Ketley Ltd.* v. *Scott and Another* [1981] I.C.R. 241.

To finance the purchase of two flats S. obtained a loan of £20,500 from K. Ltd. at 12 per cent for three months, *i.e.* at an annual rate of 48 per cent. S. had a protected tenancy of one of the flats. K. Ltd. was given a legal charge on the property.

In an action by K. Ltd. against S. for £22,960 (the principal sum plus interest at the agreed rate), S. applied for the agreement to be reopened on the ground that the credit bargain was extortionate.

The court (Foster J.) refused the application, being influenced by the following points:

Under (*a*): The rate of interest had to be compared with the prevailing rates for the *sort of transaction* in question, namely a loan which was the borrower's last resort.

Under (*b*): S., in view of his earnings and his experience in business, knew exactly what he was doing. The "financial pressure" alleged was his need to save the deposit of £2,250 and take advantage of the reduction in price arising from his protected tenancy, but he could easily have forfeited the deposit and remained in the property as a protected tenant; there was no question of his finding himself without a roof over his head. In the court's opinion there was no real "financial pressure."

Under (*c*): The degree of risk accepted by K. Ltd. was considerable: there had been no time to check S.'s financial position, and to lend 82 per cent of the value of a property worth about £25,000 was highly speculative.

Under (*e*): It was clear that S. knew the rate of interest, and to enable the purchase to be completed the money had had to be provided with extraordinary speed—within a matter of hours—with the result that it was impossible to make inquiries as to S.'s financial position.

The judge further referred to the provision in section 139 that an agreement may be reopened "if the court thinks just," and held that it would not have been just to reopen the agreement in this case, since S. had failed to disclose several material facts to K. Ltd. including his bank overdraft secured by a legal charge which, if registered, would have had priority over K. Ltd.'s charge.

Reopening of extortionate agreements

By section 139 a credit agreement may, if the court thinks just, be reopened on the ground that the credit bargain is extortionate. The application to the court for this purpose may be made by the debtor or any surety.

In reopening the agreement, the court may, for the purpose of relieving the debtor or a surety from payment of any sum in excess of that fairly due and reasonable, by order—

(1) direct an accounting to be made between any persons,

(2) set aside the whole or part of any obligation imposed on the debtor or a surety by the credit bargain or any related agreement,

(3) require the creditor to repay the whole or part of any sum paid under the credit bargain or any related agreement by the debtor or a surety, whether paid to the creditor or any other person,

(4) direct the return to the surety of any property provided for the purposes of the security, or

(5) alter the terms of the credit agreement or of any security instrument.

It is no obstacle to the making of any of these orders that the effect of the order is to place a burden on the creditor in respect of an advantage unfairly enjoyed by another person who is a party to a linked transaction. For instance, if the total charge for credit in a credit agreement relating to goods includes the cost to the creditor of having the goods serviced by a third party with whom the creditor has a maintenance contract, the court may, if it considers that the maintenance charge is extortionate, require the creditor to repay the whole or part of the sum paid under the credit agreement, even though the effect may be that the creditor has to bear the burden of paying sums due to the third party under the extortionate maintenance agreement.

V ANCILLARY CREDIT BUSINESSES

5–323 Part X of the Act brings within the scope of the Act various types of businesses which are connected with the provision of credit or hire facilities to consumers. These businesses are given the collective title of "ancillary credit businesses."

5–324 All the sections comprising Part X (*i.e.* sections 145 to 160 of the Act) have been brought into operation, at least to some extent.

5–325 Broadly the effect of Part X is to make "ancillary credit businesses"—a term requiring a statutory definition—subject to the licensing provisions of Part III of the Act, to impose on certain classes of ancillary credit business controls as to the seeking of business similar to the controls imposed by Part IV on consumer credit and consumer hire businesses, to enable regulations to be made as to the entry into ancillary credit agreements, and to protect consumers against the operation of "credit reference agencies," which maintain files of information as to the financial standing of individual consumers.

5–326 The provisions of Part X, therefore, fall under the following headings:
(a) definitions;
(b) licensing;
(c) seeking business;
(d) entry into agreements; and
(e) credit reference agencies.

(a) **Definitions**

5–327 The definitions set out in section 145, together with the exceptions stated in section 146, fix the scope of Part X.

5–328 An "ancillary credit business" is defined as "any business so far as it comprises or relates to"—
(i) credit brokerage,
(ii) debt-adjusting,
(iii) debt-counselling,
(iv) debt-collecting, or
(v) the operation of a credit reference agency.
Each of the terms in (i) to (v) is then in turn defined.

5–329 Note should be taken of the words "any business so far as it comprises or relates to" in the definition of ancillary credit business: the words imply that the person engaged in ancillary credit business may be carrying on that business within the framework of a business set up for some other purpose, *i.e.* it is the *activity* of ancillary credit business which is being brought within the scope of the Act, whether or not the activity itself constitutes a business.

5–330 An important exception made by section 146 is that solicitors and advocates in preparing for and conducting court or arbitration proceedings are not to be treated as doing so in the course of any ancillary credit business. If it were not for this exception solicitors and advocates acting regularly for creditors might be considered to be carrying on the activity of debt-collecting, while those acting regularly for debtors might be considered to be carrying on the activity of debt-adjusting or debt-counselling.

(i) *Credit Brokerage*

The definition of "credit brokerage" in section 145 is wide and complicated. In outline, the term means the effecting of introductions—

(1) of individuals desiring to obtain credit to persons carrying on a consumer credit business or (in the case of a house-purchase) to any person carrying on a business in the course of which he provides credit secured on land, or

(2) of individuals desiring to obtain goods on hire to persons carrying on a consumer hire business, or

(3) of individuals desiring to obtain credit, or to obtain goods on hire, to other credit-brokers.

The persons introduced must always be "individuals" as defined in the Act: introducing companies to sources of credit is therefore not "credit brokerage" for the purposes of the Act.

On the other hand, credit brokerage is not confined to regulated agreements: the introductions may be to creditors or owners whose agreements would be exempt or unregulated agreements.

The result is that the term "credit brokerage" embraces a wide range of activities which would not normally be described as "brokerage": "credit-brokers" for the purposes of the Act include motor dealers and retail shops introducing retail customers to finance houses for hire-purchase, credit sale, conditional sale or rental facilities or personal loans, solicitors regularly negotiating advances for clients, and estate agents introducing house purchasers to building societies.

An exception is made by section 146 for introductions effected by an individual by canvassing off trade premises either a restricted-use credit agreement to finance a transaction between debtor and creditor or a regulated consumer hire agreement, *provided* the introductions are not effected by the individual in the capacity of an employee. This exception would exclude from the definition, for example, individuals who as part-time agents for mail-order companies canvass applications from persons wishing to acquire goods on credit sale from the mail-order companies.

(ii) *Debt-Adjusting*

"Debt-adjusting" is, in relation to debts due under consumer credit agreements or consumer hire agreements,—

(1) negotiating with the creditor or owner, on behalf of the debtor or hirer, terms for the discharge of a debt, or

(2) taking over, in return for payments by the debtor or hirer, his obligation to discharge a debt, or

(3) any similar activity concerned with the liquidation of a debt (s. 145(5)).

This is a wide definition, going well beyond persons whose main business is that of debt-adjustment; it covers, for example, solicitors who, without resorting to legal proceedings, negotiate on behalf of clients who are debtors, and banks providing overdrafts to customers in place of overdrafts outstanding from the customers to other banks.

The width of the definition makes it necessary to have some exclusions; for example, it is not "debt-adjusting" where the person negotiating, *etc.*, is himself the "supplier" (s. 146(6)).

(iii) *Debt-Counselling*

5–339   "Debt-counselling" is "the giving of advice to debtors or hirers about the liquidation of debts due under consumer credit agreements or consumer hire agreements" (s. 145(6)).

5–340   Examples of debt-counsellors may include accountants, bankers, Citizens' Advice Bureaux, and free legal advice organisations.

5–341   Again, it is necessary to have some exclusions to prevent, for example, the creditor, owner or "supplier" from being himself counted as a debt-counsellor (s. 146(6)).

(iv) *Debt-Collecting*

5–342   "Debt-collecting" is "the taking of steps to procure payment of debts due under consumer credit agreements or consumer hire agreements" (s. 145(7)).

5–343   Again there are exclusions so that, for example, the creditor, owner or "supplier" who takes steps to procure payment is not to be treated as carrying on the business of debt-collecting (s. 146(6)).

(v) *Credit Reference Agency*

5–344   A "credit reference agency" is "a person carrying on a business comprising the furnishing of persons with information relevant to the financial standing of individuals, being information collected by the agency for that purpose" (s. 145(8)).

5–345   The use of the terms "person" and "individuals" should be noted: "person" includes a company (Interpretation Act 1978); "individual" includes partnerships (but not companies) (1974 Act, s. 189(1)).

5–346   The information must have been collected *for the purpose* of furnishing it to persons: the mere furnishing of information about an individual's financial standing does not amount to the operation of a credit reference agency; therefore a bank, for example, furnishing information based on its accounts between itself and one of its customers is not operating a credit reference agency.

5–347   It should be noted that the definition of "credit reference agency" makes no reference to consumer credit or consumer hire agreements, and so is not restricted to information collected and furnished in connection with such agreements.

(b) **Licensing**

5–348   The provisions of Part III of the Act ("Licensing of Credit and Hire Businesses") are extended to ancillary credit business (s. 147).

5–349   A person who carries on ancillary credit business without having the necessary licence cannot enforce any agreement for his services against the other party unless he obtains an order under section 148 from the Director General of Fair Trading. The provisions concerning applications to the Director in this connection are similar to those applicable under Part III (see 5–127 to 5–156, above); they include the right of an unlicensed person to make representations against the Director's refusal of an order and the right of the unlicensed person to appeal to the Secretary of State and, on a question of law, to the Court of Session (ss. 148 and 150). The effect is that the unlicensed person will be unable to claim his fees or commission from the person who uses his services, unless he applies for and obtains an order under section 148.

A further consequence of failure to obtain a licence for an ancillary credit business is that, by section 149, a regulated agreement itself, if made by a debtor or hirer who was introduced to the creditor or owner by an unlicensed credit-broker, is unenforceable against the debtor or hirer unless an order is obtained from the Director. An order to avoid this provision as to unenforceability of a regulated agreement may be granted to the credit-broker under section 149. The provisions for representations and appeals apply also to applications under section 149 (ss. 149 and 150). Because of section 149 those who carry on consumer credit and consumer hire businesses must be on their guard to ensure that the credit-brokers with whom they deal are duly licensed; for example, a finance company would be unable to enforce a hire-purchase agreement without an order from the Director if the supplier who introduced the finance company to the consumer was not licensed as a credit-broker.

(c) Seeking Business

Broadly the effect of sections 151 to 154 is to extend the provisions of Part IV (on advertising, canvassing *etc.*, and quotations, display of information and conduct of business—see 5–157 to 5–185, above) to persons engaged in the business of credit brokerage, debt-adjusting and debt-counselling.

In section 153 there is a definition of "canvassing off trade premises" in similar terms to the definition in section 48 (see 5–173, above), and by section 154 it is an offence to canvass off trade premises the services of a person carrying on a business of credit brokerage, debt-adjusting or debt-counselling.

Section 155 provides that a credit-broker is not entitled to more than £1[2] as a fee or commission for his services if the introduction which he has made does not result in the individual's entering into a relevant agreement within six months after the introduction. Any excess over £1 may be recovered by the individual. The provision is aimed against the abuse of commission being charged by credit-brokers, supposedly trying to procure a loan, while knowing that they were unlikely to succeed.

(d) Entry into Agreements

By section 156 regulations may make provision, in relation to agreements entered into in the course of a business of credit brokerage, debt-adjusting or debt-counselling, corresponding (with such modifications as the Secretary of State thinks fit) to the provision made under the sections in Part V ("Entry into Credit or Hire Agreements") which deal with regulations applicable to regulated agreements (see 5–187 to 5–212, above).

No regulations have yet been made under section 156.[3]

---

[2] For proposed increase in this monetary limit, see 5–09, above.

[3] Regulations are not expected to be made for the time being (see 5–05, above).

(e) **Credit Reference Agencies**

5–356   The provisions under this heading are designed to deal with the difficulties faced by a consumer who is refused credit because of erroneous information as to his financial standing supplied to prospective lenders by a "credit reference agency" (defined in section 145 as "a person carrying on a business comprising the furnishing of persons with information relevant to the financial standing of individuals, being information collected by the agency for that purpose"). These difficulties were considered by the Crowther Committee and also by the Younger Committee on Privacy whose *Report* was published in 1972 (Cmnd. 5012). The Younger Committee's recommendations were adopted in a strengthened form in the Act of 1974.

5–357   The consumer has three basic rights conferred on him:
     (i) the right to obtain from a creditor, owner or negotiator the name and address of any credit reference agency consulted;
     (ii) the right to obtain from the credit reference agency a copy of its file on him; and
     (iii) the right to require wrong information on the file to be corrected.

(i) *Name* etc. *of Agency*

5–358   By section 157 a creditor, owner or "negotiator" (*i.e.* a person who has conducted "antecedent negotiations" as defined in section 56 with the debtor or hirer) must on the written request of the debtor or hirer give him, within the prescribed period, notice of the name and address of any credit reference agency from which the creditor, owner or negotiator has, during the antecedent negotiations, applied for information about his financial standing. This provision does not apply to a request received more than 28 days after the termination of the antecedent negotiations. A creditor, owner or negotiator who fails to comply with section 157 commits an offence.

5–359   The period prescribed for the giving of the notice under section 157 is seven working days (Consumer Credit (Credit Reference Agency) Regulations 1977 (S.I. 1977 No. 329)).

(ii) *Copy of File*

5–360   By section 158 a credit reference agency, within the prescribed period after receiving a written request from the consumer and the particulars reasonably required by the agency to enable it to identify the file, and also a fee of 25p[2], must give the consumer a copy of the file relating to him kept by the agency. At the same time the agency must give the consumer a statement in the prescribed form of his rights under section 159 to have the file corrected. The word "file" means all the information about the consumer kept by the agency, regardless of how the information is stored, and "copy of the file" means, if the information kept is not in plain English (*e.g.* if it is coded), a transcript reduced into plain English. If the agency does not keep a file relating to the consumer, it must give him notice of that fact. An agency which contravenes section 158 commits an offence.

---

[2] For proposed increase in this monetary limit, see 5–09, above.

The regulations applicable are the Consumer Credit (Credit Reference Agency) Regulations 1977; they prescribe a period of seven working days for the giving of the copy of the file.

It was recognised that the right conferred by section 158 could seriously affect the ability of a credit reference agency to provide a proper service to its subscribers concerning business consumers (*i.e.* sole traders and partnerships): the copy of the file would almost certainly reveal the agency's sources of information, and these sources, while willing to give the information in confidence, would decline to do so in view of the new right conferred by section 158. An alternative procedure is therefore available under section 160 in relation to business consumers.

For the operation of the alternative procedure an application must be made to the Director General of Fair Trading by the credit reference agency, and the Director must be satisfied that—

(1) compliance with section 158 in the case of consumers carrying on a business would adversely affect the service provided by the agency to its customers, and

(2) having regard to the methods employed by the agency and to any other relevant factors, it is probable that consumers carrying on a business would not be prejudiced by the substitution of the alternative procedure.

If the application is successful, the agency has then an option when it receives a request for a copy of a file from a consumer who carries on a business: the agency may elect to comply with section 158 or, instead of giving the consumer a copy of the file, it may give the consumer such information included in or based on entries in the file as the Director may direct. If, within 28 days after receiving such information (or any longer period allowed by the Director), the consumer gives notice to the Director that he is dissatisfied with the information and satisfies the Director that he has taken reasonable steps, in relation to the agency, with a view to removing the cause of his dissatisfaction, the Director may direct the agency to give the Director a copy of the file, and the Director may then disclose to the consumer such of the information on the file as the Director thinks fit.

An agency which elects to deal with a request under section 160 and then fails to comply with the requirements of that section commits an offence.

(iii) *Correction of Wrong Information*

By section 159 a consumer who has been given a copy of his file under section 158 and considers that an entry on it is incorrect and that, if it is not corrected, he is likely to be prejudiced, may give notice to the agency requiring it either to remove the entry from the file or to amend it.

There are further elaborate provisions designed to reinforce this right: within 28 days after receiving such a notice the agency must inform the consumer that it has removed the entry from the file or amended the entry, or taken no action; the consumer then has a further 28 days in which he may, unless he has been informed by the agency that it has removed the entry, serve a further notice on the agency requiring it to add to the file an accompanying notice of correction (not exceeding 200 words) drawn up by the consumer, and include a copy of it when furnishing information included in or based on that entry; if the consumer does not then receive a notice from the agency confirming that it is to comply with the consumer's second notice, the consumer may apply to the Director; the agency also has the right to apply to the Director if it appears to the agency that the notice of correction is incorrect, defamatory, frivolous, scandalous or for any other reason unsuitable; the Director may make such order as he thinks fit, and a person who fails to comply with the order commits an offence.

5–368 These provisions in section 159 apply also to information given to business consumers under the alternative procedure of section 160 (s. 160(5)).

VI ENFORCEMENT OF THE ACT

5–369 The following are among the provisions in Part XI of the Act ("Enforcement of Act"):

Enforcement Authorities

5–370 The enforcement authorities are the Director General of Fair Trading and the local weights and measures authorities (which in Scotland are the regional and islands councils).

5–371 Every local weights and measures authority must, whenever the Director requires, report to him in such form and with such particulars as he requires on the exercise of their functions under the Act (s. 161).

Entry and Inspection

5–372 A duly authorised officer of an enforcement authority may exercise the following powers of entry and inspection at all reasonable hours and on production, if required, of his credentials:

(a) He may, in order to ascertain whether a breach of the Act has been committed, inspect any goods and enter any premises, other than premises used only as a dwelling.

(b) He may, if he has reasonable cause to suspect that a breach has been committed, require the production of business books and documents and legible reproductions of information recorded otherwise than in a legible form.

(c) He may seize and detain any goods, books or documents which he has reason to believe may be required as evidence in criminal proceedings under the Act. In this connection he may, if this is reasonably necessary, require any container to be broken open by any person having authority to do so, and, if that person does not comply, break it open himself.

5–373 Where admission to premises is likely to be refused or where an application for admission would defeat the object of the entry, a warrant may be obtained from a sheriff or justice of the peace authorising an officer of an enforcement authority to enter the premises (by force if need be).

5–374 An officer entering premises, either with or without a warrant, may take with him such other persons and such equipment as he thinks necessary.

Regulations may provide that, in cases described by the regulations, an officer of a local weights and measures authority is not to be taken as a "duly authorised" officer unless he is authorised by the Director (s. 162).

Where, in exercising the powers mentioned, an officer seizes and detains goods and their owner suffers loss because of the seizure or because of the loss, damage or deterioration of the goods during detention, then, unless the owner is convicted of an offence under the Act, the authority must compensate him for the loss suffered. Any dispute as to the right to or amount of any compensation is decided by arbitration (s. 163).

Power to Make Test Purchases, etc.

An enforcement authority may make, or authorise any of its officers to make, purchases of goods and may authorise any of its officers to procure services or facilities or enter into agreements or other transactions such as may appear to it expedient for determining whether the statutory provisions are being complied with (s. 164).

Obstruction of Authorised Officers

A person commits an offence if he wilfully obstructs an officer of an enforcement authority, wilfully fails to comply with a requirement properly made for entry and inspection under section 162, above, or without reasonable cause fails to give an officer other assistance or information which the officer reasonably requires in performing his functions under the Act.

It is also an offence for a person, in giving information, to make any statement which he knows to be false.

A person, however, need not answer any question or give any information if to do so might incriminate himself or (if he is married) his spouse (s. 165).

Notification of Convictions and Judgments to Director

Where a person is convicted of an offence or has a decree given against him by a court in the United Kingdom and it appears to the court (having regard to the functions of the Director under the Act of 1974) that the conviction or decree should be brought to the Director's attention and that it might not be brought to his attention unless the court made arrangements for that purpose, the court may make such arrangements, even after the proceedings have been finally disposed of (s. 166).

The proceedings referred to in section 166 are not necessarily proceedings (civil or criminal) *under the Act*. The purpose of the provision is to make available to the Director information which it would be relevant for him to have when exercising his licensing powers under Parts III and X of the Act.

Penalties, Defences and Onus of Proof

Schedule 1 to the Act tabulates 35 offences created by the Act, setting opposite each the mode of prosecution (summary, or solemn) and the maximum imprisonment or fine (s. 167).

5–384   In proceedings for an offence under the Act it is a defence for the person charged to prove—

(a) that his act or omission was due to a mistake, or to reliance on information supplied to him, or to an act or omission by another person, or to an accident or some other cause beyond his control, and

(b) that he took all reasonable precautions and exercised all due diligence to avoid such act or omission by himself or any person under his control.

5–385   Where this defence involves the allegation that the act or omission was due to an act or omission by another person or to reliance on information supplied by another person, the person charged is not entitled, without leave of the court, to rely on the defence unless, at least seven clear days before the hearing, he gives the prosecutor as much information as he has for the purpose of identifying the other person (s. 168).

5–386   Where at any time a body corporate (*e.g.* a company) commits an offence under the Act with the consent or connivance of, or because of neglect by, any individual, then the individual commits the same offence if at that time—

(a) he is a director, manager, secretary or similar officer of the body corporate, or

(b) he is purporting to act as such an officer, or

(c) the body corporate is managed by its members and he is one of them (s. 169).

5–387   Section 171 provides for where the onus of proof is to lie in various proceedings under section 139, the debtor or any surety alleges that the credit bargain is extortionate it is for the creditor to prove the contrary.

Statements by Creditor or Owner to be Binding

5–388   Section 172 list a number of provisions under which the creditor or owner is required to supply the debtor, hirer or surety with a statement (*e.g.* section 77(1) which requires the creditor to furnish the debtor with information as to the amounts paid and payable under a regulated agreement for fixed-sum credit), and provides that the statements given by the creditor or owner are to be binding on him.

5–389   The court has a discretion to grant relief to the creditor or owner from the operation of this provision where in court proceedings it is sought to rely on a statement and the statement is shown to be incorrect.

Contracting-out Forbidden

5–390   Section 173 prohibits contracting out of the protection given by the Act. The section provides that a term in a regulated agreement or linked transaction is void if it is inconsistent with a provision in the Act or regulations for the protection of the debtor or hirer or his associate or any surety.

VII MOTOR VEHICLES ON HIRE-PURCHASE OR CONDITIONAL SALE

The major Act on hire-purchase in Scotland has been the consolidating Hire-Purchase (Scotland) Act 1965. That Act, like the corresponding Act applicable to England—the Hire-Purchase Act 1965—is one of the Acts which will be wholly repealed when the Consumer Credit Act 1974 is fully in operation (s. 192(3)(*b*) and Sched. 5).

Part III of the Hire-Purchase Act 1964, applicable to both countries, and concerned with the protection of private purchasers of motor vehicles, is not repealed by the Act of 1974, and is reproduced, with some changes in terminology only, in Schedule 4 to the Act of 1974.

The provisions apply where a motor vehicle has been hired under a hire-purchase agreement, or has been agreed to be sold under a conditional sale agreement, and, before the property in the vehicle (*i.e.* the ownership of the vehicle) has passed to the debtor, he disposes of the vehicle to another person.

The other person may be a "private purchaser" or a "trade or finance purchaser." The latter term means a purchaser who carries on a business which consists, wholly or partly,—

(a) of purchasing motor vehicles for the purpose of offering or exposing them for sale, or

(b) of providing finance by purchasing motor vehicles for the purpose of hiring them under hire-purchase agreements or agreements to sell them under conditional sale agreements.

"Private purchaser" means a purchaser who does not carry on any such business.

Section 27 of the Act of 1964 provides that where the vehicle is disposed of to a private purchaser who purchases it in good faith without notice of the hire-purchase or conditional sale agreement affecting it the private purchaser obtains as good a title to the vehicle as he would have obtained if the debtor had been the owner. Similar protection is extended to a private purchaser in the situation where the vehicle has first been disposed of to a trade or finance purchaser from whom it has been purchased by the private purchaser.

The provisions apply even where the debtor in the hire-purchase or conditional sale agreement is a body corporate and the price exceeds £5,000.

Further Reading

Gloag and Henderson, *Introduction to the Law of Scotland,* Chapter XIX

W.A. Wilson, *The Law of Scotland Relating to Debt,* Chapters 3 and 4

David M. Walker, *Principles of Scottish Private Law,* Chapter 4.12 (part)

A.P. Dobson, *Sale of Goods and Consumer Credit,* Part Two ("Consumer Credit") (2nd ed., 1979, Sweet & Maxwell)

E.   Robert Lowe and Geoffrey Woodroffe, *Consumer Law and Practice,*
            Part IV ("Special Protection in Credit Transactions") (1980, Sweet
            & Maxwell)

E.   R.M. Goode, *The Consumer Credit Act—A Students' Guide* (1979,
            Butterworths)

E.   Aubrey L. Diamond, *Commercial and Consumer Credit: An Intro-
            duction* (1982, Butterworths)

            Current Law Statutes Annotated, Consumer Credit Act 1974, annota-
            tions by A.G. Guest and Michael G. Lloyd (1974, Sweet & Maxwell,
            Stevens & Sons, W. Green & Son)

            The following are loose-leaf works, each containing statutory pro-
            visions and kept up to date with the publication of releases:

E.   F.A.R. Bennion, *Consumer Credit Control* (1976- , Oyez Publishing)

E.   A.G. Guest and M.G. Lloyd (Editors), *Encyclopaedia of Consumer
            Credit Law* (1975- , Sweet & Maxwell)

            Enid A. Marshall (Editor), *Consumer Credit Materials—A Handbook
            for Students* (1980- , Editor)

CHAPTER 6

CARRIAGE OF GOODS BY LAND, SEA AND AIR

INTRODUCTION

A CONTRACT of carriage may be defined as a contract by which one person hires another to convey persons or goods from one place to another in a vehicle, vessel or aircraft, operated by the second party.

This contract is a species of *locatio operis faciendi* ("hiring of services"), as distinct from *locatio operarum* ("hiring of labour"). In the latter the relationship established is that of employer and employee, whereas in the former the relationship is that of employer (or hirer) and independent contractor. A carrier is not an employee working under the control or direction of the person who has engaged him, but an independent contractor who undertakes to produce a particular result—the conveyance of the persons or the goods to the specified destination—in his own way (including the use of his own conveyance and his own employees).

Theoretically the contract of carriage is a consensual contract, leaving the parties free to choose their own mode of contracting and their own contractual terms. In practice, however, the carrier almost always is the party with the opportunity to decide on the method of contracting and to fix the contractual terms. Legislation has therefore been passed to restrict freedom of contract in the interests of members of the public who engage the services of carriers. Important instances of such legislation are the Carriers Act 1830 which affects the mode of contracting and the Unfair Contract Terms Act 1977 which provides that certain terms (such as clauses excluding or restricting liability) in certain types of contracts of carriage are to have no effect unless it was "fair and reasonable" to incorporate the terms in the contract.

Carriage of goods is subject to different rules from carriage of persons. Broadly, the most prominent point of distinction is that at common law the public carrier of persons is liable for injury to his passengers only if he is proved to have been negligent, whereas the public carrier of goods is liable as an insurer of the goods, *i.e.* without proof of negligence. Only carriage of goods is within the scope of this book.

This chapter is divided into three parts:

    I.   Carriage of goods by land;
    II.   Carriage of goods by sea; and
    III.   Carriage of goods by air.

Carriage of goods by inland waterways is mainly governed by the same rules as carriage of goods by land, but necessarily has some features in common with carriage of goods by sea: *e.g.* a carrier by inland waterway impliedly guarantees that his craft is "seaworthy," *i.e.* fit for the purpose for which it is to be used. It should be noted, however, that the Carriers Act 1830 applicable to carriage by land does not apply to carriage by inland waterways.

Also excluded from further consideration is carriage of goods by post. This is governed by the Post Office Act 1969 and by post office regulations. The general rule is that no liability attaches to the Post Office or to its officers or employees for loss of or damage to goods sent by post.

There are no significant differences between Scots and English law affecting the subject-matter of this chapter. The absence of any difference between the two legal systems in the common law relating to carriage by sea has in particular been commented on (see 6–154 *et seq.*, below), and legislation for the most part applies equally in the two legal systems.

I CARRIAGE OF GOODS BY LAND

6–09 Carriage by land includes:
(a) carriage by road; and
(b) carriage by railway.
It is convenient to deal first with carriage by road, since this branch is still largely governed by the common law, whereas carriage by railway has been fundamentally altered by statute. Many of the cases, however, which illustrate the common law now applicable to carriage by road involve railway companies, having been decided at dates before carriage by railway became subject to statute.

(a) **Carriage by Road**

6–10 A division requires to be made under this heading into:
(i) inland, or non-international, carriage by road; and
(ii) international carriage by road.

(i) *Inland Carriage by Road*

6–11 There are two classes of carrier:
1. common (or public) carriers; and
2. private carriers.

6–12 A common carrier is one who holds himself out as willing to convey the goods of anyone who chooses to employ him and pay his charge, whereas a private carrier is free in every case to make or refuse to make a contract to carry goods offered to him.

6–13 The most important difference at common law between the common and the private carrier is that the common carrier is, with certain very limited exceptions, liable for any loss or damage during the carriage, whereas the private carrier is liable only if he has been negligent. A further important difference is that the Carriers Act 1830 applies to common carriers but not to private carriers.

1. **Common carriers**

6–14 The law relating to common carriers is considered below under these headings:
(a) carrier's duty to accept employment;
(b) carrier's edictal liability;
(c) carrier's charges and lien;
(d) consignor's duties;
(e) consignor's warranty;
(f) loading;
(g) deviation;
(h) delay in transit;
(i) delivery; and
(j) limitations of carrier's liability.

Many of the cases illustrating these matters involve the former railway companies. These companies were common carriers, but it should be noted that by the Transport Act 1962 the Railways Board is not a common carrier.

(a) *Carrier's duty to accept employment*

Although a common carrier is bound to carry goods for anyone who chooses to employ him, he may restrict the classes of goods which he carries and the routes and areas over which he operates; *e.g.* in *A. Siohn & Co. Ltd.* v. *R.H. Hagland & Son (Transport) Ltd.* [1976] 2 Lloyd's Rep. 428, road carriers specialising in the carriage of hanging garments in vehicles fitted with clothing rails and accompanying their advertisements with a diagram which showed that they operated from London to Liverpool and Manchester and from London to Bradford, Leeds and Sheffield were held to be common carriers (and therefore liable when one of their vehicles was hijacked even although there had been no negligence on the carriers' part).

Just as the common carrier may limit the classes of goods which he carries, so he may attach conditions when undertaking the carriage of certain goods; *e.g.* in *Wood & Co.* v. *G. & J. Burns* (1893) 20 R. 602, shipowners who operated as common carriers accepted an organ at "owner's risk," and were held not liable for damage to the organ on its removal from the ship's hold at the end of the journey, since the stipulation "owner's risk" had been validly incorporated into the contract of carriage and since it had not been proved that the damage had been caused by the fault of the shipowners or their servants.

A common carrier who refuses to accept goods of the kind which he professes to carry and for a destination within his area is liable in damages for breach of duty (*i.e.* is liable delictually) unless he can justify his refusal on one of the following grounds:

    (i) that he has no room in his vehicle; he is not bound to put on a special vehicle or to run his vehicle at a time other than its usual time;

    (ii) that the goods are dangerous, *i.e.* likely to harm the vehicle or other goods, or persons;

    (iii) that the goods are not properly packed or are in some other way not in a state which is reasonably convenient for the carriage;

    (iv) that the goods did not arrive in reasonable time for them to be loaded;

    (v) that his charges are not paid by the consignor when the goods are delivered to the carrier for carriage; or

    (vi) that the district through which the goods are to be carried is unsafe on account of riot.

(b) *Carrier's edictal liability*

The strict liability which a common carrier incurs for the loss of or damage to the goods carried, even though he is not proved to have been negligent, is referred to as "edictal" liability because it is derived from the edict of the Roman praetor, which stated:

"Nautae, caupones, stabularii, quod cujusque salvum fore receperint, nisi restituent, in eos judicium dabo."

("Sailors, inn-keepers and stable-keepers I (the praetor) shall hold liable unless they duly deliver whatever property of anyone they have undertaken will be in good order.")

The shortened form *"nautae, caupones, stabularii"* is the form commonly used in Scots law. The word *"nautae"* ("sailors") is taken to include carriers by land as well as carriers by sea.

6–20 The common carrier's liability is substantially that of an insurer of the goods. For example, he is liable, even though not proved to have been at fault, if the goods are stolen while in transit (as in *A. Siohn & Co. Ltd. v. R.H. Hagland & Son (Transport) Ltd.* (6–16, above), where the carriers were held not to have been negligent in not varying their routes or the timing of their vehicles, since they employed reputable drivers and had carried goods for many years without loss).

6–21 Under the common law of Scotland a common carrier was not liable for loss arising from accidental fire. English law was different in this respect, and to eliminate the difference the Mercantile Law Amendment Act Scotland 1856 (s. 17) provided that carriers in Scotland also were to be liable for loss arising from accidental fire.

6–22 A common carrier may be liable for goods which are no longer actually in his possession; for example, he may accept goods for carriage by a route involving both land and sea and he may not actually himself carry the goods except on land. An illustration is:

Logan & Co. v. *Highland Railway Co.* (1899) 2 F. 292: The railway company accepted delivery at Inverness of a new piano in a packing case from L. & Co. who had sold the piano to Grant of Kirkwall. The railway company undertook to forward the piano by train to Aberdeen and by steamer from Aberdeen to Orkney.

On arrival at Kirkwall, the piano was found to be spotted as if by water or steam, and much of its metallic work was deeply rusted.

Held that the railway company had, by the terms of the contract of carriage, undertaken responsibility for the whole transit and not merely for the rail journey to Aberdeen.

Lord President J.B. Balfour said (at p. 299): "A common carrier is liable to deliver goods which he has accepted for carriage in the like good order and condition in which he received them. This is a liability quite irrespective of fault, and founded upon manifest considerations of public policy. The question then is, did the piano arrive at Kirkwall in the like good order and condition in which it was delivered to the appellants for carriage, and on the evidence it is clear that it did not. The *onus*[1] is thus thrown on the appellants to prove that the damage sustained by the piano during the transit was due to some cause for which they were not responsible, such as inherent infirmity in the piano, or possibly some natural and unavoidable cause."

6–23 There are a few exceptions to edictal liability: the carrier is not liable if the goods have been lost or damaged:

(i) by act of God, *i.e.* by the operation of some natural force which could not reasonably have been anticipated;

---

[1] "burden" (of proof).

(ii) by act of the Queen's enemies, *i.e.* by enemy armed forces (not mere rioters or strikers);

(iii) by the inherent vice of the goods (including the temperament of an animal injuring itself in a way against which it was not reasonable for the carrier to take precautions, as in *Ralston* v. *Caledonian Railway Co.* (1878) 5 R. 671, where a mare fastened in the usual way in a railway horse box struggled through a feeding window into an adjoining compartment); or

(iv) by fault of the consignor, including insufficient addressing and defective packing; an illustration of insufficient addressing is:

Caledonian Railway Co. v. *Hunter & Co.* (1858) 20 D. 1097: H. & Co., warehousemen in Glasgow, delivered goods to a railway agent there. The goods were addressed to "Wm. Rae, draper, Sudbury," and were first sent along several lines of railway to Sudbury in Derbyshire, not Sudbury in Suffolk for which they were intended.

When, 36 days after their despatch, the goods were delivered to the consignee, they were refused.

Held that since the cause of the goods being mis-sent had been the insufficient address supplied by the consignor, the railway company was not liable for the loss resulting from the delay.

Lord Justice-Clerk Hope said (at p. 1100): "If the address be not ample, full, and distinct, the delay or interruption which takes place arises from fault on the part of the sender, who is the means of putting the whole thing wrong. With him the fault begins, and he is the cause of the goods not going to their proper destination."

(c) *Carrier's charges and lien*

It is an essential element in the contract of carriage that the common carrier should be entitled to some remuneration or return. So, in *Barr & Sons* v. *Caledonian Railway Co.* (1890) 18 R. 139, where B., a coal owner, had arranged with a railway company that B. should himself supply waggons for the carriage of his coal to its destination, and the railway should return the empty waggons to B. without additional charge, the railway company was held not liable for damage to B.'s waggons on their return journey because the company was not receiving any remuneration, and so was not liable as a common carrier, for that journey.

A common carrier is not entitled to charge more than a reasonable sum, and he is bound by a table of charges which he has publicly advertised. What is reasonable depends on circumstances, *e.g.* a higher charge will be deemed reasonable if the journey is through a district where the goods are particularly liable to be stolen.

The carrier is entitled to receive his fee at the time when the goods are entrusted to him for carriage. If he chooses to carry goods without pre-payment, he may exercise a lien on the goods for his charges, *i.e.* may refuse to deliver the goods until he is paid for having carried them. This lien is a special lien, not a general lien:

Stevenson v. *Likly* (1824) 3 S. 291: L., a shipping company for the conveyance of goods from Liverpool to the Clyde, was employed by S., earthenware merchants in Glasgow, to carry their goods—normally 300 or 400 parcels in the year—from Liverpool to Glasgow.

S. fell into arrears of freight, and L.'s agents at Glasgow detained particular parcels at different times in security of the general balance due by S.

Held that a carrier had no right to withhold goods for his general balance, but was entitled to refuse delivery of each parcel until the charge for the carriage *of it* was paid.

(d) *Consignor's duties*

6–27   The consignor must pack the goods in a manner reasonably sufficient for the journey, and must address them fully and distinctly. Any loss resulting from failure in packing or addressing falls on the consignor (*e.g. Caledonian Railway Co.* v. *Hunter & Co.* (6–23, above)).

6–28   The consignor must also deliver the goods to the carrier or to the carrier's agent at the appropriate place, such as the carrier's receiving office.

6–29   The stowage (*i.e.* the loading and packing of the goods on the truck or vehicle) is not the consignor's responsibility unless he actually undertakes the stowage himself.

(e) *Consignor's warranty*

6–30   The consignor impliedly warrants that the goods are not dangerous, *i.e.* are not liable to cause personal injury or to damage the carrier's vehicle or the goods of other persons which the carrier is carrying in the same vehicle. Under this implied warranty the consignor becomes liable in damages to the carrier for loss suffered by the carrier (*e.g.* the carrier may himself have incurred liability to a third party whose goods have been lost or damaged on account of the presence of the dangerous consignment in the same vehicle).

6–31   As the warranty is an implied one, it does not exist where the consignor has informed the carrier of the dangerous nature of the goods and the carrier has nevertheless accepted them for carriage. However, merely to attach a label with a word such as "dangerous" may not be sufficient notice to the carrier, as is suggested by the case of *Cramb* v. *Caledonian Railway Co.* (1892) 19 R. 1054:

A wooden box containing a number of square tins of "the Climax Weed-killer" was accepted by the railway company from a Liverpool chemical company for carriage by rail from Glasgow. The weed-killer contained arsenic and was highly poisonous. The wooden box was marked "weed-killer," but the chemical company did not inform the railway company either that the box in fact contained weed-killer or that the contents were poisonous.

During the journey the stoppers of several of the tins fell out and as a result the box leaked. At Stirling the box was placed on a waggon which contained bags of sugar addressed to McEwens, grocers in Crieff. The railway company's servants knew that the bags contained sugar, but, though they were aware of the leakage, took no precautions to prevent the weed-killer from reaching the sugar.

On delivery of the sugar at McEwens, a shop assistant noticed that one of the bags was discoloured, but thinking that this was due to rain did not separate the bag from the others.

In course of time a large number of McEwens' customers became ill, and two died, one of whom was Mrs C. Her husband and other relatives claimed damages from the railway company.

The claim was based not on the contract of carriage but on delict: the railway company had therefore to be shown to have been at fault in omitting to perform some duty which it owed to all the world. Was the railway company, in a question with the public generally, to blame, first, for having allowed the leakage to come into contact with the sugar, and, second, for not warning McEwens that the discoloured bag might be poisonous?

The court *assoilzied* that railway company, holding that (i) the primary liability lay on the consignors who had not warned the railway company of the poisonous nature of the goods, (ii) the railway company was not proved to have had reason to suspect that the contents of the box were poisonous, and (iii) the railway company was not guilty of delict in having placed the leaking box within reach of the bags of sugar or in not having informed McEwens of the leakage.

(The claim for damages was also directed against the chemical company and against McEwens. The chemical company admitted liability. McEwens were assoilzied since no fault was established against them.)

(f) Loading

The carrier must load and stow the goods in such a way that they can be carried safely. An instance of liability incurred by a railway company in this connection is *Bastable* v. *North British Railway Co.*, 1912 S.C. 555:

B., a showman, contracted with the railway company for it to convey his switchback railway on trucks attached to a passenger train from Alva to Falkirk. The charge was at a special reduced rate, and one of the conditions of the contract was that the company was not to be liable except for damage arising from the "wilful misconduct" of the company's servants.

One of the company's regulations required all loads to be gauged when there was any reason to doubt that they were not within the dimensions specified for the lines over which they had to travel.

The stationmaster at Alva, influenced by the fact that the same load had previously come safely from Dunblane, did not gauge the load, but merely judged the height of it with his eye and concluded that it did not exceed the specified dimensions.

A funnel in the load came into contact with an overhead bridge at Falkirk, and B. sued the company for damages.

Held that the damage had been caused by "wilful misconduct" of the stationmaster for which the company was liable.

The carrier is not, however, responsible if he can show that damage was due to exceptional circumstances or to the consignor's own fault.

(g) *Deviation*

6–34   The carrier must follow the usual route (which is not necessarily the shortest route), and he must not deviate unreasonably from it. If he deviates without justification, he is liable for all loss or damage to the goods unless he can prove *both*:

(i) that the loss or damage was caused by act of God, act of the Queen's enemies, inherent vice of the goods or fault of the consignor; *and*

(ii) that the loss or damage would also have occurred even if he had not deviated.

6–35   Where a special contract has been made, unjustifiable deviation deprives the carrier of the benefit of any clause exempting him from liability, even although the loss or damage was not the result of the deviation. An illustration of a railway company losing the benefit of an exemption clause because of deviation is *Lord Polwarth* v. *North British Railway Co.*, 1908 S.C. 1275:

P., the owner of three prize head of cattle, contracted with the railway company that they be sent from Maxton station, via Kelso, to Alnwick where there was an agricultural show. The contract also provided that if the cattle were not sold at the show they would be conveyed back to Maxton by the same route as that by which they had been sent; this was to be done at half-fare on condition that the railway company was not to be liable for loss or damage unless caused by wilful misconduct on the part of their servants.

On the journey to Alnwick, the cattle were despatched from Maxton via Kelso and Wooler. They were not sold at the show and were returned by another route, namely from Alnwick via Tweedmouth, the company's intention being to send them from Tweedmouth via Kelso to Maxton.

At Tweedmouth, however, the truck containing the cattle caught fire, and the cattle died. P. claimed £800 as the value of the cattle.

Held that the railway company had broken the contract in taking the cattle by Tweedmouth, and could not found on the indemnity clause in the contract.

(P.'s claim was, however, limited to £15 per animal under a provision of the Railway and Canal Traffic Act 1854, since unjustifiable deviation does not deprive the carrier of *statutory* protection.)

(h) *Delay in transit*

6–36   Edictal liability does not extend to loss or damage resulting from delay in transit. The common carrier's duty (like that of the private carrier) is to carry the goods within a reasonable time.

6–37   What is reasonable depends on the circumstances; for example, if the carrier knows that the goods are perishable, he must convey them with due speed. The extent of the carrier's liability therefore depends on, amongst other things, the information given to him by the consignor, *e.g.*:

Macdonald & Co. v. *Highland Railway Co.* (1873) 11 M. 614: M. & Co., confectioners in Inverness, delivered to the railway company perishable confectionery intended for a coming-of-age celebration to take place in Skye. The package was marked "perishable," and it was the custom of the railway company to forward goods so marked in preference to other goods.

The truck in which the package was put by the railway company was not marked "perishable," and was taken off the train at Dingwall, while goods not of a perishable nature in other trucks were forwarded.

The confectionery arrived too late for the celebration, and was also much spoiled by the delay.

Held that the railway company was liable in damages for the delay, since it had failed to forward the package with reasonable speed.

The measure of damages for delay in transit is the loss which was foreseeable by the carrier. A well-known Scottish case involved this question of measure of damages:

"Den of Ogil" Co. Ltd. v. *Caledonian Railway Co.* (1902) 5 F. 99: Owners of a steamship of 4,000 tons, which had broken one of her pistons and was lying at Plymouth, had another one cast at Port Glasgow and sent it by rail from Port Glasgow to Plymouth. The railway company received notice from the agents of the shipowners that the carriage was urgent and that any delay in delivery would cause the detention of the ship. The carriage was by passenger train at a high rate of charge. The railway company was not informed of the size of the ship, that it had a crew of 57, or that the package was a piston forming part of the ship's machinery.

The waggon containing the piston was, by a mistake of the railway, returned as an empty waggon to Scotland from Crewe, and as a result, a delay of between three and four days occurred in delivery at Plymouth.

The shipowners sued the railway company for damages including outlays and loss of profit caused by the detention of the ship amounting to £300. The railway company admitted that it had been in breach of contract, but disputed the amount of the damages claimed.

Held that the railway company was not liable for the loss of profit, and was only liable for part (estimated at £50) of the outlays caused by the detention of the ship.

If the carrier knows at the time when he receives the goods that they are likely to be delayed (*e.g.* by unusual traffic congestion), he has a duty to warn the consignor, *e.g.*:

McConnachie v. *Great North of Scotland Railway Co.* (1875) 3 R. 79: M., a fish-curer of Lossiemouth, had an arrangement with a railway company whereby the railway company forwarded consignments of fresh fish for a lower rate on condition that the company would not be liable for delay except where it was caused by the wilful fault or negligence of the company's servants.

On one occasion two of M.'s consignments were delayed and damaged. The cause of the delay was a block at a junction resulting from a diversion of traffic due to the collapse of a bridge on another company's line a few days before.

Held that the railway company was liable, since the block had been foreseeable and the company ought to have warned M. on accepting the two consignments that they were in danger of being delayed in transit; wilful negligence was held to have been proved.

Lord Justice-Clerk Moncreiff said (at p. 85): "Temporary or accidental detention from unexpected pressure of traffic is a risk incidental to railway transit, and one of which the customer must to a certain extent take his chance. But it is quite a different thing when the causes of probable detention are known and foreseen, and are not specifically disclosed to the customer when his goods are accepted."

6–40   A carrier may, expressly or by implication, undertake to deliver the goods by a certain time, *e.g.* to meet a particular market at their destination. If he does undertake such an obligation, then he may be held liable for loss of market if there is delay in transit. Such an obligation may be undertaken impliedly where the carrier is proved to have customarily provided the special service; *e.g.* in *Macdonald & Co.* v. *Highland Railway Co.* (6–37, above), as it had been the custom of the railway company to forward goods marked "perishable" in advance of other goods, the consignors were held to have been entitled to rely on the railway company's following its usual practice on the occasion in question.

6–41   Where a carrier finds that perishable goods are being damaged by delay in transit, he may, as agent of necessity, sell them, but he must first communicate with the owner of the goods, if that is reasonably practicable.

(i) *Delivery*

6–42   The place of delivery may be the consignee's business premises or his home, or may be the carrier's premises. In the latter case the carrier should notify the consignee that the goods are available for collection.

6–43   The carrier's responsibility comes to an end when he has safely delivered the goods at their destination and they have been accepted by the consignee.

6–44   For failure to deliver, the common carrier incurs stricter liability than for delay in delivery: the case of *Caledonian Railway Co.* v. *Hunter & Co.* (6–23, above) which concerned delay caused by an insufficient address, may be contrasted with *Campbell* v. *Caledonian Railway Co.* (1852) 14 D. 806, in which, where a passenger's luggage had completely disappeared, the railway company was held liable even although there were certain precautions which the passenger might have taken and did not take:

C. arrived at the railway company's Glasgow station, having with him a portmanteau and carpet bag without any address. He obtained a ticket for Edinburgh, and his luggage was put by a porter in the luggage van of the train for Edinburgh.

A change of carriages took place at Carstairs junction. C. did not inquire for his luggage at that point, and the luggage never reached Edinburgh.

Held that the railway company, having failed in its undertaking to convey the luggage to its destination, was liable for its value, and that this liability was not affected by the passenger's carelessness in not having had an address on the luggage and not having inquired for the luggage at Carstairs.

6–45   The carrier incurs liability if he fails to follow the instructions as to delivery which have been given to him, *e.g.* if he delivers the goods on board the wrong ship and that ship is lost at sea (*Gilmour* v. *Clark* (1853) 15 D. 478) or parts with the goods to someone other than the person named by the consignor (*Caledonian Railway Co.* v. *Harrison & Co.* (1879) 7 R. 151):

Gilmour v. *Clark*: G. sent a bale of goods by a carter with instructions to put them on board "The Earl of Zetland" lying at Leith and bound for Orkney. The carter, mistakenly believing that "The Earl of Zetland" had sailed, put the goods instead on "The Magnet" which with its cargo was lost at sea.

Held that, having disobeyed instructions, the carter was liable for the price of the goods.

Lord President McNeill said (at p. 479): "If a party receive express instructions, as in this case, to send a parcel by a particular ship, he takes the risk upon himself if he violates these instructions, and sends by another vessel."

Caledonian Railway Co. v. *Harrison & Co.*: C. & Co. of Newcastle contracted to supply B. of Glasgow with a quantity of old railway axles, the price to be paid on delivery. The goods were forwarded by the railway company to Greenock station with instructions from C. & Co. that they were to remain at C. & Co.'s order.

Meantime B. had resold the goods to H. & Co. of Greenock, and the railway clerk, on the order of B. and overlooking the fact that the goods were held at C. & Co.'s order, delivered them to H. & Co.

B. became bankrupt, and the railway company became liable to C. & Co. for the price of the iron.

The case reported was an action by the railway company against H. & Co. for restitution.

Held that, as H. & Co. had suffered no prejudice through the railway company's mistake, they were bound to pay to the railway company the price which the railway company had been obliged to pay to C. & Co. (a lesser price than that in the sub-sale by B. to H. & Co.).

A carrier may in certain circumstances become liable in delict if he has misdelivered goods. An illustration is *Macdonald* v. *David Macbrayne Ltd.*, 1915 S.C. 716:

A steamship company negligently delivered to M., a shopkeeper in Fort William, along with two barrels of paraffin, a third barrel containing naphtha which ought to have been delivered to someone else. The three barrels were placed in M.'s store by one of M.'s assistants, and M. was not made aware that more than two barrels had been delivered.

About three weeks later, one of M.'s assistants, desiring to obtain paraffin, went to the store with a lighted candle and tapped the barrel of naphtha. There was an explosion, and the store was set on fire and destroyed.

M. brought an action of damages against the steamship company for the loss which he had suffered as a result of the destruction of the store and its contents, and for this loss the company was held liable, *i.e.* delictually liable, because the fire had been caused by the carrier's fault.

(M. also claimed damages of £200 for personal injuries which he had suffered in falling from an adjoining roof on to which he had climbed with a hose to help to extinguish the fire, but the court held that these injuries were too remote a result of the company's negligence to give M. a valid claim for damages.)

On taking delivery, the consignee should examine the goods. If there is some damage to the goods and he does not intimate objection without delay he will find it difficult to make the carrier liable, since there is a presumption that the goods have been delivered in good order unless there is prompt intimation to the contrary. There is an instance of the operation of the presumption in *Stewart* v. *North British Railway Co.* (1878) 5 R. 426:

The railway company received from S. 77 heating batteries for carriage from Glasgow to Hull for shipment abroad. The consignee in Hull was M.

On arrival at Hull, the batteries were, according to custom, carted by the railway company to the docks and left in one of the dock sheds, which was the place of delivery agreed on between the railway company and M. for all goods addressed to M. The railway company notified M. of the arrival of the batteries.

M. made no examination of the batteries, but, relying on information supplied by the railway company's servants, wrote to the railway company on the day after the arrival of the batteries: "Please note that we find nine . . . broken, for which we must hold you responsible."

When, a fortnight later, the batteries were removed for shipment, 12 more were found to be broken. M. intimated that fact to the railway company, but the railway company declined to acknowledge any liability except for the nine previously mentioned.

S. brought an action of damages against the railway company.

Held that the railway company was liable for the price of only nine batteries.

Lord Gifford said (at p. 432): "Both on the actual receipt given, and on the presumption of law arising from the delay, I think the pursuers are barred from now saying that more than the nine were broken."

6–50   Where goods have been so badly damaged in transit that the consignee is entitled to reject them, the carrier is liable for the full value of the goods, and the consignee need not accept an offer made by the carrier to repair the goods:

Dick v. *East Coast Railways* (1901) 4 F. 178: D., a boot manufacturer in Glasgow, purchased from London a new lasting machine for £100. The machine was conveyed by the railway company from London to Glasgow, but was so badly damaged in transit that D. refused to take delivery of it.

D. sued the railway company for £100.

Evidence showed that the machine could have been repaired, at a cost of about £15 according to the railway company or £30 according to D. However, it was not clear that even when repaired the machine would have worked satisfactorily, and it was certain that it would not have been as good as new.

Held that the machine was so badly damaged that D. was entitled to reject it, and that the railway company was liable for £100.

6–51   Slight damage would not have the same legal consequence.

6–52   If the consignee cannot be found at the address given or if he refuses the goods, the carrier's responsibility as a common carrier is at an end, but he holds the goods as custodier (depositary or warehouseman) for the consignor, and may incur liability for negligence. He must redeliver the goods to, or according to the order of, the consignor and if he puts himself in such a position that he is unable to do so, he is liable to the consignor; an illustration is *Metzenburg* v. *Highland Railway Co.* (1869) 7 M. 919:

A rag-merchant in Inverness delivered to the railway company 30 bales of rags addressed to another rag-merchant in Aberdeen.

The consignee refused the rags and they were stored by the railway company.

The rag-merchant in Inverness sent a servant to Aberdeen in a vain attempt to recover the rags from the railway company there.

Held that the railway company was liable for the value of the rags and for the servant's travelling expenses.

Lord Justice-Clerk Patton said (at p. 923): "I do not think the obligation of the carrier terminates by the mere offer to deliver at the terminal point at which the address upon the goods directs them to be given. I think there is, incident to that contract, something more than a mere tender of delivery necessary. . . . It is quite plain that, incidental to the taking of these goods at Inverness for delivery at Aberdeen, there was an implied obligation upon the party, upon such a case occurring as the present, to have the goods put in such a situation that they may be at the disposal of the consigner."

(j) *Limitation of carrier's liability*

To a certain extent the common carrier's strict liability may be limited by:

  (i) statute; and
  (ii) contract.

The Carriers Act 1830, which applies only to common carriers by land, has a bearing on both of these possibilities.

(i) **Limitation of liability by statute**—Section 1 of the Carriers Act 1830 provides that the carrier is not liable for loss of or damage to a parcel or package containing certain articles of a value exceeding £10 unless at the time of the delivery to the carrier the value and nature of the articles has been declared by the consignor. The articles listed in section 1 are usually referred to as "valuables," though that word is not used in the Act. They have the common characteristic of great value in comparison to their size, and include gold and silver coins, gold, silver, precious stones, jewellery, watches, clocks, trinkets, bills of exchange, bank notes, securities for payment of money, stamps, maps, title-deeds, paintings, engravings and pictures, gold and silver plate, glass, china, silks and furs.

By section 2, it is lawful for the carrier to demand and receive an increased rate of charge for such valuables. The increased charges must be notified by a notice affixed in legible characters in a public and conspicuous part of the carrier's receiving office.

The carrier must, by section 3, grant a receipt for the increased charge. If he fails to affix the notice of increased charges or fails to sign a receipt, he loses any benefit under the Act, and must refund the increased charges.

Section 7 provides that where a parcel or package containing valuables has been duly declared and the increased charges have been paid, the person entitled to recover damages for the loss of or damage to the goods is also entitled to recover the increased charges.

6–58   There is an express provision in section 8 that the Act is not to be deemed to protect the carrier from liability for loss or damage arising from any felonious acts of his servants, or to protect any of the carrier's servants from liability for any loss or damage caused by the servant's own personal neglect or misconduct.

6–59   Section 9 provides that the declared value of the package or parcel is not conclusive against the carrier: in the event of loss or damage, he is entitled to require from the party suing proof of the actual value of the contents; the carrier is liable only for the damage proved, and is never liable for more than the declared value.

6–60   (ii) **Limitation of liability by contract**—A common carrier may enter into a special contract with a consignor by which he excludes or modifies his strict liability. However, his freedom to do so has been restricted to a certain extent by the Carriers Act 1830 and the Unfair Contract Terms Act 1977.

6–61   Before the Act of 1830, a common carrier could exclude or modify his liability simply by an advertisement or public notice displayed at his receiving office. Section 4 of the Carriers Act provides that no public notice or declaration is to be construed as limiting or in any way affecting the carrier's common law liability. By section 6 of the Act it is still open to the carrier to make a special contract with any individual consignor in any other way.

6–62   The Unfair Contract Terms Act 1977, which was passed to give effect to proposals in the Law Commissions' Second Report on Exemption Clauses (Law Com. No. 69; Scot. Law Com. No. 39), affects the content of any special contract made between the carrier and the consignor. The provisions in Part II of that Act ("Amendment of Law for Scotland") apply to their full extent to contracts for the carriage of goods by land (or air, but only to a limited extent to contracts for the carriage of goods by sea) (s. 15 of the Act). The leading provisions are in sections 16 and 17 of the Act. Their effect is that a "reasonableness" test is to be applied to the content of exemption clauses.

6–63   Section 16 relates to a term which attempts to exclude or restrict liability for "breach of duty" arising in the course of a business: such a term has no effect if it is not "fair and reasonable" to incorporate the term in the contract. The phrase "breach of duty" extends only to contractual obligations to take "reasonable care," to common law duties to take "reasonable care" and to the duty of "reasonable care" imposed by a provision of the Occupiers' Liability (Scotland) Act 1960 (1977 Act, s. 25(1)). Therefore section 16 would not affect a term in a special contract with a common carrier excluding or restricting the carrier's edictal liability because that is a strict liability and not merely a duty to take "reasonable care."

6–64   Section 17 relates to a term which attempts to exclude or restrict liability for breach of contract in the case of a "consumer contract" or a standard form contract. A "consumer contract" is a contract in which only one of the parties is acting in the course of a business, the other party being the "consumer." Many contracts of carriage would clearly be consumer or standard form contracts. The contractual term has no effect for the purpose of enabling a party who is in breach of a contractual obligation (in this context, the carrier) to exclude or restrict liability to the consumer or customer, if it was not "fair and reasonable" to incorporate the term in the contract.

Subject to these statutory provisions, the principles of the common law as developed in the "ticket" cases apply to special contracts limiting a carrier's liability. The basic principle is that the clause limiting liability must have been effectively incorporated into the contract.

An instance of effective incorporation from "Shipping Instructions" into a contract for carriage by sea occurs in *Aberdeen Grit Co. Ltd.* v. *Ellerman's Wilson Line Ltd.*, 1933 S.C. 9:

A. Ltd. engaged E. Ltd., a shipping company, to carry a consignment of grit from Aberdeen via Newcastle to Boston, U.S.A. It was understood that the cargo would be taken by coasting steamer to Newcastle, where it would be placed on board a vessel belonging to E. Ltd. for the voyage to Boston.

The contract between A. Ltd. and E. Ltd. was based upon "Shipping Instructions" containing this clause: "All goods awaiting shipment are received and carried subject . . . to the conditions . . . of any . . . persons by whom the goods may be conveyed."

During trans-shipment at Newcastle the cargo was placed on board a lighter, and was damaged through being left uncovered in heavy rain. The lighterman had accepted the cargo from E. Ltd. under a contract the terms of which exempted him from liability for his servants' negligence.

A. Ltd. brought an action of damages against E. Ltd.

Held that the clause quoted from the Shipping Instructions had imported into the contract between A. Ltd. and E. Ltd. the exemption from liability contained in the lighterman's conditions of carriage; and E. Ltd. *assoilzied.*

An exemption clause will not be held to have been incorporated into the contract where the carrier has not done what is reasonably adequate to bring the clause to the notice of the consignor:

Henderson and Others v. *Stevenson* (1875) 2 R. (H.L.) 71; (1873) 1 R. 215: A steam packet company printed on the back of its passenger tickets the following condition: "The company incurs no liability whatever in respect of loss, injury or delay to the passenger or to his or her luggage, whether arising from the act, neglect or default of the company or their servants, or otherwise."

S., a passenger on board the company's "Countess of Eglinton," lost his luggage as a result of the steamer's being wrecked off the Isle of Man, and sued the company for damages for negligence.

Held that the company was liable, since the condition had not been imported into the contract by merely being printed on the back of the ticket, S. having not actually read the condition nor had his attention directed to it by anything printed on the face of the ticket or by the carrier himself when issuing it.

The consignor may be required by the carrier to sign a document which limits the carrier's liability. It is then usually easier for the carrier to escape liability in the event of loss or damage. The difficulties facing the

carrier where no document has been signed are well illustrated by
McCutcheon v. *David MacBrayne Ltd.*, 1964 S.C. (H.L.) 28:

McC., a farm grieve in Islay, had crossed over to the mainland without
taking his car. He then desired to have the use of his car, and requested
McSporran, his brother-in-law in Islay, to send the car over. McSporran
drove the car to Port Askaig, and booked its passage to West Loch
Tarbert, paying the freight and receiving a receipt for the amount paid.

Normally, before accepting goods for carriage, the steamer company
issued a "risk-note," which set out conditions of carriage including
exemption from liability for negligence, and required the consignor to
sign this document. On this occasion, however, no risk-note was either
signed by or issued to McSporran.

Through negligence in navigation, the "Lochiel," on which the car was
being conveyed, struck a rock at the entrance to West Loch Tarbert. The
car was submerged in the sea, and became a total loss.

McC. sued the steamer company for the value of his car, which was
agreed to have been £480.

Held that (1) the contract was an oral one and that the receipt, having
been handed over after the contract had been completed, played no part
in its formation; (2) the steamer company had failed to show that by
displaying copies of their conditions of carriage they had done what was
reasonably necessary to bring them to the notice of McC. or his agent,
McSporran; and (3) any course of dealing in earlier transactions where
there *had* been a risk-note was irrelevant to the oral contract which had in
fact been made on this occasion.

The steamer company was therefore liable to McC. for the loss of his
car.

6–69   Clauses limiting liability are given a strict construction, *e.g.*:

Sutton & Co. v. *Ciceri & Co.* (1890) 17 R. (H.L.) 40; (1889) 16 R. 814:
A contract for the carriage of terra-cotta figures belonging to C. & Co.
from Leghorn to Edinburgh excluded the carriers' liability for "goods
described as statuary."

The terra-cotta figures were damaged in transit, and C. & Co. brought
an action against the carriers for damages.

Held that the burden rested on the carriers to show that the figures fell
within the description of "statuary," and that, as they had failed to do so,
they were liable for not having carried the goods in safety.

2. Private carriers

6–70   A private carrier (*i.e.* any carrier who is not a common carrier) is not
under an obligation to accept goods for carriage. On each occasion when
goods are offered to him, he is free to refuse them altogether or to
negotiate terms for accepting them; *e.g.* the contract negotiated may
incorporate the Road Haulage Association's Conditions of Carriage.

6–71   The great majority of carriers of goods by road (*e.g.* removal contractors and transport companies) are today private carriers.

6–72   A private carrier is not subject to edictal liability: he is bound only to
take reasonable care of the goods, and is liable only for loss or damage
caused by his fault or negligence. For instance, a removal contractor was

held not to have been negligent, and was therefore not liable, in *Pearcey* v. *Player* (1883) 10 R. 564:

Pearcey called at a coach-hirer's office and stated that he wished a van and two men to shift his luggage from one lodging in Edinburgh to another. A van and two men were sent in response to Pearcey's order.

The men carried the articles down a common stair at the first address, and up a common stair at the second address. Both men were occupied at the same time in the carrying process, and the van was not constantly watched. There was no list of the articles, and the men were allowed to go away without any inspection having been made by Pearcey.

Twenty-four hours later, Pearcey missed a large black portmanteau. He sued the coach-hirer for delivery of it, failing which, for payment of £45.

Held that Pearcey had failed to prove that the loss of the portmanteau had been due to the fault or negligence of the coach-hirer; in entering into the contract Pearcey had known that two men would be required for the handling of the articles, the coach-hirer, in supplying the van and two men, had exactly fulfilled Pearcey's order, and if Pearcey had wished to ensure the safe arrival of the articles he ought to have made a different contract with the coach-hirer or himself have taken precautions such as listing the articles, watching the van, and checking the articles immediately after their delivery.

As can be seen from this case, the *onus* ("burden") of proving that the carrier has been negligent rests on the consignor. If, however, goods are proved to have been handed to the carrier in good order and proved to be missing or damaged at their destination, this is *prima facie* evidence of the carrier's negligence, *i.e.* the carrier is presumed to have been negligent until the contrary is proved. This is so even where the carrier is acting gratuitously:

Copland v. *Brogan*, 1916 S.C. 277: C., a schoolmaster in Dalton near Lockerbie, asked B., a carriage-hirer, to cash three cheques for a total of about £34 for him at a bank in Lockerbie, and bring the cash back to him. B. cashed the cheques at the bank, but on his return to Dalton the package of cash was missing. There was no evidence of how the loss had occurred.

Held that B. was liable to C. for the loss of the package.

On the question of burden of proof, Lord Justice-Clerk Scott-Dickson said (at p. 282): "The packet having gone astray while it was in the defender's custody, the *onus*, in my opinion, rests on him to explain how this happened or at least to show that he exercised the necessary reasonable care."

While there is much legislation in the criminal law affecting both common and private carriers by road (*e.g.* vehicle licensing, drivers' hours and drivers' records), the contract of carriage, part of the civil law, has been left mainly to the common law, and this is even more true of private than of common carriers, since the Carriers Act 1830 does not apply to private carriers.

The only legislation which need be mentioned here as affecting the private carrier's contract of carriage is:

(a) the Mercantile Law Amendment Act Scotland 1856, section 17;

and
   (b) the Unfair Contract Terms Act 1977.

(a) *Mercantile Law Amendment Act Scotland 1856, section 17*

6–76   This section provides that *all* carriers of goods for hire are liable to make good to the owner of the goods all losses arising from accidental fire while the goods are in the carriers' custody or possession. There was at one time doubt as to whether this provision extended to private carriers. The doubt arose from the fact that the Act, as its preamble explained, was passed for the purpose of removing differences between Scots and English law, and the law of England in 1856 was that a *common* carrier was liable for loss by accidental fire, whereas a private carrier was not. The doubt was removed by two Outer House cases—*Anderson* v. *Jenkins Express Removals Ltd.*, 1967 S.C. 231 (O.H.), decided in 1944, and *James Kemp (Leslie) Ltd.* v. *Robertson,* 1967 S.C. 229 (O.H.).

   The decision in both cases was that, as the language of the section was plain and unambiguous, it had to be given effect to, even although it overshot the purpose disclosed in the preamble and, while removing one difference between Scots and English law, created another difference between them.

6–77   A condition which effectively excluded the liability imposed by section 17 of the Act of 1856 came before Lord Grieve (Ordinary) in *Graham* v. *Shore Porters Society,* 1979 S.L.T. 119 (O.H.):

   In 1976 G. accepted an estimate from private carriers for the removal of the contents of his home in Glasgow to his new home in Peterhead.

   During the journey a fire broke out in the carriers' van, resulting in the destruction of most of G.'s belongings.

   G. sued the carriers for damages for breach of contract and negligence in failing to provide a reasonably fit van. The carriers relied on an exemption clause in the contract: "Condition 7. The contractors shall not be responsible for loss and damage to furniture and effects caused by or incidental to fire."

   Held that Condition 7, being ambiguous, had to be construed *contra proferentem* ("against the party putting it forward"), and, though it was sufficient to exclude the carriers' statutory liability for *accidental* fire, it did not extend to liability for damage by fire arising from breach of contract and negligence.

(b) *Unfair Contract Terms Act 1977*

6–78   The "reasonableness" test introduced by this Act applies to any contract made by a private carrier for carriage by land in the same way as to any special contract made by a common carrier (see 6–62 *et seq.,* above).

(ii) *International Carriage by Road*

6–79   The Carriage of Goods by Road Act 1965, which was brought into operation in 1967, gave the force of law in the United Kingdom to the international Convention of Geneva of 1956, the *Convention relative au Contrat de Transport International de Marchandises par Route* ("Convention on the Contract for the International Carriage of Goods by Road"), commonly referred to as "C.M.R."

The Convention is set out in the Schedule to the Act of 1965, and in the paragraphs which follow here the Articles referred to are the Articles of the Convention as set out in that Schedule.

Some amendments were made by the Carriage by Air and Road Act 1979. In particular, section 3(3)[2] of the Act of 1979 provides that if the Government has agreed to any revision of the Convention, amendment of the Articles as set out in the Schedule to the Act of 1965 can be made by Order in Council. The object of this provision is to avoid the time lag which could otherwise emerge if Parliamentary time for an amending Act were not available at the date of any internationally agreed revision of the Convention.

The Convention applies, with three exceptions, to all contracts for the carriage of goods by road in vehicles for reward, when the place of taking over the goods and the place of delivery are situated in two different countries, *of which at least one* is a party to the Convention. The three exceptions are:

1. carriage performed under any international postal convention;
2. funeral consignments; and
3. furniture removal (Article 1).

Where the vehicle containing the goods is carried for part of the journey by sea, rail, inland waterways or air, the Convention nevertheless applies to the whole of the carriage, provided the goods are not unloaded from the vehicle (Article 2).

The United Kingdom and many other European countries are parties to the Convention. The list is kept up-to-date by the "Carriage of Goods by Road (Parties to Convention) Orders" issued from time to time. By the Protocol of Signature (see the end of the Schedule to the Act) the Convention is made not to apply to traffic between the United Kingdom and the Republic of Ireland.

From these provisions it can be seen that the Convention is of wide applicability. In particular, it applies (with the three exceptions mentioned) to all carriage of goods in a road vehicle from the United Kingdom to any foreign country (other than the Republic of Ireland), provided the vehicle goes along with the goods. It is also often adopted contractually in cases to which it would not apply under the statutory provisions.

The correct approach in the interpretation of the Convention, as explained in the House of Lords in *James Buchanan & Co. Ltd.* v. *Babco Forwarding and Shipping (U.K.) Ltd.* [1978] A.C. 141 (6–98, below), is to apply "broad principles of general acceptation," unconstrained by technical rules or by precedent, since the expressed objective of the Convention is to produce uniformity in all the States which are parties to the Convention.

The following are some of the main provisions of the Convention:

---

[2] brought into force on December 28, 1980 (Carriage by Air and Road Act 1979 (Commencement No. 1) Order 1980).

1. The consignment note

6–86   The contract of carriage is confirmed by the making out of a consignment note but the absence, irregularity or loss of the consignment note does not affect the existence or validity of the contract (Article 4).

6–87   The consignment note is made out in three original copies, signed by the sender and by the carrier—the first to be handed to the sender, the second to accompany the goods, and the third to be retained by the carrier (Article 5).

6–88   The particulars which must be contained in the note include (in addition to obvious particulars such as the identification of sender, carrier and consignee) the nature of the goods, charges relating to the carriage, and a statement that the carriage is subject, notwithstanding any clause to the contrary, to the provisions of the Convention. The note must also contain, *where applicable,* certain further particulars, *e.g.* a statement that transhipment is not allowed, a declaration of the value of the goods, and the agreed time-limit for the carriage. The parties may enter in the note any other particulars which they deem useful (Article 6).

6–89   The sender is responsible for loss sustained by the carrier through inaccuracy in particulars supplied by the sender for insertion in the consignment note (Article 7).

6–90   The consignment note is *prima facie* (*i.e.* preliminary, but non-conclusive) evidence of the making of the contract of carriage, the conditions of the contract, and the receipt of the goods by the carrier (Article 9).

2. Liability of carrier for loss, damage or delay

6–91   The general effect of the provisions of the Convention is to place the carrier in a stronger position than an inland common carrier but in a weaker position than an inland private carrier.

6–92   Under the Convention the carrier is liable for loss or damage occurring between the time when he takes over the goods and the time of delivery, as well as for delay in delivery, unless the loss, damage or delay was caused by the wrongful act or neglect of the claimant, by inherent vice of the goods, or through circumstances which the carrier could not prevent.

6–93   The carrier is not relieved of liability because of the defective condition of the vehicle used for the carriage.

6–94   The carrier is not liable for loss or damage arising from certain specified special risks:

(a) the use of open unsheeted vehicles where expressly agreed to and specified in the consignment note;

(b) defective packing;

(c) handling of the goods by the sender or by the consignee;

(d) the nature of certain kinds of goods which particularly exposes them to loss or damage, especially through factors such as breakage, rust, desiccation, leakage, moth or vermin (but this defence is not available to the carrier if the vehicle is specially equipped to protect the goods from the effects of heat, cold, or humidity, unless the carrier proves that he took all steps which he ought to have taken to maintain the vehicle in a suitable condition, and that he complied with any special instructions issued to him);

(e) inadequacy of marks or numbers on the packages; or

(f) livestock, provided the carrier proves that he took "all steps normally incumbent on him in the circumstances" and that he complied with any special instructions issued to him (Articles 17 and 18).

There is delay in delivery when the goods are not delivered within the agreed time-limit, or (if there is no agreed time-limit) within a reasonable time (Article 19).

If the goods are not delivered within 30 days after the agreed time-limit (or, if there is no agreed time-limit, within 60 days from the time when the carrier took them over), that is conclusive evidence that the goods have been lost, and the person entitled to make a claim may therefore claim the same compensation as for loss. The claimant may, on receiving such compensation, make a written request to the carrier to notify him if the goods are recovered within the next year. If then the goods are found within the year, the claimant may obtain them from the carrier, on paying charges and on returning the compensation which he received for their presumed loss (but the claimant may still be entitled to compensation for delay) (Article 20).

3. Dangerous goods

The sender must inform the carrier of the exact nature of any dangerous goods. If he fails to do so, the goods may, at any time or place, be unloaded, destroyed, or rendered harmless by the carrier, without compensation; further, the sender is liable for all expenses, loss or damage arising out of their carriage (Article 22).

4. Limitation in amount of compensation

The compensation for total or partial loss is calculated according to the value of the goods at the place and time at which they were accepted for carriage, but is limited to 8·33 "units of account" per kilogram. This amount was substituted for "25 gold francs"[3] per kilogram by section 4(2)[4] of the Carriage by Air and Road Act 1979. The "unit of account" is the special drawing right as defined by the International Monetary Fund. In addition, the carrier must refund "charges incurred in respect of the carriage of the goods" (Article 23). This last phrase fell to be construed in *James Buchanan & Co. Ltd.* v. *Babco Forwarding and Shipping (U.K.) Ltd.* [1978] A.C. 141:

B. Ltd., distillers of Scotch whisky, sold 1,000 cases of their whisky (then in one of their bonded warehouses in Glasgow) to buyers in Iran for about £7,000. B. Ltd. entered into a contract with carriers for the whisky, loaded in a container, to be driven from their warehouse to Felixstowe, where it was to be lifted on to a container ship for conveyance to Rotterdam. The carriers were then to drive it from Rotterdam to Iran and deliver it to the buyers. No excise duty was payable on the whisky since it was being exported, but if the whisky had been released on to the home market, the excise duty would have amounted to about £30,000.

---

[3] Latin Union or germinal gold francs.
[4] brought into force on December 28, 1980 (Carriage by Air and Road Act 1979 (Commencement No. 1) Order 1980).

The carriers' driver collected the container, duly sealed, from the Glasgow warehouse, but on his way to Felixstowe left his trailer with the container full of whisky unattended in a lorry park in North Woolwich over a weekend. When he returned to the lorry park the following Tuesday, he found that the container had disappeared.

B. Ltd., being unable to produce documents of export clearance, were, under the Customs and Excise Act 1952, required to pay excise duty of about £30,000 on the whisky which had presumably been stolen for release on the home market. B. Ltd.'s total loss was therefore about £37,000, and at common law B. Ltd. would have been entitled to recover that amount from the carriers on the ground of the driver's fault.

The C.M.R., however, applied to the carriage, and the decision of the case turned on the interpretation of the phrase "charges incurred in respect of the carriage" in Article 23.

Held that these words were wide enough to cover charges incurred in consequence of the way in which the goods had been carried, and the carriers were therefore liable not merely for the £7,000 (the value of the goods at the place and time at which they were accepted for carriage) but in addition for the £30,000 (the excise duty which B. Ltd. had been required to pay to the authorities because of the way in which the driver had carried the goods).

6–99   The parties may agree that, in return for a surcharge paid to the carrier, the goods have a specified value (stated in the consignment note) exceeding the limit laid down in Article 23. That specified value is then the maximum sum recoverable instead of 8·33 units of account per kilogram (Article 24).

6–100   The compensation for damage to the goods is the amount by which they have been diminished in value. This amount will never exceed the amount payable for loss (Article 25).

6–101   Compensation for delay is limited to the amount of the carriage charges (Article 23).

6–102   These limitations on the amount recoverable for loss, damage or delay do not apply if the carrier or his servants or agents have been guilty of wilful misconduct (Article 29).

5. Time-limit for claims

6–103   In the case of a claim for loss or damage, different time-limits apply according to whether or not the consignee has checked the condition of the goods with the carrier and according to whether or not the loss or damage is apparent.

6–104   (a) *The consignee takes delivery without duly checking their condition with the carrier*: If the loss or damage is apparent, then the fact of his having taken delivery is *prima facie* (*i.e.* non-conclusive) evidence that he has received the goods in the condition described in the consignment note, but if the loss or damage is not apparent, the consignee has seven days from delivery in which to give written notice to the carrier concerning the loss or damage, and it is not until the expiry of the seven days that the fact of his having taken delivery becomes *prima facie* evidence of proper condition.

(b) *The consignee duly checks the condition of the goods with the carrier*: If the loss or damage is apparent, this checking is conclusive, *i.e.* no evidence to contradict the result of the checking is admitted, but if the loss or damage is not apparent, the consignee has seven days in which to give written notice to the carrier, and until that time has elapsed there is, despite the checking, no conclusive evidence arising out of the checking.

As regards a claim for delay, no compensation is payable unless the consignee gives written notice to the carrier within 21 days after the goods have been placed at the consignee's disposal (Article 30).

Actions in respect of total or partial loss, damage or delay become barred on the lapse of one year, unless wilful misconduct is alleged, in which case the period of limitation is three years. The date from which the period of one or three years begins to run varies according to the circumstances; *e.g.* in the case of partial loss, damage or delay in delivery it begins to run from the date of delivery (Article 32).

6. Jurisdiction

Legal proceedings may be brought in the courts of any of the following countries:

(a) a country designated by the agreement of the parties, provided the country is a party to the Convention;

(b) the country where the defender is ordinarily resident, or has his principal place of business, or the agency through which the contract was made;

(c) the country where the goods were taken over by the carrier; or

(d) the country where the place designated for delivery is situated.

No legal proceedings can be brought in the courts of any other country (Article 31).

The parties may agree to refer their case to arbitration, provided the arbiter is required to apply the provisions of the Convention (Article 33).

7. Carriage by successive carriers

Where carriage governed by a single contract is performed by successive road carriers, each of them is responsible for performance of the whole operation: the second and each succeeding carrier become parties to the contract of carriage, under the terms of the consignment note, because of their acceptance of the goods and the consignment note (Article 34).

Legal proceedings for loss, damage or delay may be brought against the first carrier, the last carrier or the carrier who was performing that portion of the carriage during which the event complained of occurred. An action may be brought at the same time against more than one of these carriers (but normally not against any other carriers) (Article 36).

However, a carrier who has been required to pay compensation is entitled to recover the amount paid, or the appropriate portion of it, from other carriers who have been at fault (Article 37).

If one of the carriers is insolvent, the share of the compensation due and unpaid by him is divided among the other carriers in proportion to the payment which they receive for the carriage (Article 38).

8. Varying the provisions of the Convention

6-115   Variation of the provisions of the Convention is allowed to only a very limited extent: where there are several successive carriers, they are free to agree amongst themselves to vary the rights as to indemnity and contribution which would otherwise apply in accordance with Articles 37 and 38 (6–113 and 6–114, above), but, with that exception, any stipulation which would directly or indirectly derogate from the provisions of the Convention is null and void (Articles 40 and 41).

(b) Carriage by Railway

6-116   Carriage by railway may be treated more briefly than carriage by road for two reasons: first, some of the subject-matter (*e.g.* the distinction between common and private carriers and the provisions of the Carriers Act 1830 and the Unfair Contract Terms Act 1977) are common to both modes of carriage and need not be repeated here; secondly, carriage by railway is to a greater extent than carriage by road a matter of special contract between the parties and therefore calls for less detailed consideration in a chapter limited to the explanation of general legal principles.

6-117   As in carriage by road, a division requires to be made in carriage by railway, between:

(i) inland, or non-international, carriage; and

(ii) international carriage.

(i) *Inland Carriage by Railway*

6-118   The law which now applies to non-international carriage of goods by railway must be viewed in its historical context.

6-119   When, from 1825 onwards, railways first came to be constructed, railway companies were common carriers of goods, and their rights and liabilities were regulated by the common law supplemented by an increasing volume of legislation, including:

1. the Carriers Act 1830, applicable to all common carriers of goods by land (see 6–54 to 6–61, above);

2. the private Acts which were required for the constitution of all individual railway companies;

3. the Railways Clauses (Consolidation) (Scotland) Act 1845 (subsequently amended), which supplied clauses suitable for incorporation into the individual private Acts, so that these, though still necessary, could be much shorter; and

4. the Railway and Canal Traffic Act 1854 and much subsequent legislation of a similar character aimed at the regulation of railway traffic.

6-120   An important provision in section 7 of the Railway and Canal Traffic Act 1854 was that any special contract of carriage by which the railway company limited its liability for negligence had to be in writing signed by the owner of the goods or the consignor, and also "just and reasonable." As a result of decided cases, it came to be established that it was strong evidence that a contract limiting liability for negligence was "just and reasonable" if the railway company offered to the consignor a fair alternative of carriage under a contract in which, for a reasonable additional charge, the company *would* be liable for negligence.

This led railway companies to offer two alternative contracts to consignors:

(1) carriage at company's risk, in which (with certain exceptions) the company was liable unless it could prove that it had not been negligent; and

(2) carriage at owner's risk, in which (with certain exceptions) the company was liable only if the owner could prove that the company's servants had been guilty of wilful misconduct.

These two sets of conditions were given statutory force by the Railways Act 1921. Broadly, the effect of that Act was that, from January 1, 1928, these conditions became the "Standard Terms and Conditions," which had statutory force under the Act.

Further changes were made by the Transport Act 1962. This Act provided that the British Railways Board was no longer to be regarded as a common carrier. The Standard Terms and Conditions were abolished, and, from September 1, 1962, conditions of carriage were to be settled by contract between the parties. Consequently, the Carriers Act 1830, applicable only to *common* carriers by land, no longer applies to railway carriage.

The contractual terms now used are in several sets of "Conditions of Carriage." In content they do not differ much from the former statutory Standard Terms and Conditions, or from the pre-1928 contractual conditions for carriage at company's risk or owner's risk:

(1) In carriage at Board's risk, the Board is liable, with certain exceptions (*e.g.* act of God, war, inherent liability to wastage, insufficient packing, riot, strikes, and the consignee's failure to take delivery within a reasonable time), for loss, misdelivery or damage occurring during transit, unless the Board can prove that it used all reasonable foresight and care in the carriage; for loss proved by the trader to have been caused by delay in the carriage, the Board is liable unless it can prove that the delay arose without negligence on its part.

(2) In carriage at owner's risk, the Board is not liable for loss, misdelivery, damage or delay unless the trader proves that it was caused by the wilful misconduct of the Board.

It follows that cases decided with reference to the former statutory Standard Terms and Conditions or to the pre-1928 contractual conditions are still of value for the interpretation of the conditions now in use; *e.g. Bastable* v. *North British Railway Co.*, 1912 S.C. 555 (6–32, above) may still be referred to in the interpretation of the phrase "wilful misconduct."

Detailed consideration of contractual conditions, however, is beyond the scope of this chapter.

Passengers' luggage

In conclusion it should be noted that the historical sketch given above is concerned only with carriage of goods. The history of the law relating to liability for passengers' luggage carried in the luggage van of a passenger train followed a somewhat different course.

6–128   The position at common law was that the railway companies, as common carriers, were liable for such luggage. The companies did not make special contracts with passengers to limit this common law liability, and there were no Standard Terms and Conditions applicable. For an instance of the common law being applied to loss of a passenger's luggage, see *Campbell* v. *Caledonian Railway Co.* (1852) 14 D. 806 (6–44, above).

6–129   When the Transport Act 1962 provided that the British Railways Board was no longer to be regarded as a common carrier, the effect was that the Board became a private carrier of passengers' luggage, and therefore liable only for negligence. The Board may, by special contract, limit this liability for negligence. The terms at present contained in the Board's Conditions make the Board liable only for negligence and wilful default, and limit its liability to £500 per passenger in respect of any one claim.

6–130   If the luggage is being carried in the guard's or luggage van, the *onus* ("burden" (of proof)) is on the Board to prove that the loss, damage or delay was not caused by the Board's negligence or default; in other situations the *onus* is on the passenger to prove the Board's negligence or default.

(ii) *International Carriage by Railway*

6–131   Continental countries have in the past shown greater interest in international conventions on the carriage of goods by rail than has the United Kingdom. There has been a series of such conventions since before the 1914-18 war. The current convention is the *Convention Internationale concernant le Transport des Marchandises par Chemins de Fer* ("International Convention concerning the Carriage of Goods by Railways"), referred to as "C.I.M." or "Railway Freight Convention." It was signed in 1970 and came into effect in the United Kingdom on January 1, 1975.

6–132   There is a parallel convention on the international carriage of passengers and their luggage by rail—the *Convention Internationale concernant le Transport des Voyageurs et des Bagages par Chemins de Fer* ("International Convention concerning the Carriage of Passengers and Luggage by Railways"), referred to as "C.I.V." or "Railway Passenger Convention."

6–133   The C.I.M. has been given full legislative force in some continental countries, but in the United Kingdom its incorporation has been, apart from certain provisions about to be mentioned in the Carriage by Railway Act 1972, left as a contractual matter. However, this makes little practical difference, since all international carriage of goods by rail from this country is under a British Rail Consignment Note which provides that the goods are carried subject to the C.I.M.

6–134   The main purpose of the Carriage by Railway Act 1972, which came into operation on January 1, 1973, related to the international carriage of passengers and their luggage, not to carriage of goods. The Act provided that "the Additional Convention" set out in the Schedule to the Act was to have the force of law in the United Kingdom. The full title of "the Additional Convention" is "the Additional Convention to the International Convention concerning the Carriage of Passengers and Luggage by Rail."

The Act, however, also gave legislative effect to some parts of the other two Conventions mentioned above—the C.I.M. and the C.I.V. Only the provisions relating to the C.I.M. need be indicated here:

1. No action of any kind concerning a liability for which the C.I.M. makes provision can be brought against a railway undertaking or its servants or agents except in accordance with the C.I.M. (s. 6).

2. In any case where goods are carried under the C.I.M. (*e.g.* in the case of carriage under a British Rail Consignment Note to a foreign destination), the consignee is not entitled to enforce any right against the railway undertaking, in respect of the goods or their carriage, except in accordance with the C.I.M. (s. 7(1)).

3. If, in any case where goods are carried under the C.I.M., the consignee accepts the C.I.M. consignment note or purports to exercise some right conferred on him by the C.I.M., he must then be treated as if he had all along been a party to the contract of carriage of which the consignment note is evidence, and his rights and obligations are in accordance with the C.I.M. (s. 7(2)).

4. In any case where under the C.I.M. a railway undertaking is entitled to impose a surcharge for carriage or loading, it is treated as having a carrier's lien for that surcharge (s. 8).

Apart from provisions of sections 6 to 8 of the Act of 1972, the C.I.M. is not directly incorporated into the law of the United Kingdom. It is a lengthy document, the full text of which in French and English occupies about 200 pages in Parliamentary Papers (House of Commons and Command) Session 1965-1966, Vol. XIV, p. 373 (Cmnd. 2810). It would therefore be neither appropriate nor possible to deal fully with its provisions in this chapter. A very brief description of a few of its prominent features must suffice:

1. The consignment note

The form and content of the consignment note are specified in great detail in the Convention. The contract of carriage comes into existence when the forwarding (*i.e.* the first) railway has accepted the goods for carriage along with the consignment note duly completed and signed by the consignor.

Two types of consignment note are in use—one for fast carriage (*grande vitesse* ("great speed")) and the other for slow carriage (*petite vitesse* ("little speed")). The former is distinguished by its red borders. In the case of *grande vitesse* the goods must leave within 12 hours and then travel not less than 300 kilometres per 24-hour transit period. In the case of *petite vitesse* the despatch period extends to 24 hours and the travel rate is not less than 200 kilometres per 24-hour transit period.

2. Consignor's right to modify contract during transit

The consignor has extensive rights to alter the contract of carriage up to the time when the consignment note has been handed to the consignee or the goods have been accepted by him. These rights include the right of stoppage *in transitu* ("in transit") (not dependent, as in Scots law, on a buyer's insolvency) and the right to change the consignee, the destination and the speed of the transit.

3. Liability of railway for loss, damage or delay

6–144   The railway is liable for total or partial loss of the goods, for damage to them, and for delay (*i.e.* for exceeding the transit period) between the time of accepting the goods for carriage and the time of delivery, unless it can prove that the cause was one of the excepted perils specified in the Convention. The list of excepted perils is an extensive one.

6–145   If the goods are not at the consignee's disposal within 30 days after the expiry of the transit period, they are presumed to be lost.

4. Limitation in amount of compensation

6–146   The railway's liability for loss is limited to 100 gold francs[3] per kilogram, but the sender may make in the consignment note a declaration of interest in delivery and pay an increased charge, in which case compensation is payable up to the amount of interest declared. The railway must also refund the carriage charges, customs duties and other expenses paid for the missing goods.

6–147   Liability for damage to the goods depends on the amount by which the goods have been diminished in value; the compensation for damage will never exceed the amount payable for loss.

6–148   Liability for delay is calculated with reference to the carriage charges; in no circumstances will the compensation exceed twice the amount of the carriage charges.

6–149   These maximum limits for loss, damage or delay are doubled if the cause was gross negligence of the railway, and are removed altogether if the cause was the railway's wilful misconduct.

5. Time-limit for claims

6–150   Claims become barred if not made within one year (or three years, if wilful misconduct is alleged against the railway).

6. Jurisdiction

6–151   The forwarding railway is liable for the whole journey including delivery. The delivering railway is similarly liable, even if it never received the goods. Other railways can be made liable only for their respective sections of the transit.

6–152   The effect of these rules is to enable the consignor or consignee to choose the country in which to sue; usually the consignor will be the pursuer, and he will choose to sue the forwarding railway in his own country; however, the consignee, once he has received the consignment note, is the party with the greater interest in making a claim and he is likely to prefer to sue the delivering railway in his own country.

6–153   These rules apply only as between the railways on the one hand and the consignor or consignee on the other hand. Where the question is between two or more of the railways themselves, different rules elaborated in the Convention apply.

---

[3] Latin Union or germinal gold francs.

II CARRIAGE OF GOODS BY SEA

The law relating to the carriage of goods by sea is part of maritime law, and it is well settled that the maritime law of Scotland is the same as that of England, and that both have much in common with the maritime law of continental countries. In support of this, reference may be made to the following well-known statements:

(a) Bell's *Commentaries*, Vol. I, p. 547: "The maritime law . . . partakes more of the character of international law than any other branch of jurisprudence; and in all the discussions on this subject in our courts, the Continental collections and treatises on this subject, and the English books of reports, have been received as authority by our judges, where not unfitted for our adoption by any peculiarity which our practice does not recognise."

(b) The opinion of Lord President Inglis, who was not one to accept English law where it differed from Scots law, in *Boettcher* v. *Carron Co.* (1861) 23 D. 322, a case arising out of a collision between two vessels in the river Carron: The decision was that, both vessels having been at fault, liability for the damage had to be apportioned according to the rules of maritime law.

Lord President Inglis (then holding the office of Lord Justice-Clerk) said (at p. 330): "What, then, is the maritime law of Scotland applicable to a case of collision, where both ships are to blame for the occurrence? It is impossible to say, that there is any peculiarity in our jurisprudence in this department, which distinguishes it from the maritime law of other nations, or in particular from the admiralty law of England. In many, if not in most departments, the law of Scotland and the law of England are derived from different sources; and thus starting with different principles it is not surprising that they should, in some departments, still more widely diverge in the practice of centuries. But the admiralty law of the two countries is derived from the same source, namely, the ancient customs of the commercial nations of Europe, which have grown up into a system with the knowledge and assent of both England and Scotland, as members of the commercial community of nations, and which, within certain limits and with certain exceptions, have all the force of an international code."

The judge then referred to the fact that at the time of the Union of the Parliaments in 1707 it had not been deemed necessary to provide for the maintenance of any peculiar maritime law of Scotland, and continued (at p. 331):

"But it would be very surprising if, at the present day, ships enjoying the privileges, and subject to the conditions of British registry, should sail from the ports of the United Kingdom, under the same flag, and subject to the same statutory regulations in all respects, and yet that, in case of collision, the legal rights of the parties might vary, according as the case may be tried in one British Admiralty Court or another."

Great weight was attached in later cases to that statement.

(c) The speeches in the House of Lords in *Currie* v. *McKnight* (1896) 24 R. (H.L.) 1, which concerned a claim for a maritime lien:

The facts of the case are narrated at 8–67, below.

The House of Lords held that under Scots as under English law there was no maritime lien for damage caused by the crew of a vessel as distinct from damage caused by the instrumentality of the vessel itself (as in a collision).

Lord Chancellor Halsbury said (at p. 2): "I cannot doubt that on such questions it is the law of Great Britain that prevails, and that Scottish Admiralty Courts and English Admiralty Courts administer the same law. The Admiralty law, as we know it, differs from the common law of England, and the common law of Scotland differs from the common law of England. But the reason is obvious—the laws of England and Scotland were derived from different sources in respect of these two branches of the law. The Admiralty laws were derived both by Scotland and England from the same source. . . . It would be strange, as well as in the highest degree inconvenient, if a different maritime law prevailed in two different parts of the same island."

Lord Watson said (at p. 3): "From the earliest times the Courts of Scotland exercising jurisdiction in Admiralty causes have disregarded the municipal rules of Scottish law, and have invariably professed to administer the law and customs of the sea generally prevailing among maritime states. In later times, with the growth of British shipping, the Admiralty law of England has gradually acquired predominance, and resort has seldom been had to the laws of other states for the guidance of the Courts."

Lord Shand said (at p. 7): "The maritime law to be applied in questions like the present—Admiralty questions—is, I think, the same in Scotland as in this country [i.e. *England*]."

6–158   The passages quoted in (a), (b) and (c), above, emphasise the uniformity of Scots, English, and other foreign maritime law. Occasionally, there are conflicting authorities, which give rise to difficulties. An illustration is *Sailing Ship "Blairmore" Co. Ltd.* v. *Macredie* (1897) 24 R. 893:

This case involved the question whether, for the purposes of marine insurance, the ship was a total constructive loss or only a partial loss. The court, in holding that the loss was a partial loss, followed the rule of the English Admiralty Court in preference to an early decision of the Court of Session (*Robertson, Forsyth & Co.* v. *Stewart, Smith and Ors.*, 10 Feb. 1809, F.C.). The decision was reached despite the argument that the law of France and the United States and probably every maritime country differed from English law on the point.

Lord Trayner said (at p. 901): "There is nothing, therefore, beyond the decision of the Court of Session in *Robertson's* case which can be referred to in support of the argument that the rules of the Scotch law differ from that held in England. The law of both countries applicable to mercantile and maritime questions has been much developed since 1809, and that is another reason for declining to hold a single judgment pronounced in that year as fixing a rule binding upon us now. Second, where there is a well-settled rule on any question in the law of England, and no existing rule or principle in our law with which the English rule conflicts, it is desirable that the same rule should be followed here as there in order that there may not be conflicting rules on the same question prevailing in different parts of the same kingdom, and that even where the doctrine so settled differs from the rules of other states."

Lord Moncreiff said (at p. 907): "We are not bound by the English decisions; but looking to our close commercial relations with England, and the fact that our merchant shipping law is regulated by a code applicable to both countries, it would be unfortunate if a different rule on this point obtained in Scotland from that established in England. . . . On the whole matter, I think that, in the absence of any authority in our own law to the contrary, there are sufficiently strong reasons of expediency to lead us to adopt that of England."

(The decision of the Court of Session was reversed by the House of Lords ((1898) 25 R. (H.L.) 57) on a ground which made it unnecessary to decide whether the laws of Scotland and England were identical on the question in issue.)

The law relating to carriage of goods by sea is partly common law and partly statute. The most important legislation now is the Carriage of Goods by Sea Act 1971, which came into force in June 1977. Certain provisions of the Bills of Lading Act 1855 and of the Merchant Shipping Acts 1894 to 1981 also require to be noted.

At common law, in any case where there is no express contract, a ship-owner undertaking to carry goods by sea for reward comes within the edict *nautae, caupones, stabularii* ("sailors, inn-keepers, stable-keepers") (see 6–19, above), and so incurs the liability of a common carrier.

In practice, however, carriage by sea is always regulated by an express contract, often referred to as "the contract of affreightment."

Writing is usual, but not essential, for the formation of the contract. An instance of a contract inadvertently made orally can be seen in *McCutcheon* v. *David MacBrayne Ltd.*, 1964 S.C. (H.L.) 28 (6–68, above).

The two principal documents used in the carriage of goods by sea are:

(a) the charterparty, which is the contractual document appropriate where the whole or a principal part of the ship is let to one person; and

(b) the bill of lading, which gives evidence of the terms of the contract of carriage where, for instance, a general ship accepts parcels of goods from many different consignors.

If there is neither a charterparty nor a bill of lading, the terms of the contract of affreightment will normally be found in some other formal writing, such as the shipowner's sailing bills or an agreement entered into between shipowner and consignor.

Only the charterparty and the bill of lading need be considered in this chapter.

(a) Charterparty

The two parties to a contract of charterparty are the shipowner and the charterer. By the contract the charterer takes on hire from the shipowner the whole or a principal part of the ship.

A charterparty may be:

(i) a charterparty by demise, under which the control of the ship, and of its master and crew is transferred, for the duration of the charter, from the shipowner to the charterer;

(ii) a voyage charterparty, under which the ship is hired for a voyage or for several voyages; or

(iii) a time charterparty, under which the ship is hired for a specified period.

6–168   In (i) the master and crew become servants of the charterer, whereas in (ii) and (iii) the master and crew remain servants of the shipowner, the charterer having only the temporary use of their services along with his temporary use of the ship for the conveyance of the goods—which may be his own or may be those of other persons.

6–169   The parties to a charterparty are free to choose their own terms, but in practice standard contracts on printed forms are used. Blanks on the forms are completed, and clauses may be added, altered, or deleted, to suit the circumstances and the wishes of the parties.

6–170   Where a dispute arises between shipowner and charterer as to the terms of a charterparty, the court interprets the charterparty in such a way as to give effect, as far as possible, to the intentions of the parties as expressed in that document.

6–171   Failure by one of the parties to implement the terms of the charterparty as interpreted by the court entitles the other party to claim damages as for breach of any other contract. The remedy of rescission will also be available, if the breach is of a fundamental term. An instance of a successful claim for damages is *Gifford and Co.* v. *Dishington and Co.* (1871) 9 M. 1045:

D. & Co. were corn merchants in Leith. They had 1,800 quarters of barley lying at Caen in Normandy, and chartered the "Andalusia" from G. & Co. of Leith.

The case turned on the interpretation of a clause in the charterparty, by which the ship was to "load a *full and complete cargo* of barley, in bulk not exceeding what she can reasonably stow and carry."

After taking on 1,175 quarters of the barley, the captain declined to take more. He considered that that was all that the ship could with safety carry across the harbour bar. If, however, he had waited for a few days, there would have been a higher tide and the ship could then have taken more, if not the whole, of the barley.

The freight was about £162. Of this D. & Co. paid £80, but refused to pay the balance on the ground that the ship had not taken a *full cargo*.

G. & Co. raised an action for the balance of the freight, and D. & Co. raised a counter action to recover damages sustained through G. & Co.'s failure to implement the charterparty.

Held that the terms of the charterparty implied that the ship was to take as much grain as she could with safety carry across the bar at the highest spring tide, and that, since that had not been done, D. & Co. were entitled to damages from G. & Co. for breach of contract.

The amount due by G. & Co. to D. & Co. was about £3, calculated as follows:

Freight of a small sailing-vessel chartered to bring the remainder of the barley to Leith	£55
Loss on the barley caused by a fall in the market during the delay	30
Total damages due to D. & Co.	£85

Less balance of freight due to G. & Co.   82

Amount due to D. & Co.   £3

Some of the most important legal aspects of charterparties are considered below under these headings:
  (i) implied undertakings by shipowner;
 (ii) implied undertakings by charterer; and
(iii) usual clauses in charterparties.

(i) *Implied Undertakings by Shipowner*

The following undertakings by the shipowner are implied in a charterparty, unless they are expressly excluded:
  1. that the ship is seaworthy;
  2. that the ship will proceed with reasonable despatch; and
  3. that there will be no unjustifiable deviation.

1. Seaworthiness

In a voyage charterparty, the shipowner's implied undertaking is that
the ship is, at the time when the voyage begins, seaworthy for that voyage
and for the cargo carried. Seaworthiness is "warranted" (*i.e.* guaranteed): it is not enough for the shipowner to prove that he took due care to
make the ship seaworthy. If the charterer discovers, before the voyage
begins, that the ship is unseaworthy, he is entitled to rescind the contract
unless the defect can easily be remedied. In any other case, the charterer's
claim will be for damages for the loss caused by the unseaworthiness.

In a time charterparty, the shipowner's implied undertaking is that
the ship is seaworthy at the beginning of the period of the charter and that
he will maintain it in that condition. There is here no implied warranty
that the ship will be seaworthy at the beginning of each particular voyage
throughout the period of the charter. Unseaworthiness justifies repudiation of the contract by the charterer only if there is such long delay in
remedying the defect that the purpose of the charter is defeated.

Seaworthiness relates to the ability to withstand the ordinary perils
of the sea only, not necessarily exceptionally stormy conditions.

The two following Scottish cases decided by the House of Lords
illustrate unseaworthiness:

   (a) *Gilroy, Sons & Co.* v. *Price & Co.* (1892) 20 R. (H.L.) 1 (*rev.*
the judgment of the Court of Session at (1891) 18 R. 569): A water pipe
had been left uncased, and it was broken by the pressure of the cargo in
rough weather. The ship, the "Tilkhurst," was carrying jute from Chitta-
gong to Dundee, and as a result of the break in the pipe the cargo was
damaged by sea water. The usual practice in ships carrying jute was to
have pipes cased before the cargo was loaded.

Held that the want of casing was a defect which amounted to unseaworthiness, and that the shipowners were therefore liable to the
charterers for damages.

Lord Watson said (at p. 5): "The 'Tilkhurst' was not in a condition to
carry her cargo with reasonable safety unless and until the pipe which

eventually led to the damage was properly cased. That defect must be regarded as a breach of the shipowner's implied warranty of seaworthiness if it ought to have been remedied before the voyage began. On the other hand, if the want of casing was such a defect as is usually and may conveniently and properly be set right in the course of the voyage, the failure to case was a negligent omission on the part of the master or crew. . . . It may in some cases be a very nice question whether the defect comes within the first or the second of these categories."

The lack of casing was not a defect which could have been remedied without trouble during the voyage: the pipe was neither visible nor accessible without removal of part of the cargo; the defect was therefore a structural defect amounting to unseaworthiness because it made the ship plainly unfit for the due and safe carriage of the cargo which its owners had undertaken to carry.

6–179   (b) *A/B Karlshamns Oljefabriker* v. *Monarch Steamship Co. Ltd.*, 1949 S.C. (H.L.) 1; 1947 S.C. 179: In 1939, a Swedish firm of manufacturers purchased a quantity of soya beans to be shipped at a port in Manchuria by a British steamship.

At the time when the charterparty was entered into, there was a grave risk of war in Europe, and this risk was recognised by the shipowners. The charterparty therefore contained a clause that anything done in compliance with the orders of the British Government should not be deemed a deviation and that delivery in accordance with such orders should be a fulfilment of the contract.

The ship ought to have arrived at Karlshamn in Sweden before the end of July, but, owing to delay which had been caused by the need to have repairs done at the commencement of the voyage, the ship was still at sea when war broke out on September 3. The British Government placed an embargo on the voyage to Sweden and ordered the ship to proceed to Glasgow. There the purchasers took possession of the cargo and had it transhipped to Sweden in Swedish vessels.

Held that as it had been the ship's initial unseaworthiness which had caused the delay and had thus subjected the ship to the embargo and direction—a possibility foreseen by the shipowners—the purchasers were entitled to recover as damages from the shipowners the cost of transhipment in the Swedish vessels from Glasgow to Sweden.

2. Reasonable despatch

6–180   The ship must proceed with reasonable despatch. The shipowner's failure to do so, if it is serious, entitles the charterer to rescind the contract, and in other cases gives him a right to damages.

3. No unjustifiable deviation

6–181   The ship must proceed without deviation from the prescribed course, or, if there is no prescribed course, from the ordinary trade route.

6–182   Deviation is justifiable if it is expressly allowed by the charterparty or if it is necessary for the safe prosecution of the voyage (*e.g.* for repairs) or in order to save life (but not property).

Where there has been unjustifiable deviation, the charterer may repudiate the contract, or alternatively treat it as still binding and claim damages.

Unjustifiable deviation deprives the shipowner of the benefit of exception clauses in the charterparty, and so he becomes liable for any loss or damage to the goods unless he can prove that the loss or damage was caused by an act of God or of the Queen's enemies, the fault of the consignor, or inherent vice, and *in addition*, that the loss or damage would also have occurred even if he had not deviated.

(ii) *Implied Undertakings by Charterer*

The charterer impliedly undertakes not to ship dangerous goods. If he does, and they cause loss or damage, he will be liable.

Sections 446 to 450 of the Merchant Shipping Act 1894 relate to dangerous goods. They include the provision that the nature of dangerous goods must be distinctly marked on the outside of the package, and that the master or shipowner must be given written notice of their nature and of the name and address of the consignor before the goods are taken on board.

The shipowner or master is entitled to refuse goods which are not properly packed, as in *Keddie, Gordon & Co.* v. *North British Railway Co.* (1886) 14 R. 233:

K. & Co., tweed manufacturers at Galashiels, forwarded a bale of cloth by rail to Sutcliffe, a shipping agent at Grimsby. The bale was intended for Berlin, and had a threefold wrapper—two covers of jute and one of oilcloth.

On its arrival at Grimsby, the package was found to be frayed and some slight damage had been done to the cloth. Sutcliffe refused to take delivery, being of the opinion that the goods could not be safely forwarded in their damaged package.

The railway company thereupon returned them to K. & Co., who repacked them and forwarded them, again via Grimsby, to Germany.

On arrival in Berlin, the goods were rejected as being too late, and were returned to K. & Co., who sold them for about £32 less than the invoice price.

K. & Co. claimed £32 plus expenses of about £4 from the railway company as damages.

Held that Sutcliffe had been entitled to refuse to take delivery of the package, and that the loss of market was the direct result of the damage done to the package by the railway company, which was therefore liable to K. & Co. for the amount claimed.

In a time charterparty, the charterer in addition impliedly undertakes that he will use the ship only between good and safe ports.

(iii) *Usual Clauses in Charterparties*

The express terms in the clauses of a charterparty may to some extent state undertakings which would otherwise be implied and may to some extent vary or exclude such undertakings.

Some of the usual clauses are mentioned in the following paragraphs:

1. Specification of ship

6–191   By the leading clause the shipowner usually undertakes to provide, for a specified voyage or specified period of time, a named ship, stating its size, speed, class in Lloyd's register, *etc.*

This undertaking is treated as fundamental, and, if not implemented, entitles the charterer to rescind the charterparty. It is, however, open to the shipowner, by an express term, to reserve the right to substitute another ship. Similarly, by an express provision in a time charterparty, the charterer may have conferred on him an option to renew the charter for a further period.

2. Place and time of delivery of ship

6–192   The port and the time for delivery of the ship to the charterer will usually be specified. If the ship is not at the port of loading when the charterparty is entered into, the shipowner will usually undertake that it will proceed with reasonable despatch to that port.

6–193   Delay in delivery of the ship at the port of loading gives the charterer a claim for damages against the shipowner, but, provided it is not unreasonable, does not entitle him to rescind the contract. However, an exceptionally long delay, even although it has been caused by circumstances for which the shipowner cannot be held responsible, may be so fundamental as to put an end to the contract, in accordance with the doctrine of "frustration of the adventure." An instance is the English case *Jackson* v. *Union Marine Insurance Co. Ltd.* (1874) L.R. 10 C.P. 125:

J. contracted to send his ship with all possible speed, unless prevented by perils of the sea, from Liverpool to Newport, for the carriage of a cargo of iron rails to be used in the construction of an American railway.

The ship sailed from Liverpool on January 2, 1872, went aground upon the rocks at Carnarvon Bay the following day, and was not repaired until the month of August.

Held that the charterers had been justified in rescinding the charterparty with J. and chartering another ship for the carriage, even although the delay had been caused by "perils of the sea," for which, by the terms of the contract, J. was not to be responsible.

3. Seaworthiness

6–194   There is usually a clause guaranteeing seaworthiness, the shipowner undertaking that, for example, the ship is "tight, staunch and strong, and in every way fitted for the voyage."

6–195   Such an undertaking may, according to the words used, be the same as or different from the warranty of seaworthiness which would otherwise be implied: for instance, the clause is likely to relate to the time of the making of the charterparty or to the time when the ship sails *for* the port of loading, and not to the time at which the ship sails *from* the port of loading.

4. The route

6–196   The charterparty may, in addition to specifying the port of discharge, prescribe the route to be followed. This will displace the undertaking which would otherwise be implied that the ship is to proceed to its destination by the usual route.

Departure from a prescribed route amounts to deviation, which causes the shipowner to lose the benefit of exemption clauses.

However, express permission is often given in the charterparty for deviation such as would not be impliedly justifiable; *e.g.* the ship may have liberty to call at any ports in any order, liberty to tow and assist vessels in distress, and liberty to deviate for the purpose of saving property as well as saving life.

5. Providing a full cargo

There may be an express undertaking by the charterer to provide a full and complete cargo of a particular description.

If the charterer then fails to provide a cargo substantially corresponding to the description and in a fit state for loading, the shipowner may refuse to load the cargo.

6. The freight

The charterparty will specify the freight, *i.e.* the consideration to be paid to the shipowner for the carriage of the goods on his ship.

In the absence of provision to the contrary, payment of freight and delivery of the goods are concurrent conditions, *i.e.* freight is payable only on delivery of the cargo at its destination. There may, however, be express agreement for "advance freight," in which case freight will be payable at some earlier date than delivery (*e.g.* on loading or at a specified time after loading). In *Watson & Co.* v. *Shankland et al.* (1871) 10 M. 142, seven judges of the Court of Session held that an advance of freight was recoverable (unless the charterparty included a stipulation to the contrary) when the ship with its cargo was lost, the principle applicable being that of *condictio causa data causa non secuta* ("the action applicable where a consideration has been given and a consideration has not followed"), part of the doctrine of restitution. (On an interpretation of the terms of the particular charterparty, however, a majority of the seven judges held that the shipowners were not in that case liable to repay the advance of freight to the charterers, and on this point the Court of Session's judgment was affirmed by the House of Lords ((1873) 11 M. (H.L.) 51).)

Another qualification to the rule that freight is not payable until delivery of the goods at their destination occurs in connection with "*pro rata* ('proportionate') freight," also referred to as "freight *pro rata itineris* ('for the proportionate [*part*] of the journey')": the parties agree that delivery at an intermediate port is to be accepted as part-performance of the contract, freight being payable in proportion to the part of the voyage completed. There is no implied undertaking on the charterer's part to pay *pro rata* freight: his agreement is essential.

Where the charterer has undertaken to supply a certain quantity of goods and supplies a lesser quantity with the result that the shipowner would not receive the expected sum as freight, the shipowner may be entitled to claim "dead freight," *i.e.* an amount representing the loss caused by the charterer's failure to supply the specified quantity. The master has a duty to try to obtain goods from other sources to add to the cargo, so as to minimise the claim for dead freight against the charterer.

6–204 In a time charterparty, the sum payable by charterer to shipowner is usually a monthly sum payable in advance, with a provision that, if the ship is lost, freight paid in advance and not earned is recoverable by the charterer.

6–205 The shipowner has a lien over the goods for the freight. Part VII of the Merchant Shipping Act 1894 (ss. 492-501) extended the lien to the situation where the goods are placed in a warehouse at the port of discharge.

7. Limitation of shipowner's liability

6–206 The charterparty normally limits the shipowner's common law liability by listing various "excepted perils." Some of the phrases used in the list have required interpretation from the courts. The list is usually in a printed clause composed by the shipowner for his own protection, including protection from negligence of the master and other servants, and will therefore be strictly construed *contra proferentem* ("against the party putting it forward"). In particular, an exemption clause is assumed not to exclude the shipowner's implied undertaking of seaworthiness: the following are two illustrations:

6–207 (a) *Seville Sulphur and Copper Co. Ltd.* v. *Colvils, Lowden & Co.* (1888) 15 R. 616: The vessel was lost as a result of the breakdown of her boiler through the presence of muddy water in it, and the charterers brought an action against the shipowners for damages on account of the loss of the cargo.

The shipowners relied on a clause in the charterparty freeing them from liability for "errors or negligence of navigation, of whatsoever nature and kind, *during* said voyage."

It was proved that the muddy water had been introduced into the boiler when it was filled from the river Guadalquiver at Seville the night *before* the voyage commenced.

Held that, as the ship was thereby made unseaworthy at the time when the voyage was to start, the shipowners were not protected by the exemption clause.

6–208 (A contrasting case involving the same shipowners was *Cunningham* v. *Colvils, Lowden & Co.* (1888) 16 R. 295: In this case the vessel was lost as a result of the failure of steam power, attributable to the water having been allowed to run too low in the boiler during a voyage from Seville to Swansea.

This was held to fall within the exception "errors or negligence of navigation," and the shipowners were therefore not liable in damages to the charterers for the loss of the cargo.)

6–209 (b) *Park* v. *Duncan & Son* (1898) 25 R. 528: The vessel sailed from Hamburg to Sunderland with an insufficient supply of coals for that voyage, and had as a result to accept salvage services.

The shipowners paid the salvors, and brought an action against the charterers for relief.

The question arose of whether the circumstances fell within the clause "accidents of navigation excepted, even when occasioned by negligence, default, or error in judgment of the pilot, master, mariners, or other servants of the shipowners."

Held that the failure to provide a sufficient supply of coals was not a fault in the navigation of the vessel within the exemption clause, but a failure on the master's part to see that the vessel was seaworthy before sailing. The liability for the salvage services therefore remained with the shipowners.

If loss or damage results from an excepted peril, the master, as representing the shipowner, must still take reasonable measures to minimise the loss or damage; *e.g.* in *Adam* v. *J. & D. Morris* (1890) 18 R. 153, where, through the fault of the engineer (a matter clearly within the exceptions clause), water had made its way into the hold of the vessel and damaged the cargo of oil-cake, the shipowners were held liable on account of failure to intimate the accident to the cargo-owner so that further deterioration might be prevented.

There are statutory limitations on, and exclusions of, liability in the Merchant Shipping Acts 1894 to 1981. The provisions at present in force are those of Part VIII of the Merchant Shipping Act 1894, as amended by the Merchant Shipping (Liability of Shipowners and Others) Act 1958 and by the Merchant Shipping Act 1981. Changes have, however, been made by provisions of the Merchant Shipping Act 1979 which are not yet in operation.

(a) *Limitation and exclusion of liability (present position)*

(i) **Limitation of liability**—By section 503 of the Act of 1894, as amended by section 1 of the Act of 1958, the shipowner is not liable for loss or damage caused without his actual fault or privity to goods, merchandise, or other things on board the ship beyond an aggregate amount equivalent to 1,000 gold francs[5] for each ton of the ship's tonnage. For "1,000 gold francs" the Merchant Shipping Act 1981 (s. 1(2)) substitutes "66·67 special drawing rights" (as defined by the International Monetary Fund).

Section 3 of the Act of 1958 extended the limitation to the ship's master and all the crew and other servants of the shipowner when acting in the course of their employment, even in cases of their actual fault or privity. The same limitation was extended to charterers.

The phrase "without his actual fault or privity" has been interpreted by the courts on a number of occasions. One Scottish case which reached the House of Lords was *Standard Oil Co. of New York* v. *Clan Line Steamers Ltd.*, 1924 S.C. (H.L.) 1:

The "Clan Gordon," a ship of the turret type, had been chartered for the carriage of an oil cargo from New York to China.

Shortly after the ship left New York, the master ordered the water in two ballast tanks to be pumped out, and the result was that the ship capsized and sank, with the loss of the whole cargo.

Several years earlier, a sister turret ship had been lost in similar circumstances, and on the happening of that event the builders of the turret ships had issued instructions as to the loading of such ships,

---

[5] "Poincaré" gold francs.

including a definite warning that with a cargo of the class being carried on the "Clan Gordon" the water ballast tanks should be kept full.

The owners of the "Clan Gordon" did not themselves communicate these instructions to the master, but handed them to their chief engineer who was responsible for structural matters and who had a discretion to communicate the instructions to the master. The chief engineer did not inform the master of the instructions.

The charterers sued the shipowners for the value of the cargo, and the shipowners sought to limit their liability to £8 for each ton of the ship's tonnage (the limit then applicable under section 503 of the Merchant Shipping Act 1894).

Held that the shipowners were not entitled to the benefit of the limitation in section 503, since they could not show that the loss had occurred without their "fault or privity"; they ought to have ensured that the master was made aware of the special instructions issued by the builders.

6–215   (ii) **Exclusion of liability for fire and theft**—The following provisions apply only to British ships:

6–216   By section 502 of the Act of 1894, the shipowner is not liable to make good to any extent whatever any loss or damage happening without his actual fault or privity to goods, merchandise, or other things on board his ship, where the loss or damage is caused by fire on board. Section 3 of the Act of 1958 extended this protection to the ship's master and all the crew and other servants of the shipowner when acting in the course of their employment, and it further provided that the protection was to apply even where there was actual fault or privity on the part of the master or the other person. The protection was also extended to charterers.

6–217   By section 502 of the Act of 1894, the shipowner is not liable to make good to any extent whatever any loss or damage happening without his actual fault or privity to any gold, silver, diamonds, watches, jewels, or precious stones on board his ship, if the true nature and value of the items have not been declared in writing by the owner or shipper of them to the owner or master of the ship and if the loss or damage has been caused by "any robbery, embezzlement, making away with, or secreting thereof." Section 3 of the Act of 1958 extended this provision to the ship's master and all the crew and other servants of the shipowner when acting in the course of their employment, and also extended it to charterers. If, however, there is fault or privity on the part of the master or other person, that person is personally liable for the theft.

(b) *Limitation and exclusion of liability under the Merchant Shipping Act 1979*

6–218   The Act of 1979, when fully in force, will repeal Part VIII of the Act of 1894 and the amendments of that Part made by the Acts of 1958 and 1981, and will put in their place the provisions in sections 17 and 18 of itself, relating to limitation of liability and to exclusion of liability respectively.

6–219   (i) **Limitation of liability**—Section 17 gives the force of law in the United Kingdom to the Convention on Limitation of Liability for Maritime Claims 1976, commonly referred to as the "London Convention."

The Convention is set out in Schedule 4 to the Act. The main changes are as follows:

(1) The range of claims subject to limitation is increased: *e.g.* the privilege of limitation is extended to claims against salvors, to claims resulting from delay in the carriage, and to claims in respect of the removal, destruction or rendering harmless of the cargo.

(2) The phrase "actual fault or privity" is not used in the Convention. The formula under the Convention is that a person loses the privilege of limitation of liability "if it is proved that the loss resulted from his personal act or omission, committed with the intent to cause such loss, or recklessly and with knowledge that such loss would probably result." This new formula is designed to ensure that the limitation is unbreakable in normal cases.

(3) The limits, which have broadly been raised, are calculated in "units of account" instead of in gold francs, and are more specific, varying according to the tonnage of the ship; *e.g.* for a ship with a tonnage between 300 tons and 500 tons the limit is 167,000 units of account, and for a ship with a tonnage from 501 to 30,000, an addition is made of 167 units of account for each ton above 500 tons. The unit of account referred to is the special drawing right as defined by the International Monetary Fund.

(ii) **Exclusion of liability for fire and theft**—Section 18 of the Act of 1979 re-enacts with amendments section 502 of the Act of 1894 as amended by the Acts of 1958 and 1981. The provisions continue to apply only to British ships. The main changes are as follows:

(1) The language has been modernised and clarified; *e.g.* there is no longer the phrase "making away with" or the word "secreting": the words used are "where any gold, silver, watches, jewels or precious stones on board the ship are lost or damaged by reason of theft, robbery or other dishonest conduct."

(2) The phrase "actual fault or privity" has been discarded. The new provision is that a person's liability is not excluded if the loss or damage results from his "personal act or omission, committed with the intent to cause such loss, or recklessly and with knowledge that such loss would probably result." These words have been incorporated here from the London Convention (see 6–221, above).

8. Loading and discharge

Provision is usually made in a charterparty for loading and discharge, including the manner of loading and discharge and the time allowed for them. Where there is no express provision, loading and discharge are governed by the custom of the particular port.

The charterparty usually specifies a number of days for the loading, or discharge, of the cargo. These are known as "lay days," and normally begin to run when the charterer is notified by the shipowner that the ship is ready to receive, or discharge, the cargo as the case may be. If the charterparty does not fix lay days, a reasonable time is allowed for loading and discharge.

If the charterer fails to provide the cargo at all within the required time, the shipowner is entitled to treat the contract as repudiated. Where the cargo is provided but is not completely loaded within the required time, the shipowner has normally only the remedy of damages.

6–229   The charterparty may state a further number of days which will be allowed to the charterer for loading or discharge after the expiry of the lay days, provided additional payment, referred to as "demurrage," is made by charterer to shipowner.

6–230   Different views have been taken of the nature of demurrage:

6–231   In some cases demurrage has been treated as distinct from damages for detention of the ship, the latter being the amount for which the charterer incurs liability if he detains the ship beyond the lay days and also beyond the demurrage days. For instance, in *Gardiner* v. *Macfarlane, McCrindell & Co.* (1889) 16 R. 658, when construing a clause in a charterparty which provided "Owners to have lien on cargo for freight, dead-freight, and demurrage," the court held that the word "demurrage" did not cover damages for detention of the ship beyond the ten demurrage days allowed for in the charterparty. Similarly, in *Lilly & Co.* v. *Stevenson & Co.* (1895) 22 R. 278 (see 6–233, below), Lord Trayner observed (at p. 286):

> "Days stipulated for by the merchant, on demurrage, are just lay-days, but lay-days that have to be paid for. If a charter-party provides that the shipowner shall have ten days to load cargo, and ten days further on demurrage at a certain rate per day, the shipper has twenty days to load although he pays something extra for the last ten. Loading within the twenty days is fulfilment of the obligation to load."

6–232   On the other hand the better view appears to be that demurrage is a form of liquidate damages. This is supported by *Moor Line Ltd.* v. *Distillers Co. Ltd.*, 1912 S.C. 514:

> A charterparty allowed ten days on demurrage beyond the lay days at a certain rate. It further provided that the days for discharging should not count during the continuance of a strike, and also that in case of delay "by reason of" a strike no "claim for damages" should lie.
>
> The ship was detained at the port of discharge for four days beyond the lay days, not owing to the continuance of a strike, but owing to congestion following on the termination of a strike.
>
> The shipowners claimed demurrage for these four days.
>
> *Held* that (i) the detention was a delay "by reason of" a strike, and so no "claim for damages" could lie; and (ii) the phrase "claim for damages" was not to be interpreted as referring only to claims for damages for detention beyond the demurrage days, but included claims for demurrage. The shipowners' claim was therefore unsuccessful.
>
> Lord Salvesen said (at p. 520): "The pursuers maintained that a claim for demurrage is not a claim for damages, and that accordingly, while this provision would protect the charterer from a claim of damages for detention after the days on demurrage had expired, it confers no protection from a claim for demurrage strictly so called. . . .
>
> "The whole basis of the argument . . . depends on the view that 'demurrage' in the strict sense is not a claim for damage, but is in the nature of a payment in respect of the continued use or hire of the vessel for the charterer's purposes after the expiry of the lay days. That is a

theory of demurrage which at one time received some countenance. . . . In my opinion, however, the more correct view is that demurrage is 'agreed damages to be paid for delay of the ship in loading or unloading beyond an agreed period.' In other words, the distinction between 'demurrage' and damages for detention is that the one is liquidated damages and the other unliquidated. A claim under either head is a claim in respect of detention, and is in the nature of a claim of damages."

Lay days and demurrage days may begin, and continue, to run although the ship is not actually occupying a berth at the port where the cargo is to be loaded or discharged. An illustration is *Lilly & Co.* v. *Stevenson & Co.* (1895) 22 R. 278:

L. & Co., owners of the "Charles Steels," chartered the vessel to S. & Co. for the carriage of a cargo of coals from Bo'ness. The charterparty provided: "The charterers hereby agree to supply the said cargo. . . . The coals to be loaded in 60 hours. . . . If no longer detained, demurrage to be paid at 12s. 6d. per hour, unless detention arises from a . . . strike . . . or any cause beyond merchants' control delaying the obtaining, providing, loading, or discharging of cargo."

On November 14, the ship was put at the disposal of S. & Co. at Bo'ness, and a berth was available. However, owing to a dispute between S. & Co. and the colliery owners, there was no cargo ready to be loaded, and by the rules of the port applicable to such a situation the berth was given to another vessel.

The "Charles Steels" got a berth on November 22, but the following day a strike began at the colliery, and the loading was suspended until December 11. Loading was completed on December 15.

L. & Co. brought an action against S. & Co. for demurrage from November 16 to December 15.

Held that (i) S. & Co. had not proved that the failure to provide a cargo on November 14 had been due to a cause "beyond merchants' control," and that consequently the lay days began to run on November 14 and the demurrage days on November 16; but (ii) because of the strike exemption clause no demurrage was due for the period from November 23 to December 11.

Questions such as arose in *Lilly & Co.* v. *Stevenson & Co.* came before the House of Lords in the more recent "arrived ship" cases. In *The Aello* [1961] A.C. 135 the House held that a ship waiting at an anchorage 22 miles outside Buenos Aires could not be regarded as having "arrived" at the port, but that case was overruled by:

E.L. Oldendorff & Co. G.m.b.H. v. *Tradax Export S.A.*, *The Johanna Oldendorff* [1974] A.C. 479: The "Johanna Oldendorff" had been chartered to carry grain to one of six ports at the charterers' option. By a clause in the charterparty the time for discharge was to count "whether in berth or not."

The ship proceeded to Liverpool/Birkenhead, and anchored at the Mersey Bar, the usual waiting place for grain ships discharging at the port. This place, though within the legal limits of the port, was 17 miles from the docks. It was not until 17 days later that the ship obtained a berth.

Demurrage depended on when the ship was an "arrived ship."

Held that the "Johanna Oldendorff" when anchored at the Mersey Bar was an "arrived ship," since she had reached a position within the port where she was at the immediate and effective disposition of the charterer.

The *Johanna Oldendorff* was applied in *Federal Commerce and Navigation Co. Ltd.* v. *Tradax Export S.A., The Maratha Envoy* [1978] A.C. 1, which established the point that if the usual waiting place was outside the limits of the port a ship at anchor there was not an "arrived ship," since the voyage was not yet completed.

9. Charterer's exemption from liability for delay

6–236   There may be a clause exempting the charterer from liability for delay on his part if the delay has been caused by specified events or circumstances; *e.g.* the clause may provide that the charterer is not to be liable where "detention arises from a lock-out, strike, restriction, accident, stoppage, idle time or holidays at any works, mine or mines with which vessel may be booked, railway strikes, holidays, or idle time, or any cause beyond merchants' control" (*Lilly & Co.* v. *Stevenson & Co.*, 6–233, above).

10. Charterer's option to cancel

6–237   The charterparty may give the charterer the option to cancel it if the ship is not ready to load by a stated time or in other specified circumstances.

6–238   Where the charterer exercises such an option, he is still entitled to damages for loss which he has suffered as a result of the shipowner's breach of contract. An illustration is *Thomas Nelson & Sons* v. *Dundee East Coast Shipping Co. Ltd.*, 1907 S.C. 927:

The Edinburgh firm of publishers entered into a charterparty with the shipping company for the conveyance by the steamship "Alice" of a cargo of paper from Leith to London. The charterparty provided that the ship was expected to be ready to load about March 3, and that if it was not ready to load within seven days of March 3, the charterers were to have the option of cancelling the charter.

After entering into this charterparty, the shipping company undertook other engagements which made it impossible for the company to have the "Alice" ready to load in accordance with the publishers' charterparty.

The publishers sent their goods by other vessels at increased rates, and brought an action of damages against the shipping company.

Held that the publishers were entitled to damages, since the shipping company had, by its own act, put it out of its power to fulfil the charterparty.

11. Lien clause

6–239   The charterparty may contain a clause conferring on the shipowner a more extensive lien than he would have at common law; *e.g.* the clause may provide that the shipowner is to have a lien over the cargo for freight, advance freight, dead freight, demurrage, and general average (*i.e.* the contribution which becomes payable by a person whose property has been preserved as a result of the deliberate sacrifice of any part of the cargo or of the ship). At common law the shipowner has a lien only for freight and for general average.

12. Cesser clause

A cesser clause is one which provides that the charterer's liability under the charterparty is to cease when the cargo is loaded. Such a clause is specially appropriate where the charterer is merely an agent to fill the ship with the goods of other persons who will be liable to pay the freight. The cesser clause will protect the shipowner's right to freight by providing that he is to have a lien on the cargo for freight. In the case of ambiguity, the clause is interpreted as relieving the charterer only for breaches of the charterparty which occur after the loading, and not for breaches occurring prior to or during loading.

(b) Bill of Lading

A bill of lading is defined by Bell as "the written evidence of the undertaking to carry by sea, and deliver the goods therein described, for a certain freight" (*Commentaries*, Vol. I, p. 590).

A bill of lading differs from a charterparty in that:

(i) whereas a charterparty is itself the contract of affreightment, the bill of lading, being a document issued only after the terms of the contract have been agreed on and the goods have been put on board ship, is not itself the contract, but evidence of the contract; and

(ii) the bill of lading, besides being evidence of the terms of the contract of carriage, performs other functions—as a receipt for the goods and as a document of title to the goods—which a charterparty does not perform.

Where goods are sent by sea, it is usual for there to be both a charterparty and a bill of lading, the charterparty being the contract between the shipowner and the charterer, and the bill of lading being the document, often incorporating terms from the charterparty, issued by the master to the shipper (who may or may not be the charterer) at the time when the goods are put on board. In issuing the bill of lading the master is acting as agent for the shipowner except that in the case of a charter by demise he will be acting as agent for the charterer.

A bill of lading is usually drawn in a set of two, three or four, with the stipulation that if any one of the set is accomplished, the others are to be void. The master usually retains one, and delivers the others to the shipper, who may deliver one or more to his agent at the port of destination or to the consignee (*e.g.* a buyer who has paid for the goods).

The holder of the bill of lading, *i.e.* the person entitled to receive delivery of the goods at the port of destination, is therefore not necessarily the shipper or the agent of the shipper. The holder may be several stages removed from the shipper (*e.g.* where there have been several sub-sales).

When a bill of lading changes hands, it often requires first to be indorsed by the present holder before being delivered by him to the new holder. The new holder is then said to be the "indorsee," and he will be entitled himself to indorse the bill of lading and deliver it to a later indorsee. So the chain may continue until the goods reach the port of destination and are delivered by the carrier to the person who then is the holder of the bill of lading.

6–247   In a bill of lading under the common law there are implied undertakings corresponding to the undertakings implied in charterparties (see 6–173 *et seq.*, above): the shipowner impliedly undertakes that the ship is seaworthy, will proceed with reasonable despatch, and will not unjustifiably deviate, and the shipper impliedly undertakes not to ship dangerous goods. The common law has, however, been superseded by statutory provisions which apply to bills of lading in which the port of shipment is a port in the United Kingdom. These statutory provisions are therefore more important for the purposes of this chapter than the common law undertakings. The statutory provisions now applicable are those of the Carriage of Goods by Sea Act 1971, which gave the Hague-Visby Rules the force of law within the United Kingdom as from June 1977.

6–248   The leading aspects of the present law relating to bills of lading may therefore be considered under these headings:
- (i) bill of lading as a receipt;
- (ii) bill of lading as evidence of the contract;
- (iii) bill of lading as a document of title; and
- (iv) Carriage of Goods by Sea Act 1971.

(i) *Bill of Lading as a Receipt*

6–249   The bill of lading is a receipt given by the master, as agent for the shipowner (or, in a charter by demise, as agent for the charterer), to the shipper (the person who delivers the goods to the ship).

6–250   The bill of lading usually contains statements as to the quantity, weight, measurements, and apparent condition of the goods. The general rule is that such statements are not conclusive, but only *prima facie* (*i.e.* rebuttable) evidence:

McLean and Hope v. *Fleming* (1871) 9 M. (H.L.) 38: McL. & H. purchased a cargo of bones and arranged for it to be shipped from various ports in the East and brought to this country on board the "Persian," owned by F.

The bills of lading signed at different ports by the captain as agent for F., recorded that 701 tons of bones had been shipped, but the ship, on its arrival at Aberdeen, the port of delivery, was found to have only 386 tons on board.

McL. & H. claimed damages from F.

Evidence was brought forward to show that only 386 tons had in fact been shipped.

Held that as the bills of lading were only *prima facie* evidence that the quantity specified in them had been put on board, McL. & H. were not entitled to damages.

6–251   Similarly, in *Crawford & Law* v. *Allan Line Steamship Co. Ltd.*, 1912 S.C. (H.L.) 56, a statement in a bill of lading: "Received in apparent good order and condition" was treated as *prima facie* evidence, so that the onus of proving that damage had been caused before the goods came into the possession of the steamship company was on that company; in this case, as the company was unable to discharge that onus, the consignees were held entitled to damages.

There are, however, two important exceptions to the general rule that statements in a bill of lading are only *prima facie* evidence:

(1) The parties may expressly agree that the bill of lading is to be conclusive.

(2) Section 3 of the Bills of Lading Act 1855 provides that a bill of lading *in the hands of a consignee or indorsee for valuable consideration* is conclusive evidence *against the master or other person signing it* that the goods stated to have been shipped have in fact been shipped, unless the holder of the bill of lading had actual notice at the time of receiving it that the goods had not in fact been laden on board. There is, however, the proviso that the master or other person who has signed may free himself from liability for the misrepresentation by showing that it was caused without any default on his part and wholly by the fraud of the shipper or of the holder or some person under whom the holder claims.

If the master has made a *bona fide* ("honest") mistake about the goods which were delivered to him, that does not count as a "default," and so he is entitled to rely on the proviso for protection from liability.

It is to be noted that this section of the Bills of Lading Act makes the bill of lading conclusive evidence only against the master or other person signing it, and not against the carrier (shipowner or charterer) unless he happens to have personally signed the bill of lading. It therefore did not apply to the situation in *McLean and Hope* v. *Fleming* (6–250, above), because that was an action against the shipowner, not against the master. Lord Chancellor Hatherley said (at 9 M. (H.L.) p. 41): "The signature of the captain, however it might affect him under the statute, which renders the signature of the captain to a bill of lading conclusive against him, has not that effect as against the owner of the vessel."

A bill of lading may include some qualification; it is then described as being a "claused" (as opposed to a "clean") bill. For instance, it may include the statement: "Weight, quantity and quality unknown." The bill of lading is then not even *prima facie* evidence against the carrier or the master that the weight, quantity or quality stated in the bill of lading has been shipped. An illustration is *Craig Line Steamship Co. Ltd.* v. *North British Storage and Transit Co.*, 1921 S.C. 114:

Bills of lading signed by the master specified that a certain number of kilograms of barley had been shipped. They also contained the clause: "Weight, quality, quantity, and contents unknown to me" (the master).

Held that these bills of lading were not *prima facie* evidence against the shipowners as to the quantity of barley shipped, and that the onus was on the shippers and indorsees of the bills of lading, who alleged short delivery, to prove that the ship had received more barley than it had delivered.

(ii) *Bill of Lading as Evidence of the Contract*

The bill of lading usually records the terms of the contract of carriage. It is then available as evidence of the terms of the contract. It often incorporates terms from the charterparty.

Difficulties can arise where there is a discrepancy between the charterparty and the bill of lading. The solution to such difficulties depends partly on the relationship of the parties between whom the question arises.

6–260   (1) The question may arise *between the shipowner and the charterer* in the situation where the charterer is himself the shipper and so has received the bill of lading. The rule generally applicable here is that the terms of the contract are to be looked for in the charterparty, and that the bill of lading operates merely as a receipt. The charterparty therefore prevails. An instance is *Delaurier* v. *Wyllie* (1889) 17 R. 167, a case heard by the whole Court of Session:

Stevenson & Co. of Glasgow sold coal to D., a merchant in France, and chartered a steamer owned by W. for the carriage of the coal to France. The charterparty contained a clause exempting W. from liability for loss arising from dangers of navigation, even when occasioned by negligence of the master or crew.

Stevenson & Co., having shipped the coal on board, received a bill of lading which exempted W. from liability for loss arising from dangers of navigation but made no mention of negligence. It included the phrase "all other conditions as per charter." Stevenson & Co. insured the coal, and sent to D. the bill of lading indorsed in D.'s favour.

The steamer with its cargo was lost through the negligence of the master or crew.

Stevenson & Co. recovered the sum insured and credited D. with the price.

D., in the interest of the insurers, raised an action against W. for damages for failing to deliver the cargo in terms of the bill of lading.

Held that W. was liable under the bill of lading, since the words "all other conditions as per charter" did not incorporate the negligence clause but only such conditions in the charterparty as affected and were to be performed by the consignee (*e.g.* payment of freight and payment of demurrage at the port of discharge).

Lord Trayner, who had a high reputation in shipping law and who had been the Lord Ordinary in the case, said at the appeal stage (at p. 187):

"The defenders maintain that there was no other contract of affreightment than the charter-party, and that the bill of lading was merely a receipt. In my opinion the bill of lading . . . was something more: not, I grant, so long as the bill of lading was in the charterers' hands, and intended only to be a receipt, but when it left the charterers by indorsement. The bill of lading, then, if not contract in itself, was evidence under the hands of the defenders of the contract under which they were agreeing to carry the particular goods specified in that bill of lading. It announced to everybody into whose hands it might come that the goods were to be carried under the conditions there specified, and no other. . . . The defenders cannot fall back upon their charter-party after authorising the charterers to announce (as by granting the bill of lading to them they did) that the goods were to be carried, not on the terms of a particular charter-party, but on the terms specified in the bill of lading; and in my opinion, when the shipowner has granted bills of lading subsequent to and different from the charter-party, and which have passed out of the charterers' or shippers' hands, it is the bill of lading and not the charter-party which regulates the right and obligation both of the shipowner and the consignee."

6–261   The general rule is, however, not always applicable:

(a) It does not apply where it can be proved that the parties intended to vary their contract by the bill of lading:

Davidson v. *Bisset & Son* (1878) 5 R. 706: By a charterparty the "Mary" was to proceed with a cargo of cement from London to Aberdeen and Cruden (a small port north of Aberdeen), and was to deliver at least 100 tons at Aberdeen and the balance at Cruden. The bill of lading stated that the cement was to be delivered at Cruden and Aberdeen, the order of the ports being thus reversed. B. & Son were both charterers and shippers.

The vessel went first to Cruden with its whole cargo, but there was not sufficient depth of water at Cruden for a vessel so heavily laden to get near the shore to land the cargo. The vessel proceeded to Aberdeen, where the whole cargo was landed. D., the shipowner, acting through the master, refused to return to Cruden with any part of the cargo.

By the terms of the charterparty freight was to be at a much higher rate for the portion to be landed at Cruden than for the portion to be landed at Aberdeen, and D. brought an action against B. & Son for the freight which would have been payable under these terms if 100 tons only had been landed at Aberdeen and the balance at Cruden. B. & Son were willing to pay only the Aberdeen rate for the whole cargo.

Held that by the bill of lading the parties had intended to vary the terms of the charterparty, and that the master had duly complied with the contract by going first to Cruden. B. & Son were therefore liable to pay the amount of freight claimed by D.

Lord Justice-Clerk Moncreiff said (at p. 709): "In matters which relate to the details of the mode in which the contract of carriage is to be performed the charter-party may be varied by the bill of lading, although the substance of the contract of affreightment is to be looked for in the charter-party. If goods are delivered to a shipmaster with directions to carry and land them in a particular way, which directions are embodied in a bill of lading signed by him, I think he is entitled and bound to carry out these directions."

(b) The general rule does not apply where the question arises between the shipowner and the charterer *qua* shipper (*i.e.* in his capacity of shipper), as is shown by *Hill Steam Shipping Co. Ltd.* v. *Hugo Stinnes Ltd.*, 1941 S.C. 324:

This was an action by shipowners against charterers, who were also shippers, for payment of freight. The bills of lading stipulated for payment of freight "as per charter-party." The charterers put forward as their defence the cesser clause in the charterparty, which provided that the charterers' liability was to cease as soon as the cargo had been shipped.

Held that as the charterers were being sued as shippers, their liability was to be found in the bills of lading, and that the stipulations in the bills of lading for payment of freight "as per charter-party" incorporated the conditions of the charterparty concerning the reception of the cargo at the port of discharge, but not the cesser clause, which was for the protection of charterers, not shippers.

(2) The question may arise *between the shipowner and the indorsee of the bill of lading* or some other holder of it who is not the charterer. There are divergent views in relation to this situation.

6–265   According to what appears to be the more authoritative view, the bill of lading is in this situation the ruling document and is *prima facie* ("rebuttable") evidence of the terms of the contract. See the passage quoted from Lord Trayner's opinion in *Delaurier* v. *Wyllie* (6–260, above): referring to the stage when the bill of lading was indorsed and left the charterers' hands, Lord Trayner said: "The bill of lading, then, if not contract in itself, was evidence under the hands of the defenders of the contract under which they were agreeing to carry the particular goods specified in that bill of lading."

6–266   The alternative view is that the bill of lading is itself the contract of carriage and not merely evidence of it.

6–267   (3) The question may arise *between the master or other person who has actually signed the bill of lading and a consignee or indorsee for valuable consideration.* By the provision in section 3 of the Bills of Lading Act 1855 already noticed (see 6–254, above), the bill of lading is then conclusive evidence that the goods stated to have been shipped have in fact been shipped, unless the holder of the bill of lading had actual notice at the time of receiving it that the goods had not in fact been laden on board.

(iii) *Bill of Lading as a Document of Title*

6–268   The bill of lading is regarded as a symbol of the goods while they are on board ship, and so transfer of the bill of lading from one party to another has, by "symbolical delivery," the effect of transferring the ownership of the goods from the transferor to the transferee. Having received the bill of lading from the master, the shipper may enter into transactions in which he uses the bill of lading as a document of title to the goods; for example, he may sell the goods outright, receiving the price from the purchaser in exchange for the bill of lading, or he may obtain a loan of money on handing over the bill of lading to the lender as security for the loan. The transferee may similarly use the bill of lading as a document of title for his own purposes.

6–269   When the goods reach the port of destination, the person who then is the holder of the bill of lading is entitled, on presenting it to the master, to delivery of the goods which it represents. The shipowner is discharged of liability once the master as his agent has delivered the goods to the holder of the bill of lading. This applies even if the holder of the bill of lading is not the person truly entitled to the goods, provided the delivery is made in good faith and without notice of any defect in the holder's title. Production of the bill of lading is essential: the shipowner is not discharged if the master delivers the goods to a person who does not produce the bill of lading. An illustration is *Pirie and Sons* v. *Warden et al.* (1871) 9 M. 523:

Wynands chartered the ship "Emily and Jessie" for the carriage of a cargo of Esparto grass from Spain to Aberdeen. The shipper, Corredor, received a bill of lading from the master.

Corredor sold the cargo to Noble of London, and handed over the bill of lading in exchange for the acceptance of a bill of exchange. Noble had agreed to supply Esparto grass to P. & Sons, papermakers in Aberdeen, and so the bill of lading passed into the hands of P. & Sons.

Meantime Wynands, who claimed that he had advanced money to Corredor on account of the cargo on board the "Emily and Jessie" and other cargoes, considered that he was the owner of the cargo, and as he had agreed to supply Tait & Sons, papermakers at Inverurie, with Esparto grass, urged Tait & Sons to take delivery of the cargo on the ship's arrival at Aberdeen.

The master, acting on the instructions of Wynands, delivered the cargo to Tait & Sons.

P. & Sons as indorsees and holders of the bill of lading claimed damages from the shipowners.

Held that delivery of the cargo by the master to Tait & Sons in the absence of a bill of lading had been wrongful and that P. & Sons, as onerous indorsees of the bill of lading, had a good title to sue the shipowners for damages.

A bill of lading, when operating as a document of title to the goods, resembles, but is not, a negotiable instrument. It is sometimes described as a "semi-negotiable instrument."

It resembles a negotiable instrument in that the contract of which it is evidence may be assigned by delivery, or by indorsement and delivery, without intimation being given to the other party to the contract, *i.e.* to the master who, as agent for the shipowner, is by the bill of lading under an obligation to deliver the goods. The printed form of bill of lading usually contains an undertaking by the master to deliver the goods "to   or to his assigns," words which indicate that the bill of lading is intended to be a transferable document.

The blank before the words "or to his assigns" may be filled up at the time when the bill of lading is issued. Where the goods are made deliverable to a named consignee or to his order or to his assigns, transfer is made by indorsement by the consignee followed by delivery. Where no consignee is named or where the goods are made deliverable to bearer, no indorsement is required: delivery of the bill of lading is all that is required to transfer the right to the goods.

An indorsement may be a special indorsement, *i.e.* one which names the transferee, or it may be an indorsement in blank, the effect of the latter being that the goods become deliverable to the bearer of the bill. A bill which has been indorsed in blank may later be specially indorsed by the insertion of a transferee's name.

A bill of lading differs from a negotiable instrument in the strict sense in that the transferee obtains no better title than the transferor had; *e.g.*:

Craig & Rose v. *Delargy &c.* (1879) 6 R. 1269: A merchant in Algeria shipped a cargo of olive oil in casks, and obtained a bill of lading from the master. The merchant sold the oil to C. & R., oil merchants in Leith, and transferred the bill of lading to C. & R.

On arrival of the ship at Leith, much of the oil was found to have leaked from the casks, and C. & R. claimed damages from the shipowners.

The leakage was proved to have been caused by the fault of the shipper in supplying insufficient casks.

Held that C. & R. could have no higher right than the shipper; and shipowners *assoilzied*.

(iv) *Carriage of Goods by Sea Act 1971*

6–275   Until 1925 bills of lading were governed mainly by the common law subject to the provisions of the Bills of Lading Act 1855 and some provisions of the Merchant Shipping Act 1894. From January 1, 1925, however, bills of lading issued at a United Kingdom port became subject to the Hague Rules.

6–276   In 1922, an international conference had been held in Brussels for the purpose of removing some of the difficulties which arose out of the lack of uniformity in the laws of various countries concerning bills of lading. The view of the conference was that a set of rules should be drawn up, suitable for adoption by the national laws of the various countries. The rules which fulfilled this purpose were known as the Hague Rules because they had originally been drafted by the International Law Association at a conference held at The Hague in 1921.

6–277   The Hague Rules were incorporated into the national laws of most trading nations. In the United Kingdom the Hague Rules were given statutory force by the Carriage of Goods by Sea Act 1924, which came into operation on January 1, 1925. The Rules were set out in the Schedule to that Act.

6–278   In the course of years some weaknesses became apparent in the Hague Rules, and in 1968 amended rules were introduced under a Protocol signed at Brussels. These amended rules are known as the Hague-Visby Rules to distinguish them from the original Hague Rules.

6–279   The Hague-Visby Rules were incorporated into the law of the United Kingdom by the Carriage of Goods by Sea Act 1971, which came into operation in June 1977, repealing the Act of 1924 and substituting the Hague-Visby Rules, set out in the Schedule to the Act of 1971, for the Hague Rules scheduled to the Act of 1924. The Act of 1971 provides that the Hague-Visby Rules "shall have the force of law" (s. 1(2)). The effect of this provision, according to the judgment of the House of Lords in *The Hollandia* [1982] 3 W.L.R. 1111, is that the Rules have supremacy over every other provision of the bill of lading: there can be no contracting out of the Rules. This marks an important change from the position existing before the Act of 1971 came into operation.

The case related to a bill of lading for the shipping of a road-finishing machine from Leith on a Dutch vessel for carriage to the Dutch West Indies. Since the port of shipment was a port in the United Kingdom, the Hague-Visby Rules applied (see 6–282, below). However, a clause in the bill of lading specified that the law of the Netherlands, which incorporated the old Hague Rules, applied to the contract. This would have restricted the carrier's liability to about £250, whereas under the Hague-Visby Rules the liability would have come to over £11,000. This lessening of liability was "null and void and of no effect" under Article III, 8 (see 6–320, below).

Lord Diplock said (at p. 1116): "The provisions of section 1 of the Act . . . appear to me to be free from any ambiguity perceptible to even the most ingenious of legal minds. The Hague-Visby Rules, or rather all those of them that are included in the Schedule, are to have the force of law in the United Kingdom; they are to be treated as if they were part of directly enacted statute law. But since they form part of an international convention which must come under the consideration of foreign as well as English courts, . . . they should be given a purposive rather than a narrow literalistic construction particularly wherever the adoption of a literalistic construction would enable the stated purpose of the international convention, viz., the unification of domestic laws of the contracting states relating to bills of lading, to be evaded by the use of colourable devices that, not being expressly referred to in the Rules, are not specifically prohibited."

The Hague-Visby Rules are, it is proposed, to be superseded by the Hamburg Rules on Bills of Lading, which were accepted by a conference of the United Nations held at Hamburg in 1978. The Hamburg Rules would apply to *all* contracts for the carriage of goods by sea between two different States, *other than charterparties,* even if the carriage was not carried out under a bill of lading. They are less weighted in the carrier's favour than the Hague-Visby Rules.

Some idea of the importance and nature of the Hague-Visby Rules may be gathered from a consideration of:

(1) the circumstances in which the Hague-Visby Rules apply (to be found in the Act of 1971 and also in some of the Articles of the Rules themselves); and

(2) the substantive Articles of the Hague-Visby Rules (as distinct from the Articles to be considered under (1)).

Under these two headings, references to sections are to sections of the Carriage of Goods by Sea Act 1971, and the phrase "the Rules" means, as in that Act, "the International Convention for the unification of certain rules of law relating to bills of lading signed at Brussels on 25th August 1924, as amended by the Protocol signed at Brussels on 23rd February, 1968" (s. 1(1)).

(1) **Circumstances in which the Hague-Visby Rules apply**

Although the Rules arose out of the need to improve the regulation of international carriage, the law of the United Kingdom does not restrict the application of the Rules to international carriage: the Rules have the force of law in carriage of goods by sea where the port of shipment is a port in the United Kingdom, whether or not the carriage is between ports in two different States (s. 1(3)). This provision of the Act overrides Article X of the Rules which provides that the Rules are to apply to carriage of goods between ports *in two different States.* The Rules therefore apply to United Kingdom coastal traffic, as well as to carriage from a United Kingdom port to a port in another State.

The Act enables the Rules to be extended by Order in Council to contracts where the port of shipment is in the Isle of Man, any of the Channel Islands, some colonies, any associated State, or any country in which the United Kingdom Government has jurisdiction. Any Order in Council would specify the territory concerned, and could be varied or revoked by a later Order in Council (ss. 4 and 5).

The Rules do not compulsorily apply unless the contract of carriage expressly or by implication provides for the issue of a bill of lading or any similar document of title (s. 1(4)). The underlying reason for this provision is that the purpose of the International Convention was to clarify the rights of holders of bills of lading who took the bills, as documents of title, in good faith and for value; where there is no bill of lading or other similar document of title, the legal position of a third party purchasing in good faith and in reliance on such a document does not arise.

6–285   The Rules may voluntarily, by agreement of the parties, be made to apply to contracts to which they would not compulsorily apply: *any* bill of lading may contain an express provision that the Rules are to govern the contract of carriage, and any non-negotiable document may contain a similar provision. The agreement of the parties then gives the Rules the force of law (s. 1(6)).

6–286   The Rules do not apply to those cases of carriage by sea to which, by the Carriage of Goods by Road Act 1965, the C.M.R. applies, *i.e.* where the goods are not unloaded from the road vehicle during their sea transit (see 6–82, above).

6–287   The Articles of the Rules which require to be noted in considering the circumstances in which the Rules apply are Articles I, and V to X.

Article I (definitions)

6–288   Article I defines the terms "carrier," "contract of carriage," "goods," "ship," and "carriage of goods."

6–289   (a) **"Carrier"**—"Carrier" includes the owner or the charterer who enters into a contract of carriage with a shipper.

6–290   The Rules therefore apply to bills of lading issued under a charterparty by demise as well as to those issued under the more usual voyage or time charterparties. Where the charterparty is a charterparty by demise, the "carrier" will be the charterer, whereas in relation to a voyage or time charterparty, the "carrier" is the shipowner.

6–291   (b) **"Contract of carriage"**—This term applies only to contracts of carriage "covered by" a bill of lading (or any similar document of title), *including any bill of lading* (or similar document) *issued under or pursuant to a charterparty*, from the moment at which such bill of lading (or similar document of title) regulates the relations between a carrier and a holder of the document.

6–292   This provision must be taken along with Article V of the Rules, which states that the Rules are not applicable to charterparties, but that if bills of lading are issued in the case of a ship under a charterparty, they must comply with the terms of the Rules.

6–293   In the quite usual situation, therefore, where there is a charterparty containing the contract of carriage between shipowner and charterer, and also a bill of lading issued by the shipowner (or on his behalf by the master as agent) to the charterer (the charterer being himself the shipper of the goods), the Rules are not normally applicable as between the shipowner and the charterer because, as has been already explained (6–260, above), the general rule in such a situation is that the terms of the contract are to be looked for in the charterparty. If, however, the shipowner and the charterer intended by the bill of lading to alter the terms of the contract as contained in the charterparty, then the Rules will apply because the contract of carriage will be "covered by" the bill of lading. The Rules also apply as between the shipowner and any shipper of goods other than the charterer, and between the shipowner and an indorsee of the bill of lading.

(c) **"Goods"**—The term "goods" includes:

"Goods, wares, merchandise, and articles of every kind whatsoever except live animals and cargo which by the contract of carriage is stated as being carried on deck and is so carried."

Where the carrier is merely authorised to carry the goods on deck if he so chooses, the Rules *will* apply.

It is open to the parties to agree that the Rules are to apply to carriage of live animals and to a deck cargo (s. 1(7)).

(d) **"Ship"**—"Ship" means any vessel used for the carriage of goods by sea.

(e) **"Carriage of goods"**—"Carriage of goods" covers the period from the time when the goods are loaded on, to the time they are discharged from, the ship.

However, Article VII of the Rules allows the carrier and the shipper to enter into an agreement regarding the liability of the carrier for loss or damage occurring prior to the loading on, and subsequent to the discharge from, the ship.

Article V (special agreement enlarging carrier's liability)

In addition to providing that the Rules are not applicable to charter-parties (see 6–292, above), Article V enables the carrier to enlarge (but not to diminish) his liability; Article V provides:

"A carrier shall be at liberty to surrender in whole or in part all or any of his rights and immunities or to increase any of his responsibilities and obligations under these Rules, provided such surrender or increase shall be embodied in the bill of lading issued to the shipper."

Article V also expressly permits any lawful provision regarding general average to be inserted in a bill of lading, *e.g.* a provision that the rights and liabilities of the parties with regard to questions of general average are to be governed by the York-Antwerp Rules (instead of by the common law).

Article VI (special agreement limiting carrier's liability)

Article VI relates to the possibility that the carrier and the shipper may enter into some special agreement affecting the carrier's liability and containing provisions which conflict with the Rules. The scope for such an agreement is strictly limited: in particular, there can be no such agreement in "ordinary commercial shipments made in the ordinary course of trade"; such an agreement can have full legal effect only where the character or condition of the property to be carried or the circumstances, terms and conditions under which the carriage is to be performed are such as reasonably to justify a special agreement.

Article VII (special agreement relating to time outside duration of carriage)

This Article enables the carrier and shipper to enter into an agreement concerning the time before or after the duration of the carriage (see 6–296, above).

Article VIII (limitation of liability under other statutes)

6–301   Article VIII provides that the Rules are not to affect the rights and obligations of the carrier under any statute relating to the limitation of the liability of owners of sea-going vessels.

The provisions of the Merchant Shipping Act 1894, Part VIII, as amended by the Merchant Shipping (Liability of Shipowners and Others) Act 1958 and by the Merchant Shipping Act 1981, therefore, where they are applicable, take precedence over the Rules (see 6–211 *et seq.*, above).

Article IX (nuclear damage)

6–302   Article IX provides that the Rules are not to affect the provisions of any international convention or national law governing liability for nuclear damage.

Article X (bills of lading to which Rules apply)

6–303   This Article provides that the Rules apply to every bill of lading relating to the carriage of goods between ports in two different States if:

(a) the bill of lading is issued in a contracting State (*i.e.* a State which has become a party to the International Convention and the Protocol); or

(b) the carriage is from a port in a contracting State; or

(c) the contract contained in, or evidenced by, the bill of lading provides that the Rules are to govern the contract. The nationality of the ship, of the carrier, of the consignee or of any other interested person is immaterial.

6–304   As has already been noticed (6–282, above), in the law of the United Kingdom the Rules are not restricted to carriage of goods between ports in two different States, but extend also to carriage between United Kingdom ports.

(2) The substantive Articles of the Hague-Visby Rules

6–305   The leading Article of the Hague-Visby Rules is Article II. It summarises the content of the substantive Rules as follows:

"Subject to the provisions of Article VI, under every contract of carriage of goods by sea the carrier, in relation to the loading, handling, stowage, carriage, custody, care and discharge of such goods, shall be subject to the responsibilities and liabilities, and entitled to the rights and immunities hereinafter set forth."

Article VI, as has been seen (6–299, above), does not apply to ordinary commercial shipments. The Rules are therefore of great practical value, since they establish uniformity in the rights and obligations arising out of bills of lading used in the ordinary course of trade.

6–306   The detailed provisions of which Article II is a summary are set out in Articles III, IV and IV *bis* of the Rules. A brief description of the contents of these three Articles is given below. Article III may be regarded as concerned with positive matters, *i.e.* the responsibilities and liabilities of the carrier, whereas Articles IV and IV *bis* (the latter added by the Protocol of 1968) are of a negative character being concerned with exemptions, exceptions, limitations and defences.

Especially important is the question of seaworthiness. The Act itself abrogates the common law on this matter by providing:

"There shall not be implied in any contract for the carriage of goods by sea to which the Rules apply by virtue of this Act any absolute undertaking by the carrier of the goods to provide a seaworthy ship" (s. 3).

Under the Rules the carrier is bound only to exercise due diligence to make the ship seaworthy (Article III). Neither the carrier nor the ship is liable for loss or damage resulting from unseaworthiness which has been caused by any other factor than the lack of the due diligence referred to in Article III, but whenever loss or damage has resulted from unseaworthiness, the burden of proving that due diligence has been exercised lies on the carrier or other person claiming the exemption (Article IV).

Article III (responsibilities and liabilities of carrier)

1. **Due diligence as regards the ship**—The carrier is bound *before and at the beginning of the voyage* to exercise due diligence to:

(a) make the ship seaworthy;
(b) properly man, equip and supply the ship; and
(c) make the holds, refrigerating and cool chambers, and all other parts of the ship in which goods are carried, fit and safe for their reception, carriage and preservation.

Since the carrier's undertaking relates only to the time "before and at the beginning of the voyage," he would not be liable under (a) if the ship became unseaworthy during the course of the voyage.

The meaning of "seaworthy" (in the context of the Hague Rules) was considered by the Court of Appeal in the English case *Actis Co. Ltd.* v. *Sanko Steamship Co. Ltd. (The Aquacharm)* [1982] 1 W.L.R. 119:

The owners of the vessel "Aquacharm" let her to Japanese charterers on a time charter to carry a cargo of coal from Baltimore to Tokyo through the Panama Canal.

The master was at fault in taking on too heavy a load for safe passage through the Canal. As a result part of the cargo had to be discharged into another vessel at the entrance to the Canal and then reloaded at the other end. This involved a delay of nearly nine days and an additional hire charge of over $86,000.

The case raised the question whether the charterers could recover that amount as damages from the owners. The answer depended on whether the vessel was seaworthy or not when she left Baltimore. If she was seaworthy, the owners were exempted from liability under Article IV of the Rules because the loss arose from the neglect of the master in the "management" of the ship (see 6–323, below).

Held that the vessel was seaworthy, and that the charterers could therefore not recover damages for having to pay the additional hire.

Lord Denning M.R. said (at p. 122): "I think the word 'seaworthy' in the Hague Rules is used in its ordinary meaning, and not in any extended or unnatural meaning. It means that the vessel—with her master and crew—is herself fit to encounter the perils of the voyage and also that she is fit to carry the cargo safely on that voyage. . . . This vessel was so fit. It may be that she had to be lightened to pass through the Panama Canal, but that did not make her unfit. . . . There is no case in which a ship has been held to be unseaworthy merely because she has to lighten in order to get into port. So also if she has to lighten in order to get through a canal."

6–311   2. **Proper and careful carriage of the goods**—Subject to Article IV, the carrier must properly and carefully load, handle, stow, carry, keep, care for, and discharge the goods carried.

6–312   A Scottish case founded on an alleged breach of this undertaking (as contained in the Hague Rules) was *Albacora S.R.L.* v. *Westcott & Laurence Line Ltd.*, 1966 S.C. (H.L.) 19; 1965 S.C. 203:

A consignment of fish, which had been shipped in apparent good order and condition, was discharged damaged, and the indorsees of the bill of lading brought an action against the shipowners for damages for breach of contract.

It was proved that the damage had been caused by bacteria in the fish when shipped. The bacteria were dormant below a temperature of 41°F., but had been activated when that temperature was exceeded on the voyage. There was no evidence that the shipowners knew or ought to have known of this danger. The ship had no refrigerating plant.

Held that a breach of Rule 2 of Article III had not been established: the obligation to carry "properly" was an obligation to carry in accordance with a system sound in the light of the knowledge which the shipowners had or ought to have had.

6–313   3. **Issue of bill of lading**—After receiving the goods the carrier (or the master or agent of the carrier) must, on demand of the shipper, issue to the shipper a bill of lading showing:

(a) the leading marks necessary for identification of the goods;

(b) the number of packages or pieces, or the quantity, or weight, as the case may be; and

(c) the apparent order and condition of the goods.

Items (a) and (b) must be furnished in writing by the shipper. No carrier, master or agent of the carrier need state these items if he has reasonable ground for suspecting that the information supplied by the shipper is not accurate or if he has had no reasonable means of checking the information.

6–314   4. **Bill of lading as evidence**—The bill of lading is *prima facie* (*i.e.* first, but non-conclusive) evidence of receipt by the carrier of the goods as described in the bill. Where the bill of lading has been transferred to a third party in good faith, the bill is conclusive evidence of such receipt.

6–315   5. **Shipper's guarantee of accuracy**—The shipper is deemed to have guaranteed to the carrier the accuracy at the time of shipment of the marks, number, quantity and weight as furnished by him, and must indemnify the carrier against all loss, damages and expenses caused by any inaccuracies.

6–316   The effect is that the carrier is unable to "falsify" (*i.e.* contradict the terms of) the bill of lading in a question with a third party holding it in good faith, but that if the carrier thus incurs liability to the third party, he may have recourse against the shipper for reimbursement.

6–317   6. **Time-limits on claims**—Notice of any loss or damage and of the general nature of such loss or damage should be given in writing to the carrier or his agent at the port of discharge before or at the time of the removal of the goods into the custody of the person entitled to delivery of them, or, if the loss or damage is not apparent, within three days; otherwise the removal is *prima facie* (but not conclusive) evidence of the delivery by the carrier of the goods as described in the bill of lading. Any legal proceedings must be brought within one year after the delivery date, unless the parties agree to an extension of that time-limit.

6 *bis* (added by the Protocol of 1968). **Special time-limit for actions for indemnity**—An action for indemnity against a third person may be brought even after the expiry of a year. The limitation will depend on the law of the court before which the case is brought, but the time allowed must be not less than three months after the date of the claim made against the pursuer himself.

7. **"Shipped" bill of lading**—After the goods are loaded the shipper may demand that the bill of lading to be issued to him be a "shipped" bill of lading. If the shipper already has a document of title to the goods, he must surrender that document as against the issue of the "shipped" bill of lading, but the carrier has the option of having the existing document of title "noted" at the port of shipment with the name of the ship and the date of shipment; that document then (provided it states the particulars required by Article III, paragraph 3 (6—313, above)), constitutes a "shipped" bill of lading.

8. **Contracting out prohibited**—Any agreement relieving the carrier or the ship from liability for loss or damage arising from negligence, fault or failure in the duties and obligations of Article III or lessening such liability in some way contrary to the Rules is "null and void and of no effect." A benefit of insurance in favour of the carrier falls within this provision.

Article IV (exemptions, exceptions, limitations and defences)

Some of the Rules in this Article are for the protection of the carrier or shipowner, and others for the protection of the shipper.

1. **No absolute undertaking of seaworthiness**—Neither the carrier nor the ship is liable for loss or damage due to unseaworthiness unless caused by want of the diligence required to be exercised by the carrier under Article III, paragraph 1(a), (b) and (c) (see 6–308, above). The burden of proving the exercise of due diligence is on the carrier or other person claiming exemption.

2. **Excepted causes**—Neither the carrier nor the ship is responsible for loss or damage arising or resulting from any of 17 listed circumstances:

(a) act, neglect, or default of the master, mariner, pilot, or the servants of the carrier *in the navigation or in the management of the ship;*

(The phrase in italics gives rise to difficult questions of interpretation. As the phrase was also in the original Hague Rules, cases decided in relation to these Rules give some guidance. Pre-1924 cases have also some value, since the phrase was commonly used in bills of lading. A distinction is drawn between management of the ship itself (covered by the exception) and management of the cargo (not covered by the exception). It follows that for negligence in the management of the cargo the carrier will be liable; *e.g.* in *Gosse Millerd Ltd.* v. *Canadian Government*

Merchant Marine Ltd. [1929] A.C. 223, where rain had damaged a cargo of tinplates because, by the negligence of the shipowner's servants, hatches had been left open with the result that rain penetrated the hold, the House of Lords held that as negligence in the management of the hatches was not negligence in the "management of the ship," the shipowner was liable in damages for the injury done to the tinplates. On the other hand, in another English case, *The Glenochil* [1896] P. 10, where the phrase had been used in a similar context in a bill of lading, the court held that the shipowner was exempt from liability because the damage to a cargo of corn-seed oil-cake had resulted from a fault in the "management" of the vessel: the situation had been that during discharge of the cargo it had become necessary to stiffen the ship and for that purpose the engineer had run water into a ballast tank, negligently overlooking a breakage which had been caused by heavy weather during the voyage; the result had been that water reached the cargo and damaged it.)

    (b) fire, unless caused by the actual fault or privity of the carrier;

(This is similar to the provision in section 502 of the Merchant Shipping Act 1894 (see 6–216, above), but is wider in scope in that it is not restricted to a fire on board the ship.)

    (c) perils, dangers and accidents of the sea or other navigable waters;

    (d) act of God;

    (e) act of war;

    (f) act of public enemies;

    (g) arrest or restraint of princes, rulers or people, or seizure under legal process;

    (h) quarantine restrictions;

    (i) act or omission of the shipper or owner of the goods, his agent or representative;

    (j) strikes or lockouts or stoppage or restraint of labour from whatever cause, whether partial or general;

    (k) riots and civil commotions;

    (l) saving or attempting to save life or property at sea;

    (m) wastage in bulk or weight or any other loss or damage arising from inherent defect, quality or vice of the goods;

    (n) insufficiency of packing;

    (o) insufficiency or inadequacy of marks;

    (p) latent defects not discoverable by due diligence; and

    (q) any other cause arising without the actual fault or privity of the carrier, and without the fault or neglect of the agents or servants of the carrier, but the burden of proof is on the person claiming the benefit of this exception to show that neither the actual fault or privity of the carrier nor the fault or neglect of the agents or servants of the carrier contributed to the loss or damage.

6–324   3. **Shipper's exemption from liability**—The shipper is not responsible for loss or damage sustained by the carrier or the ship if it has been caused without the act, fault or neglect of the shipper, his agents or his servants.

6–325   4. **Deviation**—Any deviation in saving or attempting to save life or property at sea or any reasonable deviation is not to be deemed to be an infringement or breach of the Rules or of the contract, and the carrier is not liable for any loss or damage resulting from the deviation.

(Observations on the meaning of "reasonable deviation" in the same context in the original Hague Rules are to be found in *Stag Line Ltd.* v. *Foscolo Mango & Co. Ltd.* [1932] A.C. 328; [1931] 2 K.B. 48:

The "Ixia" was loaded at Swansea with a cargo of coal to be carried to Constantinople. The ship had been fitted with a "superheater," and had on board two engineers to observe whether this new equipment was working efficiently. The intention was that the engineers should be landed at Lundy, but when the ship reached that island no satisfactory trial had been obtained and the engineers remained on board and were later landed in St. Ives Bay, which was off the usual course. Before the ship had returned to the usual course, it was stranded on the Cornish coast, and both ship and cargo were lost.

The owners of the cargo claimed damages from the shipowners.

The trial judge and the Court of Appeal held that the deviation was not a "reasonable deviation" within the meaning of the Hague Rules, and the House of Lords refused to disturb that finding.

In the House of Lords, Lord Atkin observed (at p. 343): "A deviation may, and often will, be caused by fortuitous circumstances never contemplated by the original parties to the contract; and may be reasonable, though it is made solely in the interests of the ship or solely in the interests of the cargo, or indeed in the direct interest of neither: as for instance where the presence of a passenger or of a member of the ship or crew was urgently required after the voyage had begun on a matter of national importance; or where some person on board was a fugitive from justice, and there were urgent reasons for his immediate appearance. The true test seems to be what departure from the contract voyage might a prudent person controlling the voyage at the time make and maintain, having in mind all the relevant circumstances existing at the time, including the terms of the contract and the interests of all parties concerned, but without obligation to consider the interests of any one as conclusive.")

5. **Limitation in amount of damages**—Unless the nature and value of the goods have been declared by the shipper before shipment and inserted in the bill of lading, neither the carrier nor the ship is liable for loss or damage in an amount exceeding 10,000 gold francs[5] per package or unit or 30 gold francs[5] per kilo of gross weight of the goods lost or damaged, whichever is the higher.

The Merchant Shipping Act 1981 (s. 2(3)) substitutes for "10,000 gold francs" and "30 gold francs" the amounts "666·67 units of account" and "two units of account," respectively; a unit of account is a special drawing right as defined by the International Monetary Fund.

The limitation of liability provided for in this paragraph does not apply where it is proved that the damage resulted from an act or omission of the carrier done with intent to cause damage, or recklessly and with knowledge that damage would probably result.

A declaration of the nature and value of the goods, if embodied in the bill of lading, is *prima facie* evidence, but is not binding or conclusive on the carrier.

By agreement between the carrier, master or agent of the carrier and the shipper other maximum amounts than those stated in this paragraph

---

[5] "Poincaré" gold francs.

of the Rules may be fixed, but any amounts so fixed must not be lower than the statutory amounts.

If the nature or value of the goods has been knowingly mis-stated in the bill of lading, neither the carrier nor the ship is responsible for any loss or damage.

6–327   6. **Inflammable, explosive or dangerous goods**—Goods of this nature to the shipment of which the carrier, master or agent of the carrier has not consented with knowledge of their nature, may at any time before discharge be landed at any place, or destroyed or made harmless by the carrier without compensation, and the shipper of such goods is liable for all damages and expenses directly or indirectly arising out of or resulting from the shipment.

If any such goods shipped with knowledge and consent become a danger to the ship or cargo, they may in the same way be landed at any place, or destroyed or made harmless by the carrier without liability on the carrier's part except for general average (if any).

Article IV bis *(additions made to Article IV by the Protocol of 1968)*

6–328   This Article makes it clear that the Rules apply both to claims based on contract and to claims based on delict, and it extends the limitation of liability to servants and agents of the carrier. The provisions are:

6–329   1. The defences and limits of liability provided for in the Rules apply in any action against the carrier for loss or damage to goods covered by a contract of carriage, whether the action is founded on contract or on delict.

6–330   2. If an action is brought against a servant or agent of the carrier (such servant or agent not being an independent contractor), the servant or agent is entitled to avail himself of the defences and limits of liability which the carrier is entitled to invoke under the Rules.

6–331   3. The aggregate of the amounts recoverable from the carrier and such servants and agents must in no case exceed the limit provided for in the Rules.

6–332   4. A servant or agent is not entitled to avail himself of the provisions of this Article if it is proved that the damage resulted from an act or omission of the servant or agent done with intent to cause damage or recklessly and with knowledge that damage would probably result.

III CARRIAGE OF GOODS BY AIR

6–333   The common law has been of slight importance in relation to carriage of goods by air, and since June 1, 1967, all contracts for carriage by air have been governed by statutory provisions.

6–334   Four Acts require attention:

the Carriage by Air Act 1932, which gave effect in the United Kingdom to the Warsaw Convention of 1929;

the Carriage by Air Act 1961, which gave effect in the United Kingdom to the Warsaw Convention as amended at The Hague in 1955;

the Carriage by Air (Supplementary Provisions) Act 1962, which gave effect in the United Kingdom to the supplementary Convention adopted at Guadalajara, Mexico, in 1961; and the Carriage by Air and Road Act 1979, which, when fully in force, will give effect in the United Kingdom to Protocols signed at Montreal in 1975 further amending the Warsaw Convention as amended at The Hague.

In addition, account must be taken of delegated legislation in the form of Orders in Council, the most important of which at present is the Carriage by Air Acts (Application of Provisions) Order 1967.

As the short titles of the Acts suggest, the statutory provisions deal with carriage of passengers as well as with carriage of goods. What follows here is restricted to carriage of goods.

In order to understand the applicability of the various statutory provisions it is necessary first to appreciate:

(a) the distinction between international and non-international carriage; and

(b) the historical context of the statutory provisions.

There then follows an account in outline of the substantive provisions of:

(c) the Warsaw Convention and its amendments.

In conclusion, shorter notice is taken of:

(d) the supplementary Convention adopted at Guadalajara; and

(e) the Non-International Carriage Rules of 1967.

(a) Distinction between International and Non-International Carriage

The distinction between international and non-international carriage by air depends on the definition of "international carriage" contained in the Warsaw Convention, which is set out in the First Schedule to the Carriage by Air Act 1932. The definition was not substantially altered by the amendment of the Warsaw Convention made at The Hague in 1955 and is therefore also to be found in the First Schedule to the Carriage by Air Act 1961, which Schedule comprises the English and French texts of the Warsaw Convention as amended at The Hague in 1955. No change was made in this matter by the Montreal Protocols of 1975, and so the same definition appears in the First Schedule to the Carriage by Air and Road Act 1979.

The definition of "international carriage" is:

"any carriage in which, according to the agreement of the parties, the place of departure and the place of destination, whether or not there be a break in the carriage or a transhipment, are situated either within the territories of two High Contracting Parties or within the territory of a single High Contracting Party if there is an agreed stopping place within the territory of another State, even if that State is not a High Contracting Party" (Article 1 as stated in the English text in the Schedules to the 1961 and 1979 Acts).

Carriage between two points within the territory of a single High Contracting Party without an agreed stopping place within the territory of another State is not international carriage for the purposes of the Convention (Article 1).

Carriage to be performed by several successive air carriers is deemed, for the purposes of the Convention, to be one undivided carriage if it has been regarded by the parties as a single operation (whether it takes the form of a single contract or the form of a series of contracts), and it does not lose its international character merely because one contract or a series of contracts is to be performed entirely within the territory of the same State (Article 1).

6–340 The Convention extends to carriage performed by the State or by legally constituted public bodies (Article 2), but the parties to the Convention may avail themselves of an Additional Protocol which is printed at the end of the Convention. This Additional Protocol enables a party to the Convention to exempt its state-operated aircraft from the provisions of the Convention.

6–341 The Convention as stated in the Schedules to the Acts of 1932 and 1961 does not extend to mail and postal packages. Under the Act of 1979, the Convention will apply to the carriage of postal items but only so as to make the carrier liable to the relevant postal administration in accordance with the rules applicable to the relationship between the carriers and the postal administrations; with that exception, the Convention as stated in the First Schedule to the Act of 1979 will not apply to the carriage of postal items (Article 2).

(b) Historical Context of the Statutory Provisions

6–342 The Warsaw Convention, a convention for the unification of certain rules relating to international carriage by air, was signed on behalf of the United Kingdom government in 1929, and, as from May 15, 1933, was given statutory effect in the United Kingdom by the passing of the Carriage by Air Act 1932. In course of time, most countries ratified the Warsaw Convention, with the result that the provisions of the Convention became applicable to most cases of "international" carriage by air, *i.e.* to carriage between *either:*

(a) places in two different States provided both States were parties to the Convention; and

(b) places in the same State provided that State was a party to the Convention and provided also that there was an agreed stopping place in another State (whether or not that other State was itself a party to the Convention).

6–343 The Act of 1932 had, however, the further aim of applying the rules of the Convention, with exceptions, adaptations and modifications, to carriage by air which was *not* "international" carriage within the meaning of the Convention. Section 4 of the Act provided that such an extension could be made by Order in Council. It was not until 1952 that this power was exercised: the Carriage by Air (Non-International Carriage) (United Kingdom) Order 1952 then applied the "Non-International Carriage Rules" (a modification of the Warsaw Convention) to cases of carriage by air which was not "international" carriage for the purposes of the Convention.

6–344 In 1955, a further international Convention, signed at The Hague, amended the Warsaw Convention of 1929, and this amended Convention was given statutory force in the United Kingdom by the Carriage by Air Act 1961. Most other countries similarly ratified the amended Convention. A notable exception was the U.S.A.

6–345 Section 1 of the Act of 1961 provided that the Act was to come into operation on a date fixed by an Order in Council. From that date the whole of the Carriage by Air Act 1932 would be repealed. The Act of

1961, like its predecessor, also enabled the provisions of the amended Convention to be extended by Order in Council to carriage which was not "international" carriage (s. 10 of the 1961 Act).

It was not until 1967 that the necessary Order in Council was promulgated—the Carriage by Air Acts (Application of Provisions) Order 1967. In the interval another international Convention—the international Convention of Guadalajara—had come into existence in 1961 and had been given the force of law in the United Kingdom by the Carriage by Air (Supplementary Provisions) Act 1962 which was brought into operation in 1964.

As from June 1, 1967, the Order in Council had the following three effects:

(i) It made the amended Convention applicable to cases of "international" carriage as defined by the amended Convention (*i.e.* to cases of carriage between places in different States both of which were parties to the amended Convention and also to cases of carriage between places in the same State provided that State was a party to the amended Convention and provided also there was an agreed stopping place in the territory of another State (not necessarily a party to the amended Convention)).

(ii) It made the original Warsaw Convention applicable to those cases of "international" carriage which were not within (i) because the place of departure or of destination or of both was not within a State which was a party to the amended Convention, though the State was a party to the original Convention. This provision was made necessary by the repeal of the Act of 1932 by the Act of 1961.

(iii) It made new Non-International Carriage Rules (a modified form of the amended Convention) applicable to all other cases of carriage by air.

A few illustrations may make the position clearer:

(i) (a) Both France and the United Kingdom have ratified the amended Convention. Therefore carriage by air from Paris to London is governed by the amended Convention.

(i) (b) Carriage from London to Glasgow with an agreed stop at Dublin is also governed by the amended Convention, because it is carriage between two places in a State (the United Kingdom) which is a party to the amended Convention with an agreed stopping place in the territory of another State (Eire). The fact that Eire has ratified the amended Convention is of no consequence in this connection.

(ii) The U.S.A. is a party to the Warsaw Convention but has not ratified the amended Convention. Therefore carriage by air from New York to London is governed by the original Warsaw Convention (see *Corocraft Ltd.* v. *Pan American Airways Inc.* [1969] 1 Q.B. 616 (6–380, below)).

(iii) (a) Carriage from London to Edinburgh direct is governed by the Non-International Carriage Rules, being carriage between two places within the same State without an agreed stopping place in the territory of another State.

(iii) (b) "Non-international" is a term which depends on the definition of "international" for the purposes of the Convention: it is not restricted to inland carriage but extends to carriage to distant parts overseas, provided the territory is part of the same State and there is no agreed stopping place in the territory of another State. A British colony is not a State known to public international law. Therefore carriage by air from London to Gibraltar is governed by the Non-International Carriage Rules. (An agreed stop in Spain would convert the carriage into "international" carriage, and the amended Convention would then apply to it.)

6–349 Orders in Council published from time to time, list the States which are deemed to be parties to the original Warsaw Convention and to the Convention as amended at The Hague. These Orders in Council (entitled "Carriage by Air (Parties to Convention) Orders") are conclusive evidence of the matters which they certify (1961 Act, s. 2).

6–350 The Carriage by Air and Road Act 1979, which is not yet fully in force, substitutes a new Schedule 1 to the Carriage by Air Act 1961. This new Schedule, which is itself Schedule 1 to the Act of 1979, contains the English and French texts of the Warsaw Convention (already amended at The Hague) as further amended by provisions of Protocols No. 3 and No. 4 which were signed at Montreal in 1975.

6–351 An Order in Council under section 7 of the Act of 1979 is required before the Convention with these further amendments will be operative in the law of the United Kingdom.

6–352 The Convention with the new amendments may, like its predecessors, be extended by Order in Council to non-international carriage with such modifications as may be specified in the Order in Council (s. 6 of the 1979 Act).

6–353 Section 3 of the Act of 1979 introduces a new device designed to avoid the time lag which, owing to shortage of Parliamentary time, is prone to follow between the Government's agreement to a revision of an international convention such as the Warsaw Convention and the date of the passing of the Act which gives the revision statutory force in the United Kingdom: by adding new sections to the Acts of 1961 and 1962 (as well as to the Carriage of Goods by Road Act 1965—see 6–81, above), section 3 of the Act of 1979 enables effect to be given to revisions by an Order in Council approved by a resolution of each House of Parliament.

(c) The Warsaw Convention and its Amendments

6–354 The original Warsaw Convention, the formal title of which is the "Convention for the Unification of Certain Rules relating to International Carriage by Air," consists, as printed (in English translation only) in the First Schedule to the Carriage by Air Act 1932, of 41 Articles, grouped into five Chapters as follows:

Chapter I: Scope—Definitions (Articles 1-2);
Chapter II: Documents of Carriage (Articles 3-16);
Chapter III: Liability of the Carrier (Articles 17-30);
Chapter IV: Provisions Relating to Combined Carriage (Article 31); and
Chapter V: General and Final Provisions (Articles 32-41).

6–355 The amended Convention of 1955 is referred to in the Carriage by Air Act 1961 as "the Warsaw Convention as amended at The Hague, 1955." The First Schedule to the Act, which sets out the amended

Convention, is headed "the Warsaw Convention with the Amendments made in it by The Hague Protocol."

The Convention is printed both in English and in French—Part I of the Schedule being the English text and Part II being the French text. Section 1 of the Act provides that if there is any inconsistency between the text in English and the text in French, the text in French is to prevail. An interesting illustration of a possible inconsistency in the original Convention came before the Court of Appeal in *Corocraft Ltd.* v. *Pan American Airways Inc.* [1969] 1 Q.B. 616 (see 6–380, below): the Court of Appeal there held that although the original Convention was printed in English translation only in the First Schedule to the Act of 1932 and although there was no express provision such as that in section 1 of the Act of 1961 as to inconsistency, Parliament had intended in the Act of 1932 that the official French text should prevail if it were inconsistent with the English translation in the schedule. The most authoritative comments on section 1 of the Act of 1961 are those made in the House of Lords in *Fothergill* v. *Monarch Airlines Ltd.* [1981] A.C. 251 (see 6–440, below). Lord Wilberforce said (at p. 272):

"Here it is not only permissible to look at a foreign language text, but obligatory. What is made part of English law is the text set out *in Schedule 1, i.e.* in both Part I and Part II, so both English and French texts must be looked at. Furthermore, it cannot be judged whether there is an inconsistency between the two texts unless one looks at both. So, in the present case the process of interpretation seems to involve:

1. Interpretation of the English text, according to the principles upon which international conventions are to be interpreted. . . .

2. Interpretation of the French text according to the same principles but with additional linguistic problems.

3. Comparison of these meanings."

The general arrangement of the Convention as amended at The Hague does not differ from that of the original Convention. There are some changes in terminology (*e.g.* the substitution of "air waybill" for "air consignment note," and of "cargo" for "goods").

The Convention as further amended by the Protocols signed at Montreal in 1975 is headed in Schedule 1 to the Carriage by Air and Road Act 1979 "The Warsaw Convention as amended at The Hague in 1955 and by Protocols No. 3 and No. 4 signed at Montreal in 1975." As in the Act of 1961, Part I of the Schedule gives the English text of the Convention and Part II gives the French text, and the provision of the Act of 1961 that the text in French is, in the event of inconsistency, to prevail over the text in English will also apply to the Convention as further amended, once the new provisions have been substituted under section 1 of the Act of 1979 for the present First Schedule to the Act of 1961.

The general arrangement still remains substantially unaltered from that of the original Warsaw Convention.

The following is an outline of the leading provisions of the original Warsaw Convention (still applicable to certain cases of international carriage—see 6–347, above), with an indication of the main changes which were made by the amendment at The Hague in 1955 (now applicable to most cases of international carriage, and also, with modifications, to non-international carriage), and subsequently made by the Protocols signed at Montreal in 1975 (not yet applicable).

Chapter I: Scope—Definitions

Article 1

6–361   The Convention is made applicable to all international carriage performed by aircraft for reward, and also to gratuitous carriage by aircraft performed by an air transport undertaking.

6–362   The Article then proceeds to define "international carriage" for the purposes of the Convention (see 6–338, above).

Article 2

6–363   The Convention applies to carriage performed by the State or by legally constituted public bodies provided it falls within the conditions laid down in Article 1. (However, this part of Article 2 does not apply to the States which have availed themselves of the Additional Protocol (see 6–340, above).)

6–364   The Convention does not apply to carriage performed under any international postal Convention. The Convention as amended at The Hague similarly makes the Convention inapplicable to mail and postal packages. The amendment made by the Montreal protocols has been already noted (see 6–341, above). (By the Carriage by Air Acts (Application of Provisions) Order 1967, all carriage of postal packets, whether international or not, is governed by the Non-International Carriage Rules of 1967.)

Chapter II: Documents of Carriage

6–365   Articles 3 and 4, which relate to passenger and luggage tickets (referred to as "passenger tickets" and "baggage checks" in the later versions of the Convention), are not further considered here.

6–366   The remaining Articles (5-16) all relate to the document which is relevant for carriage of goods—the "air consignment note," or the "air waybill." The first of these alternative terms was used in the original Warsaw Convention as printed in Schedule 1 to the Act of 1932. However, the term "air waybill" is used in the Carriage by Air Acts (Application of Provisions) Order 1967, and since the application of the original Warsaw Convention now depends on the Order of 1967 "air waybill" is now the preferable term even for cases of carriage to which the original Warsaw Convention applies.

6–367   The term "air waybill" is used in the Schedules to the Acts of 1961 and 1979.

Article 5

6–368   Every carrier of goods has the right to require the consignor to make out and hand over to him an air waybill, and every consignor has the right to require the carrier to accept this document. Absence, irregularity or loss of this document does not affect the validity of the contract of carriage; the contract will still be governed by the Convention. This provision is, however, qualified to some extent by Article 9.

This Article is amended in the Schedule to the Act of 1979. Any other means which would preserve a record of the carriage may, with the consignor's consent, be substituted for the delivery of an air waybill, and if this other means is used, the carrier must, on the consignor's request, deliver to the consignor a receipt for the cargo and allow him access to the record. Failure to comply with Article 5 does not affect the validity of the contract and there is in this latest amendment no qualification whatsoever to that in Article 9.

Article 6

The air waybill must be made out by the consignor in three parts and be handed over with the goods.

The first part is marked "for the carrier," and is signed by the consignor. The second part is marked "for the consignee," and is signed by the consignor and by the carrier; it accompanies the goods. The third part is signed by the carrier and handed by him to the consignor after the goods have been accepted. Signatures may be stamped.

Article 7

The carrier has the right to require the consignor to make out separate air waybills when there is more than one package.

The only alteration made to this Article is that if, under the Act of 1979, the alternative to the air waybill (see Article 5, above) is used, the consignor has the right to require the carrier to deliver separate receipts.

Article 8

This Article lists the particulars which must be contained in the air waybill:
  (a) the place and date of its execution;
  (b) the place of departure and of destination;
  (c) the agreed stopping places;
  (d) the name and address of the consignor;
  (e) the name and address of the first carrier;
  (f)   the name and address of the consignee, if the case so requires;
  (g) the nature of the goods;
  (h) the number of the packages, the method of packing and the particular marks or numbers upon them;
  (i)   the weight, the quantity and the volume or dimensions of the goods;
  (j)   the apparent condition of the goods and of the packing;
  (k) the freight, if it has been agreed upon, the date and place of payment, and the person who is to pay it;
  (l)   if the goods are sent for payment on delivery, the price of the goods, and, if the case so requires, the amount of the expenses incurred;
  (m) the amount of the value declared in accordance with Article 22 (see 6–422, below);
  (n) the number of parts of the air waybill;
  (o) the documents handed to the carrier to accompany the air waybill;
  (p) the time fixed for the completion of the carriage and a brief note of the route to be followed, if these matters have been agreed upon; and

(q) a statement that the carriage is subject to the rules relating to liability established by the Convention.

Items (a) to (i) and item (q) are of particular importance as will be seen from Article 9.

6–375 The list is much shorter in the amended versions.

6–376 Under the Schedule to the Act of 1961, the air waybill must contain:

(a) an indication of the places of departure and destination;

(b) if the places of departure and destination are within the territory of a single party to the Convention, there being one or more agreed stopping places within the territory of another State, an indication of at least one of these places; and

(c) a notice to the consignor to the effect that, if the carriage involves an ultimate destination or stop in a country other than the country of departure, the Warsaw Convention may be applicable and that the Convention governs and in most cases limits the liability of carriers in respect of loss of or damage to cargo.

Item (c) is of particular importance in connection with Article 9.

6–377 In the Schedule to the Act of 1979, (a) and (b) are unchanged, but (c) has been removed, and in its place there is:

(c) an indication of the weight of the consignment.

Article 9

6–378 If the carrier accepts goods without an air waybill having been made out, or if the air waybill does not contain all the particulars set out in Article 8(a) to (i) inclusive and (q), the carrier is not entitled to avail himself of the provisions of the Convention which exclude or limit his liability.

6–379 Article 9 was strictly interpreted in *Westminster Bank Ltd.* v. *Imperial Airways Ltd.* [1936] 2 All E.R. 890, a decision of Lewis J.:

The defendants had consigned to them three bars of gold for carriage from London to Paris. The gold was placed in the strong room of the airport at Croydon. On the following morning the door of the strong room was found open, and the gold was missing.

The plaintiffs claimed the value of the consignment—over £9,000.

On the back of the consignment note was a statement that the conditions of carriage were "based upon the Convention of Warsaw."

Held that this statement was not a sufficient compliance with the requirement of Article 8(q) because "based on " was not identical to "subject to."

The defendants were therefore not entitled to avail themselves of the provisions of the Convention which would have limited their liability for the loss of the gold.

6–380 On the other hand, in the more recent decision of the Court of Appeal in *Corocraft Ltd.* v. *Pan American Airways Inc.* [1969] 1 Q.B. 616, a liberal interpretation of Article 9 was preferred, this being the correct approach in the reading of international conventions.

The case related to item (i) in the list in Article 8—"the weight, the quantity and the volume or dimensions of the goods."

A carton of topaz jewels valued at £1,194 was delivered to the airway company in New York for delivery to C. Ltd. in London. The consignment note gave the weight as "7 lbs. (3.1 kgs.)," but the space headed "Dimensions or volume" was blank.

The jewels were stolen by an employee of the airway company, and C. Ltd. sued the company for their value.

Because the U.S.A. had not ratified the amended Convention, the original Warsaw Convention applied.

The airway company claimed that its liability was limited under Article 22 to £19 (the sterling equivalent of 250 gold francs per kilogram (see 6–422, below). C. Ltd., however, contended that the right to that limitation had been excluded by the omission of volume and dimensions in the consignment note.

The Court compared the English and the French texts: the English text—"the weight, the quantity and the volume or dimensions of the goods"—suggested that three out of four matters required to be stated, whereas the French text—"le poids, la quantité, le volume ou les dimensions de la marchandise"—suggested that only one out of four matters required to be stated.

Held (i) that Parliament had intended in the Act of 1932 that the official French text should prevail if there was inconsistency between that text and the English text (which alone was printed in the Schedule to the Act), (ii) that the Articles should be interpreted so as to make good commercial sense, (iii) that, on such an interpretation, Article 8(i) had been sufficiently complied with and (iv) that the airway company was therefore entitled to the limitation of liability claimed.

Lord Denning M.R. said (at p. 655): "The article does not require that the consignment note should state every particular, no matter how useless or irrelevant. It only requires those particulars to be stated so far as they are necessary or useful for the purpose in hand."

The Act of 1961 introduced a less stringent Article 9.

The Article as amended at The Hague provides that if, with the carrier's consent, cargo is loaded on board the aircraft without an air waybill having been made out, or if the air waybill does not include the notice required by Article 8(c), the carrier is not entitled to avail himself of the provisions of Article 22, paragraph (2) (*i.e.* the provision which limits liability to 17 special drawing rights per kilogram (see 6–421 *et seq.*, below)).

The carrier is therefore entitled to avail himself of the other provisions of the Convention which exclude or limit his liability.

The Act of 1979 completely removes the stringency.

The Article as amended by the Montreal Protocols provides that non-compliance with the provisions of Articles 5 to 8 is not to affect the existence or the validity of the contract of carriage, which shall, nonetheless, be subject to the rules of the Convention including those relating to limitation of liability.

Article 10

The consignor is responsible for the correctness of the particulars and statements relating to the goods which he inserts in the air waybill, and is liable for all damage suffered by the carrier or any other person as a result of the irregularity, incorrectness or incompleteness of the particulars and statements.

6–386   Article 10 in the Schedule to the Act of 1979 makes reference in addition to the situation where the alternative to the air waybill is being used: the consignor is responsible for the correctness of the particulars and statements furnished by him for insertion in the receipt or for insertion in the record. The carrier for his part is liable to indemnify the consignor for damage suffered by the consignor or any other person to whom the consignor is liable, on account of the irregularity, incorrectness or incompleteness of the particulars and statements inserted by the carrier in the receipt or in the record.

Article 11

6–387   The air waybill is *prima facie* (preliminary, but rebuttable) evidence of the conclusion of the contract, of the receipt of the goods and of the conditions of carriage.

6–388   The statements in it as to weight, dimensions and packing, as well as those as to the number of packages, are *prima facie* evidence of the facts stated, but the statements as to quantity, volume and condition of the goods do not constitute evidence against the carrier except in so far as:

(a) they have been checked by him in the presence of the consignor *and* the air waybill states that this has been done; or

(b) they relate to the *apparent* condition of the goods.

6–389   In the Schedule to the Act of 1979 the receipt for the cargo, as an alternative to the air waybill, is declared to be *prima facie* evidence of the conclusion of the contract, of the acceptance of the cargo and of the conditions of carriage, but otherwise the Article is unaltered.

Article 12

6–390   This relates to the consignor's right of stoppage *in transitu* ("in transit"). The provisions of the Convention are distinct from the United Kingdom legislation on the "unpaid" seller's right of stoppage in transit.

6–391   Article 12 provides that the consignor has the right to dispose of the goods by withdrawing them at the aerodrome of departure or destination or by stopping them in the course of the journey on any landing, or by calling for them to be delivered to a person other than the consignee named in the air waybill, or by requiring them to be returned to the aerodrome of departure. He must not exercise this right in such a way as to prejudice the carrier or other consignors, and he must repay any expenses incurred.

6–392   The carrier, in obeying such instructions, must take the precaution of having the consignor's part of the air waybill produced to him; otherwise he may find himself made liable for damage caused to a person who is lawfully in possession of that part of the air waybill.

6–393   The consignor's right under this Article ceases at the moment when the consignee's right under Article 13 begins, except that if the consignee declines to accept the air waybill or the goods, or if he cannot be communicated with, the consignor resumes his right of disposal.

6–394   There are no substantial changes in this Article; under the Schedule to the Act of 1979, the document to be delivered up by the consignor when exercising his right of stoppage *in transitu* may be the receipt instead of his part of the air waybill.

Article 13

Except in the circumstances set out in Article 12, the consignee is entitled, on arrival of the goods at the place of destination, to require the carrier to hand over to him the air waybill and to deliver the goods to him, on payment of the charges due and on complying with the conditions of carriage set out in the air waybill.

Unless it is otherwise agreed, it is the duty of the carrier to give notice to the consignee as soon as the goods arrive.

If the carrier admits the loss of the goods, or if the goods have not arrived at the expiration of seven days after the date on which they ought to have arrived, the consignee is entitled to put into force against the carrier the rights which flow from the contract of carriage (*e.g.* bring legal proceedings for loss of the goods).

There are no amendments to be noted.

Article 14

The consignor and the consignee can respectively enforce all the rights given them by Articles 12 and 13, each in his own name, whether he is acting in his own interest or in the interest of another, provided that he carries out the obligations imposed by the contract.

There are no amendments.

Article 15

Articles 12, 13 and 14 do not affect either the relations of the consignor and the consignee with each other or the mutual relations of third parties whose rights are derived either from the consignor or from the consignee.

The provisions of Articles 12, 13 and 14 can only be varied by express provision in the air waybill.

A new paragraph was added to this Article in the Convention as amended at The Hague, namely the provision that nothing in the Convention prevents the issue of a negotiable air waybill. This provision does not have the effect of making an air waybill a "negotiable instrument," in the strict sense of a document which can be sued on by the holder of it despite any defect in the title of the person from whom he received it. It merely makes it clear that the way is open for an air waybill to acquire a negotiable character *if* mercantile custom supports such a development.

The additional paragraph was removed by the Montreal Protocols.

Article 16

The consignor must furnish the information and documents necessary to meet the formalities of customs, octroi or police, and is liable to the carrier for any damage caused by his failure in this respect, unless the damage is due to the fault of the carrier or his agents.

6–405   The carrier is under no obligation to inquire into the correctness or sufficiency of the information or documents.

6–406   There are no substantial amendments.

Chapter III: Liability of the Carrier

Article 18

6–407   The broad principle of the carrier's liability is stated in this Article and in the immediately following Article. The liability is qualified by the provisions of later Articles.

6–408   Article 18 provides that the carrier is liable for damage sustained in the event of the destruction or loss of, or of damage to, the goods, if the occurrence causing the damage took place during the carriage by air, *i.e.* during the period when the goods are in charge of the carrier, whether in an aerodrome (as in *Westminster Bank Ltd.* v. *Imperial Airways Ltd.*, 6–379, above) or on board an aircraft, or, in the case of a landing outside an aerodrome, in any place whatsoever.

6–409   The period of carriage by air does not extend to any carriage by land, by sea or by river performed outside an aerodrome. If, however, such a carriage takes place in the performance of a contract for carriage by air, for the purpose of loading, delivery or transhipment, any damage is presumed, until the contrary is proved, to have been the result of an event which took place during the carriage by air. The effect of this last provision is to place the onus of proof that the damage occurred outwith the period of carriage by air on the party (usually the carrier) who alleges that it did.

6–410   In the Schedule to the Act of 1979, Article 18 has an additional paragraph providing that the carrier is not liable if he proves that the destruction, loss of, or damage to, the cargo resulted solely from one or more of the following:

(a) inherent defect, quality or vice of that cargo;

(b) defective packing of that cargo performed by a person other than the carrier or his servants or agents;

(c) an act of war or an armed conflict;

(d) an act of public authority carried out in accordance with the entry, exit or transit of the cargo.

This additional paragraph should be linked with the restricted scope of Article 20 in the Schedule to the Act of 1979.

Article 19

6–411   The carrier is liable for damage caused by delay in the carriage.

Article 20

6–412   This Article qualifies Article 18 by providing that the carrier is not to be liable at all in certain circumstances. The onus of proof lies on the carrier.

6–413   The Article provides that the carrier is not liable if he proves that he and his agents have taken all necessary measures to avoid the damage or that it was impossible for him or them to take such measures.

The carrier is also not liable if he proves that the damage was caused by negligent pilotage or negligence in the handling of the aircraft or in navigation *and* that, in all other respects, he and his agents have taken all necessary measures to avoid the damage.

The negligence which is mentioned in this Article must be distinguished from the "wilful misconduct" referred to in Article 25.

In the Schedule to the Act of 1961, Article 20 is restricted in scope: the provision is that the carrier is not liable if he proves that he and his servants or agents have taken all necessary measures to avoid the damage or that it was impossible for him or them to take such measures; the part of the original Article relating to negligent pilotage, and to negligence in the handling of the aircraft or in navigation has been removed.

The scope of the Article is further narrowed in the Schedule to the Act of 1979: as there amended, the Article relates only to exemption from liability for damage *occasioned by delay*: the carrier is not liable if he proves that he and his servants and agents have taken all necessary measures to avoid the damage or that it was impossible for them to take such measures. (See, however, the excepted causes added in this Schedule to Article 18.)

Article 21

This Article is concerned with contributory negligence, which may wholly or partly exonerate the carrier from his liability. The wording of the original Warsaw Convention refers to the damage as being caused by or contributed to by the negligence "of the injured person," and this is appropriate for carriage of passengers. The provision is that if the carrier proves that the damage was caused by or contributed to by the negligence of the injured person the court may, in accordance with the provisions of its own law, exonerate the carrier wholly or partly from his liability.

The wording was not altered in the amendment at The Hague, but there had by that time been a change in the law of the United Kingdom with the passing of the Law Reform (Contributory Negligence) Act 1945 which allowed apportionment both in personal and in property claims. It appears that the effect of that Act has been to admit apportionment under Article 21 in claims for damaged goods as well as in claims for personal injuries.

In the Schedule to the Act of 1979, Article 21 has separate provisions for passengers and their baggage and for cargo respectively. As regards cargo, if the carrier proves that the damage was caused by or contributed to by the negligence or other wrongful act or omission of the person claiming compensation, the carrier is wholly or partly exonerated from his liability to the claimant to the extent that the negligence or wrongful act or omission caused or contributed to the damage. There is no longer any reference to the law of the country before whose courts the case is taken.

Article 22

This Article qualifies Article 18 by providing an upper limit on the damages for which the carrier may be held liable.

6–422   The carrier's liability is limited to a sum of 250 gold francs[5] per kilogram, unless the consignor has made, at the time when the package was handed over to the carrier, a special declaration of the value at delivery and has paid a supplementary sum if the case so requires. In that case the carrier is liable to pay a sum not exceeding the declared sum, unless he proves that that sum is greater than the actual value to the consignor at delivery.

6–423   The sterling equivalents of the sums such as 250 gold francs laid down in the Convention are specified from time to time in statutory instruments entitled "Carriage by Air (Sterling Equivalents) Orders."

6–424   This Article had additions made to it by the amendment at The Hague. These include the provision that the limit prescribed by the Article is not to prevent the court from awarding the whole or part of the court costs and of the other expenses of the litigation incurred by the pursuer, but that if the carrier has made a written offer to the pursuer of an amount equal to or greater than the damages awarded by the court the pursuer will not be awarded costs or expenses.

6–425   As amended by the Montreal Protocols, Article 22 relates only to passengers and their baggage, and Article 22A has been added to deal with cargo. For the reference to 250 gold francs there is substituted a reference to 17 special drawing rights per kilogram. Special drawing rights are defined by the International Monetary Fund, and conversion into national currencies is, in a court case, made according to the value of such currencies at the date of the decision of the case. By section 5 of the Act of 1979 a certificate given by the Treasury stating the sterling equivalent on a particular day of a special drawing right is conclusive evidence.

Article 23

6–426   Any provision tending to relieve the carrier of liability or to fix a lower limit than that which is laid down in Article 22 is declared to be null and void. The nullity affects only the provision in question, and the rest of the contract remains subject to the provisions of the Convention.

6–427   This Article also had an addition made to it by the amendment at The Hague, namely that this Article is not to apply to provisions governing loss or damage resulting from the inherent defect, quality or vice of the cargo carried. The carrier is therefore under the amended Convention enabled to exclude his liability or to place a lower limit on it where the loss or damage results from the factors mentioned.

Article 24

6–428   In the cases covered by Articles 18 and 19 any action for damages, however founded, can only be brought subject to the conditions and limits set out in the Convention.

6–429   As amended by the Montreal Protocols, Article 24 is in wider terms, removing all doubts as to the possibility of contracting out of the provisions of the Convention: in the Schedule to the Act of 1979 this Article makes no specific reference to Articles 18 and 19, and provides that any

---

5 "Poincaré" gold francs.

action for damages, however founded, whether under the Convention or in contract or in delict or otherwise, can only be brought subject to the conditions and limits of liability set out in the Convention, and that the limits of liability constitute maximum limits and may not be exceeded whatever the circumstances which gave rise to the liability.

Article 25

This Article provides that the carrier is not entitled to avail himself of the provisions which exclude or limit his liability, if the damage is caused by his wilful misconduct or by such default on his part as is considered by the court which is dealing with the case to be equivalent to wilful misconduct. Similarly, the carrier is not entitled to avail himself of the provisions referred to, if the damage has been caused by the wilful misconduct (or its equivalent) of any agent of the carrier acting within the scope of his employment. Since this Article makes the interpretation of "wilful misconduct" a matter for the court before which the case comes, it would appear that the courts of this country could look for assistance to the railway cases in which the interpretation of this phrase featured (see 6–125, above). An air carriage case involving Article 25 was *Rustenburg Platinum Mines Ltd.* v. *South African Airways and Pan American World Airways Inc.* [1979] 1 Lloyd's Rep. 19 (C.A.):

Two boxes of platinum were to be carried by air from South Africa to U.S.A. with a change from a South African aircraft to an American aircraft at Heathrow. One of the boxes was stolen at Heathrow after it had been loaded on to the American aircraft but before that aircraft took off.

The owner of the platinum was successful in an action brought against the American company: since the loader, entrusted with the task of loading the box carefully, had placed it in such a position that it could be easily abstracted and with a view to its being abstracted, there had been theft within the scope of the loader's employment and that was "wilful misconduct."

The language of Article 25 was altered by the amendment at The Hague: the phrase "wilful misconduct" was removed, and in its amended form the Article provides that the limits of liability specified in Article 22 are not to apply if it is proved that the damage resulted from an act or omission of the carrier, his servants or agents, done with intent to cause damage or recklessly and with knowledge that damage would probably result, and if it is further proved, in the case of an act or omission of a servant or agent, that the servant or agent was acting within the scope of his employment.

In the Convention as amended by the Montreal Protocols, Article 25 has been completely removed; it has been superseded by the revised Article 24.

Article 25A

This Article was added to the Convention by the amendment at The Hague. It relates to the situation where an action is brought against a servant or agent of the carrier.

6–434   The Article provides that if the servant or agent proves that he acted within the scope of his employment, he is entitled to avail himself of the limits of liability which the carrier himself is entitled to invoke, and that the aggregate of the amounts which the pursuer can recover from the carrier, his servants and agents, must, in that case, not exceed the limits laid down in the Convention.

6–435   The Article further provides that these provisions are not to apply if it is proved that the damage resulted from an act or omission of the servant or agent done with intent to cause damage or recklessly and with knowledge that damage would probably result.

6–436   In Article 25A of the Convention as amended by the Montreal Protocols this last paragraph has been removed from the Article.

Article 26

6–437   This Article, like Articles 20 and 21, is for the carrier's protection since it imposes time-limits on the complaints which are a necessary preliminary to actions against the carrier.

6–438   The Article provides that receipt by the person entitled to delivery of the goods without complaint is *prima facie* ("rebuttable") evidence that the goods have been delivered in good condition and in accordance with the document of carriage.

"In the case of damage," the person entitled to delivery must complain to the carrier immediately the damage is discovered, and, at the latest, within seven days from the date of receipt. In the case of delay the complaint must be made, at the latest, within 14 days from the date on which the goods have been placed at his disposal.

Every complaint must be in writing.

Failing complaint within the times specified, no action can be brought against the carrier except in the case of fraud on his part.

6–439   In this Article as amended at The Hague, the periods allowed for complaints are extended, with the substitution of 14 days for seven days, and, in the case of delay, 21 days for 14 days.

6–440   The Article was not further amended by the Montreal Protocols, but section 2 of the Act of 1979—the only section of that Act which came into force at the date when the Act was passed—deals with the interpretation of the phrase "in the case of damage," as used in this Article in its original and amended forms. Section 2 provides that the reference to damage is to be construed as including loss of part of the cargo. This statutory provision had its historical source in the case of *Fothergill* v. *Monarch Airlines Ltd.*:

Returning from holiday in Italy in an aircraft of M. Ltd., F. found, on arrival at Luton Airport, that a suitcase which was part of his luggage was badly torn. He immediately reported the fact to a representative of M. Ltd.

After reaching his home in Colchester, F. became aware that some of his personal effects were missing from the suitcase. He notified his own insurers of this, and they passed on F.'s claim to M. Ltd. about four weeks later.

M. Ltd. accepted liability for the torn suitcase (£12), but denied liability for the value of the missing articles (£16·50) on the ground that F. had not complained of that "damage" within seven days (the time allowed by Article 26, as amended at The Hague, for baggage claims).

Kerr J. ([1978] Q.B. 108) gave judgment for F., holding that the paragraph in Article 26 beginning with the words "in the case of damage" did not require notice to be given where there was a partial loss of the contents of the baggage.

This decision led to the inclusion in the Act of 1979 of the provision in section 2 referred to. The Act was passed on April 4, 1979.

M. Ltd. appealed to the Court of Appeal against Kerr J.'s judgment, and the Court of Appeal ([1980] Q.B. 23), by a majority, dismissed the appeal. Although section 2 of the Act of 1979 was by that time in force, it did not assist M. Ltd.'s appeal, since the section was expressly declared not to apply to loss which occurred before the passing of the Act.

The Court of Appeal treated the question of interpretation as one of discovering the meaning of the English text, and held that as a matter of ordinary English the term "damage" in Article 26 referred only to physical injury to baggage and did not extend to partial loss of contents.

The airline appealed to the House of Lords.

Held ([1981] A.C. 251) that, although on a literal interpretation in an English legal context "damage" would not extend to cover "loss," the appropriate method of interpretation of an international convention was a purposive interpretation, and that since the purpose of Article 26 was to ensure that the airline received prompt notice, the Article applied to loss as well as to damage in the ordinary English sense.

F. had therefore not lodged his complaint for the lost articles within the required time and the airline's appeal was allowed.

Article 28

This Article deals with jurisdiction.

The pursuer has the option of bringing his action of damages, in the territory of one of the States which are parties to the Convention, either:

(i) before the court which has jurisdiction where the carrier is ordinarily resident, or has his principal place of business, or has an establishment by which the contract has been made; or

(ii) before the court which has jurisdiction at the place of destination.

Questions of procedure are governed by the law of the court before which the case comes.

Article 29

This Article is concerned with limitation of actions.

The right to damages is extinguished if an action is not brought within two years, reckoned from the date of arrival at the destination, or from the date on which the aircraft ought to have arrived, or from the date on which the carriage stopped.

This Article has remained unchanged, but section 5(1) of the Act of 1961 itself expressly extends the same limitation of two years to actions brought against the carrier's servants or agents who have been acting within the scope of their employment.

Article 30

6–446   This Article relates to the situation where the carriage is to be performed by various successive carriers, but is regarded by the parties as a single operation and so is deemed to be one undivided carriage for the purposes of the Convention (see 6–339, above).

6–447   In such cases, each carrier who accepts the goods is subjected to the Convention, and is deemed to be one of the contracting parties to the contract of carriage in so far as the contract deals with that part of the carriage which is under his supervision.

6–448   The consignor has a right of action against the first carrier, and the consignee who is entitled to delivery has a right of action against the last carrier, and further, each may take action against the carrier who performed the carriage during which the destruction, loss, damage or delay took place. These carriers are jointly and severally liable to the consignor or consignee.

Article 30A

6–449   This Article was added by the Montreal Protocols.

6–450   It states that nothing in the Convention is to prejudice the question whether a person liable for damage in accordance with its provisions has a right of recourse against any other person.

Chapter IV: Provisions Relating to Combined Carriage
Article 31

6–451   The single Article in this Chapter of the Convention provides that in the case of combined carriage performed partly by air and partly by any other mode of carriage, the Convention applies only to the carriage by air.

6–452   This does not prevent the parties from inserting in the document of air carriage conditions relating to other modes of carriage, provided that the provisions of the Convention are observed as regards the carriage by air.

Chapter V: General and Final Provisions

6–453   In this Chapter of the Convention, the first two Articles are of importance in relation to the question of the extent to which it is permissible to contract out of the provisions of the Convention.

Article 32

6–454   By Article 32, any clause contained in the contract and all special agreements entered into before the damage occurred by which the parties purport to infringe the rules laid down by the Convention, whether by deciding the law to be applied, or by altering the rules as to jurisdiction, are null and void. One exception is provided for: arbitration clauses are allowed, provided the arbitration is to take place within one of the jurisdictions referred to in Article 28.

Article 33

6–455   This Article declares that nothing in the Convention is to prevent the carrier either from refusing to enter into any contract of carriage, or from making regulations which do not conflict with the provisions of the Convention.

The interpretation of "regulations" in this context is doubtful: the word might be restricted to regulations which the carrier was authorised to make by some statutory power conferred on him.

When taken along with Article 32, this Article would seem to allow the insertion of terms concerning matters about which the Convention is silent (*e.g.* the carrier's lien), but not the variation of the provisions of the Convention itself (*e.g.* the substitution of a different limit for the carrier's liability).

Article 34

This Article provides that the Convention does not apply to carriage performed by way of experimental trial by air navigation undertakings with the view to the establishment of a regular line of air navigation, nor to carriage performed in extraordinary circumstances outside the normal scope of an air carrier's business.

In the amendment made at The Hague, this Article was shortened and restricted. There is in the amended version no reference to carriage by way of experimental trial, and only certain Articles of the Convention are made inapplicable, instead of the whole Convention.

As amended, the Article provides that Articles 3 to 9 inclusive relating to documents of carriage do not apply to carriage performed in extraordinary circumstances outside the normal scope of an air carrier's business.

Consequently even carriage performed in such "extraordinary circumstances" is subject to the provisions of the amended Convention other than the provisions in Articles 3 to 9.

Article 34 in the Schedule to the Act of 1979 is to substantially the same effect.

Article 35

The word "days" when used in the Convention means current days, not working days.

Articles 36-41

These Articles relate to such matters as the drawing up of the Convention and its ratification.

(d) Supplementary Convention Adopted at Guadalajara

The Convention adopted at Guadalajara in September 1961 was given the force of law in the United Kingdom by the Carriage by Air (Supplementary Provisions) Act 1962. The Convention, which is supplementary to the Warsaw Convention as amended at The Hague, is set out in the Schedule to the Act, Part I of the Schedule being the English text and Part II being the French text. The Act provides that if there is any inconsistency between the two texts, the text in French is to prevail (s. 1(2)).

By an Order in Council this Act of 1962 was brought into operation on May 1, 1964, at which date the Convention was supplementary to the original Warsaw Convention, as the Carriage by Air Act 1961 had not then been brought into operation. The Convention was also extended to non-international carriage by the Carriage by Air (Non-International Carriage) (United Kingdom) Order 1964. Its applicability is now governed by the Carriage by Air Acts (Application of Provisions) Order 1967.

6–465   The Convention consists of ten Articles. Only the general purpose and effect of the Convention are noted here.

6–466   The word "carrier" was used in the Warsaw Convention without being defined, and doubts consequently arose, in those cases where a contract for carriage by air was performed by a carrier other than the contracting carrier, as to whether the word "carrier" denoted the contracting carrier or the actual carrier.

6–467   The Convention defines "contracting carrier" as "a person who as a principal makes an agreement for carriage governed by the Warsaw Convention with a . . . consignor or with a person acting on behalf of the . . . consignor." "Actual carrier" is defined as "a person, other than the contracting carrier, who, by virtue of authority from the contracting carrier, performs the whole or part of the carriage . . . but who is not with respect to such part a successive carrier within the meaning of the Warsaw Convention."

6–468   The general effect of the Supplementary Convention is to extend the provisions of the Warsaw Convention to both the contracting carrier and the actual carrier. The Supplementary Convention gives the owner of the goods the same rights against both carriers as the Warsaw Convention gives to him against the "carrier"; and similarly both carriers are entitled under the Supplementary Convention to the same exemptions from, and limits of, liability as the "carrier" enjoys under the Warsaw Convention.

(e) Non-International Carriage Rules of 1967

6–469   Only one set of Non-International Carriage Rules requires notice—those of 1967, brought into force, as from June 1, 1967, by the Carriage by Air Acts (Application of Provisions) Order 1967. This Order in Council was made under section 10 of the Carriage by Air Act 1961 and section 5 of the Carriage by Air (Supplementary Provisions) Act 1962. A notable amendment was made to the Order of 1967 by the Carriage by Air Acts (Application of Provisions) (Second Amendment) Order 1979: as from August 1, 1979, special drawing rights were substituted for gold francs as the unit in which the limits of the carrier's liability are expressed in non-international carriage.

6–470   The Non-International Carriage Rules are, by the Order of 1967, made applicable to all carriage by air which is not subject to the Warsaw Convention in either its original or its amended form. They extend to, amongst other things, mail and postal packets.

6–471   The Rules are for the most part the same as the provisions of the Warsaw Convention as amended at The Hague, coupled with the Guadalajara Convention. The main differences are as follows:

(i) *Air Waybill not Required*

6–472   The Rules do not require the issue of an air waybill. There is no list of particulars as in Article 8 of the Convention, and no legal consequences follow from the absence of an air waybill or from the failure to include specified particulars in it if the parties choose to have one. (Contrast Article 9 of the Warsaw Convention in its original form and as amended at The Hague, but compare that Article as further amended by the Montreal Protocols (see 6–378 *et seq.*, above).)

(ii) *Stoppage* in Transitu *and Delivery*

The provisions of Articles 12 and 13 of the Convention concerning stoppage of the goods in transit and concerning delivery are not included in the Rules.

(iii) *Jurisdiction*

The provisions of Article 28 of the Convention concerning jurisdiction are not included in the Rules. Matters of jurisdiction therefore depend on the ordinary municipal law of the United Kingdom.

(iv) *Carriage Performed in "Extraordinary Circumstances"*

The provision in Article 34 of the amended versions of the Convention is not included in the Rules, since it refers to Articles 3 to 9 of the Convention, and these Articles are in any case inapplicable to non-international carriage.

Further Reading

Gloag and Henderson, *Introduction to the Law of Scotland,* Chapters XIX, XX and XXI

David M. Walker, *Principles of Scottish Private Law,* Chapters 4.17, 4.18 and 4.19

J.J. Gow, *The Mercantile and Industrial Law of Scotland,* Chapter 8

Jasper Ridley, *The Law of The Carriage of Goods by Land, Sea and Air,* 6th ed. by Geoffrey Whitehead (1982, Shaw & Sons Ltd.)

Malcolm A. Clarke, *International Carriage of Goods by Road: CMR* (1982, Stevens and Sons)

Schmitthoff's Export Trade—The Law and Practice of International Trade, 7th ed. by Clive M. Schmitthoff (1980, Stevens & Sons)

D.M. Day, *The Law of International Trade* (1981, Butterworths)

International Transport Conventions Bill (Parliamentary session 1982-83) (Royal Assent: April 11, 1983)

CHAPTER 7

BILLS OF EXCHANGE, CHEQUES AND PROMISSORY NOTES

INTRODUCTION

THE law relating to bills of exchange, cheques and promissory notes was codified by the Bills of Exchange Act 1882, which, with a few exceptions, applies equally to Scotland and England. In this chapter references to sections are, except where the context otherwise requires, references to sections of that codifying Act. The only major amendments of the Act are those concerning cheques, and are now to be found in the Cheques Act 1957.

Bills of exchange, cheques and promissory notes are the principal (but not the only) instances of "negotiable instruments," *i.e.* they are documents having the quality of "negotiability," which enables them to pass from one person to another with much the same effect as that with which cash passes from one person to another.

The 100 sections of the Act of 1882 substantially codified the then existing common law of Scotland and England on the subject. In *McLean* v. *Clydesdale Bank Ltd.* (1883) 11 R. (H.L.) 1; (1883) 10 R. 719, a case decided under the common law shortly after the Act of 1882 had received the royal assent, Lord Blackburn said (at 11 R. (H.L.) p. 3):

"The general law merchant for many years has in all countries caused bills of exchange to be negotiable. That is a common ground which belongs to all, or almost all, countries, and it has been adopted as the law in all civilized countries. There are in some cases differences and peculiarities which by the municipal law of each country are grafted upon it, and which do not affect other countries; but the general rules of the law merchant are the same in all countries, and before the recent Act (the Bills of Exchange Act) which received the royal assent in August 1882, the general law of Scotland and the general law of England were the same. Some peculiarities there were in the municipal law of Scotland as to the mode in which it was to be enforced. . . . Upon the general question of negotiability the law has always been the same in both countries, and we have always been in the habit of treating the authorities of each country as authorities in the other."

The Act provides that the rules of common law including the law merchant, except in so far as they are inconsistent with the express provisions of the Act, continue to apply to bills of exchange, cheques and promissory notes (s. 97(2)).

This chapter has three divisions:

I. Bills of exchange;

II. Cheques; and

III. Promissory notes.

These divisions correspond to Parts II to IV of the Act.

Parts I and V of the Act consist of preliminary and supplementary provisions respectively, equally applicable to bills of exchange, cheques and promissory notes (*e.g.* the definition of terms such as "bearer," "holder," and "indorsement" (s. 2), and rules concerning good faith (s. 90), signature (s. 91) and the calculation of time (s. 92)).

Part II (on bills of exchange) is by far the longest Part of the Act (ss. 3 to 72). The statutory provisions applicable to cheques (ss. 73 to 82 of the Act of 1882 along with the eight sections of the Cheques Act 1957) and to promissory notes (ss. 83 to 89 of the Act of 1882) appear at first sight to be much shorter. It must, however, be kept in view that a cheque is by definition a "bill of exchange drawn on a banker payable on demand," with the result that, except where the sections expressly applicable to cheques provide otherwise, the provisions of Part II of the Act apply to cheques (s. 73), and that by section 89 the provisions of Part II are, with some necessary modifications and exceptions, made to extend also to promissory notes.

7–05   To assist in the appreciation of the subject-matter of this chapter, a brief explanation is first given of:

(a) negotiable instruments in general; and

(b) some functions of a bill of exchange.

(a) Negotiable Instruments in General

7–06   Negotiable instruments form one category of incorporeal moveable property and so have some affinity with other incorporeal moveable property such as policies of life assurance, shares in companies, claims of damages, goodwill, and patents. The distinctive feature of negotiable instruments is the quality of "negotiability," by which they are exceptions to two rules which are generally applicable to the transfer of incorporeal moveable property. A policy of life assurance, for instance, may be transferred by the policy-holder to another person by an assignation, the policy-holder being the cedent and the person to whom the policy is assigned being the assignee. The debtor (*i.e.* the party liable to pay the proceeds of the policy on the cedent's death) continues to be the assurance company. According to the general rules:

(i) the assignation must be intimated to the assurance company in order to enable the assignee to collect the proceeds of the policy from the company on the cedent's death; and

(ii) the assignee cannot obtain any better right to payment from the assurance company than the cedent had, the maxim applicable being *assignatus utitur jure auctoris* ("the assignee enjoys (only) the right of his cedent"); *e.g.* if the policy was voidable as between the original policy-holder and the company on account of misrepresentation by the former as to his state of health, the policy remains voidable after the assignation.

In contrast, where a negotiable instrument is transferred:

(i) no assignation or intimation is necessary; if the document is payable to "bearer," the mere handing over of the document is sufficient, while if the document is payable to "order" the mere indorsement (signature on the back of the document) followed by handing over is sufficient; and

(ii) the person to whom the transfer is made, provided he takes the document in good faith, for value and without notice of any defect in the transferor's title, obtains a good title to the obligation, although the transferor may have had no title or only a defective title.

Examples of negotiable instruments are bills of exchange (including cheques), promissory notes (including bank notes), share warrants issued to bearer (which entitle the bearer to the shares specified), debentures payable to bearer, and dividend warrants. The following are not negotiable instruments—postal orders, deposit receipts, share certificates, and bills of lading. The class of negotiable instruments is not closed: other documents may, by statute or by decisions of the courts giving effect to mercantile usage, be added to the class. It is not, however, permissible for contracting parties to create a new form of negotiable instrument by mere agreement unsupported by mercantile usage: any isolated agreement of this kind would be binding only on the parties to it and would not affect the rights of subsequent holders of the document; but if the agreement were of a type in common use in mercantile circles, the courts might hold that the document in question should be added to the class of negotiable instruments (*e.g.* "negotiable sterling certificates of deposit," first issued in London in 1968 and modelled on U.S. certificates of deposit which had long been recognised as fully negotiable instruments in the U.S.A., would probably be held by the courts to be a new form of negotiable instrument in our law).

(b) Some Functions of a Bill of Exchange

Bills of exchange developed in medieval Europe to meet the needs of merchants engaged in foreign trade. Such documents enabled the merchants to overcome the difficulty of transmitting coins from one country to another. In Scotland by the end of the seventeenth century bills of exchange were in use for both foreign and inland trading, as is proved by the passing of a Scots Act in 1681 providing for summary diligence on foreign bills, followed by a further Scots Act in 1696 extending summary diligence to inland bills.

With the expansion of trade, the use of bills of exchange increased, so that by 1882 the law relating to bills had emerged as a sufficiently important and well-defined branch of commercial law as to merit the codification of that year.

Bills of exchange other than cheques are seldom encountered now in inland transactions. Even in foreign trade they are now used in fewer transactions than formerly, though a significant part of foreign trade is still conducted by transactions which *include* the use of bills of exchange (*e.g.* a bill of exchange may be one of the documents specified in a "documentary credit"). The chief importance of the law relating to bills of exchange at the present day, at least in inland transactions, is that it includes the law relating to cheques. Since a cheque is by definition "a bill of exchange drawn on a banker payable on demand," and since the statutory provisions applying to bills of exchange are made to apply (with some modifications) to cheques (s. 73), the law relating to cheques, obviously of supreme importance to the present-day business community, must be approached via the law relating to bills of exchange in general.

7–11   Bills of exchange have fulfilled various functions, and have often featured in complex transactions as can be seen from reported cases. The question of whether or not a particular document is a bill of exchange depends on whether or not it satisfies the statutory definition (7–16, below). A preliminary glance at some of the functions of a bill of exchange will make the study of the precise terms of that definition more meaningful. Two situations, shorn of all the complexities which often beset actual practice and decided cases, are here given as illustrations:

7–12   (i) A bill of exchange may be used in conjunction with a bill of lading to ensure that a seller who ships goods to a buyer will obtain, by the time when the goods are delivered to the buyer, either immediate payment or at least an easily enforceable written undertaking by the buyer to pay.

For example, B, a seller in Brazil, will receive on shipping a cargo to G, a buyer in Glasgow, a bill of lading from the master of the ship (in practice usually from the master's agent). This is both a receipt for the goods and a document of title to them. The master will deliver the cargo only to the person who, at Glasgow, presents the bill of lading to him.

B sends the bill of lading to his own agent in Glasgow, attaching to it a bill of exchange for the price of the goods. In the bill of exchange B orders G to pay to some specified person, such as B's Glasgow agent, the sum of money which is the price of the goods. The Glasgow agent will hand over the bill of lading to G (putting G in a position to collect the cargo from the ship) only if G pays, or at least accepts, the bill of exchange.

This is an over-simplification of what happens in practice: the transactions are conducted through banks as agents for the parties themselves. Accordingly, B would not normally send the bill of lading with the bill of exchange attached direct to a Glasgow agent: he would hand over the documents to his bank in Brazil, and that bank would then transmit them to its Glasgow agent (usually a Scottish bank).

7–13   (ii) A bill of exchange, although it may not be payable until some future date, can be used by its holder to provide immediate cash. This is accomplished where the holder "discounts" the bill at his bank.

For example, one merchant, X, who has sold goods to another merchant, Y, may wish to allow Y three months' credit, and so he will draw on Y a bill of exchange payable three months after its date. When Y accepts this bill, X may obtain immediate cash for it by having it discounted at his bank. X will receive the sum for which the bill was drawn, less a discount.

I BILLS OF EXCHANGE

7–14   A bill of exchange has three principal characteristics:

(i) It contains an obligation to pay money. The person who holds it has therefore a document, of at least potential value, which he may use to obtain cash or credit for himself. If the bill has been accepted by the drawee, it is the acceptor who is primarily liable to pay it, but there are circumstances in which other parties to the bill, provided they have signed the bill, are liable to pay it. Hence the liability of the drawer and of indorsers, as well as that of the acceptor, must be taken into account.

(ii) It is a negotiable instrument. The results are that: (1) it may be transferred by one holder to another holder without the need for intimation to the acceptor or other person liable on the bill; and (2) the second, or subsequent, holder acquires a good title to the bill (provided certain conditions are fulfilled), so that his rights against the acceptor or other person liable are unaffected by any defects in the title of a previous holder.

(iii) It operates as an assignation of funds held by the drawee, when it is intimated to the drawee. This characteristic is of practical importance where the holder presents the bill to the drawee at a time when the drawee has insufficient funds in his hands to pay the full amount of the bill, and because of that does not accept the bill. Such funds as he has are, by the mere fact that the bill has been presented to him, assigned to the holder. The presentment takes effect as an intimated assignation. In this respect there is a distinction between Scots and English law: the common law of Scotland is expressly preserved by section 53 (2). On this see also 7-97 *et seq.*, below. Under English law a bill does not, of itself, operate as an assignment of funds in the hands of the drawee (s. 53(1)).

These three major characteristics underlie the specific statutory provisions of Part II of the Act, which are considered below under these headings:

(a) definitions of bills;
(b) acceptance of a bill;
(c) issue of a bill;
(d) holder in due course;
(e) negotiation of a bill;
(f) presentment for acceptance and presentment for payment;
(g) procedure on dishonour;
(h) liabilities of parties;
(i) measure of damages on dishonour;
(j) enforcement of liability by summary diligence;
(k) discharge of bill;
(l) acceptance and payment for honour *supra* protest;
(m) miscellaneous statutory provisions (lost bills, bill in a set and conflict of laws).

(a) Definitions of Bills

The Act defines a bill of exchange as follows: "A bill of exchange is an unconditional order in writing, addressed by one person to another, signed by the person giving it, requiring the person to whom it is addressed to pay on demand or at a fixed or determinable future time a sum certain in money to or to the order of a specified person, or to bearer" (s. 3(1)). A document which does not comply with these conditions, or which orders any act to be done in addition to the payment of money, is not a bill of exchange (s. 3(2)).

Before some explanatory comments are made on this definition, it is appropriate to set out the statutory definitions of inland and foreign bills.

"An inland bill is a bill which is or on the face of it purports to be

(*a*) both drawn and payable within the British Islands, or

(*b*) drawn within the British Islands upon some person resident therein.

Any other bill is a foreign bill." "British Islands" mean any part of the United Kingdom, the islands of Man, Guernsey, Jersey, Alderney, and Sark, and the islands adjacent to any of them if they are part of Her Majesty's dominions (s. 4(1)).

7–18 The only important legal distinction between an inland bill and a foreign bill is that, if a foreign bill is dishonoured, it must be "protested" for non-acceptance or for non-payment; this procedure is not necessary if the bill is an inland bill (s. 51(1) and (2)). Unless the contrary appears on the face of the bill, the holder of the bill may treat it as an inland bill (s. 4(2)).

7–19 The wording of the definition of a bill of exchange will now be examined with reference to the following fictitious specimen bill:

Glasgow,
£1,000   November 6, 1981
At sight pay to Peter Piper or order the sum of One thousand pounds. Value received.
Derek Driver
To Arthur Dee,
      15 High Street,
            Edinburgh.

Alternatives to "At sight" would be "On demand," "Three months after date," "Six months after sight," *etc.*, and instead of "Peter Piper or order" one might have "Peter Piper or bearer," "me" or "bearer."

This specimen includes some items which, though usual, are not essential to the validity of the bill. A bill is not invalid if it is not dated ("November 6, 1981"), or if it does not include the words "Value received," or if it does not specify the place where it is drawn ("Glasgow"). A bill may specify the place where it is payable (*e.g.* "at the Bank of Scotland Head Office" or (more usually) at a particular branch), but this is also not essential (s. 3(4)). Nor is a bill invalid merely because it is ante-dated or post-dated, or bears a date which is a Sunday (s. 13(2)).

"Unconditional Order in Writing"

7–20 This is the word "pay," an order given by Derek Driver to Arthur Dee. If conditions could be attached to the order, the document would not serve the needs of the commercial community, because investigation would be necessary to ascertain whether or not the conditions had been fulfilled.

An instance of a conditional order is an order to pay out of a particular fund. It is, however, permissible to have an unqualified order to pay, coupled with either:

(i) an indication of a particular fund out of which Arthur Dee is to reimburse himself or a particular account to be debited with the amount; or

(ii) a statement of the transaction which gave rise to the bill.

Such an order is regarded as "unconditional" (s. 3(3)).

"Writing" includes print (s. 2). A bill may therefore be partly printed.

"Addressed by One Person to Another"

The order is addressed by Derek Driver, who is referred to as the "drawer," to Arthur Dee, who is referred to as the "drawee."

The drawee must be named or otherwise indicated in the bill with reasonable certainty (s. 6(1)). The purpose is to ensure that the holder of the bill will know to whom he is to present the bill for acceptance or payment.

A bill may be addressed to two or more drawees (*e.g.* to partners), but an order addressed to two drawees in the alternative or to two or more drawees in succession is not within the definition of a bill (s. 6(2)).

"Signed by the Person Giving it"

Derek Driver must sign the bill. If, and as long as, his signature is the only signature on the bill, he is the only party liable to pay the bill. He may, however, insert an express stipulation in the bill negativing or limiting his own liability (s. 16(1)).

The requirement that the drawer must sign the bill is part of the wider principle applicable to bills of exchange (and also to cheques and promissory notes) that signature is essential for liability: no person is liable as drawer, indorser, or acceptor unless he has signed the bill (s. 23). Other statutory provisions as to signature may be conveniently noted here, although they are not restricted to the drawer's signature.

It is not necessary that the drawer (or the other person concerned) should sign the bill (or cheque or promissory note) with his own hand: it is sufficient if the signature is written by some other person by or under his authority (s. 91(1)). In the case of corporations (including limited and other registered companies) sealing with the corporate seal is sufficient as a signature, but sealing is not essential (s. 91(2)). By the Companies Act 1948 (s. 33), a bill of exchange or promissory note is deemed to have been made, accepted or indorsed on behalf of a company if made, accepted, or indorsed in the name of, or by or on behalf or on account of, the company by any person acting under its authority.

Where a person signs a bill in a trade or assumed name, he is liable on the bill as if he had signed it in his own name (s. 23, proviso (1)). The signature of the name of a firm is equivalent to the signature of all the partners, provided the person signing the firm's name has the necessary express or implied authority to bind the firm (s. 23, proviso (2)). The circumstances may be such that the person who takes the bill ought to suspect that a partner signing the firm's name has no authority to do so (*cf. Paterson Brothers* v. *Gladstone* (1891) 18 R. 403 (2-64, above), in which a partner who had signed the firm name on promissory notes was held not to have been acting in the ordinary course of the firm's business, with the result that the firm (and so ultimately the other partners) could not be held liable to pay the notes).

An unauthorised signature is not the same as a forged signature: the former may be ratified and so become binding on the party on whose behalf it purported to be made, whereas a forged signature cannot be ratified. That distinction apart, however, the statutory rule applicable to forged and to unauthorised signatures on bills is the same: subject to the provisions of the Act, the signature is wholly inoperative, and no right to retain the bill or to give a discharge for it or to enforce payment of it against any party can be acquired through that signature, unless the party against whom the bill is being retained or enforced is barred from saying that the signature was forged or unauthorised (s. 24). An instance of such a bar is given in section 54: the acceptor against whom the bill is being enforced is barred from saying that the drawer's signature was forged. *Greenwood* v. *Martins Bank Ltd.* [1933] A.C. 51 supplies another instance:

G.'s wife repeatedly forged her husband's signature on cheques, and drew out money which she applied to her own uses. G. became aware of the forgeries in October 1929, but his wife begged him not to inform the bank; she said that she had used the money to help her sister in legal proceedings relating to a house. In the hope of a favourable outcome to the sister's legal proceedings and for his wife's sake, G. said nothing to the bank.

In June 1930 G. discovered that his wife had deceived him, there being no legal proceedings. He said that he would go at once to the bank, and he went out. He did not actually go to the bank, but on his return home his wife shot herself.

G. brought an action against the bank to recover the sums paid out on the forged cheques.

Held that G. had owed a duty to the bank to disclose the forgeries when he became aware of them so as to enable the bank to recover the sums wrongfully paid, and that since his failure to fulfil this duty had prevented the bank from bringing an action against G. and his wife for the tort (wrong) committed by the wife until after her death, G. was "estopped" (the English equivalent of "personally barred") from saying that the signatures were forgeries, and so was not entitled to recover the sums from the bank.

(According to the law applicable at the date of the case, a husband was liable for the torts of his wife and the liability ceased on the wife's death. The Law Reform (Married Women and Tortfeasors) Act 1935 (s. 3) abolished a husband's liability for his wife's torts.)

Lord Tomlin said (at p. 58): "The respondents' case is that the duty [*to disclose the forgeries*] ought to have been discharged by the appellant immediately upon his discovery in October, 1929, and that if it had been then discharged they could have sued the appellant's wife in tort and the appellant himself would have been responsible for his wife's tort. They claim that his silence until after his wife's death amounted in these circumstances to a representation that the cheques were not forgeries and deprived the respondents of their remedy. . . .

"The appellant's silence . . . was deliberate and intended to produce the effect which it in fact produced—namely, the leaving of the respondents in ignorance of the true facts so that no action might be taken by them against the appellant's wife. The deliberate abstention from speaking in those circumstances seems to me to amount to a representation to the respondents that the forged cheques were in fact in order, and assuming that detriment to the respondents followed there were, it seems to me, present all the elements essential to estoppel."

A signature may be a signature "by procuration." This occurs where, expressly or by implication, one person makes another person his "procurator" (agent) for the purpose of signing. In practice the words "per pro" are often used to indicate that the signature is of this character. By section 25 of the Act a signature by procuration operates as notice that the agent has only a limited authority to sign, and the principal is only bound by such signature if the agent in signing was acting within the actual limits of his authority.

It is also possible that a person who signs his own name may add to his signature words which indicate that he is *signing* for or on behalf of a principal, or in a representative character. A drawer, indorser, or acceptor who adds such words to his signature is not personally liable. However, the mere addition of words *describing* the person as an agent, or as filling a representative character, does not exempt him from personal liability (s. 26(1)). For example, in *Brebner* v. *Henderson*, 1925 S.C. 643, where a promissory note was signed:

"JAS. R. GORDON Director
ALEX HENDERSON, Secretary
The Fraserburgh Empire Limited,"

the words added to the two signatures were held to be no more than descriptive and not to indicate that the signature was "for or on behalf of" the company. In determining whether a signature on a bill is that of the principal or that of the agent by whose hand it is written, the interpretation most favourable to the validity of the document is adopted (s. 26(2)).

"To Pay on Demand or at a Fixed or Determinable Future Time"

The time at which a bill falls due is referred to as the "maturity" of the bill. A bill which is not paid at its maturity becomes "overdue".

A bill is payable "on demand" if it is expressed to be payable "on demand," or "at sight," or "on presentation," or if no time for payment is expressed (s. 10(1)).

A "fixed future time" is some specified future date.

A bill is payable at a "determinable future time" if it is expressed to be payable at a fixed period after date or sight (*e.g.* "three months after date" and "six months after sight"), or on or at a fixed period after the occurrence of a specified event which is certain to happen, though the time of happening may be uncertain (*e.g.* on the death of a named individual or six months after the death of a named individual). A document which is expressed to be payable on a "contingency" (an event which may or may not happen, *e.g.* the arrival of a named ship) is not within the definition of a bill of exchange even if the event happens (s. 11).

There may have been an omission to insert a date which is necessary for fixing the maturity of the bill: this occurs if a bill expressed to be payable at a fixed period after date is in fact undated, or if the drawee in accepting a bill which is payable at a fixed period after sight does not date his acceptance. Any holder is then entitled to insert the true date of issue or acceptance as the case may be, and the bill is then payable accordingly. If the holder in good faith and by mistake inserts a wrong date, and in every case where a wrongly dated bill comes into the hands of a "holder in due course" (7–47 *et seq.*, below), the bill is payable as if the wrong date were the true date (s. 12).

7–30   Where a bill or an acceptance or any indorsement is dated, that date is, unless the contrary be proved, deemed to be the true date of the drawing, acceptance, or indorsement, as the case may be (s. 13(1)).

7–31   Where the drawee chooses to accept a bill which is already overdue he becomes liable on the bill as if it were a bill payable on demand (s. 10(2)).

7–32   The rules for calculation of the time of payment are in section 14, as amended by the Banking and Financial Dealings Act 1971:

(1) A bill is due and payable on the last day of the time of payment as fixed by the bill or, if that is a "non-business day," on the succeeding business day. Days of grace, formerly allowed in the payment of bills other than those payable on demand, were abolished by the Act of 1971. By section 92, as amended by the Act of 1971, where the time limited for doing any act or thing is less than three days, "non-business days" are excluded. "Non-business days" are:

(*a*) Saturday, Sunday, Good Friday, Christmas Day;

(*b*) a bank holiday under the Act of 1971;

(*c*) a day appointed by royal proclamation as a public fast or thanksgiving day;

(*d*) a day declared by an order under the Act of 1971 to be a non-business day.

Any other day is a business day.

(2) Where a bill is payable at a fixed period after date, or after the happening of a specified event, the time of payment is determined by excluding the day from which the time is to begin to run and by including the day of payment.

(3) Where a bill is payable at a fixed period after sight, the time begins to run from the date of the acceptance, or, if the bill is dishonoured by non-acceptance, from the date of "noting" or "protest."

(4) The term "month" in a bill means calendar month.

"A Sum Certain in Money"

7–33   The sum payable still qualifies as a "sum certain" although it is required to be paid:

(*a*) with interest;

(*b*) by stated instalments;

(*c*) by stated instalments, with a provision that upon default in payment of any instalments the whole will become due; or

(*d*) according to an indicated rate of exchange (s. 9(1)).

Where a bill is expressed to be payable with interest, then, unless there is provision to the contrary, interest runs from the date of the bill, and if the bill is undated, from the issue of the bill (s. 9(3)).

As the specimen bill indicates, the amount of the bill may be expressed both in words and in figures. If there is a discrepancy between the two, the sum expressed in words is the amount payable (s. 9(2)). In the case of a cheque, the banking practice is to return the cheque unpaid, with the remark "words and figures differ."

By the Decimal Currency Act 1969, a bill of exchange (or promissory note) drawn (or made) after February 15, 1971 ("Decimal Day") is invalid if the sum payable is an amount wholly or partly in shillings or pence.

"To or to the Order of a Specified Person, or to Bearer"

These words refer to the payee of the bill. If a bill is not payable to bearer, the payee must be named or otherwise indicated with reasonable certainty (s. 7(1)).

A bill may be made payable to two or more payees jointly, or it may be made payable in the alternative to one of two, or one or some of several, payees. It may also be made payable to the holder of an office for the time being (s. 7(2)).

Where the payee is a fictitious or non-existing person, the bill may be treated as payable to bearer (s. 7(3)).

A bill may be an "order bill" (e.g. payable to "Peter Piper or order," or payable to "me or my order"), or a "bearer bill" (e.g. payable to "Peter Piper or bearer"). In practice bearer bills are rare. Either type of bill is "negotiable" (i.e. may be transferred by the payee to another person as a negotiable instrument) (s. 8(2)). If, however, a bill contains words prohibiting transfer, or indicating an intention that it should not be transferable, it is valid as between the parties to it, but it is not negotiable (s. 8(1)).

The words "or order" need not appear in an order bill. Any negotiable bill which is expressed to be payable to a particular person counts as an order bill (s. 8(4)). It is also of no consequence whether the phrase used is "to the order of Peter Piper" instead of "to Peter Piper or order": in either case Peter Piper has the option of enforcing payment himself or "negotiating" (transferring) the bill to another person (s. 8(5)).

A bill which is not originally a bearer bill may become one in the process of negotiation. This occurs where the indorsement (signature on the back by the specified payee) is a blank indorsement (i.e. does not name the new payee) (s. 34(1)). Hence a bill on which the only or the last indorsement is a blank indorsement is considered to be payable to bearer (s. 8(3)).

(b) Acceptance of a Bill

The acceptance of a bill is "the signification by the drawee of his assent to the order of the drawer" (s. 17(1)).

In order to be valid an acceptance must comply with the following conditions:

(i) It must be written on the bill and be signed by the drawee. The mere signature of the drawee without additional words is sufficient.

(ii) It must not express that the drawee will perform his promise by any other means than the payment of money (s. 17(2)).

A bill need not always be presented to the drawee for acceptance (see 7–69, below). However, the drawer or holder of the bill may wish to obtain the drawee's acceptance because its effect is to make the acceptor primarily liable to pay the bill when it becomes due.

In normal cases the acceptance would be obtained soon after the bill had been signed by the drawer and well before the time when it was due to be paid, but it is permissible for a bill to be accepted:

(i) before it has been signed by the drawer, or while it is otherwise incomplete; or

(ii) when it is overdue, or after it has been dishonoured by a previous refusal to accept, or by non-payment (s. 18).

7–39   An acceptance may be either general or qualified (s. 19(1)).

A general acceptance is one by which the drawee assents, without any qualification, to the order of the drawer. A qualified acceptance varies the effect of the bill as drawn. In particular an acceptance is qualified if it is:

(i) conditional, *i.e.* makes payment by the acceptor dependent on the fulfilment of a condition;

(ii) partial, *i.e.* to pay part only of the amount for which the bill is drawn;

(iii) local, *i.e.* to pay *only* at a particular specified place; an acceptance to pay at a particular place is a general acceptance, unless it expressly states that the bill is to be paid there only and not elsewhere;

(iv) qualified as to time; or

(v) the acceptance of some one or more of the drawees, but not of all (s. 19(2)).

The holder of the bill may refuse to take a qualified acceptance (s. 44(1)).

(c) Issue of a Bill

7–40   The "issue" of a bill is defined as "the first delivery of a bill, complete in form, to a person who takes it as a holder" (s. 2). Three terms in this definition should be noted:

(i) "delivery";

(ii) "complete in form"; and

(iii) "holder."

The liabilities of the various parties to the bill and the rights and duties of the holder of the bill arise only after the bill has been issued.

(i) *"Delivery"*

7–41   "Delivery" means transfer of possession, actual or constructive, from one person to another (s. 2). Every contract on a bill, whether it be the drawer's, or the acceptor's, or an indorser's contract, is incomplete and revocable until there is delivery. Where, however, an acceptance is written on a bill and the drawee gives notice to the person who is entitled to the bill that he has accepted it, the acceptance then becomes complete and irrevocable (s. 21(1)). In most cases the transfer takes the form of the physical delivery of the bill from one person to another. A "constructive" delivery occurs where, for instance, a person who originally held the bill as agent for another party comes to hold the bill for himself.

In order to be effectual the delivery must be made either by or under the authority of the party drawing, accepting, or indorsing the bill, as the case may be, and the delivery may be shown to have been conditional or for a special purpose only (and not for the purpose of transferring the ownership of the bill). A "holder in due course" (see 7–47 *et seq*., below), however, has special protection in this connection: if the bill is in the hands of a "holder in due course" there is a conclusive presumption that the bill was validly delivered by all parties prior to him so as to make them liable to him (s. 21(2)).

Where a bill is no longer in the possession of a party who has signed it as drawer, acceptor, or indorser, the bill is presumed, until the contrary is proved, to have been validly and unconditionally delivered (s. 21(3)). This presumption, which is not a conclusive presumption, gives some assistance to a holder who is not a "holder in due course."

(ii) *"Complete in Form"*

For an explanation of "complete in form," reference must be made to the definition of a bill (7–16, above). It follows from the definition that the bill will have at least one signature—that of the drawer—and will identify the drawee and the payee. If the bill has already been accepted by the drawee, it will also bear the acceptor's signature, and if it is an order bill and has already been indorsed by the payee, it will also bear the signature of the payee as indorser. As has been noticed, signature is essential for liability (s. 23); hence a "bearer" who has parted with possession of a bill by merely handing it over to another "bearer" is not liable on the bill.

However, liability on a bill may arise although the bill is not "complete in form" but merely "inchoate." This occurs where a simple signature on a blank paper is delivered by the signer in order that it may be converted into a bill; the person to whom it is delivered has a *prima facie*[1] authority to fill it up as a complete bill for any amount using the signature for that of the drawer, or the acceptor, or an indorser. Similarly, when a bill is wanting in any material particular, the person in possession of it has a *prima facie*[1] authority to fill up the omission in any way he thinks fit (s. 20(1)). For the bill to be enforceable against prior parties to it, it must be filled up within a reasonable time and strictly in accordance with the authority given, except that if, after completion, the bill is negotiated to a "holder in due course" it is valid and effectual for all purposes in his hands, and he may enforce it as if it had been filled up within a reasonable time and strictly in accordance with the authority given (s. 20(2)).

An instance of the application of section 20 is *Kinloch, Campbell & Co. &c.* v. *Cowan* (1890) 27 S.L.R. 870, in which acceptors of a bill who had delivered it blank in the name of the drawer were held not entitled to have a charge at the instance of the drawer (who claimed that he had given value for the bill) suspended without finding caution.

Lord President Inglis said (at p. 871): "It appears to me that when a man sends acceptances blank in the name of the drawer into circulation he must take all the consequences of his rashness, which enables anyone to sign as drawer and become creditor of the acceptor."

(iii) *"Holder"*

"Holder" means either:
    (1) the payee or indorsee of a bill who is in possession of it; or
    (2) the bearer of it.

---

[1] "until the contrary is proved."

"Bearer" is defined as the person in possession of a bill which is payable to bearer (s. 2). Possession is therefore essential: an indorsee who is no longer, or not yet, in possession of the bill is not a "holder," nor is a person who has been, but no longer is, in possession of a bearer bill a "holder."

7–46   A holder is entitled to sue on the bill in his own name all or any of the parties who are liable to pay it (s. 38(1)), but the party being sued may be able to put forward some defence which would not be available to him if the holder were a "holder in due course" (7–48, below).

See also 7–57 and 7–58, below.

(d) **Holder in Due Course**

7–47   The definition of "holder in due course" is of central importance, since it is only in the hands of a holder in due course that a bill of exchange is fully a negotiable instrument, *i.e.* the holder in due course holds the bill free from any defect of title of prior parties, as well as free from mere personal defences available to prior parties among themselves, and he may enforce payment of the bill against any party who is liable on it (s. 38(2)).

7–48   A "holder in due course" is defined as a holder who has taken a bill, complete and regular on the face of it, under the following conditions:

(*a*) that he became the holder of it before it was overdue, and without notice that it had been previously dishonoured, if such was the fact; and

(*b*) that he took the bill in good faith and for value, and that at the time the bill was negotiated to him he had no notice of any defect in the title of the person who negotiated it (s. 29(1)).

With regard to condition (*b*), the Act includes further provisions as to the meaning of:

(i)   "good faith";
(ii) "value"; and
(iii) "defect in title."

(i) *"Good Faith"*

7–49   A thing is deemed to be done in good faith provided it is in fact done honestly, whether it is done negligently or not (s. 90).

(ii) *"Value"*

7–50   "Value" means "valuable consideration" (s. 2), and in this connection the Act was framed to match the doctrine of consideration which is part of the common law of contract in England but has no place in that of Scotland.

7–51   The Act provides that "valuable consideration" for a bill may be constituted by:

(a) any consideration sufficient to support a "simple contract" (a term of English law, which distinguishes between simple contracts and contracts under seal); or

(b) an antecedent debt or liability (which, according to English law, would not normally count as consideration because of the rule that "consideration must not be past") (s. 27(1)).

Under the common law of Scotland a bill of exchange could be enforced although it was gratuitous. An acceptor, therefore, could not put forward as a defence to an action against him by the drawer that the drawer had given him no consideration for the bill (*Law* v. *Humphrey* (1875) 3 R. 1192). The Act gives no separate explanation of how "valuable consideration" may be constituted for Scots law, but from the definition of "holder in due course" it may be inferred that valuable consideration is now essential if a bill is to take full effect as a negotiable instrument.

Where a holder of a bill has a "lien" on it (*i.e.* a right to retain it in security for a debt due to him by the owner of the bill), he is deemed to be a holder for value to the extent of the sum for which he has the lien (s. 27(3)).

Although a holder in due course must, to satisfy the definition, have given value for the bill, he is not required to prove that he has done so; the "onus" (burden) of proof lies on the defender (the acceptor or other party being sued as liable on the bill) to prove that he (the holder) did not in fact give value; every party whose signature appears on a bill is *prima facie*[1] deemed to have become a party to the bill for value (s. 30(1)). This rule is in accordance with the common law of Scotland: "onerosity of a bill is to be assumed" (*per* Lord President Inglis in *Law* v. *Humphrey* (1875) 3 R. 1192, at p. 1193). However, the Act altered the common law with regard to the method by which this assumption could be proved wrong: by the common law, non-onerosity could be proved only by writ or oath, but by section 100 of the Act "parole evidence" (the oral evidence of witnesses) is now allowed for the proof of any fact relevant to liability on a bill.

While the holder in due course must, by definition, have given value for the bill to his immediate predecessor, it does not follow that the person from whom he seeks payment (the acceptor or other party whose signature is on the bill) has received value when he parted with the bill. The bill may have passed through a series of transactions before payment is demanded, and it could be that in one or more of these transactions no value was given for the transfer of the bill. The Act provides that where value has at any time been given for a bill, the holder is deemed to be a holder for value as regards the acceptor and all parties to the bill who became parties to the bill before the stage at which value was given (s. 27(2)).

A person who has received no value for a bill may be an "accommodation party," defined as a "person who has signed a bill as drawer, acceptor, or indorser, without receiving value therefor, and for the purpose of lending his name to some other person" (s. 28(1)). An accommodation party is liable to a holder for value, and it makes no difference whether or not the holder knew, when he took the bill, that it was in fact an accommodation bill (s. 28(2)).

(iii) *"Defect in Title"*

The title of the person who is transferring the bill is "defective" if he himself obtained the bill (or the acceptance of the bill) by fraud, duress, or force and fear, or other unlawful means, or for an illegal consideration, or

---

[1] "until the contrary is proved."

when he is acting in breach of faith, or under circumstances amounting to a fraud (s. 29(2)).

7–57   A holder (whether for value or not), who derives his title to a bill through a holder in due course, and who is not himself a party to any fraud or illegality affecting it, has all the rights of that holder in due course as regards the acceptor and all parties to the bill prior to that holder (s. 29(3)).

7–58   A holder whose title is defective and who is therefore not himself a holder in due course, may negotiate the bill to another holder, who may, if he satisfies the definition, be a holder in due course, with a good and complete title to the bill (s. 38(3)).

7–59   Every holder of a bill is *prima facie*[1] deemed to be a holder in due course; but if in an action on a bill it is admitted or proved that the acceptance, issue, or subsequent negotiation of the bill is affected with fraud, duress, or force and fear, or illegality, the burden of proof is shifted, unless and until the holder proves that, subsequent to the alleged fraud or illegality, value has in good faith been given for the bill (s. 30(2)).

(e) Negotiation of a Bill

7–60   A bill is negotiated when it is transferred from one person to another in such a manner as to make the transferee the holder of the bill (s. 31(1)). A bill payable to bearer is negotiated by delivery (s. 31(2)). A bill payable to order is negotiated by the indorsement of the holder (*i.e.* the holder's signature, usually on the back of the bill) completed by delivery (s. 31(3)). Thus, if the specimen bill (7–19, above) is again referred to, the first indorser would be Peter Piper; if the bill were payable to "me," the first indorser would be Derek Driver. The indorsement would in both cases require to be completed by delivery of the bill to the indorsee (the new holder indicated in the indorsement). If the bill were payable to "Peter Piper or bearer" or simply to "bearer," no indorsement would be required in order to negotiate the bill: mere delivery of the document by Derek Driver to another holder would be sufficient.

7–61   Where the holder of a bill payable to his order transfers the bill for value without indorsing it, the transfer gives the transferee the title which the transferor had, and the transferee in addition acquires the right to have the indorsement of the transferor (s. 31(4)). This provision was considered by the court in *Hood* v. *Stewart* (1890) 17 R. 749, in which the transferee, who had given value for the bill, was held entitled to recover payment from the acceptor, on the ground that section 31(4) conferred on the transferee a title as complete as that of the transferor had been, *i.e.* the transferee had a title equivalent to a duly intimated assignation (although there had in fact been no intimation). Lord Justice-Clerk J.H.A. Macdonald explained the distinction between negotiation and mere transfer as follows (at p. 753):

"The title obtained by transference is not necessarily the same as the title obtained by indorsement. It is well known that an indorser may

---

[1] "until the contrary is proved."

confer on an indorsee a better title than he himself possessed. This cannot happen in the case of mere transference. The transferee acquires the title of the transferor, and nothing more. Hence such exceptions[2] may be stated to the pursuer's title as might have been stated against the title of the transferor. As in an assignation, *utitur jure auctoris*[3], and if the title of his author is bad, his own is no better."

An indorsement, in order to operate as a negotiation, must comply with the following conditions:

(1) It must be written on the bill itself and be signed by the indorser. The simple signature of the indorser, without additional words, is sufficient, and the indorsement may be written on an "allonge" (a piece of paper attached to the bill to allow room for more indorsements) or on a copy of the bill issued or negotiated in a country where copies are recognised.

(2) It must be an indorsement of the entire bill, and not a partial indorsement attempting to transfer part only of the amount to the indorsee or attempting to divide the bill between two separate indorsees.

(3) Where the bill is payable to the order of two or more payees or indorsees who are not partners, all must indorse, unless the one indorsing has authority to indorse for the others (s. 32(1)-(3)).

Where, in a bill payable to order, the payee or indorsee is wrongly designated, or his name is mis-spelt, he may indorse the bill according to the description in the bill, adding, if he thinks fit, his proper signature (s. 32(4)).

Where there are two or more indorsements on a bill, each indorsement is deemed to have been made in the order in which it appears on the bill, until the contrary is proved (s. 32(5)).

Where a bill purports to be indorsed conditionally, the condition may be disregarded by the payer, and payment to the indorsee is valid whether the condition has been fulfilled or not (s. 33).

An indorsement may be "in blank" or it may be "special." An indorsement "in blank" specifies no indorsee (*e.g.* where the indorser simply signs his name on the back of the bill). A bill indorsed in this way becomes payable to bearer. A "special" indorsement specifies the person to whom, or to whose order, the bill is to be payable (*e.g.* where the indorser writes on the back of the bill "pay Ina McNee or order" followed by his signature). The indorsee under a special indorsement ("Ina McNee") is then in the position of payee of the bill. The holder of a bill may convert a blank endorsement into a special indorsement by writing above the indorser's signature a direction to pay the bill to or to the order of himself or some other person (s. 34).

It is also possible to have a "restrictive" indorsement, *i.e.* an indorsement which prohibits the further negotiation of the bill, or which expresses that it is a mere authority to deal with the bill in the way directed and not a transfer of the ownership of the bill (*e.g.* "Pay D only," or "Pay D for the account of X," or "Pay D or order for collection"). A restrictive indorsement gives the indorsee the right to receive payment of the bill and to sue any party whom his indorser could have sued, but gives

---

[2] defences.
[3] "He enjoys the right of his author."

him no power to transfer his rights as indorsee unless it expressly authorises him to do so. Where a restrictive indorsement authorises further transfer, all subsequent indorsees take the bill with the same rights and subject to the same liabilities as the first indorsee under the restrictive indorsement (s. 35).

7–66   A bill which is negotiable in its origin continues to be negotiable until it has been either restrictively indorsed or discharged by payment or otherwise. However, if an overdue bill is negotiated, it can only be negotiated subject to any defect of title affecting it at its maturity: no person who takes the bill thereafter can acquire or give a better title than that which the person from whom he took it had. A bill which is payable on demand is deemed to be "overdue" for this purpose when it appears on the face of it to have been in circulation for an unreasonable length of time, and what is an unreasonable length of time is a question of fact. Except where an indorsement is dated after the maturity of the bill, every negotiation is *prima facie* deemed to have been effected before the bill was overdue. Where a bill which is not overdue has been dishonoured, any person who takes it with notice of the dishonour takes it subject to any defect of title attaching to it at the time of dishonour (s. 36). These provisions are to be linked to the definition of "holder in due course" (7–48, above): a holder in due course must have become the holder of the bill before it was overdue and without notice that it had been previously dishonoured (if such was the fact) (s. 29(1)).

(f) Presentment for Acceptance and Presentment for Payment

7–67   In certain circumstances it is the duty of the holder, if he is to exercise his full rights on a bill, to present the bill for acceptance and to present it for payment.

(i) *Presentment for Acceptance*

7–68   It is *advisable* for the holder to present the bill to the drawee for acceptance. If the drawee accepts the bill, the holder thus obtains the right to enforce payment of the bill against the acceptor and is in a position to pass on to a new holder a document of better currency. If the drawee refuses to accept the bill, the holder will acquire an immediate right to hold other parties who have signed the bill (drawer and indorsers) liable to pay it.

7–69   Presentment for acceptance is, however, not *necessary*, except in the three following cases:

(1) where a bill is payable "after sight" (*e.g.* "six months after sight," *i.e.* six months after the drawee sees it): presentment for acceptance is necessary in this case in order to fix the maturity of the bill; a holder to whom a bill payable after sight has been negotiated must either present it for acceptance or himself negotiate it within a reasonable time (regard being had to the nature of the bill, the usage of trade and the facts of the particular case); if he does not do so, the drawer and all prior indorsers are discharged;

(2) where a bill expressly stipulates that it must be presented for payment; and

(3) where a bill is drawn payable elsewhere than at the residence or place of business of the drawee; in this case, if the holder has not time

(with the exercise of reasonable diligence) to present the bill for acceptance before presenting it for payment on its due date, the delay caused by presenting the bill for acceptance is excused and does not discharge the drawer and indorsers (ss. 39 and 40).

Rules as to presentment for acceptance

The Act sets out the following rules as to presentment for acceptance:

(a) The presentment must be made by or on behalf of the holder to the drawee or to some person authorised to accept or refuse acceptance on his behalf at a reasonable hour on a business day and before the bill is overdue.

(b) Where a bill is addressed to two or more drawees who are not partners, presentment must be made to them all, unless one has authority to accept for all, in which case presentment may be made to him only.

(c) Where the drawee is dead, presentment *may* be made to his personal representative.

(d) Where the drawee is bankrupt, presentment *may* be made to him or to his trustee.

(e) Where authorised by agreement or usage, a presentment through the post office is sufficient (s. 41(1)).

Excuses for non-presentment for acceptance

Presentment in accordance with these rules is excused, and a bill may be treated as dishonoured by non-acceptance:

(a) where the drawee is dead or bankrupt, or is a fictitious person or person not having capacity to contract by bill;

(b) where, after the exercise of reasonable diligence, presentment in accordance with the rules cannot be effected; or

(c) where, although the presentment has been irregular, acceptance has been refused on some other ground (s. 41(2)).

The fact that the holder has reason to believe that the bill, on presentment, will be dishonoured does not excuse presentment (s. 41(3)).

When a bill is duly presented for acceptance and is not accepted within the customary time, the person presenting it must treat it as dishonoured by non-acceptance. If he does not, the holder loses his right of recourse against the drawer and indorsers (s. 42). The common law, which was to the same effect, is to be found expressed in *Martini & Co.* v. *Steel & Craig* (1878) 6 R. 342. The "customary" time is usually 24 hours.

As has been noted (7–39, above), the holder of a bill may refuse to take a qualified acceptance. If he does not obtain an unqualified acceptance, he may treat the bill as dishonoured by non-acceptance. Where the holder takes a qualified acceptance and the drawer or an indorser has not authorised him to do so and does not subsequently assent to his having done so, the drawer or indorser is discharged from his liability on the bill, unless the qualified acceptance is a "partial" acceptance (*i.e.* to pay part only of the amount for which the bill is drawn) and due notice has been given. When the drawer or an indorser receives notice of a qualified acceptance, and does not within a reasonable time express his dissent to the holder, he is deemed to have assented to the taking of the qualified acceptance (s. 44).

(ii) *Presentment for Payment*

7–75   Subject to the provisions of the Act a bill must be "duly presented" for payment (s. 45). When a bill has been accepted generally, presentment for payment is not necessary in order to make the acceptor liable (s. 52(1)). The effect of not duly presenting a bill for payment is that the drawer and indorsers (but not the acceptor) are discharged (s. 45). Another effect, applicable only to Scotland, is that a bill which has not been duly presented for payment cannot be enforced by summary diligence (see 7–118 *et seq.*, below) even against the acceptor; this follows from section 98 of the Act which left the law of Scotland on summary diligence unaltered (*Neill* v. *Dobson, Molle & Co. Ltd.* (1902) 4 F. 625).

Rules as to presentment for payment

7–76   A bill is "duly presented" for payment if it is presented in accordance with rules set out in section 45 of the Act:

(1) Where the bill is not payable on demand, presentment must be made on the day it falls due (not, for example, on September 10 if it had become payable on July 8 as in *Neill* v. *Dobson, Molle & Co. Ltd.*, above).

(2) Where the bill is payable on demand, presentment must be made within a reasonable time after its issue in order to make the drawer liable, and within a reasonable time after its indorsement in order to make the indorser liable. In deciding what is a reasonable time, regard must be had to the nature of the bill, the usage of trade and the facts of the particular case.

(3) Presentment must be made by the holder or by some person authorised to receive payment on his behalf at a reasonable hour on a business day, at the "proper place" (as defined in rule (4)), either to the person specified in the bill as the payer, or to some person authorised to pay or refuse payment on his behalf, if with the exercise of reasonable diligence such person can there be found.

(4) A bill is presented at the "proper place":

(*a*) where a place of payment is specified in the bill and the bill is there presented;

(*b*) where no place of payment is specified, but the address of the drawee or acceptor is given in the bill, and the bill is there presented;

(*c*) where no place of payment is specified and no address given, and the bill is presented at the drawee's or acceptor's place of business if known, and if not, at his ordinary residence if known;

(*d*) in any other case if presented to the drawee or acceptor wherever he can be found, or if presented at his last known place of business or residence.

In *Neill* v. *Dobson, Molle & Co. Ltd.*, above, the bill, which specified no place of payment, was addressed to "Mr J. Neill, 1 Morrison Place, Piershill, Edinburgh" (Neill's private address). The bill, which had been accepted by Neill, was presented for payment at his place of business in George Street, Edinburgh, and, by an application of rule (4) (*b*), this was held not to be presentment at the "proper place." Summary diligence could therefore not be used to enforce the bill against Neill.

(5) Where a bill is presented at the proper place, and after the exercise of reasonable diligence no person authorised to pay or refuse payment can be found there, no further presentment to the drawee or acceptor is required.

(6) Where a bill is drawn upon, or accepted by, two or more persons who are not partners, and no place of payment is specified, presentment must be made to them all.

(7) Where the drawee or acceptor is dead, and no place of payment is specified, presentment *must* be made to a personal representative, if there is one and with the exercise of reasonable diligence he can be found.

(8) Where authorised by agreement or usage, a presentment through the post office is sufficient.

Excuses for delay or non-presentment for payment

Delay in making presentment for payment is excused when the delay is caused by circumstances beyond the control of the holder and not due to his default, misconduct or negligence. When the cause of delay ceases to operate, presentment must be made with reasonable diligence (s. 46(1)).

The fact that the holder has reason to believe that the bill will, on presentment, be dishonoured, does not dispense with the necessity for presentment. Presentment for payment is dispensed with:

(*a*) where after the exercise of reasonable diligence presentment cannot be effected;

(*b*) where the drawee is a fictitious person;

(*c*) as regards the drawer, where the drawee or acceptor is not bound, as between himself and the drawer, to accept or pay the bill, and the drawer has no reason to believe that the bill would be paid if presented;

(*d*) as regards an indorser, where the bill was accepted or made for the accommodation of that indorser (see 7–55, above), and he has no reason to expect that the bill would be paid if presented; or

(*e*) by waiver of presentment, express or implied (s. 46(2)).

The effect of (*c*) and (*d*) is that the drawer (in (*c*)) and the indorser (in (*d*)) are, contrary to the general rule, not discharged by the fact that there has been no presentment for payment.

The question of waiver of presentment was considered in *Mactavish's Judicial Factor* v. *Michael's Trustees*, 1912 S.C. 425: A bill, which had been indorsed, was not presented for payment, and no notice of its dishonour was given to the indorser. The indorser paid part of the bill, but was proved to have done so under the erroneous belief that she was not an indorser, but a joint acceptor.

Held that the part payment gave rise to a presumption that the indorser had waived presentment for payment and notice of dishonour, but that this presumption had been rebutted by proof that the payment had been made in error; and that the indorser was therefore free from liability because the holder had not complied with the statutory requirements.

(g) **Procedure on Dishonour**

7–78   On the dishonour of a bill by non-acceptance or non-payment the holder obtains an immediate "right of recourse" against the drawer and indorsers (ss. 43(2) and 47(2)), but in order to preserve this right of recourse the holder must comply with statutory procedure as to:

(i) notice of dishonour; and

(ii) protest.

(i) *Notice of Dishonour*

7–79   When a bill has been dishonoured by non-acceptance or by non-payment, the general rule is that notice of dishonour must be given to the drawer and each indorser and that any drawer or indorser to whom notice is not given is discharged. Exceptions to the general rule are:

(1) Where a bill is dishonoured by non-acceptance, and notice of dishonour is not given, the rights of a holder in due course subsequent to the omission are not prejudiced by the omission.

(2) Where a bill is dishonoured by non-acceptance and due notice of dishonour is given, it is not necessary to give notice of a subsequent dishonour by non-payment unless the bill has in the meantime been accepted (s. 48).

Rules as to notice of dishonour

7–80   Notice of dishonour in order to be valid and effectual must be given in accordance with 15 rules set out in section 49:

(1) The notice must be given by or on behalf of the holder, or by or on behalf of an indorser who, at the time of giving it, is himself liable on the bill.

(2) The notice may be given by an agent either in his own name or in the name of any party entitled to give notice.

(3) Where the notice is given by or on behalf of the holder, it enures for the benefit of all subsequent holders and all prior indorsers who have a right of recourse against the party to whom notice is given.

(4) Similarly, where the notice is given by or on behalf of an indorser, it enures for the benefit of the holder and all indorsers subsequent to the party to whom notice is given.

(5) The notice may be given in writing or by personal communication, and may be given in any terms which sufficiently identify the bill and intimate its dishonour.

(6) The return of a dishonoured bill to the drawer or an indorser is deemed a sufficient notice of dishonour.

(7) A written notice need not be signed, and an insufficient written notice may be supplemented and made valid by verbal communication. A misdescription of the bill does not vitiate the notice unless the party to whom the notice is given is in fact misled by the misdescription.

(8) The notice may be given either to the party himself or to his agent.

(9) Where, to the knowledge of the party giving the notice, the drawer or indorser is dead, the notice must be given to a personal representative, if there is one and with the exercise of reasonable diligence he can be found.

(10) Where the drawer or indorser is bankrupt, notice may be given either to the party himself or to the trustee.

(11) Where there are two or more drawers or indorsers who are not partners, notice must be given to each, unless one has authority to receive notice for the others.

(12) The notice may be given as soon as the bill is dishonoured, and must be given within a reasonable time. In order to satisfy the standard of "reasonable time," the notice must, if the parties giving and receiving the notice reside in the same place, be given in time to reach the recipient on the day after the dishonour, and if the parties reside in different places, be sent off not later than the day after the dishonour (or if there is no convenient post on that day, by the next post).

(13) When the bill is, at the time of its dishonour, in the hands of an agent, he may either give notice to the parties liable on the bill, or he may give notice to his principal. If the agent chooses the latter alternative, the principal will then have the same "reasonable time" for giving notice to the parties liable on the bill.

(14) Where a party receives due notice of dishonour, he has then the same "reasonable time" for giving notice to prior parties.

(15) Where a notice of dishonour is duly addressed and posted, the sender is deemed to have given due notice of dishonour, notwithstanding any miscarriage by the post office.

Excuses for delay or non-notice

Delay in giving notice of dishonour is excused where the delay is caused by circumstances beyond the control of the party giving the notice, and not due to his default, misconduct, or negligence. When the cause of delay ceases to operate, notice must be given with reasonable diligence (s. 50(1)).

Notice of dishonour is dispensed with:

(*a*) when, after the exercise of reasonable diligence, it cannot be given to or does not reach the drawer or indorser;

(*b*) by waiver, express or implied (which may be either before the time of giving notice has arrived, or after the omission to give due notice);

(*c*) as regards the drawer, in the following cases:
(1) where drawer and drawee are the same person;
(2) where the drawee is a fictitious person or a person lacking capacity to contract;
(3) where the drawer is the person to whom the bill is presented for payment;
(4) where the drawee or acceptor is, as between himself and the drawer, under no obligation to accept or pay the bill; or
(5) where the drawer has countermanded payment (*i.e.* given notice that the bill should not be paid);

(*d*) as regards the indorser, in the following cases:
(1) where the drawee is a fictitious person or a person lacking capacity to contract;
(2) where the indorser is the person to whom the bill is presented for payment; or
(3) where the bill was accepted or made for his accommodation (see 7–55, above) (s. 50(2)).

(ii) Protest

7–82 As well as giving notice of dishonour, the holder of a bill which appears on the face of it to be a foreign bill must "protest" the bill when it is dishonoured by non-acceptance or by non-payment, and if it is not duly protested, the drawer and indorsers are discharged (s. 51(2)). The purpose of protest is to provide proof, in a form acceptable to any court at home or abroad, that the bill has been duly presented and has been dishonoured.

In the case of an inland bill, the holder may, if he thinks fit, protest it on its dishonour, but, if he chooses not to do so, he does not thereby lose his right of recourse against the drawer or indorsers (s. 51(1)). However, where it is desired to enforce a bill by the process of summary diligence (available only in Scotland and not altered by the Act of 1882 (see s. 98)), protest is essential.

7–83 The procedure for protesting a bill has two stages:

(1) noting, which is informal; and

(2) protest, which is formal.

Both stages require the services of a notary public, but the Act provides that if the services of a notary cannot be obtained at the place where the bill is dishonoured, any householder or "substantial resident" of the place may, in the presence of two witnesses, give a certificate, signed by them all and narrating the presentment and dishonour of the bill. A form suitable for use in these circumstances is set out in the First Schedule to the Act. Such a certificate operates as if it were a formal protest (s. 94), but it is doubtful whether summary diligence could follow on such a certificate—a question which was raised, but did not require to be decided, in *Sommerville* v. *Aaronson* (1898) 25 R. 524, below.

(1) Noting

7–84 Noting takes place when a notary presents the bill to the drawee for acceptance or payment, and notes on the bill the date, the fact that the bill is protested for non-acceptance ("P.N.Ac.") or non-payment ("P.N.P."), and his own initials followed by the abbreviation "N.P."

7–85 The place at which this proceeding must normally be carried out is the place where the bill is dishonoured, but when a bill is presented through the post office and is returned by post dishonoured, the noting may be at the place to which the bill is returned (s. 51(6)). In *Sommerville* v. *Aaronson*, a promissory note, expressed to be payable at Bradford, was duly presented there and was dishonoured. Some months later the note was presented to the maker of it personally at Millport, in Bute, and, there being no notary resident at Millport, a householder's certificate was obtained. *Held* that, as the place of payment and of dishonour was Bradford, the householder's certificate issued at Millport was of no effect.

7–86 By the Act of 1882, as amended by the Bills of Exchange (Time of Noting) Act 1917, the noting must take place either on the day of dishonour or on the next succeeding business day (or, in the case of a bill returned by post, on the day of its return or on the next business day after that). When a bill has been duly noted, the protest (the second and formal stage) may be left until later but will take its date from that of the noting (s. 51(4) and (6)).

(2) Protest

The document referred to as a "protest" is a formal notarial certificate, based on, and bearing the date of, the noting, but in practice drawn up at the notary's office at a convenient later date.

The protest must contain a copy of the bill, must be signed by the notary, and must specify:

(a) the person at whose request the bill is protested; and

(b) the place and date of protest, the cause or reason for protesting the bill, the demand made, and the answer given (if any), or the fact that the drawee or acceptor could not be found (s. 51(7)). These statutory provisions were applied in *Bartsch* v. *Poole & Co.* (1895) 23 R. 328:

A bill, accepted by B., was expressed to be payable at the office of P. & Co., the drawers. The bill was dishonoured and was protested for non-payment. The protest stated that the notary "presented the said bill at the place where payable to a clerk there, who made answer that no funds had been provided to meet said bill, and payment was refused accordingly."

Held that, since the clerk, being an employee of P. & Co., could not be regarded as agent for B., the protest was invalid because it did not state, as required by section 51(7)), that the acceptor could not be found. By accepting the bill payable at P. & Co.'s office, B. had undertaken to be at that office with the money on the date when the bill was due. (It is, however, familiar practice for a bill to be made payable at a named bank, and in that case the bank would be considered to be the agent for the acceptor.)

The protest must exactly conform to the noting: for example, if the noting is dated September 24, the date included in the formal certificate must also be September 24, and if the notary substitutes September 25 (even though that may have been the true date of the noting), the protest is invalid (*McPherson* v. *Wright* (1885) 12 R. 942).

Excuses for delay or non-protest

These are the same as the excuses for delay in giving notice of dishonour, and for dispensing with notice of dishonour (see 7–81, above) (s. 51(9)).

(h) Liabilities of Parties

The normal function of a bill is to enable the holder of it to obtain payment of the amount of the bill when the bill becomes due. In an ordinary transaction, it is most likely that the holder, on presenting the bill to the drawee (who will be the acceptor, if the bill has been accepted) will be duly paid the amount of the bill. However, the Act necessarily includes provisions to cover the situation where the transaction does not follow the ordinary course. Hence the frequent references in the Act to dishonour of the bill, which in practice is exceptional.

The general principle is that all parties to the bill (*i.e.* all persons who have signed the bill) are liable, jointly and severally, to pay the amount of the bill to a holder in due course (see 7–47 *et seq., above*). The effect is that not only the acceptor but also the drawer and the indorsers may be held liable to pay the bill to a holder in due course, and that, on the other hand, no liability to pay the bill attaches to the drawee who has not yet accepted the bill or to a person who transfers a bearer bill to another bearer by simple delivery without indorsing it.

7–92   This does not mean that the holder is in every case completely free to choose from among the signatories any one particular person whom he is to hold liable to pay the bill. A distinction must be drawn between primary liability and secondary liability. If the bill has been accepted, the person primarily liable to pay it is the acceptor, and the other parties are only secondarily or subsidiarily liable. If the bill has not yet been accepted, the person primarily liable to pay it is the drawer, and the indorsers have only a secondary liability. Once the holder has duly received payment from the person who is primarily liable to pay the bill, the liability of all the other parties is at an end. It is only where the party primarily liable to pay fails to do so that the holder can have recourse to the parties who are secondarily liable. Further, as can be seen from the sections above on presentment for acceptance and presentment for payment (7–67 et seq., above), and on procedure on dishonour (7–78 et seq., above), the holder may lose his right of recourse against such parties if he fails to comply with the statutory requirements.

7–93   On presenting a bill for payment the holder must exhibit the bill to the person from whom he demands payment, and, when it is paid, the holder must immediately hand it over to the person paying it (s. 52(4)).

7–94   Where a bill has been dishonoured by non-acceptance by the drawee or by non-payment by the acceptor, the holder may naturally turn to the person from whom he obtained the bill, hold that party liable to him and, on receiving payment, hand over the bill to him. In this way the dishonoured bill may pass backwards through a chain of parties, each indorsee holding his own indorser liable to reimburse him for what he has had to pay to the later party, until ultimately the bill reaches the party who, as drawer or acceptor, is primarily liable to pay. Such procedure is not essential: the holder is entitled to choose from among the prior parties which party he is to hold liable to himself on the dishonoured bill, or he may himself immediately enforce payment from the party who is primarily liable.

7–95   The main provisions of the Act relating to the liabilities of the various parties are as follows:

(i) Liability of Drawee

7–96   The drawee, not having signed the bill, is not liable as a party to the bill.

7–97   Where, however, the drawee has in his hands funds available for the payment of the bill, the bill operates as an "assignment" of the sum for which it is drawn in favour of the holder, from the time when the bill is presented to the drawee (s. 53(2)). This provision of the Act applies to Scotland only and is derived from the common law of Scotland.

7–98   There is a dearth of cases actually decided on section 53(2), but the following five cases, all relating to cheques, have at least some bearing on it. For a comprehensive study of the provision and its common law background see D.J. Cusine, "The Cheque as an Assignation" (1977) 22 J.R. 98.

(1) *British Linen Co. Bank* v. *Carruthers and Fergusson* (1883) 10 R. 923: David F. gave a cheque for £161 drawn on his current account with the B. Bank to John F. The cheque was handed by John F. to his own bank, which presented it to the B. Bank for payment. As the balance at the credit of David F.'s current account was only £135 13s. 10d., the B. Bank refused payment.

A few months later David F. became bankrupt, and C. was appointed the trustee in his sequestration. The B. Bank had then in its hands £156 8s. belonging to David F., and competing claims were made, John F. claiming that he was entitled to at least £135 13s. 10d. because the presentation of the cheque had operated as an assignation to him of the funds then at the credit of David F.'s account, and C. on the other hand claiming that the whole fund was to be treated as part of the sequestrated estate to be divided amongst David F.'s creditors.

An action of multiplepoinding was raised—the type of action used to settle disputed claims in such a situation.

Held that John F. was entitled to £135 13s. 10d. out of the funds held by the B. Bank.

"The result of the presentation of the cheque was to give a right to the funds of the drawer which the banker had in his hands at the time" (*per* Lord Shand at p. 928).

Since the transaction had taken place before the passing of the Act of 1882, the case was decided under the common law, but the observation was made that "the statute only carries out what it is understood was intended—a consolidation of the existing Scotch law. There is nothing new in it" (*per* Lord Shand at p. 927).

(2) *Bank of Scotland* v. *Reid and Others* (1886) 2 Sh. Ct. Rep. 376: On March 2, 1886, Stewart, a joiner, granted to Knox, a glazier, a cheque for £14 drawn on the Bank of Scotland. Knox passed the cheque to his own bank—the Royal Bank—which paid him cash for it. The cheque was then presented, through the clearing-house, to Stewart's bank on March 4.

Stewart, however, had died on March 3, and his death had been intimated to his bank before the cheque was presented.

Stewart's estate was bankrupt, and Reid, as trustee on that estate, claimed £83 18s., which was the sum lying at Stewart's credit in the Bank of Scotland. The Royal Bank claimed £14 out of that amount, and an action of multiplepoinding was raised to settle the competing claims.

Held (i) that the cheque from its date was an incomplete "assignment" to Knox and through him to the Royal Bank of the £14, (ii) that that assignment did not fall by Stewart's death and so it became operative as an assignment on being presented to Stewart's bank after his death, and (iii) that, although by section 75 of the Act of 1882 the bank's duty and authority to pay the cheque were terminated by notice of Stewart's death, that did not prevent the Royal Bank from proving its right to the fund in a legal action.

Sheriff-Substitute Erskine Murray, referring to section 53(2) of the Act, said (at p. 379): "The words 'operates as an assignment' must be held equivalent to 'become a completed and thus operative assignment.'"

If so, it just means that the assignment is incomplete without presentation or intimation; but, as an unintimated assignation is good though intimated after death, the intimation subsequent to death completed the Royal Bank's right, though section 75 barred the Bank of Scotland from paying without legal process."

7–101   (3) *Kirkwood & Sons* v. *Clydesdale Bank Ltd.*, 1908 S.C. 20: This case is the highest reported authority on the application of section 53(2), and will be considered more fully in connection with the banker's duty to honour cheques (see 7–166, below).

The court held that a cheque presented after the customer's death did not operate as an assignment under section 53(2) of any part of the credit balance on the customer's current account, because on a combination of all the customer's accounts the bank had no "funds available" for the payment of the cheque within the meaning of the statutory provision.

7–102   (4) *Dickson* v. *Clydesdale Bank Ltd.*, 1937 S.L.T. 585 (O.H.): D. was a customer of the C. Bank, and occasionally sent Taylor to the bank to cash her cheques.

On one occasion Taylor obtained from D. a cheque for £166 payable to Mrs Taylor. On July 20, 1933, Taylor attempted to obtain cash for it from the C. Bank, but the bank refused his request.

The following day Taylor returned with the same cheque, but with the letter "s" deleted from "Mrs" and with the date altered from July 20 to July 21. The alterations were initialled "M.L.D." The C. Bank then paid Taylor £166.

D. claimed that the bank was not entitled to debit her account with the £166.

Held that the cheque was a forgery and therefore not a good mandate to the bank to debit D.'s account.

One of the arguments put forward by counsel for the bank was that on presentation the cheque had operated as an assignment on July 20 in favour of someone—either Mrs Taylor or Mr Taylor—and that D. could therefore not challenge the debiting of her account.

Lord Carmont (Ordinary) rejected that argument, saying (at p. 586) with reference to section 53(2): "It must not be overlooked that the statute says that the assignment is *in favour of the holder.* . . . When John Taylor sought to obtain cash for the cheque payable to 'Mrs Taylor' on 20th July he was not the holder although he was in physical possession of it. . . . It was only the following day that on the footing that Taylor was himself the holder as payee . . . presentation was recognised by the defenders. But as the cheque was then a forged document the defenders cannot put it forward as having operated a valid assignment of the pursuer's funds."

7–103   (5) *Williams* v. *Williams*, 1980 S.L.T. (Sh. Ct.) 25: W. made out a cheque for £250 in favour of his son and handed it to him, but before the son presented the cheque for payment the father had countermanded payment.

The son raised an action of payment against his father, one of the grounds being that presentment of the cheque operated as an assignment in his favour in terms of section 53(2) of the Act of 1882.

Held that if the father was not liable by virtue of his making out and delivering the cheque, he would not become liable by virtue of section 53(2).

The Sheriff Principal (G.S. Gimson) said (at p. 25): "The pursuer's third plea appears to be put forward on the supposition that as an assignee by virtue of s. 53(2) of the Act he had an alternative ground of action. It appears that that was the basis on which the pursuer claimed to be entitled to sue the defender 'on the cheque.' I consider that the argument on assignation does not assist the pursuer. I reserve my opinion on the question whether s. 53(2) is operative in the case of a cheque which has been countermanded before presentation since it appears to me that that question can only arise and is only relevant in proceedings between the payee of the cheque and the bank upon which it is drawn."

A point on which the cases give no guidance is whether the words "when the bill is presented to the drawee" in section 53(2) cover presentment for acceptance as well as presentment for payment. There is no express exclusion of presentment for acceptance, but a view which appears to be generally held in banking circles is that the presentment referred to in the provision is restricted to presentment for payment and that presentment for acceptance would not operate as an "assignment," *i.e.* would not attach funds. The question is unlikely to arise in connection with those bills of exchange which are cheques because they are not usually, and perhaps could not competently be, presented for acceptance in any case: Lord Wright, delivering the judgment of the Privy Council, in *Bank of Baroda Ltd.* v. *Punjab National Bank Ltd.* [1944] A.C. 176 (a case in which the marking or certification of a cheque as "good for payment" was held not to be an acceptance in the statutory sense) said (at p. 184): "So far as their Lordships know, there is no case in the books of the acceptance of a cheque." Further, there is no doubt that on present-ment of any bill of exchange for *payment*, funds would be attached. The only remaining situation then is where a bill of exchange other than a cheque is presented for acceptance. There seems to be no authority available either to support or to challenge the practice which would be followed if such a situation arose, *viz.*, that funds would not be attached.

(ii) *Liability of Acceptor*

Where a bill is accepted "generally" (see 7–39, above), presentment for payment is not necessary in order to make the acceptor liable (s. 52(1)).

Where, by the terms of a qualified acceptance, presentment for pay-ment is required, the acceptor is not discharged by the mere omission to present the bill for payment on the day on which it matures: an express stipulation would be required for such a discharge (s. 52(2)).

In order to make the acceptor liable, it is not necessary to protest it, or that notice of dishonour should be given to him (s. 52(3)).

The acceptor, by accepting the bill, engages that he will pay it according to the tenor of his acceptance, and he is barred from denying to a holder in due course:

(a) the existence of the drawer, the genuineness of the drawer's signature, and the drawer's capacity and authority to draw the bill;

(b) in the case of a bill payable to drawer's order, the then capacity of the drawer to indorse (but not the genuineness or validity of his indorsement);

(c) in the case of a bill payable to the order of a third person, the existence of the payee and his then capacity to indorse (but not the genuineness or validity of his indorsement) (s. 54).

On the liability of an "acceptor for honour" see 7–137 *et seq.*, below.

(iii) *Liability of Drawer*

7–107 The drawer, by drawing the bill, engages that on due presentment it will be accepted and paid according to its tenor, and that, if it is dishonoured, he will compensate the holder or any indorser who is compelled to pay it, provided that the necessary proceedings on dishonour are duly taken. He is barred from denying to a holder in due course the existence of the payee and the payee's then capacity to indorse (s. 55(1)).

7–108 However, it is open to the drawer to insert in the bill an express stipulation negativing or limiting his own liability to the holder (*e.g.* the words "without recourse"). Another option open to the drawer is to waive as regards himself some or all of the holder's duties (*e.g.* as to notice of dishonour) (s. 16).

7–109 On a general view, the drawer may be regarded as cautioner for the drawee or acceptor.

(iv) *Liability of Indorser*

7–110 The indorser, by indorsing the bill, engages that on due presentment it will be accepted and paid according to its tenor, and that, if it is dishonoured, he will compensate the holder or a subsequent indorser who is compelled to pay it, provided that the necessary proceedings on dishonour are duly taken. He is barred from denying to a holder in due course the genuineness and regularity in all respects of the drawer's signature and all previous indorsements, and he is barred from denying to his immediate or a subsequent indorsee that the bill was at the time of his indorsement a valid and subsisting bill and that he had then a good title to it (s. 55(2)).

7–111 An indorser has the same ability as the drawer to negative or restrict his liability by an express stipulation, and to waive, as regards himself, some or all of the holder's duties (s. 16).

7–112 On a general view, the indorser may be regarded as in the position of a cautioner to later parties (including the holder) for those who are already parties to the bill. Ultimate liability does not lie with the indorser: his liability is secondary only, and he is entitled to recover from prior parties the whole of what he has himself paid out to the holder or other later party.

7–113 Where a person signs a bill otherwise than as a drawer or acceptor, he incurs the liabilities of an indorser to a holder in due course (s. 56).

(v) *Liability of Transferor by Delivery*

7–114 A "transferor by delivery" is a holder of a bill payable to bearer, who negotiates it by delivery without indorsing it.

A transferor by delivery is not liable *on the bill* (signature being essential for such liability), but he "warrants" (*i.e.* guarantees) to his immediate transferee, provided that transferee is a holder for value, that the bill is what it purports to be, that he has a right to transfer it, and that at the time of transfer he is not aware of any fact which makes it valueless (s. 58).

(vi) *Liability of Referee in Case of Need*

The drawer and any indorser may insert in the bill the name of a person to whom the holder may resort in case of need, *i.e.* in case the bill is dishonoured by non-acceptance or non-payment. Such person is called "the referee in case of need." The holder has an option to resort to the referee in case of need or not, as he thinks fit (s. 15).

(i) Measure of Damages on Dishonour

Where a bill is dishonoured, the measure of damages, which will be deemed to be liquidate damages, is as follows:

(1) The holder may recover from any party liable on the bill:
(*a*) the amount of the bill;
(*b*) interest from the time of presentment for payment if the bill is payable on demand, and from the maturity of the bill in any other case;
(*c*) the expenses of noting, or, where protest is necessary and the protest has been drawn up, the expenses of protest.
Similarly, the drawer who has been compelled to pay the bill may recover those amounts from the acceptor, and an indorser who has been compelled to pay the bill may recover those amounts from the acceptor or from the drawer, or from a prior indorser.

(2) Where by the Act interest may be recovered as damages, the interest may, if justice require it, be withheld wholly or in part, and where a bill is expressed to be payable with interest at a given rate, interest as damages may or may not be given at the same rate as interest proper (s. 57).

(j) Enforcement of Liability by Summary Diligence

Liability on a bill may be enforced by an ordinary action for payment founded on the bill as the document of debt. An alternative method of enforcement is the procedure of summary diligence, which dispenses with the need to bring an action in court. The procedure is peculiar to Scotland, and is governed by two Scots Acts—the Bills of Exchange Act 1681 and the Inland Bills Act 1696—and by the Bills of Exchange (Scotland) Act 1772, along with decided cases. Nothing in the Act of 1882 in any way alters or affects the Scots law and practice in regard to summary diligence (s. 98).

The bill must be duly presented, noted and protested. If, therefore, the place at which the bill has been presented for payment is not the proper place, the bill cannot be enforced by summary diligence (*Neill* v. *Dobson, Molle & Co. Ltd.* (1902) 4 F. 625 (7–75 *et seq.,* above)), and it may be that the householder's certificate cannot take the place of the formal notarial certificate for this purpose (*Sommerville* v. *Aaronson*

(1898) 25 R. 524). However, the rule in the Act of 1882 (s. 45) that where a bill is not payable on demand presentment for payment must be made on the day it falls due need not be complied with where summary diligence is being used against the acceptor; it is enough if the whole procedure has been completed within six months of the date when the bill was dishonoured; this was held to be so in *McNeill & Son* v. *Innes, Chambers & Co.*, 1917 S.C. 540, on the ground that this had been the established practice before the Act of 1882 and the Act expressly saved the then existing law and practice in regard to summary diligence (s. 98).

7–120   The formal protest once it has been drawn up is registered in the Books of Council and Session in Edinburgh or in the books of the sheriff court of the sheriffdom which has jurisdiction over the person who is to be charged. An "extract" (*i.e.* a certified copy) may then be obtained by the holder of the bill, and this contains a warrant to charge the party liable on a six or 14 days' induciae, *i.e.* the party liable must pay the amount due within six days if he resides in Scotland[4] or within 14 days if he resides "furth of" (outside) Scotland.

7–121   Summary diligence is therefore a speedy and simple procedure enabling the creditor in the bill, without raising a court action, to obtain a warrant which is equivalent to a decree of the court ordering the debtor to pay the amount due. The creditor has also the right at once to arrest in the hands of third parties any money or goods belonging to the debtor. If the debtor fails to pay by the end of the induciae, the creditor may proceed to poind and sell the debtor's goods, or he may petition the court for the debtor's sequestration.

7–122   If the debtor considers that he has grounds for avoiding liability, he may present a "note of suspension" in the Court of Session to have the summary diligence suspended, but in order to succeed in having the note passed he is usually required to find caution (*e.g. Simpson* v. *Brown* (1888) 15 R. 716).

7–123   There are some restrictions on the use of summary diligence:

(i) Summary diligence may be used only to obtain payment of the amount of the bill and interest: for the recovery of damages and expenses, an ordinary action is required (Erskine, *An Institute of the Law of Scotland*, III, 2, 36).

(ii) It may be used only against a person who is subject to the jurisdiction of the Scottish courts (*Charteris* v. *Clydesdale Banking Co.* (1882) 19 S.L.R. 602 (O.H.), in which summary diligence was held incompetent against an acceptor who was resident in Manchester, though the bills were payable in Leith).

(iii) It cannot be used if there is an alteration or vitiation in some essential part of the bill (*e.g.* where a bill has been torn into three pieces and pasted together again: *Thomson* v. *Bell* (1850) 12 D. 1184).

(iv) It cannot be used where the liability of the person charged does not appear *ex facie* ("on the face") of the bill but would require to be proved by extrinsic evidence.

---

[4] Orkney and Shetland are no longer exceptional: the Act 1685, c. 43 ("Act in favours of the Inhabitants of Orkney and Zetland") was wholly repealed by the Statute Law Revision (Scotland) Act 1964 (s. 1 and Sched. 1).

(v) It cannot be used to enforce payment of an unpaid cheque (*Glickman* v. *Linda*, 1950 S.C. 18 (O.H.)): under the Acts of 1681 and 1696 it applied only to bills of exchange other than cheques, and it was extended to promissory notes by the Act of 1772.

(k) Discharge of Bill

The Act provides for five methods of discharge of a bill:

   (i) payment in due course;
  (ii) acceptor becoming holder;
 (iii) renunciation or waiver;
 (iv) cancellation; and
  (v) alteration.

A bill may also be discharged under the Prescription and Limitation (Scotland) Act 1973 by:

 (vi) prescription.

It is possible for one or more of the parties to a bill to be discharged without the bill itself being discharged: for instance, where a bill has been dishonoured by non-payment and notice of dishonour has not been given to one of the indorsers, that indorser is discharged (s. 48) but the parties to whom notice of dishonour has been duly given (the drawer and other indorsers) remain liable and the bill continues to be enforceable as a bill.

(i) *Payment in Due Course*

A bill is discharged by payment in due course *by or on behalf of the drawee or acceptor*. "Payment in due course" means payment made at or after the maturity of the bill to the holder of the bill in good faith and without notice that his title to the bill is defective (s. 59(1)).

When a bill is paid *by the drawer or an indorser*, it is not discharged, but:

   (*a*) Where the bill is payable to, or to the order of, a third party, and is paid by the drawer, the drawer may enforce payment against the acceptor, but is not permitted to re-issue the bill. (In this case the drawer is not an indorser, and the only right which the drawer has is to claim payment from the acceptor.)

   (*b*) Where the bill is paid by an indorser, or where it is a bill payable to, or to the order of, the drawer and is paid by the drawer (who in this case is an indorser), the party paying it is remitted to his former rights as regards the acceptor or antecedent parties to the bill, and he may, if he thinks fit, strike out his own and subsequent indorsements, and again negotiate the bill (s. 59(2)).

An accommodation bill (see 7–55, above) is an exception to these provisions of section 59(2)): where an accommodation bill is paid in due course *by the party accommodated* the bill is discharged (s. 59(3)).

For proof of the payment of a bill of exchange writ or oath is still required according to the rule of the common law: the provision in section 100 of the Act allowing parole proof of any fact "relevant to any question of liability" on a bill has been held not to make parole proof of payment competent (*Nicol's Trustees* v. *Sutherland*, 1951 S.C. (H.L.) 21).

(ii) *Acceptor Becoming Holder*

7–129 When the acceptor is or becomes the holder of the bill at or after its maturity, in his own right, the bill is discharged (s. 61). This is discharge *confusione* ("by merging").

(iii) *Renunciation or Waiver*

7–130 When the holder of a bill *at or after its maturity* absolutely and unconditionally renounces his rights against the acceptor, the bill is discharged. The renunciation must be in writing, unless the bill is delivered up to the acceptor (s. 62(1)).

The liability of any party to a bill may similarly be renounced by the holder, and this may be done before as well as at or after its maturity (s. 62(2)).

However, the rights of a holder in due course are not affected by any renunciation of which he has no notice (s. 62(2)).

(iv) *Cancellation*

7–131 Where a bill is *intentionally* cancelled by the holder or his agent and the cancellation is *apparent,* the bill is discharged (s. 63(1)).

Similarly, any party liable on a bill may be discharged by the intentional cancellation of his signature by the holder or the holder's agent. In such a case any indorser who would have had a right of recourse against the party whose signature is cancelled, is also discharged (s. 63(2)).

A cancellation made unintentionally, or under a mistake, or without the authority of the holder is inoperative, but where a bill or any signature on it appears to have been cancelled the burden of proof lies on the party who alleges that the cancellation was made unintentionally, or under a mistake, or without authority (s. 63(3)).

(v) *Alteration*

7–132 Where a bill or acceptance is *materially* altered without the assent of all parties liable on the bill, the bill is avoided (*i.e.* is of no effect) except as against a party who has himself made, authorised, or assented to the alteration, and as against subsequent indorsers, but there is this exception made to protect a holder in due course: where a bill has been materially altered *and the alteration is not apparent* (compare cancellation, above), a holder in due course may avail himself of the bill as if it had not been altered and may enforce payment of it according to its original tenor (s. 64(1)).

The following alterations are material—any alteration of the date, the sum payable, the time of payment, the place of payment, and, where the bill has been accepted generally, the addition of a place of payment without the acceptor's assent (s. 64(2)).

7–133 The acceptor of a bill of exchange is not under a duty to take precautions against fraudulent alterations in the bill after acceptance:

Scholfield v. *Earl of Londesborough* [1896] A.C. 514: Sanders drew a bill for £500 on Scholfield, and Scholfield accepted it. The stamp on the bill was of much larger amount than was necessary, and there were spaces in the bill.

Sanders fraudulently inserted the figure "3" between "£" and "5" in the figures section and the words "three" at the end of the second line and "thousand" at the beginning of the third line before the words "five hundred" in the body of the bill, thus converting the bill into one which purported to be for £3,500.

Sanders negotiated the bill, and it came into the hands of a holder in due course, who brought an action against Scholfield for £3,500. Scholfield paid £500 into court.

Held that Scholfield was liable for no more than £500, because he owed no duty to the holder to take precautions against fraudulent alterations and so was guilty of no negligence.

Cheques differ from other bills of exchange on this point: bank customers have a duty to take reasonable precautions in drawing cheques (see 7–175, below).

(vi) *Prescription*

Under the Bills of Exchange (Scotland) Act 1772, a bill of exchange ceased to be an enforceable document of debt on the lapse of six years from the date when it became payable. This sexennial prescription was replaced under the Prescription and Limitation (Scotland) Act 1973, as from 1976, by a five-year prescription, which also wholly extinguishes the bill.

A condition which must be satisfied for the operation of this prescription is that the creditor has for five years made no "relevant claim" (*i.e.* he must not have brought court or arbitration proceedings, or lodged a claim in the debtor's sequestration or liquidation or executed any form of diligence). Bills of exchange (and promissory notes) are exceptions to the general rule that for the operation of the prescription there must also have been no "relevant acknowledgment" of the subsistence of the debt by the debtor during the five-year period. It is therefore possible in the case of bills of exchange and promissory notes for the prescriptive period to continue to run even where the debtor has clearly indicated, by conduct or by an unequivocal written admission, that the obligation still subsists.

(l) **Acceptance and Payment for Honour supra Protest**

When a bill has been dishonoured by non-acceptance or by non-payment, the holder has the option of resorting to the "referee in case of need" if the drawer or any indorser has inserted the name of such a person on the bill (s. 15) (see 7–116, above). Where a dishonoured bill contains a reference in case of need, it must be protested for non-payment before it is presented for payment to the referee in case of need (s. 67(1)).

It is also possible that the holder may be entitled to avail himself of either:

(i) an acceptance for honour *supra* protest (after protest); or
(ii) payment for honour *supra* protest.

(i) *Acceptance for Honour* supra *Protest*

Where a bill has been protested for dishonour by non-acceptance and is not overdue, any person who is not a party already liable on it may, with

S.M.L.—14

the consent of the holder, intervene and accept the bill *supra* protest, for the honour of any party liable on it, or for the honour of the person for whose account the bill is drawn (s. 65(1)).

An acceptance for honour *supra* protest in order to be valid must be written on the bill, must indicate that it is an acceptance for honour, and must be signed by the acceptor for honour (s. 65(3)).

Where an acceptance for honour does not expressly state for whose honour it is made, it is deemed to be an acceptance for the honour of the drawer (*i.e.* the party primarily liable to pay a bill which has no acceptance on it) (s. 65(4)).

7–138   The undertaking of the acceptor for honour is that he will, on due presentment, pay the bill if it is not paid by the drawee, provided it has been duly presented for payment and protested for non-payment, and that he receives notice of these facts (s. 66(1)). The protest for non-payment must precede the presentment for payment to the acceptor for honour (s. 67(1)). The acceptor for honour is liable to the holder and to all parties to the bill subsequent to the party for whose honour he has accepted (s. 66(2)).

7–139   If a bill is dishonoured by the acceptor for honour, it must be protested for non-payment by him (s. 67(3)).

(ii) *Payment for Honour* supra *Protest*

7–140   Where a bill has been protested for non-payment, any person may intervene and pay it *supra* protest for the honour of any party liable on it, or for the honour of the person for whose account the bill is drawn (s. 68(1)).

Payment for honour *supra* protest must be attested by a "notarial act of honour," which may be appended to the protest or form an extension of it (s. 68(3)). The notarial act of honour must be founded on a declaration made by the payer for honour declaring his intention to pay the bill for honour and for whose honour he pays (s. 68(4)).

Where a bill has been paid for honour, all parties subsequent to the party for whose honour it is paid are discharged, but the payer for honour obtains for himself the rights which the holder had as regards the party for whose honour he pays and as regards all parties liable to that party (s. 68(5)). The payer for honour on paying to the holder the amount of the bill and the notarial expenses connected with its dishonour is entitled to receive both the bill and the protest (s. 68(6)).

(m) **Miscellaneous Statutory Provisions**

7–141   At the end of Part II of the Act there are sections on:
   (i)   lost bills;
   (ii) bill in a set; and
   (iii) conflict of laws.

(i) *Lost Bills*

7–142   Where a bill has been lost before it is overdue, the person who was the holder of it may apply to the drawer to give him another bill of the same tenor. The drawer may be compelled to give a replacement, but he may, as a condition of complying, require the holder to indemnify him against all persons whomsoever in case the bill alleged to have been lost should be found again (s. 69). If the drawer does not take this precaution, the possible result is that the acceptor or (if the bill has not been accepted) the drawer may find himself liable to pay the amount of the bill twice over—once to the holder of the original bill and again to the holder of the bill which replaces the "lost" bill.

(ii) *Bill in a Set*

A bill may be drawn "in a set," *i.e.* there may be more than one copy of it. Each part of the set is numbered (*e.g.* "first of exchange," "second of exchange," *etc.*) and contains a reference to the other parts. In practice the use of bills in a set is confined to overseas trade, the object being to ensure that at least one of the set will duly and at a conveniently early date reach the desired destination. The whole of the two, three or more parts of a bill in a set constitute only one bill (s. 71(1)).

The acceptance may be written on any part, and it must be written on *one* part only. If the drawee accepts more than one part, and these different parts get into the hands of different holders in due course, the acceptor is liable on every part as if it were a separate bill (s. 71(4)).

The general principle is that where any one part of the bill is discharged by payment or otherwise, the whole bill is discharged (s. 71(6)). Accordingly, where the acceptor pays one part, he ought to require the part bearing his acceptance to be delivered up to him, and if he does not do so and that part at maturity is outstanding in the hands of a holder in due course, the acceptor is liable to that holder (s. 71(5)).

A holder who indorses two or more parts to different persons is liable on each part, and every indorser subsequent to him is liable on the part which he has himself indorsed as if the parts were separate bills (s. 71(2)).

(iii) *Conflict of Laws*

The rules of private international law are of particular importance in relation to bills of exchange, since these documents (apart from cheques) are mostly confined to the foreign trading scene.

Section 72 of the Act sets out a number of rules, but these are not exhaustive; rather they form a basis, and they have been augmented by decided cases which have applied general principles of private international law. Full treatment of this subject is beyond the scope of this work: only the provisions of section 72 are noted here:

(1) As regards form, the general rule is that the validity of the bill is determined by the law of the place of issue, and the validity of later contracts, such as acceptance and indorsement, is determined by the law of the place where that contract was made (s. 72(1)). The place at which a contract is "made" is the place of delivery, not necessarily the place of signing, because of the rule that every contract on a bill is revocable until delivery (s. 21(1)).

There are two exceptions to this general rule:

(a) Where a bill is issued out of the United Kingdom it is not invalid merely because it is not stamped as required by the law of the place of issue.

(b) Where a bill, issued out of the United Kingdom, conforms to the law of the United Kingdom, it may, for the purpose of enforcing payment, be treated as valid as between all persons who negotiate, hold, or become parties to it in the United Kingdom (s. 72(1)).

(2) As regards essential validity, the interpretation of the drawing, indorsement or acceptance is determined by the law of the place where the contract is made, except that where an inland bill is indorsed in a foreign country the indorsement is, as regards the payer, interpreted according to the law of the United Kingdom (s. 72(2)).

(3) Presentment for acceptance or payment, protest and notice of dishonour are governed by the law of the place where the act is done or the bill is dishonoured (s. 72(3)).

(4) Where a bill is drawn in one country and is payable in another, its due date is determined according to the law of the place where it is payable (s. 72(5)).

II CHEQUES

7–146   A cheque is defined as a "bill of exchange drawn on a banker payable on demand." The provisions of the Act of 1882 applicable to bills of exchange payable on demand apply to cheques except where there is some provision to the contrary, either in the Act of 1882 or in the Cheques Act 1957 (s. 73).

7–147   The definition calls for some examination of the term "banker," and the statutory provisions which are peculiar to cheques relate mainly to presentment for payment, to crossing of cheques and to the protection of bankers. These matters are considered below under the headings:

(a)   relation of banker and customer;
(b)   presentment of cheque for payment;
(c)   crossed cheques; and
(d)   protection of bankers.

7–148   As has been seen (7–123, above), summary diligence—a process unaffected by the Act of 1882 (s. 98)—cannot be used to enforce payment of an unpaid cheque (*Glickman* v. *Linda,* 1950 S.C. 18 (O.H.)).

(a) Relation of Banker and Customer

7–149   The relation of banker and customer is principally a contractual one, but, because of the variety of services provided by bankers, the contract is not the same category of contract in every situation. Thus, where the customer has placed money in the hands of his banker on deposit or current account, there is a contractual relationship of creditor and debtor as between customer and banker. Where, on the other hand, the banker has advanced money to the customer, the relationship is the reverse one of creditor and debtor as between banker and customer. In paying cheques drawn by the customer and in collecting payment of cheques on behalf of the customer, the banker is in the position of agent for his customer, and the principles of the law of agency govern their relationship. Again, where the banker accepts articles (such as jewellery) and documents (such as share certificates) from his customer for safe keeping, the relationship between the parties is governed by the law of deposit.

The law on the relation of banker and customer is mainly to be found in decided cases rather than in specific statutory provisions. Some of the more important aspects of the relation are indicated below under the headings:

    (i) who is a "banker";

    (ii) who is a "customer";

    (iii) banker's duties to customer; and

    (iv) customer's duties to banker.

(i) *Who is a "Banker"*

The Act of 1882 provides that "banker" includes a body of persons whether incorporated or not who carry on the business of banking (s. 2). The Cheques Act 1957, which must be construed along with the Act of 1882 (Cheques Act 1957, s. 6(1)), makes no advance on that definition. Some other statutes have supplied definitions of "banker," each for its own purposes.

The most notable of the statutory definitions is in the Banking Act 1979, an Act passed mainly to control deposit-taking. A central provision of the Act of 1979 is that a "recognised bank" is exempt from the general prohibition placed by the Act on the acceptance of deposits (1979 Act, s. 2). For "recognition" as a bank for the purposes of the Act, application must be made to the Bank of England, and before granting an institution recognition as a bank the Bank of England must be satisfied that the criteria in Part I of Schedule 2 to the Act are fulfilled (1979 Act, s. 3). There are six detailed criteria specified in Part I of Schedule 2. They include the requirement that the institution must provide either a wide range of banking services or a highly specialised banking service, and the Schedule stipulates that an institution shall not be regarded as providing a "wide range of banking services" unless it provides five specialised services, which in outline are:

    (1) current or deposit account facilities;

    (2) overdraft or loan facilities;

    (3) foreign exchange services;

    (4) finance through the medium of bills of exchange and promissory notes; and

    (5) financial advice or investment management services and facilities for arranging purchase and sale of securities.

The case-law relating to the definition of "banker" culminated in the Court of Appeal case *United Dominions Trust Ltd.* v. *Kirkwood* [1966] 2 Q.B. 431, which gave support to the traditional view that an essential characteristic of a banker was that he paid cheques drawn on himself. The question in the case was whether the plaintiff finance company ("U.D.T.") carried on the business of banking (and so would have been exempt from provisions of the Moneylenders Act 1900). All three members of the Court of Appeal described the characteristics of banking as being:

    (1) the acceptance of money from, and collection of cheques for, customers, and the placing of them to the customers' credit;

(2) the honouring of cheques or orders drawn on the bank by their customers when presented for payment, and the debiting of the customers accordingly; and

(3) the keeping of some form of current or running accounts for the entries of customers' credits and debits.

(The Court of Appeal held that the evidence in this case did not establish that U.D.T.'s conduct of its business had the usual characteristics of banking, but the Court, by a majority, further held that the evidence of the company's reputation of carrying on the business of banking was sufficient to prove that it carried on the business of banking.'

(ii) *Who is a "Customer"*

7–154   The Act of 1882 did not define "customer," although it used the word in section 82 (now replaced by section 4 of the Cheques Act 1957). Nor is there any definition of "customer" in the Cheques Act 1957.

7–155   The leading English case is *Great Western Railway Co. v. London and County Banking Co. Ltd.* [1901] A.C. 414, in which the House of Lords held that to make a person a "customer" of a bank for the purposes of section 82 of the Act of 1882 "there must be some sort of account, either a deposit or a current account or some similar relation" (*per* Lord Davey at p. 420). The decision in the case was therefore that a person who had for 20 years been in the habit of having cheques cashed for him by the bank but who had no account with the bank was not a "customer" (the result being that the bank did not enjoy the protection which it would otherwise have had under section 82 of the Act).

7–156   The general rule as stated by Lord Davey in that case may require to be qualified in the light of a more recent English case—*Woods v. Martin Bank Ltd.* [1959] 1 Q.B. 55:

On May 9, 1950, W. was induced to invest £5,000 in shares of Brock Refrigeration Ltd. ("B.R."), following advice given by the manager of a branch of Martins Bank Ltd. that B.R., a customer of the bank, was financially sound and that the investment was a wise one to make.

On June 1, 1950, the bank opened a current account for W., and W. made further investments in B.R. after that date.

There were no grounds on which the branch manager could reasonably have advised that B.R. was in a sound or strong financial position, and still less could the investment be reasonably recommended as a wise one.

W. lost all the £14,800 which he had invested in B.R., and brought an action against the bank and the branch manager.

Held that it was within the scope of the bank's business to advise on all financial matters and the bank owed a duty to W. to advise him with reasonable care and skill, that from May 9 the relationship of banker and customer existed, and that W. had made out his case in negligence both against the bank and against the manager.

Salmon J., in considering what was and what was not within the scope of the bank's business, looked at the bank's own publications and concluded (at p. 71): "I find that it was and is within the scope of the defendant bank's business to advise on all financial matters and that, as they did advise him, they owed a duty to the plaintiff to advise him with reasonable care and skill."

In dealing with the point taken by the bank that W. was not a customer of the bank at the date of the first transaction in May 1950, in that no current account had then been opened, Salmon J. held that W. was a customer of the bank on May 9, 1950.

The case suggests two possible alternative qualifications to Lord Davey's statement: *either* a person may be a customer if he is about to open an account *or* a person may be a customer if he avails himself of facilities offered by the bank other than deposit or current account facilities (in this case advice on investments). The second qualification is the more radical of the two.

A "customer" does not require to have had habitual dealings with the bank: he becomes a customer from the moment he opens an account. This may be illustrated by the Privy Council case *Commissioners of Taxation* v. *English, Scottish and Australian Bank Ltd.* [1920] A.C. 683:

On June 7, a person giving his name as "Thallon" opened a current account with the bank and paid £20 in cash into it.

On the following day, a cheque for some £786, which had been stolen from the Commissioners of Taxation, was handed into the bank with a pay-in slip to be credited to Thallon's account.

Held that Thallon was a customer of the bank.

Lord Dunedin, giving the judgment, said (at p. 687): "The word 'customer' signifies a relationship in which duration is not of the essence. A person whose money has been accepted by a bank on the footing that they undertake to honour cheques up to the amount standing to his credit is . . . a customer of the bank in the sense of the statute, irrespective of whether his connection is of short or long standing."

(iii) *Banker's Duties to Customer*

The banker's duties to his customer depend on the terms of the contract between them: if the customer has a deposit or savings account, the banker will be bound to pay him the agreed interest on the credit balance of that account and to repay the amount deposited when required to do so; if money has been lodged on deposit receipt, the banker will be bound to pay the money deposited with interest to the person named in the deposit receipt (who is not necessarily the person who deposited the money); where the contract is for the safe keeping of the customer's property, either for a charge or gratuitously, the banker will incur the obligations of an onerous or gratuitous depositary as the case may be.

Of special importance are:
(1) the banker's duty of secrecy; and
(2) the banker's duty to honour cheques.

1) **Banker's duty of secrecy**

The relation of banker and customer is of a confidential nature, and so, as a general rule, the banker has a duty not to disclose his customer's affairs.

This duty was considered and given effect to by the Court of Appeal in *Tournier* v. *National Provincial and Union Bank of England* [1924] 1 K.B. 461. Bankes L.J. said (at pp. 472-473) that the duty was not absolute but qualified, and he classified the qualifications under four heads:

(a) where disclosure is compelled by law (*e.g.* where a court requires a banker to give evidence in legal proceedings);

(b) where there is a duty to the public to disclose (*e.g.* where, in wartime, the customer is transacting with the enemy);

(c) where the interests of the bank require disclosure (*e.g.* where the bank brings an action in court claiming repayment of the customer's overdraft); and

(d) where the disclosure is made by the express or implied consent of the customer (*e.g.* where the customer has requested the banker to act as a referee concerning the customer's financial position).

It is an established practice that bankers give information about their customers to other bankers without asking for permission from the customers. This practice may perhaps be justified on the ground that, on opening an account, a customer impliedly consents to such disclosure.

7–162   Other points included in Bankes L.J.'s judgment were that the duty of secrecy did not cease the moment the customer closed his account—the information gained during the currency of the account remained confidential—and that the confidence was not confined to the actual state of the customer's account but extended to information derived from the keeping of the account.

(2) Banker's duty to honour cheques

7–163   "The relation between banker and customer is that of debtor and creditor, with a superadded obligation on the part of the banker to honour the customer's cheques if the account is in credit. A cheque drawn by a customer is in point of law a mandate to the banker to pay the amount according to the tenor of the cheque" (*per* Lord Finlay, L.C., in *London Joint Stock Bank Ltd.* v. *Macmillan and Arthur* [1918] A.C. 777, at p. 789). This concise quotation involves a number of considerations:

(a) *"If the account is in credit"*

7–164   The banker is under no obligation to allow an overdraft. Where, however, a banker has insufficient funds to meet a cheque which is presented to him for payment, he must set aside such funds as he has, since, by section 53(2), the presentment of the cheque has the effect in Scotland of assigning these funds to the holder of the cheque (see 7–97 *et seq.*, above).

7–165   The question can arise of whether a banker is entitled, without prior notice to his customer, to mass several current accounts kept by the customer, at one or more branches of the bank, in order to ascertain whether there are funds to meet a cheque. The question would usually be covered by an agreement made between banker and customer, as in the English case of *National Westminster Bank Ltd.* v. *Halesowen Presswork & Assemblies Ltd.* [1972] A.C. 785:

In February 1968 H. Ltd.'s current account was overdrawn to the extent of £11,339. An agreement was made between the bank and H. Ltd. that in order to support H. Ltd.'s business so that it could be disposed of as a going concern, the current account, to be called the "No. 1 account," would be frozen and that a new account, the "No. 2 account," would be opened and be maintained in credit.

In June 1968 H. Ltd. went into liquidation, and the liquidator claimed from the bank the sum of about £8,611, then standing at the credit of the No. 2 account. The bank on the other hand claimed to be entitled to set off this amount against H. Ltd.'s indebtedness on the No. 1 account.

Held, on an interpretation of the agreement, that the parties had not contemplated that the agreement should continue in force after liquidation; the bank was therefore entitled to consolidate the two accounts and exercise the right which existed on a winding up to set off the balance on the No. 2 account against H. Ltd.'s debt on the No. 1 account.

The case was alternatively decided on section 31 of the Bankruptcy Act 1914 as applied by section 317 of the Companies Act 1948—provisions not applicable to Scotland. In Scotland the common law rules of compensation would apply.

Lord Kilbrandon (of Scottish origin) said (at p. 820): "The main question in the case, and on one view the only question, is whether as a matter of construction the agreement between the bank and the company was intended to, and did, provide that in the event which happened, *i.e.*, a winding up of the company, the bank were to be deprived of the power, which they would in the absence of agreement have had, to combine the No. 1 and the No. 2 accounts. This depends on a construction of the agreement. I have formed the opinion that such was not the intention or the effect of the agreement.

". . . . But a great deal of the argument was directed to section 31 of the Bankruptcy Act 1914, as applied to liquidations by section 317 of the Companies Act 1948, and it is necessary to deal with the points which were raised. . . .

"An interesting feature of this controversy is that, while by section 318 of the Companies Act 1948 the provisions of the Bankruptcy (Scotland) Act 1913 relating to ranking of claims are imported into the Scottish liquidation code, there is no equivalent to section 31 to be found in the latter Act. The right of set off, or, as Bell calls it in his *Commentaries on the Laws of Scotland*, 5th ed. (1826), vol. II, p. 124, 'the balancing of accounts in bankruptcy,' stands on the common law of compensation or retention, expanded in cases of bankruptcy to include debts which would not be susceptible of set off in the case of a solvent creditor. For example, in bankruptcy, the debts need not be of the same nature, or both due at the same time, or both liquid. *Bell's Commentaries*, vol. II, at pp. 119-121, supply an illuminating account of the parallel development of the law in England and Scotland respectively. It would hardly be possible to maintain in Scotland that set off is mandatory, and independent of the act or agreement of parties, since 'it must be pleaded by the debtor who wishes to take advantage of it.' . . . So, if set off be mandatory in England, this seems to be one of the fields in which the law relating to British companies varies according as they are registered in England or in Scotland."

Where no event such the customer's liquidation or death has occurred to stop the current accounts, the generally accepted view, based on the English case of *Garnett* v. *McKewan* (1872) L.R. 8 Ex. 10, is that, in the absence of any agreement or course of dealing to the contrary, the banker is entitled without prior notice to mass the customer's several current accounts even if kept at different branches of the bank.

7–166   If the several accounts are of a different kind (*e.g.* a deposit account and a current account), the banker is not entitled to combine them without prior notice to the customer. This was taken to be an established rule in *Kirkwood & Sons* v. *Clydesdale Bank Ltd.*, 1908 S.C. 20:

Moffatt, a Glasgow stockbroker, had a current account, a loan account and several cash accounts with his bank. A cheque drawn by Moffatt in favour of K. & Sons was presented to the bank at a time when the credit balance on the current account was more than sufficient to meet it, but payment was refused on the ground that Moffatt had died earlier the same day. K. & Sons argued that the cheque had the effect of assigning funds under section 53(2).

Held that (i) the cheque, as a cheque, lapsed at Moffatt's death; and (ii) the cheque did not operate as an "assignment" under section 53(2) because, on a combination of all Moffatt's accounts, he was indebted to the bank and so the bank had no "funds available" for the payment of the cheque, within the meaning of that subsection.

(b) *"Drawn by a customer"*

7–167   The customer's signature must be genuine. If the banker pays a cheque on which the drawer's signature has been forged, he is not entitled to debit the customer's account with the amount because he has no mandate (authority) to do so. The loss therefore falls on the banker.

(c) *"A mandate to the banker to pay"*

7–168   In paying cheques the banker is the agent for the customer whose funds he holds.

7–169   This mandate or agency is terminated in various circumstances either by statute or at common law. These circumstances include:

(i) countermand of payment (*i.e.* where the drawer, before the cheque has been paid, instructs the banker not to pay it) (s. 75); however, presentment of the cheque for payment will operate, under section 53(2) of the Act (see 7–97 *et seq.*, above), as an assignation of funds in the banker's hands available for payment, and the banker will therefore transfer the amount of the cheque (or the whole credit balance if that is less than the amount of the cheque) to a suspense account; where the holder of the cheque and the drawer of it do not then agree as to the disposal of the funds, the matter will be settled by a court process known as a "multiplepoinding"; cheques which have been issued along with production of a cheque card cannot, according to the usual terms of the agreement between banker and customer, be countermanded;

(ii) notice of the customer's death (s. 75); presentment of a cheque after notice of the customer's death will again operate as an assignation under section 53(2) (*Bank of Scotland* v. *Reid and Others* (1886) 2 Sh. Ct. Rep. 376 (7–100, above)), but in this situation all the customer's accounts are taken into consideration in the decision of whether the banker has any "funds available" (*Kirkwood & Sons* v. *Clydesdale Bank Ltd.* (7–166, above));

(iii) the drawer's sequestration (Bankruptcy (Scotland) Act 1913, s. 107); any credit balance vests in the trustee as at the date of the sequestration (1913 Act, s. 97); section 53(2) of the Act of 1882 may operate here also: if, before sequestration, a cheque has been presented and payment of it has been refused on account of there being insufficient funds to meet it, the holder of the cheque and not the trustee is entitled to any funds which, on the occasion of the presentment of the cheque, were at the credit of the account;

(iv) notice given by either party of the closing of the account, but a banker giving notice to his customer is bound to pay cheques drawn prior to, though not presented until after, the date of receipt of the notice (*King v. British Linen Co.* (1899) 1 F. 928); and

(v) appointment of a *curator bonis* ("guardian") on the mental incapacity of the drawer (*Mitchell & Baxter v. Cheyne* (1891) 19 R. 324).

(d) *"According to the tenor of the cheque"*

The banker must follow the instructions of his principal, the customer. He must, therefore, observe any crossing which there may be on the cheque (see 7–180 *et seq.*, below), and if the customer has postdated the cheque, the banker must not pay it until that date has arrived.

A banker who wrongfully fails to honour his customer's cheques commits a breach of contract, and is liable in damages measured by the actual loss sustained by the customer on the transaction and by the injury to his credit and reputation. If the customer is in business he is entitled to substantial damages under the latter head without proving actual injury (*e.g.* £100 to a hay and grain merchant in *King v. British Linen Co.* (1899) 1 F. 928), but a person who is not in business must prove his actual injury; otherwise he is entitled only to nominal damages (*e.g.* £2 for wrongful dishonour of a cheque payable to a landlord in *Gibbons v. Westminster Bank Ltd.* [1939] 2 K.B. 882). In both of the cases mentioned the claim was founded on breach of contract.

An alternative ground would be delict, since it is defamatory to cast unjustifiable doubts upon a person's financial soundness. An English case which is an example of a successful claim for libel (corresponding to written slander in Scots law) is *Davidson v. Barclays Bank Ltd.* [1940] 1 All E.R. 316: A cheque for £2 15s.8d. drawn by a credit bookmaker had been dishonoured by his bank because the bank had not given effect to a stop order placed by the customer on a previously-drawn cheque for £7 15s.9d. The customer obtained damages of £250. Hilberry J. in that case said that he could not imagine anything much more damaging to a credit bookmaker than a statement which suggested that he could not meet a cheque for such a small amount as £2 15s.8d. "Substantial damage," he continued (at p. 325), "is done, for the very good reason that nothing about a man travels so fast as that which is to his discredit. . . . The sum to be given as a reasonable compensation for the injury which has been done to the plaintiff . . . must be sufficient to mark beyond a shadow of doubt the complete lack of justification for making the aspersion which was made by this means on the plaintiff's credit."

In the cases concerning damages for dishonour of a cheque (whether founded on breach of contract or founded on delict) the emphasis placed on damage to the customer's credit in his business cannot readily be reconciled with the provision in section 57(1) of the Act of 1882 that the measure of damages for the dishonour of any bill of exchange is to be the amount of the bill, plus interest from the time of presentment for payment and the expenses of noting and of protest (where protest is necessary) (David M. Walker, *Civil Remedies*, p. 413).

(iv) *Customer's Duties to Banker*

7–174 In relation to cheques, the customer has a duty towards the banker:
  (1) to take reasonable precautions to prevent fraudulent alteration of cheques drawn; and
  (2) to notify the banker timeously of any forgeries known to the customer.

(1) Reasonable precautions in drawing cheques

7–175 "It is beyond dispute that the customer is bound to exercise reasonable care in drawing the cheque to prevent the banker being misled. If he draws the cheque in a manner which facilitates fraud, he is guilty of a breach of duty as between himself and the banker, and he will be responsible to the banker for any loss sustained by the banker as a natural and direct consequence of this breach of duty" (*per* Lord Finlay, L.C., in *London Joint Stock Bank Ltd.* v. *Macmillan and Arthur* [1918] A.C. 777). The facts of the case referred to are a memorable illustration:

"On the morning of February 9, 1915, one of the plaintiff partners, Mr. Arthur, was going out to lunch about mid-day. He had his hat on and was leaving the office when the clerk came up to him and said he wanted £2 for petty cash and produced a cheque for signature. The clerk had repeatedly presented cheques for signature to get petty cash, but usually for £3, and Mr. Arthur asked him why it was not £3 on this occasion. The clerk replied that £2 would be sufficient. Mr. Arthur thereupon signed the cheque. . . . On the next day the clerk did not come to business. . . .

". . . Mr. Arthur was in a great hurry when he signed the cheque, and . . . when he signed it there were no words at all in the space left for words; that space was a blank. There were the figures '2. 0 0' in the space left for figures. The clerk, having obtained Mr. Arthur's signature to the cheque in this condition properly dated and payable to 'ourselves,' added the words 'one hundred and twenty pounds' in the space left for words, and the figures '1' and '0' on either side of the figure '2.'"[5]

The clerk had absconded with the £120, and Macmillan and Arthur brought an action claiming a declaration that the bank was not entitled to debit the plaintiffs' account with the £120.

The House of Lords held that the bank was entitled to do so on the ground of the customer's failure to take reasonable and ordinary precautions against forgery.

(2) Timeous notification of forgeries

7–176 The customer has a duty to notify the banker of forged cheques known to the customer: otherwise, the customer may be barred from objecting

---

[5] narrative adopted by Lord Finlay L.C. (at p. 787) from the judgment of Sankey J.

when further forged cheques are debited to his account. An illustration is *Greenwood* v. *Martins Bank Ltd.* [1933] A.C. 51 (7–25, above).

(b) Presentment of Cheque for Payment

In all but exceptional cases a cheque is intended to operate as an immediate payment out of the drawer's funds to the payee. While in theory the cheque is an "order" on the banker to pay to the payee, in reality it is an appropriation to the payee by the drawer of what the drawer regards as his own funds. Primary liability, therefore, lies with the drawer, and presentment to the banker for acceptance would be inappropriate.

There is, however, the possibility of certification (or "marking") of a cheque. In certifying a cheque the banker undertakes that the customer has sufficient funds to meet it. The banker might write on the face of the cheque words such as "This cheque is good for payment," accompanied by an authorised signature and a date, but the usual Scottish practice is to stamp the back of the cheque with a rubber stamp stating that if the cheque is presented within 10 days it will be paid. This procedure can enhance the creditworthiness of the drawer in the eyes of the payee. Though certification does not amount to "acceptance" in the statutory sense (*Bank of Baroda Ltd.* v. *Punjab National Bank Ltd.* [1944] A.C. 176), it is an undertaking binding on the banker, and in order to protect himself the banker immediately, at the time of granting the certification, debits the customer's account with the amount of the cheque and places the amount at the credit of another account such as "Sundry Credits"; on presentation of the cheque, the amount is then recredited to the customer's account and the cheque is paid out of his account. Certified cheques are in common use in some Commonwealth countries, but in this country bankers' drafts are preferred. (A banker's draft is a document in the form of a cheque drawn by the banker on himself. It is issued at the customer's request, is payable to a named payee, and the amount of the draft is debited, at that time, to the customer's account. Funds are thus available in the banker's hands to pay the draft to the payee when it is presented.)

Presentment for payment is one of the matters on which the Act of 1882 differentiates between cheques and other bills of exchange. The rule applicable to bills of exchange in general is that where a bill is payable on demand (as a cheque always is), presentment for payment must be made within a reasonable time after its issue in order to make the drawer liable, and within a reasonable time after its indorsement, in order to make the indorser liable (s. 45, rule (2)). In the case of a cheque, however, the extent to which the drawer is discharged by the holder's failure to present the cheque for payment within a reasonable time is much more limited: the Act provides that where a cheque is not presented for payment within a reasonable time of its issue and the drawer suffers actual damage through the delay, he is discharged to the extent of that damage, *i.e.* to the extent to which he is a creditor of the banker to a larger amount than he would have been had his cheque been paid (s. 74(1)). The effect of this provision is that the drawer will be discharged only if the banker becomes insolvent. As the failure of a bank is an event of very rare occurrence, the practical result is that a drawer remains liable to pay the cheque until the lapse of the prescriptive period of five years. As a matter of Scottish banking practice, however, a cheque which is over six months old when it is presented for payment is returned by the banker to the person presenting it, in order that it may be confirmed by the drawer before it is paid.

The Act further provides that where the unusual circumstances mentioned in section 74(1), above, do occur, the holder of the cheque becomes a creditor of the banker for the amount of which the drawer has been discharged (s. 74(3)).

(c) Crossed Cheques

7–180 The effect of crossing a cheque is to give a direction to the banker on whom it is drawn (the "paying banker") that payment of it should only be made to another banker (the "collecting banker"). The advantage of crossing is that it helps to ensure that the cheque will be paid only to the person for whom it is intended.

7–181 The normal procedure is for the recipient of the cheque to pay the cheque into his own banking account, and his banker will then collect the amount of the cheque by presenting the cheque to the banker on whom it is drawn. If the recipient of the cheque does not himself have a bank account, he will require to enlist the help of another person who does have a bank account and who will obtain payment of the cheque by presenting it, through his bank account, to the banker on whom the cheque is drawn. It would be exceptional for the recipient of a crossed cheque to present it for payment in cash to the banker on whom it is drawn; the banker would be under no obligation to pay it in cash, but if he chose to do so, he would not be acting illegally: he would be without the statutory protection conferred on paying bankers who observe crossings (see 7–202 *et seq.*, below) and he might incur liability under section 79(2) to the true owner of the cheque for any loss sustained by the true owner as a result of the cheque having been paid in disregard of the crossing. A more likely occurrence is where the payee of a crossed cheque hands it to the paying banker along with a giro credit slip, thus transferring the amount of the cheque to his own account at another bank. The use of giro credits is becoming increasingly common, but there is doubt as to how the statutory provisions apply to that system: in particular, is the banker who ultimately receives the proceeds of the crossed cheque a collecting banker enjoying the same protection as that conferred on a banker collecting a crossed cheque? Other questions which are still open are whether the handing in of the giro credit slip and the cheque to the drawee bank is effective as a presentment of the cheque for the purposes of section 53(2) (assignation of funds—see 7–97 *et seq.*, above), and whether the cheque is paid at the moment of the handing in of the giro credit slip, so that countermand of payment would thereafter be impossible.

7–182 The statutory provisions are considered under these headings:

  (i)   general and special crossings;
  (ii) who is entitled to cross a cheque;
  (iii) effect of crossing; and
  (iv) effect of addition of "not negotiable."

A note is also included on:

(v)   effect of addition of "account payee only."

(i) *General and Special Crossings*

A cheque may be crossed generally or specially.

A cheque is crossed generally if it bears across its face an addition of:

(1) the words "and company," or any abbreviation of these words, between two parallel transverse lines, either with or without the words "not negotiable"; or

(2) two parallel transverse lines simply, either with or without the words "not negotiable" (s. 76(1)).

The following are therefore general crossings:

A cheque is crossed specially if it bears across its face an addition of the name of a banker, either with or without the words "not negotiable" (s. 76(2)). The Act does not require two parallel transverse lines in this case, but such lines are commonly used.

Examples of special crossings are:

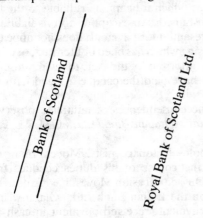

(ii) *Who is Entitled to Cross a Cheque*

A cheque may be crossed generally or specially by the drawer. Where a cheque is uncrossed, the holder may cross it generally or specially, and where a cheque is already crossed generally, the holder may cross it specially. Where a cheque is crossed generally or specially, the holder may add the words "not negotiable" (s. 77(1)-(4)).

Where an uncrossed cheque, or a cheque crossed generally, is sent to a banker "for collection," *i.e.* in order that he may obtain payment of it from the banker on whom it is drawn, he may cross it specially to himself (s. 77(6)).

7–188   There is only one situation in which a cheque may be crossed specially to more than one banker, namely, where the banker to whom the cheque is crossed specially again crosses it specially to another banker for collection (s. 77(5)). If in any other situation a cheque is crossed specially to more than one banker, the banker on whom it is drawn must refuse payment of the cheque (s. 79(1)).

7–189   Crossing as authorised by the Act is a material part of a cheque, and it is not lawful for any person to obliterate or (with the exceptions mentioned above) to add to or alter the crossing (s. 78).

(iii) *Effect of Crossing*

7–190   Crossing imposes certain duties on, and gives some protection to, the drawee bank, *i.e.* the bank on which the cheque is drawn. The duties imposed are considered here, and the protection conferred is dealt with later (see 7–195 *et seq.*, below).

If a cheque is uncrossed, the holder of it may himself present it to the bank on which it is drawn and obtain cash for it. Alternatively, he may request his own bank to collect payment on his behalf from the bank on which the cheque is drawn.

In the case of a crossed cheque, only the second alternative is open to the holder. If the crossing is a general crossing, the cheque must be presented for payment through a bank, and if the crossing is a special crossing, the cheque must be presented for payment through the bank which is specially named in the crossing.

7–191   If the banker on whom the cheque is drawn pays it in contravention of the general or special crossing which it bears, he is liable to the true owner of the cheque for loss sustained. An exception to this liability is made where a cheque, when presented for payment, does not appear to be crossed or to have had a crossing which has been obliterated, or added to or altered in some way not authorised by the Act: to avail himself of this exception the banker must have paid the cheque in good faith and without negligence (s. 79(2)).

There is an illustration of the consequences of failure to observe a crossing in *Godfrey Phillips Ltd.* v. *Italian Bank Ltd.*, 1934 S.L.T. 78 (O.H.):

P. Ltd. of London were wholesale tobacconists. Moyes, one of P. Ltd.'s travellers, obtained in the course of his duties cheques from customers in favour of P. Ltd. On one occasion Moyes, having obtained three crossed cheques drawn on the Italian Bank Ltd., Glasgow, presented them to the bank for payment, received payment in cash and applied the proceeds to his own purposes.

Held, on an application of section 79(2), that P. Ltd. were entitled to recover the amount of the three cheques from the bank.

(iv) *Effect of Addition of "Not Negotiable"*

7–192   When a person takes a crossed cheque which bears on it the words "not negotiable," he does not himself obtain, and is not capable of giving, a better title to the cheque than that which the person from whom he took it had (s. 81). The cheque can still be transferred, but each transferee will take the cheque subject to any defects in the title of previous parties.

(v) *Effect of Addition of "Account Payee Only"*

It is a common practice for the words "account payee only" to be added to a general crossing. These words have no statutory meaning. They are not properly part of the crossing (which is an instruction to the banker *on whom the cheque is drawn*), but are a direction to the banker *who collects the proceeds* as to how he is to deal with them. The words do not make the cheque not negotiable.

(d) **Protection of Bankers**

Statutory protection is given to both:

(i) the paying banker (*i.e.* the banker on whom the cheque is drawn); and

(ii) the collecting banker (*i.e.* the banker who, as agent for the holder of the cheque, collects payment of it from the paying banker).

(i) *Protection of Paying Banker*

The statutory provisions under this heading modify, as regards cheques, the rule of section 24 applicable to bills of exchange in general, *viz.*, that where a signature on a bill is forged or unauthorised, the forged or unauthorised signature is wholly inoperative and no right to retain the bill or to give a discharge for it or to enforce payment of it against any party can be acquired through or under that signature, unless the party against whom it is sought to retain or enforce payment of the bill is barred from saying that there has been forgery or want of authority (see 7–25, above).

Where it is the drawer's signature which is forged or unauthorised, the paying banker has no statutory protection. He is not permitted to debit his customer's account with the amount of the cheque, unless the drawer has himself in some way so materially contributed to the forged or unauthorised signature that he is barred from saying to the banker that it ought not to have been paid.

The statutory protection is therefore confined to the situation where the cheque has one or more indorsements which have been forged or made without authority.

Before the statutory provisions themselves are considered, it is first necessary to distinguish "bearer" cheques (those payable to a named payee "or bearer") from "order" cheques (those payable to a named payee "or order").

Bearer cheques, like any other bills of exchange payable to bearer, may be transferred from one person to another by simple delivery without any indorsement. If in fact a bearer cheque is indorsed, it is not the indorsement which gives the holder of the cheque his title to it: his title is derived from the delivery of the cheque to him. If, therefore, a bearer cheque has a forged or unauthorised indorsement and the banker on whom the cheque is drawn pays it to the holder, the banker will be considered as having paid the cheque in due course, the cheque will be discharged and the amount will be properly debited to the drawer's account. The rule in section 24 does not apply in such a case because the holder has not acquired his right "through or under" the forged or unauthorised signature, but by delivery.

7–200   As regards order cheques, there are three statutory provisions giving protection to the paying banker:

(1) Bills of Exchange Act 1882, section 60

7–201   This applies to any bill payable to order on demand and drawn on a banker. Provided the banker pays the bill *"in good faith and in the ordinary course of business,"* he need not show that the indorsement of the payee or any subsequent indorsement was made by or with the authority of the person whose indorsement it purports to be, and he is deemed to have paid the bill in due course, although the indorsement has in fact been forged or made without authority.

Both crossed and uncrossed cheques would come within this provision. If, however, the banker paid a crossed cheque over the counter, that would not be payment "in the ordinary course of business," and he would not be able to rely on section 60; nor would he be protected by this provision if he paid a cheque which bore an irregular indorsement.

(2) Bills of Exchange Act 1882, section 80

7–202   This applies only to crossed cheques. Provided the banker *"in good faith and without negligence"* pays the cheque in accordance with its general or special crossing, the banker is entitled to the same rights and is placed in the same position as if payment of the cheque had been made to the true owner of it.

This provision is differently worded from that in section 60, and there is some overlapping of the two provisions. The explanation appears to be that section 80 is a reproduction of an earlier statutory provision relating to cheques in the Crossed Cheques Act 1876.

(3) Cheques Act 1957, section 1

7–203   Neither section 60 nor section 80 gave the paying banker protection if an indorsement on the cheque was missing or was irregular on its face. It was therefore necessary for the banker to check all indorsements to verify that they were apparently regular. This time-taking procedure may be dispensed with under section 1 of the Cheques Act 1957, the effect of which is to extend the paying banker's protection to cheques, whether crossed or uncrossed, which are unindorsed or which are irregularly indorsed.

The provision is that where a banker *"in good faith and in the ordinary course of business"* pays a cheque which is not indorsed or is irregularly indorsed, he does not, in doing so, incur any liability merely because of the absence of, or irregularity in, indorsement, and he is deemed to have paid the cheque in due course.

7–204   Questions can arise as to whether the banker has acted "in the ordinary course of business" within the meaning of (1) and (3), above, and as to whether he has acted "without negligence" within the meaning of (2), above. In interpreting these phrases, the courts look to banking practice. It is, for instance, banking practice for a banker to require a cheque to be indorsed if it is presented for payment over the counter and not through a bank. If, therefore, a paying banker were to disregard that practice and pay the cheque over the counter, he would not be protected. Similarly, a cheque marked "R" on its face is, by banking practice, a combined cheque and receipt requiring indorsement, and the paying banker must verify that there is an apparently regular indorsement on it; otherwise he will not be protected if the indorsement turns out in fact to have been forged or unauthorised.

(ii) *Protection of Collecting Banker*

The banker who collects the proceeds of a cheque may incur liability if the person from whom he takes the cheque has in fact no title or only a defective title to the cheque. The purpose of the statutory provision under this heading is to protect the collecting banker from such liability on certain conditions.

The statutory provision used to be section 82 of the Act of 1882:

"Where a banker *in good faith and without negligence receives payment for a customer* of a cheque crossed generally or specially to himself, and the customer has no title or a defective title thereto, the banker shall not incur any liability to the true owner of the cheque by reason only of having received such payment."

That provision was amended by section 1 of the Bills of Exchange (Crossed Cheques) Act 1906 as a result of the decision of the House of Lords in the English case *Capital and Counties Bank Ltd.* v. *Gordon* [1903] A.C. 240. The case established that bankers were protected by section 82 of the Act of 1882 *only where they received payment of a crossed cheque as agents for collection for a customer* and were not protected by the section when they received payment as holders of the cheque on their own account. An outline of the facts is as follows:

Gordon was the holder for value of various crossed cheques. His clerk, Jones, forged indorsements on these cheques and took the cheques to the C. Bank, where Jones had an account. Jones also indorsed the cheques in his own name, and the C. Bank credited his account with the amounts. Jones then drew on his account. The bank manager dealt in perfect good faith and without negligence. The vital point was that the bank did not wait until the cheques paid in by Jones had been passed through the clearing-house before their amounts were placed to his credit: they were placed to his credit when he paid the cheques in, and he was allowed to draw upon his account as increased by them. The C. Bank received the amounts in due course from the banks on which the several cheques had been drawn.

Jones' frauds were later discovered and he was prosecuted and convicted.

Gordon, who had been robbed of the cheques and wrongfully deprived of the money represented by them, brought an action against the C. Bank to recover the money which that bank had received.

Gordon was successful since the House of Lords, on an interpretation of section 82 of the Act of 1882, held that it was impossible to say that the bank had received payment of the cheques *for their customer* (Jones). Observations were made on the desirability of amending section 82 so that protection would be extended to collecting bankers acting in the way that the C. Bank had acted in the case.

7–208   Amendment took the form of section 1 of the Bills of Exchange (Crossed Cheques) Act 1906:

"A banker receives payment of a crossed cheque for a customer within the meaning of section 82 of the Bills of Exchange Act 1882 notwithstanding that he credits his customer's account with the amount of the cheque before receiving payment thereof."

7–209   Both section 82 of the Act of 1882 and the amendment of it in the Act of 1906 were repealed in 1957, and replaced by section 4(1) of the Cheques Act 1957. The protection conferred by section 4(1) of the Act of 1957 applies not only to cheques, whether crossed or uncrossed, but to certain other documents for the payment of money, including bankers' drafts (1957 Act, s. 4(2)).

7–210   The statutory protection for the collecting banker now is that where a banker, *"in good faith and without negligence"*:

(a) *"receives payment for a customer"* of the cheque or other document; or

(b) *"having credited a customer's account"* with the amount, receives payment for himself,

and the customer has no title, or a defective title, to the document, the banker does not incur any liability to the true owner of the document merely because he has received payment of it (1957 Act, s. 4(1)).

7–211   A further provision in section 4 of the Act of 1957 had the effect of enlarging the area of a collecting banker's protection. Before the Act of 1957, if the cheque being collected was not properly indorsed the banker was considered to be acting negligently and so was not protected by section 82 of the Act of 1882. Section 4(3) of the 1957 Act changed the law on this point by providing that a banker is not to be treated as having been negligent merely because he has failed to concern himself with absence of, or irregularity in, indorsements. The provision has relieved bankers of the need to check indorsements in the majority of ordinary transactions involving the collection of cheques for customers, namely those in which the customer pays into his own account cheques which have been drawn in favour of the customer himself. As a matter of banking practice, however, a collecting banker still requires indorsement of cheques in certain circumstances, namely:

(1) where the payee of the cheque is not the customer into whose account the cheque is being paid (the banker would look for the indorsement of the payee and at any subsequent indorsements up to the stage when his own customer became the holder); if a cheque is specially indorsed to the customer for whose account it is tendered for collection, no further indorsement is necessary (but the banker may write on the customer's name for easy reference);

(2) where the payee's name is mis-spelt, or the payee is incorrectly described, and the surrounding circumstances are suspicious; or

(3) where the cheque is payable to joint payees and is being paid into an account to which they are not all parties.

Section 4(3) of the Act of 1957 is so worded that a court, looking to banking practice for guidance, could still hold that a banker who failed to observe these usual precautions would be liable to the true owner of the cheque if his customer had no title or a defective title to it.

There is a dearth of Scottish case-law on the statutory provisions relating to the protection of the collecting banker, and the assumption may have been too readily made that the statutory provisions apply in the same way to Scotland as to England. English case-law, however, has this importance, that it has been the basis for standard banking practice in both countries, and it is likely that in any Scottish case relating to the statutory provisions the court would look to standard banking practice. There would therefore appear to be some value in referring to English cases particularly those concerned with the interpretation of the central phrase "without negligence." The following are two instances of how the English courts have relied on banking practice in interpreting the phrase:

(1) *Lloyds Bank Ltd.* v. *E.B. Savory & Co.* [1933] A.C. 201: In this case the House of Lords held that the practice of the bank in question had been defective in certain respects.

A clerk employed by a firm of stockbrokers had opened a private account with the bank, but had not been asked for the name of his employers.

He stole numerous crossed cheques from his employers and paid them into his private account.

The bank was held to have failed to prove that it had acted "without negligence," and so it was not entitled to the benefit of the statutory protection then in section 82 of the Act of 1882.

Lord Warrington of Clyffe said (at p. 221): "There is here no special duty, contractual or otherwise, towards the true owners of the cheque. The standard by which the absence, or otherwise, of negligence is to be determined must in my opinion be ascertained by reference to the practice of reasonable men carrying on the business of banking, and endeavouring to do so in such a manner as may be calculated to protect themselves and others against fraud."

(2) *Marfani & Co. Ltd.* v. *Midland Bank Ltd.* [1968] 1 W.L.R. 956: In this case, decided by the Court of Appeal under section 4 of the Cheques Act 1957, reference was made to the standard of the "reasonable banker." The bank was in this case held not to have been guilty of negligence.

Diplock L.J. explained (at p. 972): "Where the customer is in possession of the cheque at the time of delivery for collection and appears upon the face of it to be the 'holder,' *i.e.* the payee or indorsee or the bearer, the banker is, in my view, entitled to assume that the customer is the owner of the cheque unless there are facts which are, or ought to be, known to him which would cause a reasonable banker to suspect that the customer was not the true owner."

Reasonable care was, he said (at p. 975), to be judged by "the practice of careful bankers."

The ground of liability which a collecting banker would incur if he were not protected by the statutory provision now in section 4(1) of the

Cheques Act 1957 is different in Scots law from what it is in English law. For a full account of the distinction reference should be made to the article "The Collecting Banker's Protection in Scots Law" by D.J. Cusine (1978) 23 J.R. 233.

As explained in that article, the statutory provisions were enacted to give the collecting banker protection from liability for the tort of conversion, by which the true owner could under English law sue a *bona fide* intermediary who had obtained stolen property and parted with it again.

7–216   Scots law has no equivalent to the tort of conversion: in Scots law if a person who has parted with possession of property is to be made liable to the true owner it will be on the ground of restitution, and liability on that ground will arise only if the intermediary made a profit from the disposal or if he acted in bad faith. The collecting banker in Scotland, therefore, stood in no need of special statutory protection.

7–217   A case governed by the common law of Scotland was *Clydesdale Banking Co.* v. *Royal Bank of Scotland* (1876) 3 R. 586:

The case concerned a crossed cheque for £4,800 purporting to be drawn upon the Clydesdale Bank by Dixon Brothers, who were customers of that bank, in favour of Paul, who was a customer of the Royal Bank.

Paul's clerk presented the cheque, apparently indorsed by Paul, to the Royal Bank, and that bank, regarding the cheque as in order, paid its contents to the clerk. The cheque was then presented by the Royal Bank through the Clearing House to the Clydesdale Bank, and paid by that bank. The Royal Bank retained the cash thus received.

It was then discovered that both the drawer's signature and the indorsement were forged, and the question was, on which of the two innocent banks was the loss to fall.

Held that the loss fell on the Clydesdale Bank.

The position was thus described by Lord Ardmillan (at p. 590): "The cheque was drawn on the Clydesdale Bank and presented to the Royal Bank, and the Royal Bank merely acted as the medium for cashing it. . . . There is no ground for holding that the Royal Bank acted otherwise than in regular course, and in good faith, and they merely were the hands through which the crossed cheque, drawn on the Clydesdale Bank by their customer, found its way to the Clydesdale Bank."

A passage in the opinion of the Lord Ordinary (Rutherfurd Clark) is still more illuminating as to the position of the collecting banker under the common law of Scotland (at p. 589): "The Royal Bank were . . . the mere agents for recovering payment of the cheque. That they paid in anticipation does not . . . affect the position. They took the risk of the cheque being honoured by the pursuers. But when it was honoured, they received the money on account of the person who presented it to them; and having already paid him the money, they are in the same position as if they had first presented the cheque for payment, received the money, and then handed it over to him. *There is no allegation that they were not in good faith, or that they were in any way richer by the transaction.*"

(A sequel to this case gives some further information as to the facts: *Clydesdale Banking Co.* v. *Paul* (1877) 4 R. 626, in which the Clydesdale Bank successfully sued Paul for the amount of the forged cheque, shows that the clerk had represented his employer in Stock Exchange transactions, Paul being a member of the Stock Exchange, that the clerk had engaged in speculative transactions unauthorised by Paul, and that on settling-day the clerk had used the proceeds of the cheque (on which he had himself forged both the drawer's signature and the indorsement) to pay the adverse balance on Paul's Stock Exchange account which would otherwise have led to Paul's being deprived of his membership of the Stock Exchange. The ground on which the action succeeded was that Paul was liable to the extent to which he had been benefited by the fraud of his agent (the clerk).)

The common law as applied in *Clydesdale Banking Co.* v. *Royal Bank of Scotland* may be regarded as having been re-stated in section 82 of the Act of 1882, the main possible difference being that the common law required the collecting banker to have *acted only as an agent*, whereas the statutory provision required that the collecting banker was *receiving payment for a customer*.

Further, in view of the decision in *Clydesdale Banking Co.* v. *Royal Bank of Scotland*, there was no need in Scotland for the amendment of section 82 of the Act of 1882 made by the Act of 1906.

The final paragraph of the article referred to (7–215, above) states:

"The author's conclusion is that there is no Scottish equivalent of conversion, and, for that reason, the English cases are of little assistance in an assessment of the collecting banker's protection. It is sufficient to examine the common law as enunciated in *Clydesdale Bank* v. *Royal Bank*, the ratio of which found expression in section 82 of the 1882 Act, the amendments to which have created confusion in Scotland because they are otiose and in England because there is still considerable doubt about the decision in the *Gordon* case."

It appears that in practice claims are quite frequently made in Scotland against collecting bankers, probably the main reason being that many cheques are now issued by bodies such as Government departments to persons who do not have bank accounts and who therefore negotiate the cheques through the local grocer or public house. In the event of such a claim the collecting banker puts forward section 4 of the Cheques Act 1957 as a defence. However, it would be exceptional for a case to come to court, since (1) the amount is usually quite small and (2) it is usually quite obvious where any negligence lies; the result would normally be a fairly amicable settlement out of court.

In practice, therefore, it seems that the position in Scotland is much the same as that in England and if a case did come to court in Scotland the leading modern English case *Baker* v. *Barclays Bank Ltd.* [1955] 1 W.L.R. 822 would be highly persuasive:

Baker and Bainbridge were trading in partnership under the name "Modern Confections." Bainbridge misappropriated nine cheques amounting to about £1,160 payable to the partnership, by indorsing the cheques and handing them to Jeffcott who paid them into his account at Barclays Bank. Jeffcott also paid into his account cheques payable to, and indorsed by, Bainbridge.

On the occasion when the second of the nine cheques was being paid in, the bank manager asked Jeffcott for an explanation, and Jeffcott's reply was that Bainbridge was the sole partner in Modern Confections and that he, Jeffcott, was assisting Bainbridge with the financial side of the business with a view to going into partnership with him later.

Baker eventually brought an action against Barclays Bank for damages for conversion in respect of the nine cheques.

Held that the bank's defence under section 82 of the Act of 1882 failed because the bank could not show that it had acted without negligence.

Devlin J. said (at p. 825): "Of course, cheques are indorsed over to third parties, but usually for small sums and only occasionally. When the bank manager sees it happening for large sums and quite regularly, I think that he is put on inquiry. . . .

"The explanation which Jones, the bank manager, received when he asked for one was not, I think, one which should have satisfied a bank manager. . . . I do not think that he appreciated the significance of a number of indorsed cheques coming in one after the other, or also the significance that the payments out included substantial sums for cash. If he had, I think that he would have found Jeffcott's story less convincing, for within less than a month Bainbridge had received from people who were presumably his customers cheques amounting to £2,000 or £3,000. Surely a man whose business was on that scale and was done in cheques might have been expected to have a bank account of his own?"

III PROMISSORY NOTES

7–223   A promissory note is defined as "an unconditional promise in writing made by one person to another signed by the maker, engaging to pay, on demand or at a fixed or determinable future time, a sum certain in money, to, or to the order of, a specified person or to bearer" (s. 83(1)). A document which, in addition to the promise to pay a sum of money, included a promise to employ and pay the staff of a business was held not to be a promissory note in *Dickie* v. *Singh,* 1974 S.L.T. 129 (O.H.).

7–224   A simple specimen promissory note might take the form:

"£500   Glasgow,
                                                                  December 1, 1981.
On demand I promise to pay to Peter Piper or order the sum of Five hundred pounds. Value received.

                                                    Mark Anthony"

Alternatives to "On demand" and "Peter Piper or order" would be respectively "Three months after date" and "Peter Piper or bearer."

7–225   An ordinary bank note comes within the definition: it is made by a banker and is payable to bearer on demand.

7–226   A document in the form of a note payable to maker's order is not within the statutory definition unless and until it is indorsed by the maker (s. 83(2)).

7–227   A note is not invalid merely because it contains also a pledge of collateral security with authority to sell or dispose of the security (s. 83(3)). The maker may therefore confer on his creditor a right in security over property, to which the creditor may wish to have recourse if the maker fails to fulfil his promise to pay.

An "inland note" is "a note which is, or on the face of it purports to be, both made and payable within the British Islands." Any other note is a "foreign note" (s. 83(4)).

The provisions of the Act of 1882 relating to bills of exchange apply, with some necessary modifications, to promissory notes (s. 89(1)). There are also some provisions in Part IV of the Act which relate only to promissory notes.

The modifications referred to are as follows:

(a) In applying to promissory notes the provisions of Part II of the Act (*i.e.* the provisions relating to bills of exchange) the maker of a note is deemed to correspond to the acceptor of a bill, and the first indorser of a note is deemed to correspond to the drawer of an accepted bill payable to drawer's order (s. 89(2)).

(b) The following provisions as to bills do not apply to notes, namely, provisions relating to:

(i) presentment for acceptance;
(ii) acceptance;
(iii) acceptance *supra* protest; and
(iv) bills in a set (s. 89(3)).

(c) Where a foreign note is dishonoured, protest of it is unnecessary (s. 89(4)).

The provisions in Part IV of the Act relating only to promissory notes are considered below under these headings:

(a) delivery;
(b) joint and several notes;
(c) note payable on demand;
(d) presentment for payment; and
(e) liability of maker.

The process of summary diligence (7–118 *et seq.*, above), which is left untouched by the Act of 1882 (see s. 98), may be used to enforce payment of a promissory note.

(a) Delivery

A promissory note is "inchoate" (*i.e.* not yet of legal effect) and incomplete until it is delivered to the payee or bearer (s. 84). This differs from the provision as to delivery of a bill of exchange: by section 21 (see 7–41, above) a party to a bill of exchange may *revoke his contract* on the bill until he delivers it, but the bill itself is not inchoate or incomplete.

(b) Joint and Several Notes

A promissory note may be made by two or more makers, and their liability will be "joint" (*i.e.* each will be liable for only his *pro rata* ("proportionate") share) or "joint and several" (*i.e.* each will be liable for the whole amount), according to the tenor of the note (s. 85(1)).

Where a note runs "I promise to pay," and is signed by two or more persons, it is deemed to be their joint and several note (s. 85(2)). This is an instance of a statutory provision rebutting the presumption which is generally applicable in Scots law to debts undertaken by more than one party, namely that *prima facie* ("until the contrary is proved") each party is liable only *pro rata*.

(c) Note Payable on Demand

7–235   A bill of exchange which is payable on demand is normally intended to be presented for payment almost immediately, but a promissory note, though it may be expressed to be payable on demand, is often intended to operate as a continuing security. Special provision is therefore made in section 86 with the twofold purpose of:

(i) protecting an indorser from liability to pay a note if an unreasonably long time has elapsed since he indorsed it; and

(ii) enabling the full negotiability of the note to continue even although an unreasonably long time has elapsed since the note was issued.

7–236   The first purpose is achieved by the provision that where a note payable on demand has been indorsed, it must be presented for payment within a reasonable time after the indorsement; otherwise the indorser is discharged (s. 86(1)). In deciding what is a reasonable time, one must look to the nature of the document, the usage of trade, and the facts of the particular case (s. 86(2)).

7–237   For the full negotiability of the note to exist, the note must be in the hands of a "holder in due course" (see 7–48, above), for only such a person will be unaffected by defects of title. However, one of the conditions which, by definition, a holder in due course must satisfy is that he became the holder of the document *before it was overdue*—a condition which the holder of a note would often be unable to satisfy if the same rules applied to promissory notes as to bills of exchange. The Act therefore provides that where a note payable on demand is negotiated, it is not deemed to be overdue, for the purpose of affecting the holder with defects of title of which he had no notice, merely because it appears that a reasonable time for presenting it for payment has already elapsed since its issue (s. 86(3)). The effect is that the holder of the note may still qualify as a holder in due course, although by the time he received the note it appeared to have been an unreasonably long time in circulation.

(d) Presentment for Payment

7–238   Presentment for payment is not necessary in order to render the *maker* liable to pay the note except in one case, namely, where the note is in the body of it made payable at a particular place; it must then be presented for payment at that place (s. 87(1)). The presentment at that particular place need not be on the day when payment is due (*Gordon* v. *Kerr* (1898) 25 R. 570).

7–239   Presentment for payment, however, is necessary in order to make an *indorser* liable (s. 87(2)). Where a note is in the body of it made payable at a particular place, presentment at that place is necessary in order to make an indorser liable, but if the place of payment is indicated only by way of memorandum, an alternative is available—either presentment at that place or presentment to the maker elsewhere (s. 87(3)).

(e) Liability of Maker

7–240   The maker of a promissory note by making it:

(i) engages that he will pay it according to its tenor; and

(ii) is barred from denying to a holder in due course the existence of the payee and the payee's then capacity to indorse (s. 88).

Further Reading

Scots Mercantile Law Statutes (annual reprint from *The Parliament House Book*) (W. Green & Son) for Bills of Exchange Act 1882 and Cheques Act 1957

Gloag and Henderson, *Introduction to the Law of Scotland*, Chapter XXVI

David M. Walker, *Principles of Scottish Private Law*, Chapters 4.23 and 4.24

J.J. Gow, *The Mercantile and Industrial Law of Scotland*, Chapter 7

Campbell B. Burns, *The Law of Banking* (1976, William Hodge & Co. Ltd.), Chapters 1, 2, 6 and 7

W.A. Wilson, *The Law of Scotland Relating to Debt*, Chapters 5 and 6

Byles on Bills of Exchange, 24th ed. by Maurice Megrah and Frank R. Ryder (1979, Sweet & Maxwell)

J. Milnes Holden, *The Law and Practice of Banking, Vol. 1: Banker and Customer* (3rd ed., 1982, Pitman)

CHAPTER 8

RIGHTS IN SECURITY OVER MOVEABLES

INTRODUCTION

8–01   THE term "right in security," as explained by the leading authority on this branch of Scots law, denotes "any right which a creditor may hold for ensuring the payment or satisfaction of his debt, distinct from, and in addition to, his right of action and execution against the debtor under the latter's personal obligation" (Gloag and Irvine, *Law of Rights in Security, Heritable and Moveable, including Cautionary Obligations*, p. 1).

8–02   "Whatever the special form of the right in security may be, its effect is in all cases to put the party entitled to it in a position of advantage, and to render his power of realising payment of his debt more sure" (*op. cit.,* p. 2). In other words, a creditor holding a right in security is better protected than his debtor's other creditors (referred to as "general" or "ordinary" creditors) because he has at his disposal some means of obtaining payment or performance of the obligation due to him, distinct from, and in addition to, the means—available to the general creditors also—of relying on the debtor's personal credit only.

8–03   From this description of the general nature of rights in security, two immediate consequences follow:

(a) There must be a principal obligation to which the right in security is accessory or subsidiary.

(b) The test of the validity of a right in security is the debtor's bankruptcy: as long as the debtor remains solvent (*i.e.* able to pay his debts), the creditor will have no need to resort to any right in security; he will be content to rely, in common with all the other creditors, on the debtor's personal credit; once, however, it becomes clear that the debtor is insolvent (*i.e.* unable to pay all his creditors in full) the creditor who holds a right in security emerges in an advantageous position; it follows that the general creditors will then, since they will be at a corresponding disadvantage, have an interest to challenge and to have set aside any right in security which has not been validly created.

There are two major classes of rights in security:

First, there are the rights in security which create a *nexus* ("bond") over property—usually over the debtor's property. These give the creditor a *jus in re* ("real right") over the property, and in the event of the debtor's bankruptcy the creditor will be entitled to use the property in payment of the debt which the debtor is personally unable to pay; general creditors will have no share in that property (unless there is a surplus left after full payment of the secured creditor's debt).

Secondly, there are the rights in security which are known in Scots law as "cautionary[1] obligations." These give the creditor a *jus in personam* (literally, "right against a person") or *jus ad rem* (literally, "right with reference to a thing"), *i.e.* a personal right, against some person other than the debtor. In the event of the debtor's bankruptcy the creditor will be entitled to go against that other person for the payment which the debtor himself is unable to make; the general creditors, in contrast, have no such right: they can look only to the debtor himself and his property, and that will mean that, if the debtor is bankrupt, they will get only part-payment of the debts due to them.

This chapter is concerned with rights in security in the first class. Rights in security in the second class are dealt with in Chapter 9, below.

The most important general principle relating to the creation of rights in security over property is that there must be some form of delivery of the property to the creditor—some overt act which will make other parties such as potential general creditors aware of the preference being conferred on the secured creditor: a mere agreement between the debtor and the favoured creditor that the debtor *will* make delivery of the property concerned is not enough to create a valid right in security.

The form of delivery varies according to the type of property. In the case of heritable property delivery has taken the form of registration of the document creating the security (now a "standard security" in accordance with the Conveyancing and Feudal Reform (Scotland) Act 1970) in the Register of Sasines. Under the registration of title system, now being extended area by area under the Land Registration (Scotland) Act 1979, delivery takes the form of an entry on the title sheet in the Land Register of Scotland. In the case of corporeal moveable property (*e.g.* furniture, stock-in-trade and personal effects) delivery normally involves an actual physical transfer of the articles, while in the case of incorporeal moveable property (*e.g.* the right to a debt due, or a fund held by a third party)

---

[1] pronounced "káy-shun-ary."

delivery takes the form of an intimation to the third party that the property in question has been assigned to the creditor.

8–10   There are some exceptions to the general principle as to delivery: in particular, there are, under the common law, hypothecs (see 8–30 *et seq.*, below) which enable a creditor to exercise rights in security over moveable property of which he does not have possession, and various statutes have created exceptions, of which the most important is the floating charge affecting heritable and moveable property of companies, introduced in 1961 and now governed by the Companies (Floating Charges and Receivers) (Scotland) Act 1972.

8–11   Rights in security which are not exceptional are said to be "founded on possession," because they comply with the general principle mentioned above. It is usual to divide securities founded on possession into two classes—those created by express contract and those implied by law. Into the first class fall the standard security over heritable property, and the pledge of moveable property, while securities implied by law are lien and retention.

8–12   Rights in security over heritable property are outside the scope of this book. They are regulated by the Heritable Securities (Scotland) Act 1894, the Conveyancing and Feudal Reform (Scotland) Act 1970 and the Land Registration (Scotland) Act 1979, and are generally regarded as part of the topic of Conveyancing. This chapter is therefore confined to consideration of rights in security over moveables, and is divided as follows:

    I. The general principle—the need for possession;
    II. Exceptions to the general principle—hypothecs and statutory charges;
    III. Securities founded on possession and created by express contract; and
    IV. Securities founded on possession and implied by law—lien and retention.

8–13   The subject-matter is largely common law. Its origins are in Roman law as brought to Scotland principally through the Netherlands and France during the formative era of Scots law.

8–14   English authorities are not a reliable guide, the main distinguishing feature being the insistence of Scots law on the need for delivery. There has, however, been some English influence; for example the term "lien" has been imported from English law. Moreover, the provisions of the Consumer Credit Act 1974 on security provided in relation to "regulated agreements" within the meaning of that Act are almost identical in the two legal systems; they comprise Part VIII of the Act (see 5–261 *et seq.*, above).

I THE GENERAL PRINCIPLE—THE NEED FOR POSSESSION

8–15   The general principle is that there must be some form of delivery of the property to the security holder: mere agreement is not enough to give him the "real" right which will put him in an advantageous position on the debtor's bankruptcy. The general principle is expressed in the maxim *"traditionibus, non nudis pactis, dominia rerum transferuntur"* ("by delivery, not by mere agreements, are real rights in property transferred").

A well-known illustration of the general principle is *Clark &c.* v. *West Calder Oil Co. Ltd. &c.* (1882) 9 R. 1017:

C. and others were the trustees for debenture-holders who had lent money to W. Ltd. As security for the loans, W. Ltd. had assigned to the trustees certain mineral leases in which it was tenant, together with the moveables on the ground.

The assignation was duly intimated to the landlords, but the trustees took no steps to enter into possession of the leases or of the moveables. W. Ltd. went into liquidation.

Held that the trustees had no priority over the leases or moveables, since no possession had followed on the assignation.

"There is no principle more deeply rooted in the law than this, that in order to create a good security over subjects delivery must be given. If possession be retained no effectual security can be granted" (*per* Lord Shand at p. 1033).

(At the date of this case floating charges were not valid rights in security in Scotland.)

Various attempts have been made to avoid the application of the general principle, *e.g.*:

(a) *The trust theory*: The theory was put forward that if the debtor had *agreed* to transfer some specific thing to a particular creditor by way of security, the debtor then held the thing *in trust for* that creditor, the result being that if the debtor became bankrupt the specific thing would not be counted part of the bankrupt's estate but would be made available to the creditor for whom it was supposed to be held in trust.

This theory was finally rejected in *Bank of Scotland* v. *Liquidators of Hutchison, Main & Co. Ltd.*, 1914 S.C. (H.L.) 1; 1913 S.C. 255:

H. Ltd. arranged with its bank, to which it was indebted, that the bank would surrender golf balls to the value of £2,000 belonging to H. Ltd. and held by the bank in security, and would take instead as security a debenture which H. Ltd. was to obtain from J. Ltd., a company indebted to H. Ltd.

The golf balls were duly surrendered, and the debenture was issued by J. Ltd. to H. Ltd., but, before H. Ltd. had assigned the debenture to the bank, H. Ltd. went into liquidation.

The bank claimed the debenture on the ground that H. Ltd. held it merely as a trustee for the bank.

Held that H. Ltd. had, at most, come under a contractual obligation to assign the debenture to the bank, and it was an inaccurate use of language to describe H. Ltd. as a "trustee" of the debenture. The bank's claim was therefore rejected.

The debenture was part of H. Ltd.'s property at the date of the liquidation: the bank had no *jus in re* ("real right"), but only a personal right to compel H. Ltd. to assign the debenture to the bank. Since the assignation had not been obtained by the date of the liquidation, the debenture formed part of the estate for equal distribution among all H. Ltd.'s creditors.

8–20   (b) *Fictitious sale*: The statutory provisions considered under this heading formed part of the codifying Sale of Goods Act 1893 and are now to be found in the consolidating Sale of Goods Act 1979.

8–21   In a contract for the sale of specific or ascertained goods, the property in (*i.e.* the ownership of) the goods passes from seller to buyer at whatever time the parties intend it to pass (Sale of Goods Act 1979, s. 17(1)). In a sale, therefore, the buyer may have a real right (namely, the right of ownership) in goods which still are in the possession of the seller: it is all a matter of the intention of the parties, as gathered from "the terms of the contract, the conduct of the parties and the circumstances of the case" (Sale of Goods Act 1979, s. 17(2)).

8–22   The legislation on sale of goods does not extend to what are here called "fictitious sales," *i.e.* "sales" in which the true position is that the "seller" is obtaining a loan from the "buyer" under a contract which provides that the ownership of the goods is to pass immediately to the "buyer" though the goods are to remain in the "seller's" possession. The express statutory provision which prevents the sale of goods legislation from applying to fictitious sales is:

"The provisions of this Act about contracts of sale do not apply to a transaction in the form of a contract of sale which is intended to operate by way of mortgage, pledge, charge, or other security" (Sale of Goods Act 1979, s. 62(4)).

8–23   The following are two instances of fictitious sales, which were held to be struck at by the corresponding provision in the Sale of Goods Act 1893 (s. 61(4)):

8–24   (i) *Jones & Co.'s Trustee* v. *Allan* (1901) 4 F. 374: J., a bicycle dealer, applied to A., an agent of the Royal Bank of Scotland Ltd., for a loan of £40. A. stipulated for some security as a condition of making the loan. J. offered six bicycles. A. lent the £40 to J. on receiving from J. a promissory note for that amount, payable in three months' time. J. delivered to A. a receipt as for six bicycles amounting to £72 12s. The six bicycles listed in the receipt were not set apart in any way but remained in J.'s shop along with 20 or 30 other bicycles.

After J. had granted a trust-deed for creditors, his salesman sold five of the six bicycles and paid the proceeds to A.

Not many days later J.'s estates were sequestrated, and the trustee in the sequestration successfully claimed repayment of the proceeds from A. on the ground that the transaction was truly an attempt to create a security without giving possession of the goods to the creditor.

8–25   (ii) *Hepburn* v. *Law*, 1914 S.C. 918: L. was pressing his debtor Rev. J.S. Weir for payment of £130. Weir offered security over his furniture. An inventory was made of certain articles of furniture estimated to be of the value of £130 and was incorporated in a document which stated: "Received from L. . . . the sum of £130, in payment of the following specified articles of furniture belonging to me in the Manse of Rayne and sold to him at date hereof." No money passed, nor was possession taken by L. of the furniture.

H., another of Weir's creditors, having obtained a decree against Weir, proceeded to poind Weir's moveables including the furniture specified in the inventory.

Held that L. was not entitled to have the articles in the inventory withdrawn from the poinding.

"The reality of the transaction was . . . nothing but a security, and a bad security, over the furniture. The transaction is exactly struck at by section 61(4) of the statute" (*per* Lord Johnston at p. 921).

(c) *Fictitious hire-purchase transaction*: Section 61(4) of the Sale of Goods Act 1893 was held to have the effect of defeating a fictitious hire-purchase transaction in *Scottish Transit Trust Ltd.* v. *Scottish Land Cultivators Ltd.*, 1955 S.C. 254:

The defenders were public works contractors who were short of money to cover their operating costs. They suggested to the pursuers, whose business included the financing of hire-purchase transactions, that the pursuers should purchase some of the defenders' vehicles and then hire these out to the defenders under an ordinary hire-purchase agreement. The effect was that the defenders received a cheque for £4,000 and became liable to pay to the pursuers £4,600 by 24 monthly instalments with an option to purchase the vehicles for 10s. when all instalments had been paid. The vehicles never at any time left the possession of the defenders.

Payments of the instalments became irregular, and the pursuers brought an action for delivery of the vehicles and payment of the instalments in arrear.

Held that as the transaction had been intended to operate by way of security for a loan, the provisions of the 1893 Act did not apply, that the property in the vehicles had not passed to the pursuers, and that their claim for delivery failed. The pursuers were, however, entitled to repayment of the advances which they had made, under deduction of the instalments received.

(d) *Fictitious lease*: In a genuine lease the landlord has a right in security for the rent over the tenant's *invecta et illata* (literally, "things brought in and things carried in," *i.e.* the tenant's moveables). In *Heritable Securities Investment Association Ltd.* v. *Wingate & Co.'s Trustee* (1880) 7 R. 1094, the lease was a fictitious one: W. & Co. had purported to transfer their shipbuilding yard to H. Ltd., and then to become tenants of H. Ltd. at an annual rent of £4,800. The value in the valuation-roll was only £1,800. In reality, the transaction was a loan by H. Ltd. to W. & Co. of £55,000, repayable in annual instalments of £4,800.

W. & Co. became bankrupt, and H. Ltd. sought to exercise the landlord's right in security over the *invecta et illata*.

Held that the relationship of landlord and tenant never truly existed and that the supposed lease was only an attempt to create a security over moveables which Scots law did not recognise.

(e) *Sasine and other ineffectual procedures*: The ceremony of sasine was used for the transfer of, and granting of security over, heritable property, but it was ineffectual when applied to moveables. An instance is *Stiven* v. *Cowan & Ors.* (1878) 15 S.L.R. 422:

W., of Pitscottie cotton spinning-mills, had obtained an advance of £2,000 from his bank. C. and another were cautioners (*i.e.* were guaranteeing repayment of the advance). In order to give the cautioners a security over the mills and machinery, a ceremony of sasine took place at the mills and deeds were recorded in the Register of Sasines.

In W.'s sequestration the court held that a valid security had been created over the mills themselves and the fixed machinery, but that the transaction as regarded the moveables was an attempt to create a security over moveables *retenta possessione* ("with possession retained")—a form of security not recognised in Scots law.

8–29   Other ineffectual procedures have included an inventory of furniture (*Fraser* v. *Frisbys* (1830) 8 S. 982) and a ceremony of delivery and "instrument of possession" for moveables on a farm (*Roberts* v. *Wallace* (1842) 5 D. 6).

II EXCEPTIONS TO THE GENERAL PRINCIPLE— HYPOTHECS AND STATUTORY CHARGES

8–30   A hypothec is "a real right in security, in favour of a creditor, over subjects which are allowed to remain in the possession of the debtor" (Gloag and Irvine, *op. cit.*, p. 406). It is an exception to the general rule that for the creation of a real right in security (as opposed to a personal right against the debtor), the creditor must have possession of the property.

8–31   In some early authorities the term "hypothec" has a wider meaning, extending to rights in security founded on possession; *e.g.* in Morison's *Dictionary* cases on a solicitor's lien appear under the heading of "hypothec."

8–32   Hypothecs in the now accepted sense of rights in security without possession are recognised by the common law in a limited number of situations. Several statutes have enlarged the exceptions to the general rule by permitting similar rights in security to be created in other situations as defined in the statutes. Such statutory rights are usually termed "charges"; *e.g.* the solicitor's common law hypothec has been extended by statute so that the solicitor may also have a "charge" in certain other circumstances. The most prominent of these charges created by statute is the floating charge by which a company may now grant security over all or any of its heritable and moveable property for the time being.

8–33   Hypothecs are either:

(a) "conventional," *i.e.* created by contract; or
(b) "legal" or "tacit," *i.e.* implied by law.

(a) Conventional Hypothecs

8–34   The only conventional hypothecs recognised by Scots law are bonds of bottomry and bonds of respondentia.

8–35   A bond of bottomry creates a right in security over a ship, whereas a bond of respondentia creates a right in security over a ship's cargo.

8–36   Such bonds can be granted by the master of a ship when the ship is in a foreign port and is unable to proceed on its voyage without an advance of money (*e.g.* to pay for essential repairs or for supplies). The master's first duty is to obtain the advance on the personal credit of the shipowners, and it is only when this fails that the master is entitled to resort to the far more costly mode of raising money on a bond of bottomry or respondentia (*Miller & Co.* v. *Potter, Wilson & Co.* (1875) 3 R. 105, *per* Lord Gifford at p. 111).

Before granting such bonds the master must communicate with the owner of ship or cargo as the case may be, if that is possible. If communication is impossible, the master may act as agent of necessity (see 1–28 *et seq.*, above).

A bond of bottomry entitles the lender to arrest the ship and have it sold so that he may be repaid out of the proceeds of sale. The enforceability of the bond depends on the safe arrival of the ship at its port of destination; if that condition is not fulfilled the lender has no right in security.

Where two or more bottomry bonds have been granted by the master at different stages of the same voyage, the latest bond has priority over the earlier ones, since it was presumably the last loan which enabled the voyage to be completed.

A bond of respondentia entitles the lender to have the cargo attached and sold so that he may be repaid out of the proceeds of sale. The bond can be enforced only if the cargo arrives at the port of destination, but it is not necessary that the ship itself should arrive at that port.

Where a bond of respondentia has been enforced, the shipowner is liable to the cargo-owner for the value of the cargo. An illustration is *Anderston Foundry Co.* v. *Law &c.* (1869) 7 M. 836:

The "Black Eagle" owned by L. and others sailed from Glasgow for Bombay via Melbourne with a cargo including railway chairs shipped by the A. Co. for delivery to an Indian railway company at Bombay.

Having encountered tempestuous weather the vessel put into Rio de Janeiro in a disabled condition. There the master, being unable otherwise to pay the debt of £5,230 incurred for repairs, granted a bond of bottomry and respondentia, payable ten days after the arrival of the vessel at Melbourne.

The holders of the bond failed to obtain payment at Melbourne, and as a result ship and cargo were sold.

Held that the shipowners were liable to indemnify the owners of the railway chairs for the loss caused to them by the sale of the railway chairs at Melbourne under the bond.

Bonds of bottomry and respondentia have become virtually obsolete owing to improvement in communications.

(b) Legal Hypothecs

The recognised legal or tacit hypothecs are those of the landlord, the superior, and the solicitor, and certain maritime hypothecs (also referred to as maritime "liens").

(i) *Landlord's Hypothec for Rent*

A landlord has a hypothec over certain moveables of his tenant called the "*invecta et illata*" (literally, "things brought in and things carried in").

8–45   By the Hypothec Abolition (Scotland) Act 1880 this hypothec was abolished in the case of agricultural property over two acres in extent.

What are invecta et illata?

8–46   The *invecta et illata* are the ordinary corporeal moveables in the premises—the furniture in the tenant's house and the equipment and stock-in-trade in the case of business premises. Money and incorporeal moveables such as stocks and shares, bonds and bills of exchange are not included in the *invecta et illata*.

8–47   The general rule is that the hypothec covers only moveables belonging to the tenant and not moveables belonging to other persons. Thus in *Bell* v. *Andrews* (1885) 12 R. 961 the landlord B. was held not to have a hypothec over a piano belonging to his tenant A.'s minor daughter who had received it as a gift from her grandmother, and in *Pulsometer Engineering Co. Ltd.* v. *Gracie* (1887) 14 R. 316 pumps belonging to P. Ltd. and placed in a tenant's premises for exhibition purposes were held not to be subject to a hypothec in favour of the landlord of the premises. Similarly articles which are on the premises for the purposes of repair do not fall under the landlord's hypothec. On the other hand, in *Scottish & Newcastle Breweries Ltd.* v. *Edinburgh District Council*, 1979 S.L.T. (Notes) 11 (O.H.), kegs belonging to a brewery company and kept temporarily but regularly at a public house were held to be subject to the hypothec on the ground that they were part of the ordinary equipment and stock-in-trade of the public house.

8–48   Difficulties have arisen over articles hired by the tenant. The authorities were reviewed in *Dundee Corporation* v. *Marr*, 1971 S.C. 96:

The Corporation of the City of Dundee, owners of the Scrambled Egg Café in High Street, Lochee, let the premises to M. at a rent payable monthly. The rent fell into arrear, and the Corporation wished to avail itself of its hypothec.

The question was whether a record player belonging to the Ditchburn Organisation (Sales) Ltd. and hired out by that company for four years to M. and his partner fell under the landlord's hypothec.

Held that the record player did fall under the hypothec.

8–49   The early case of *Penson and Robertson, Petitioners*, June 6, 1820, F.C., relating to a hired musical instrument, was taken as clear authority by the court in *Dundee Corporation* v. *Marr*.

8–50   On the other hand, in *Edinburgh Albert Buildings Co. Ltd.* v. *General Guarantee Corporation Ltd.*, 1917 S.C. 239, the landlord's hypothec was held not to extend to a hired piano in a furnished let where the rent was payable in advance: the fact that the hall was let furnished showed that the landlord did not intend it to be furnished by the tenant with articles which would be subject to the landlord's hypothec, and the fact that the rent was payable in advance indicated that the landlord was relying on the tenant's personal credit without contemplating that he would have a right in security over property brought in by the tenant.

8–51   By the Consumer Credit Act 1974 (s. 104) goods comprised in a hire-purchase or conditional sale agreement are in certain circumstances not to be treated as subject to the landlord's hypothec (see 5–260, above).

Rents covered

The hypothec covers one year's rent but not prior arrears:

Young v. *Welsh* (1833) 12 S. 233 (decided before the abolition of the hypothec in agricultural property over two acres in extent): The rent for two farms for the year 1830 was payable at Candlemas and Whitsunday, 1831. In September 1830, when the rent for part of 1828 and the whole of 1829 was still unpaid, the landlord took proceedings to enforce his hypothec in security of the rent for 1830.

The proceeds of the resulting sale of crop and stock considerably exceeded the rent for 1830. W., a creditor of the tenant, arrested purchase money in the hands of Y. and others, who had not yet paid the price of their purchases.

Held that the landlord was not entitled to apply the proceeds of the sale except to the rent for 1830, and that the surplus could be arrested by W.

The usual practice is for the landlord to enforce the hypothec for the rent actually due and in security of the rent to become due at the next term.

Enforcing the hypothec

The procedure for enforcing the hypothec is known as "landlord's sequestration for rent." This type of diligence, which takes the form of an "initial writ" in the sheriff court, must be used within three months of the last term at which the rent to be recovered fell due. The landlord applies to the sheriff court for a warrant, the articles are inventoried and valued by a sheriff-officer, and are ultimately sold by auction under another warrant from the sheriff. Once the inventory has been made, the articles are regarded as being *in manibus curiae* ("in the hands of the court"), and must not be removed by the tenant or by anyone else.

The jurisdiction of the sheriff court in landlord's sequestration for rent is privative (*i.e.* exclusive): proceedings brought in the Court of Session would be dismissed as incompetent. In *Duncan* v. *Lodijensky* (1904) 6 F. 408, therefore, a Russian, who was tenant of business premises in Sauchiehall Street, Glasgow, was held not entitled to argue that the sheriff court at Glasgow had no jurisdiction to grant a warrant in a sequestration for rent brought against him by his landlord.

Warrant to carry back

Where *invecta et illata* have been removed from the premises before the landlord has commenced his sequestration for rent, he may obtain a warrant to have them brought back. An instance is *Nelmes & Co.* v. *Ewing* (1883) 11 R. 193:

E. let premises to Neilson to be occupied as a billiard-room. Neilson obtained on hire from N. & Co. a billiard-table and its equipment, but a few years later fell into arrear with the hire charges payable to N. & Co., with the result that N. & Co. removed these furnishings.

E. then came forward, applying for a sequestration for rent and a warrant to carry back to the premises the items which had been removed.

Held that E. was entitled to enforce the hypothec against the items carried back.

8–57   A warrant to carry back is, however, regarded as an extraordinary warrant, only to be granted with great care and after full consideration of the circumstances said to make it necessary. In particular, only in exceptional circumstances would it be granted without notice being given to the opposite party. *Johnston* v. *Young* (1890) 18 R. (J.) 6 is an instance of a warrant being recalled on an appeal to the High Court of Justiciary from the former small debt court:

Y., tenant of a house owned by J. at Leith, removed in January 1890 to a house in Greenock, where he had obtained work at better wages, and took his furniture with him. His tenancy of the Leith house did not expire until Whitsunday 1890, and J. raised a summons of sequestration in security of the rent to become due and sought a warrant to carry back the furniture. No notice of these proceedings was given to Y.

The sheriff granted the warrant, and a sheriff-officer proceeded to Y.'s new abode and brought back the furniture to J.'s house at Leith.

Held that no circumstances had been set forth to justify the sheriff in granting the warrant without notice to Y.

8–58   A landlord who wrongly executes a warrant to carry back is liable in damages to the tenant. This can occur where there is a genuine dispute as to the amount of the rent due (as in *Jack* v. *Black*, 1911 S.C. 691) or where the circumstances do not justify such extreme measures (as in *Gray* v. *Weir* (1891) 19 R. 25).

(ii) *Superior's Hypothec for Feu-Duty*

8–59   A superior has a hypothec, similar to that of a landlord, over the *invecta et illata* of the owner of the feu. It takes priority over a landlord's hypothec.

8–60   As it is not mentioned in the Hypothec Abolition (Scotland) Act 1880, it probably exists over agricultural as well as over urban property.

8–61   In *Yuille &c.* v. *Lawrie &c.* (1823) 2 S. 155, the court refused to grant an interdict which would have prohibited the execution of a superior's hypothec:

Herbertsons were the owners of heritable property which included a wood-yard and a house. The feu-duty on the property was £276, payable to L. as superior.

Herbertsons became bankrupt and Y. and others purchased materials which Herbertsons had procured for repairing houses belonging to these parties. By Whitsunday 1820 all the materials had in this way been removed from the yard, and L. applied to the sheriff for warrant to bring back and sell the materials on the ground that they were subject to his right of hypothec for the feu-duty due at Whitsunday. The warrant was granted.

Y. and others sought to interdict the execution of the superior's hypothec on the grounds that the superior had no hypothec in urban property and that they had, at any rate, purchased the materials fairly and in good faith.

Held that the superior in urban property did possess a hypothec, and that that right could not be defeated by a sale of the moveables.

(iii) *Solicitor's Hypothec for Costs of Action*

At common law a solicitor who has incurred costs in connection with court proceedings which he has conducted on his client's behalf has a hypothec over any expenses awarded by the court to the client. Expenses are normally awarded to the successful party in an action.

The solicitor can make this right effectual by asking the court to grant the decree for expenses in his own name as "agent-disburser" instead of in the name of the client.

In certain circumstances the solicitor is entitled to be sisted as a party to the action (*i.e.* take his client's place in the action, as pursuer or defender) in order to make his hypothec effectual. The need for this can arise where the parties to the action settle their dispute out of court, with the result that the court proceedings would terminate before reaching the stage at which a decree for expenses would finally be made. An instance is *Ammon* v. *Tod*, 1912 S.C. 306:

A., whose headquarters were in Manchester, was the sole export agent for a U.S. company. A. engaged T. to represent him in Scotland.

T. went to America and there succeeded in filching the agency which A. held from the American company. T. then intimated to A. that he would cease to represent A. in Scotland, and terminated the then current agreement between himself and A., which had still four months to run.

A. raised an action against T. in the sheriff court at Glasgow for interdict, accounting and damages, and obtained a decree for £68 in the accounting and for £100 as damages, with expenses.

T. appealed to the Court of Session, and, while the case was awaiting hearing, A. and T. settled their case without the knowledge or consent of A.'s solicitors, A. agreeing to take £70 in full settlement of all claims of principal and expenses. In accordance with this settlement T. lodged a note craving the Court of Session to assoilzie (*i.e.* discharge) him and to find no expenses due to or by either party.

A.'s solicitors, however, lodged a minute craving that they might be sisted as parties to the action as agents-disbursers in order that a decree might be pronounced against T. in their favour as agents-disbursers.

Held that the solicitors were entitled to be sisted in that way.

At common law a solicitor had no hypothec over property recovered for his client, but a statutory charge, introduced by the Law Agents and Notaries Public (Scotland) Act 1891, improved the solicitor's position in this respect. The statutory provision, now in section 62 of the consolidating Solicitors (Scotland) Act 1980, is that where a solicitor has been employed by a client in an action, the court may declare the solicitor entitled to a charge upon, and a right to payment out of, any property which has been recovered or preserved on behalf of the client in the action. The court has a discretion whether to grant or refuse an application by a solicitor for such a declaration. The Act further provides that where a declaration is made any subsequent acts and deeds of the client, *unless they are in favour of a bona fide purchaser or lender,* are absolutely void as against the charge or right; the effect of this further provision is that the statutory charge is not a full right in security.

(iv) *Maritime Hypothecs or Maritime "Liens"*

8–66 These rights in security over a ship, though often referred to as "liens," are properly hypothecs, because the creditor does not have possession of the ship. They are enforced by a "judicial sale" of the ship (*i.e.* a sale authorised by a warrant from the court). Creditors holding a hypothec have priority over mortgagees of the ship.

8–67 Seamen have a maritime hypothec for their wages, the master of a ship for his wages and disbursements, and a salvor for the amount found due to him for salvage. Where there has been a collision, the owner of the damaged ship has a maritime hypothec over the ship for damages, but there is no such right where one ship has been injured, without any actual collision, through the action of the master and crew of another ship, as was decided in the well-known case *Currie* v. *McKnight* (1898) 24 R. (H.L.) 1; (1895) 22 R. 607:

Three vessels were moored alongside an open quay in the Sound of Islay. The "Dunlossit" was in the centre, and the "Easdale," owned by C., was moored outside the "Dunlossit" by ropes passing over the deck of the "Dunlossit."

One night when, owing to a violent gale, the "Dunlossit" was in danger of being damaged from contact with the other two vessels, her crew cut the mooring ropes of the "Easdale" and stood out to sea. The "Easdale" was driven ashore and damaged.

The "Dunlossit" was sold by McK., who held a mortgage over her, and a competition then arose between McK. and C., the latter claiming a maritime hypothec for the damages due to him as a result of the wrongful action of the crew.

Held that, as there was no hypothec where damage had been done by the crew and not by the vessel itself, C. had no preferable claim on the proceeds of sale.

8–68 The case is especially noted for the observations made in the House of Lords to the effect that the maritime law to be applied in Admiralty questions, such as maritime hypothecs, was the same in Scotland as in England.

8–69 There is no maritime hypothec for repairs executed or necessaries supplied in a home port: *Clydesdale Bank Ltd.* v. *Walker & Bain*, 1926 S.C. 72:

The bank had lent money to the Stevens, owners of the "Arbonne," a ship registered at Leith, and in security for the loan the Stevens had granted a mortgage over the ship in favour of the bank.

Ultimately, when the Stevens were bankrupt, the ship was sold, and shipbrokers at Grangemouth claimed that they had a hypothec over the proceeds of sale for disbursements made on behalf of the Stevens as owners when the ship was lying at that port.

Held that as the services had been rendered in a home port (though not the port where the ship was registered), the shipbrokers had no hypothec.

8–70 The earlier Outer House case of *Constant* v. *Christensen*, 1912 S.C. 1371 (O.H.), is authority for the statement that there is no maritime hypothec for necessaries even when these have been supplied to the ship in a foreign port:

The "Baltic" was owned by Klompus, a Russian, and was registered at a Russian port. The vessel had been mortgaged to Constant, a London shipowner, in security of an advance of £2,400. Klompus failed to pay instalments in accordance with his agreement with Constant, and ultimately the vessel was sold by judicial warrant. The proceeds were £1,255.

Christensen, a coal merchant in Copenhagen, claiming £150 for coal supplied and cash advanced to the master for the purchase of necessaries when the vessel had been in Copenhagen, maintained that he was entitled to be ranked preferably on the proceeds because he had a maritime hypothec.

Held, applying English authorities, that Christensen had no hypothec.

An extensive review of English authorities is to be found in *Bankers Trust International Ltd.* v. *Todd Shipyards Corporation (The Halcyon Isle)* [1981] A.C. 221, which was an appeal to the Privy Council from the judgment of the Court of Appeal in Singapore where English Admiralty law applied:

"The Halcyon Isle," a British ship, had repairs executed on her in New York by T. Later she was arrested in Singapore by B. Ltd., an English bank which held a mortgage on her. She was then sold for a sum insufficient to satisfy all creditors' claims in full, and the question was whether in the distribution of the proceeds T. had a claim preferable to that of B. Ltd.

Held that the question fell to be decided by the *lex fori* (literally, "law of the court") of the country whose court was distributing the proceeds, *i.e.* by the Singapore Admiralty law, which, unlike United States law, did not recognise a maritime hypothec for repairs, and that B. Ltd. had therefore priority over T.

There is no maritime hypothec where the creditor has relied on the personal credit of the shipowner:

Clark v. *Bowring & Co.*, 1908 S.C. 1168: The owners of the ship "Abbey Holme" became bankrupt, and the ship was sold at Glasgow. Shipbrokers B. & Co. claimed a hypothec for payments made in New York for repairs, for the supply of necessaries and for wages due to the crew.

Held that (1) the question whether any claimants had a hypothec over the ship had to be decided by the *lex fori* (*i.e.* Scots law) and not by American law, and (2) the payments made in New York had been made on the credit of the owners and not of the ship and were therefore not secured by any hypothec.

III SECURITIES FOUNDED ON POSSESSION AND CREATED BY EXPRESS CONTRACT

Rights in security which adhere to the general principle of being founded on possession take different forms according to whether the moveables over which they exist are corporeal (*i.e.* physical objects which can be seen and touched such as furniture, stock-in-trade and jewellery) or incorporeal (*i.e.* rights which have no physical substance (though they may be *represented by* documents of title) *e.g.* stocks and shares and claims under policies of insurance). It is appropriate, therefore, to consider separately:

(a) securities over corporeal moveables; and

(b) securities over incorporeal moveables.

8–74   In addition, a brief account is included of certain principles applicable to both corporeal and incorporeal property:

(c) the two general forms of constituting security and their effects; and

(d) the obligations of the security holder.

(a) Securities over Corporeal Moveables

8–75   Securities over ships are subject to special provisions contained in the Merchant Shipping Act 1894. By section 31 of that Act a ship may be mortgaged by an "instrument" (document) modelled on Form B in Part I of Schedule 1 to the Act and recorded by the registrar of the ship's port of registry in the register book. Where several mortgages have been granted over the same ship, priority depends on the order of entry in the register (1894 Act, s. 33). The Act also provides a statutory form for the transfer of a mortgage—Form C in Part I of Schedule 1 to the Act (s. 37).

8–76   Mortgaging of aircraft is also governed by statutory provisions—the Mortgaging of Aircraft Order 1972 (S.I. 1972 No. 1268) and the Mortgaging of Aircraft (Amendment) Order 1981 (S.I. 1981 No. 611), both made under section 16 of the Civil Aviation Act 1968: a Register of Aircraft Mortgages is kept by the Civil Aviation Authority, and priority depends on the order of entry in that register.

8–77   As regards corporeal moveables other than ships and aircraft, the usual mode of creating security is pledge. The general law of pledge is common law, but the form of pledge known as "pawn" has been governed by statute—the Pawnbrokers Acts 1872 and 1960 and the Moneylenders Act 1927, all to be replaced by provisions of the Consumer Credit Act 1974 which are not yet fully in force. The word "pawn" in the Act of 1974 has a wide definition: it means "any article subject to a pledge" (1974 Act, s. 189(1)). It must be kept in mind, however, that these provisions of the 1974 Act apply only where the article is pledged under a "regulated agreement" as defined by the 1974 Act (see 5–50 *et seq.*, above). For an account of the provisions of the 1974 Act (sections 114 to 122) on "pledges," see 5–270 to 5–283, above. In the present chapter only some of the general principles of the common law on pledge will be noted.

Pledge

8–78   Pledge is a contract by which the owner of a corporeal moveable deposits it with a creditor for it to be retained by the creditor until payment or satisfaction of the debt or other obligation due to the creditor. The person who owns the moveable is called the "pledger," and the creditor who obtains the moveable in security is called the "pledgee."

8–79   "The creditor has no right of use during his possession; and the security expires with loss of possession" (Bell's *Principles*, § 206). This passage was considered in *Wolifson* v. *Harrison*, 1977 S.C. 384, to support the view that loss of possession by the pledgee would amount to a material breach of the contract of pledge whereas the pledgee's use of the moveable would not do so:

H. lent money to a company of which W. was a director and principal shareholder. W.'s wife gave to H. four items of diamond jewellery as a pledge for the loan to the company.

W., alleging that H. donated items of the jewellery to his wife and daughter, sought delivery of the jewellery on the ground that the donation and permitted use of the jewellery amounted to fundamental breaches of the contract of pledge.

H. denied that he had donated the jewellery and claimed that he had never regarded the jewellery as being out of his possession and control when worn by his wife or daughter.

Held that (i) in view of H.'s denial of donation and of loss of possession and control, an inquiry, by way of "proof before answer," was required in order to ascertain the facts; and (ii) use of the jewellery did not of itself constitute such a material breach of the contract of pledge as to terminate the contract.

In relation to the second point reference was made to a surprisingly apposite passage in Baron Hume's *Lectures* (Stair Society Publication, vol. 4, pp. 2 and 3). Lord Justice-Clerk Wheatley said (at p. 391):

"This passage exempts from breach of contract of pledge use of the pledge which is in the interest of all concerned. Examples of this are said to be milking of cows or shearing of sheep. On the other hand Hume states that in the absence of a permissive condition to do so the pledgee is not entitled for example to wear the watch or give the jewels to his wife or daughters to appear with at public places and the like. 'If he does otherwise, he must pay a hire for the jewels.' This clearly indicates that in Hume's view such a breach of the contract of pledge is not a fundamental one terminating the contract, which . . . continues to exist subject to an accounting. . . . As I read and apply Hume's view the use of the jewellery *per se*[2] does not constitute a fundamental breach warranting the termination of the contract."

Delivery is essential for the proper constitution of a pledge. A mere "assignation" of furniture, for instance, creates no effective right in security (*Pattison's Trustee* v. *Liston* (1893) 20 R. 806).

The delivery required for pledge may be:

   (i)   actual delivery;
  (ii) symbolical delivery; or
 (iii) constructive delivery.

(i) Actual delivery

There is actual delivery where the pledger physically transfers the moveables to the pledgee. It can also take place where the moveables are confined in a space which can be locked and the key to which is handed to the pledgee; *e.g.* in *Pattison's Trustee* v. *Liston*, above, it seems that the handing over by the debtor P. of the house keys to the lender L. would have given L. a good security over the furniture, had it not been that L. was acting as house-agent for the purpose of letting the house and was

---

[2] "of itself."

held to be in possession of the keys merely in his capacity of house-agent for A.

(ii) Symbolical delivery

8–83   The main instance of symbolical delivery is the bill of lading, which is regarded as a symbol of the goods shipped: transfer of the bill of lading has the same legal effect as actual delivery of the goods themselves; intimation to the master of the ship is not required. See *Hayman & Son* v. *McLintock*, 1907 S.C. 936 (8–91, below).

8–84   A wider form of symbolical delivery is provided for by the Factors Act 1889, extended to Scotland by the Factors (Scotland) Act 1890: a "mercantile agent," who is in possession of "documents of title" to goods with the consent of the owner of the goods, may make as valid a pledge of the documents of title as if he were expressly authorised by the owner of the goods, provided:

(1) he is acting in the ordinary course of business of a mercantile agent when making the pledge;

(2) the pledgee is acting in good faith and has given valuable consideration; and

(3) the pledge is not for a debt already due by the mercantile agent to the pledgee.

In this statutory context the expression "mercantile agent" means "a mercantile agent having in the customary course of his business as such agent authority either to sell goods, or to consign goods for the purpose of sale, or to buy goods, or to raise money on the security of goods," and the expression "document of title" includes "any bill of lading, dock warrant, warehouse-keeper's certificate, and warrant or order for the delivery of goods, and any other document used in the ordinary course of business as proof of the possession or control of goods, or authorising or purporting to authorise, either by endorsement or by delivery, the possessor of the document to transfer or receive goods thereby represented." It is expressly provided that a pledge of the documents of title is to be deemed to be a pledge of the goods.

8–85   Symbolical delivery may be confined to these two instances: certainly other attempts to create rights in security over corporeal moveables by the use of symbols have proved unsuccessful (*e.g. Stiven* v. *Cowan & Ors.* (1878) 15 S.L.R. 422 (8–28, above)).

(iii) Constructive delivery

8–86   The term "constructive delivery" is used where goods are in a store, and the pledger delivers them by addressing a delivery-order to the storekeeper or by indorsing the storekeeper's warrant.

8–87   Constructive delivery is effectual only if the following conditions are satisfied:

8–88   (1) The transfer must be intimated to the storekeeper; a delivery-order or storekeeper's warrant is not, apart from the statutory provision mentioned in 8–84, above, regarded as a symbol of the goods as is a bill of lading. The effect of intimation to the storekeeper is to convert him from a holder for the pledger into a holder for the pledgee. An illustration is *Inglis* v. *Robertson & Baxter* (1898) 25 R. (H.L.) 70; (1897) 24 R. 758:

Goldsmith, the owner of certain whisky in a bonded warehouse in Glasgow, held a warrant granted by the warehouse-keepers, stating that they held the whisky to order of Goldsmith "or assigns by indorsement hereon." He borrowed £3,000 from I. on the security of the whisky and indorsed and delivered the warrant to I. This assignation was not intimated to the warehouse-keepers.

R. & B., creditors of Goldsmith, arrested the whisky in the hands of the warehouse-keepers, and an action of multiplepoinding was raised to decide between the competing claims of I. and R. & B.

Held that as the assignation had not been intimated to the warehouse-keepers, the real right remained in Goldsmith and so was subject to the diligence of his creditors R. & B.

(2) Intimation must be to an actual storekeeper, not merely to an excise officer who holds a key to a bonded warehouse:

Rhind's Trustee v. *Robertson & Baxter* (1891) 18 R. 623: R. was the tenant of a bonded warehouse in Edinburgh. He used the warehouse entirely for his own goods. The warehouse could not be entered without the use of two keys, one of which remained throughout in the possession of R. and the other in the possession of an excise officer.

When R. had a large quantity of wines and spirits in the warehouse, he obtained a loan from R. & B., and as security gave R. & B. delivery-orders addressed to the excise officer. R. & B. intimated these delivery-orders to the excise officer, who then entered R. & B.'s name in his register as transferees of the goods.

R. became bankrupt.

Held that R. & B. had no valid security over the goods since the goods had remained in the possession of R. down to the date of his sequestration.

(3) The storekeeper must be an independent third party, not an employee of the pledger:

Anderson v. *McCall* (1866) 4 M. 765: Jackson & Son were grain-merchants and storekeepers whose foreman, Angus, had the management of their store. They obtained from McC. an advance of £1,250 giving to McC. as security a document which they had obtained from Angus stating that a certain quantity of wheat had been transferred to the account of McC.

Jackson & Son became bankrupt, and the trustee on their sequestrated estate claimed the wheat.

Held that as Angus was an employee of Jackson & Son, the transfer in Angus's books did not amount to delivery.

(4) The goods pledged must be sufficiently identified, *e.g.* by being set apart or separately marked. A case which illustrates this condition and also suggests a possible distinction between symbolical and constructive delivery in this respect is *Hayman & Son* v. *McLintock*, 1907 S.C. 936:

This was an action of multiplepoinding raised for the purpose of determining the right to 1,174 sacks of "Golden Flower" flour lying in H.'s store. The sacks were the balance of various lots of flour which had been purchased by McNairn & Co. from America and then shipped to Glasgow.

McNairn & Co. became bankrupt, and the trustee in the sequestration claimed that all the sacks belonged to McNairn & Co. and therefore formed part of the sequestrated estate, but his claim was resisted by (a) holders of bills of lading (relating in all to 750 sacks), who had lent money to McNairn & Co. on the security of the bills of lading, and (b) holders of delivery-orders (relating in all to 321 sacks) who had purchased and paid for but not yet taken delivery of these sacks, though they had intimated the delivery-orders to H.

Held that (a) the holders of the bills of lading had obtained a good security and were therefore entitled to delivery out of H.'s store of, in all, 750 sacks in preference to the trustee, but (b) the holders of the delivery-orders were not entitled to any such preference since the 321 sacks, not having been separately marked, were unascertained goods, the ownership of which could not, by section 16 of the Sale of Goods Act 1893, pass to the buyers.

Lord McLaren said (at p. 952): "It is perfectly true that a delivery-order is worthless as passing specific property until the goods have been ascertained, but that is exactly the distinction between the effect of a delivery-order for goods on shore and a bill of lading. . . . Such bills, expressed to be for so many bags of flour or quarters of grain on board a particular ship, would pass by blank indorsation from hand to hand while the ship was at sea. How is it possible, consistently with such a state of the law, that the goods could be specifically ascertained, or that the various persons who took such bills of lading could examine and verify the goods while the ship was in mid-ocean?"

8–92 A contrasting case is *Price & Pierce Ltd.* v. *Bank of Scotland*, 1912 S.C. (H.L.) 19; 1910 S.C. 1095:

A limited company of timber merchants borrowed money on the security of delivery-orders for quantities of logs lying in a store. The delivery-orders were intimated to and acknowledged by the storekeepers, and the logs were identified by marks being stamped on them by the storekeepers.

The company went into liquidation and was hopelessly insolvent.

Held that the logs transferred by the delivery-orders had been sufficiently identified, and that the holders of the delivery-orders had therefore a claim prior to that of the liquidators.

(b) Securities over Incorporeal Moveables

8–93 Incorporeal moveables may be transferred in security by a written assignation followed by intimation to the debtor. The word "debtor" here denotes the person who is liable to pay the debt over which security is being granted; *e.g.* where the holder of a life policy wishes to borrow money on the security of his policy, the "debtor" to whom intimation must be given is the insurance company, and where shares in a company are transferred in security, the "debtor" is the company. Merely depositing with a lender a document such as a life policy or a share certificate gives him no valid right in security. Two illustrations are:

8–94 (i) *Strachan* v. *McDougle* (1835) 13 S. 954: In 1825 S. took out a policy of insurance for £1,000 upon his life. In 1830, when he was liable to pay £1,000 to Miss McD., he sent to her a promissory note for £1,000 and the life policy which he intended, as was clear from a covering letter, to be a security for due payment of the promissory note.

In March 1832 S. granted a promissory note for £1,621 10s. in favour of his son, and the following month the son, for the purpose of enforcing payment of this promissory note, arrested the proceeds of the life policy in the hands of the insurance company. Not many days later S. died.

It was not until June 1832 that Miss McD. intimated her right to the insurance company.

Held that the son's arrestment had priority over Miss McD.'s unintimated assignation.

(ii) *Gourlay* v. *Mackie* (1887) 14 R. 403: On December 23, 1885, a firm of coalmasters obtained a loan from M., and in exchange granted to M. a promissory note and a letter stating that they were handing over as security 100 shares of £6 paid in the Holmes Oil Company and were binding themselves to transfer the shares at any time desired by M. The share certificate was at that date delivered to M.

On January 14, 1886, a circular was issued intimating that the coalmasters were in financial difficulties. On the following day M. obtained a transfer of the shares from the coalmasters, and this transfer was immediately intimated to the Holmes Oil Company.

The estates of the coalmasters were sequestrated on January 28, 1886, and G., the trustee in the sequestration, raised an action against M. for reduction of the transfer and for delivery of the share certificate.

Held that the transfer, having been granted within 60 days before bankruptcy to secure a pre-existing debt, was reducible under the Bankruptcy Act 1696.

(The period of 60 days has since been altered to six months (Companies Act 1947, s. 115(3)).)

Life insurance policies and stocks and shares are commonly used as security. Much less usual was the situation in *Liquidator of the Union Club Ltd.* v. *Edinburgh Life Assurance Co.* (1906) 8 F. 1143, where a club, which was a registered limited company, gave to its landlord as security for the lease of its premises an assignation of its uncalled capital of 5s. per share on each of its issued £1 shares; the same general principle as to intimation applied: as the assignation had not been intimated to the individual shareholders who might be called on to pay up the 5s. on their shares, the landlord had no valid right in security and so no preference over the general body of creditors in the liquidation of the club.

Stocks and Shares

There is a marked difference between Scots and English law in relation to the constitution of security over stocks and shares of a company. English law recognises both a legal mortgage (*i.e.* where there is a transfer of the shares to the mortgagee (the lender) and the transfer is registered by the company) and an equitable mortgage (*i.e.* where the share certificate is deposited with the lender, usually accompanied by a "blank" transfer (a transfer signed by the borrower but with the transferee's name left blank so that the transfer may, if necessary, be later completed by the lender and then registered with the company)). The English equitable mortgage does not give the lender absolute security, because the borrower is still registered as the holder in the company's register of members and so might fraudulently sell the shares to a third party who would then, by registering his transfer with the company, become, as far as the company would be concerned, the undisputed owner of the shares.

8–98   Scots law does not recognise any form of "equitable mortgage": the only effective way of granting security over shares corresponds to the "legal mortgage" of English law, *i.e.* the borrower hands over to the lender the share certificate accompanied by a completed transfer which is registered with the company so as to substitute the lender's name for that of the borrower in the company's register of members. This procedure involves expense and publicity (since the company's register of members is open to public inspection), and it is particularly unsuitable in the now rare instances where the shares are only partly paid (since the lender, being himself registered as the holder of the shares, will then be liable to pay to the company any calls made by it on the shares). Alternative procedures are therefore sometimes followed, but none of these is completely satisfactory from the lender's point of view:

8–99   (i) The borrower may merely deposit his share certificate with the lender and give an undertaking to execute a transfer whenever required by the lender to do so. For the time being the lender has no valid right in security at all; the only immediate value of the procedure is that it places an obstacle in the way of the borrower's selling his shares or granting security over them to some other party, but that obstacle is not an insurmountable one, particularly if the borrower is fraudulent.

8–100   The lender has the right to call on the borrower to execute a transfer at any time, and may decide to exercise this right if he sees the borrower getting into financial difficulties. The lender may thereby convert himself from an unsecured creditor into a secured creditor. The chances are, however, that other creditors of the borrower also will become aware of the borrower's financial difficulties about the same time, the borrower will become "notour bankrupt" and a sequestration will follow within the next six months. The transfer of the shares to the lender will then be reducible under the Bankruptcy Act 1696 (as amended by the Companies Act 1947, s. 115(3)) as a "fraudulent preference" (namely, giving security for a previously unsecured debt), and the lender will revert to being an unsecured creditor (see *Gourlay* v. *Mackie*, 8–95, above).

8–101   (ii) The borrower may hand over to the lender not only his share certificate but also a duly executed transfer, ready to be registered with the company whenever the lender wishes to send it in. The understanding between borrower and lender then is that the transfer will not be registered unless the borrower fails to implement his obligations to the lender. In the event of such a failure the lender will be in a position to acquire a right in security over the shares by having them registered in his own name; no further act of the borrower will be required at that stage.

8–102   An instance is *Guild* v. *Young* (1884) 22 S.L.R. 520 (O.H.): Duly executed transfers had been delivered to the creditor, enabling him to register the shares in his own name without further intervention of the debtor. In fact the transfers were not registered until the debtor was on the eve of sequestration.

Held that the transfers were not reducible under the Bankruptcy Act 1696, because the date of the grant of the security was taken to be the date of the delivery of the transfers to the creditor, not the date of their registration with the company.

(iii) The borrower may deposit with the lender, along with his share certificate, a "blank" transfer, in accordance with English practice (see 8–97, above). The intention of the parties is that, so long as the borrower implements his obligations to the lender no further steps will be taken in relation to the shares, but that in the event of the borrower's failure to implement his obligations the lender may then proceed to complete the transfer by inserting his own or another party's name and having it registered with the company.

In Scotland the validity of blank transfers is doubtful because the Blank Bonds and Trusts Act 1696 declares null "bonds, assignations, dispositions or other deeds" subscribed blank in the name of the person or persons to whom they have been granted.

(c) The Two General Forms of Constituting Security and their Effects

The express contracts by which securities founded on possession are constituted may take one or other of two general forms:

(1) The contract may take the form of a transfer to the creditor expressly as a security. Pledge belongs to this category. The creditor obtains possession of the moveables but the right of ownership remains with the person who is granting the security.

(2) The contract may take the form of an *ex facie* ("apparently") absolute transfer to the creditor, so that he appears to become the owner, not merely the possessor, of the moveables. The true nature of the transaction will be explained in a separate document—a "back-letter" or other agreement—in which the creditor will undertake to retransfer the moveables to the debtor when the debt has been repaid.

The two forms have different effects in relation to:

 (i) the creditor's power to sell; and
 (ii) the scope of the security.

(i) *Creditor's Power to Sell*

A creditor to whom moveables are transferred expressly in security (*e.g.* a pledgee) has no implied power to sell them. In order to sell he must either have an express power to do so conferred on him by the transferor or he must obtain a power of sale from the court.

If, on the other hand, the creditor has had the moveables transferred to him *ex facie* absolutely, he does have a power of sale, which he may exercise even without giving notice to the debtor. In the "back-letter" or other agreement the creditor may have undertaken not to sell the moveables or to follow a specified procedure in selling them, and if he violates any such undertaking, he will be liable in damages to the debtor for breach of contract, but the title of the purchaser will not be affected.

(ii) *Scope of Security*

A security which is an express security (*e.g.* pledge) covers only the debt for which it was granted, not debts subsequently incurred. This rule was applied in *National Bank of Scotland* v. *Forbes &c.* (1858) 21 D. 79:

Laing assigned a policy of insurance for £1,000 on his own life as security for a debt of £500 owed by him to F. Laing later incurred a further debt of £700 to F., but in that second transaction no mention was made of the insurance policy.

Laing died a bankrupt, and the proceeds of the policy were claimed by F. as security for both debts.

Held that F.'s title to the proceeds was limited to security for the £500 debt, because the assignation was an assignation specially in security of that one particular debt.

8–112 Where, on the other hand, the security has taken the *ex facie* absolute form, the creditor has a right of retention which enables him to use the security to cover other debts incurred to him by the debtor. An instance is *Hamilton* v. *Western Bank of Scotland* (1856) 19 D. 152 (see 8–185, below).

(d) The Obligations of the Security Holder

8–113 The obligations of the security holder have been more fully developed, both by statutory provisions and by decided cases, in relation to heritable property than in relation to moveable property. The most general of the obligations apply to both types of property. These are:

8–114 (i) The security holder must take reasonable care of the property while it is in his possession. A case which illustrates this principle as applied to shares held in security is *Waddell* v. *Hutton*, 1911 S.C. 575:

By an agreement between W. and H., 599 shares of a limited company came to be held by H. as security for certain advances which he had made to W.

While the shares were standing in H.'s name, the company made an issue of new shares at par, offering proportional quantities of the new shares to persons then on its register. The par value of the shares was £10 and their market value was £20. H. declined to take up more than a certain small number of the new shares offered to him, and he did not inform W. of the offer which had been made.

W. averred that he had thus lost the opportunity of taking up at par 101 shares of £10 each, and brought an action against H. for £1,010 as damages for H.'s breach of duty as security holder.

Held that W.'s averments were relevant, and proof *allowed*.

8–115 The security holder is not, however, liable for the accidental loss or destruction of the property, and neither of these eventualities prevents him from recovering the debt due to himself.

8–116 (ii) On payment of the debt for which the security was given, the security holder must restore to the debtor the exact property which was given in security. If, therefore, the property given in security was a holding of shares in a company, the specific shares (and not merely the corresponding quantity of shares) will require, according to the strict rule, to be restored. If, however, the practice is to the contrary and the debtor knows of and acquiesces in that practice, he cannot insist on specific shares being restored to him. Such was the position in *Crerar* v. *Bank of Scotland*, 1922 S.C. (H.L.) 137; 1921 S.C. 736:

C. obtained advances from her bank and in security transferred to the bank and its nominees numbered shares of J. & P. Coats Ltd. According to its usual practice the bank credited C. with the appropriate quantity of shares without preserving the identifying numbers. This practice was known to and approved by C.'s stockbrokers.

C. brought an action against the bank for an accounting and averred that the bank had sold her shares without her authority, in breach of its obligation to retain the specific shares and to retransfer the identical shares on repayment of the loan.

Held that as C. had to be deemed to have known and acquiesced in the bank's practice, she was barred from insisting in the action.

If the security holder is, on account of his own fault, unable to restore the property, he cannot demand payment of the debt.

(iii) Where the security holder has power to sell the property, he must in the exercise of that power proceed exactly according to the authority conferred on him and with due regard for the interests of the debtor.

(iv) Special rules apply where there are catholic and secondary securities. A catholic creditor is one who holds security over two or more subjects while the secondary creditor holds security over only one of these subjects.

The underlying principle is that a catholic creditor is not entitled to act in such a way as to harm the interests of the secondary creditor without obtaining any advantage for himself.

The main rule is therefore that where the catholic creditor, A, holds a prior security over two items of the debtor's property, X and Y, and the secondary creditor, B, holds a postponed security over item X only, A must use item Y before item X in satisfying the debt due to him, or, alternatively, if he chooses to use item X, must assign to B his own security over item Y. The main rule does not apply where the catholic creditor can obtain some advantage for himself by using item X first; *e.g.* if A held item Y as security for two debts and item X as security for only one of these debts, he would be quite entitled to use item X himself, disregarding the interests of B in that item.

An illustration of the main rule is *Littlejohn* v. *Black* (1855) 18 D. 207:

Robert Black was the owner of heritable property and also of three ships. The Scottish Provident Institution for money advanced to him held security over both the heritable property and the ships. John Black held a postponed security over the heritable property only.

Robert Black became bankrupt and L. was appointed trustee on his estate.

Held that John Black was entitled to insist that the Institution should make good its debt in the first instance out of the ships and should have a claim against the heritable property only for the balance, the effect being to make the heritable property, as far as possible, available for the claims of the secondary creditor.

Lord President McNeill said (at p. 212): "In the ordinary case of a catholic creditor—*i.e.*, a creditor holding security over two subjects, which for the sake of simplicity I shall suppose to be heritable subjects—and another creditor holding a postponed security over one of them, there can be no doubt that the catholic creditor is entitled to operate payment out of the two subjects as he best can for his own interest, but he is not entitled arbitrarily or nimiously to proceed in such a manner as to injure the secondary creditor without benefiting himself—as, for instance, capriciously to take his payment entirely out of the subjects over which there is a second security, and thereby to exhaust that subject, to the detriment of the second creditor, leaving the other subject of his own security unaffected or unexhausted. The second creditor will be protected against a proceeding so contrary to equity, and the primary creditor will be compelled either to take his payment in the first instance out of that one of the subjects in which no other creditor holds a special interest, or to assign his right to the second creditor, from whom he has wrested the only subject of his security."

IV SECURITIES FOUNDED ON POSSESSION AND IMPLIED BY LAW—LIEN AND RETENTION

8–120   The law on this topic is complicated by the lack of uniformity in the definitions of the terms "lien" and "retention." The term "lien" was adopted from English law, and the original Scottish term was "retention," which denoted a wide variety of rights in security including the liens of English law.

8–121   The three categories to be considered are:
   (a) liens;
   (b) retention on property title; and
   (c) retention of debt.

(a) Liens

8–122   A lien is "the right of a creditor to retain moveable property, belonging to the debtor but entrusted to the creditor's possession for some purpose, until the creditor's claims against the debtor are satisfied" (David M. Walker, *Principles of Scottish Private Law* (3rd ed.), Vol III, p. 408).

8–123   According to this definition a lien may be either created by express contract or implied by law. Where created by express contract, a lien comes very near to being a pledge: the point of distinction is that lien will arise out of another contract collateral to it or associated with it, whereas pledge will be a transaction in its own right. Thus *Gloag and Irvine* (after defining "retention") explains (at p. 303): "It is distinguished . . . from an express pledge or other right in security, because it is not, generally speaking, a part of the express contract between the parties, but is implied by law as a tacit condition or corollary of that contract."

8–124   Support for the contractual basis of lien is also to be found in the opinion of Lord Young in *Miller* v. *Hutcheson & Dixon* (1881) 8 R. 489, a case in which a firm of auctioneers was held to have a lien over horses for a balance due to the firm on a series of transactions (*i.e.* a general, as opposed to a special, lien). Lord Young said (at p. 492): "Lien is just a contract of pledge collateral to another contract of which it is an incident. . . . People can contract as to liens as they please."

8–125   Normally, however, liens are not created by an express contract, but are implied by law from various contractual relationships established between parties for other purposes; *e.g.* where the owner of goods hands them over to a person who is to repair them, the repairer has by implication of law a special lien over the goods for his charges, and where parties stand in the relationship of solicitor and client, the solicitor has, by implication of law, a general lien over the client's documents for payment of legal fees.

A lien merely entitles the holder of it to *retain* the moveables; he has no right to sell them unless authorised by the court.

The other main points arising in connection with liens are:

  (i) the need for possession; and

  (ii) the distinction between special and general liens.

(i) *Need for Possession*

Lien is described as a "possessory" right because it exists only where the person claiming it has possession of the moveables.

The following points have been established by decided cases:

(1) Mere custody, as distinct from possession, is not enough. The distinction between possession and custody is brought out in *Gladstone* v. *McCallum* (1896) 23 R. 783:

McC. had been secretary of a limited company until its liquidation, at which time a sum of £17 11s. was due to McC. for his services as secretary. McC. claimed a lien over the company's minute-book. The court, however, ordered him to deliver the minute-book to the liquidator.

Lord McLaren explained (at p. 785): "I think there is no foundation in the facts . . . for any claim either of retention or of lien. Retention, as I understand it, is the right of an owner of property to withhold delivery of it under an unexecuted contract of sale or agreement of a similar nature, until the price due to him has been paid, or the counter obligation fulfilled. Lien, again, is the right of a person who is not the owner of property but is in possession of it on a lawful title, and whose right of lien, if it is not a general one—of which class of liens there are not many examples—is a right to retain the property until he has been compensated for something which he has done to it. In this case there is no right of retention, because the books belong to the company, and there is no right of lien, because they are not in the possession of the respondent but of the company."

It does not matter whether the secretary does his work on the books in the company's premises or in his own private office: the latter situation is covered by *Barnton Hotel Co. Ltd.* v. *Cook* (1899) 1 F. 1190, in which an Edinburgh accountant, who had been secretary of B. Ltd. and whose private office had been registered as the company's registered office, was held not entitled to retain the company's books and papers as security for payment of the amount due to himself for his services as secretary.

(2) The possession must be actual possession, not mere constructive or fictitious possession. In some situations there can be doubts as to whether this requirement is satisfied, *e.g.*:

(a) *Paton's Trustee* v. *Finlayson*, 1923 S.C. 872: P., a potato merchant, entered into contracts with farmers, by which P. acquired the right to use the farmers' ground for growing potatoes, P. supplying the seed potatoes and artificial manure and lifting the crop, and the farmers doing the horse work, supplying straw for covering pits and carting the potatoes to the railway station. P. was to pay £15 per acre to the farmers for the use of the ground.

P. became bankrupt at a time when potatoes were in pits on the farms and P. had not yet paid the agreed sums to the farmers.

Held that the farmers had under the contracts acquired possession of the potatoes, either at the time of planting or at the time of pitting, and that they had therefore a lien over the potatoes until payment of the sums due by P. for the use of the ground.

(There was no doubt about the *ownership* of the potatoes: both parties accepted that the property in (*i.e.* the ownership of) the potatoes had passed to P. when his servants removed them from the soil; the crucial question was whether the farmers had *possession*, an essential factor if they were to be entitled to exercise a lien. If the property in the potatoes had still remained with the farmers, the right which they would have claimed would have been a right of retention (see the passage quoted from Lord McLaren's opinion in *Gladstone* v. *McCallum* (8–130, above) and section (b)—"Retention on Property Title" (8–176 *et seq.*, below)).)

8–134   (b) *Ross & Duncan* v. *Baxter & Co. &c.* (1885) 13 R. 185: Engineers contracted with shipbuilders to put engines into a vessel which was in the course of being built. The engineers claimed a lien over the vessel, and for this purpose they required to establish that they were in possession of the vessel.

Held that the engineers had never obtained possession, because (i) the contract provided that the vessel was to continue in charge of the shipbuilders while the engines were being put in; and (ii) the shipbuilders kept a representative on board during the whole of the time when the work was being done.

Lord Mure said (at p. 197): "This action is laid expressly on an alleged right of lien . . .; and the question depends upon whether the pursuers had obtained actual and exclusive possession of the ship during the time her engines were being fitted in. If they had, then the lien is good, if they had not, it is bad."

8–135   (3) The possession must be lawful possession: it must not have been acquired by fraud, or under a void contract, or by mere accident or mistake. An illustration of the last is *Louson* v. *Craik* (1842) 4 D. 1452:

C., junior, purchased for his father, C., senior, a quantity of yarn which was to be sent by the seller in Montrose to C., senior, in Forfar. C., junior, was a cautioner for his father in the transaction.

By mistake the carrier delivered the yarn to the premises of C., junior.

A few days later, C., senior, became bankrupt, and L., the trustee in his sequestration, applied to the court to have C., junior, ordered to hand over the yarn as part of the sequestrated estate of C., senior. C., junior, proposed to retain the yarn as security for his liability as cautioner.

Held that since the possession of C., junior, was not lawful possession but had only been acquired by mistake, he had no lien.

8–136   (4) The ground of the possession must not be inconsistent with the creation of a lien. An illustration is *Brown* v. *Sommerville* (1844) 6 D. 1267:

Sutherland, the publisher of a periodical entitled "Wilson's Tales of the Borders," delivered stereotype plates to B., a printer, for the purpose of printing from them.

Sutherland became bankrupt, and the trustee in his sequestration sought to have the plates delivered up to him. B. resisted, however, on the ground that he had a lien over the plates for £800 which he alleged was due to him by the bankrupt.

Held that B. had no lien; the plates had been put into his possession for a special and limited purpose and not in order that he might expend work upon them.

(5) When possession is lost, the lien is at an end unless the loss of possession has been due to error or fraud.

The holder of a lien may be compelled by the court to give up possession under reservation of his lien, and the court may authorise the owner to sell the moveables if they are deteriorating in the creditor's hands:

Parker &c. v. *Brown & Co.* (1878) 5 R. 979: Maize belonging to P. in B. & Co.'s stores deteriorated in value through heat and contamination with weevils. P. alleged that the deterioration had been caused by B. & Co.'s negligence. B. & Co. claimed a lien for their charges.

Held that P. was entitled to a warrant from the court authorising him to sell the maize on condition that he consigned the proceeds as the court should direct.

(ii) *Distinction between Special and General Liens*

A special lien is one which entitles the holder of the moveables to retain them until satisfaction of an obligation arising out of the contract through which he obtained possession of them. A general lien, on the other hand, entitles the holder of the moveables to retain them until a balance due to him on a whole course of dealing is discharged. For instance, a carrier, whose lien is a special lien, is entitled to retain a parcel until he receives payment of his charge for the carriage of that particular parcel (but not any outstanding charges for the carriage of parcels previously carried), whereas a solicitor, whose lien is a general lien, is entitled to retain his client's papers until his business account and ordinary outlays for a whole series of transactions are met.

Normally only special liens are allowed; general liens are recognised only in a limited number of situations, and the law does not favour their extension to new situations. Hence, in *Laurie* v. *Denny's Trustee* (1853) 15 D. 404, a store-keeper was held not entitled to retain grain as security for payment of the balance on a whole account but only for payment of the charges applicable to the particular grain then in his store, and there are observations in *Findlay (Liquidator of Scottish Workmen's Assurance Co. Ltd.)* v. *Waddell*, 1910 S.C. 670, and other cases, to the effect that an auditor or other accountant has no general lien comparable to that of a solicitor but is only entitled to retain papers until he is paid for the particular piece of work for which he obtained possession of the papers.

Examples of special liens

The ordinary rule in any contract for the performance of services is that, by the doctrine of mutuality, if the party performing the services has obtained possession of moveables belonging to the employer, he is entitled to retain them until he is paid for the work which he has done. The rule does not apply where the relationship between the parties is that of employer and employee (arising out of a contract *of service*), since an employee has merely custody and not possession of his employer's property: the relationship must be that between employer and independent contractor (arising out of a contract *for services*).

8–142   *Meikle & Wilson* v. *Pollard* (1880) 8 R. 69 is a well-known illustration of special lien: M. & W. were "accountants and business agents" who were employed by Smith, a baker, to recover debts for him. For this purpose books and documents belonging to Smith were handed over to M. & W.

When Smith became bankrupt and P., the trustee in the sequestration, sought delivery of the books and documents, M. & W. were held entitled to refuse to deliver them until their account for the work which they had done was paid.

8–143   This case was followed in *Robertson* v. *Ross* (1887) 15 R. 67—a case in which a bank-agent who had acted as factor for a landed proprietor had in that capacity obtained possession of documents relating to the estate.

8–144   *Meikle & Wilson* v. *Pollard* was also referred to in *Findlay (Liquidator of Scottish Workmen's Assurance Co. Ltd.)* v. *Waddell* (8–140, above), but the decision in that case was that under the Companies (Consolidation) Act 1908 the liquidator was entitled to an order for the delivery to himself of the company's books and papers in the accountant's possession, "without prejudice to any lien" which the accountant might have.

8–145   For another instance of a special lien, see *Paton's Trustee* v. *Finlayson* (8–133, above).

Examples of general liens

8–146   General liens are recognised by usage of trade in a limited number of situations.

8–147   English cases may be referred to in this connection: if a general lien is in a particular situation clear and well-established in England, comparatively slight proof of the practice in Scotland will be enough to establish its existence also in Scotland: such was the attitude taken by the Court of Session in *Strong* v. *Philips & Co.* (1878) 5 R. 770:

A firm of Turkey red dyers in Glasgow had been in the habit of employing a firm of packers there to pack goods.

When the dyers became bankrupt and S., the trustee in the sequestration, claimed delivery of yarn which was in the packers' hands, the packers were held entitled to a lien on the yarn for the general balance due to them by the dyers, such a general lien being seemingly recognised by usage of trade in Glasgow and being well settled in England.

8–148   Although usage of trade is the normal basis for claiming a general lien, it is possible for such a lien to be created by the express terms of a contract. An instance is *Anderson's Trustee* v. *Fleming* (1871) 9 M. 718: bleachers employed by manufacturers to bleach and finish goods were held in that case to have a general lien constituted by a notice sent out on each occasion when the bleachers returned goods; the notice stated: "N.B.—All goods received by us are subject to a lien, not only for the work done thereon, but also for the general balance of our accounts." (According to observations made by the judges, the court would have held (if that had been necessary) that by usage of trade the bleachers had a general lien extending to charges for all goods sent to them within the previous year.)

The most prominent of the general liens recognised by usage of trade are those of the factor or mercantile agent, the banker, and the solicitor.

Lien of factor or mercantile agent

A factor or mercantile agent has a general lien over all the property of his principal which has come into his possession in the course of his employment. It covers the amount due by the principal to the agent as a result of the agency (including the agent's salary or commission and any liabilities incurred by the agent on the principal's behalf). An instance of a corn factor having a general lien, so that he was able to retain commission for an earlier transaction out of the proceeds of sale in a later transaction, occurred in *Sibbald* v. *Gibson* (1852) 15 D. 217 (see 1–132, above).

The lien of a factor or mercantile agent does not extend to a debt due to him by his principal but arising out of a transaction other than an agency transaction: an illustration is *Miller* v. *McNair* (1852) 14 D. 955:

Clarke employed Miller, commission merchant in Glasgow, to sell certain goods to Smith. Miller instructed Smith not to pay the price to Clarke but to hold it on behalf of himself, Miller.

Shortly afterwards Clarke became bankrupt, and there was a competition for the price between McNair, the trustee in the sequestration, and Miller who claimed that he had a lien for a debt due to him by Clarke on a distinct transaction.

Held that Miller had no such lien, and the trustee's claim was therefore preferred.

An auctioneer is classified as a mercantile agent and so has a general lien (*e.g. Miller* v. *Hutcheson & Dixon* (1881) 8 R. 489 (8–124, above)). It is not necessary that the articles should be brought to the auctioneer's own premises: he is entitled to exercise a lien even if he conducts the sale in his principal's premises (*e.g. Mackenzie* v. *Cormack*, 1950 S.C. 183, where a sale of furniture by auction took place in the seller's castle).

A stockbroker has a similar general lien, entitling him to retain his principal's documents in security of a general balance, and not merely in security of the amount due for the particular transaction to which the documents relate (*Glendinning* v. *Hope & Co.*, 1911 S.C. (H.L.) 73).

A factor managing an estate is not within the category of factor or mercantile agent, and he does not have a general lien. Hence, in *Macrae* v. *Leith*, 1913 S.C. 901, L. who had acted as a factor on an estate was held to have no lien on leases and other estate documents which he held.

Lien of banker

A banker has a general lien over negotiable instruments, such as bills of exchange (including cheques) and promissory notes, belonging to his customer, provided they have come into the possession of the banker in his capacity of monetary agent; it does not cover documents which are non-negotiable (*e.g.* share certificates) or negotiable instruments which have been lodged with the banker for some specific purpose inconsistent with the creation of a lien (*e.g.* bills of exchange lodged for safe-keeping only).

8–156   The lien may, in circumstances where it would otherwise exist, be excluded by agreement, express or implied, *e.g.*:

Robertson's Trustee v. *Royal Bank of Scotland* (1890) 18 R. 12: R. had from time to time deposited certain bonds, which were negotiable instruments, with his bank, and had received receipts from the bank stating that the bonds were held "for safe-keeping on your account and subject to your order." There was, however, evidence to show that on each occasion when a bond was deposited R. was seeking an overdraft or additional overdraft corresponding to the exact amount of the bond deposited.

Held in R.'s sequestration that the terms of the receipts were not sufficient to exclude the creation of a lien in view of the inference which could be drawn from the other evidence; the bank was therefore entitled to retain the bonds as security for payment of the balance due to it by R.

Lien of solicitor

8–157   A solicitor has a general lien over his client's papers in his possession, for payment of amounts due to him by his client.

8–158   The early case which is regarded as having established the solicitor's lien is *Ranking of Hamilton of Provenhall's Creditors* (1781) Mor. 6253, in which the "hypothec" of Wilson, a writer to the signet, on the papers of a bankrupt was found to be preferable to another creditor's infeftment on the bankrupt's lands, although the infeftment was prior in date to the writer's account. (This particular aspect of the solicitor's lien has since been altered by statute: by the Conveyancing (Scotland) Act 1924 (s. 27), where there is a creditor with an existing heritable security already recorded, a solicitor acting for the owner or for other creditors with postponed securities cannot acquire a lien which will be effective against the first-mentioned creditor.)

8–159   There is a wealth of Scottish cases on the solicitor's lien; some of the points established by them are as follows:

8–160   *Over what papers does the lien exist?* It exists over title-deeds (*Ranking of Hamilton of Provenhall's Creditors*, above), and in general over all other deeds and documents, including share certificates. It exists over the client's will, even when both client and solicitor are dead:

Paul v. *Meikle* (1868) 7 M. 235: Mrs Duncan by her will, which had been prepared by her solicitor, M., conveyed heritable property to her son. She owed M. £35 10s.2d. for professional services.

On Mrs Duncan's death, her son conveyed the property to P. by a disposition containing the usual assignation of writs clause, but M.'s representatives claimed that they were entitled to retain Mrs Duncan's will until the business account was paid.

Held that they were entitled to do so.

8–161   The lien does not extend to a company's register of members, because it would interfere with the public's right of access to the register (*Liquidator of the Garpel Haematite Co. Ltd.* v. *Andrew* (1866) 4 M. 617).

What does the lien give the solicitor security for? It gives him security for his business account and for outlays made in the ordinary course of business, such as fees to counsel, but not for cash advanced to the client:

Christie v. *Ruxton* (1862) 24 D. 1182: C. entered into a contract to sell his heritable property for £300, and the title-deeds were handed over to R., a solicitor, to enable him to carry the contract into effect on behalf of the purchaser.

Before the price was paid, the purchaser became bankrupt, and C. brought an action against R. for the return of the title-deeds.

Held that R. had a lien for the business account incurred to him but not for £35 advanced to the purchaser.

In *Liquidator of Grand Empire Theatres Ltd.* v. *Snodgrass,* 1932 S.C. (H.L.) 73, the House of Lords held that a solicitor's lien did not extend to accounts incurred by the solicitor on his client's behalf to English solicitors and auctioneers, at least where the solicitor had not himself paid the accounts or become personally liable to pay them.

Is the solicitor entitled to a lien where he acts for both lender and borrower? Where a solicitor acts for both lender and borrower he is bound to reveal to the lender any lien which he has over the borrower's title-deeds; otherwise he is barred from afterwards setting up that claim against the lender:

Gray v. *Graham et al.* (1855) 2 Macq. 435; 18 D. (H.L.) 52 (*sub nom. Gray* v. *Wardrop'a Trustees* (1851) 13 D. 963):

Gray, a solicitor, was in possession of the title-deeds of his client Charles Cunningham, who owed him £609 12s.7d. Part of that amount consisted of Gray's fee for preparing a heritable security over the client's house for £700 borrowed from the client's sister, Janet Cunningham. Gray had acted for both Charles and Janet in the transaction.

Charles Cunningham died bankrupt, and Gray claimed a preference on account of his lien over the title-deeds.

Held that, as Gray had never communicated to Janet Cunningham that he held a lien over the title-deeds, he was barred from claiming a preference as against her.

It is, however, only in a question with the lender that the solicitor is barred from claiming his lien:

Drummond v. *Muirhead & Guthrie Smith* (1900) 2 F. 585: Waldie purchased heritable property, and the title-deeds were delivered to his solicitors, M. & G.S. Waldie then borrowed money from trustees, who were also clients of M. & G.S.

Waldie became bankrupt, with a large business account owing to M. & G.S. D., the trustee in the sequestration, raised an action against M. & G.S. to have it declared that M. & G.S. had no lien against him over the title-deeds.

Held that D. was not entitled to challenge M. & G.S.'s lien: only the trustees, as lenders, could have challenged the lien.

What is the effect of the lien? A peculiarity of the solicitor's lien is that it exists over papers which cannot be made available for payment of the debt due to the solicitor: *e.g.* the fact that the solicitor has title-deeds in his possession does not entitle the solicitor to sell the client's heritage and obtain payment out of the proceeds. Title-deeds and other documents over which the lien exists are said to be *extra commercium* ("outside commerce"), *i.e.* they are not articles which can be traded in.

8–167   The practical value to the solicitor of his lien is that by retaining the documents in his possession he will cause inconvenience to his client (because the client will be unable to produce evidence of his right to heritable or moveable property to other parties) and thus may induce the client to pay what is due to himself.

8–168   In some situations, however, the solicitor is deprived of the right even to retain the documents:

8–169   (1) The solicitor is not entitled to stop the procedure in a litigation by withholding the documents relating to that litigation from his client:

Callman v. *Bell* (1793) Mor. 6255: C. employed B., a writer to the signet, to raise an action of declarator of marriage and other proceedings. The court decided against C., and B., on her behalf, appealed. While the action was at the appeal stage, C. notified B. that she was to change her solicitor and insisted that B. should deliver to her all the papers relating to the court proceedings. B. refused to comply on the ground that he had a "hypothec" over the papers in his possession until he obtained payment of his account.

Held that B. was not entitled to withhold the papers from C.

8–170   (2) If the client is sequestrated, the solicitor is not entitled to withhold documents from the trustee in the sequestration. However, on surrendering the documents to the trustee, the solicitor becomes entitled to a preference in the division of the estate.

8–171   The position under the common law is seen in *Skinner* v. *Henderson* (1865) 3 M. 867, in which a solicitor was held bound to deliver up to the trustee in his client's sequestration all the deeds in his possession affecting the bankrupt's estate, but was entitled in doing so to reserve all the rights which he would have had against the estate by retaining the deeds.

8–172   The statutory provisions which would now apply to the trustee in a sequestration in relation to title-deeds and other papers in the hands of the bankrupt's solicitor are the Bankruptcy (Scotland) Act 1913, section 76 (which directs the trustee to take possession of the title-deeds and other papers and documents), and section 97 (which vests the estate in the trustee subject to existing securities). The combined effect of these provisions is that express reservation of the lien is not necessary (*per* Lords Sorn and Guthrie in *Garden Haig Scott & Wallace* v. *Stevenson's Trustee*, 1962 S.C. 51, a case in which for different reasons the court held that a firm of solicitors was not entitled to a lien giving them preference in a client's sequestration).

8–173   A solicitor would similarly require to surrender documents to a liquidator if the client were a company which was being wound up (Companies Act 1948, ss. 243 and 258).

8–174   There is little authority on the precise preference to which the solicitor becomes entitled on surrendering the documents: *Miln's Judicial Factor* v. *Spence's Trustees*, 1927 S.L.T. 425 (O.H.) (a case concerning surrender of a trust deed for creditors to a judicial factor), suggests that expenses of administration of the sequestration or liquidation would have priority over the solicitor's claim, but it is an open question whether the solicitor would rank before other preferential creditors.

(3) The court has an equitable control on the exercise of a lien, and this control enables the court to intervene to prevent an abuse of the solicitor's lien (*e.g.* where the estate would be likely to suffer great prejudice if the lien were exercised or where the solicitor unreasonably refused to surrender the papers in return for a good substituted security). There are observations to that effect in *Ferguson and Stuart* v. *Grant &c.* (1856) 18 D. 536, though in the circumstances of that case the court found no sufficient grounds to intervene so as to compel the solicitor to accept the security of caution in place of his lien.

(b) Retention on Property Title

This right is based on property (*i.e.* on ownership), not on possession; it may be exercised by a creditor who owns the moveables, even though they are in the possession of another party. It may be explained in this way (David M. Walker, *Principles of Scottish Private Law* (3rd ed.), Vol. III, p. 414): "Where one party has a title of property to some subject, heritable or moveable, but is under a personal obligation to transfer or convey it to another, he is entitled to retain it in security of the payment of any debt, or the performance of any obligation, due to him by the party to whom he is bound to convey."

Illustrations of this right in relation to corporeal moveable property fall into two main categories:

(i) contracts for the sale of goods where the property in the goods does *not* pass to the buyer at the time when the contract is made; and

(ii) rights in security created by an express contract which is *ex facie* ("apparently") absolute, though truly in security (see 8–107, above).

(i) *Sale of Goods*

The rule of the common law was that goods which parties had agreed should be sold remained the property of the seller until they were delivered. In the interval between the agreement and the delivery the seller was therefore in a position which satisfied the requirements of the right of retention as described in the quotation given above: he had a "title of property" to a moveable subject but was "under a personal obligation to transfer or convey it" to the buyer. He was therefore entitled to "retain it in security of the payment of *any* debt, or the performance of *any* obligation due to him" by the buyer.

The statutory rules now applicable under the Sale of Goods Act 1979 to the passing of property from seller to buyer usually have the effect of denying to the seller this right of retention which the common law allowed him. The Act (re-enacting provisions of the Sale of Goods Act 1893) provides that where there is a contract for the sale of specific or ascertained goods the property in them is transferred to the buyer at such time as the parties to the contract intend it to be transferred (s. 17(1)), and that, *unless a different intention appears*, the rule to be applied, where there is an unconditional contract for the sale of specific goods in a deliverable state, is that the property passes to the buyer when the contract is made, and that it does not matter that the time of payment or of delivery or both be postponed (s. 18). The "terms of the contract, the conduct of the parties and the circumstances of the case" must always be looked at (s. 17(2)): a "different intention" may then appear: *e.g.* the parties may have agreed that the property is not to pass to the buyer until delivery. A right of retention can therefore still arise, provided the contract is such that it expressly or by implication excludes the ordinary statutory rule. The use of retention of title clauses in contracts of sale has in recent years become much more common as a result of the Court of Appeal's judgment in the *Romalpa* case (*Aluminium Industrie Vaassen B.V.* v. *Romalpa Aluminium Ltd.* [1976] 1 W.L.R. 676—see 4–129, above).

8–180 A simple illustration of the common law position is *Mein (Landale and Company's Trustee)* v. *Bogle and Company* (1828) 6 S. 360: B. sold to L. three lots of sugar. L. received delivery, but did not pay the price. L. then bought a fourth lot of sugar from B. and paid the greater part of the price for that lot but became bankrupt before the lot was delivered to him.

Held that B. was entitled to retain the fourth lot of sugar in security for payment of the price of the first three lots. The court emphasised that its judgment did not rest on the special point that the full price for the fourth lot had not been paid but on the general ground that B. had a right of retention over the fourth lot in security of the balance due by L. to B. in respect of all four lots.

8–181 Two further cases, also decided under the common law, may be mentioned for the purpose of illustrating how this right of retention operates where third parties have become involved (*e.g.* through sub-sales):

8–182 (1) *Melrose* v. *Hastie* (1851) 13 D. 880: H. sold to Bowie 1,533 bags of sugar which were at that time held by a store-keeper as H.'s property. Bowie then re-sold 761 of the bags to M., and M. obtained delivery of 170 of them, which left 591 bags still in the warehouse in H.'s name. The price was duly paid both in the sale to Bowie and in the sub-sale to M., but the delivery-orders used in the transactions were not intimated to the store-keeper.

On two further occasions H. sold quantities of sugar to Bowie, and these had been only partly paid for when Bowie became bankrupt, with a balance due to H. for the second and third purchases of £4,000.

Held that H. was entitled to retain the 591 bags as security for payment of the balance of £4,000. As there had been no actual or constructive delivery, H. had remained the undivested owner of these bags, and his right was a right of retention on a property title, and not a lien.

8–183 (2) *Distillers Co. Ltd.* v. *Russell's Trustee* (1889) 16 R. 479: D. Ltd. sold certain lots of whisky which were lying in D. Ltd.'s warehouse. Several sub-sales followed over the next few years, and on the occasion of each transaction a delivery-order was intimated to D. Ltd.

R., a wine-merchant, was the last subvendee in the chain. He became bankrupt, and the trustee in his sequestration demanded delivery of the whisky, which had continued to lie in D. Ltd.'s warehouse. D. Ltd. claimed a right to retain the whisky, which was valued at some £200, to set it off against the outstanding balance of some £2,000 which D. Ltd. claimed was due to it on its account with R.

Held that D. Ltd. had continued to be the undivested owner of the whisky and therefore had a right of retention over it for the balance due by R.

(Intimation of the delivery-orders did not operate as constructive delivery in this case, because the warehouse was D. Ltd.'s own warehouse, not that of an independent party. The effect of the intimation was merely to notify D. Ltd. that the right to demand delivery had passed from the original or earlier purchaser to the next subvendee in the chain.)

(ii) Ex Facie *Absolute Transfer*

The effect of an *ex facie* absolute transfer is to make the security-holder apparently the owner of the goods, though in a separate document he will declare that the transaction is truly a transfer in security and not an absolute transfer, and so he will undertake to retransfer the goods when they are no longer required as security. The transferee, as apparent owner, has a right to retain the goods for a general balance: his right is not restricted to the particular transaction for which the security was first given.

An illustration of how a right of retention can arise from an *ex facie* absolute transfer of a delivery-order is *Hamilton* v. *Western Bank of Scotland* (1856) 19 D. 152:

In December 1853 Miller applied to the bank to discount a bill of exchange for £650 which was payable in May 1854. Having discounted the bill, the bank required security from Miller for the advance which it was thus making, and Miller gave the bank a delivery-order for 300 cases of brandy to be "collateral security" until the bill matured.

In May 1854, Miller arranged with the bank for a renewal of the bill to the extent of £500 until August and for the continuation of the collateral security until then. In July 1854 Miller obtained a further £400 from the bank.

In September 1854 Miller became bankrupt, and H., the trustee in the sequestration, raised an action against the bank for delivery of the brandy and for damages for wrongful detention of it after payment of the bill for £500 in August. The bank claimed that it was entitled to retain the brandy as security for the advance of £400 which was still outstanding.

Held that as the transaction had not been one of pledge but had been the transfer of a right of ownership, the bank was entitled to retain the brandy until *all* advances were repaid.

The distinction between retention on a property title and lien is explained by Lord Curriehill (at p. 163) thus: "Retention entitles a party who is the owner, or *dominus* of property, to withhold performance of some personal obligation to transfer his right of ownership to another, until the latter perform a counter obligation; whereas lien entitles a party who is in possession of what is another's property, to continue to withhold it from its real owner, until the latter perform a counter obligation. And, on the other hand, the corresponding right to demand possession of the property, on the counter obligation being performed, is, in the former case, merely a personal right, or *jus crediti;* while, in the latter case, it is the real right of property."

8–187 On the difference in principle applicable to a case of pledge and to the case of an *ex facie* absolute transfer, Lord Deas observed (at p. 166): "In a case of pledge the property remains with the pledger, and, consequently, if the article be pledged for a specific debt, the right to withhold it is limited to that debt. But in a transference like this the property passes to the transferee, subject only to a personal obligation to reconvey, and consequently the right of retention for the general balance, competent by the law of Scotland to a party in whose favour the property has been transferred, comes to be applicable—just as happens in the case of an absolute disposition to heritage, or an intimated assignation to a debt, qualified by a back-bond."

8–188 (Most of the cases on *ex facie* absolute transfers have been concerned with heritable property; by the Conveyancing and Feudal Reform (Scotland) Act 1970, however, the *ex facie* absolute disposition is no longer a permissible form for creating a heritable security.)

(c) Retention of Debt

8–189 This right is based on the doctrine of mutuality in the law of contract: a party who has not performed his part of a contract cannot insist on the other party's paying what is due under the contract. "In the exercise of a right of retention a party to a mutual contract may withhold payment due to the other in security of performance by the other of the obligations due by him" (David M. Walker, *Principles of Scottish Private Law* (3rd ed.) Vol. III, p. 416).

8–190 Exercise of this type of retention brings compensation (also called "set off") into operation: the lesser claim will be extinguished and the greater claim will be diminished *pro tanto* ("to the extent of so much," *i.e.* to the extent of the lesser claim).

8–191 The following are two illustrations:

8–192 (i) *Johnston* v. *Robertson* (1861) 23 D. 646: J. contracted with a parochial board to erect a poor-house for £1,742. By the contract J. undertook to complete the work by March 31, 1856, under a "penalty" of £5 for every week during which the work remained unfinished after that date.

J. brought an action against the board for an alleged balance of the contract price and also for payment for extra work. The board alleged that, since the work had not been completed by March 31, 1856, J. was, under the "penalty" clause, liable to the board for a greater sum than the sum sued for.

Held that (1) the stipulated "penalty" was liquidate damages and not penalty, and was therefore enforceable; and (2) in a mutual contract the principle applicable was that one party was not entitled to enforce performance without showing that he had himself performed his part of the contract.

8–193 (ii) *Gibson and Stewart* v. *Brown and Co.* (1876) 3 R. 328: G. & S., storekeepers, received from B. & Co., grain importers, a quantity of corn to be stored.

After re-delivering the greater part, G. & S. presented a petition to the sheriff for warrant to sell the remainder and apply the proceeds towards payment of their charges, which B. & Co. refused to pay.

B. & Co. stated as a counterclaim damage to a greater amount done to the corn re-delivered, owing to the neglect of G. & S. B. & Co., by minute, restricted their counterclaim to the amount of G. & S.'s claim.

Held that set off was competent, since both claims arose out of the same contract; and objection that this was an attempt to set off an illiquid against a liquid claim *repelled.*

The general rule is that, for the operation of retention, both claims must arise out of the same contract; retention was not allowed, for instance, in *Smart* v. *Wilkinson,* 1928 S.C. 383:

S. sold his medical practice to W. for £500, payable in three instalments. W. paid the first two instalments, but when sued for the balance of the price, *viz.,* £200, he pleaded that he had been induced to enter into the contract by false and fraudulent misrepresentations made by S. regarding the practice, and he counterclaimed for £500, his estimate of the loss which he had suffered as a result of S.'s representations.

Held that as W.'s claim did not arise out of the contract, but out of an alleged delict which had preceded the making of the contract, it could not be pleaded as a defence and was not a competent counterclaim.

The right of retention is not an absolute right but is subject to equitable control by the court. It may be excluded by the court where it would produce an inequitable result, and on the other hand it may be extended, in the interests of equity, to situations where the claims do not arise out of the same contract; *e.g.* in bankruptcy, if a debtor of the bankrupt has an illiquid claim against him he is entitled to withhold payment of a liquid debt which he owes to the bankrupt, even though the debts arise out of different contracts: it would be inequitable that the debtor of the bankrupt should be required to pay his own debt in full to the bankrupt and then receive only a dividend on the debt due to himself by the bankrupt.

Further Reading

Gloag and Henderson, *Introduction to the Law of Scotland,* Chapters XIII (part) and XX

David M. Walker, *Principles of Scottish Private Law,* Chapters 5.30 and 5.40

W.A. Wilson, *The Law of Scotland Relating to Debt,* Chapters 7, 8 and 13

David M. Walker, *The law of Contracts and related obligations in Scotland* (1979, Butterworths), Chapter 33 (part)

J.J. Gow, *The Mercantile and Industrial Law of Scotland,* Chapter 4

Gloag and Irvine, *Law of Rights in Security, Heritable and Moveable, including Cautionary Obligations,* Chapters I and VII-XVIII (1897, William Green & Sons)

Enid A. Marshall, *Scottish Cases on Rights in Security over Moveables* (1981, Author)

CHAPTER 9

CAUTIONARY OBLIGATIONS

INTRODUCTION

9–01 A CAUTIONARY[1] obligation may be shortly described as an obligation of guarantee. Its purpose is to protect a creditor from loss if his principal debtor fails to pay or fails to perform some other obligation: the cautionary obligation gives the creditor the right to recover his loss from a person other than his principal debtor, that other person being referred to as a cautioner.[2]

9–02 As with rights in security over a debtor's property (see Chapter 8, above), the ultimate test of the validity of cautionary obligations comes with the bankruptcy of the principal debtor, but whereas the creditor holding security over some item of his debtor's property has a real right (*i.e.* a *jus in re* ("right in a thing")), the creditor who is protected by a

---

[1] pronounced "káy-shun-ary."
[2] pronounced "káy-shun-er."

cautionary obligation has a personal right (*i.e.* a *jus in personam* ("right against a person")) against the cautioner. Just as the value to the creditor of his right in security over property depends on the price at which the property may be sold, so the value of a cautionary obligation depends on the solvency of the cautioner.

The word "cautionry"[3] is used to denote the branch of the law relating to cautionary obligations.

The law on this subject is mainly common law; a few statutory provisions, notably those of the Mercantile Law Amendment Act Scotland 1856, are mentioned below at the appropriate points.

Three parties are involved in a cautionary obligation:

A, the creditor, a person to whom a debt must be paid or for whom some service must be performed;

B, the principal debtor, the person who has incurred the debt or who is to perform the service; and

C, the cautioner, the person who guarantees that if B fails to pay or perform, he, C, will be liable to A.

Other terms which are used are "principal obligant" for B, and "guarantor" or "surety" for C. The last-mentioned is the usual English law equivalent of the Scots law term "cautioner," just as "suretyship" in English law corresponds to "cautionry" in Scots law. However, the terminology in this branch of the law is not kept rigidly distinct in Scottish legal literature; see, *e.g.*, the use of "surety" in the definitions quoted below from Bell's *Principles* (9–15) and from *Gloag and Irvine* (9–16).

The Scots law of cautionry is founded on the Roman law contract of *fidejussio* ("guarantee").

As to the value of English decisions Lord Justice-Clerk Cooper in *Aitken's Trustees* v. *Bank of Scotland*, 1944 S.C. 270 (see 9–108, below) commented (at p. 279):

"Now I readily agree, as was pointed out by George Joseph Bell in his Commentaries ((7th ed.) vol. I, p. 364), that the general principles of the Scots Law of cautionary obligations are 'nearly the same' as those of the English Law of suretyship, and that this statement is as true to-day as when it was first made. I also agree that, in so far as it is related to these general principles, the *ratio decidendi*[4] of a decision in the one country may have value, and even persuasive authority, in the other; and for this limited purpose many English decisions are cited in our Scottish works on rights in security. But it is only for this limited purpose that English decisions may be used, and through our unfamiliarity with a different legal system we shall incur the risk of being misled if we attempt to follow English decisions not merely when they enunciate general principles common to the two countries but when they apply these principles to the specialties of other branches of English Law and to the special facts of individual cases."

Cautionary obligations are part of the law of contract, and are therefore subject to the general principles of the law of contract. Only the specialties affecting cautionary obligations as distinct from other

---

[3] pronounced "káy-shun-ry."
[4] basic reasoning.

contractual obligations are dealt with in this chapter. They come under the following headings:

    I. General nature of cautionary obligations;
   II. Kinds of cautionary obligations;
  III. Constitution and form;
  IV. Validity;
   V. Extent of cautioner's liability;
  VI. Rights of cautioners; and
 VII. Termination of cautionary obligations.

I GENERAL NATURE OF CAUTIONARY OBLIGATIONS

9–10   It is of the essence of a cautionary obligation that it is accessory to another obligation. There must always be a principal obligation either already in existence or contemplated at the time when the cautionary obligation is undertaken, and it is essential for the continuance of the cautionary obligation that the principal obligation should also continue. Accordingly, if the principal obligation is a nullity, there can be no valid cautionary obligation. Similarly, if the principal obligation which was contemplated never in fact comes into existence, there will be no cautionary obligation, and if the principal obligation is brought to an end (*e.g.* by prescription or novation), the cautionary obligation will automatically terminate with it.

9–11   If, however, a cautioner knows, at the time when he undertakes his cautionary obligation, that the principal obligation is invalid, he will be bound by the cautionary obligation:

Stevenson v. *Adair* (1872) 10 M. 919: Mackenzie, a minor, entered into an indenture of apprenticeship with S. A., as cautioner, bound himself to indemnify S. to the extent of £50 for Mackenzie's omissions or defaults during the apprenticeship. A. knew that Mackenzie's father was alive and had not consented to the indenture.

Mackenzie abandoned his apprenticeship.

Held that S. was entitled to recover damages from A. in accordance with the cautionary obligation.

The case may be explained by the principle of personal bar.

9–12   For the fuller understanding of the general nature of a cautionary obligation, consideration is given below to:

  (a) some definitions of cautionary obligation; and

  (b) some obligations which are in some respects similar to, and in other respects different from, cautionary obligations.

(a) Definitions of Cautionary Obligation

9–13   There is no statutory definition. The following are amongst the best-known definitions appearing in books of authority:

9–14   (i) "By a cautionary obligation one becomes bound that the principal debtor shall pay to the creditor the debt which, by the principal obligation, he engages to pay; or that he shall deliver or perform what, by that principal obligation, he has undertaken"—Bell's *Commentaries*, Vol. I, p. 364.

(ii) Cautionry is "an engagement or obligation, as surety for another, that the principal obligant shall pay the debt or perform the undertaking for which he has engaged"—Bell's *Principles,* § 246.

(iii) "A cautionary obligation or guarantee is an obligation accessory to a principal obligation, to answer for the payment of some debt or the performance of some duty, in case of the failure of another person, who is himself, in the first instance, liable to such payment or performance. . . . The person who gives the promise is the cautioner, surety, or guarantor; the person to whom the promise is given is the creditor; and the person whose liability is the foundation of the contract is the principal debtor"— Gloag and Irvine in their authoritative *Law of Rights in Security, Heritable and Moveable, including Cautionary Obligations* (published in 1897), p. 642.

(b) **Similar Obligations**

It is sometimes difficult but important to distinguish between a cautionary obligation and:

- (i)   an independent obligation;
- (ii) delegation;
- (iii) indemnity; and
- (iv) representation as to credit.

(i) *Independent Obligation*

Cautionary obligations are always accessory, never independent, obligations, but the distinction is sometimes narrow.

One party, X, may for the benefit of another party, Y, undertake an obligation to a third party, Z, without necessarily becoming a cautioner for Y. X's obligation would be an independent obligation unless the circumstances showed that it was intended that Y was to be primarily liable.

The question of whether X's obligation is a cautionary obligation or an independent one becomes important when Z wishes to enforce X's obligation. If X is a cautioner, Z will require to produce writing to prove the existence of the cautionary obligation, and he will require to allow to X the rights to which cautioners are entitled. The test to be applied is: "On whose credit did Z rely?" If the answer is that he relied solely on X's credit, the obligation will be held to be an independent one, whereas if he relied on the credit of both X and Y, and primarily on the credit of Y, the obligation will be held to be a cautionary one.

Stevenson's Trustee v. *Campbell & Sons* (1896) 23 R. 711: A builder who had certain building contracts in hand became unable to complete them without financial assistance. Arrangements were made by which the builder became the servant of S., a property speculator who was to pay for the materials to be ordered by the builder for the completion of the contracts.

C. & Sons, metal merchants, supplied material to the builder on the understanding that S. was to pay for it.

S. died before payment was made, and S.'s estate was sequestrated. The trustee in the sequestration rejected C. & Sons' claim for the price of the material on the ground that S. had been merely a cautioner and that there was no valid evidence of the cautionary obligation.

Held that C. & Sons had a claim in the sequestration on the basis that S. had been the buyer of the material.

Lord President J.P.B. Robertson said (at p. 714): "The present case is in substance and very nearly exactly that stated by the Court in *Birkmyr* v. *Darnell* (1 Smith's Leading Cases, 10th ed. 287), 'If two come to a shop and one buys and the other . . . says, Let him have the goods, I will be your paymaster . . . this is an undertaking as for himself and he shall be intended to be the very buyer, and the other to act but as his servant.'"

(ii) *Delegation*

9–22 Delegation (the substitution of a new debtor with the creditor's consent) is distinct from cautionry because in delegation the obligation of the original debtor is extinguished, whereas in cautionry the creditor gains the benefit of an additional obligant against whom he may have recourse on the failure of the principal debtor, who remains primarily liable.

9–23 There is a presumption against delegation, *i.e.* until the contrary is proved, the new party is regarded as an additional obligant.

(iii) *Indemnity*

9–24 A contract of indemnity is one by which one party undertakes to relieve another of loss incurred by that other in certain circumstances. For instance, X may in a contract of indemnity undertake to relieve Z of any liability which Z may incur in his transactions with Y. The contract of indemnity between X and Z is not accessory to the contract governing the transactions between Y and Z, and is therefore distinct from a cautionary obligation.

9–25 Guarantee policies issued by insurance companies are contracts of indemnity which come very close to cautionry. The insurance company agrees to pay any loss which may be incurred by the insured through the default of the insured's debtor. The distinction between such a policy and a cautionary obligation is important when the question arises of whether all material facts have been disclosed by the insured to the insurance company. A contract of insurance, being a contract *uberrimae fidei* ("of the utmost good faith"), will be voidable unless full disclosure has been made, whereas there is no such rule generally applicable to cautionary obligations. A further point of distinction is that a guarantee policy is an arrangement made by the *creditor* with the insurance company, whereas in cautionry it is usual for the arrangements for the guarantee to be made by the principal debtor.

(iv) *Representation as to Credit*

9–26 A representation as to credit may be briefly described as a statement made by one party, X, to another party, Z, as to the trustworthiness of a third party, Y. This brings out the similarity between such a representation and a cautionary obligation. A fuller description of a representation as to credit, based on section 6 of the Mercantile Law Amendment Act Scotland 1856, is:

a representation or assurance "as to the character, conduct, credit, ability, trade, or dealings of any person, made or granted to the effect or for the purpose of enabling such person to obtain credit, money, goods, or postponement of payment of debt, or of any other obligation demandable from him."

"Ability" in that context has been construed as referring to financial ability (*Irving* v. *Burns*, 1915 S.C. 260, in which a statement relating to a company commencing business that £3,000 of the capital had been subscribed was held to be a representation as to credit within the statutory definition).

The Act requires such representations, as well as cautionary obligations, to be in writing.

A representation as to credit, unlike a cautionary obligation, does not give rise to liability on the part of the person making it, merely because the person obtaining credit comes to be in default. The person making the representation will incur no liability for a representation honestly and carefully made, even although it may in fact be false. Where liability is incurred, it will be on the ground of delict, not contract, and will take the form of damages for fraud or for negligence.

II KINDS OF CAUTIONARY OBLIGATIONS

There are three kinds of cautionary obligations:

    (a) those constituted by a contract of cautionry to which the creditor is a party;

    (b) those constituted by a contract of cautionry to which the creditor is not a party; and

    (c) those arising by implication of law.

(a) Contract of Cautionry to which Creditor is Party

Here a distinction must be made between proper and improper cautionry.

In proper cautionry the cautioner is bound to the creditor expressly as cautioner for the principal debtor.

In improper cautionry the cautioner is bound to the creditor as a co-obligant jointly and severally with the principal debtor. This enables the creditor to hold either the cautioner or the principal debtor liable *in solidum* ("for the full amount"). The true relationship of principal debtor and cautioner will rest on some other provision; *e.g.* one of the parties may be described expressly as "cautioner and co-principal," or the contract may contain a clause of relief conferring on one of the apparent co-principals (the cautioner) the right to recover from the other (the principal debtor) the amount which he has had to pay to the creditor, or in the case of a cash credit bond one of the apparent co-principals (the principal debtor) may have the sole right to operate the account though both are made liable for the sum advanced. Wherever it can be established that one of the co-obligants is truly a cautioner for the other, he is entitled to the rights of a cautioner (see 9–80, below).

(b) Contract of Cautionry to which Creditor is not Party

9–33 The relation of principal debtor and cautioner may be constituted in an agreement separate from the agreement between these two parties on the one hand and the creditor on the other hand. As long as the creditor does not know the true relationship between his two debtors, he need not treat the one as cautioner for the other: he simply has two debtors. If, however, he comes to know of the true relationship of the two debtors, he must observe all the duties which are imposed on a creditor in a cautionary obligation.

(c) Implication of Law

9–34 Cautionry arises by implication of law where, without there being any contract of cautionry, two parties are liable for the same debt, the liability of one party being primary and the liability of the other being secondary.

9–35 Instances of this type of cautionry occur in the law of partnership and in the law relating to bills of exchange: in partnership the individual partners are in the position of cautioners for the debts of the firm, *i.e.* they are liable to pay the firm's debts if the firm itself fails to do so; in the case of a bill of exchange which has been accepted, the acceptor is in the position of principal debtor, and the drawer and indorsers are in the position of cautioners, liable to pay the amount of the bill to the holder if the acceptor fails to pay.

III CONSTITUTION AND FORM

9–36 The constitution of cautionary obligations is governed by the principles of the common law of contract, but their form depends partly on statute.

(a) Constitution

9–37 The rules of offer and acceptance apply.

9–38 The offer may be an undertaking, addressed by the intending cautioner to a particular creditor, to guarantee the debt or actings of a third party (the principal debtor). The contract will be concluded by either an express acceptance, addressed by the creditor to the cautioner, or an acceptance implied by actings, such as the giving of credit by the creditor to the principal debtor on the faith of the cautioner's undertaking.

9–39 Alternatively, the offer may be contained in a letter or other document, not addressed to anyone in particular, but handed by the intending cautioner to the prospective principal debtor on the understanding that the latter will show it to a prospective creditor, *e.g.*:

"The bearer, Mr Fortune, we have known for a long number of years, and have pleasure in testifying as to his good and straightforward character, and guarantee that his financial standing is all in order . . . to the extent of from £1,600 to £1,800" (*Fortune* v. *Young*, 1918 S.C. 1 (9–48, below)).

Actings by the creditor on the faith of such document then constitute acceptance.

(b) **Form**

By section 6 of the Mercantile Law Amendment Act Scotland 1856 all cautionary obligations must be in writing and must be subscribed by the person undertaking them or by some person duly authorised by him; otherwise they have no effect.

The Act does not state that the writing must be probative. Probably it does not require to be probative, but the point is undecided. It is, however, clear that:

(i) If there is an improbative writing and the creditor has acted in reliance on it, a binding cautionary obligation will have been formed:

National Bank of Scotland Ltd. v. *Campbell* (1892) 19 R. 885: A bank agreed to make advances to a firm of builders in Oban on their obtaining a guarantee from C., a shipmaster in Oban.

A formal letter of guarantee was prepared by the bank and handed to the builders so that they would have it executed by C.

The builders obtained C.'s signature and afterwards got two persons to sign as "witnesses" although these persons had neither seen C. sign or nor heard him acknowledge his signature.

The builders then returned the document to the bank, and the bank advanced money to them on the faith of the guarantee.

Later, when the bank sought to enforce the guarantee against C., C. pleaded that he was not bound because the document was not probative.

Held that as C. had signed the document and delivered it to the builders who were acting as agents for the bank in this matter, the guarantee was binding on C. in accordance with the doctrine of *rei interventus* ("actings following on" (an informal document)).

(ii) If the cautionary obligation is *in re mercatoria* ("on a commercial matter"), the writing need not be probative:

B.O.C.M. Silcock Ltd. v. *Hunter*, 1976 S.L.T. 217: A company supplying feedstuffs to grain merchants obtained from H., the individual principally interested in a company of grain merchants, a document by which H. personally guaranteed all such sums as should be due by his company to the suppliers. The document was signed in the presence of one witness only.

Feedstuffs to the value of £45,198·91 were supplied, and the grain merchant company failed to discharge its indebtedness. H. refused to pay under the guarantee on the ground that the document was neither holograph nor tested.

Held that, being a writ *in re mercatoria*, the document was binding on H.

The opinion of the First Division was that (at p. 224):

"Before a guarantee will be held to qualify as a writing *in re mercatoria* it must be granted in a course of dealing between merchants. Further, . . . it must . . . be seen from all the circumstances which surrounded its origin to be an informal writing of the kind which merits its treatment as a mercantile writing."

IV VALIDITY

Questions as to the validity of cautionary obligations are mostly decided according to the general principles of the law of contract. The following matters, however, call for special attention:

(a) capacity and authority of the cautioner;
(b) disclosure by the creditor; and
(c) the situation where there are several cautioners for the same debt.

(a) Capacity and Authority of Cautioner

9–45 The ordinary rules as to capacity and authority are applied with a greater strictness.

9–46 Accordingly, a minor (who either has no curator or acts with his curator's consent) has the capacity to enter into a cautionary obligation, but there is a strong presumption that in doing so he has suffered lesion, which makes the obligation reducible within the *quadriennium utile* (literally, "the useful four-year period," *i.e.* the four years after the attainment of majority).

9–47 Similarly, an agent usually requires express authority if he is to undertake a cautionary obligation on behalf of his principal. Authority would be implied only if the granting of guarantees was part of the ordinary business (*e.g.* if the principal were a guarantee association). An ordinary commercial agent has no such authority.

9–48 Partners, as agents of their firm, and directors, as agents of their company, likewise normally require special authority for the undertaking of a cautionary obligation which will be binding on the firm or company. An instance relating to partnership is *Fortune* v. *Young,* 1918 S.C. 1:

Y., a partner of the firm James Tait & Co., signed the firm name, without the authority of the firm, on a letter guaranteeing the financial standing of an applicant for the lease of a farm.

As a result of the letter, the farm was let to the applicant.

On the subsequent bankruptcy of the applicant, an action was brought against Y. as an individual to enforce the guarantee.

Held that Y. was liable.

Lord Justice-Clerk Scott Dickson said (at p. 6): "It is not suggested that this cautionary obligation was within the scope of the business of the firm. . . . If it had been sought to make the firm or the partner other than the one who signed the firm-name liable, there might have been a good defence. . . . A partner who signs an obligatory document outwith the scope of his copartnery does not bind the firm, but he undoubtedly binds himself."

9–49 The Partnership Act 1890 (s. 7) provides that where one partner pledges the credit of the firm for a purpose apparently not connected with the firm's ordinary course of business, the firm is not bound, unless he is in fact specially authorised by the other partners, but that provision does not affect any personal liability incurred by an individual partner.

(b) Disclosure by Creditor

9–50 When a cautionary obligation is being undertaken, the creditor must ensure that he makes such disclosure to the cautioner as the law requires, so that the cautioner will be able to assess the degree of risk which he is to run as cautioner.

9–51 In this connection a distinction is made between:
(i) the guarantee of a debt; and
(ii) a fidelity guarantee.

(i) *Guarantee of a Debt*

Where the principal obligation is the payment of a sum of money, the creditor need not give the cautioner any information or warning as to the extent of the risk which he is undertaking; *e.g.* a bank is not bound to disclose to a prospective cautioner the state of the principal debtor's bank account which the cautioner is to guarantee:

Young v. *Clydesdale Bank Ltd.* (1889) 17 R. 231: Y., who had been in the habit of granting accommodation bills to his brother for sums between £300 and £400, gave a letter to his brother's banker in which he guaranteed "payment of any advances made and which may hereafter be made" to his brother. Y. had signed the letter without reading it, and the bank-agent had not informed Y. that his brother's account was overdrawn to the amount of about £5,000.

The bank sued Y. for £5,303 0s.9d. under the letter of guarantee, and Y. brought an action of reduction of the letter.

Held that there had been no duty on the bank-agent to inform Y. of the state of his brother's account.

Lord Adam (at p. 240) said: "It is well settled that it is not the duty of a bank to give any information to a proposed cautioner as to the state of accounts with the principal. That is quite settled. If the cautioner desires to know the state of accounts with the principal it is his duty to ask and to inform himself, but no duty lies upon a party seeking security to give any information of that kind."

If, however, the creditor spontaneously or in answer to questions gives information to the cautioner, his statement must be true; otherwise the cautioner will be freed from liability.

(ii) *Fidelity Guarantee*

In a fidelity guarantee the creditor is usually an employer, the principal debtor is usually his employee, and the cautioner is guaranteeing that the employee is honest: the cautioner's liability will arise if the employee proves dishonest. The cautionary obligation here, therefore, is in substance an insurance against the employee's dishonesty, and the same rule of law applies to fidelity guarantees as to contracts of insurance, namely, that full disclosure of material facts must be made. For instance, an employer who knows that an employee has not been trustworthy in the past must disclose that fact to the prospective cautioner; the result of non-disclosure would be that the cautioner would not be liable:

French v. *Cameron* (1893) 20 R. 966: F. engaged Jamieson as a commercial traveller.

After his first journey Jamieson was about £32 short in his cash account, and his explanation was that his pocket had been picked at a procession in Dublin. F. accepted that excuse, and an arrangement was made for retention off wages to make up the deficiency.

Jamieson then left for a second journey. At first he sent the proper returns, but on the latter part of the journey he failed to do so, and on his return he was found to be about £30 short. He admitted that he had been "drinking and misbehaving himself," and he begged forgiveness. F. consented to give him another chance out of sympathy for his wife, but only on condition that he found security for his deficiency and for his future transactions.

Jamieson approached C. and B., stating that F. had resolved to promote him to a position of greater trust and responsibility on condition that he procured cautioners. C. and B. then signed a cautionary obligation for £50.

Thereafter Jamieson again misconducted himself and was dismissed. F. raised an action against the cautioners.

Held that because of F.'s failure to disclose the circumstances in which the cautionary obligation was demanded the cautioners were not bound.

9–55   The duty of full disclosure continues throughout the course of the fidelity guarantee: if, for instance, the employee is guilty of some dishonesty after the guarantee has been given, the employer must inform the cautioner of that fact; otherwise the cautioner would cease to be liable:

Snaddon v. *London, Edinburgh and Glasgow Assurance Co. Ltd.* (1902) 5 F. 182: By a bond of guarantee S., a publican, of Devonside Inn, Tillicoultry, became cautioner to an insurance company for Jack, who was appointed the company's superintendent at Alva in December 1896.

The following year these events took place: on August 11 Jack embezzled £25 by putting a forged indorsement on a cheque which had been entrusted to him by the company so that he might hand it over to a policy-holder. He also sent to the company a forged receipt by the policy-holder for the money. On September 25 he confessed the crime to the company, and was suspended. On October 8 he absconded. On October 11 the company intimated to S. that he was liable for £25 under the bond of guarantee.

Held that the company had failed to intimate Jack's criminal conduct timeously to S., and was therefore barred from claiming against S. under the bond of guarantee.

Lord Young said (at p. 186): "On the general rules of law if any company of this kind employs an employee whose honesty is guaranteed by another, and if the employee commits a crime such as forgery, and his employers get to know of it, they are not entitled to retain him a day in their employment under the guarantee, unless they inform the cautioner, and he is prepared to continue the guarantee on the footing that the employee remains in their service."

9–56   These rules as to disclosure by the creditor in a fidelity guarantee are justified on the ground that an employer, both before he engages an employee and during the course of the employment, has a greater opportunity than the cautioner has of discovering any faults in the employee.

(c) Obligations by Several Cautioners

9–57   There may be several cautioners guaranteeing the same principal debt. If so, the creditor must ensure that, after one cautioner has undertaken liability, the co-cautioners also do so, since there is an implied condition that each of the several co-cautioners undertakes liability only if the others do so. The underlying reason is that the co-cautioner who undertook liability would be deprived of his expected right of relief against co-cautioners if they did not sign (see 9–96 *et seq.*, below).

The rule applies even where the co-cautioners are jointly and severally liable to the creditor (provided the creditor knows that they are really cautioners):

Paterson v. *Bonar* (1844) 6 D. 987 (a majority decision of the whole Court of Session): A bond in favour of a bank stated that M. (who was the principal debtor), C., P. and W. (who were cautioners) were bound "conjunctly and severally" to pay £1,500 to the bank in respect of advances to be made by the bank to M. W. did not sign the bond.

M. became bankrupt, owing the bank upwards of £2,000, and the bank sued P. for £1,500.

Held that since one co-cautioner had not signed the bond, the others were not liable for the advances made under it.

"None are bound until all have subscribed" (*per* Lord Jeffrey at p. 1015).

The result is the same if the signature of a co-cautioner has been forged:

Scottish Provincial Assurance Co. v. *Pringle and Others* (1858) 20 D. 465: The S. Co. agreed to give a loan of £150 to X upon a personal bond to be granted by X and four other persons, P., V., K., and M., as joint and several obligants. The bond was given to X so that he might obtain the signatures of the other obligants.

P., V., and K. signed the bond. M. did not sign it, but X forged M.'s signature and that of two witnesses.

X then returned the bond to the S. Co., and the money was paid to him.

X became bankrupt, and the forgeries were discovered.

The S. Co. sued P., V., and K.

Held that P., V., and K. were not liable.

Judicial cautionry (*i.e.* cautionary obligations required in various court proceedings) is an exception: in that case a cautioner is bound even though the signature of his co-cautioner is forged (*Simpson* v. *Fleming* (1860) 22 D. 679).

V EXTENT OF CAUTIONER'S LIABILITY

A cautioner is never liable for more than the whole loss actually resulting from the principal debtor's failure. The whole loss would include not only the capital sum due by the principal debtor but also unpaid interest and any expenses reasonably incurred by the creditor in trying to enforce the debt against the principal debtor (*Struthers* v. *Dykes* (1847) 9 D. 1437).

Apart from that general principle, the extent of the cautioner's liability depends on the terms of his undertaking. Three matters call for special attention:

(a) the interpretation of cautionary obligations;

(b) the situation where the cautionary obligation is limited as to amount; and

(c) the situation where the cautionary obligation is limited as to time.

(a) Interpretation of Cautionary Obligations

A cautionary obligation is construed in the narrowest sense which the words will reasonably bear.

9–64   An illustration of how a cautionary obligation will not be extended to transactions which, according to a strict interpretation, are outside its scope is:

North of Scotland Banking Co. v. *Fleming* (1882) 10 R. 217: F. had been appointed a bank-agent by the North of Scotland Banking Co. F.'s brother and another party became cautioners for the faithful discharge by F. of his duties. One of the terms of their bond of caution was that they were to be jointly and severally liable for loss resulting to the bank from overdrafts allowed by F. without the bank's consent.

F. opened a current account in his own name, and, with the bank's knowledge, allowed overdrafts on that account.

Held that the cautioners were not liable to the bank for the overdrafts on F.'s own account, since these were truly advances made by the bank to F. as an individual, whereas the risk intended to be covered by the bond of caution related to overdrafts allowed by F. to customers without the bank's consent.

9–65   Similarly, in *Ayr County Council* v. *Wyllie*, 1935 S.C. 836, W., the cautioner for a sheriff officer, was held not liable for sums embezzled by the sheriff officer when the officer was acting not in his official capacity as sheriff officer but as debt collector for the county council.

9–66   The interpretation of cautionary obligations often is *contra proferentem* ("against the party putting them forward"), the obligation being contained in a formal document issued by the creditor (*e.g.* a guarantee of a bank overdraft contained in a printed form supplied by the bank, as in *Aitken's Trustees* v. *Bank of Scotland*, 1944 S.C. 270 (9–108, below).

(b) Cautionary Obligations Limited as to Amount

9–67   Where there is a limitation on the amount for which the cautioner is to be liable, a distinction must be made between:

(i) a cautionary obligation which guarantees only a part of the principal debtor's debt; and

(ii) a cautionary obligation which guarantees the whole of the principal debtor's debt, though placing a limit on the amount which the cautioner is liable to pay.

Obligations of category (i) are favourable to the cautioner, those of category (ii) are favourable to the creditor.

9–68   The distinction is of practical importance when the principal debtor becomes bankrupt, and the cautioner pays the creditor the full amount of his guarantee. The question then is: "Is the cautioner entitled to rank on the bankrupt principal debtor's estate to recover a dividend on the amount which he has paid to the creditor?" If the cautionary obligation falls into category (i), the answer to that question will be in the affirmative, and if the obligation falls into category (ii), the answer will be in the negative.

9–69   Because of the stringent interpretation applied to cautionary obligations, precise and definite language is required for the creation of obligations in category (ii).

9–70   The following cases will clarify the distinction:

(i) *Harmer & Co.* v. *Gibb,* 1911 S.C. 1341: M. was starting business as a retail clothier. H. & Co., wholesale clothiers, agreed to supply him with goods provided G. granted a letter of guarantee in their favour.

The letter signed by G. was in these terms: "I, G., hereby undertake to guarantee to you the due payment of all such goods as you may from time to time sell and deliver to M. up to the value of £200."

Several years later, M. sold off his business and disappeared, leaving H. & Co. unpaid to the extent of about £300. In addition to the guarantee, H. & Co. held as security a policy of insurance on M.'s life, the surrender value of the policy being £116.

H. & Co. sued G. under the guarantee for £200.

Held, on an interpretation of the terms of the guarantee, that G. had guaranteed only the first £200 of M.'s debt to H. & Co., and that in paying to H. & Co. under the guarantee, G. was therefore entitled to deduct from £200 that proportion of the value of the policy which £200 bore to the whole debt due by M. to H. & Co. (*i.e.* approximately two-thirds of £116 had to be deducted from H. & Co.'s claim against G.).

(ii) *Harvie's Trustees* v. *Bank of Scotland &c.* (1885) 12 R. 1141: This case gives an example of an "ultimate loss clause," which entitles the creditor to regard the cautioner as having guaranteed the whole of the principal debtor's debt, not merely the debt up to the stated limit of the guarantee. The effect of such a clause is to deprive the cautioner of his right of relief against the principal debtor.

H. granted a letter of guarantee to a bank, guaranteeing "due payment of all sums for which M. is or may become liable to you, the amount which I am to be bound to pay under this guarantee not to exceed £15,000, . . . and I further declare that I shall not be entitled to demand from you an assignation of this guarantee, so long as the same M. is indebted to you in any such sums such as aforesaid."

The estates of M. were sequestrated. Shortly afterwards, on February 28, H. paid £10,000 into the bank. On March 14 he paid a further £5,000. On March 18 he died.

H.'s trustees claimed a ranking for £15,000 in M.'s sequestration. The bank claimed to be ranked for £44,000, the amount due to it by M. at the date of the sequestration, without deduction of the £15,000 paid by H. (*Both* claims could not be allowed, since this would have amounted to double ranking, to the extent of £15,000.)

The trustee in M.'s sequestration rejected the claim of H.'s trustees, and sustained that of the bank. H.'s trustees appealed against that decision.

Held that, in view of the terms of the letter of guarantee, H.'s trustees were not entitled to interfere with the bank's ranking for the full £44,000.

Lord Shand said (at p. 1146): "It appears to me that the case does not raise any question of general principle, but must be determined on a construction of the particular terms of the letter of guarantee.

"The words which occur towards the close of the document, 'and I further declare that I shall not be entitled to demand from you an assignation of this guarantee so long as the said Andrew Hislop Maclean is indebted to you in any sums such as aforesaid,' are quite conclusive of the present question. . . . The plain meaning of these words is that so long as any sum whatever is due by Maclean to the bank the claims of the cautioner shall not come into conflict with theirs."

9–73   A case to be contrasted with *Harvie's Trustees* v. *Bank of Scotland &c.* is *Veitch* v. *National Bank of Scotland Ltd.*, 1907 S.C. 554: This case indicates the careful choice of language which must be made when the parties intend to create an effective "ultimate loss clause": in particular, the use of a phrase such as "a covering security for the creditor's ultimate loss" is not of itself sufficient. While the case emphasises again that each case turns entirely on the construction of the actual terms of the cautionary obligation, the inclusion of a provision, as in *Harvie's Trustees* v. *Bank of Scotland &c.*, that the cautioner is not to be entitled to demand an assignation of the guarantee from the creditor as long as any indebtedness is outstanding emerges as being of vital importance:

R., V. and H. granted a bond of cash-credit in favour of a bank. The current account was in the name of R.; V. and H. were truly cautioners. The bond stated that the bank had agreed to allow credit to the extent of £1,500, and that the parties bound themselves, conjunctly and severally, to repay all sums advanced to R. not exceeding £1,500 in all, "it being the express meaning of these presents that this bond shall to the extent foresaid be a covering security to said bank against any ultimate loss that may arise on the transactions of R. with the said bank."

R. ultimately granted a trust deed for creditors. The sum then due by R. to the bank was £5,855, upon which the bank received a dividend of 13s.4d. in the £ from R.'s estate, leaving £1,951 as the balance still due.

The bank claimed repayment of this balance to the extent of £1,500 from V.

Held that, on a sound construction of the bond, V.'s guarantee was limited to repayment of an advance of £1,500 to be made to R. by the bank, and that as the bank had already recovered (by receiving 13s.4d. in the £) £1,000 of that advance, V. was liable only for repayment of the remaining £500.

(If V. had paid the £1,500 to the bank, he would have been entitled in relief to an assignation of the bank's right to rank on R.'s estate for that sum.)

Lord Stormonth-Darling said (at p. 560): "The judgment in *Harvie's Trustees* proceeded entirely on the ground that by the express words of the guarantee the cautioner had given up the right to demand an assignation so long as the principal debtor was indebted to the bank in any sum whatever."

9–74   An ultimate loss clause such as that in *Harvie's Trustees* v. *Bank of Scotland &c.* operates only on the bankruptcy of the principal debtor:

Mackinnon's Trustee v. *Bank of Scotland*, 1915 S.C. 411: In 1907 for the purpose of guaranteeing M.'s bank account Zollner had signed a letter of guarantee in the same terms as that signed by Harvie except that the maximum amount was not to exceed £2,500.

In 1912 Zollner desired to terminate his liability, which he did by paying £2,500 to the bank and then realising property which M. had assigned to him as security for the guarantee.

In 1913 M. became bankrupt, and the bank claimed that it was entitled to rank for the full amount of M.'s indebtedness without deducting the amount paid to it by Zollner.

Held that as the payment by Zollner had been made before M.'s bankruptcy, the bank was entitled to rank on M.'s estate only for the balance due to it after deduction of Zollner's payment.

(c) Cautionary Obligations Limited as to Time

A cautionary obligation may be either limited as to its duration or continuing and indefinite as to its duration.

A limitation on duration may arise:

(i) from an express term specifying the limited duration; or

(ii) by inference from other terms in the obligation, from the general nature of the obligation, and from its surrounding circumstances.

Scott v. *Mitchell* (1866) 4 M. 551: In 1853 M. granted to S. a letter of guarantee in the following terms: "As you have become security to Clydesdale Bank for £150, on account of Mr James Wood, for the purpose of assisting him in his business, I hereby guarantee you against any loss by your so doing." The "security" referred to was a cautionary obligation, to the extent of £150, undertaken by S. to the bank in respect of Wood's cash-credit account with the bank.

Wood operated on his account with the bank between 1853 and 1861. In the latter year the balance due to the bank was £151 17s. 1d.

The bank obtained a decree against S. for £150, and S. brought an action of relief against M.

Held that M.'s letter of guarantee was to be construed as a guarantee against loss in respect of one advance of £150 and not as a continuing guarantee with reference to all advances on Wood's cash-credit account.

Lord Cowan said (at p. 553): "This letter has no reference to a cash-credit account such as the pursuer undertook. It refers to a single transaction, and by its terms the defender became security for £150. . . . It would be contrary to the principles on which such obligations are to be construed, to enlarge the scope of the obligation undertaken beyond what its terms fairly import."

M.'s obligation had terminated at the time when Wood, in operating on the account, paid into it sufficient to wipe out the original debit of £150.

There was no doubt that S.'s obligation to the bank in respect of Wood's cash-credit account was a continuing guarantee.

It is natural that a cautionary obligation attached to a current account with a bank should be of a continuing nature and not restricted to a single advance only. There was held to be such a continuing obligation in *Caledonian Banking Co.* v. *Kennedy's Trustees* (1870) 8 M. 862, although the ultimate decision in the case was that the cautioner had been liberated by transactions between the creditor and the principal debtor, such as the giving of time to the principal debtor. Lord Justice-Clerk Moncreiff made the following observations concerning continuing guarantees (at p. 867):

"I am of opinion that there is no presumption either way in regard to the construction of the document, but that it must be fairly construed according to its terms, read in the light of the subject-matter of it, and of the surrounding circumstances. . . . The question is, whether, so read, the granter meant to bind himself for one advance, or for the balance of continuous transactions. I do not think much assistance is to be derived from precedent on this matter, as each case must be judged of by the words used, and the circumstances in which they were used."

9–79   A cautioner in a continuing guarantee may withdraw his undertaking as regards future transactions by giving notice to the creditor; in practice the length of notice required would be specified in the guarantee.

VI RIGHTS OF CAUTIONERS

9–80   The rights or privileges of cautioners fall under these headings:

    (a) *beneficium ordinis* ("benefit of discussion");
    (b) *beneficium divisionis* ("benefit of division");
    (c) right of relief against principal debtor;
    (d) right of relief against co-cautioners;
    (e) *beneficium cedendarum actionum* ("benefit of having rights of action assigned"); and
    (f) right to share in securities held by co-cautioners.

9–81   These rights may be varied or waived by agreement of the parties concerned. For instance, as regards (c), there could be an agreement between cautioner and principal debtor that the cautioner would have no right of relief against the principal debtor unless the principal debtor's financial circumstances allowed it (*Williamson* v. *Foulds*, 1927 S.N. 164 (O.H.)), and, as regards (f), there may be agreement amongst co-cautioners that one of their number is to have the sole benefit of a security which he has obtained over the principal debtor's estate (*Hamilton & Co.* v. *Freeth* (1889) 16 R. 1022), while the ultimate loss clause in *Harvie's Trustees* v. *Bank of Scotland* (9–72, above), by which the cautioner agreed that he was not to be entitled to demand an assignation from the creditor involved a surrender of right (e).

9–82   Rights (a) and (b) arise only in proper cautionry. The other rights arise in both proper and improper cautionry.

(a) Beneficium Ordinis ("Benefit of Discussion")

9–83   "Discuss" in this context means "sue" or "bring a legal action against."

9–84   The common law relating to this right was altered by section 8 of the Mercantile Law Amendment Act Scotland 1856.

9–85   At common law the cautioner in proper cautionry was entitled to insist that the creditor should first discuss and do diligence against the principal debtor before calling upon the cautioner.

9–86   The Act made it competent for the creditor to proceed against both the principal debtor and the cautioner or against either of them for payment of the debt covered by the cautionary obligation, except where the cautioner had stipulated in the document containing the cautionary obligation that the creditor was to be bound, before proceeding against him, to discuss and do diligence against the principal debtor.

9–87   The Act refers only to cautionary obligations for the payment of a debt. It would appear therefore that where the principal debtor's obligation is *ad factum praestandum* ("for the performance of an act"), the common law would still apply, the result being that the cautioner would be liable only when the creditor had failed to recover from the principal debtor the full amount of damages.

The benefit of discussion has never existed in improper cautionry.

(b) Beneficium Divisionis ("Benefit of Division")

Where, in proper cautionry, there are two or more cautioners, each cautioner is liable to the creditor only for his *pro rata* ("proportionate") share.

If any cautioner is insolvent, then each solvent co-cautioner is liable *pro rata* ("proportionately") for the insolvent's share.

In improper cautionry, on the other hand, the creditor is entitled to hold any one co-cautioner liable *in solidum* ("for the whole debt").

(c) Right of Relief against Principal Debtor

A cautioner who has had to pay to the creditor is entitled to recover what he has paid from the principal debtor.

The law protects this right of relief in two ways:

(i) The cautioner is treated as having an implied mandate to pay the principal debt. As soon, therefore, as any sum has become due by the principal debtor to the creditor, the cautioner is entitled to pay the sum, so terminating his own liability, and then sue the principal debtor for the amount paid.

(ii) If the principal debtor is *vergens ad inopiam* ("tending towards insolvency"), the cautioner may take steps to secure his right of relief, even although the time for payment of the debt has not arrived; *e.g.* he may attach goods belonging to the principal debtor or retain funds belonging to him.

In proper cautionry there may be, in the document which expressly binds the cautioner as cautioner, a clause by which the principal debtor expressly undertakes to relieve the cautioner, but this is not essential, since the right of relief is implied by the express constitution of the cautionary obligation.

In improper cautionry the cautioner claiming his right of relief must be able to establish that he is in fact a cautioner, though expressly bound to the creditor as a co-obligant with the principal debtor. Parole evidence is permissible to prove the true relationship.

(d) Right of Relief against Co-Cautioners

Where there are several cautioners, each is liable, in a question with his co-cautioners, only for his *pro rata* ("proportionate") share, although his liability in a question with the creditor may be *in solidum* ("for the whole debt"). Any cautioner, therefore, who has paid more than his *pro rata* share is entitled to relief from his co-cautioners to the extent of the excess:

Marshall & Co. v. *Pennycook*, 1908 S.C. 276: McDonald entered into a contract to construct water-works for Selkirk Town Council. M. and P. were bound jointly and severally as cautioners for the due performance of the contract.

McDonald became unable to continue the contract, and M., who himself owned a building and contracting business, after consulting P.

and with the consent of the town council, completed the contract. In doing so M. sustained loss.

Held that P. was bound to pay to M. one-half of the loss sustained by M., including one-half of the fee of £75 claimed by M. for having personally superintended the work.

9–97　　In calculating the amount of relief due, any co-cautioner who is insolvent is not counted:

Buchanan v. *Main* (1900) 3 F. 215: In 1894 by a letter of guarantee Buchanan, Brown, Main and two other persons, all directors of a certain limited company, jointly and severally guaranteed to the Bank of Scotland payment of all sums up to a maximum of £12,500 for which the company might become liable to the bank.

In 1896 Main, who had resigned his office of director, intimated to the bank that he withdrew from the guarantee. The bank thereupon closed the company's current account which was overdrawn. The company then went into liquidation.

Buchanan and Brown paid £4,306 17s. 11d. to the bank under the guarantee, and then brought an action against Main for relief to the extent of one-third, *i.e.* £1,435 12s. 8d. They led evidence to prove that the two other guarantors were insolvent. Main denied that the insolvency of either of the two other guarantors had been proved, and pleaded that he was liable in relief to the extent of only one-fifth of the sum paid by the pursuers.

Held that, whether the two other guarantors were insolvent or not, the pursuers were not bound to bear the whole risk of their insolvency, and that therefore Main was liable in relief to the extent of one-third of the sum paid by the pursuers.

Lord Trayner said (at p. 221): "There were five guarantors all jointly and severally liable. Two of these guarantors, as the pursuers say, and, as I think, have fairly established, are insolvent, in which case the defender must bear with the pursuers the whole claim under the guarantee. But whether the other two guarantors are insolvent or not, I think the same result follows. The pursuers are no more liable than the defender; he must therefore share their burden, with the same rights and the same risk as the pursuers of obtaining relief from the other two guarantors of the amount due by them."

9–98　　This right of relief does not apply where each of the co-cautioners is bound for a specific part only of the whole debt, as in *Morgan* v. *Smart* (1872) 10 M. 610 (see 9–148, below).

(e) Beneficium Cedendarum Actionum (Right to Assignation)

9–99　　A cautioner who has paid the creditor is entitled to obtain from the creditor an assignation of the debt, of any security held for it, and of any diligence done on it, so that he may be in a position to enforce his right of relief against the principal debtor or against co-cautioners.

9–100　　This right exists only where the cautioner has made *full* payment: it does not belong to a cautioner who is himself bankrupt, and able to pay only a dividend on the debt:

Ewart v. *Latta* (1865) 3 M. (H.L.) 36: Christie, a cautioner, became bankrupt, and L., the trustee in his sequestration, declared a dividend of 7s.6d. in the £ on Christie's estate. The principal debtor was also bankrupt.

E., the creditor in the cautionary obligation, lodged a claim in Christie's sequestration, and L. required that E., before drawing his dividend, should execute in favour of L. an assignation of securities held by him.

Held (reversing the judgment of the Court of Session) that (i) the cautioner was not entitled, without making full payment, to demand from the creditor an assignation of securities held by the creditor, and (ii) payment of a dividend by the trustee in the cautioner's sequestration was not full payment for that purpose.

The rule as to assignation of securities applies to securities over the principal debtor's estate, not to securities granted to the creditor by a third party:

Thow's Trustee v. *Young*, 1910 S.C. 588: Y., M., and T., in security for advances to be made to Y., granted a cash-credit bond to a bank, in which they bound themselves conjunctly and severally to repay to the bank the sums advanced on Y.'s current account.

The bond also contained an assignation in security to the bank by Y. and his brother and three sisters of their interest in their grandfather's trust-estate.

Y. received advances and was unable to repay them. The bank called upon M. and T. to pay under the bond. M. was bankrupt, and T. paid the full amount due, receiving from the bank an assignation of its rights against Y. and M., and also of the interest in the grandfather's trust-estate.

Some years later, T. died, and his representative claimed relief out of the grandfather's trust-estate.

Held that, on a sound construction of the bond, Y.'s brother and sisters were not co-cautioners with T., but had merely conveyed their interest in the trust-estate in security of the obligation undertaken by Y., M. and T. to the bank, and that T. was not entitled to relief out of that interest in the trust-estate but only out of Y.'s own interest (one-fifth). The mere fact that T. had obtained an assignation of the whole security from the creditor could not alter the substantial rights of the parties.

Lord President Dunedin said (at p. 596): "Nor can Mr Thow's trustee crave in aid the doctrine known as the *beneficium cedendarum actionum*, which, if amplified, means not only the assigning of the right to sue, but also the giving over of any security held by the creditor. Here again I examined the cases and I find that 'security' always means security over the estate of the debtor."

(f) Right to Share in Securities held by Co-Cautioners

A cautioner is entitled to share in the benefit of any securities granted to any of his co-cautioners over the principal debtor's estate.

The right does not extend to securities granted to one co-cautioner by a third party:

Scott v. *Young*, 1909 1 S.L.T. 47 (O.H.): S. and Y. were co-cautioners for M.'s cash credit account with the Bank of Scotland. M. failed to pay interest on the account, and S. and Y. were compelled to make equal payments to the bank.

Later it came to S.'s knowledge that Y. had had an assignation granted to him by M.'s wife of her interest in her father's estate.

Held that S. was not entitled to have one-half of the benefit of that security made over to him by Y.

9–104 According to the decision in *Hamilton & Co.* v. *Freeth* (1889) 16 R. 1022, it is competent for a cautioner to prove by parole evidence that his co-cautioners have orally agreed that, contrary to the general rule, he has the exclusive benefit of a security obtained from the principal debtor.

VII TERMINATION OF CAUTIONARY OBLIGATIONS

9–105 The ways in which a cautionary obligation may be terminated may be considered under two headings:

(a) termination resulting from extinction of the principal obligation; and

(b) other modes of termination.

(a) Termination resulting from Extinction of Principal Obligation

9–106 Since cautionry is an accessory obligation, it is terminated if the principal obligation is extinguished. The ways in which the principal obligation may be extinguished include:

(i) discharge;

(ii) novation;

(iii) compensation;

(iv) operation of the rule in *Clayton's Case;* and

(v) prescription.

(i) *Discharge*

9–107 The general rule is that if the principal debtor is discharged by the creditor without the cautioner's consent, the cautioner's liability is at an end. There is an exception to this in section 52 of the Bankruptcy (Scotland) Act 1913: if the creditor draws a dividend in the sequestration of the principal debtor or assents to the discharge of the bankrupt principal debtor, this does not free the cautioner from his liability.

9–108 There is an illustration of the general rule in *Aitken's Trustees* v. *Bank of Scotland*, 1944 S.C. 270:

A father entered into a guarantee, limited to £500, of his son's bank overdraft. The guarantee, which was on a printed form supplied by the bank, authorised the bank to grant to the son "any time or other indulgence," and to "compound" with him without discharging the father's liability. At the bank's request, the father lodged the £500 with the bank.

Later the bank brought an action against the son for the whole sum due under the overdraft—about £2,000. The son arranged with another bank to take over the overdraft. About £1,500 was paid to the first bank, which then consented to an unqualified decree of absolvitor being pronounced in its action against the son. The father's consent was not asked.

The first bank then applied the father's £500 to the balance of the overdraft, and the father brought an action against the bank for payment of the £500.

Held that (1) the guarantee had to be construed *contra proferentem* (see 9–66, above), (2) on that construction there had been no "compounding" with the son in the sense of the guarantee, and (3) by its unqualified discharge of the son, the bank had simultaneously extinguished the liability of his father as cautioner.

A discharge must be distinguished from a *pactum de non petendo* ("agreement not to sue"). A discharge extinguishes the principal obligation and frees the cautioner from liability, whereas in a *pactum de non petendo* the creditor gives up his right to sue the principal debtor but reserves his claim against the cautioner. Such an agreement does not deprive the cautioner of his right of relief against the principal debtor. The cautioner, therefore, if he is required to pay to the creditor, may demand from the creditor an assignation of the debt and may then sue the principal debtor to recover what he has paid. There is an instance of a *pactum de non petendo* in *Muir* v. *Crawford* (1875) 2 R. (H.L.) 148 (affirming *Crawford* v. *Muir* (1873) 1 R. 91):

The Scottish Granite Co. Ltd. accepted a bill of exchange payable to Cleland of London, by which the company undertook to pay £200 to Cleland on a specified date.

Cleland indorsed the bill to Holmes of London, Holmes indorsed it to Muir of Glasgow, and Muir indorsed it to Crawford of Edinburgh. The object of these indorsations was to give increased security to Crawford who agreed to discount the bill if Holmes and Muir indorsed it.

Crawford discounted the bill, paying the proceeds to Cleland.

The bill was dishonoured when it became due, and all the obligants on the bill were duly notified of the dishonour.

Crawford granted a discharge to the company, reserving his claims against the other obligants. He then sued Muir for the amount of the bill with interest from the date of dishonour.

Held that the discharge had not extinguished the debt, but was merely an agreement not to sue the acceptor, and that the indorser was liable to pay since his right of recourse against the acceptor had not been prejudiced.

Lord Chancellor Cairns said (at p. 149): "There is no doubt that by proper and apt instrument it is competent for the holder of a security of this kind to agree with the principal debtor not to enforce his remedies against the principal debtor; and, if he does that in an instrument, which at the same time reserves his rights against those who are liable in the second degree, there will be no discharge of those persons so liable.... If, on looking at the discharge, you find that there is nothing inconsistent in it with a proceeding by the surety afterwards against the principal debtor, then the surety is not in any way discharged."

(ii) *Novation*

The cautioner is liberated where there is novation of the principal debt, *i.e.* where the original principal debt is discharged and a new one substituted for it.

(Assignation of the principal debt to a new creditor does not liberate the cautioner.)

(iii) *Compensation*

9–111 If the principal debt is extinguished by compensation, the cautioner is liberated. This would occur where the creditor sues the principal debtor and the latter successfully puts forward the defence that a debt due by the pursuer to the defender must be set off against the pursuer's claim.

9–112 Compensation must, however, be pleaded in an action: a cautioner is not liberated merely because the principal debt might have been extinguished by the plea of compensation if an action had been brought.

(iv) *Rule in* Clayton's Case

9–113 According to the rule in *Clayton's Case* (which was part of the English case *Devaynes* v. *Noble* (1816) 1 Mer. 529, 572; 35 E.R. 767, 781), where there is a continuous account such as a current account at a bank, payments into the account extinguish items on the debit side in order of date. If it happens that the cautioner's obligation in connection with such an account is terminated by his giving notice of withdrawal or by an event such as his sequestration, the guarantee crystallises at that point of time and any subsequent payments into the account go towards reducing the amount for which the cautioner is liable. The cautioner's liability may thus ultimately disappear, even although the account continues to show as great a debit balance as it did at the time when the guarantee crystallised:

9–114 *Cuthill* v. *Strachan* (1894) 21 R. 549: Strachan, one of the cautioners for a cash-credit account with a bank, was sequestrated. The balance against the principal debtor, George Cuthill, was then £599. The bank made no claim in the sequestration, and the principal debtor continued to operate on the account until he granted a trust deed for creditors. The bank then closed the account, the balance due by George Cuthill being £615.

William Cuthill, another cautioner, paid £615 to the bank, and then made a claim of relief against Strachan, who had carried through a composition arrangement with his creditors.

In defence, Strachan maintained that the balance due to the bank at the date of his sequestration had been extinguished by subsequent payments by George Cuthill into the bank. The debit balance on the account from day to day had never been reduced below about £550.

Held that the payments into the account were to be appropriated according to the order of the debit items in the account, and that Strachan's cautionary obligation had therefore been extinguished.

9–115 In practice, the termination of a cautionary obligation by the operation of the rule in *Clayton's Case* is avoided by the closing of the principal debtor's existing account and the opening of a new account for him.

(v) *Prescription*

9–116 Where the principal debt has been allowed to prescribe, the cautioner is freed from liability (*e.g. Halyburtons* v. *Graham* (1735) Mor. 2073).

(b) **Other Modes of Termination**

A cautionary obligation may be extinguished, without extinction of the principal obligation, in any of the following ways:
   (i) by discharge of the cautioner;
  (ii) by revocation by the cautioner;
 (iii) by death;
  (iv) by change in a firm;
   (v) by conduct of the creditor; or
  (vi) by prescription.

(i) *Discharge of Cautioner*

If the cautioner is expressly discharged by the creditor, he is freed from liability.

(ii) *Revocation by Cautioner*

A cautionary obligation may be limited as to time (see 9–75 *et seq.*, above). The cautioner's liability will then be at an end once the period of his guarantee has expired without fault on the part of the principal debtor.

The question of revocation can arise if the cautioner wishes to withdraw *before* the fixed period of his guarantee has expired, and it can also arise where the guarantee is a *continuing* one.

The rules which apply depend on whether the cautionary obligation is:
 1. a guarantee for payment of a debt; or
 2. a fidelity guarantee.

The effect of revocation, where it is permissible at all, is, of course, to free the cautioner from liability only in respect of future transactions or misconduct: where liability has already been incurred, the cautioner must meet it.

1. **Guarantee for payment of debt**

If the guarantee is for a fixed period, the cautioner is not entitled to withdraw before the expiry of that period unless he "takes the debtor into his own hand," *i.e.* pays the debt to the creditor and himself becomes creditor.

If, on the other hand, the guarantee is for an indefinite period, the cautioner is entitled at any time to give notice to the creditor that he will not be responsible for future transactions.

In order to free himself from liability for past transactions, the cautioner may, on giving reasonable notice, require the principal debtor to relieve him of all liability already incurred. The principal debtor must then obtain from the creditor and deliver to the cautioner a discharge by the creditor of the cautioner's liability:

Doig v. *Lawrie* (1903) 5 F. 295: In November 1898, by a letter of guarantee addressed to the Bank of Scotland, D. became cautioner for advances made or to be made, not exceeding £6,500, by the bank to L. The letter stated that the guarantee was to remain in force until recalled in writing.

In March 1901, D. intimated to L. that he desired his name to be removed from the guarantee. L., however, failed to make any arrangement with the bank for the release of D., and in August 1901 D. raised an action of relief against L.

Held that L., having been given reasonable notice, was bound to relieve D. of his liability by making payment to the bank of all sums due under the guarantee and obtaining from the bank and delivering to D. a discharge of D.'s liability.

2. Fidelity guarantee

9–125   The cautioner may revoke the guarantee for the future if the person whose trustworthiness is being guaranteed becomes guilty of misconduct. It is the duty of the employer to notify the cautioner timeously of the misconduct, and if he fails in this duty, he loses his right to hold the cautioner liable (*Snaddon* v. *London, Edinburgh and Glasgow Assurance Co. Ltd.* (9–55, above)).

9–126   If the employment to which the fidelity guarantee relates is for a fixed period, the cautioner is not entitled to withdraw before the expiry of that period unless there is misconduct.

9–127   If the employment is for an indefinite period, the cautioner may revoke the guarantee for the future by giving reasonable notice of revocation to the creditor. The length of notice which will be considered reasonable depends on the circumstances including the length of notice required to terminate the contract of employment.

(iii) *Death*

9–128   The death of the principal debtor fixes the cautioner's liability: unless the contract of cautionry is to the contrary effect, the cautioner will not be liable for any debt not then due:

Woodfield Finance Trust (Glasgow) Ltd. v. *Morgan*, 1958 S.L.T. (Sh. Ct.) 14: In August 1954 Peter Flaherty rented a television set from a finance company for 139 weeks at a weekly rental of 15s.6d. Two relatives, M. and Festus Flaherty, agreed in writing jointly and severally to guarantee payment of all sums due by Peter Flaherty.

In December 1954 Peter Flaherty died. The rent was then in arrear. Festus Flaherty had disappeared. The finance company sued M. for the arrears due at Peter Flaherty's death and for sums becoming due thereafter.

Held that M. was not liable for sums which had become due after Peter Flaherty's death.

9–129   Similarly, the death of the creditor causes the cautioner's obligation to cease to run. Accordingly, in a fidelity guarantee, the employer's death terminates the guarantee, even although the employee is kept on by the deceased's representatives.

9–130   The death of the cautioner does not affect his existing liability: his estate will be liable to the same extent as the cautioner himself. Further, if the guarantee is a continuing guarantee, the cautioner's representatives will continue to become liable for debts incurred after the cautioner's death unless they withdraw the guarantee; it is not the duty of the creditor to inform them of the guarantee, and so they must be held liable even although they were not aware of the guarantee:

British Linen Co. v. *Monteith and Others* (1858) 20 D. 557: A Court of Session judge, Lord Fullerton, had a current account with a commercial bank. He was allowed a credit of £600 on the account under a cash-credit bond by which McDowall and Monteith, who were truly cautioners, were bound conjunctly and severally along with him.

McDowall died in 1840, Monteith in 1848, and Lord Fullerton in 1853.

In 1854 the bank raised an action against the representatives of McDowall and Monteith for payment, jointly and severally, of £600, which was composed of sums advanced to Lord Fullerton after Monteith's death. The bank did not notify McDowall's or Monteith's representatives of the existence of the bond.

Held that the representatives were liable under the bond.

Lord Deas said (at p. 562): "But it is said there is great hardship in holding representatives liable who may never have heard of the obligation. It may be so. But who is to blame for this? The granter of the obligation, who left no trace of it in his repositories? or the Bank officers, who may or may not have heard of his death? I think the duty lies on the debtor, who binds his representatives, to keep them informed that he has done so, rather than upon the creditor, who receives and relies upon the obligation."

However, a prudent creditor, on learning of the cautioner's death, would inform the representatives of the guarantee; otherwise he might find himself barred from enforcing the guarantee in court; *e.g.*, in *Caledonian Banking Co.* v. *Kennedy's Trustees* (1870) 8 M. 862, there were circumstances in which a cautioner's representatives were held to be liberated from the guarantee by transactions between the creditor and the principal debtor.

(iv) *Change in a Firm*

A cautionary obligation in which a firm is either the creditor or the principal debtor is, in the absence of agreement to the contrary, revoked as to future transactions by any change in the constitution of the firm (Partnership Act 1890, s. 18, re-enacting Mercantile Law Amendment Act Scotland 1856, s. 7, which itself substantially reproduced the common law).

The change in the constitution of the firm may be the introduction of a new partner or the retiral or death of an existing partner.

(v) *Conduct of Creditor*

Acts of the creditor which affect the cautioner's liability or his rights of relief terminate the cautionary obligation unless they are done with the cautioner's consent. Such acts are:
1. giving time to the principal debtor;
2. otherwise altering the principal contract;
3. releasing co-cautioners; and
4. giving up securities.

1. **Giving time to principal debtor**

"Giving time" has a technical meaning: it denotes some act by which the creditor deprives himself of the right to sue the principal debtor when the debt is due, *e.g.* where the creditor takes a bill of exchange payable at a future date in payment of a debt immediately due. By giving time the creditor is postponing the time at which the cautioner may exercise his right of relief against the principal debtor.

9–136 Mere delay on the creditor's part in enforcing payment against the principal debtor does not amount to "giving time": the cautioner is entitled in that case to settle with the creditor and then claim against the principal debtor.

9–137 There are instances of giving time in the two following cases:

9–138 (a) *Richardson* v. *Harvey* (1853) 15 D. 628: R., proprietor of an estate, let two farms to Baird. H., a friend of Baird, by letter guaranteed to R. "full and regular payment of the current year's rent of £373 5s., as it falls due at Martinmas and Whitsunday."

R., without H.'s knowledge, took two bills from Baird, the one in payment of a balance of the rent which had become due at Martinmas, and the other for the rent which was to become due at Whitsunday. The bills were not payable until dates later than the terms of Martinmas and Whitsunday respectively.

Baird became bankrupt before Whitsunday, and R. brought an action against H. for payment of the balance of the Martinmas rent and for the whole of the Whitsunday rent.

Held that R., by taking the bills from Baird, had freed H. of his cautionary obligation.

Lord President McNeill said (at p. 632): "The broad principle of the matter is, that when a person becomes cautioner for a debt payable at a given time, and especially when it is one with certain rights in the original creditor against the debtor, such as a landlord has against his tenant, if the creditor gives time without concurrence of the cautioner, that liberates the cautioner, because that amounts to an alteration of the contract."

9–139 (b) *C. & A. Johnstone* v. *Duthie* (1892) 19 R. 624: In March 1888 D., a retail grocer in Aberdeen, disposed of his business to Cormack, his brother-in-law, who had been his manager. In April, in order to start Cormack in business, D. granted a letter of guarantee to J., wholesale merchants in Aberdeen, undertaking to see J. duly paid for all goods to be supplied by J. to the order of Cormack.

J. supplied goods to Cormack until April 1890, when the account was closed.

In September 1890, when there was still a balance due to J. on the account, J., without D.'s knowledge, drew two bills on Cormack, payable at three months from their date, for the outstanding balance.

In November 1890, Cormack became bankrupt, and J. sued D. under the letter of guarantee for the balance.

Held that D. had been liberated by J.'s action in taking the bills.

Lord Adam said (at p. 628): "All transactions under the letter of guarantee came to an end in April 1890.

"The account was closed, and the amount alleged to be due by the defender was then ascertained. . . .

". . . [*The pursuers*] could not have sued Cormack, the principal debtor, during the currency of these bills, and so they gave him time. . . .

". . . It is quite settled law that if the creditor gives time to the principal debtor the cautioner is free. Neither is it necessary for the cautioner to shew that he has been thereby *de facto*[5] prejudiced."

A distinction is made between a cautionary obligation which guarantees a specific transaction and one which is continuing or "general," *i.e.* relates to a course of dealing. In the case of the latter it is less likely that the cautioner will be liberated by arrangements between the creditor and the principal debtor for postponing payment: in particular, the allowance of a period of credit which is in accordance with usage of trade will not free the cautioner:

Stewart, Moir and Muir v. *Brown* (1871) 9 M. 763: B., a grocer in Glasgow, granted a letter of guarantee to S., muslin manufacturers there, becoming security for goods supplied by S. to Ramsay & Co. of Glasgow.

S. took a bill payable one month after its date from Ramsay & Co. in payment of an account for goods supplied, and later brought an action against B. under the letter of guarantee.

Held that B. had not been liberated, because the taking of the bill had not been at variance with the ordinary custom of merchants.

Drawing the distinction between a cautionary obligation attached to a specific transaction and one attached to a course of dealing, Lord Justice-Clerk Moncreiff said of the latter (at p. 766):

"The cautioner, if there be nothing to the contrary expressed in his obligation, is not presumed to grant it on the faith of any specific conditions, but rather to have contemplated the general usage of trade, and the ordinary credit given among merchants. Where one guarantees all goods which may be furnished to a trader, or all bills which may be discounted by a banker, as a cautioner, he necessarily, by the generality of the obligation, leaves the principal debtor and creditor free to arrange the details of their transactions as they think fit, provided these are not at variance with the ordinary custom of merchants. This is the principle of a general guarantee, and it has been frequently applied."

Similarly, in *Calder & Co.* v. *Cruikshank's Trustee* (1889) 17 R. 74, Cruikshank, whose guarantee related to whisky supplied by distillers to McLaren & Co. over a period of years, was held not to have been liberated by bills taken, without his consent, by the distillers from McLaren & Co. and payable five months after their date.

Lord President Inglis said (at p. 80): "There is a broad distinction taken in all the cases between the guarantee of a particular debt of a certain amount, to be paid at a certain time, and a general guarantee for the price of goods sold or for money advanced or the like.

"In the former case if a creditor innovates or alters the relation of debtor and creditor in any essential point, he liberates the cautioner. In the latter case that result by no means follows. Many general guarantees are intended to extend far beyond the guarantee of a particular debt. This case seems to me to belong to the latter category."

Giving time must be distinguished from a *pactum de non petendo* ("agreement not to sue"), which preserves the cautioner's right of relief against the principal debtor and therefore does not terminate the cautionary obligation (see 9–109, above).

---

[5] "in fact."

2. Otherwise altering the principal contract

9–143   Alteration of the contract between the creditor and the principal debtor may adversely affect the cautioner's position, and so, if done without the cautioner's consent, may terminate the cautionary obligation. Giving time is one instance of such an alteration. Another is where the principal debtor materially increases his liability, *e.g.*:

9–144   *N.G. Napier Ltd.* v. *Crosbie*, 1964 S.C. 129: Mrs C., a domestic help, entered into a personal credit agreement with N. Ltd., by which, for the purpose of purchasing a television set, she was granted credit facilities up to £200 and undertook to make weekly payments of 17s.6d. to N. Ltd. In security of this contract, N. Ltd. entered into a contract of guarantee with Reid.

Shortly afterwards, Mrs C. agreed with N. Ltd. to increase her weekly payments to 20s. Reid was not informed of this change.

Held that the increase in the weekly payments was in the circumstances a material alteration of the principal contract, and that since it had been made without the knowledge of the cautioner, he was discharged from the guarantee.

9–145   Similarly, in a fidelity guarantee the cautioner is released if the creditor fails to make the checks on the employee's conduct which were stipulated for in the contract of employment and relied on by the cautioner. An instance is:

Haworth & Co. v. *Sickness and Accident Assurance Association Ltd.* (1891) 18 R. 563: Slater was employed by H. & Co., tea-merchants, as a traveller. An assurance company undertook, in return for payment of a premium, to guarantee H. & Co. against loss by embezzlement on the part of Slater. The assurance company had been informed that there were to be monthly settlements between H. & Co. and Slater, and that, as a check on the accuracy of Slater's accounts, statements were to be sent by H. & Co. direct to customers every three months.

Slater was guilty of embezzlement, and H. & Co. sued the assurance company for £87. It was proved that there had not been monthly settlements between H. & Co. and Slater and that the three-monthly statements for customers had been sent through Slater and not direct to the customers.

Held that as the employer had failed to comply with the specified precautions, the assurance company was not liable.

9–146   Where the employee's duties are materially altered, the cautioner is released unless he has been informed of the alteration and has agreed to continue as cautioner:

Bonar v. *McDonald* (1850) 7 Bell's App. 379; (1847) 9 D. 1537: Bird was appointed teller in the Edinburgh and Leith Bank in 1839, and McD. T. and B. were cautioners for his faithful performance of the duties of teller.

A few months later, Bird was appointed manager of a branch of the bank at Dalkeith, and the cautioners were informed of this and consented to continue as cautioners.

In April 1840, however, an alteration was made in the terms of Bird's appointment: he was to be liable for one-fourth of the losses arising from discounts to customers, and, to reflect this additional possible liability is salary was to be increased to what was then a large figure (£130 per annum). The cautioners were not informed of this alteration.

A year later Bird was dismissed for various banking irregularities committed by him, especially in connection with a customer Moffat, who became bankrupt.

Bonar, the manager of the bank, brought an action against Bird and his cautioners for the losses incurred by the bank in its business with Moffat.

Held that, although these losses were unconnected with the alteration of April 1840 in Bird's terms of appointment, the cautioners were not liable, since they had not consented to that material alteration.

Lord Mackenzie said (at 9 D. p. 1551): "A person . . . asked to be cautioner for a bank agent might most naturally and reasonably say, 'I am willing to be cautioner for A B if he is to be a mere salaried agent; but if he is to run the risk of loss by discounts, I will have nothing to do with it.' If that be true, however, then on that ground a bank cannot have right to change a cautionry of the one kind into a cautionry of the other, without the consent of the cautioner."

The legal position is different if the fidelity guarantee is separate from the contract of employment and the cautioner is unaware of the terms of that contract: *e.g.* in *Nicolsons* v. *Burt &c.* (1882) 10 R. 121, a cautioner who had in such circumstances bound himself in general words "for the due and punctual payment of all sums of money collected by" a traveller was held not to have been liberated by the renewal of the traveller's employment for a second period of three years on the expiry of the first three years.

3. Releasing co-cautioners

Section 9 of the Mercantile Law Amendment Act Scotland 1856 provides that where there are co-cautioners, a discharge granted by the creditor to any one cautioner without the consent of the other cautioners is to be deemed to be a discharge granted to all the cautioners, unless the cautioner being discharged by the creditor is bankrupt. This applies only where the co-cautioners are bound jointly and severally, each being liable for payment of the full debt: it does not apply where each is bound for a separate sum as in *Morgan* v. *Smart* (1872) 10 M. 610:

M., an Edinburgh grocer, agreed to sell his stock-in-trade to McDonald provided McDonald found security to the extent of £105.

Two letters of guarantee were handed to M. By one of these Banks became a cautioner for £70, and by the other S. became a cautioner for £35.

Held that the discharge by M. of Banks did not affect the liability of S. for his proportion of the debt.

4. Giving up securities

A cautioner is entitled, on paying the debt, to an assignation of securities held by the creditor (see 9–99 *et seq.*, above); his position is therefore prejudiced if the creditor voluntarily gives up securities. The cautioner is released from his obligation only to the extent of the value of the security which has been given up.

9–150   The same result follows where the creditor fails to take the steps necessary to make his security effectual, *e.g.* fails to record a heritable security in the Register of Sasines.

(vi) *Prescription*

9–151   Formerly the Cautioners Act 1695 provided for the extinction of certain cautionary obligations on the lapse of seven years from the date when they were undertaken. This septennial prescription was abolished, with effect from July 25, 1976, by the Prescription and Limitation (Scotland) Act 1973.

9–152   Under section 6 of the Act of 1973 any cautionary obligation is extinguished on the lapse of five years after "the appropriate date" provided no relevant claim and no acknowledgment of its existence has been made during the five years. The Act expressly provides that this five-year prescription applies even where the cautionary obligation is in the form of a probative writing (1973 Act, Sched. 1).

9–153   Difficult questions can arise concerning the date from which the prescriptive period is to run. "The appropriate date" in relation to certain kinds of obligations is specified in Schedule 2 to the Act and in relation to all other kinds of obligation it is the date when the obligation became "enforceable" (1973 Act, s. 6).

9–154   The interpretation of these statutory provisions came before the Inner House of the Court of Session in *Royal Bank of Scotland Ltd.* v. *Brown and Others* (1982, unreported):

On May 23, 1979, a bank raised an action against cautioners who had guaranteed a loan by the bank to a company. The cautioners contended that their obligation had been extinguished under the Act of 1973, since "the appropriate date" was at latest September 1, 1969, when the bank had made a claim in the liquidation of the company.

The bank, on the other hand, maintained that prescription did not start to run until May 27, 1974—the date on which the bank had by letter demanded payment under the guarantee.

Held that (1) "the appropriate date" in relation to cautionary obligations was not to be found in Schedule 2 to the Act: cautionary obligations were neither expressly mentioned in that Schedule nor could they be covered by the category "any obligation to repay the whole, or any part of, a sum of money lent to . . . the debtor under a contract of loan," since "debtor" in that context denoted a principal debtor; and (2) because the guarantee required the cautioner to make full and final payment "on demand" of all sums due to the bank by the company, the cautionary obligation did not become "enforceable" until the date of the demand, *i.e.* May 27, 1974.

9–155   The case shows that it is vitally important for banks to ensure that their guarantee forms are so worded as to make a demand for payment a condition precedent to the enforcing of the guarantee.

9–156   Care must similarly be exercised in relation to the obligation of a person guaranteeing a standard security: if the guarantee took the form of the cautioner becoming a co-obligant jointly and severally in the standard security, the guarantee would prescribe in five years from the creation of the security; it is therefore advisable for the guarantee to be a separate deed with the effect that prescription will not start to run on the guarantor's obligation until there has been a default by the principal debtor (see John M. Halliday, *Conveyancing and Feudal Reform (Scotland) Act 1970* (2nd ed.), pp. 127-128).

Further Reading

Gloag and Henderson, *Introduction to the Law of Scotland*, Chapter XXI

David M. Walker, *Principles of Scottish Private Law*, Chapter 4.21

W. A. Wilson, *The Law of Scotland Relating to Debt*, Chapter 10

J. J. Gow, *The Mercantile and Industrial Law of Scotland*, Chapter 5

Gloag and Irvine, *Law of Rights in Security, Heritable and Moveable, including Cautionary Obligations*, Chapters I and XIX—XXV (1897, William Green & Sons)

CHAPTER 10

BANKRUPTCY

INTRODUCTION

THE term "bankruptcy" has itself no precise technical meaning. It may denote one of three things:

(a) insolvency, *i.e.* a person's inability to pay his debts;

(b) "notour bankruptcy," *i.e.* a state of insolvency which has become notorious in the sense of being public knowledge; or

(c) sequestration, a court process by which the insolvent person's assets are gathered in and sold, the net proceeds (after payment of administration expenses) being then divided, as far as they will go, amongst the creditors, according to their various priorities, in payment or part-payment of the debts due to them.

The principal Act relating to the Scots law of bankruptcy is the Bankruptcy (Scotland) Act 1913, which was passed to consolidate and amend earlier statutory provisions on sequestration dating back to the Act of 1772 (12 Geo. III, c. 47) which introduced that process, limiting it to the moveable estate of a living debtor engaged in trade. Prior to the Act of 1913, the principal Act on bankruptcy was the Bankruptcy (Scotland) Act 1856. Cases decided when the Act of 1856 was in force are still of authority in so far as provisions have been carried forward without amendment from that Act into the Act of 1913.

In this chapter, references to sections are to sections of the Bankruptcy (Scotland) Act 1913 unless the context indicates otherwise.

Later statutory provisions have amended the Act of 1913 in certain respects. The most noteworthy of these provisions are in the Companies Act 1947 and in the Insolvency Act 1976.

The Act of 1913 is concerned mainly with sequestration. As regards insolvency and notour bankruptcy, two Scots Acts which are still in force are of supreme importance, namely, the Bankruptcy Act 1621 (c. 18) and the Bankruptcy Act 1696 (c. 5), respectively.

Instead of resorting to sequestration, the insolvent and his creditors often in practice prefer to have recourse to a private arrangement, usually a trust deed for creditors. From the standpoint of the creditors such arrangements may save expense (with the result that there will be more funds available to meet the debts due to the creditors), and the debtor has the advantage of avoiding the greater publicity and the statutory disqualifications and disabilities involved in the sequestration process. Private arrangements are described as "extra-judicial," because, unlike sequestration, they are not conducted under "judicial" (*i.e.* court) authority.

The topic of bankruptcy is considered in this chapter under the following headings:

   I. Insolvency;

  II. Notour bankruptcy;

 III. Sequestration; and

 IV. Extra-judicial settlements.

The subject-matter of the chapter is confined to individuals and partnerships. The Act of 1913 makes it competent to sequestrate a "company" (s. 11)—a term defined in the Act (s. 2) as including "bodies corporate, politic or collegiate, and partnerships" (no mention being made of registered companies). The identical definition in the

Bankruptcy (Scotland) Act 1856 was held, in *Wotherspoon and Hope* v. *Magistrates of Linlithgow* (1863) 2 M. 348, to make it competent to sequestrate a royal burgh. Registered companies may become insolvent and (as was decided in *Clark &c.* v. *Hinde, Milne & Co.* (1884) 12 R. 347) be made notour bankrupt, but they cannot be sequestrated (*Standard Property Investment Co. Ltd.* v. *Dunblane Hydropathic Co. Ltd.* (1884) 12 R. 328) or enter into extra-judicial settlements such as a trust deed for creditors (Companies Act 1948, s. 320(2)); the appropriate procedure is liquidation or one of the schemes for reconstruction provided for in the Companies Acts.

10–09   The English law of bankruptcy is quite distinct, the principal Act applicable to England being the Bankruptcy Act 1914. Of all branches of commercial law, bankruptcy is the one in which least assistance may be obtained from decisions of the English courts.

10–10   The Scots law of bankruptcy was the subject of an intensive study by the Scottish Law Commission for some 13 years from 1968. The resulting *Report* (*Report on Bankruptcy and Related Aspects of Insolvency and Liquidation* (Scot. Law Com. No. 68)) was published in February 1982. It makes a large number of proposals for changes in the law on matters both of principle and of detail, and includes in an Appendix a draft Bankruptcy (Scotland) Bill, which, if introduced to and passed by Parliament, would repeal the Acts of 1621 and 1696 and substantially the whole of the Act of 1913 and replace them with new statutory provisions in accordance with the Commission's recommendations. The questions of whether and, if so, when the proposed legislation will be enacted are at present unanswerable. Meantime the *Report,* in addition to its being of obvious interest for the future, has the immediate practical usefulness of providing a comprehensive and up-to-date review of the present law of bankruptcy.

I INSOLVENCY

10–11   Insolvency may be either absolute or practical.

10–12   A person is absolutely insolvent if his total liabilities exceed his total assets, even though he may be able to meet demands as they are made on him. The common law regards a person who is absolutely insolvent as bound to administer his affairs on behalf of his creditors generally: he is no longer free to make gifts, nor is he entitled to favour one creditor at the expense of other creditors.

The principle is described thus in Bell's *Commentaries* (7th ed.), Vol. II, p. 170: "From the moment of insolvency a debtor is bound to act as the mere trustee, or rather as the *negotiorum gestor,* [1] of his creditors, who thenceforward have the exclusive interest in his funds. He may, as long as he is permitted, continue his trade, with the intention of making gain for his creditors and for himself; but his funds are no longer his own, which he can be entitled secretly to set apart for his own use, or to give away as caprice or affection may dictate."

---

[1] "manager of affairs."

Similarly, Lord Dunedin in *Caldwell* v. *Hamilton*, 1919 S.C. (H.L.) 100, at p. 107, said: "After insolvency a man is truly, *quoad*[2] his property, a trustee for his creditors."

A more recent case, *Nordic Travel Ltd.* v. *Scotprint Ltd.*, 1980 S.C. 1, made it clear, however, that the description of the insolvent as being a trustee for his creditors is not to be taken too literally:

In the liquidation of N. Ltd. the liquidator attempted to set aside as "fraudulent preferences" certain cash payments which had been made by N. Ltd. to S. Ltd., a closely associated company, in respect of debts due by N. Ltd. to S. Ltd. Counsel for the liquidator argued that since a person who was absolutely insolvent, and knew it, was a trustee for all his creditors, he would, *prima facie* ("until the contrary were proved") be in breach of trust even if he merely paid to one of his creditors in cash a debt which was past due and payable.

The court rejected that argument.

Lord President Emslie said (at p. 9): "It is of course the fact that in a number of passages in Bell's Commentaries it is suggested that the doctrine that an insolvent with knowledge of his absolute insolvency is a trustee for all his creditors, is at the root of the common law on fraudulent preferences. When all these passages are read together, however, it is quite evident that the suggestion is not to be taken literally. In particular, nowhere in Bell's Commentaries nor in any other authority or decided case is it for the moment suggested that it is, even *prima facie*, a breach of trust for an insolvent person who knows of his absolute insolvency to fulfil obligations which are due and prestable and, in particular, to pay in cash debts which are past due. There are no doubt certain acts which, in the interests of all his creditors, such an insolvent person is obliged not to do, but to say that he is, literally, a trustee for his creditors is unwarranted in authority and wholly misleading."

A state of practical insolvency exists where a person either has ceased to pay his debts in the ordinary course of business or cannot pay his debts as they become due, even though his total assets may exceed his total liabilities. What a creditor is primarily concerned with and entitled to in commercial transactions is to receive payment when it is due. Hence the definition of insolvency for the purposes of the Sale of Goods Act 1979 is a definition of practical insolvency: "A person is deemed to be insolvent within the meaning of this Act if he has either ceased to pay his debts in the ordinary course of business, or he cannot pay his debts as they become due, whether he has . . . become a notour bankrupt or not" (Sale of Goods Act 1979, s. 61(4)). For the purposes of the Bankruptcy Act 1696 practical insolvency is all that is required (*Teenan's Trustee* v. *Teenan* (1886) 13 R. 833). Again, in section 5 of the Bankruptcy (Scotland) Act 1913, one of the ways in which notour bankruptcy may be constituted is by "insolvency" coupled with various forms of completed diligence; of the word "insolvency" in the same context in the Debtors (Scotland) Act 1880 Lord Adam in *McNab* v. *Clarke* (1889) 16 R. 610 said (at p. 613) that it "just means present inability to pay. If a man cannot meet his obligations he is insolvent, and it is no answer for him to say that if he is given

---

[2] "as regards."

time to realise his means he will some day be able to pay." In that case th court held that production of an expired charge on an undisputed deb neither paid nor offered to be paid, raised a presumption of "insolvency

10–14 Consequences of insolvency are that:
(a) gratuitous alienations and
(b) fraudulent preferences
may be reduced (*i.e.* set aside).

(a) Reduction of Gratuitous Alienations

10–15 Gifts and other gratuitous alienations by an insolvent out of his asse may be reduced either:
(i) at common law; or
(ii) under the Bankruptcy Act 1621.

(i) *At Common Law*

10–16 The underlying principle is the fiduciary position which an insolve person occupies at common law in relation to his creditors.

10–17 The challenge may be made by any creditor, whether his debt w incurred before or after the alienation. Under the Act of 1913 the truste in a sequestration has also the right to make the challenge on behalf of th whole body of creditors (s. 9).

10–18 The transaction challenged may be any type of alienation, direct indirect, and whether effected by writing or by simple delivery of mone or property.

10–19 The challenger must prove that:
(1) the debtor was absolutely insolvent at the date of the alienation (was made insolvent by the alienation), and has continued in that sta until the date of the challenge;
(2) the alienation was gratuitous, *i.e.* the insolvent received no co sideration, in money or money's worth, for it; and
(3) the alienation prejudiced lawful creditors.

10–20 Provided the challenger proves these points, it will be inferred tha the alienation was "fraudulent" in the sense that it was unfair to th lawful creditors; it is not essential to prove that the debtor was active and consciously defrauding his creditors or even, it seems, that he ha insolvency in contemplation (*Goudy on the Law of Bankruptcy* (4th ed. p. 24).

10–21 The following are three instances of reduction of gratuitous alienatio at common law:

10–22 (a) *Dobie* v. *Mitchell* (1854) 17 D. 97: The allegations in this case we that McFarlane, shortly before absconding, had collected various deb which were due to him and had handed over to his sister, without an consideration, £500 which she immediately deposited in a bank; that that time, to the knowledge of both McFarlane and his sister, D. was creditor of McFarlane; and that the transaction was a scheme entered int between brother and sister for the purpose of defeating D.'s right t receive payment.

The court held that if these allegations were true the deposit-receip which was the only title by which the sister held the money, would b reduced.

(b) *Main* v. *Fleming's Trustees* (1881) 8 R. 880: From 1865 F. spent rge sums in permanently improving an estate which was held by his itenuptial marriage-contract trustees for the benefit of his children. In 371 F. became to his knowledge insolvent but continued to spend large ims in improving the estate.

Held that the trustee in F.'s sequestration was entitled to a declarator iat in so far as the estate had been benefited by F.'s expenditure after his solvency, the marriage-contract trustees held it on behalf of the trustee F.'s sequestration.

The effect of F.'s insolvency was explained thus by Lord President iglis (at p. 886):

"If he had remained solvent nobody could have found any fault with m for increasing the funds in the hands of the trustees, and so increasing e provision in favour of his children. And down to the year 1871 every iilling that he spent on the estate of Keill does go to increase the value of ie estate in the hands of these trustees, and so to enlarge the children's ovisions. But . . . Mr Fleming was not entitled to go on expending oney in this way after he became insolvent, because that was simply creasing the provision to his children at the expense of his creditors; . . . far as this expenditure was made after he became insolvent it was at immon law an unlawful thing for him to do—a fraud upon his creditors the technical sense of the term, although I am not at all inclined to ippose that any actual fraud was intended. Still it is what the common w calls a fraud against his creditors, because it is taking the money that ight to have gone to pay them to increase gratuitously the provision in vour of his own children. . . . If the defenders as trustees are *lucrati*[3] by at expenditure, or, in other words, if the value of the children's pro- sions is, in point of fact, enhanced by the expenditure of that money, en I apprehend to that extent the pursuer, upon the part of the editors, has a perfectly equitable claim to participate in the trust-estate hich is held by them."

(c) *Obers* v. *Paton's Trustees* (1897) 24 R. 719: P., a Scotsman, after : had been declared bankrupt in France where he carried on business, ecuted a discharge of legitim at a time when his father was on his athbed. The effect of the discharge was, on the father's death, to ejudice P.'s creditors by depriving them of several thousand pounds id to benefit to that extent other persons entitled to share the legitim nd (P.'s brothers and sisters).

Although at the time of the discharge P.'s claim to legitim was a mere *es successionis* ("expectation of succession") which would have been feated if P. had died before his father, the court held that the discharge uld be reduced on behalf of the creditors in P.'s French bankruptcy.

On considering whether P. had had the power to discharge his legitim id so prevent that valuable right from coming into the possession of his editors, Lord McLaren said (at p. 733):

"There is this difference between a fraud on creditors and fraudulent ts of the ordinary type, that an act may be a fraud on creditors which is rfectly innocent in itself or even laudable if done by a solvent person,

---

enriched."

because the fraud consists in the violation of the principle that an insolvent is a virtual trustee for his creditors, and is disabled from dealing with his estate so as to defeat or imperil their right to distribution.

". . . The right of creditors to restoration against fraudulent alienation is independent of statute, and I think that the principle has sufficient strength and consistency to prevail over any device by which an insolvent person seeks to secure a benefit to himself, his relatives, or other favoured persons, by putting away funds which, but for his interference, would be available for the liquidation of his debts."

(ii) *Under the Bankruptcy Act 1621*

10–25 The Act of 1621 had the effect of facilitating the challenge of gratuitous alienations by introducing presumptions which in certain common situations lessen the heavy burden of proof which otherwise rests on the challenger.

10–26 In some respects the Act is not so widely applicable as the common law: the challenger under the Act must be either a prior creditor (*i.e.* a creditor whose debt existed at the time of the alienation) or the trustee in sequestration, whether representing prior creditors or not (Bankruptcy (Scotland) Act 1913, s. 9); only alienations to persons closely connected with the insolvent by ties of relationship or otherwise are within the Act; and it is doubtful whether the Act applies to mere transfers of property where there is no writing, and in *Gilmour, Shaw & Co.'s Trustee* v. *Learmonth*, 1972 S.C. 137 (O.H.), it was held not to apply to a cash payment made to a fiancée in order to purchase the matrimonial home.

10–27 The challenger must prove that:

(1) he is a prior creditor or the trustee in sequestration;

(2) the alienation was made to a "coniunct Or confident" person; the preamble to the Act mentiones "wyiffes Childrene kynnismen alleyis and vther confident and Interposed persounes"; and

(3) the debtor is absolutely insolvent at the date of the challenge.

10–28 It is then presumed that:

(4) the debtor was absolutely insolvent at the date of the alienation;

(5) the alienation was gratuitous, or, as the Act puts it, was "without trew Just and necessarie causes and without a Just pryce realie payit"; and

(6) the alienation prejudiced prior creditors.

10–29 The defender may rebut the presumptions (4), (5) and (6), but if he is unable to do so, the challenger is in the same position as he would have been in at common law after actually proving all the points necessary for a reduction at common law, *i.e.* it is inferred that the alienation was a "fraud" on lawful creditors.

10–30 The way in which the Act operates to assist a reduction of a gratuitous alienation may be illustrated by the two following cases:

10–31 (a) *Dawson* v. *Thorburn* (1888) 15 R. 891: D., the owner of a lodging-house in Bridge of Allan, had borrowed first £850 from Baird's trustees and later £125 from T., on the security of the house.

In 1886, interest having fallen into arrear, Baird's trustees sold the house at a price which barely covered the loan which they had made to D. The purchaser was D.'s daughter.

In March 1887 D. in writing transferred the furniture in the house to his daughter stating that this was her remuneration, estimated at £100, for having assisted him as housekeeper in the house for the previous 15 years.

In May 1887 T. raised an action against D. for the £125 due to him, obtained a decree against D., and proceeded to poind the furniture on the footing that it still belonged to D.

D.'s daughter petitioned the court for interdict against the sale of the furniture, but the only evidence brought forward by her in support of her claim to the furniture was her own statement that she had acted as D.'s housekeeper without remuneration for 15 years.

Held that she had failed to prove that the transfer had been made for a true, just and necessary cause; and petition *dismissed*.

Lord Rutherfurd Clark said (at p. 895): "It is quite possible that for services such as these a daughter may become a creditor of her father, but it must be proved, and considering that the granter was insolvent at the date of granting, and she was conjunct with him, it lies upon the person standing on the deed to prove by sufficient evidence the existence of the true, just, and necessary cause, which alone will sustain it. In this I think the pursuer has entirely failed."

(b) *North British Railway Co.* v. *White & Ors.* (1882) 20 S.L.R. 129: This was an action of multiplepoinding to have the right to a quantity of furniture in the hands of a railway company determined. The furniture was claimed by White and others as creditors of Seton. It was also claimed by Roberts, Seton's brother-in-law, on the ground that Seton had sold it to him for £135 10s.

Held that, as Seton was at the time insolvent, the burden of proof lay with Roberts to show that there had been a *bona fide* sale, with the price being really paid. Roberts had failed to overcome the presumption against him.

On the other hand, in *Hodge* v. *Morrisons* (1883) 21 S.L.R. 40, where a tenant had, 18 months before dying insolvent, assigned the lease of his house to his three daughters, the court, on the evidence, held that the daughters had given value for the lease in the form of money contributed by them from their own earnings while living in family with their father, and that the presumption of insolvency at the date of the assignation had been overcome.

Lord Young said (at p. 43): "I think the reasonable conclusion from the whole evidence is that the cedent was solvent in June 1879, the date of the assignation, and that the insolvency of his estate ascertained after his death in 1881 is accounted for by circumstances supervening after the assignation."

Transactions which have been reduced as gratuitous alienations under the Act of 1621 include the discharge of a debt due by an uncle (*Laing* v. *Cheyne* (1832) 10 S. 200), a promissory note granted to a sister-in-law (*Thomas* v. *Thomson* (1865) 3 M. 1160), the lease of a shop by father to son at a rent of £7 per annum when the shop was of the annual value of £10 (*Gorrie's Trustee* v. *Gorrie* (1890) 17 R. 1051), the sale of a business by a person in financial difficulties to his wife for an inadequate price (*Tennant* v. *Miller* (1897) 4 S.L.T. 318), and a gratuitous disposition by an insolvent husband to his wife of his half-share of a house previously in the couple's joint ownership (*Lombardi's Trustee* v. *Lombardi*, 1982 S.L.T. 81 (O.H.)).

10–35 "Conjunct" persons are close relatives of the insolvent, whether by blood, *e.g.* father and son (*Gorrie's Trustee* v. *Gorrie* (10–34, above)), or father and daughter (*Dawson* v. *Thorburn* (10–31, above)), or by affinity, *e.g.* step-father and step-son (*Mercer* v. *Dalgardno* (1695) Mor. 12563), or brother-in-law and sister-in-law (*Thomas* v. *Thomson* (10–34, above)). Persons engaged to be married were admitted to be "conjunct" in *Gilmour, Shaw & Co.'s Trustee* v. *Learmonth* (10–26, above).

10–36 "Confident" persons are persons in whom the insolvent is presumed to place an unusual degree of trust, *e.g.* a business partner, a senior employee or a confidential clerk. In *Laing* v. *Cheyne* (10–34, above) a person who had acted as tutor, curator, or trustee for the illegitimate son of his deceased brother was held to be a "conjunct and confident" person, with the result that a discharge of a debt granted to that person by his insolvent nephew could be reduced under the Act. In *Edmond* v. *Grant* (1853) 15 D. 703 the deeds being challenged by the trustee in a sequestration had been granted by the bankrupt to the maternal aunt of his wife who was his wife's next-of-kin and was over eighty years of age. The bankrupt was stated to be her "law-agent, confidential adviser, and intimate friend." This was held to be a relevant statement of confidentiality for the purposes of the Act of 1621. The relationship between an insurance company and a policy holder has been held not to be a confidential relationship for the purposes of the Act, with the result that a discharge granted by the policy holder to the company could not be reduced as a gratuitous alienation under the Act, although challenge would be competent at common law (*Ritchie* v. *Scottish Automobile and General Insurance Co.*, 1931 S.N. 83 (O.H.), and *Todd* v. *Anglian Insurance Co. Ltd.*, 1933 S.L.T. 274 (O.H.)).

10–37 An alienation is not reduced if it can be proved to have been made for a "true, just and necessary cause." A legal obligation already existing at the time of the alienation would be such a cause. In *McLay* v. *McQueen* (1899) 1 F. 804, the court held that an antenuptial marriage-contract entered into by McQ. with his future wife and by which he transferred certain heritable property to marriage-contract trustees for the benefit of his wife and children was not reducible under the Act of 1621, as it could not be regarded as having been made without "true, just and necessary cause." "A contract of marriage, . . . according to the custom of this country, is regarded as a proper protection of the interests of wife and family against the possibility of the supervening bankruptcy of the husband" (*per* Lord McLaren at p. 811). Similarly, in *Gilmour, Shaw & Co.'s Trustee* v. *Learmonth* (10–26, above) a payment made by an insolvent to his fiancée to enable her to purchase their future home was held not to be open to challenge, since it had been made in consideration of the forthcoming marriage.

10–38 On the other hand, reduction was granted in *McManus's Trustee* v. *McManus*, 1979 S.L.T. (Notes) 71 (O.H.), where a husband had simply made a gift of the family home to his wife at a time when the marriage was in danger of breaking down and the wife, as a condition of an attempt at reconciliation, wished to secure a roof for her children and herself.

Although the statutory wording is "true, just *and* necessary," the words are construed "disjunctively," so that if *either* there was a prior obligation (in which case the cause would be "necessary") *or* there was a true and just cause (*e.g.* the payment to the fiancée for the future home) the transaction is not reducible (*Gilmour, Shaw & Co.'s Trustee* v. *Learmonth* (10–37, above).

(b) Reduction of Fraudulent Preferences

It is a consequence of the fiduciary relationship in which an insolvent stands towards his creditors as a body that he must not show favour to particular creditors at the expense of other creditors. Transactions which have that effect are referred to as "fraudulent preferences" or "illegal preferences," and may be reduced at common law.

Fraudulent preferences may also be reduced under the Bankruptcy Act 1696 when granted *either* within six months before, *or* after, the constitution of notour bankruptcy (see 10–63, below). For the present, only reduction at common law, which is on the ground of insolvency, is being considered.

The challenge may be made by a prior creditor, *i.e.* a creditor who was already a creditor of the insolvent at the date of the transaction, and perhaps also by a creditor whose debt was contracted after the transaction, although the point is not free from doubt (*Goudy on the Law of Bankruptcy* (4th ed.), p. 42). Under the Bankruptcy (Scotland) Act 1913 the trustee in a sequestration, whether he represents prior creditors or not, is also entitled to make the challenge on behalf of the whole body of creditors (s. 9).

The underlying principle is that the rights of the creditors become fixed *inter se* ("as among themselves") at the time of the insolvency, and the insolvent must treat all his creditors equally according to their rights as then established: he must not, for instance, voluntarily grant a security to a creditor who is at that time an unsecured creditor.

The challenger must prove that:

(i) the debtor was absolutely insolvent at the date of the transaction and knew himself to be so;

(ii) the transaction was a voluntary act of the debtor; and

(iii) the transaction was "fraudulent" in the sense that it conferred a preference on one creditor to the prejudice of the others.

The following are two instances of reduction of fraudulent preferences at common law:

(1) *Wylie, Stewart & Marshall* v. *Jervis*, 1913 1 S.L.T. 465 (O.H.): A father had lent money to his son to enable the son to purchase a house. Later the son, knowing himself to be insolvent, transferred the house by an *ex facie* ("apparently") absolute disposition to his father so as to put it beyond the reach of his other creditors.

Held that the disposition was reducible at the instance of the other creditors.

(2) *Bank of Scotland* v. *Faulds* (1870) 7 S.L.R. 619: F., a waggonbuilder, when insolvent, entered into an arrangement with his creditors to pay a composition of 7s. 6d. in the £ with a condition attached

empowering the creditors to make an additional call of 2s. 6d. in the £ The additional call was not made and F. was discharged.

Between the date of the agreement and the discharge F. made a arrangement with Rowan & Co., iron merchants, his largest creditor: which resulted in his granting to them a promissory note for £1,732 3s.6d being 2s.6d. in the £ on their claim. Rowan & Co. discounted the not with the Bank of Scotland, and the bank brought an action against F. fo the amount of the note.

Held that the transaction constituted an illegal preference and that th bank, as coming in the place of Rowan & Co., could not recover.

10–48 It is particularly difficult to prove that the insolvent knew of hi insolvency at the date of the transaction, though the courts have readil allowed the debtor's knowledge of his insolvency to be inferred fror circumstances. A case in which a challenge failed for lack of evidence o this point is *Macdonald (Logan's Trustee)* v. *David Logan & Son Ltd* (1903) 11 S.L.T. 32 and 369:

In 1898 L. sold his colliery business to L. Ltd. In August 1901 there wa a debit balance of £7,460 standing in L. Ltd.'s books against L., and L disponed to the company in security of his indebtedness certain superiori ties of the value of £2,000. In February 1902 the estates of L. wer sequestrated, and the trustee in the sequestration brought an actio against the company for reduction of the disposition.

Held that there was no evidence to show that at the date of th disposition sought to be reduced L. knew that he was insolvent; his viev of his financial situation, though sanguine, was such as he might no unreasonably have been expected to take.

10–49 It is not, however, essential for the challenger of a fraudulent pre ference to prove that the favoured *creditor* knew of the debtor' insolvency: the "fraud" does not necessarily involve complicity on th creditor's part; it is inferred from the creditor's acceptance of the *debtor*' fraudulent act. This point was fully explained in *McCowan* v. *Wrigh* (1853) 15 D. 494, a case concerned with the reduction of a number o deeds "fraudulently" granted by an insolvent to his brother-in-law i order to give his brother-in-law security for large sums previousl advanced by the brother-in-law.

Lord Justice-Clerk Hope said (at p. 498) in considering reduction o securities on the ground of fraud: "It plainly is the act of the debtor whicl is injurious to the other creditors. His act creates the security. Then th fraud consists in this—that, being insolvent, or in circumstances whicl must end in hopeless insolvency, he creates that security to the effect o favouring one creditor, and to the prejudice of the rights of his othe creditors, by withdrawing all the funds which he can, or which ar necessary for the preference, from distribution among the creditor generally, and giving them to the favoured creditor. . . . The creditors ar equally injured—the prejudice to them is the same, whether the receive at the time knew that the security was a fraud against them or not; and if i was a fraud against them to give him that security, it does not become less so, that he did not at the time know that it was a fraud. The character anc effect of the debtor's act is not thereby altered."

A more recent authority on the same point is *Nordic Travel Ltd.* v. *Scotprint Ltd.*, 1980 S.C.1 (see 10–12, above), a case concerned with challenge of a fraudulent preference in the winding up of a registered company (see Companies Act 1948, s. 320(1), (3), by which both the common law and the statutory grounds of challenge are made to extend to registered companies).

The court held that N. Ltd., though absolutely insolvent, was entitled to pay, in cash and in the ordinary course of business, debts which were due and payable.

Lord President Emslie said (at p. 14): "The creditor's knowledge of his debtor's absolute insolvency at the time when the debtor performs an act in his favour is quite irrelevant in deciding whether or not the act is a fraudulent preference. If a particular act by an insolvent debtor to his creditor is *per se*[4] unobjectionable and lawful I am unable to see how his creditor's mere knowledge of his insolvency can make it objectionable and unlawful."

Three categories of voluntary acts of the debtor are exempt from challenge unless actual fraud is proved. These are:
  (i) payments in cash;
  (ii) transactions in the ordinary course of business; and
  (iii) *nova debita* ("new debts").
The same three categories are exempt from challenge under the Bankruptcy Act 1696.

(i) *Payments in Cash*

An insolvent who has funds in his hands sufficient to meet a debt which is immediately due is, if he pays that debt in cash, doing no more than he is bound to do. His act is not considered to be a voluntary act, and it is therefore necessarily exempt from challenge. A cheque drawn by the debtor on his bank is regarded as payment in cash in this connection.

An instance of a payment in cash is *Whatmough's Trustee* v. *British Linen Bank*, 1934 S.C. (H.L.) 51; 1932 S.C. 525:

W. was a motor omnibus proprietor whose business was being carried on at a loss. He sold the business, and, knowing himself to be insolvent, paid the cheque for £7,300 representing the price into his bank account which was then overdrawn to the extent of about £8,000. This cheque together with certain securities held by the bank was sufficient to pay off the overdraft. The bank was unaware of W.'s insolvency and no collusion on its part to obtain an illegal preference was shown to have existed.

About a month later W.'s estates were sequestrated, and the trustee sued the bank for £7,300 on the ground that the payment of that amount into the bank account had been an illegal preference both at common law and under the Act of 1696.

Held that the payment of the £7,300, being a payment in cash of an existing debt, made without collusion on the part of the creditor, was not reducible either at common law or under the Act.

The speech of Lord Thankerton in this case (1934 S.C. (H.L.) at pp. 55–65) has a full and authoritative review of the significance of "payments

---

[4] "of itself."

in cash" as well as of "transactions in the ordinary course of business," and Lord President Clyde's opinion (1932 S.C. at p. 543) is regarded as providing "the clearest summary of settled law on the matter of cash payments of debts by insolvent persons" (*per* Lord President Emslie in *Nordic Travel Ltd.* v. *Scotprint Ltd.*, 1980 S.C. 1, at p. 17 (see 10–12 and 10–50, above)).

(ii) *Transactions in the Ordinary Course of Business*

10–54 Even where an insolvent is conscious of his insolvency, he remains free at common law to continue in business, and so transactions which are in the ordinary course of that business are protected from challenge. If, however, financial difficulties cause him to depart from the ordinary course of business, the transactions are reducible.

10–55 Questions have arisen in relation to payment by cheque. Where the debtor makes payment by drawing a cheque on his own bank account this is clearly recognised as a transaction in the ordinary course of business. Equally, where, in *Whatmough's Trustee* v. *British Linen Bank* (10–53, above), the debtor indorsed a cheque to his bank so that the bank might collect the amount of the cheque from the bank on which it had been drawn, there was held to have been a transaction in the ordinary course of business. The position is different where the debtor resorts to negotiating cheques received from his own debtors. For instance, in *Horsburgh* v. *Ramsay & Co.* (1885) 12 R. 1171, where a boot manufacturer had been carrying on business in financial difficulties, paying his suppliers in cash when he had cash but more often by indorsing to them bills of exchange granted to him by the customers who bought his manufactured goods, such indorsations were held to be reducible under the Act of 1696 on the ground that they were not transactions in the ordinary course of trade. Similarly, in *Carter* v. *Johnstone* (1886) 13 R. 698, where a bankrupt paid a creditor by indorsing to him cheques on which the bankrupt was named as the payee, the indorsations were held reducible under the Act of 1696 as being neither cash payments nor transactions in the ordinary course of business.

(iii) Nova Debita

10–56 What is objectionable during insolvency is that the debtor should show favour to one of his existing creditors to the prejudice of his other existing creditors. There is no objection to his contracting new debts and granting to the creditor concerned a right in security or a preference in respect of the new debts, provided the reciprocal obligations (*e.g.* the creditor's obligation to lend money and the debtor's obligation to grant security for the loan) are created simultaneously.

10–57 An example of a transaction coming within this third category occurred in *Cowdenbeath Coal Co. Ltd.* v. *Clydesdale Bank Ltd.* (1895) 22 R. 682: A merchant obtained an advance from a bank, and on the following day indorsed and delivered to the bank in security of this advance a bill of lading for a cargo of coal. A creditor in an action against the bank sought to have the security set aside on the ground that it was an illegal preference under the Act of 1696. It was, however, proved that the bank had, in making the advance, relied on the bill of lading being delivered to it, and the court accordingly held that the security had been granted for a present advance and not for a prior debt and was therefore not struck at by the Act.

Similarly, in *Thomas Montgomery & Sons* v. *Gallacher,* 1982 S.L.T. 138 (O.H.), a standard security granted by a trader to one of his suppliers, who was becoming restive about the trader's credit-worthiness, was held to be good security to the extent of the value of goods supplied between the date of his undertaking to grant the standard security and the date of sequestration.

II NOTOUR BANKRUPTCY

The concept of "notour bankruptcy" was introduced by the Bankruptcy Act 1696. Proof of absolute insolvency (necessary for the reduction of fraudulent preferences at common law) was difficult: there was a need for a statutory provision which would eliminate this difficulty and make the legal consequences of inability to pay one's debts follow on a status or condition which could be easily recognised and proved. Hence "notour bankruptcy" may be defined in general terms as being a "status or condition fixed by legislative provision; in which insolvency accompanied by certain steps of diligence is held to be no longer doubtful, but public, proclaimed, or notorious" (Bell, *Commentaries* (7th ed.), Vol. II, p. 154).

The specific definition of "notour bankruptcy" now applicable is that in section 5 of the Bankruptcy (Scotland) Act 1913: notour bankruptcy is constituted by the following circumstances:

(a) by sequestration (in Scotland), or by the issuing of an adjudication of bankruptcy or the granting of a receiving order in England or Northern Ireland; or

(b) by insolvency, concurring with one of the following:

(i) a duly executed charge for payment, where a charge is necessary, followed by the expiry of the days of charge without payment;

(ii) where a charge is not necessary, the lapse without payment of the days which must elapse before poinding or imprisonment can follow on a decree or warrant for payment of a sum of money (a possibility removed when the small debt procedure authorised by the Small Debt (Scotland) Act 1837 was replaced, as from September 1, 1976, by the summary cause procedure introduced by the Sheriff Courts (Scotland) Act 1971, since a charge is essential in all cases in the latter procedure);

(iii) a poinding or seizure of any of the debtor's moveables for non-payment of rates or taxes;

(iv) a decree of adjudication of any part of the debtor's heritable estate for payment or in security; or

(v) sale of any of the debtor's effects under a sequestration for rent.

As regards (a), sequestration (or one of the other procedures mentioned) is a matter which, if it has occurred, is easy to prove. Also, as regards (b), any one of the five instances of diligence is easy to prove. The "insolvency" required for (b) is more difficult to prove, but there are two aids available to the person seeking to establish this mode of notour bankruptcy:

First, the insolvency is merely practical or commercial insolvency and not absolute insolvency (*Teenan's Trustee* v. *Teenan* (1886) 13 R. 833, in which the days of charge on a bill of exchange had expired without payment being made).

Secondly, insolvency is presumed if one of the five forms of diligence is proved, and it is then for the debtor to rebut the presumption by proving that he was in fact solvent. A case in which a debtor was successful in rebutting the presumption was *Michie* v. *Young,* 1962 S.L.T. (Notes) 70 (O.H.), where, in a petition for the recall of a sequestration, the debtor was able to show that he had had funds sufficient to pay a debt on which the charge had expired but had been prevented from paying the debt because of arrestments.

10–60 Notour bankruptcy of a partnership may be constituted in the same way as notour bankruptcy of an individual, and in addition it may be constituted by any of the partners being made notour bankrupt for a debt of the firm (s. 6).

10–61 Once constituted, notour bankruptcy continues, in case of a sequestration, till the debtor obtains his discharge, and in other cases until insolvency ceases (s. 7).

10–62 The legal effects of notour bankruptcy are that:

(a) it enables fraudulent preferences to be challenged under the Bankruptcy Act 1696;

(b) it equalises diligences; and

(c) it makes the debtor liable to sequestration at the instance of a creditor.

(a) Reduction of Fraudulent Preferences

10–63 The Act of 1696 facilitated the challenge of fraudulent preferences by declaring "voyd and null" "all and whatsomever voluntar dispositions assignations or other deeds which shall be found to be made or granted directly or indirectly" by a debtor, either at or after his becoming notour bankrupt or in the space of 60 days before notour bankruptcy, in favour of any of his creditors for their "satisfaction or farther Security in preference to other Creditors." The Companies Act 1947 (s. 115) substituted the period of six months before notour bankruptcy for the period of 60 days before notour bankruptcy.

10–64 The person making the challenge under the Act of 1696 must be either a prior creditor or the trustee in the debtor's sequestration, whether representing prior creditors or not (Bankruptcy (Scotland) Act 1913, s. 9).

10–65 The challenger must prove that:

(i) the debtor is notour bankrupt;

(ii) the deed was voluntary and in satisfaction or further security of a prior debt; and

(iii) the deed was granted at, or after, or within six months before, notour bankruptcy.

The challenger need not prove that the debtor was insolvent at the date of the transaction; nor need he prove that the transaction was fraudulent.

10–66 As at common law, cash payments, transactions in the ordinary course of business and *nova debita* are exempt from challenge unless actual fraud is proved (see 10–52—10–57, above).

The following are three instances of transactions which were held to be reducible under the Act of 1696:

(1) *McFarlane* v. *Robb and Co.* (1870) 9 M. 370: On August 23, William Marshall & Co. ("M. & Co.") chartered a vessel from R. & Co. for a voyage from Glasgow to Melbourne. The freight stipulated for in the charterparty was £4,500, of which £1,250 was payable after loading and £3,250 at the port of discharge. R. & Co. became doubtful of the credit of M. & Co., and on September 3, before any part of the freight had become due, M. & Co. accepted and paid a bill of exchange for £1,000 drawn on them by R. & Co.

On October 26, the estates of M. & Co. were sequestrated. McF., the trustee in the sequestration, brought an action against R. & Co. for the reduction of the bill and recovery of the £1,000.

Lord Neaves said (at p. 376): "Here the bill was accepted in security of the freight to become payable. . . . It is given as a pre-payment, before payment was prestable, as a security, in fact, to make Robb and Company safe in the transaction. There was not . . . a *novum debitum*[5] under a new contract. The money was truly deposited in the hands of Robb and Company till the period of payment under the contract should arrive, if it ever did arrive. It was not an absolute payment in present extinction of any claim, but was an anticipation of what was expected to become payable afterwards."

(2) *Gourlay* v. *Mackie* (1887) 14 R. 403: On December 23, 1885, John Millen & Co. ("M. & Co.") obtained a loan from Mackie, and as security handed over to Mackie a share certificate and undertook to transfer the shares to Mackie if and when Mackie so desired.

On January 15, 1886, Mackie procured a transfer of the shares from M. & Co., immediately registered the transfer with the company and obtained a new share certificate in his own name.

On January 28 next, the estates of M. & Co. were sequestrated, and G., the trustee in the sequestration, raised an action against Mackie for reduction of the transfer.

Lord Justice-Clerk Moncreiff said (at p. 408): "The money here was not advanced on the faith of a present or instant security. It was advanced without security and in the knowledge that there was none, but under a promise from the debtor that if and when the creditor desired it the shares in question should be transferred to him. The meaning of this was quite plain. It was a transaction separate from the advance, and was not absolute but conditional. So far as the parties were concerned, neither desired that any present or instant security should be then given."

(3) *Newton & Sons' Trustee* v. *Finlayson & Co.*, 1928 S.C. 637: In July 1924, the firm of N. & Sons was engaged in doing building work for the trustees of Cardonald parish church. The price for the work was payable by instalments on the architect's certificates. The firm was insolvent, and arrestments had been used in the hands of the church trustees by F. & Co.

N. & Sons arranged that the church trustees should pay the next instalment, when due, to F. & Co., in return for which F. & Co. would

---

[5] "new debt."

withdraw the arrestments. Effect was given to this arrangement by the end of July, F. & Co. receiving £200.

On August 7, the estates of N. & Sons were sequestrated, and the trustee in the sequestration brought an action for repayment of the £200 received by F. & Co.

Lord President Clyde said (at p. 645): "There was nothing whatever beyond the pressure of insolvency to compel the bankrupts in the present case to make or carry out the agreement described above, whereby the defenders were enabled to obtain satisfaction or further security for the bankrupts' indebtedness to them."

(b) Equalisation of Diligences

10–71 The object of the provisions considered under this heading is to prevent a "race of diligence," which would otherwise be likely to occur when it becomes known that a person is insolvent, each creditor attempting to attach some property belonging to the debtor towards the payment of the debt owed by the debtor to him. The statutory provisions, now in the Bankruptcy (Scotland) Act 1913, relate to arrestments and poindings, *i.e.* to the diligences which are appropriate for attaching moveable property which is in the hands of, respectively, a third party and the debtor himself. Arrestment would, for instance, be appropriate for attaching an employee's wages in the hands of his employer before payment is made and poinding would be appropriate for attaching furniture in the debtor's house.

10–72 Section 10 of the Act of 1913 provides that arrestments and poindings used within 60 days before, or four months after, the constitution of notour bankruptcy are ranked *pari passu* ("equally," "rateably") as if they had all been used of the same date. If the arresting or poinding creditor takes a further step towards completing his diligence (*i.e.* by bringing an action of forthcoming (or "furthcoming") in the case of arrestment or an action of poinding and sale in the case of poinding), any other creditor who then produces to the court liquid (*i.e.* "clear" and ascertained) grounds of debt or a decree for payment is entitled to rank as if he had executed an arrestment or a poinding. The effect is to give that other creditor a ranking equal to the ranking of arresting and poinding creditors. If the diligence has already reached its later stage where the arresting creditor obtains a decree of forthcoming and preference or a poinding creditor carries through a sale, that creditor is accountable for the sum recovered to those who are eventually found to have a right to a *pari passu* ranking with him.

10–73 These provisions in section 10 must be taken along with section 104 which provides that sequestration (though not itself a diligence, but rather a conglomeration of legal actions) is equivalent to an arrestment in execution and decree of forthcoming and to an executed or completed poinding. Section 104 further provides that no arrestment or poinding executed on or after the 60th day prior to the sequestration shall be effectual, and that the proceeds of such diligences must be handed over to the trustee in the sequestration. The only exception is that any arrester or poinder *before* the date of the sequestration who is, by this provision deprived of the benefit of his diligence is entitled to a preference for the expense *bona fide* incurred by him in executing the diligence.

The combined effect of section 10 and section 104 is seen in *Stewart v. Jarvie,* 1938 S.C. 309:

On October 12, 1936, S. brought an action against the Craigelvin Coal and Fireclay Co. for £273, and on October 16 used arrestments which attached the sum of £136. On November 27, notour bankruptcy was constituted against the firm by the expiry of a charge without payment.

Sequestration of the firm's estates was awarded on January 4, 1937.

Held that the only preference to which S. was entitled was the preference for his expenses in executing the arrestment.

Lord Fleming said (at p. 312): "It is important to note that, on the one hand, the appellant's arrestment was used within 60 days prior to the constitution of notour bankruptcy, and that, on the other hand, sequestration took place within four months thereafter. . . .

"Applying sections 10 and 104 to the case in hand, the result is that, as at 4th January 1937, the sequestration is to be regarded as equivalent to an arrestment used for behoof of all the creditors equally. And, accordingly, the appellant's claim for a preference over the other creditors must be dealt with on the footing that, in addition to the arrestment which he used on 16th October, 1936, there was also used, for behoof of the general body of the creditors, an arrestment on 4th January 1937. . . . The appellant is not entitled to any preference over the other creditors, for his arrestment and their arrestment are equalised under section 10. The appellant is entitled to be ranked on the arrested fund for the amount of his claim, but, equally, all the other creditors are entitled to be ranked thereon *pari passu* with him for the amount of their respective claims. . . .

"The trustee appears, however, to have taken the view that, under section 104, the appellant was entitled to a preference for the expense incurred by him in procuring his warrant and executing the diligence, and I think that the trustee was well founded in so holding."

(c) Liability to Sequestration

Notour bankruptcy enables creditors to take proceedings for the sequestration of their debtors' estates (s. 11).

III SEQUESTRATION

Most of the Bankruptcy (Scotland) Act 1913 is taken up with the details of the process of sequestration. For a general description of the purpose and nature of sequestration, reference may be made to the following three passages:

(i) Bell's *Commentaries* (7th ed.), Vol. II, p. 283: "Sequestration may be said to be a judicial process for attaching and rendering litigious the whole estate, heritable and moveable, real and personal, of the bankrupt, wherever situated, in order that it may be vested in a trustee selected by the creditors, to be recovered, managed, sold, and divided by him, according to certain rules of distribution."

10–78 (ii) Lord Dunedin in *Caldwell* v. *Hamilton,* 1919 S.C. (H.L.) 100 (a case in which future instalments of a bankrupt's salary, so far as they exceeded what was required for his reasonable maintenance, were held to vest in the trustee in the sequestration), at p. 107: "The principle of sequestration is that it is a process by which the whole property of a bankrupt person is ingathered by a trustee for the purpose of division *pari passu*[6] among the creditors."

10–79 (iii) Lord Kinnear in *Sinclair* v. *Edinburgh Parish Council,* 1909 S.C. 1353 (a case in which the word "sequestration" in the context "poinding, sequestration, or diligence whatever" in the Revenue Act 1884 was held to refer to the diligence of sequestration for rent and not to a sequestration under the bankruptcy statutes), at p. 1358: "It is said that sequestration under the Bankruptcy Act is also a diligence. But that is inaccurate. A petition for sequestration is not a diligence, it is an action. . . . It is a totally different thing to say that a trustee who has been confirmed is to have the same rights as if a diligence had been executed, and to say that the award of sequestration is itself a diligence. It is in fact the declaration of a Bankruptcy Court that the estates of a bankrupt debtor are set apart for the benefit of his creditors. . . .

". . . It is a judicial process for rendering litigious the whole estate of the bankrupt in order that no part of it may be carried away by a single creditor for his own benefit, but that the whole may be vested in the trustee, to be administered by him and distributed among the creditors according to certain fixed rules of distribution. Nothing could be more different from a diligence carried out by an individual creditor for his own benefit than a statutory process of that kind."

10–80 A point of terminology should be noted at the outset. It is evident from the passages quoted that sequestration is a process affecting the *estate* of the bankrupt. Therefore, strictly one should not refer to the sequestration of a *person,* but to the sequestration of the *estate of a person.* The former expression, however, is commonly used as a convenient and generally acceptable ellipsis.

10–81 Two sequestration procedures are provided for in the Act of 1913. These, as amended by the Insolvency Act 1976, are:

(a) sequestration, which, for the purpose of distinction, may be referred to as "ordinary sequestration"; and

(b) summary sequestration, which is available where a debtor's assets do not exceed £4,000 in value (s. 174, as amended by Insolvency Act 1976 (s. 1(1) and Sched. 1)).

10–82 Both procedures lay great emphasis on publicity. Applications and reports to the court are required at several stages. Most steps must be advertised, particularly in the *Edinburgh Gazette.* Entries must be made in public registers—the Register of Inhibitions and Adjudications and the Register of Sequestrations, the latter being a book kept by the Accountant of Court in the form set out in Schedule G to the Act (s. 156). The trustee administering the sequestrated estate, though appointed by the creditors, has no title to act without the court's authority. While the sequestration continues he is required to make a return annually to the

---

[6] "equally," "rateably."

sheriff clerk (s. 157), and his conduct in the sequestration, as that of the commissioners (creditors or their agents appointed to act along with him), is subject to the supervision of the Accountant of Court who may report any matter to the court (ss. 158-160). Each year a return must be made by each sheriff clerk to the Accountant of Court of all sequestrations then current in the sheriffdom, and these returns may be inspected by any interested party in the Accountant's office (s. 157).

This publicity, necessarily involving considerable expense, persuades many a bankrupt and also his creditors to shun sequestration and resort instead to a private trust deed for creditors (see 10–353 *et seq.*, below).

Another general aspect of the sequestration procedures which may be mentioned here is the rigidity of the statutory provisions. This has in many cases resulted in applications to the *nobile officium* ("equitable power") of the Inner House of the Court of Session, and will be illustrated later, once an outline of the procedure has been looked at (10–97 *et seq.*, below).

(a) Ordinary Sequestration

First to be considered are:

(i) the circumstances in which sequestration is competent.

One must then know:

(ii) the courts which may award sequestration.

The various steps in the procedure are laid down in great detail in the Act: in particular there are numerous time-limits which must be carefully observed. It will, therefore, be useful to set out:

(iii) a timetable of events in a sequestration,

before a description is given of:

(iv) the main steps in the sequestration process.

(i) *Circumstances in which Sequestration is Competent*

Sequestration may be awarded of the estate of any individual in the following cases:

(1) In the case of a living debtor who is subject to the jurisdiction of the supreme courts of Scotland, it may be awarded either:

(a) on his own petition,[7] with the concurrence of a "qualified" creditor; or

(b) on the petition of a "qualified" creditor, provided the debtor is notour bankrupt and has at any time within the year before the presentation of the petition resided or had a dwelling-house or place of business in Scotland.

(2) In the case of a deceased debtor who at the date of his death was subject to the jurisdiction of the supreme courts of Scotland, it may be awarded either:

(a) on the petition of a "mandatory" (*i.e.* an authorised person) to whom he had granted a "mandate" (*i.e.* authority) to apply for sequestration; or

---

[7] The word "petition" is used throughout the Act; in practice, however, where the application is to a sheriff court, it is made by "initial writ" and not by "petition" in the usual sense.

(b) on the petition of a "qualified" creditor (s. 11, as amended by Law Reform (Miscellaneous Provisions) (Scotland) Act 1980, s. 12(*a*)).

10–87 For the sequestration of the estate of a partnership the requirements are the same as for the sequestration of a living debtor's estate except that (1)(b), above, becomes:

on the petition of a "qualified" creditor, provided the debtor is notour bankrupt and has within the year before the presentation of the petition either:

(i) carried on business in Scotland, with at least one partner residing or having a dwelling-house in Scotland; or

(ii) had a place of business in Scotland (s. 11).

One of the ways in which the notour bankruptcy of a partnership may be constituted is, as has already been noticed, by any of the partners being made notour bankrupt for a debt due by the partnership (s. 6).

10–88 A "qualified" creditor is one to whom the debtor owes at least £200[8]. The debt may be liquid (*i.e.* ascertained in amount) or illiquid, but must not be contingent (*i.e.* dependent on the fulfilment of a condition) (s. 12, as amended by Insolvency Act 1976, s. 1(1) and Sched. 1). On the authority of Bell's *Commentaries* (7th ed., Vol. II, p. 289) and *Goudy on the Law of Bankruptcy* (4th ed., p. 121) a future debt payable on a day which is certain to arrive forms a good ground for a petition—a view which produces the anomaly that a creditor may be in a position to use a debt as a ground for a sequestration though he is not yet entitled to raise an action for payment of the debt. Several creditors may be joined together for the purpose of satisfying the qualification of £200.

10–89 Where a petition for the sequestration of a living debtor is presented without his concurrence (*i.e.* falls within (1) (b), above), it must be presented within four months of the date of his notour bankruptcy. A petition for the sequestration of a deceased debtor may be presented by a creditor at any time after the debtor's death, but sequestration cannot be awarded until six months from the death unless either the debtor was notour bankrupt at the time of his death or his successors concur in the petition or renounce the succession (s. 13).

(ii) *Courts which may Award Sequestration*

10–90 Sequestration may be awarded either by the Court of Session or by the sheriff court. In the latter case the debtor must either:

(a) have resided or had a dwelling-house or place of business in the sheriffdom concerned at the date of presentation of the petition; or

(b) have resided or carried on business within the sheriffdom for any period of 40 days or more during the year before the presentation of the petition.

No sequestration can be awarded by any court if evidence is produced that a sequestration has already been awarded in another court and is still undischarged (s. 16, as amended by Law Reform (Miscellaneous Provisions) (Scotland) Act 1980, s. 12(*b*)). Similarly, it has been held that where a person has been adjudicated bankrupt in England and the English bankruptcy is still alive, there is no room for a Scottish

---

[8] This amount may be altered by statutory instrument (Insolvency Act 1976, s. 1(2)).

sequestration (*Bank of Scotland* v. *Youde* (1908) 15 S.L.T. 847 (O.H.)).
It is, however, competent for a second sequestration to be awarded *in the
same court*—as in *Cook* v. *McDougall*, 1923 S.C. 86: McD., a Glasgow
publisher, had had his estates sequestrated in the sheriff court of Lanarkshire in 1900. He had never been discharged, but had continued to carry
on business and incurred new debts. In 1922 one of his new creditors
obtained a new award of sequestration in the same court.

If two petitions have been presented to different courts, the court to
which the later petition has been presented *may* remit the petition to the
other court (s. 16).

Where sequestration has actually been awarded by the sheriffs of two
or more sheriffdoms, the later sequestration or sequestrations *must* be
remitted to the sheriff who first awarded sequestration, and intimation of
that fact must be given in the *Edinburgh Gazette*. If all the sequestrations
are of the same date, an appeal could be made to the Court of Session.
Where sequestration has been awarded by the Court of Session and also
by one or more sheriff courts, the Court of Session must remit the
sequestration to such sheriff court as in the whole circumstances it deems
expedient; notice of the remit must be given in the *Edinburgh Gazette* (s.
17). Sequestrations awarded by the Court of Session alone must also be
remitted by that court to a sheriff court (s. 17), but, according to the
decision in *West of Scotland Refractories Ltd., Petitioners*, 1969 S.C. 43,
such a remit need not be intimated in the Gazette.

It is competent, at any time, to bring a sequestration before the Court
of Session so that that court may transfer the sequestration from one
sheriff court to another sheriff court (s. 19).

(iii) *Timetable of Events in Sequestration*

This timetable is intended to be complementary to the narrative in (iv),
below. Some words may be unfamiliar, *e.g.* "deliverance" (meaning a
pronouncement by the court), and "abbreviate" (meaning a summary or
note). Further explanation will be found in (iv), below. References to the
"Gazette" are in this timetable, as in the Act itself, references to the
Edinburgh Gazette unless otherwise stated (s. 2).

1. Presentation of petition to court (ss. 11-13).
2. In same petition or in separate petition, possible application by creditor to court for
   interim preservation of the estate (s. 14).
3. Court's first deliverance (which may or may not actually award sequestration, but is
   in either case taken as fixing the commencement of the sequestration) (ss. 28, 29 and 41).
4. Within 2 days of first deliverance, presentation by petitioner of abbreviate of petition
   and first deliverance for recording in Register of Inhibitions and Adjudications (s. 44
   and Sched. A).
5. Award of sequestration (if not awarded by first deliverance) (s. 29).
6. Within 40 days of award, possibility of recall of sequestration (s. 30).
7. Within 4 days of award, notice in Gazette of award and of date of forthcoming first
   statutory meeting (s. 44 and Sched. B).
8. Within 6 days of award, similar notice in *London Gazette* (s. 44 and Sched. B).
9. Within 6-12 days of appearance of Gazette notice (see 7, above), first statutory meeting:
   submission by bankrupt of state of affairs; election by creditors of trustee and commissioners; possibility of bankrupt's offer to pay a composition being "entertained"
   (ss. 63, 77, 64, 72 and 134).
10. Possibility of winding up under deed of arrangement (s. 34).

11. With least possible delay, declaration by sheriff of trustee's election (ss. 65-67).
12. Within 7 days of sheriff's declaration, lodging by trustee of bond of caution with sheriff clerk (s. 69 and Sched. C).
13. Confirmation by sheriff of trustee's election, and issue by sheriff clerk of trustee's act and warrant (s. 70 and Sched. D).
14. Within 3 days of issue of act and warrant, transmission by sheriff clerk of copy of act and warrant to Accountant of Court for entry of trustee's name in Register of Sequestrations (s. 70).
15. Within 8 days of act and warrant, application by trustee to sheriff to fix date of public examination of bankrupt and for issue by sheriff of warrant for bankrupt's attendance (s. 83).
16. Publication by trustee in Gazette of notice giving date for public examination and date of second statutory meeting; sending by trustee of same notice to each creditor (s. 83 and Sched. F).
17. Within 10 days of confirmation of trustee's election (see 13, above), presentation by trustee of abbreviate of his act and warrant for recording in Register of Inhibitions and Adjudications (s. 75 and Sched. E).
18. As soon as may be after appointment, trustee to take possession of bankrupt's estate, make up inventory and valuation, and immediately transmit copies of inventory and valuation to Accountant of Court (s. 76).
19. Within 7-14 days of sheriff's warrant (see 15, above), public examination of bankrupt (ss. 83-91).
20. Within 7-14 days of public examination, second statutory meeting: consideration of trustee's report on bankrupt's affairs and trustee's estimate of what estate may produce; possibly directions given by creditors to trustee concerning management *etc.* of estate; possibly also acceptance of offer of composition to be paid by bankrupt (see 9, above) (ss. 83 and 92).
21. Immediately on expiry of 4 months from actual award of sequestration, account by trustee of his intromissions (s. 121).
22. Within next 14 days, commissioners meet to audit the account and to decide what dividend may be paid (s. 121).
23. On or before the first lawful day after the 14 days referred to in 22, above, trustee to post to each creditor a letter specifying the dividend which is proposed to be paid on his claim (s. 124).
24. Within 8 days after the expiry of the 14 days referred to in 22, above, trustee to give notice in Gazette of time and place of payment of dividend (s. 124).
25. Before expiry of 6 months from actual award of sequestration, scheme of division to be drawn up by trustee as directed by commissioners, and notification by trustee to each creditor of amount of dividend to which he may be entitled (s. 125).
26. On first lawful day after expiry of 6 months from actual award of sequestration, payment of first dividend (s. 126).
27. On expiry of 8 months from actual award of sequestration, another account by trustee of his intromissions, followed by repetition of steps 22 to 25, above, leading up to payment of second dividend on first lawful day after expiry of 10 months from actual award of sequestration (ss. 127 and 128).
28. Possibility of further dividends after similar procedure to that in 22 to 25, above, each dividend being paid on first lawful day after expiry of 3 months from payment of previous dividend (s. 129).
29. Possibility of discharge of bankrupt on composition (ss. 134-142).
30. Discharge of bankrupt without composition—
    after second statutory meeting and before expiry of 2 years from actual award of sequestration, petition by bankrupt to court with concurrence of varying majorities of creditors; *or*
    after expiry of 2 years from actual award of sequestration, petition by bankrupt to court without any consents of creditors;
    trustee's report, not demandable till expiry of 5 months from actual award of sequestration;
        petition intimated in Gazette and to each creditor;
        bankrupt's declaration of full and fair surrender of estate;
        at least 21 days after publication in Gazette, court deliverance finding bankrupt entitled to discharge;

abbreviate of deliverance of discharge recorded in Register of Inhibitions and Adjudications (ss. 143 and 145 and Sched. E).

31. Trustee's discharge—
　　final division of funds;
　　meeting of creditors to be advertised in Gazette and intimated to each creditor by letter;
　　holding of meeting at least 14 days after Gazette notice;
　　application to court by trustee for discharge;
　　court's decree of exoneration;
　　transmission by sheriff clerk of extract decree to Accountant of Court for entry in Register of Sequestrations;
　　trustee's bond of caution delivered up (s. 152).

(iv) *Main Steps in Sequestration Process*

The detailed statutory procedure must be strictly observed at every stage; otherwise the sequestration will be invalid, *e.g.*:

George Younger & Son Ltd. v. *Cronin*, 1926 S.N. 36 (O.H.); 1926 S.L.T. 238 (O.H.): Under sections 20 and 21 of the Act of 1913 an oath containing certain specified particulars must be produced in a petition for sequestration.

Y. Ltd. presented a petition for the sequestration of C., and produced an oath which did not comply with the statute in that it did not specify that Y. Ltd. held certain securities.

Y. Ltd. lodged an amended oath.

The Lord Ordinary, however, dismissed the petition, holding that a petitioner must produce the oath in its final and proper form along with the petition.

In some situations a defect in the procedure may be cured by an application to the *nobile officium* ("equitable power") of the Inner House of the Court of Session. Most of the recent reported cases on bankruptcy have been applications of this type.

In particular, there is under the Act no way by which a bankrupt may obtain his discharge if the statutory machinery has broken down. This is regarded as a *casus improvisus* ("unforeseen occurrence") for which one may invoke the *nobile officium, e.g.*:

Laings, Petitioners, 1962 S.C. 168: The estates of Mr and Mrs L. as individuals and as partners in a firm were sequestrated in 1953. The trustee appointed failed to lodge a bond of caution within seven days of his election being declared as is required by section 69 of the Act of 1913, and the sheriff therefore refused to confirm the trustee's election under section 70.

No further steps were taken in the sequestration for eight years.

Mr and Mrs L. were unable to obtain a discharge under section 143 of the Act since that section required a report by a trustee whose election had been duly confirmed.

No dividend had been paid, but creditors representing over 95 per cent of the debts due had waived their claims.

The bankrupts petitioned the *nobile officium* of the Court of Session for their discharge, and the prayer of their petition was *granted*.

A similar case was that of *Black, Petitioner*, 1964 S.C. 276.

In *Fraser* v. *Glasgow Corporation*, 1967 S.C. 120, a sheriff court had awarded sequestration, but no creditors attended the first statutory meeting and so no trustee was elected. No further steps were taken in the sequestration. Several years later the bankrupt obtained his discharge under the *nobile officium.*

10–102　　Applications to the *nobile officium* for other purposes have included the two following cases:

10–103　　(1) *Kippen's Trustee, Petitioner,* 1966 S.C. 3: The abbreviate recorded in the Register of Inhibitions and Adjudications under section 44 of the Act lasts for five years, but, if the trustee has not been discharged within these five years, he must renew the abbreviate by recording a memorandum in a statutory form.

This case was a successful application by a trustee to the *nobile officium* for authority to record such a memorandum five years after it ought to have been recorded.

10–104　　(2) *Law Society of Scotland, Petitioners,* 1974 S.L.T. (Notes) 66: The date for the holding of the first statutory meeting is, by section 63 of the Act, six to 12 days after the appearance of the Gazette notice of the award of the sequestration.

In this case concerning the sequestration of a solicitor, while the notice had appeared timeously in the *Edinburgh Gazette,* the notice in the *London Gazette* had, owing to an industrial dispute at the press of the *London Gazette,* not appeared until two days before the meeting. The sheriff refused to confirm the trustee's election.

The petition was presented to the *nobile officium* for a declaration that the notice which had appeared in the *London Gazette* was to be equivalent to a notice appearing within the time-scale required by the Act.

10–105　　The main steps in a sequestration are as follows:

The petition

10–106　　For the circumstances in which a petition for sequestration may be presented and the courts which have jurisdiction, see (i) and (ii), above (10–86—10–93).

10–107　　The creditor who presents the petition (or who concurs in it if it is presented by the debtor himself) must produce along with the petition an oath and also the account and vouchers of the debt; otherwise the petition will be dismissed (s. 20). The oath referred to is an oath as to the "verity" (genuineness) of the debt claimed. It must be taken by the creditor before a judge or justice of the peace or notary public. The creditor must state in the oath what other persons are, besides the debtor, liable for the debt and must specify any security which he holds over the estate of the debtor or of other persons (s. 21). If the oath does not comply with the statutory requirements, the petition will be dismissed (*George Younger & Son Ltd.* v. *Cronin* (10–96, above)). The term "voucher" is not explained in the Act. In *Samson* v. *Campbell* (1851) 13 D. 1395 an account which contained lump sums for "postages and cash" and amounts claimed as disbursements for the bankrupt was held not to be "vouched," though it had been marked as "correct" by the bankrupt himself. In modern practice a statement or description included in an ordinary trade account is regarded as being of itself a sufficient "voucher."

Interim preservation of estate

08 Once the petition has been presented, the court may if it thinks proper take immediate measures for the preservation of the estate, either by the appointment of a judicial factor or by other proceedings (s. 14).

09 Circumstances in which a judicial factor was appointed were present in *J. & G. Stewart* v. *Waldie,* 1926 S.L.T. 526 (O.H.): A creditor of a deceased debtor had presented a petition for sequestration. Under section 13 of the Act sequestration could not be awarded until six months after the death. A judicial factor was appointed to administer the deceased's estate until a trustee in the sequestration could be appointed.

10 At any time after the presentation of the petition, warrant may be granted for possession to be taken of money, cheques and other moveable property belonging to or in the possession of the debtor, and, if necessary, for lock-fast places to be opened and for the house or other premises and the person of the debtor to be searched (s. 15).

Award of sequestration

11 Before sequestration can be awarded, citation *may* first be necessary, *i.e.* the court in its "first deliverance" will grant warrant to cite the debtor (or if he is dead, his successor) to appear in court within a specified period to show cause why sequestration should not be awarded. This procedure of citation is necessary where the petition is presented without the consent of the debtor (or, in the case of sequestration of a deceased debtor, without the consent of his successor) (s. 25). The specified period, referred to as the "induciae of citation," must be not less than six nor more than 14 days (s. 27).

12 When the petition is presented by or with the concurrence of the debtor (or, in the case of a deceased debtor, with the concurrence of his successor or if the successor renounces the succession), the court *must forthwith* award sequestration (s. 28). The "first deliverance" in this case is therefore the actual award of sequestration.

13 Where the petition is not by or with the concurrence of the debtor (or, if he is dead, of his successor), there must first be citation, as explained above, and the court then awards sequestration only if the debtor (or his successor, as the case may be) does not appear and show cause why sequestration cannot be awarded, or if the debtor does appear but does not instantly pay the debts or produce written evidence that they have been satisfied (s. 29).

14 If a creditor who has petitioned for sequestration or concurred in such a petition withdraws or becomes bankrupt himself or dies, any other creditor may be "sisted" (*i.e.* made to stand, or substituted) in his place to continue the proceedings (s. 33).

15 The petitioning or concurring creditor is entitled to payment of the expenses incurred by him in obtaining the sequestration out of the first of the funds which come into the hands of the trustee (s. 40).

16 The sequestration commences on and from the date of the first deliverance: that date is taken as the date of the sequestration, although the sequestration may not actually have been awarded until a later date (s. 41).

10–117   For the preservation of the estate, the sheriff has power if he thinks fit, at any time after the date of the sequestration and before the election of a trustee, to cause the books and papers of the bankrupt to be sealed up and put under safe custody and to lock up the bankrupt's shop or other repositories and keep the keys until a trustee is elected and confirmed (s. 15). This is additional to the steps which may be taken for interim preservation of the estate *before* the date of the sequestration (see 10–108, above).

Registration of sequestration (section 44)

10–118   The party who applied for sequestration must, before the expiry of the second lawful day after the first deliverance, present or send an abbreviate of the petition and deliverance to the Keeper of the Register of Inhibitions and Adjudications at Edinburgh. The abbreviate must be in the form set out in Schedule A, No. 1:

> "Petition for sequestration of *A.B.* [*name and designation*].
> Date of first deliverance   day of
>   (Signed) *C.D.* [*if an agent, state so.*]
> Date   ''

10–119   The Keeper must forthwith record the abbreviate in the Register and write a certificate on the abbreviate in the form specified in Schedule A, No. 2. The person who lodged the abbreviate may then have it returned to him.

10–120   The abbreviate, once recorded, takes effect from the *date of the first deliverance.* From that date it has the effect of an inhibition and of a citation in an adjudication of the debtor's estate at the instance of all the creditors who are afterwards ranked on the estate, *i.e.* all these creditors are placed in the same position as if they had done diligence against the debtor's estate. This effect cannot be stopped by payment of the debts for which the sequestration has been awarded.

10–121   The effect of the recorded abbreviate expires on the lapse of five years from the date of its recording, but it may be renewed by recording a memorandum in the form of Schedule A, No. 4. If the trustee has not been discharged, he *must* record such a memorandum before the lapse of the five years. The same procedure applies on the lapse of every subsequent period of five years.

10–122   Where there has been failure to comply with these statutory provisions as to the recording of an abbreviate or a memorandum, the document in question does not take effect as an inhibition or citation in an adjudication. An application may be made to the *nobile officium* of the Court of Session for a remedy (*e.g. White Cross Insurance Association Ltd. and Another, Petitioners,* 1924 S.C. 372, in which, where the original abbreviate had been transmitted to the Keeper after the statutory period had expired, the court authorised a fresh abbreviate to be transmitted for recording, and *Kippen's Trustee, Petitioner* (10–103, above), in which there had been failure to renew the abbreviate before the expiry of five years from the date of its having been recorded.

10–123   In addition to these requirements for recording in the Register of Inhibitions and Adjudications which apply to the *first deliverance* (whether that awards sequestration or not), section 44 provides for notices to be inserted in the *Edinburgh* and *London Gazettes* within a specified time from the date of the *deliverance awarding sequestration.* The responsibility for inserting these notices lies on the person who applied for the sequestration. The notices are in the form set out in Schedule B; they state:

1. the fact that the estates of *"A.B."* were sequestrated on a specified date by the Court of Session or a specified sheriff court, as the case may be;

2. the date of the first deliverance;

3. the hour, date and place of the "first statutory meeting" (at which the trustee and commissioners are to be elected); and

4. the fact that all future advertisements relating to the sequestration will be published in the *Edinburgh Gazette* alone.

The time for insertion of the notice in the *Edinburgh Gazette* is a maximum of four days after the date of the award of the sequestration if it was awarded by the Court of Session, or, if it was awarded by a sheriff court, a maximum of four days after a copy of the deliverance could be received in course of post in Edinburgh. The time for insertion in the *London Gazette* is a maximum of six days after the same dates. Failure to comply with these time-limits may involve an application to the *nobile officium* of the Court of Session, as in *Law Society of Scotland, Petitioners* (10–104, above).

Recall, reduction and annulment of sequestration

No appeal can be made to a higher court against an award of sequestration (s. 30). The Act, however, does enable a sequestration to be "recalled" in certain circumstances (ss. 30, 31 and 43). A sequestration may also be "reduced" (set aside), and it may be annulled under the *nobile officium* of the Court of Session:

1. *Recall under section 30*

This is usually competent only within 40 days after the deliverance awarding sequestration. The procedure is for a petition to be presented to the Outer House of the Court of Session, setting forth the grounds for the recall. The petition may be at the instance of:

(a) the debtor (but only if his estate has been sequestrated without his consent); or

(b) in the case of a deceased debtor who has not authorised his own sequestration, the successors of the deceased debtor, provided they have neither renounced the succession nor consented to the sequestration; or

(c) any creditor.

An exception is provided for the situation where the successor of a deceased debtor whose estate has been sequestrated has been "edictally cited" (a reference to the type of citation applicable where the successor is outside Scotland or his address is unknown): in that situation the successor, or any person having interest, may present a petition for recall at any time before the publication of the advertisement for payment of the first dividend.

The Lord Ordinary must order a copy of the petition for recall to be served on the parties who petitioned or concurred in the petition for sequestration and on the trustee (if appointed), must require these parties to answer within a specified short time, and must order publication in the Gazette of a notice of the presentation of the petition for recall. If he decides to recall the sequestration, the recall must be entered in the Register of Sequestrations, and an abbreviate extract of his deliverance recalling the sequestration must be recorded in the Register of Inhibitions and Adjudications. The form for this abbreviate extract is Schedule E, No. 5.

10–128 The ground for a recall may be any ground which could have been stated to oppose the award (*e.g.* that notour bankruptcy was not properly constituted, as in *Michie* v. *Young,* 1962 S.L.T. (Notes) 70 (O.H.) (10–59, above)), or any ground which has since emerged.

2. *Recall under section 31*

10–129 Section 31 provides that "excepting as hereinafter provided" no petition for recall is competent after the expiration of the 40-day period or after the advertisement for payment of the first dividend as the case may be. The section then goes on to provide that nine-tenths in number and value of the creditors may at any time apply for recall by presenting a petition to the Outer House of the Court of Session.

10–130 The Lord Ordinary must order publication in the Gazette of a notice requiring all concerned to appear within the next 14 days to show cause why the sequestration should not be recalled.

10–131 No ground for recall need be established by the petitioners. The onus is on those appearing to oppose the recall to satisfy the court that a recall should not be granted (*Livingstone's Creditors* v. *Livingstone's Trustee,* 1937 S.L.T. 391 (O.H.)).

3. *Recall under section 43*

10–132 Section 43 provides for recall on the special ground that a majority of the creditors in number and value reside in England or [Northern] Ireland and that from the situation of the property or other causes the estate ought to be distributed under the laws of England or [Northern] Ireland. The petition must be presented within three months after the date of sequestration, and may be at the instance of the Accountant of Court or any creditor or any other person who has an interest. According to section 43 the petition may be presented to either the Inner or the Outer House of the Court of Session, but according to Court of Session practice it would be an Outer House petition (R.C. 189).

10–133 An instance of a recall on this ground is *Cooper* v. *Baillie &c.* (1878) 5 R. 564:

B., a Scotsman by origin, had resided and traded in England. His assets consisted chiefly of shares in English mining companies, and these shares had been pledged by him to certain of his creditors in security of the debts due to them.

B. returned to Scotland, and with the concurrence of a creditor obtained sequestration in Scotland. All his debts, which amounted to over £80,000, had their origin in England, except for a small claim for house rent in Oban. With two or three exceptions his creditors resided in England.

C. of London, to whom B. owed £5,492, presented a petition for the recall of the sequestration under the statutory provision which is now section 43 of the Act of 1913.

The petition for recall was opposed by B. and by a large majority of his creditors, whose claims amounted to about £67,000.

Holding that the bankruptcy was essentially an English bankruptcy, the court *recalled* the sequestration.

4. Reduction

Reduction of a sequestration is competent at common law. The action for reduction—which would be in the Outer House of the Court of Session—must be brought timeously:

Central Motor Engineering Co. v. *Galbraith*, 1918 S.C. 755: Partners in a firm, having become aware of an irregularity in the citation of the petition for the firm's and their own sequestration, delayed for two and a half years before bringing an action for reduction.

Held that they were not entitled to succeed in their action.

5. Annulment

A sequestration which cannot be recalled under 1. to 3., above, and which cannot be reduced under 4., above, may be annulled by the Inner House of the Court of Session in the exercise of its *nobile officium*. This is a last resort:

Central Motor Engineering Co. v. *Gibbs*, 1917 S.C. 490: A petition was presented under the *nobile officium* to have a sequestration declared void because of irregularities in citation of the debtors and in the oath of the petitioning creditor.

Held that the petition was incompetent or premature since the petitioners had failed to show that they could not obtain their remedy by an action of reduction.

Ranking of claims

The way in which creditors make their claims in the sequestration, their rights of voting at creditors' meetings and their rights to be ranked on the bankrupt estate when dividends are being paid are regulated principally by sections 45 to 62 of the Act of 1913 (as amended by the Insolvency Act 1976, s. 5(3)). Also to be noted in this connection are sections 96 and 105.

Section 96 provides that all questions at any meeting of creditors are to be decided by the *majority in value* of those present and entitled to vote, except where there is some other express provision. Section 96 further provides that where under the Act creditors are required to be counted in number, no creditor whose debt is under £20 is to be reckoned in number, but his debt is to be computed in value. That latter part of section 96 would apply where for some step in the proceedings the Act required, *e.g.*, "nine-tenths in number and value of the creditors ranked on the estate" (s. 31—see 10–129, above) or "a majority in number and three-fourths in value of the creditors present" (s. 34—see 10–164, below).

10–138   Section 105 provides for the interruption of prescription: when a creditor presents or concurs in presenting a petition for sequestration or lodges a claim in the sequestration, prescription ceases to run on the debt due to him.

10–139   The rules in sections 45 to 62 and in sections 96 and 105 of the Act of 1913 apply also to liquidations of registered companies (Companies Act 1948, s. 318).

10–140   There are three groups of rules in sections 45 to 62: first, there are general rules as to voting and ranking for payment of dividends (ss. 45-54—see 1. to 5., below); secondly, there are special rules as to voting (ss. 55-60—see 6., below); and thirdly, there are special rules as to ranking for payment of dividends (ss. 61 and 62—see 7., below).

10–141   The main rules are as follows:

10–142   1. A creditor wishing to vote or draw a dividend formerly had to produce at the meeting concerned or lodge with the trustee an oath in the same form as the oath which is still required in the case of the petitioning creditor (s. 45). Formalities were lessened by the Insolvency Act 1976: a creditor wishing to vote or draw a dividend is now normally bound to produce at the meeting or lodge with the trustee merely a *"notice of claim"* (in a form set out in a statutory instrument) along with the account and vouchers necessary to prove the debt claimed, though the trustee is entitled in any case to require an oath instead of a notice of claim (s. 45, as substituted by Insolvency Act 1976, s. 5(3)).

10–143   2. A creditor who has a debt due to him is entitled to vote and rank for the accumulated sum of *principal and interest to the date of the sequestration,* but not for any interest accruing after that date. If the debt is not payable until after the date of the sequestration, he must deduct interest from that date. He must also deduct any special discount applicable to his debt by usage of trade or by the contract or course of dealing between himself and the bankrupt (s. 48).

10–144   3. When the claim of a creditor depends on a *contingency* which is unascertained at the date of the lodging of the claim, the creditor is not entitled to vote or draw a dividend unless and until he has applied to the trustee (or, if the trustee has not yet been elected, to the sheriff) to put a value on the debt; he will then be entitled to vote and draw dividends in respect of the value fixed by the trustee or the sheriff, as the case may be, but for no more (s. 49).

10–145   4. Similarly, where the bankrupt has granted an *annuity,* the creditor in the annuity must first have the annuity valued before he is entitled to vote and draw a dividend (s. 50).

10–146   5. This rule relates to *co-obligants* of the bankrupt. Where a creditor ("C") has a right to receive payment of his debt from another person ("A") along with the bankrupt ("B"), then A is not freed from his liability for the debt merely because C votes or draws a dividend in B's sequestration or consents to B's discharge, but if A pays the amount of the debt to C, then A is entitled to obtain from C an assignation to the debt, and A may then make a claim on B's estate and vote and draw dividends in place of C (s. 52).

10–147   6. The first of the *special rules as to voting* is that if a creditor holds a security for his debt over part of the bankrupt's estate, he must, before voting, put a specific value on the security and deduct that value from his debt; he is then entitled to vote in respect of the balance and no more, except that in questions as to the disposal or management of the estate subject to his security he is entitled to vote as a creditor for the full amount of his debt without making any such deduction (s. 55). Similarly, where there is a co-obligant who is bound to relieve the bankrupt, the creditor must put a value on the obligation of that co-obligant and must deduct that value from his debt; he is then entitled to vote only in respect of the balance (s. 56). It is only in the case of a co-obligant who is bound to relieve the bankrupt that valuation and deduction require to be made under this provision: for example, where the claim is being made on the estate of a cautioner, the value of the principal debtor's obligation must be deducted, but in the converse situation where the claim is being made on the estate of the principal debtor, no value requires to be put on the cautioner's obligation.

In the bankruptcy of a firm, a creditor is not bound, for the purpose of voting on the firm's estate, to deduct from his claim the value which he may be entitled to draw from the estates of the partners, but if he claims on the estate of a partner, he must, before voting, value and deduct his claim against the firm's estate and also his claim against the other partners in so far as they are liable to relieve that partner (s. 57).

To dissuade a creditor from specifying too low a value in any of the circumstances covered by this sixth rule, the Act provides that the trustee (with the consent of the commissioners) or the majority of the other creditors at any creditors' meeting may require the creditor to transfer the security or obligation or claim to the trustee on payment to the creditor of the specified value plus 20 per cent (s. 58).

7. For the purpose of *ranking for dividends,* a creditor who holds a security over any part of the bankrupt's estate must similarly value and deduct his security, but in this case the trustee (with the consent of the commissioners) is entitled to have the security transferred to him at the specified value without any increase; the creditor is ranked for and receives a dividend only on the balance left after deduction of his security (s. 61).

In the bankruptcy of a firm, if a creditor claims on the estate of a partner for a debt due by the firm, the trustee in the partner's sequestration must, before ranking the creditor, put a valuation on the firm's estate, make the necessary deduction from the creditor's claim and pay to him a dividend only on the balance (s. 62). Where the firm has been dissolved at an earlier date than the date of the partner's sequestration, the trustee must take the earlier date for the purposes of his valuation (*Clydesdale Bank Ltd.* v. *Morison's Trustee,* 1983 S.L.T. 42).

First statutory meeting

The Lord Ordinary or the sheriff, in the deliverance which awards sequestration, must fix the time for the creditors' meeting at which the trustee in the sequestration will be elected and certain other business will be transacted. This meeting is commonly referred to as the "first statutory meeting," though that term is not used in the Act. The date of the meeting must be not earlier than six nor later than 12 days from the date of the appearance in the Gazette of the notice of the award of sequestration. The place of the meeting must be a "convenient place" within the sheriffdom in which the sequestration has been awarded or to which it has been remitted (s. 63). According to *A* v. *B* (1847) 10 D. 245, decided under earlier legislation, the meeting should be held "in some public place, such as an inn or the Sheriff-Clerk's office, and not in the chambers of law-agents or accountants, as was sometimes the practice."

10–153   At this meeting the bankrupt must deliver to the clerk of the meeting a state of his affairs, specifying his whole property, wherever situated, and the names and designations of his creditors and debtors and the debts due by and to him (s. 77).

10–154   If two or more creditors give notice to the sheriff, he must attend and preside at the meeting. The sheriff clerk or his depute must then also attend and write the minutes in the presence of the meeting, entering in the minutes the names and designations of the creditors present and the amount of their claims, and any other circumstances which the presiding sheriff considers fit. The sheriff must sign the minutes (s. 64). In practice the sheriff is seldom called upon to attend the meeting.

10–155   If the sheriff is not present, the creditors must elect a "preses" (chairman) and (if the sheriff clerk or a depute is not present) a clerk.

10–156   The creditors who have produced their claims and documents of debt and who have been entered in the minutes must then and there elect a fit person to be trustee, or two or more trustees, to act in succession, in case the first does not accept or dies or resigns or is removed or is disqualified (s. 64).

The words relating to the election of a substitute trustee have been interpreted as having only a limited scope and not as enabling the substitute to act automatically if at any time during the sequestration the first trustee dies or resigns or is removed; the argument is that if that wider interpretation were accepted, there would then be an inconsistency between the words in section 64 and section 71, which refers to the holding of a creditors' meeting for devolving the estate on the trustee next in succession (see 10–181, below). *Goudy on the Law of Bankruptcy* states (at p. 203):

"It is only in cases where the failure of the first named trustee has arisen, from non-acceptance, etc., prior to the Sheriff's declaration,[9] that the subsidiary trustee will be declared elected; in other cases . . . the creditors must again meet, either to devolve the estate on the trustee next in succession, or to elect a new trustee."

Goudy's view, however, seems open to the criticism that it does not differentiate between (1) the provisions in section 71 which relate to removal of a trustee by the court on the petition of one-fourth of the creditors and (2) the provisions which relate to removal by a majority in number and value of creditors present at a meeting and to death and resignation: in (1) the provision for a meeting is mandatory—the court "*shall* remove the trustee, and appoint a meeting of the creditors to be held for devolving the estate on the trustee next in succession, or electing a new trustee," but in (2) the provision for a meeting is permissive—"any

---

[9] See 10–173 *et seq.*, below.

commissioner, or any creditor . . . *may* apply to the [*court*] for an order to hold a meeting for devolving the estate on the trustee next in succession or electing a new trustee."

In the case of the sequestration of a firm and its individual partners, one trustee may be appointed for all the estates or separate trustees may be appointed for the different estates.

It is not lawful to elect as trustee the bankrupt, or any person "conjunct or confident" with him, or who holds an interest opposed to the general interest of the creditors, or whose residence is not within the jurisdiction of the Court of Session (s. 64).

Further procedure is necessary before the trustee is in a position to commence his duties in the sequestration. That further procedure is detailed in sections 65 to 70 of the Act (see 10–170 *et seq.*, below).

After the election of the trustee, the creditors elect three commissioners, who must be either creditors or "mandatories" (agents) of creditors. No person is eligible as a commissioner if he is disqualified from being a trustee, and any mandatory who has been elected a commissioner loses that office if the creditor concerned recalls the mandate (s. 72).

Here again further procedure is required before the commissioners are entitled to act in the sequestration (see 10–179, below).

Other business which may be transacted at the first statutory meeting includes a resolution that the estate be wound up under a deed of arrangement (s. 34—see 10–163 *et seq.*, below), the fixing of an allowance for the bankrupt (s. 74—see 10–184, below), and the "entertaining" of an offer of composition (s. 134—see 10–306, below).

Deed of arrangement

It is possible for the sequestration to be brought to an end before it has proceeded even as far as the election of the trustee. This happens if a winding up under a deed of arrangement is substituted for the sequestration in accordance with sections 34 to 39 of the Act.

First there must be a resolution passed by *a majority in number and three-fourths in value of the creditors present* at a meeting to the effect that the estate ought to be wound up under a deed of arrangement and that an application should be presented to the court to "sist" (stop) procedure in the sequestration for up to two months. The meeting may be either the first statutory meeting or any later meeting called for the purpose. In the former case, if the resolution is carried, election of a trustee is unnecessary (s. 34).

Secondly, the bankrupt or any person appointed by the meeting reports the resolution to the court within the next four days, and applies for a sist of the sequestration. The court may hear any party having interest, and, if it finds that the resolution was duly carried, *and that the application is reasonable,* may grant the sist (s. 35). Any creditor may then apply to the court for it to make any reasonable and necessary arrangements for the interim management of the estate (s. 36).

Thirdly, at any time within the period of the sist, the creditors produce to the court a deed of arrangement subscribed by a majority in number and three-fourths in value of *all* the bankrupt's creditors (not merely of those present at any meeting). The court makes such intimation as it thinks proper, may hear parties having interest, and may make any inquiry it thinks necessary. If it is satisfied that the deed of arrangement was duly entered into and executed *and is reasonable,* it must approve of it and declare the sequestration at an end. The deed is then binding on all the creditors as if they had all acceded to it. The sequestration, however, continues to have full effect so far as may be necessary for the purpose of preventing, challenging or setting aside preferences over the estate (s. 37).

10–167 The court is not entitled to hold that a deed of arrangement is "reasonable" unless it has evidence before it which explains in a satisfactory way how the deficiency in the bankrupt's estate arose: the fact that the necessary majority of creditors is in favour of the deed is not in any way conclusive upon the question of reasonableness (*Stone* v. *Woodhouse Hambly & Co.,* 1937 S.C. 824).

10–168 If the winding up under a deed of arrangement fails to pass through any of the stages described above, the sequestration proceeds, and the court may make all necessary orders, by calling meetings of creditors and otherwise, for resuming the sequestration procedure (s. 38).

10–169 If the sequestration is declared to be at an end, an abbreviate extract of that judgment must be recorded in the Register of Inhibitions and Adjudications, in the form of Schedule E, No. 5 (s. 39).

Issue of trustee's act and warrant

10–170 The further procedure which is required before the trustee elected by the creditors at the first statutory meeting can commence his duties in the sequestration culminates in the issue to the trustee by the court of an "act and warrant."

10–171 Commissioners also may not commence their duties without some further procedure.

10–172 The procedure culminating in the issue of the trustee's act and warrant depends partly on whether the sheriff has been chairman at the first statutory meeting or not. In outline, it is as follows:

10–173 If the sheriff has been present at the election and there is no competition or objection, the sheriff immediately *declares* the person chosen by the creditors to be trustee. Where there is competition or objection, the sheriff may either decide the matter forthwith or may, if necessary, make a note of the objections and answers and hear the parties within four days after the meeting before giving his decision and stating the grounds for it (s. 65).

10–174 If the sheriff has not been present at the election, the preses of the meeting must (whether there is competition or objection or not) immediately report the proceedings to the sheriff. Where there is no competition or objection, the sheriff *declares* the person elected trustee. Where there is competition or objection, the parties must, within four days after the meeting, lodge with the sheriff clerk short notes of objections, and the sheriff then forthwith hears the parties and gives his decision, stating the grounds for it in a note (s. 66).

10–175 Whichever procedure is applicable, the sheriff's declaration of the trustee's election must be given with the least possible delay. The decision is final and not open to review in any court or in any other way (s. 67).

The trustee must, within seven days of his election being declared by the sheriff, lodge with the sheriff clerk a bond of caution in the form of Schedule C to the Act. It is signed by the trustee and by the cautioner, both parties undertaking that the trustee will faithfully discharge his duties. The sum for which the cautioner undertakes liability must have been fixed by the creditors at the first statutory meeting. The bond of caution may take the form of a bond issued by a guarantee society on payment of a premium. Such a premium is a legitimate charge on the sequestrated estate (s. 69).

Once the bond of caution has been duly lodged, the sheriff must *confirm* the trustee's election. This confirmation also is final and not open to review in any way.

The sheriff clerk must then issue an act and warrant in the form of Schedule D to the Act, and within three days thereafter transmit a copy of it to the Accountant of Court who enters the trustee's name and designation in the Register of Sequestrations. The act and warrant gives the trustee his title to perform his statutory duties, and it is evidence of his right to the sequestrated estate. It entitles the trustee to recover property belonging or debt due to the bankrupt, and to maintain actions, in the same way as the bankrupt might have done if his estate had not been sequestrated (s. 70).

In the case of the commissioners, their election must be *declared* by the sheriff, and they are then entitled to act without further confirmation. They are not bound to find security (s. 72).

Resignation and removal of trustee and commissioners

The Act does not enable a trustee to resign of his own free will but provides that *a majority in number and value* of the creditors present at any meeting called for the purpose may either remove him or *accept* his resignation. The court has also power to remove a trustee if a petition for removal is presented by *one-fourth in value of all the creditors* and the court is satisfied that sufficient reason has been shown.

If the trustee has resigned or been removed, or has died, been discharged or remained for three months out of Scotland, any commissioner or creditor may apply to the court for a meeting to be held to devolve the estate on the trustee next in succession or to appoint a new trustee. The same procedure, including the lodging of a bond of caution and the issue of an act and warrant, must then be followed as for the election of the first trustee (s. 71).

Where a commissioner has declined to act, resigned, become incapacitated or died, the trustee must call a meeting of creditors to elect a new commissioner (s. 72). A commissioner may also be removed, and another elected in his place, by a majority of the creditors at any meeting called for that purpose (s. 73). "Majority" in this context means majority in value (s. 96—see 10–137, above) and is in contrast to the requirement of a "majority in number and value" required for the removal of the trustee (10–180, above).

Election of new commissioners requires to be declared by the sheriff in the same way as the election of the first commissioners (ss. 72 and 73).

Allowance to bankrupt

10–184   Payment to the bankrupt of a sum out of the estate for his sustenan
may be authorised by *four-fifths in value* of the creditors present at th
first or second statutory meeting or at any meeting called for the purpos
Since, however, the maximum allowance under this provision has r
mained at £3 3s. (£3·15) per week, an adequate allowance for sustenan
can now be obtained out of the estate only by recourse to the provisio
that a "special" allowance may be made to the bankrupt if the majority
the creditors at a meeting consider that it is for the interest of the esta
that the special allowance be made *and* the Accountant of Court repor
in its favour, *and* the court awards it (s. 74).

10–185   The bankrupt may be in a position to maintain himself on his ov
earnings or other income, but if he is not, he is likely in practice to l
dependent on State funds for his sustenance.

Duties of trustee

10–186   For assistance in carrying out his statutory duties a trustee will refer
*Notes by the Accountant of Court for the Guidance of Trustees in Seque
trations,* which enlarge on the statutory provisions and set out specime
accounts. In the preliminary part of these *Notes* the Accountant explai
that he has no right to interfere with the *administration and manageme*
of bankrupt estates, that his power is one of *control* of trustees ar
commissioners, and that this power is *official* rather than *judicial* and
exercised subject to the directions of the court.

10–187   The following account is confined to the statutory provisions:

10–188   1. The trustee, within ten days after his election has been confirm
by the sheriff (see 10–177, above), must present an *abbreviate* to th
Keeper of the Register of Inhibitions and Adjudications for recordin
The abbreviate must be in the form of Schedule E, No. 1:

> "The whole estates and effects, heritable and moveable, and real and person
> wherever situated, of *A.B.* [*name and designation*], are transferred and belong to *E.*
> [*name and designation*], as trustee on his sequestrated estate, conform to act a
> warrant of confirmation dated the   day of   , issued in terms of t
> Bankruptcy (Scotland) Act 1913.
>
> [*Signed by the trustee or his agent.*

10–189   The Keeper must forthwith record the abbreviate in the Register ar
write a certificate on the abbreviate in the form specified in Schedule I
No. 2 (s. 75).

10–190   2. The trustee must, as soon as may be after his appointment, *tal
possession* of the bankrupt's estate and effects, and of his title deed
books, and papers, and must also make up an *inventory* of the estate ar
effects, and a *valuation* showing the estimated value and the annu
revenue. He must immediately transmit copies of the inventory ar
valuation to the Accountant of Court (s. 76).

10–191   The state of affairs prepared by the bankrupt for the first statuto
meeting (see 10–153, above) will by this stage be in the trustee's hands.
addition the bankrupt must at all times give every information ar
assistance necessary to enable the trustee to execute his duty. Th
bankrupt's failure to do so may lead to his imprisonment (s. 77).

3. The trustee must *manage, realise and recover* the bankrupt's estate, wherever situated, and *convert it into money,* according to directions given by the creditors at any meeting (or, if there are no such directions, then with the advice of the commissioners). He must *lodge all money in a bank* in his official character as trustee (s. 78).

If he keeps in his hands more than £100 belonging to the estate for more than ten days, he must pay interest to the creditors at 20 per cent on the excess over £100 [10] for as long as he keeps it in his hands beyond ten days. Unless his breach of duty has been due to innocent causes, he must, if any creditor petitions the court, be dismissed from his office, and he will have no claim for remuneration (s. 79, as amended by Insolvency Act 1976, s. 1(1) and Sched. 1).

The trustee in recovering the property must follow the usual procedure for recovery. He has no general authority to sell book-debts due to the bankrupt, as was finally settled (in relation to the corresponding provisions of the Bankruptcy (Scotland) Act 1856) in *Stewart* v. *Crookston,* 1910 S.C. 609, a decision of seven judges. Lord President Dunedin said (at p. 613):

"It is, I think, quite certain that the word 'recover' is the word appropriate to the ingathering of debts due to the bankrupt. Now, the natural way of recovering a debt is to get it paid, voluntarily if possible, if not then by process, and the very act of recovery converts it into money. To sell a debt to another person is not only not a usual process, but is one which almost postulates a loss, because no one is going to buy debts at the full face value, simply because there would be no profit in such a transaction."

Book-debts may, however, eventually be sold under section 133 provided:

(a) at least 12 months have elapsed from the date of the actual award of sequestration;

(b) the trustee and commissioners think it expedient;

(c) a meeting of creditors is duly convened and three-fourths in value of the creditors assembled decide in favour of the sale; and

(d) the sale is by a public auction which has been suitably advertised.

The policy underlying section 133, which relates to all heritable and moveable estate which has not been disposed of by 12 months from the award, is, as explained by Lord Dunedin in *Stewart* v. *Crookston* (at p. 613), "not to allow sequestration to be indefinitely protracted simply because the assets of the bankrupt are hard to realise."

4. The trustee must keep a *sederunt book,* recording all minutes of creditors and commissioners, accounts, reports, and all the proceedings necessary to give a correct view of the management of the estate. He must also keep regular accounts of the affairs of the estate, and transmit copies of his accounts at specified intervals to the Accountant of Court. He must also transmit to the Accountant copies of all circulars which he issues.

The sederunt book and accounts are open to inspection by the commissioners and by the creditors or their agents at all times.

If a document is of a confidential nature (*e.g.* the opinion of counsel on any matter affecting the interest of the creditors), the trustee is not

This amount may be altered by statutory instrument (Insolvency Act 1976, s. 1(2)).

bound to insert it in the sederunt book or to exhibit it to any person other than the commissioners or the Accountant of Court (s. 80).

Duties of commissioners

10–200   The commissioners' duties are:
1. to superintend the proceedings of the trustee;
2. to concur with him in submissions and transactions;
3. to give their advice and assistance concerning the management of the estate; and
4. to decide as to paying or postponing a dividend.

10–201   They may meet at any time to ascertain the situation of the bankrupt estate, and any one commissioner is entitled to make a report to a general meeting of the creditors (s. 81).

10–202   Their duties and powers under the Act are gathered together and commented on in *Notes by the Accountant of Court for the Guidance of Commissioners in Sequestrations.*

Public examination of bankrupt

10–203   Within eight days after the date of his act and warrant, the trustee must apply to the sheriff to name a day for the public examination of the bankrupt. The sheriff issues a warrant for the bankrupt to attend for this examination within the sheriff court house on a specified day not sooner than seven days nor later that 14 days from the date of the warrant. The trustee must then publish an advertisement, in the form of Schedule F, in the Gazette and send special notice to every creditor who has lodged a claim or who may be named in the bankrupt's state of affairs, intimating his own election as trustee, the time and place for the examination of the bankrupt and also the date of the second statutory meeting (s. 83).

10–204   The sheriff has power to grant a warrant to apprehend the bankrupt and bring him before the sheriff for examination. He has also power, if the bankrupt is prevented by lawful cause from attending at the time and place fixed, to grant commission for the examination to be taken otherwise, and he may, on the application of the trustee, order the bankrupt to be examined as often as he sees fit (s. 84).

10–205   At any time, on the application of the trustee, the sheriff may order an examination of the bankrupt's wife and family, clerks, servants, factors, solicitors, and others, who can give information concerning his estate. They also may be apprehended if they fail to attend when summoned (s. 86).

10–206   The bankrupt and any other person being examined must answer all lawful questions concerning the bankrupt's affairs. The sheriff may also order these persons to produce for inspection books of account and papers in their custody and have these or copies of them delivered to the trustee (s. 87).

10–207   The examination (except where a commission has been granted) takes place on oath before the sheriff and, if the trustee so applies, in open court (s. 88). In practice the examination is almost always conducted in open court (*i.e.* in public) but it often happens that the sheriff will preside throughout the examination only if the trustee has first indicated that the bankrupt is likely to prove unco-operative: it is quite usual for the sheriff

o place the bankrupt on oath in court and then for the bankrupt, trustee
and commissioners to proceed to some other room (e.g. the court library)
or the actual examination.

Questions may be put by the sheriff or trustee or by any creditor with
the sanction of the sheriff. The bankrupt or other person being examined
s liable to imprisonment if he refuses to answer lawful questions or fails,
without lawful cause, to produce books or papers (s. 89).

Before the close of his examination, the bankrupt may add to or alter
the state of his affairs (previously submitted to the first statutory
meeting), so that it may give a full view of his affairs. The state is then
signed by the sheriff and the bankrupt, and the bankrupt takes an oath to
the effect that:

1. the state of affairs which he has signed contains a full and true
account, to the best of his knowledge and belief, of all debts due to him,
and of all his assets and effects (except wearing apparel), and also
contains a full and true account of all debts due by him;

2. he has delivered up all books and papers relating to his affairs;

3. he has made a full disclosure of every particular relating to his
affairs; and

4. he will forthwith reveal all matters which subsequently come to his
knowledge and which may tend to increase or diminish the estate in which
his creditors may be interested (s. 91).

Second statutory meeting

The meeting of creditors commonly referred to as the "second statutory
meeting" is held within seven to 14 days after the bankrupt's examination. It is advertised in the Gazette, and notified to creditors individually,
at the same time as the bankrupt's public examination is advertised and
notified (s. 83).

Before this meeting the trustee must prepare a report setting out the
state of the bankrupt's affairs, and an estimate of what the estate may
produce. He must exhibit this report to the meeting and give all explana-
tions concerning it.

At this meeting the creditors may also give directions for the recovery,
management, and disposal of the estate; e.g. they may decide on the
method by which the bankrupt's heritable property is to be sold.

At this meeting also the creditors may receive an offer of composition
(see 10–309, below) (s. 92).

Other meetings of creditors

In the course of the sequestration a meeting of the creditors may be
called at any time by the trustee or by any commissioner with notice to the
trustee. The trustee *must* call a meeting when required to do so by
one-fourth in value of the creditors ranked on the estate, or by the
Accountant of Court (s. 93).

Notice of all meetings must be advertised in the Gazette at least seven
days before the day of the meeting (s. 94).

No notification need be sent by post to any creditor whose debt is under
£20 unless he has given special directions for notification to be sent. No

notification is sent to any creditor who has directed that none be sent (s. 95).

10–216   All questions at creditors' meetings are decided by the majority in value of those present and entitled to vote, except where the Act otherwise provides. When, by some provision, creditors are required to be counted in number, no creditor whose debt is under £20 is reckoned in number, but his debt is computed in value (s. 96) (see also 10–137, above).

Extent of trustee's right

10–217   The trustee is said to take the estate *tantum et tale* ("to such an extent and of such quality") as it belonged to the bankrupt, *i.e.* his right is as great as, but no greater than, the bankrupt's right.

10–218   The trustee may continue the bankrupt's business. In practice the situation will often be that the bankrupt himself will actually continue the business under the general authority of the trustee, as in *Mackessack & Son* v. *Molleson* (1886) 13 R. 445:

The owners of the vessel the "Jeanie Hope" were sequestrated. After the sequestration the vessel continued to make voyages and earn freight, the proceeds being paid into the sequestrated estates.

On one voyage, through the fault of the master, the cargo was damaged, and the cargo-owners brought an action of damages against the trustee in the sequestration.

Held that as the contract of carriage had been entered into with the master under the general authority of the trustee and for the benefit of the sequestrated estates, the trustee was liable to the cargo-owners.

10–219   The trustee may adopt current contracts of the bankrupt other than contracts which involve *delectus personae* ("choice of person," *i.e.* personal qualities or skills). He must do so within a reasonable time. In *Anderson* v. *Hamilton and Co.* (1875) 2 R. 355, for example, the trustee made an offer, 21 days after the sequestration of a firm, to implement the bankrupt firm's contract to supply iron to certain shipbuilders, and this offer was held not to have been made *tempestive* ("timeously"), the result being that the shipbuilders were not liable in damages to the trustee.

10–220   If the trustee chooses not to adopt a current contract of the bankrupt, the sequestrated estate is liable in damages for breach of contract. Since, however, the party entitled to damages would receive only a dividend in respect of the amount of any award, it will often not be worth his while to bring an action for damages.

10–221   The trustee may bring or continue actions to enforce patrimonial rights of the bankrupt (*e.g.* where the bankrupt has a right to damages for breach of contract), but he has no title to initiate an action for a purely personal claim (*e.g.* a claim for *solatium* ("comfort for wounded feelings") caused by a motor accident, as in *Muir's Trustee* v. *Braidwood*, 1958 S.C. 169).

10–222   If the bankrupt himself raises an action of damages for personal injuries, the ordinary rule is that he must find caution for expenses. An instance is *Clarke* v. *Muller* (1884) 11 R. 418, in which C., an undischarged bankrupt, was suing M., the landlord of the farm of which C. was the tenant, for damages for defamation of character. The ordinary rule would be relaxed only in exceptional cases at the court's discretion.

If a sum of damages has been recovered by the bankrupt in an action which he has personally brought, that sum falls into the sequestrated estate for the benefit of the creditors. Thus, in *Jackson* v. *McKechnie* (1875) 3 R. 130, a sum of £400 recovered by the bankrupt for slander uttered during his sequestration was held to be vested in the trustee as *acquirenda* ("after-acquired property") under the statutory provision which is now section 98(1) of the Act of 1913 (see 10–235, below).

The statutory provisions relating to the extent of the trustee's right are in sections 97 to 102 of the Act. The main ones are outlined here under these headings:

1. vesting of the bankrupt's property in the trustee;
2. *acquirenda* (literally, "things to be acquired," *i.e.* property acquired by the bankrupt during the course of the sequestration);
3. alimentary provisions;
4. taking property out of the sequestration; and
5. title to heritable property.

1. *Vesting of the bankrupt's property in the trustee*

Section 97 provides that the act and warrant *ipso jure* ("by mere operation of law") transfers to and vests in the trustee, for the benefit of the creditors, absolutely and irredeemably, as at the date of the sequestration (*i.e.* the date of the first deliverance (s. 41)), all the moveable and heritable property of the bankrupt.

The act and warrant has the effect of completing the trustee's title to the bankrupt's corporeal moveables as if actual delivery or possession has been obtained. It also completes his title to those incorporeal moveables whose transfer is completed by assignation followed by intimation to the debtor in the obligation; *e.g.* if a life insurance policy has been assigned, but intimation of the assignation has not been made, before the cedent's sequestration, the trustee has a right to the policy preferable to that of the assignee. These effects of the act and warrant are expressly provided for in section 97(1).

If, however, the incorporeal moveable is of a type whose transfer can be completed only by entry on a register (*e.g.* shares, ships, patents and trade-marks), the trustee does not have a real right to the property until his title is registered. The authority for this is *Morrison* v. *Harrison &c.* (1876) 3 R. 406 (10—232, below).

As regards heritable property in Scotland owned by the bankrupt, section 97(2) provides that the act and warrant has the same effect as if a decree of adjudication had been pronounced in favour of the trustee and recorded at the date of the sequestration. This is a reference to recording in the Register of Inhibitions and Adjudications, and the effect is therefore to give the trustee only a personal title to the property: to fortify his title against competitors he will require to record it in the Register of Sasines or register it in the Land Register of Scotland.

An illustration of the application of section 97 is *White* v. *Stevenson*, 1956 S.C. 84:

S., the owner of Hatton Estate, was sequestrated, and W., the trustee in the sequestration, sold the estate in lots, lot 1 being the mansion-house in which S. and his wife were residing.

S. refused to move out of the mansion-house, and an action was brought against him by W. and the purchasers to have him summarily ejected.

Held that as the effect of the act and warrant had been to vest the property in W., S. had no right to occupy or possess or deal with it in any way, and therefore the action of summary ejection was competent.

Lord President Clyde said (at p. 89): "The consequence of the act and warrant was to vest in the trustee the whole rights of the bankrupt in Lot 1 and to reduce him to the position of a squatter in that property without any right or title to remain there. The essential objects of the Bankruptcy Act would be defeated upon any other view, for the essence of a sequestration is to make the whole estates of the bankrupt available for the creditors according to their several rights and preferences through the medium of the trustee. If a bankrupt could at will continue to occupy any part of the property which vests in his trustee, this would defeat the whole object of the Act."

10–230 The act and warrant also vests in the trustee all "real" (equivalent to "heritable" in Scots law) estate belonging to the bankrupt in other parts of the United Kingdom and in any of Her Majesty's dominions, but for this purpose the act and warrant must be registered in the chief court of bankruptcy for the country in which the property is situated (s. 97(3)).

10–231 The act and warrant also has the effect of transferring to the trustee rights to property which at the date of the sequestration have not yet vested in the bankrupt but are still "contingent" (dependent on the fulfilment of a condition). The bankrupt may, for instance, have such non-vested contingent right under a trust set up by a person who has died or under a marriage contract. The trustee in the sequestration is in the same position as if he had received an assignation of the right from the bankrupt and the assignation had been intimated to the holder of the property at the date of the sequestration (s. 97(4)).

10–232 It is, of course, quite likely that some creditors will have obtained for themselves rights in security over parts of the bankrupt's property. Provided these rights existed at the date of the sequestration and are not null or reducible, the trustee takes the property *subject to* the rights. Creditors holding valid rights in security are, therefore, protected, to the extent of their securities, from loss on their debtor's sequestration. This is precisely the purpose for which rights in security are created. Where however, a creditor has at the date of sequestration merely a personal right to some part of the bankrupt's property, he cannot as a general rule then proceed to convert his personal right into a real right so as to obtain valid security. There is an exception to the general rule in the situation where the conversion takes the form of entry in a register; for example, a person holding a duly executed transfer of shares can complete his title to the shares by having his own name entered in the company's register of members (*Morrison* v. *Harrison &c.* (1876) 3 R. 406), and similarly a creditor holding a heritable security may obtain priority over the trustee by recording his security in the Register of Sasines or registering it in the Land Register of Scotland as the case may be.

Property which *ex facie* ("apparently") belongs to the bankrupt but which he truly holds merely as a trustee is not "property of" the bankrupt for the purposes of section 97 (*Heritable Reversionary Co. Ltd.* v. *Millar* (1892) 19 R. (H.L.) 43, a case decided under the corresponding provision of the Bankruptcy (Scotland) Act 1856).

By the Married Women's Policies of Assurance (Scotland) Act 1880 a policy of assurance taken out by a married man on his own life for the benefit of his wife or children or both is considered to be a trust for her or them, and his creditors have no right to the proceeds of the policy except that if the policy has been taken out in order to defraud creditors or if the bankruptcy occurs within two years of the date of the policy the creditors are entitled to the amount paid as premiums under the policy. The provisions of that Act were extended, by the Married Women's Policies of Assurance (Scotland) (Amendment) Act 1980, to policies taken out by a married woman on her own life for the benefit of her husband or children or both.

2. Acquirenda

The term *"acquirenda"* is used of property which comes to the bankrupt after the date of his sequestration and before he has obtained his discharge. This property *ipso jure* ("by mere operation of law") falls under the sequestration. On acquiring such property, the bankrupt must immediately notify the trustee; otherwise he will forfeit all the benefits of the Act (*i.e.*, in particular, he will be unable to obtain his discharge). The trustee, on coming to know about the after-acquired property, must present a petition to the court. Intimation is made in the Gazette, and if no cause is shown to the contrary, the court, after a specified time, declares all right and interest in the property to be vested in the trustee as at the date of the acquisition (s. 98(1)).

This provision enables the trustee to claim part of a bankrupt's earnings during the sequestration for the benefit of the creditors, as in *Caldwell* v. *Hamilton*, 1919 S.C. (H.L.) 100; 1918 S.C. 677:

H. at the date of his sequestration was earning, and thereafter continued to earn, a salary of £500 under a contract of service to a company. H.'s total annual income was £670.

Held that the instalments of salary as they fell due from time to time (in so far as they exceeded what was required for H.'s reasonable maintenance) vested in C., the trustee in the sequestration, under section 98(1) of the Act, as *acquirenda* of H., and that it was competent for the court to order payment to C. of future instalments, reserving to H., C., and any other interested persons the right to apply to the court in the event of a change of circumstances.

In that case the bankrupt was ordered to pay £150 a year to the trustee.

If, in the course of a sequestration, a succession opens owing to the death of, for instance, the bankrupt's father and an election requires to be made between a claim to a legal right (which in this case would be the right of legitim) and a benefit conferred by the deceased's will, it is the trustee and not the bankrupt who is entitled to make the election (*Wishart* v. *Morison* (1895) 3 S.L.T. 29 (O.H.)). A mere *spes successionis* ("expectation of succession"), such as exists where the bankrupt, if he survives, will be entitled to succeed to the estate of a person who is still living, does not come within the sequestration.

See also *Jackson* v. *McKechnie* (10–223, above).

3. *Alimentary provisions*

10–238 Where the bankrupt has a right to an alimentary provision, the trustee may present a petition to the court for the court to decide whether the amount of the provision is in excess of a suitable aliment to the bankrupt in view of his existing circumstances, and, if the court decides that it is, to fix the amount of the excess and order that amount to be paid to the trustee as part of the property falling under the sequestration. The trustee or the bankrupt may later apply to court for such an order to be reconsidered and altered in the event of any change of circumstances (s. 98(2)).

10–239 An instance of the application of this provision is *Inglis's Trustee* v. *Inglis,* 1924 S.C. 226:

The bankrupt had an alimentary income, partly from his marriage-contract trust and partly from his father's testamentary trust, of about £721 per annum. His wife, his daughter aged 17, and a son attending the University of Glasgow were dependent on him; his other son, who was being educated at a boarding-school (the fees being paid by a relative), was partly dependent on him. The bankrupt had been well educated but had never worked except at one time in the business of his father who had been a wealthy engineer and shipbuilder. At the time of this, his second, sequestration, the bankrupt was 45 years of age, and it was questionable whether he could earn anything at any occupation. His debts amounted to £27,000, and the probable dividend was under 10d. in the £.

The trustee's petition under section 98(2) of the Act was opposed by the bankrupt who maintained that the alimentary provisions were necessary to keep him in the same style of life as that to which he had been accustomed.

Held that the alimentary provisions were in excess of a suitable aliment in view of his existing circumstances by £300.

Lord Justice-Clerk Alness said (at p. 229): "I regard as quite inadmissible the [*bankrupt's*] leading . . . contention, viz., that no part of this sum should be set aside to his trustee in bankruptcy. I think that would be tantamount to offering judicial encouragement to profligate bankruptcy. . . . It is a bad bankruptcy. At the same time, in the existing circumstances, and, particularly having regard to the dependants upon the bankrupt, . . . I suggest that we should fix the excess at £300 instead of £400, which is the figure fixed by the Sheriff-Substitute."

10–240 A contrasting case is *Young* v. *Turnbull,* 1928 S.N. 46 (O.H.):

The bankrupt, T., was an unmarried police constable in Glasgow, with a pay of £5 1s.6d. per week.

He was ordered to pay over to Y., the trustee in his sequestration, 30s. per week, this being held to be in excess of a suitable aliment to him in view of his existing circumstances.

4. *Taking property out of the sequestration*

10–241 Any person who claims that he has a right to estate which has been included in the sequestration may present a petition to the court for the property concerned to be taken out of the sequestration. The trustee may lodge answers, and it is then for the court to decide between the competing claims (s. 99). Recourse may be had to this provision, for instance, where the bankrupt has received property as agent, and has wrongly immixed it with his own property: the principal may have what belongs to him taken out of the sequestration, as long as it is still distinguishable. Thus, in *Macadam* v. *Martin's Trustee* (1872) 11 M. 33, under the corresponding provision of the Act of 1856, clients who had sent £1,000 to a law-agent to be invested in a heritable security were held entitled in the law-agent's sequestration to have the £1,000 repaid to them.

5. *Title to heritable property*

The act and warrant does not operate as infeftment: the bankrupt's heritable property continues to be feudally vested in him. The Act therefore provides that the bankrupt must, if required, grant all deeds necessary for recovering his property and for feudally vesting his heritable estate in the trustee. If the bankrupt's title to any estate has not been completed, the trustee may complete the title either in his own person or in the person of the bankrupt. It is also permissible for the trustee, without making up a feudal title in his own person, and without concurrence of the bankrupt, to grant any conveyance of the bankrupt's heritable estate which the bankrupt might competently have granted: a purchaser receiving such a conveyance is in as good a position as he would have been in had the conveyance been granted by the bankrupt with the concurrence of the trustee (s. 100).

Most of these provisions in section 100 are no longer of any consequence in view of the enabling provisions of the nineteenth century conveyancing legislation and of the Conveyancing (Scotland) Act 1924: the act and warrant can competently be specified under the last-mentioned Act as a link of title in a clause of deduction of title, and the normal procedure would now be for the conveyance of the bankrupt's heritable estate to be granted by the trustee and to incorporate such a clause.

In the case of a sequestration of a deceased person, the trustee may require heritable property to be transferred to him by the person who has succeeded to it (s. 101).

Effect of sequestration on ranking of creditors

Sequestration is not itself a diligence, but by the Act is made "equivalent" to the various diligences which are appropriate for different categories of property in varying circumstances: see the quotation from Lord Kinnear's opinion in *Sinclair* v. *Edinburgh Parish Council* (10–79, above). The effect of the provisions of the Act is to discourage a "race of diligence," in which each individual creditor would attempt to salvage for himself at the last moment some item of the bankrupt's property which could be attached. One of the principal objectives of sequestration is that all creditors who are creditors at the date of the sequestration (other than secured and preferential creditors) should be evenly treated, each receiving the same proportion of his debt as any other creditor.

10–246   The detailed rules are in sections 103 to 107 of the Act. In outline they are as follows:

10–247   1. As regards the *heritable property* of the bankrupt, the sequestration is equivalent to a decree of adjudication for payment of the whole debts of the bankrupt, principal and interest, accumulated at the date of the sequestration, and, if an actual adjudication has taken place within a year and a day before the sequestration, the property attached by that adjudication forms part of the sequestrated estate (*i.e.* the creditor who has resorted to adjudication within that period before sequestration is not allowed to keep for himself the benefit of his diligence). Often the bankrupt's heritable property will be subject to a right in security in favour of a particular creditor (*e.g.* a building society or a bank which has lent the purchase price to the bankrupt); the rights of such a heritable creditor are not affected by this provision of the Act: his right in security confers on him a power of sale which is preferable to the powers of the trustee (s. 103). The landlord's right of hypothec is also expressly preserved by the Act (s. 115).

10–248   2. As regards the *moveable property* of the bankrupt, the sequestration is equivalent to an arrestment in execution and decree of forthcoming (*i.e.* to an arrestment which has been carried to completion by the subsequent step of forthcoming (commonly spelt "furthcoming")), and to an executed or completed poinding. No arrestment or poinding on or after the 60th day before the sequestration is effectual, and funds and effects (or, if the effects have been sold, their proceeds) must be handed over to the trustee. The only exception is that any arrester or poinder before the date of the sequestration who has in this way been deprived of the benefit of his diligence is given a preference out of the funds or effects for the expense *bona fide* incurred by him in carrying out his diligence (s. 104).

For an application of this provision, see *Stewart* v. *Jarvie* (10–74, above).

10–249   3. *Prescription* of a debt is *interrupted* when the creditor concerned presents or concurs in a petition for his debtor's sequestration or when he lodges a claim in the sequestration (s. 105).

10–250   4. In the case of a *deceased* debtor, provided the sequestration is dated within seven months after his death, any preference acquired by an individual creditor within 60 days *before the death* is of no effect in competition with the trustee (except that he will be entitled to a preference for expenses *bona fide* incurred in obtaining the preference) (s. 106).

10–251   5. All *payments* made, and all acts done or deeds granted, by the bankrupt in relation to his estate *after* the date of the *sequestration* and before his discharge are, unless the trustee consents, null and void.

10–252   Third parties are, however, protected in the following circumstances:

(a) If a *bona fide* purchaser is in possession of moveable effects received from the bankrupt after sequestration, but in ignorance of it, and if he has paid or is ready to pay the price, he is not obliged to restore the effects.

(b) If a debtor of the bankrupt, in ignorance of the sequestration, has paid his debt *bona fide* to the bankrupt, he is not obliged to pay it a second time to the trustee.

(c) If a person holding a security for a debt due by the bankrupt has received payment of his debt from the bankrupt in ignorance of the sequestration, and has given up the security to the bankrupt, that person is not liable to repay the amount received to the trustee unless the trustee replaces him in the situation in which he stood or reimburses him for any loss or damage (s. 107).

Realisation of heritable estate

It has already been noted (10–192, above) that the trustee has a general duty under section 78 of the Act to realise the bankrupt's estate and convert it into money, according to directions given by the creditors at any meeting (or, if there are no such directions, then with the advice of the commissioners).

When any part of the estate consists of heritable property, creditors at the second statutory meeting have the option of deciding as to the method by which that property is to be sold (s. 92—10–212, above).

Sections 108 to 116 further regulate the realisation of the bankrupt's heritable property, dealing especially with the questions which arise where one or more creditors hold security over the property. The main rules are as follows:

1. A *creditor* who holds a security which is preferable to the right of the trustee and who has, under the terms of his security, a power to sell, is entitled to sell. The trustee or any posterior heritable creditor who is preferable to the trustee may present a petition to the court to compel the selling creditor and the purchaser to account for any reversion of the price (*i.e.* any amount by which the price exceeds the debt due to the selling creditor) (s. 108).

2. The *trustee* may sell the property in his own name, *with the concurrence of a creditor* who holds a security and has, under the terms of his security, a power to sell. The conveyance is then executed by the trustee with the consent of the creditor and the commissioners, and the price is paid by the purchaser to the parties legally entitled to it. This payment of the price frees the property sold from the security of the consenting creditor (whether his debt is satisfied or not) and from all securities postponed to the security of that creditor (s. 109).

3. The *trustee* may sell the property *by public auction* at an upset price fixed by him with the consent of the commissioners. Such a sale takes place if the creditors at the second statutory meeting or at any other meeting called for the purpose resolve on this method, and no heritable creditor with a power to sell has at the time begun proceedings for sale. A heritable creditor is not entitled to interfere with the trustee's sale, but, for his protection, the upset price must not be less than sufficient to pay his debt in full (s. 110).

It is lawful for any creditor, but not for the trustee or commissioners or any solicitor employed by the trustee, to purchase the property if it is sold in this way (s. 116).

10–260   4. The *trustee* may sell the property *by private bargain,* but for this he requires not only the concurrence of a majority of the creditors in number and value but also the concurrence of any heritable creditors and of the Accountant of Court (s. 111).

10–261   5. Whichever way the property is sold, the trustee must make up a *scheme of ranking and division* of the claims of the heritable creditors and other creditors on the price, and report that scheme to the court. The purchaser will then be required to pay the price in accordance with the court's judgment on the scheme (s. 112).

10–262   On cause shown, the court may authorise an interim scheme of division or may grant an interim warrant for payment of preferable claims out of the price (s. 113).

10–263   6. A heritable creditor's *right to poind the ground is limited*: if the poinding has not been carried into execution by sale of the moveables 60 days before the date of the sequestration, it is of limited effect in competition with the trustee: a creditor who holds a security over the heritable estate preferable to the right of the trustee is not prevented from executing a poinding but it can be used only to cover the interest on the debt for the current half-year and for the previous year (s. 114).

10–264   The landlord's hypothec for rent is not affected by any provision in the Act of 1913 (s. 115).

Classification of creditors

10–265   Creditors fall into the following categories:

1. secured;
2. privileged or preferential;
3. ordinary; and
4. postponed.

1. *Secured creditors*

10–266   A secured creditor is one who holds a right in security over the whole or part of the bankrupt's estate for the whole or part of the debt which the bankrupt owes to him. The very object of a right in security is to protect the holder of it from loss in the event of the debtor's bankruptcy. If the subjects held in security can be sold by the creditor for an amount which covers his debt, then the creditor will suffer no loss at all, and he will have no claim against the sequestrated estate. If, however, the subjects held in security are not sufficient to cover the secured creditor's claim in full, then the creditor has a claim on the sequestrated estate for the difference between the amount of the debt due to him and the amount which can be realised by the sale of the security subjects.

10–267   The Act gives effect to these principles by the rule, already noted (10–150, above), that, for the purpose of ranking for dividends, a secured creditor must value and deduct his security, and this rule is reinforced by the provision that the trustee with the consent of the commissioners is entitled to have the security subjects transferred to him at the valuation placed on them by the creditor (s. 61), the objective being to discourage the creditor from under-valuing the security which he holds.

A secured creditor therefore receives full payment of his debt up to the extent covered by the value of the security subjects. For any unsecured balance, he ranks as an ordinary creditor.

2. *Privileged or preferential creditors*

The following claims have priority, and in the following order:
(i) the trustee's charges and commission (s. 117);
(ii) in the case of a deceased debtor, death-bed and funeral expenses (s. 118(5));
(iii) "preferential payments" listed in section 118(1), as amended by later legislation including the Companies Act 1947 (s. 115) and the Insolvency Act 1976 (s. 1(1) and Sched. 1). All these rank equally among themselves and must be paid in full, unless the assets are insufficient to meet them, in which case they abate in equal proportions. Many of the preferential payments are debts due to the Crown. Under the common law of Scotland, Crown debts as such have no priority (*Admiralty* v. *Blair's Trustee,* 1916 S.C. 247).

By an addition to section 118 made by the Insolvency Act 1976 (s. 5(4)), the trustee may, with the consent of the commissioners, pay any of these preferential debts before the period for the payment of the first dividend (s. 118(3A)).

The main "preferential payments" listed in section 118(1) as amended are:
(a) all *local rates* which have become due and payable by the bankrupt within *12 months* before the award of sequestration (or, in the case of the sequestration of a deceased debtor, the date of death);
(b) all *assessed taxes,* such as income tax and Class 4 contributions under the Social Security Acts, assessed on the bankrupt up to April 5 before the same date, but not more than *one year's* assessment (a provision which enables the Inland Revenue to claim preference for the largest assessment outstanding);
(c) all *wages or salary* of any clerk, servant, workman or labourer for service rendered to the bankrupt during *four months* before the same date, but not more than £800[10] to any one person; certain payments (*e.g.* guarantee payments) owed by an employer under employment protection legislation are treated as wages in this connection (Employment Protection (Consolidation) Act 1978, s. 121); and
(d) debts under *social security* legislation for the previous 12 months.

There are also other statutory provisions which confer preferences in a sequestration, *e.g.* under the Betting and Gaming Duties Act 1981 a preference is conferred on the Commissioners of Customs and Excise for betting and bingo duties which have become due within the period of 12 months before the sequestration.

3. *Ordinary creditors*

Ordinary creditors are those who are not entitled to any preferential ranking. This class will include secured creditors for the balance due after

---

[10] This amount may be altered by statutory instrument (Insolvency Act 1976, s. 1(2)).

realisation of security subjects, and will include preferential creditors for amounts claimed by them over and above the amounts for which they are entitled to a preference.

10–274   All ordinary creditors rank equally *inter se* ("amongst themselves"). They will seldom be paid in full: each will receive only a dividend of so much in the £ on the debt due to him. It is possible for the preferential claims to swallow all the estate, and in such a case the ordinary creditors will receive no dividend at all.

4. *Postponed creditors*

10–275   Postponed creditors have their claims paid only if all ordinary creditors have been paid in full. In practice, postponed creditors seldom receive anything from the sequestrated estate.

10–276   Postponed creditors are (a) the bankrupt's wife for any money or other estate which she has lent or entrusted to her husband, or which is immixed with his funds (Married Women's Property (Scotland) Act 1881, s. 1(4)), and (b) a person who either has lent money on condition that he is to receive a rate of interest varying with the profits, or a share of the profits, of the borrower's business, or has sold the goodwill of a business in return for a share of the profits to be made by the new owner of the business (Partnership Act 1890, s. 3).

Rule against double ranking

10–277   The property of which the bankrupt has been divested through sequestration is a fund available for part-payment of the bankrupt's debts *pari passu* ("proportionately"), *i.e.* each debt will be met by the same dividend of so much in the £. It is a fundamental rule that there must be no double ranking, *i.e.* the same debt must not be ranked twice (or more times). If double ranking were allowed, the sequestrated estate would be paying twice as much on some debts as on others.

10–278   The rule against double ranking is of practical importance where there are co-obligants of whom the bankrupt is one:

10–279   A typical case is where the debt due by the bankrupt has been guaranteed by a cautioner: the creditor is entitled, on the sequestration of the principal debtor, to lodge his claim in the sequestration and receive a dividend of, say, 30p in the £, and then to go against the cautioner claiming from him the balance of 70p in the £; it is then not open to the cautioner to claim relief out of the sequestrated estate for what he has been required to pay to the creditor, since, as far as the sequestrated estate is concerned, that particular debt has already been satisfied to the same extent as other debts by the payment of the dividend of 30p in the £ to the creditor; an alternative course for the creditor to take is to go immediately to the cautioner for payment of the full debt, and the cautioner is then, on payment of the full debt, entitled to rank in relief on the sequestrated estate and receive the 30p dividend, since the creditor, having received full payment from the cautioner, will in this case not be claiming in the sequestration. See also the cases of *Harvie's Trustees* v. *Bank of Scotland &c.* (1885) 12 R. 1141, and *Veitch* v. *National Bank of Scotland Ltd.*, 1907 S.C. 554 (9–72 and 9–73, above).

Another situation is where more than one party is liable to pay a bill of exchange:

Anderson v. *Mackinnon* (1876) 3 R. 608: Crawford accepted certain bills of exchange for accommodation of the firm Watson and Campbell. The firm discounted the bills at banks. Subsequently both Crawford and Watson and Campbell became bankrupt, and the banks ranked on both sequestrated estates for the full amount of the bills. M. who was the trustee in Crawford's sequestration claimed that he was entitled to a dividend from A., the trustee in Watson and Campbell's sequestration, on the amount which he, M., had paid to the banks.

Held that as the banks had already been ranked on Watson and Campbell's estate for the full amount of the bills, M. could not also be ranked on that estate for the same debt.

Lord President Inglis said (at p. 613): "It is clear that if Crawford had been solvent he would have been obliged to pay the amount of the bills to the banks, and would have been entitled to rank on the estate of Watson and Campbell for the full amount. But . . . the banks have claimed dividends on this £4,000 from Crawford's estate, . . . and also from Watson and Campbell's estate. . . . If Crawford's trustee had been entitled to rank on Watson and Campbell's estate . . . it would be a double ranking for the same debt. The bills for £4,000 have been ranked on the estate of Watson and Campbell by the banks. They have received a dividend, and when a bankrupt estate pays a dividend it pays the debt."

Payment of first dividend

The date for the payment of the first dividend is "the first lawful day" after the expiry of six months from the date of the deliverance actually awarding sequestration (s. 126).

The trustee and commissioners, with the consent of the Accountant of Court, may accelerate the payment, if that is found to be expedient, but not so as to make it earlier than four months from that deliverance (s. 130), and the commissioners may postpone payment of the first dividend until the time for payment of the second dividend arrives, if they consider that there ought to be such postponement (s. 131).

Where the sequestrated estate consists chiefly of land, and in any other cases where it may be necessary, the trustee and commissioners may make a special application to the court for a suitable alteration in the date of payment (s. 132).

A creditor, in order to be entitled to payment of the first dividend, must produce his oath or notice of claim at least two months before the time fixed for payment (or, if payment has been accelerated, at least one month before the time fixed for payment). If he comes too late for the first dividend, but in time for the second dividend, he is entitled to receive out of the first of the funds then available an equalising dividend corresponding to the dividend which he would have drawn if he had claimed in time for the first dividend (s. 119, as amended by Insolvency Act 1976, s. 5(3)).

There is an instance of a creditor obtaining an equalising dividend under this provision in *Commercial Bank of Scotland Ltd.* v. *Muirhead's Trustee*, 1918 1 S.L.T. 132 (O.H.), in which it was said that the bank had not lodged its claim in time for the first dividend because it had then considered itself to be sufficiently secured. The Lord Ordinary (Sands), observing that section 119 did not require the creditor's delay to have been due to excusable ignorance or error, said that the rule might be unwholesome and might in certain cases operate inequitably.

10–286   A creditor who is resident abroad is entitled to share in the funds available for the first dividend provided he lodges his oath or notice of claim 14 days before the time fixed for payment (s. 120).

10–287   The procedure leading up to the payment of the first dividend is as follows:

1. *Trustee's state and account*

10–288   Immediately on the expiry of four months from the date of the deliverance actually awarding sequestration (unless there is to be acceleration of payment) the trustee must proceed to make up a state of the whole of the bankrupt's property and also an account of his own intromissions and management.

2. *Meeting of commissioners*

10–289   Within 14 days after the expiry of the four months referred to in 1., above, the commissioners must meet, examine the state and account, audit the accounts, settle the trustee's commission or fee, and declare how much, if any, is to be divided among the creditors (s. 121).

3. *Intimation of trustee's commission or fee*

10–290   The trustee must intimate the amount of his commission or fee by circular to every creditor and also to the bankrupt, and objections to its amount as fixed by the commissioners may be made by the trustee or by the bankrupt or by any creditor to the Accountant of Court. If the Accountant's suggestion is not acceptable to all parties, an appeal may be made to the sheriff or Lord Ordinary, whose decision will be final (s. 122).

4. *Trustee's decision on claims*

10–291   Meantime, within the same period of 14 days after the expiry of the four months from the award of sequestration, the trustee must examine the creditors' claims, and must in writing reject or admit them, or require further evidence in support of them. He must complete the list of the creditors entitled to draw a dividend, distinguishing whether they are ordinary creditors or preferable or contingent, and he must make up a separate list of any creditors whose claims he has rejected in whole or in part (s. 123).

5. *Notification of payment of dividend*

10–292   On or before the first lawful day after the expiry of the same 14 days the trustee must post to each creditor a letter notifying him of the proposed dividend on his claim, or of the rejection of his claim, and within eight days of the expiry of the 14 days he must give notice in the Gazette of the time and place of the payment of the dividend.

A creditor has 14 days from the publication of that Gazette notice in which he may lodge an objection in court against the trustee's decision on his claim; otherwise, the trustee's decision is final and conclusive as regards the first dividend. If a claim has been rejected in whole or in part, the creditor may make a new claim in reference to future dividends, but that will not disturb the first dividend (s. 124).

6. Trustee's scheme of division

Before the expiry of six months from the award of sequestration the trustee must make up a scheme of division of the fund which the commissioners have directed to be divided. The scheme shows how the fund is to be apportioned among the various creditors according to their rights, and must be open to all concerned. The trustee must also send notice to each creditor of the amount of the dividend to which he may be entitled (s. 125).

7. Payment to creditors

On the first lawful day after the expiry of six months from the award the trustee pays to the creditors the dividends allotted to them in accordance with his scheme of division. Where an apportioned amount is not yet payable (e.g. where a claim is still under appeal or where the debt is a contingent one), it must be lodged by the trustee in a separate bank account (s. 126).

Payment of second and subsequent dividends

The date for the payment of the second dividend is "the first lawful day" after the expiry of ten months from the date of the deliverance actually awarding sequestration (s. 128).

The procedure is the same as for the payment of the first dividend, except that it starts with the making up by the trustee of a state on the expiry of *eight* months from the award (s. 127).

Subsequent dividends, if any, are paid on "the first lawful day" after the expiry of three months from the day of payment of the immediately preceding dividend. The same procedure is followed on each occasion (s. 129).

The times for payment of the second and subsequent dividends may be accelerated or postponed or altered in the same way as the payment of the first dividend (10–282, above).

Disabilities and offences of undischarged bankrupt

A person whose estate has been sequestrated continues to be an "undischarged bankrupt" until he receives his discharge from the court (s. 2).

An undischarged bankrupt is under certain disabilities. For all payments and property transactions he requires the consent of the trustee (s. 107). If he obtains credit to the extent of £50[10] or upwards from any person without informing that person that he is an undischarged

---

[10] This amount may be altered by statutory instrument (Insolvency Act 1976, s. 1(2)).

bankrupt, he is guilty of an offence for which he may be imprisoned for up to two years (s. 182, as amended by Insolvency Act 1976 (s. 1(1) and Sched. 1)). He is disqualified from sitting in the House of Lords, from being elected to the House of Commons, and from being appointed a J.P. (s. 183 and Bankruptcy Act 1883, s. 32). He is disqualified from being a member of a local authority (Local Government (Scotland) Act 1973, s. 31(1)). He must not act as director of a company or be concerned in the management of a company without the leave of the court under penalty of two years' imprisonment or a fine of £500 or both (Companies Act 1948, s. 187(1)).

10–302 Further, section 178 of the Act of 1913 lists 12 offences which make an undischarged bankrupt liable to up to two years' imprisonment, and for six of these the onus of proof, contrary to the general principle of the criminal law, lies on the bankrupt: the section provides that the bankrupt is to be *deemed guilty unless* he proves to the satisfaction of the court that he had no intent to defraud. In outline these six are:

1. failing to disclose the state of his affairs fully and truly;
2. failing to deliver up to the trustee all his property and papers, or failing to dispose of these according to the trustee's directions;
3. concealing or destroying books or papers relating to his property or affairs (and this extends back to four months before the presentation of the petition for sequestration);
4. making false entries in books or papers relating to his property or affairs (and this also extends back to falsification within four months before the presentation of the petition);
5. within four months before the presentation of the petition, pledging or disposing of, in some way other than in the ordinary course of trade, any property which he has not paid for; and
6. having failed, for the three years before the petition or for the time for which he has carried on business, whichever is the less, to keep books or accounts sufficient to explain his transactions (but this applies only where the debts in the sequestration exceed £2,500[11]).

An illustration of the sixth is *Adair* v. *Isaacs,* 1946 J.C. 84:

Isaacs had commenced business less than three years before his sequestration. For the first 17 months he had kept adequate books, but during the next 10 months he had failed to do so.

Held that an offence was committed under section 178 if the bankrupt failed to keep the necessary books during *any part of* the three years during which he had carried on business before his sequestration.

10–303 The other six offences of an undischarged bankrupt listed in section 178 include:

1. failing to inform the trustee that a claim being made in the sequestration is false;
2. attempting to account for part of his property by fictitious losses or expenses;
3. fraudulently obtaining property on credit;

---

[11] substituted for £200 by the Insolvency Act 1976 (s. 1(1) and Sched. 1). The figure may be altered by statutory instrument (Insolvency Act 1976, s. 1(2)).

4. absconding from Scotland to avoid his creditors or taking with him property valued at £250[12] or more which ought to be divided among his creditors; and

5. making gifts or transferring property, with the intention of defrauding his creditors.

Discharge of bankrupt

Discharge is the main privilege which the bankrupt may obtain from the sequestration process. It is not a right on which the bankrupt may insist: the court has a discretion as to whether it will grant or refuse the discharge. The bankrupt's conduct during the sequestration is an important factor.

The statutory provisions governing discharge of the bankrupt depend partly on whether the discharge is:

1. on composition; or
2. without composition.

There are in addition:

3. provisions applicable to both modes of discharge.

1. *On composition*

At the first statutory meeting the bankrupt or his friends may offer a composition to the creditors on the whole debts, with security for payment of the composition. If the *majority of the creditors in number and three-fourths in value present at the meeting* resolve that the offer be "entertained for consideration," the trustee must immediately advertise the offer in the *Edinburgh Gazette* and notify each creditor by letter (s. 134).

The decision on whether to *accept* the offer is then taken at the second statutory meeting. Again, a majority in number and three-fourths in value of the creditors present is required, and a bond of caution for payment of the composition, executed by the bankrupt and the proposed cautioner, must be immediately lodged with the trustee, who transmits it to the court along with a report of the resolution.

If the court, after hearing any objections by creditors, finds that the offer has been "duly made" and is "reasonable," it pronounces a deliverance approving of it (s. 135).

Alternatively, an offer of a composition may be made at the second statutory meeting or at any subsequent meeting specially called for the purpose. The procedure is essentially the same:

(a) There must be *two* meetings, one to "entertain" the offer and the second to accept it.

(b) The majority in favour must at both meetings be *a majority in number and three-fourths in value of the creditors present*.

(c) The court must approve of the offer (s. 136).

The bankrupt must in every case where the court has approved of the offer make a declaration before the court that he has fully and fairly surrendered his estate and has not entered into any secret agreement to

---

[12] substituted for £20 by the Insolvency Act 1976 (s. 1(1) and Sched. 1). The amount may be altered by statutory instrument (Insolvency Act 1976, s. 1(2)).

obtain the consent of any creditor to the offer. The court then, if satisfied with the bankrupt's declaration, pronounces a deliverance discharging him of all debts for which he was liable at the date of his sequestration, and declares the sequestration to be at an end and the bankrupt reinvested in his estate (reserving to the creditors their claims for the agreed composition against the bankrupt and the cautioner). The clerk of the court transmits an extract of the court's deliverance to the Accountant of Court who then enters the discharge in the Register of Sequestrations (ss. 137 and 156).

10–311　If an offer of composition has been made and been rejected or become ineffectual, no other offer of composition can be entertained unless *nine-tenths in number and value of all the creditors ranked on the estate assent in writing* to the offer. If such assent is obtained, a meeting is called. Acceptance requires a *majority in number and nine-tenths in value of those present at that meeting.* Only then can the approval of the court be sought (s. 142).

10–312　The sequestration continues up to the time when the court's approval of the composition is pronounced (s. 139). It is, however, not open to any of the parties—bankrupt, cautioner or creditors—to withdraw in the interval between acceptance of the offer and the court's approval of it: all parties are treated as having bound themselves irrevocably, subject only to the condition that the court will approve of the composition (*Lee* v. *Stevenson's Trustee* (1883) 11 R. 26, a case decided under the Act of 1856 with reference to an attempted withdrawal by the cautioner).

10–313　The general nature of a composition contract is described by Lord President Inglis in *Macbride* v. *Stevenson* (1884) 11 R. 702, at p. 705, as follows:

"The offer by the bankrupt, the acceptance by the creditors, and the judicial approval, are all steps of procedure in the sequestration. They have the effect of putting an end to the sequestration, and of restoring his estate to the bankrupt, but they are none the less sequestration proceedings, and have a reference to the rules of sequestration law. The essence of a composition contract is that the bankrupt buys from his creditors the estate which is in the hands of the trustee, and which would fall to be divided among all the creditors, and the consideration which the bankrupt gives for the purchase is the value, on a fair estimate, in the opinion of the parties to the contract, of what the creditors would have drawn in the shape of dividends. But a composition is not merely a contract with the whole body of creditors; it is, in effect, also a contract between the bankrupt and each creditor who would be entitled to a dividend, and therefore what each creditor is surrendering or selling is his prospect of a dividend, and the consideration is the sum which he considers a fair equivalent payable, it may be, immediately or in instalments, secured by caution."

The case concerned a claim for a composition made by a secured creditor without valuing and deducting his security. The court held that the same rules of ranking applied to his claim as operated where dividends were claimed in the ordinary course of a sequestration, and that he was therefore bound to value and deduct his security and claim only for the balance.

14 On the other hand, the court, in considering whether an offer of composition is "reasonable," may look beyond the property which has actually fallen into the sequestrated estate:

Bradshaw v. *Kirkwood & Sons* (1904) 7 F. 249: B., the bankrupt, offered a composition of 5s. in the £. The offer was duly entertained and accepted at meetings of creditors.

K. & Sons, creditors, objected that the offer was unreasonable because it took no account of a valuable *spes successionis* ("expectation of succession"), namely, B.'s share in his deceased father's estate which would vest in him if he survived his mother who was then over 80 years of age and infirm.

Held that, in view of the value of the *spes successionis*, the offer of 5s. in the £ was not reasonable.

2. *Without composition*

15 The bankrupt may at any time after the second statutory meeting present a petition to the court for his discharge, but in order to do so he must ensure that two conditions are satisfied:

16 (a) There must be produced in the proceedings a *report prepared by the trustee* with regard to the conduct of the bankrupt, and as to how far he has complied with the statutory provisions, and whether the bankruptcy has arisen from innocent misfortunes or losses in business, or from "culpable or undue conduct"; the trustee is under a duty to prepare this report as soon as may be after the bankrupt's public examination, but the bankrupt is not entitled to demand it from him till the expiry of five months from the actual award of sequestration.

17 (b) Any necessary *consents of creditors* have been obtained:

Time of presenting petition	Consent of creditors required
Within 6 months after award	Every creditor
6-12 months after award	Majority in number and four-fifths in value
12-18 months after award	Majority in number and two-thirds in value
18-24 months after award	Majority in number and value
After 2 years from award	None.

18 The petition is intimated in the *Edinburgh Gazette* and to each creditor, and at least 21 days are allowed for objections, which may be made by creditors or by the trustee.

19 The court may then, after judging any objections, grant the discharge or refuse it, or postpone consideration of it, or annex conditions to it (s. 143). There is an instance of a condition being attached to a discharge in:

Leslie v. *Cumming & Spence* (1900) 2 F. 643: L., a parish minister in Orkney, six years after his sequestration and after a dividend of 5s.6d. in the £ had been paid to his creditors, petitioned for his discharge.

Some of his creditors objected to the discharge being granted except on the condition of his assigning part of his future stipend for the benefit of his creditors.

Held that L. was entitled to his discharge on condition that he assigned to his creditors £80 per annum out of his annual income of £273.

20 If the bankrupt is found entitled to his discharge, he must make a declaration before the court that he has fully and fairly surrendered his estate and has not entered into any secret agreement to obtain the concurrence of any creditor to his discharge. The court, if satisfied with the bankrupt's declaration, pronounces a deliverance discharging him of all debts for which he was liable at the date of his sequestration. The clerk of the court transmits an extract of the court's deliverance to the Accountant of Court who then enters the discharge in the Register of Sequestrations (ss. 143 and 156).

3. *Provisions applicable to both modes of discharge*

10–321   The final stage in the procedure for discharge is the issue by the clerk of the court of an abbreviate of the court's deliverance of discharge (whether following on a composition or not) and its recording in the Register of Inhibitions and Adjudications. The form of the abbreviate is set out in Schedule E, No. 4 (s. 145).

10–322   The Act provides that a bankrupt is not at any time to be entitled to be discharged unless it is proved to the court that *either*:

(a) a dividend or composition of not less than 25p in the £ has been paid, or security for payment of that amount has been found to the satisfaction of the creditors; *or*

(b) failure to pay 25p in the £ has, in the court's opinion, arisen from "circumstances for which the bankrupt cannot justly be held responsible" (s. 146).

10–323   Two contrasting cases may be given to illustrate this provision:

10–324   (i) *Clarke* v. *Crockatt & Co.* (1883) 11 R. 246: A bankrupt who had paid only 2s.2½d. in the £ petitioned for his discharge, and some of his creditors lodged objections.

The bankrupt was found by the court to have begun a very precarious and speculative business without capital and to have pursued it recklessly on a large scale. The trustee reported that he was unable to say that the bankruptcy had arisen from innocent losses.

Application *refused*.

10–325   (ii) *Bremner, Petitioner* (1900) 2 F. 1114: The bankrupt, B., a cycle dealer, had paid no dividend to his creditors. The trustee reported favourably. It appeared that at the time of sequestration the trustee estimated that a dividend of 8s. in the £ would be paid, and that the failure to pay a dividend was due to depression in the cycle trade.

Held that B. was entitled to his discharge.

10–326   A discharge does not free the bankrupt from liability for debts due to the Crown (s. 147).

10–327   The court may refuse a discharge, even although two years may have elapsed from the date of the sequestration and no creditor opposes the discharge, if it appears from the report of the Accountant of Court or from other sufficient evidence that the bankrupt has fraudulently concealed any part of his property or has wilfully failed to comply with any of the provisions of the Act (s. 149).

Trustee's discharge

10–328   The procedure for the discharge of the trustee is independent of that for the discharge of the bankrupt. Much may still remain to be done in the sequestration after the bankrupt's discharge, and conversely a trustee who has finished his work in the sequestration may obtain his discharge although the bankrupt may still be undischarged.

The trustee's discharge, like that of the bankrupt involves an application to the court. The procedure is as follows:

After a final division of the funds, the trustee calls a meeting of creditors, by an advertisement in the *Edinburgh Gazette* and by letters posted to all creditors, to consider the trustee's application for his discharge. The date of the meeting must be at least 14 days after the publication of the Gazette notice.

At the meeting the trustee must lay before the creditors the sederunt book and accounts, with a list of unclaimed dividends, and the creditors may then declare their opinion of his conduct as trustee.

The court, in considering the trustee's petition, with the minutes of the meeting, hears any objecting creditor, and may then pronounce or refuse "decree of exoneration" (s. 152). In *Hamilton's Trustee* v. *Caldwell,* 1918 S.C. 190, for instance, the court *refused* the petition for the trustee's discharge on the ground of a creditor's objection that the trustee had failed to ingather part of the bankrupt's salary, which, by a condition attached to the bankrupt's discharge, fell into the sequestrated estate.

If decree of exoneration is granted, the clerk of the court immediately transmits an extract of the decree to the Accountant of Court for entry in the Register of Sequestrations, and the bond of caution for the trustee is delivered up (s. 152).

Unclaimed dividends, etc.

Before his discharge the trustee must transmit the sederunt book to the Accountant of Court, deposit the unclaimed dividends and any unapplied balances in a bank, and send the deposit receipts for these to the Accountant of Court who keeps in his office a book entitled "The Register of Unclaimed Dividends," listing all the creditors entitled to unclaimed dividends and specifying the banks in which these dividends are deposited. This register is open to public inspection (s. 153(1)).

Within the next seven years a person producing evidence of his right to any unclaimed dividend may obtain from the Accountant of Court a warrant authorising the bank to pay the dividend with any interest which may have accrued on it (s. 153(2)).

On the expiry of seven years from the date of deposit of any unclaimed dividend or unapplied balance, the Accountant of Court hands over the deposit receipt or other voucher to the Secretary of State for Scotland, who obtains payment of the principal and interest from the bank on behalf of the Crown (s. 153(3), as amended by the Transfer of Functions (Treasury and Secretary of State) Order 1974 (S.I. 1974 No. 1274)).

Any surplus remaining, after all the charges of the sequestration have been met and all the bankrupt's debts have been paid with interest, must be paid to the bankrupt, or to his successors or assignees (s. 155).

(b) Summary Sequestration

Summary sequestration was introduced by the Act of 1913 (see s. 177) to make available a speedier process for the sequestration of small estates. It does not apply to deceased debtors or to partnerships. The debtor's estate of every description must not exceed in the aggregate

£4,000[13] (this being the amount substituted by the Insolvency Act 1976 (s. 1(1) and Sched. 1) for the limit of £300 in section 174 of the Act of 1913).

10–339   Summary sequestration is subject to all the provisions of the Act of 1913 relating to ordinary sequestration, except where sections 175 (as amended by the Law Reform (Miscellaneous Provisions) (Scotland) Act 1980 (s. 12(c))) and 176 of the Act of 1913 provide otherwise (s. 174).

10–340   The major differences are as follows:

(i) Section 175 (as amended)—The Petition

10–341   1. The petition may be presented either:
(a) by the debtor himself, without the concurrence of any creditor; or
(b) by a creditor whose claim amounts to at least £120. [14]
In the case of (b), the debtor must be notour bankrupt and the petition must be presented within four months after the constitution of notour bankruptcy.

10–342   2. The petition must always be presented to a sheriff court. The appropriate court is that of the sheriffdom in which the debtor either:
(a) resides or has a dwelling-house or place of business; or
(b) has resided or carried on business for any period of 40 days or more during the past year.
If the petitioner does not possess sufficient information to enable him to decide which sheriff court is appropriate or if the debtor is furth of Scotland, the petition may be presented to the sheriff court at Edinburgh.

10–343   3. If the petition is at the instance of the debtor (falling under 1(a), above), the debtor must lodge with the petition a short state of his affairs (similar to the state which he must in an ordinary sequestration make up for the first statutory meeting).

If the petition is at the instance of a creditor (falling under 1(b), above), the first deliverance contains, in addition to the warrant to cite, an order on the debtor to lodge in court within six days a short state of affairs of the same kind.

10–344   4. The judge to whom the petition is presented *may* award sequestration. He has a full discretion to refuse the petition. There is no such discretion in an ordinary sequestration (see 10–112, above). Even where the estate does not exceed £4,000, there may be circumstances which, in the judge's opinion, make it not expedient to order that the sequestration should proceed as a summary sequestration.

(ii) Section 176—The Procedure

10–345   1. Some time-limits are shortened (*e.g.* the trustee's application to the sheriff to fix the public examination of the bankrupt must be within seven days of the deliverance declaring the trustee's election), and other time-limits are removed altogether (*e.g.* there is no fixed time for the holding of the second statutory meeting, it being contemplated that the estate will normally be ready for distribution by that stage).

10–346   2. Various applications and reports to the court may be made orally, instead of in writing.

---

[13] This amount may be altered by statutory instrument (Insolvency Act 1976, s. 1(2)).
[14] substituted for £10 by the Insolvency Act 1976 (s. 1(1) and Sched. 1). The amount may be altered by statutory instrument (Insolvency Act 1976, s. 1(2)).

3. The trustee must report on summary sequestrations to the Accountant of Court every six months, instead of annually.

4. If there are no funds for division, the sheriff may, in writing, dispense with any further procedure in the sequestration, and the bankrupt may then at any time petition the sheriff for his discharge.

5. On the final division of the funds, or in any case where the sheriff has dispensed with further procedure under 4., above, the trustee, without calling a meeting of creditors as is required in an ordinary sequestration, applies to the Accountant of Court for a certificate that he is entitled to his discharge. On obtaining that certificate the trustee reports the fact to the sheriff, and, after a Gazette notice and consideration of any objections, the sheriff may grant the trustee his discharge.

IV EXTRA-JUDICIAL SETTLEMENTS

In order to avoid the publicity, formality and expense of sequestration, creditors, as well as the debtor himself, often prefer to enter into some private arrangement which will achieve much the same practical results as sequestration—*pari passu* ("rateable") distribution of the debtor's estate, as far as it will go, among the creditors, and for the debtor the opportunity to make a fresh start free from his crippling burden of debt.

The main obstacle with private arrangements is that they may be defeated by any one creditor who is opposed to the arrangement.

The commonest forms of extra-judicial settlements are:

(a) the private trust deed for creditors; and
(b) the extra-judicial composition contract.

(a) Private Trust Deed for Creditors

The debtor may by a trust deed transfer his whole estate to a named trustee for realisation and distribution among his creditors.

Although the trustee under such a trust deed represents the creditors and holds the estate on their behalf, he does not have the statutory position of a trustee in a sequestration. In particular:

(i) He has no act and warrant, and must therefore complete title to each item in the debtor's estate in the appropriate way (*e.g.* by recording in the Register of Sasines, by taking possession, or by intimation); otherwise it may be attached by the diligence of a non-acceding creditor or a subsequent creditor (*i.e.* a creditor to whom the debtor has become indebted after the date of the trust deed).

(ii) He has no statutory right to challenge gratuitous alienations or fraudulent preferences (contrast section 9 of the Act of 1913). An illustrative case is *Fleming's Trustees* v. *McHardy* (1892) 19 R. 542:

F. granted a trust deed for his creditors in favour of two trustees. McH. was a creditor who did not accede to the trust deed.

The trustees brought an action against McH. for reduction of certain preferences which they alleged to be illegal at common law and under the Act of 1696.

Held that the trustees had no title to sue.

Lord McLaren said (at p. 545): "The right to reduce preferences flows from the particular creditors who have acceded. If the deed contains such a power they by their accession are held to have conferred it on the trustee, but if the deed contains no such power, then their accession does not imply their assent to anything beyond what is contained in the deed."

10–355 In the absence of contrary provisions in the trust deed, the trustee's powers and position are governed by the Trusts (Scotland) Acts 1921 to 1961.

10–356 However, it is usual for the trust deed expressly to confer on the trustee the powers of a trustee in sequestration, and to stipulate that the rights of creditors are to be the same as they would be in a sequestration (so that, *e.g.*, a secured creditor will not be entitled to rank for the full amount of his debt without deducting the value of the security which he holds).

10–357 A creditor who does not accede to the trust deed is nevertheless entitled to receive from the trustee the same rate of dividend on his debt as the acceding creditors receive, and he may recover his share by direct action against the trustee (*Ogilvie & Son* v. *Taylor* (1887) 14 R. 399).

10–358 A non-acceding creditor may sue the debtor for his debt, may obtain a preference for himself by diligence, may challenge the trust deed as a fraudulent preference under the Bankruptcy Act 1696, and may petition for sequestration, which will supersede the trust deed.

10–359 An acceding creditor may also petition for sequestration where the object of the trust deed is being defeated by the action of non-acceding creditors (as in *Campbell and Beck* v. *Macfarlane* (1862) 24 D. 1097, where non-acceding heritable creditors who had executed a poinding of the ground were about to carry off the moveable estate). A trust deed often expressly confers on the trustee the right to apply for sequestration.

10–360 On the award of sequestration, the trust deed automatically falls, and the trustee under the trust deed is bound to account to the trustee in the sequestration.

10–361 A trust deed usually provides that the debtor will be discharged of his debts on payment of the dividend which the estate yields. Such a provision does not have the effect of discharging the debtor of a debt due to a non-acceding creditor even where that creditor has received the same rate of dividend as the other creditors (*Ogilvie & Son* v. *Taylor*, above).

10–362 A trust deed may provide for the appointment of a committee of creditors whose duties will correspond to those of commissioners in sequestration. In particular, the audit of the trustee's accounts and the fixing of the trustee's remuneration will often by the trust deed be the duty of such a committee. The only provision of the Act of 1913 relating to trust deeds is to the effect that where a trust deed does not require the trustee's accounts to be audited and his remuneration to be fixed by a committee of creditors or where such a committee is not appointed or does not act, then the trustee, before making a final division of the estate, must submit his accounts to the Accountant of Court, who will audit the accounts and fix the trustee's remuneration. A trustee who fails to observe that provision forfeits all claim to remuneration for his services as trustee (s. 185).

(b) **Extra-Judicial Composition Contract**

This is a private agreement entered into between the debtor and his creditors by which the creditors agree to accept from the debtor a composition, which will be distributed rateably among them, and on payment of which the debtor will usually be discharged. As the debtor is not divested of his property, this type of extra-judicial settlement is more appropriate than the trust deed for the situation where the debtor is in business and it is intended that he should continue his business instead of having it sold and the proceeds distributed.

The payment of a composition under an extra-judicial composition contract is to be distinguished from the payment of a composition in the course of a sequestration (see 10–306 *et seq.*, above). The former is governed only by the common law (except in so far as the parties to the contract voluntarily incorporate statutory provisions), whereas the latter necessarily involves strict adherence to the Act of 1913.

An extra-judicial composition contract is not binding on a creditor who has not acceded to it. Such a creditor may, therefore, use diligence against the debtor's property, and may petition for sequestration.

It is an implied condition in any extra-judicial composition contract that all creditors will be treated rateably. If one favoured creditor is to receive an additional instalment, this will constitute an illegal preference (see *Bank of Scotland* v. *Faulds* (1870) 7 S.L.R. 619 (10–47, above)).

If the debtor fails to pay the composition, his original debts revive:

Horsefall v. *Virtue & Co.* (1826) 5 S. 36: V. & Co. entered into an extra-judicial composition contract with their creditors by which they agreed to pay 6s.6d. in the £ on their debts, in three instalments at six, 12 and 18 months from September 1, 1821. H., a creditor for £500, accordingly received three bills of exchange each for £54 3s.4d. V. & Co. duly paid the first two bills, but failed to pay the third.

Held that, in V. & Co.'s sequestration, H. was entitled to lodge a claim for £500 less the amount of the two composition bills which had been paid.

The composition contract may provide security for payment of the composition. A cautioner will be freed from liability if material alteration is made without his consent (as in *Allan, Buckley Allan & Milne* v. *Pattison* (1893) 21 R. 195, where, on the debtor's failure to pay the first of two instalments of a composition, his creditors took from him a trust deed under which the debtor's estate was realised).

Further Reading

Scots Mercantile Law Statutes (annual reprint from *The Parliament House Book*) (W. Green & Son) for Bankruptcy (Scotland) Act 1913, as amended, Bankruptcy Act 1883 and Companies Act 1947

Gloag and Henderson, *Introduction to the Law of Scotland,* Chapter XLIX

David M. Walker, *Principles of Scottish Private Law,* Chapter 10.1

J. J. Gow, *The Mercantile and Industrial Law of Scotland,* Chapter 12

W. A. Wilson, *The Law of Scotland Relating to Debt*, Chapters 18 and
    22
Goudy on the Law of Bankruptcy, 4th ed. by T.A. Fyfe (1914, T. & T.
    Clark)
Scottish Law Commission, *Report on Bankruptcy and Related Aspects
    of Insolvency and Liquidation* (Scot. Law Com. No. 68) (1982,
    H.M.S.O.)

CHAPTER 11

INSURANCE

INTRODUCTION

THERE is no statutory definition of "insurance," and both judges and textbook writers have usually avoided stating a definition. In *Medical Defence Union Ltd.* v. *Department of Trade* [1980] Ch. 82 Sir Robert Megarry V.-C. said (at p. 95):

"I do not know whether a satisfactory definition of 'a contract of insurance' will ever be evolved. Plainly it is a matter of considerable difficulty. It may be that it is a concept which it is better to describe than to attempt to define." In that case the Medical Defence Union Ltd. was held not to be an insurance company carrying on an insurance business within the meaning of the Insurance Companies Act 1974. The work of the Union included indemnifying its members against claims for damages and costs, but members had no *right to receive money or money's worth*, but only to have applications for help with claims fairly considered by the Union.

A modern textbook definition which takes this and earlier cases into account is: "A contract of insurance is any contract whereby one party assumes the risk of an uncertain event, which is not within his control, happening at a future time, in which event the other party has an interest, and under which contract the first party is bound to pay money or provide its equivalent if the uncertain event occurs" (John Birds, *Modern Insurance Law*, p. 7).

For the purposes of the elementary account of the law of insurance given in this chapter it may be sufficient to explain that insurance is a contract by which one person, called the "insurer" or (especially in marine insurance) the "underwriter," undertakes, in return for a money consideration called the "premium," to indemnify another person, called the "insured" or the "assured," against possible loss, or to make a payment on the happening of a specified event which involves some uncertainty. The indemnity referred to in the first branch of this definition need not take the form of a sum of money: it may be reinstatement of property or some other benefit in kind (*e.g.* in *Department of Trade and Industry* v. *St. Christopher Motorists' Association Ltd.* [1974] 1 W.L.R. 99 an association which undertook to provide chauffeur services for any member who became unable to drive was held to be carrying on insurance business).

11–02 There are many different types of insurance contracts, and several classifications are possible. This chapter does not deal separately with the various types of insurance, but is confined to a consideration of those broad principles of law which operate throughout the insurance field, or at least in large areas of it. It is sufficient, therefore, to note at this stage two major dividing lines:

11–03 First, there is the division into contracts of indemnity and contracts not of indemnity. This division is apparent in the explanation of insurance suggested above. In a contract of indemnity the amount which can be recovered from the insurer is limited to the amount of loss suffered by the insured, whereas if the contract is not one of indemnity the insurer is bound to pay whenever the specified event happens, whether or not the insured suffers a loss. All insurance contracts except those for life insurance, some personal accident insurance and some sickness insurance are contracts of indemnity. The principle of indemnity is therefore of great importance in the law of insurance, and will be returned to later in this chapter.

11–04 Secondly, there is the division into marine and non-marine insurance. Marine insurance was codified by the Marine Insurance Act 1906. Non-marine insurance includes life, fire, accident and liability insurance, and is governed mainly by the common law, though several important statutes have been passed from time to time affecting aspects of non-marine insurance. The principles of insurance law have been more fully worked out in relation to marine insurance, and some provisions of the Marine Insurance Act 1906 can often be referred to as affording a statement of a principle generally applicable to non-marine as well as to marine insurance. This chapter will also include some incidental mention of other statutory provisions on insurance.

A central topic in insurance law is that of insurable interest. The need for insurable interest is recognised both at common law and in statutory provisions. It is the subject-matter of the first part of this chapter:

    I. Insurable interest.

It is then appropriate to describe the general nature of an insurance contract, starting with:

    II. Formation of the contract.

This brings in a consideration of proposal forms, cover notes and slips, and above all the principle that insurance is a contract *uberrimae fidei* ("of the utmost good faith"), involving not merely an absence of misrepresentation but full disclosure of material facts. Under the same heading there is a brief account of the meaning and effect of warranties in insurance law.

The next part of the chapter deals with the formal document in which the terms of the insurance are set forth:

    III. The policy.

This is the document to be looked to for a statement of the premium, for any value agreed to be placed on the items insured, for the risk which is insured against, for the exceptions to that risk, and for the conditions to be observed during the continuance of the contract. The major principle applied in the interpretation of this formal document is that it is to be construed, in the event of ambiguity, *contra proferentem* ("against the party putting it forward"), *i.e.* in the sense which is less favourable to the insurer. The possibility of assigning a policy is also noted at this point.

The next matter for consideration is:

    IV. The claim.

The "proximity rule," also referred to as the "doctrine of proximate cause," requires explanation here, as do also the terms "subrogation," "contribution" and "reinstatement," (in marine insurance) "constructive total loss," "notice of abandonment," "average" and "suing and labouring clause" and (in motor insurance) a "knock-for-knock" agreement.

Following on the simple account in parts II, III and IV of how insurance operates, attention is directed to the principle described as the "fundamental principle of insurance":[1]

    V. The principle of indemnity.

Finally, an indication is given, without going into details, of the extent to which the common law of insurance has been affected by statute; this comes under the heading:

    VI. Statutory provisions.

The short account of basic insurance law contained in this chapter should not be allowed to obscure the vastness and complexity of the

---

[1] *per* Brett L.J. in *Castellain* v. *Preston* (1883) 11 Q.B.D. 380, at p. 386.

insurance market in practice. For instance, the term "insurer" will usually denote, not an individual, but a limited company with substantial financial resources, perhaps quoted on the Stock Exchange, and probably having a widespread business conducted through numerous branches and agencies; the insured for his part, though he may very well be an individual, may choose to transact his insurance business, not by a direct approach to any of the insurer's branches or agencies, but by engaging the services of an insurance intermediary, such as a Lloyd's broker or other insurance broker. It can be seen, therefore, that the principles of the law of agency will often require to be invoked, and in addition there is statutory supervision of insurance brokers under the Insurance Brokers (Registration) Act 1977. Again, it should be noted that, by the practice of reinsurance, the ultimate liability for the insured's loss may not rest fully on the shoulders of his own insurer, because the risk will have been spread by that insurer over a number of other insurers.

11–12   The subject-matter of this chapter is restricted to contractual insurance: wholly excluded is the compulsory social insurance system under which the State levies contributions and pays benefits in respect of unemployment, sickness, industrial injuries, *etc*.

11–13   The Scots law of insurance is not derived from Roman law. Its origins lie in maritime law, and it is believed to have been introduced into England by the Lombards in the Middle Ages. Marine insurance first assumed importance with the establishment of the London coffee houses (including Lloyd's Coffee House) after the Great Fire of 1666. There was rapid development in the law relating to various forms of insurance, but again particularly marine insurance, in the latter part of the eighteenth and early part of the nineteenth century, an outstanding contribution being made (as in other branches of commercial law) by Lord Mansfield, the Scot who was Chief Justice of the King's Bench in England from 1756 to 1788 and who, by admitting evidence of mercantile custom, incorporated into the common law many of the principles widely accepted in commercial circles. Several statutes were passed about the end of the eighteenth century to prohibit wagering policies, and the Life Assurance Act 1774 was aimed principally against life policies fraudulently taken out by persons who had no insurable interest in the life insured and who could consequently do nothing but benefit from his death. By the end of the nineteenth century, marine insurance had developed to such a stage that it was considered ripe for codification, and this was achieved, as already mentioned, by the Marine Insurance Act 1906.

11–14   There are no substantial differences at common law or in the statutes between the Scots and the English law of insurance, and English decided cases and books of authority may accordingly be justifiably cited and relied on.

I INSURABLE INTEREST

11–15   The requirement for an insurable interest may arise out of a statutory provision or out of a principle of the common law. It is important to distinguish between the insurable interest required by the Life Assurance

Act 1774, and the insurable interest required through the application of the common law principle of indemnity; this is because these two different types of insurable interest differ from one another in respect of time: under the 1774 Act the time at which the insurable interest must exist is the time when the contract of insurance is made, whereas if the insurable interest is required under the principle of indemnity, the material time is the time when the loss occurs.

(a) Insurable Interest Required by Life Assurance Act 1774

The title of the 1774 Act in full is: "An Act for regulating Insurances upon Lives, and for prohibiting all such Insurances except in cases where the Persons insuring shall have an Interest in the Life or Death of the Persons insured." This suggests, as the short title also does, that the Act is concerned only with life insurance; the actual provisions of the Act, however, are not so restricted: they extend to insurance on life *or any other event,* but *bona fide* insurance on "ships, goods, or merchandises" is expressly excluded. The Act is a short one, consisting of only four sections:

(i) No insurance can be made on the life of any person or on any other event whatsoever if the person for whose use or benefit or on whose account the policy is made has no interest, or by way of gaming or wagering; every insurance which infringes this provision is declared "null and void to all intents and purposes whatsoever" (s. 1).

(ii) Every policy on the life of any person or other event must have inserted in it the name of the person interested in it or of the person for whose use or benefit or on whose account the insurance has been made (s. 2). This is not to have the effect of invalidating a group policy (*e.g.* for a group of employees) provided the group is described in the policy in such a way as to make it possible to identify all the persons who at any given time are entitled to benefit under the policy (Insurance Companies Amendment Act 1973, s. 50).

(iii) No greater sum can be recovered or received from an insurer than the value of the interest of the insured in the life or other event (s. 3).

(iv) Nothing in the Act extends to insurances *bona fide* made on "ships, goods, or merchandises"; all such insurance is declared to be as valid and effectual in the law as if the Act had not been passed (s. 4).

The reference to "other event" has been held to bring accident insurance within the scope of the Act (*Shilling* v. *Accidental Death Insurance Co.* (1857) 2 H. & N. 42; 157 E.R. 18); most of the decided cases, however, have been concerned with life insurance, and in particular with the question whether or not there was sufficient insurable interest to satisfy the requirements of the Act. It has been submitted that "not only does the 1774 Act not apply to 'ships, goods or merchandises,' and fire insurance but that it has no application whatsoever to any insurance which is, in nature, an indemnity" (J.N. Quar, "Insurable Interest and the Life Assurance Act 1774", 1971 S.L.T. (News) 141, at p. 142).

The following points as to the application of the Act have been established:

11–23   (i) No question of insurable interest arises where a person is insuring his own life; the Act does not apply to that situation, and a person may insure his own life for any sum he pleases.

11–24   (ii) The interest required by the Act is a real interest: a mere expectancy, such as an heir may have before the death has occurred, is not enough.

11–25   (iii) The interest must be a pecuniary interest, which may arise either (1) out of contract, or (2) out of relationship:

11–26   (1) Where the interest arises out of contract, the person taking out the insurance must have a reasonable expectation of advantage from the continuance in life of the person whose life is being insured. For example, a creditor has an interest in the life of his debtor, a cautioner in the life of the principal debtor, an employer in the life of an employee, and an employee in the life of his employer. The interest is limited according to the terms of the contract; *e.g.* the creditor's interest is limited to the amount of the debt due to him.

11–27   (2) Where the interest arises out of relationship, the party insuring must be entitled to aliment from the person whose life is insured. Husband and wife have an insurable interest in each other's lives, a child in the life of his parent, and probably a parent in the life of his child. The last-mentioned example (which would not apply in English law) is supported by observations in a court of seven judges in *Carmichael* v. *Carmichael's Executrix*, 1919 S.C. 636:

A father had taken out a policy upon the life of his son. The policy provided that during the son's minority the father would be entitled to the surrender value of the policy and that, if the son died before attaining majority, the premiums would be repaid to the father, but that, if the son attained majority and continued to pay the premiums, the sum insured would be paid on his death to his executors.

The son attained majority, but died before the next premium fell due. He had known of the existence of the policy, but it had not been delivered or intimated to him by his father. Both the father and the son's executrix (an aunt to whom he had bequeathed all his estate by a holograph will) claimed the proceeds of the policy.

The Court of Session held that the father was entitled to the proceeds because the gift of the policy by father to son had not been completed by the necessary delivery.

Lord Dundas said (at p. 646): "The question whether or not a father has, according to the law of Scotland, an insurable interest in his son's life does not . . . here arise, as no point is taken by the Assurance Company. But . . . I may say that, as at present advised, I see no reason to doubt that he has such an interest. By our law a parent has right to claim aliment from his children, and this seems to me sufficient to give the parent an insurable interest in the child's life."

(The Court of Session's judgment was later reversed by the House of Lords (1920 S.C. (H.L.) 195) on the ground that, although the policy had never been delivered to the son, its terms, taken along with all the circumstances of the case, showed that the son had a *jus quaesitum tertio* ("right acquired by a third party") under it, with the result that the proceeds fell to his executrix.)

(iv) Provided the interest exists at the time when the insurance is taken out, the policy can be continued after the interest has lapsed; *e.g.* if a creditor has insured the life of his debtor, and the debt has been paid before the debtor dies, the insurer is still liable to pay the proceeds of the policy to the creditor on the debtor's death. A policy may also be assigned to a person who has no insurable interest in the life insured.

(v) Absence of insurable interest gives the insurance company a defence to a claim on the policy, but if the company waives the defence, then, according to the Scottish case of *Hadden* v. *Bryden* (1899) 1 F. 710, the court will not refuse to decide the question of who is entitled to the proceeds of the policy:

Robert Hadden, when a minor, took out an insurance policy on his own life for £500, payable to his executors on his death. The policy immediately passed into the possession of Robert's father, James Hadden, who paid all the premiums until his own death, 25 years later. In his trust-disposition and settlement James described the policy as "belonging to me," and directed his trustees to pay future premiums necessary to keep the policy in force.

When, some six years later, Robert died, competing claims to the proceeds of the policy were made by James's representatives and Robert's representatives, and one argument put forward by the latter was that the policy would have been void under the 1774 Act if it had belonged to the father James, because a father had no insurable interest in a son's life.

The court did not accept this argument. Lord President J.P.B. Robertson said (at p. 715): "The answer is, that it has been decided on grounds which are clearly valid that the statute merely furnishes a defence to the insuring company against a claim on the policy, but that, if the company waive the defence, the question who is entitled to the proceeds of the policy falls to be determined as if the statute did not exist. Accordingly, as the insurance company have paid the money, the plea disappears."

Robert's representatives won their case on another ground.

(For observations that the father would in any case have had an insurable interest, see *Carmichael* v. *Carmichael's Executrix* (11–27, above).)

There is an English decision which is contrary to *Hadden* v. *Bryden*— *Re London County Commercial Reinsurance Office Ltd.* [1922] 2 Ch. 67, decided by P.O. Lawrence J.

(b) Insurable Interest in Contracts of Indemnity

Most insurance contracts (life, some personal accident and some sickness being exceptions) are contracts of indemnity, in which the insured can recover no more than the amount of his loss. The time at which an insurable interest is essential is therefore the time when the loss occurs and the claim arises. The requirement may be waived by the insurer. The principle of indemnity does not require that there should be any insurable interest at the time when the contract is entered into (but the 1774 Act will require an insurable interest at that time also, unless the insurance comes within one of the exceptions provided for by the Act, namely, "ships, goods or merchandises").

11–32   The principle of indemnity is a common law principle, but in the case of marine insurance it has been given statutory expression in the codifying Marine Insurance Act 1906.

11–33   Several persons may each have an insurable interest in the same property at the same time; their separate interests arise out of the different capacities in which they are connected with the property; *e.g.* one person may be the owner, and another a tenant or a person holding the property in security, or a carrier. Each interest may be separately insured, and the extent of the insurable interest is not necessarily the same; *e.g.*, since a stipulation in a lease binding the tenant to keep the property in repair does not bind him to repair damage by fire (*Duff* v. *Fleming* (1870) 8 M. 769), tenants of the Plaza Ballroom in Stirling, who were under a duty to maintain the building and who insured it against damage or destruction by fire, were held not to have an insurable interest in the full value of the building at the time of its destruction by fire (*Fehilly* v. *General Accident Fire and Life Assurance Corporation Ltd.*, 1983 S.L.T. 141 (O.H.)).

11–34   A creditor has no insurable interest in the property of his debtor, and it is a corollary of this principle that a shareholder has no insurable interest in the property of the company, even although he holds all the shares in the company: *Macaura* v. *Northern Assurance Co. Ltd.* [1925] A.C. 619 (3–143, above).

11–35   The most prominent of the indemnity insurances are fire insurance and marine insurance.

(i) *Insurable Interest in Fire Insurance*

11–36   In fire insurance an insurable interest must exist not only at the time when the fire occurs but also, in situations where the Life Assurance Act 1774 applies, at the time when the contract of insurance is entered into.

11–37   A well-known English case which illustrates how the principle of indemnity prevents the insured from making a profit out of his loss is *Castellain* v. *Preston* (1883) 11 Q.B.D. 380:

On March 25, 1878, P., owner of certain lands and buildings in Liverpool, took out insurance on the buildings against loss by fire. On July 31 following, P. contracted to sell the land and buildings to his tenants Messrs. Rayner for £3,100. On August 15, a fire damaged part of the buildings, and as a result of a claim being made under the policy, £330 was paid to P. on September 25 by the insurance company, which did not at that time know of the existence of the contract of sale.

In December 12, 1879, the conveyance was executed, and the purchase-price was paid in full by Messrs Rayner to P.

Held, in an action by the insurance company against P., that the company was entitled to recover from P. the amount of the insurance-money, on the ground that fire insurance was a contract of indemnity under which no more could be recovered by the insured than the full amount of his loss (see also 11–210 and 11–249 *et seq.*, below).

(ii) *Insurable Interest in Marine Insurance*

11–38   A contract of marine insurance is by definition a contract of indemnity: the Marine Insurance Act 1906 starts with this definition:

"A contract of marine insurance is a contract whereby the insurer undertakes to indemnify the assured, in manner and to the extent thereby agreed, against marine losses, that is to say, the losses incident to marine adventure" (s. 1).

The provisions of the Act as to insurable interest are in sections 4 to 15. The most important of them are:

(1) Every contract of marine insurance by way of gaming or wagering is void. A contract of marine insurance is deemed to be a gaming or wagering contract—

(a) where the assured has not an insurable interest, *and* the contract is entered into with no expectation of acquiring such an interest; or

(b) where the policy is made "interest or no interest," or "without further proof of interest than the policy itself," or "without benefit of salvage to the insurer," or subject to any other similar term (except that where there is no possibility of salvage, a policy may be effected without benefit of salvage to the insurer) (s. 4).

(2) In general, every person has an insurable interest if he is "interested in a marine adventure," and he will satisfy that description if he "stands in any legal or equitable relation to the adventure or to any insurable property at risk therein, in consequence of which he may benefit by the safety or due arrival of insurable property, or may be prejudiced by its loss, or by damage thereto, or by the detention thereof, or may incur liability in respect thereof" (s. 5).

(3) The assured must be interested in the subject-matter insured at the time of the loss (though he need not be interested when the insurance is effected). There is an exception to this provision: where the subject-matter is insured "lost or not lost," the assured may recover under the policy even although he may not have acquired his interest until after the loss, unless at the time of effecting the insurance the assured was aware of the loss and the insurer was not. The assured cannot acquire an interest after he is aware of the loss (s. 6).

(4) The following are amongst those who have an insurable interest— the lender of money on a bond of bottomry or respondentia (see 8–34 *et seq.*, above) up to the amount of the loan (s. 10), the master or any member of the crew to the extent of his wages (s. 11), and a person who has advanced the freight in so far as such freight is not repayable in the event of loss (s. 12).

The Marine Insurance (Gambling Policies) Act 1909 made contracts of marine insurance entered into without a *bona fide* interest or a *bona fide* expectation of acquiring an interest an offence on the part of the insurer, the insured and the broker.

However, in spite of these statutory provisions of the civil and criminal law, "p.p.i." policies (policies proof of interest) are common in marine insurance practice. They are described as "honour" policies, because, though they are not legally binding, any claims which arise under them will be paid by the insurers as a matter of honour. In *"Gunford" Ship Co. Ltd.* v. *Thames and Mersey Marine Insurance Co. Ltd.,* 1911 S.C. (H.L.) 84, the existence of honour policies which over-insured a ship was held to be a material fact which ought to have been disclosed to the insurance company which was to issue a legally enforceable policy; as it was, since there had been no disclosure of the honour policies, the later insurance contract was voidable.

II FORMATION OF THE CONTRACT

11–46 There is no definite authority as to whether the contract of insurance is by the common law of Scotland one of the *obligationes literis* ("written obligations") for the constitution of which formal writing is necessary, but the view that it does fall within that category has the support of an *obiter dictum* ("remark by the way") of Lord McLaren in *McElroy* v. *London Assurance Corporation* (1897) 24 R. 287, at p. 290: "As I have always understood,—indeed I think it is perfectly settled in the law of Scotland,—a contract of insurance can only be made in writing. . . . Either a policy or some informal writing followed by *rei interventus*[2] is requisite. A policy is the proper mode of constituting the contract. . . . But the parties may be bound by a preliminary contract in terms of the formal deed which is afterwards executed." The decision in the case was that the court could not entertain a claim under a fire insurance policy because the insured did not aver that the policy had been delivered or that the premium had been paid to the insurance company prior to the date of the fire.

On the other hand there is the following support for the proposition that at common law a contract of insurance may be constituted orally and proved *prout de jure* ("by any evidence, including parole evidence"):

(a) In *Christie and Others* v. *North British Insurance Co.* (1825) 3 S. 519 (see 11–56, below) Lord Justice-Clerk Boyle said (at p. 522):

"It is impossible to assent to the doctrine, that without a delivered policy there is no insurance. If the premium in this case had been agreed on, the insurance would have been effected, although no policy was delivered."

(b) In an early marine insurance case, *Mills and Others* v. *Albion Insurance Co.* (1826) 4 S. 575, the court held that where a policy was not delivered, the extent of the risk actually insured against could competently be proved by parole evidence.

(c) *Parker & Co. (Sandbank) Ltd.* v. *Western Assurance Co.*, 1925 S.L.T. 131 (O.H.): P. Ltd., boat and launch builders, brought an action against insurance companies in respect of a fire loss in its premises. P. Ltd. averred that an oral contract of insurance had been concluded, and the insurance companies denied this.

Held that P. Ltd. had failed to prove the existence of the contract in question beyond reasonable doubt; the insurance companies were therefore assoilzied.

The opinion of the Lord Ordinary (Constable) assumes that a contract could be constituted orally.

11–47 The Scottish Law Commission has suggested that the uncertainty be removed by the introduction of a rule requiring all contracts of insurance to be constituted in writing (Scottish Law Commission, *Memorandum*

---

[2] literally, "actings following on"—a form of personal bar.

No. 39 ("Constitution and Proof of Voluntary Obligations: Formalities of Constitution and Restrictions on Proof"), para. 69 et seq.).

The Marine Insurance Act 1906 makes the issue of a marine policy essential in a contract of marine insurance: section 22 of the Act provides that a contract of marine insurance is "inadmissible in evidence unless it is embodied in a marine policy" in accordance with the Act.

In non-marine insurance there is no general statutory requirement that there must be writing, but attention must be paid to the revenue provisions in the Stamp Act 1891, as amended by later Finance Acts, which imposed penalties for failure to issue stamped policies; since the Finance Act 1970 the only remaining provision is that in life insurance the insurer must issue a stamped policy within one month of receiving the first premium.

In practice, in both marine and non-marine insurance, there always is a formal policy, either issued or at least contemplated, and that policy will provide evidence of the terms of the insurance.

In addition to these matters relating to formalities and proof, the formation of a contract of insurance involves a consideration of:

(a) proposal forms;
(b) cover notes and slips;
(c) disclosure and representations; and
(d) warranties.

(a) Proposal Forms

A contract of insurance, like any other contract, requires *consensus in idem* ("mutual agreement"), *i.e.* the acceptance must meet the offer in every material respect.

The normal procedure is for the offer to be made by the completion of a "proposal form," a document supplied by an insurance company and consisting of a number of questions to be answered by the person who is seeking insurance. The completed proposal form is lodged with the company, and if the company gives an unqualified acceptance of the proposal, the contract is then complete. In marine insurance a "slip" may be used instead of a proposal form (see 11–69 *et seq.,* below).

As long as there are still material terms to be settled, there can be no *consensus in idem,* the parties are still at the stage of negotiation, and there will be no binding contract of insurance. For instance, it may very well be that the amount of the premium is not fixed until the insurance company has considered the answers given in the proposal form; the contract will not then be complete until the proposer has agreed to the premium asked by the company.

The following are two illustrations of absence of *consensus in idem:*

(i) *Christie and Others* v. *North British Insurance Co.* (1825) 3 S. 519: Stead decided to insure his wire-mill for £5,000. He applied to the Phoenix Insurance Co.'s agent in Edinburgh to take the risk to the extent of £2,000, and the question of the amount of the premium was referred by the Edinburgh agent to the directors in London. Stead also applied to the N.B. Co. of Edinburgh to take the remaining £3,000, and that company agreed to insure at the same premium as the Phoenix Co. would charge.

Before the premiums had been fixed, the mill was destroyed by fire. The Phoenix Co. paid its share of the loss, as a favour and not because it considered itself bound to do so, but the N.B. Co. refused to pay. Stead raised an action against the latter company, and the action was carried on by his executors.

Held that the mill was not insured, because the premiums had never been fixed, and that the conduct of the Phoenix Co. in paying its share of the loss could not affect the question with the N.B. Co.

11–57　(ii) *Star Fire and Burglary Insurance Co. Ltd.* v. *C. Davidson & Sons Ltd.* (1902) 5 F. 83: D. Ltd. wished to insure its paper works against fire with S. Ltd. The negotiations leading up to the issue of the policy made no mention of the fact that S. Ltd. was a mutual company, *i.e.* one in which the policy-holders were members of the company. The policy narrated that D. Ltd. had agreed to become a member of S. Ltd.—a position which would have made D. Ltd. liable to contribute to the assets of S. Ltd. in the event of its liquidation.

D. Ltd. refused to accept the policy, and S. Ltd. brought an action for payment of the premium.

Held that D. Ltd. was not liable for the premium, because it had not agreed to become a member of S. Ltd.

11–58　The acceptance which completes the contract of insurance may take the form of an express written communication from the insurance company to the proposer, or it may be inferred from actings; the issue of a policy, for instance, or the acceptance by the company of the payment of the premium usually implies that the company has accepted the proposer's offer.

11–59　A number of cases have related to "coupon" insurance, by which an offer is made in an advertisement and is capable of being accepted by any member of the public who chooses to fill in the coupon and send it with the stipulated premium to the insurance company. A well-known case is *Hunter* v. *General Accident Fire and Life Assurance Corporation Ltd.*, 1909 S.C. (H.L.) 30; 1909 S.C. 344:

A coupon policy of insurance in a Letts's diary stated that £1,000 would be paid to the executors of any owner of the diary fatally injured in a railway accident provided the owner had caused his name to be registered at the insurance company's head office and provided the claim was made within 12 months of the registration. H. applied for registration on December 25, 1905, and received from the company a letter dated January 3, 1906, with which was enclosed an official acknowledgment dated December 29, 1905.

H. was injured in a railway accident on December 28, 1906, and died the following day. His executrix made a claim under the policy on January 2, 1907, and the decision in the case turned on the date of registration.

Held that the burden was on the company to prove the date of registration and that upon a balance of probabilities registration was subsequent to the sending of the acknowledgment on January 3, 1906; the claim had therefore been made within 12 months of the registration, and the company was liable under the policy.

11–60　Insurance advertisements are now subject to statutory regulations under the Insurance Companies Act 1982 (s. 72).

A contract of insurance gives rise to contractual rights and obligations. A document which excludes such rights and obligations is not a contract of insurance:

Woods v. *Co-operative Insurance Society Ltd.*, 1924 S.C. 692: An advertisement in the newspaper *John Bull* invited readers to obtain the benefits of a "free insurance scheme" by filling up two coupons, one to be sent to *John Bull* and the other to be handed to a newsagent as an order for a regular weekly delivery of the newspaper. Along with the newspaper there was also circulated a printed document containing the conditions of the scheme, and one of the conditions stated: "This free insurance scheme does not involve any contractual liability."

Held that a reader who had followed the procedure indicated had no valid contract of insurance under the scheme.

A proposal form usually includes a "basis clause," *i.e.* a clause by which the proposer agrees that the proposal form as completed by him is to be the basis of the contract between him and the company. The effect of such a clause is explained under "Warranties," below. The basis clause is normally repeated, for extra clarity, in the policy, but repetition is not essential: the policy does not supersede the contractual documents preceding it in the same way as a disposition supersedes the missives in a transfer of heritable property: "the policy differs from a disposition of heritage in being an acceptance of the proposer's offer, and unless it fails to meet the offer . . . the terms stated in the offer form part of the resulting contract" (*per* Lord Fraser (Ordinary) in *McCartney* v. *Laverty*, 1968 S.C. 207 (O.H.)).

(b) Cover Notes and Slips

Cover notes are used in non-marine insurance, and slips in marine insurance, in order to provide insurance cover during the period of negotiation.

Cover notes are common in fire and accident insurance. They are not used in life insurance.

A cover note is usually a printed document signed on behalf of the insurance company by the agent with whom the proposal form is lodged. It gives temporary protection only. If the proposal is accepted, the cover note is then superseded by the policy. If the insurer rejects the proposal, the duration of the cover note depends on the terms contained in it; *e.g.* the cover note may state that it is to remain in force for 14 days with the right reserved to the insurer to terminate it at an earlier date by intimation of the rejection.

A cover note is itself a contract of insurance and is enforceable according to its own terms, which are not necessarily the same as the terms of the policy. Usually, however, the cover note will expressly incorporate all the usual terms of the type of policy which is being sought.

Neil v. *South East Lancashire Insurance Co. Ltd.*, 1932 S.C. 35: On February 9, 1927, an agent of the insurance company S. Ltd. issued to MacKellar a cover note for comprehensive insurance of a bus owned by MacKellar. It stated: "The Undernoted Insurance is held covered subject to the usual terms and conditions of the Company's Policy and payment of the premium pending preparation of the policy or until notice in writing declining the risk be given from the Head Office of the Company."

On February 18, a proposal form was filled up and signed by Mac-Kellar. There was an error in the answer to one of the questions asked. The proposal form included the clause "I warrant the truth of the foregoing," and the policy, issued on March 2, stated that the insured had agreed that the proposal should be the basis of the contract of insurance contained in the policy.

Meantime, on February 16, N. had been knocked down and injured by MacKellar's bus. N. brought an action against MacKellar, and S. Ltd. undertook the defence of the action. The claim was settled at £300, and a decree was pronounced for that amount in N.'s favour.

S. Ltd. then discovered the error in the answer in the proposal form, and refused to pay the £300.

Held that the liability of S. Ltd. depended on the cover note, which contained the only contract of insurance in force at the date of the accident; the reference to the "usual terms and conditions of the Company's Policy" did not have the effect of incorporating into the cover note the warranty contained in the proposal form; S. Ltd. was therefore bound to meet the claim.

11–68   (Under the Road Traffic Act 1972 a third party may have a valid claim against the insurance company, even where the company would, in a question with the insured, be entitled to avoid the policy on account of some misrepresentation or concealment on the part of the insured.)

11–69   In marine insurance a document called a "slip" may correspond to the cover note in non-marine insurance. Alternatively—in those classes of marine insurance where proposal forms are not used—the slip takes the place of both the proposal form and the cover note in non-marine insurance.

11–70   A slip states briefly who the insured is, the amount proposed to be insured, the subject-matter of the insurance, the risk insured against, and the date of commencement and duration of the contract. It is prepared by a broker and is submitted by him to the various underwriters with whom he normally does business. Each underwriter who wishes to accept the proposed insurance, initials the slip, adding opposite his initials the amount for which he is willing to be responsible. The initialling of the slip by the underwriter amounts to acceptance of the insured's proposal.

11–71   By section 21 of the Marine Insurance Act 1906 a contract of marine insurance is deemed to be concluded when the proposal of the assured is accepted by the insurer, whether the policy be then issued or not, and for the purpose of showing when the proposal was accepted, reference may be made to the slip. The policy need not be executed until some time after the contract is concluded, but no contract of marine insurance is admissible in evidence unless it is embodied in a marine policy in accordance with the Act (s. 22). Even after the policy has been duly issued, reference may still be made to the slip in any legal proceedings (s. 89).

11–72   In marine insurance practice, slips are regarded as binding the underwriters to issue policies, but the case of *Clyde Marine Insurance Co. Ltd.* v. *Renwick & Co.*, 1924 S.C. 113, shows that because of the statutory provisions the obligation to issue a policy is an honourable, and not a legally enforceable, obligation:

A marine insurance company had initialled a number of slips, but before any policies had been issued the company went into liquidation. The liquidator subsequently issued policies to some of the holders of the initialled slips.

Held that (i) the company had been under no legal obligation to issue policies to holders of initialled slips; (ii) although the company might have been under an honourable obligation to issue policies, the liquidator was not bound, or even entitled, to do so; and (iii) the policies which the liquidator had issued were *ultra vires* ("beyond his powers") and had to be cancelled, with the premiums being refunded.

"Notwithstanding all this," Lord President Clyde said (at p. 123), "in the practical conduct of marine insurance business the slip plays a part of the greatest importance. It is by means of the slip that the actual business of the broker and the underwriter is done; and . . . the honourable obligations . . . between underwriter and broker to carry through the piece of insurance business to which the slip refers are of the highest kind, and are sanctioned by the penalty of exclusion from professional intercourse which brokers and underwriters alike mete out to anyone who fails in the strict observance of them. But while such exclusion may be no more unlawful than the contracting of the honourable obligations themselves, both those obligations and their sanction are wholly extra-legal."

(c) Disclosure and Representations

Each party to a contract of insurance must, up to the time of the formation of the contract, not only refrain from material misrepresentations— fraudulent or innocent—but spontaneously disclose to the other party all material facts known to himself. The effect of failure to disclose material facts or of material misrepresentation is that the contract of insurance is voidable.

The principle as applied to non-marine insurance is a principle of the common law. As regards marine insurance, it has been given statutory expression in sections 17 to 21 of the Marine Insurance Act 1906.

In the common situation where the contract of insurance is made between the proposer and an agent for an insurance company, the knowledge of the agent is taken as the knowledge of the company, with the result that the company can be barred from treating the contract as voidable for non-disclosure or misrepresentation, *e.g.:*

Cruikshank v. *Northern Accident Insurance Co. Ltd.* (1895) 23 R. 147: C., when taking out a policy for accidental death, was asked in the proposal form: "Are there any circumstances which render you peculiarly liable to accident?" His answer was: "Slight lameness from birth." He had in fact been *extremely* lame.

C. died as a result of burns sustained when he fell into a fireplace in his house, and his widow claimed payment under the policy.

The evidence showed that the proposal form had been filled up by the insurance company's agent at a hotel where C. was staying, and that the agent had seen C. walking across the room.

Held that as the agent must have seen the extent of C.'s lameness, the insurance company was not entitled to take advantage of any misdescription of the lameness in the proposal form, and the widow's claim therefore succeeded.

11–76 The central point in relation to disclosure and representations is that the contract is voidable only if the fact not disclosed or the misrepresentation, as the case may be, is *material*. It is therefore appropriate to consider first:

  (i) what is meant by "material,"

before looking separately at:

  (ii) disclosure, and
  (iii) representations.

A brief indication then follows of how the harshness of the present law on disclosure and representations has led to:

  (iv) mitigation in insurance practice and proposals for reform.

11–77 The well-known case of *The "Spathari,"* 1925 S.C. (H.L.) 6; 1924 S.C. 182, makes a suitable introduction to each of (i), (ii) and (iii):

Demetriades, a Greek resident in Glasgow, purchased a Finnish ship with the intention of selling it to a syndicate of Greeks in Samos. He arranged with Borthwick, an impecunious British subject, that the ship be transferred by the Finnish owners to Borthwick, be registered and insured in Borthwick's name, sail to Samos under the management of Demetriades, and be transferred at the end of the voyage by Borthwick to Demetriades. At the time when the insurance was taken out, Greek ships were either uninsurable or only insurable at exceptionally heavy premiums.

The ship sank, and a claim was made against the insurance company for total loss.

Held that the company was not liable, because of (i) the misrepresentation that the ship was sailing under the British flag and was therefore entitled to be registered as a British ship, and (ii) the failure to disclose the Greek interest in the ship—a fact material to the risk in view of the attitude of underwriters towards Greek-owned ships at the time.

(i) What is Meant by "Material"

11–78 The best known definition of "material" is that of the Marine Insurance Act 1906. Section 18 of that Act, which deals with disclosure of material circumstances, provides that "every circumstance is material which would influence the judgment of a prudent insurer in fixing the premium, or determining whether he will take the risk." Similarly, section 20, which requires every material representation made at the negotiating stage to be true, provides that "a representation is material which would influence the judgment of a prudent insurer in fixing the premium, or determining whether he will take the risk."

11–79 Another statutory definition of "material" is that of the Road Traffic Act 1972 (s. 149(5)): "'material' means of such a nature as to influence the judgment of a prudent insurer in determining whether he will take the risk and, if so, at what premium and on what conditions."

11–80 These statutory provisions apply the "prudent insurer" test, and this is now generally recognised to be the proper test also at common law. For example in *Glicksman* v. *Lancashire and General Assurance Co. Ltd.* [1927] A.C. 139, at p. 143, Lord Dunedin in the House of Lords described a material consideration as being "any consideration which would affect the mind of the ordinary prudent man in accepting the risk," and in *Lambert* v. *Co-operative Insurance Society Ltd.* [1975] 2 Lloyd's Rep. 485 (C.A.) the Court of Appeal held that what was material was that which would influence the mind of a prudent insurer. (Each of these English cases is referred to later (11–93 and 11–107, below).)

When this "prudent insurer" test is being applied, any inquiry as to what actually would influence the particular insurer is irrelevant, as is also the insured's own opinion as to whether a fact is material or not.

Another possible test is the "reasonable insured" test. According to this test no fact would be deemed material unless it would be considered material by a reasonable insured. The test was applied by Lord President Inglis in *Life Association of Scotland* v. *Foster* (1873) 11 M. 351 (see 11–113, below). The Lord President said (at p. 360):

"My opinion is . . . that the swelling which is proved to have existed at the date of the contract of insurance has not been shewn to be such a fact as a reasonable and cautious person, unskilled in medical science, and with no special knowledge of the law and practice of insurance, would believe to be of any materiality or in any way calculated to influence the insurers in considering and deciding on the risk."

It could be argued, on the strength of that opinion, that the "reasonable insured" test is the correct test to apply to life insurance in Scots law, but it seems likely that such argument would be unable to withstand the statutory definitions of "material" (11–78 *et seq.,* above) and the persuasive authority of the later English cases (11–80, above). On the uncertainty of Scots law on the matter see *Fourth Report of the Law Reform Committee for Scotland* (1957: Cmnd. 330), paras. 5-8.

Suggestions have been made for the reform of the law, so that this test would be adopted instead of the "prudent insurer" test, which is harsh to the insured and operates in favour of the insurer, who will usually be able to draw on a large fund of experience, not available to the insured, in judging what is material. However, the Law Reform Committee for Scotland found "very substantial practical difficulties" in the way of introducing the "reasonable insured" test (Cmnd. 330, para. 9).

Materiality is in each case a question of fact, depending on the type of insurance and on the other circumstances: the decision in one case is no sure guide as to the decision in another.

In normal practice the insurer, by the specific questions asked in the proposal form, indicates what he considers to be material; *e.g.* in a proposal for life insurance the insurer will normally ask, and require evidence of, the age of the life insured, and will normally ask questions as to medical history and dangerous pursuits. The proposal form, however, is not conclusive: a fact about which no question is asked may be material, and conversely a fact about which a question is asked may be non-material, *e.g.*:

(1) *Schoolman* v. *Hall* [1951] 1 Lloyd's Rep. 139 (C.A.): S., a well-established and respected retail jeweller in London, made a claim against H., an underwriting member of Lloyd's, in respect of a burglary at the shop.

S. had answered 15 questions in a proposal form, but had not stated in addition that some 15 years earlier he had had a criminal record.

Held that H. was entitled to refuse to pay S.'s claim, on the ground that S. had failed to disclose a material fact about which the proposal form had asked no specific question.

11–86 (2) *Dawsons Ltd.* v. *Bonnin,* 1922 S.C. (H.L.) 156: The proposal form for a comprehensive motor vehicle policy included the request: "State full address at which the vehicles will usually be garaged." The answer given was untrue.

Held that the misrepresentation was not material. (The case was decided in the underwriters' favour, however, on the ground that the parties had expressly made the proposal the "basis" of their contract.)

(The modern practice in motor insurance of fixing different premiums according to the locality in which a vehicle is kept would justify a court in now reaching a different conclusion about the materiality of such a misrepresentation as occurred in this case.)

11–87 If the proposer omits to give an answer to a question in the proposal form and the insurer raises no objection to the omission, the question is deemed to relate to a non-material fact.

11–88 The following facts are usually held to be material:

(1) Exposure to more than ordinary danger

11–89 In life insurance the nature of a person's occupation or hobbies can be material on this ground, while in fire insurance the situation of a building and the items stored in it can be material.

(2) Special motive of the insured

11–90 Facts suggesting that the insured has some special motive and is not acting out of mere ordinary prudence can be material; *e.g.* in *"Gunford" Ship Co. Ltd.* v. *Thames and Mersey Marine Insurance Co. Ltd.,* 1911 S.C. (H.L.) 84, over-insurance of a ship was held to be a material fact, even although the policies involved were honour policies and therefore not legally enforceable.

(3) Greater liability of insurer

11–91 Facts which indicate that the liability of the insurer would be greater than would normally be expected can be material; *e.g.* where the insured entrusts his goods to a carrier and makes a special contract with the carrier by which he relieves the carrier of the liability which would normally attach to the carrier in respect of the goods, that special contract could be a material fact.

(4) "Moral hazard"

11–92 The term "moral hazard" is used of facts relating to the character of the insured which suggest that a contract of insurance with him is specially likely to give rise to more than ordinary claims against the insurer. "Character" in this context has a wide meaning: it covers such factors as a history of previous losses and claims under other policies, refusals of insurance by other insurers, in motor insurance convictions for motoring offences, convictions for dishonesty, and nationality (as in *The "Spathari"* (11–77, above)).

The burglary insurance case of *Glicksman* v. *Lancashire and General Assurance Co. Ltd.*, already mentioned (11–80, above), is an instance of failure to disclose a refusal by another insurer:

Sapsy Glicksman, a small ladies' tailor, was asked in the proposal form: "Has any company declined to accept, or refused to renew, your burglary insurance? If so, state name of company." In his answer he referred to one refusal by the "Yorkshire" but not to a previous refusal by that same company.

Held that the earlier refusal was a material fact which he ought to have disclosed, and that the insurance company was therefore entitled to resist a claim under the policy.

An instance of motor insurance made voidable by a material misrepresentation is *Zurich General Accident and Liability Insurance Co. Ltd.* v. *Leven*, 1940 S.C. 406:

The insured had been asked in the proposal form whether she, or any other person who to her knowledge would drive the car, had been convicted of any offence in connection with any motor vehicle. She answered "No" to the question. At the time of signing she knew that her father would drive the car, but she did not know that about six years previously he had been convicted of reckless driving.

Held that the conviction was material, and that consequently the insurance company was entitled to avoid the policy.

For instances of failure to disclose a criminal record, see *Schoolman* v. *Hall* (11–85, above), and *Lambert* v. *Co-operative Insurance Society Ltd.* [1975] 2 Lloyd's Rep. 485 (C.A.) (11–107, below).

However, the law relating to disclosure of a criminal record was modified by the Rehabilitation of Offenders Act 1974. That Act provides that certain convictions are to be treated as "spent" after a "rehabilitation period," and that a person is not required to disclose a spent conviction. A conviction which has resulted in a sentence of imprisonment of more than 30 months never becomes "spent," but for lesser sentences the "rehabilitation period" varies according to the length of the sentence; *e.g.* the maximum length of the period is 10 years from the date of conviction and for a sentence of imprisonment for a term not exceeding six months the period is seven years.

In practice the difficulties which can arise out of doubts and arguments as to whether a particular fact is material are usually avoided by the use of warranties (see 11–132, below).

(ii) *Disclosure*

A contract of insurance is the most prominent of the contracts *uberrimae fidei* ("of the utmost good faith")—the category which is an exception to the general rule of the law of contract that neither party to an intended contract is under a duty to disclose material facts to the other.

An explanation of why insurance should be included in this category was given by Scrutton L.J. in *Rozanes* v. *Bowen* (1928) 32 Ll. L.R. 98 (C.A.), at p. 102:

"It has been for centuries in England the law in connection with insurance of all sorts, marine, fire, life, guarantee and every kind of policy that, as the underwriter knows nothing and the man who comes to him to ask him to insure knows everything, it is the duty of the assured, the man who desires to have a policy, to make a full disclosure to the underwriters without being asked of all the material circumstances, because the underwriter knows nothing and the assured knows everything. That is expressed by saying that it is a contract of the utmost good faith—*uberrima fides*.[3]"

That case concerned a claim by a Paris jeweller (R.) against an underwriting member of Lloyd's (B.) for a loss of £10,000 worth of jewellery from R.'s shop. In an answer to a question in the proposal form R. had disclosed one previous theft, but had failed to disclose two other previous thefts. As the proposal form stated that it was to be the basis of the policy, B. was entitled to avoid the policy (*i.e.* treat it as voidable and set it aside).

11–100 Most instances of the principle of *uberrima fides* arise out of the *insured's* failure to disclose, and so are covered by Scrutton L.J.'s explanation. However, the principle applies also to the insurer. Accordingly, the Marine Insurance Act 1906 provides: "A contract of marine insurance is a contract based upon the utmost good faith, and, if the utmost good faith be not observed by either party, the contract may be avoided by the other party" (s. 17).

11–101 The rule on disclosure, as expressed in the leading provision of section 18 of the Marine Insurance Act 1906, is: "The assured must disclose to the insurer, before the contract is concluded, every material circumstance which is known to the assured, and the assured is deemed to know every circumstance which, in the ordinary course of business, ought to be known by him. If the assured fails to make such disclosure, the insurer may avoid the contract." More shortly expressed, the rule is: "A failure on the part of the assured to disclose a material fact within his actual or imputed knowledge renders the policy voidable at the option of the insurers" (E. R. Hardy Ivamy, *General Principles of Insurance Law* (3rd ed.), p. 139).

11–102 In addition to the question of what is "material" (see 11–78 *et seq.*, above), the following aspects of the rule call for some comment:
(1) the time of disclosure;
(2) what must be disclosed; and
(3) what need not be disclosed.

(1) The time of disclosure

11–103 Disclosure must be made before the contract is formed. Once the insurance is current, the risk lies with the insurer, and the insured is not required to disclose to the insurer the fresh emergence of material circumstances.

11–104 In the normal situation the time for disclosure will be the signing of the proposal form, but as this is not the point of time for conclusion of the

---

3 "*Uberrima fides*" is Latin nominative (translated "utmost good faith"); "*uberrimae fidei*" is Latin genitive (translated "of the utmost good faith").

contract, any material change occurring between the signing of the proposal form and the acceptance of the proposal by the insurer must be disclosed.

It is important to remember that many policies, including fire and accident policies, usually last only for one year, at the end of which they are renewable for a further year. The usual procedure is for no proposal form to be filled in on the occasion of a renewal, but the legal position is that the "renewal" is a new contract by which cover is granted on the understanding that the answers in the original proposal form continue to be a true and full representation of material facts.

An illustration is *Law Accident Insurance Society Ltd.* v. *Boyd*, 1942 S.C. 384:

In February 1935, B. took out a car insurance policy, making a statement in the proposal form that he had not been convicted during the previous five years of any offence in connection with any motor vehicle. He made a series of annual renewals, the last of which was in February 1940. He did not disclose that in July 1939 he had been convicted of driving while under the influence of drink.

In November 1940 B. was involved in a motor accident.

Held that the insurance company was entitled to avoid the policy because of B.'s failure to disclose at the renewal in February 1940 the material change in circumstances resulting from the conviction of July 1939.

Another illustration is *Lambert* v. *Co-operative Insurance Society Ltd.* [1975] 2 Lloyd's Rep. 485 (C.A):

In 1963 L. signed a proposal form to cover her own and her husband's jewellery. Her husband had been convicted some years earlier of receiving 1,730 cigarettes knowing them to have been stolen, but this was not disclosed in the proposal. There were annual renewals, the last being in March 1972, and on that occasion there was no disclosure of a second conviction for dishonesty, incurred in December 1971.

In April 1972 L. made a claim under the policy for seven items lost or stolen.

Held that the insurance company was entitled to repudiate the claim on the ground of L.'s failure to disclose the first conviction in 1963 and on the further ground that she had failed to disclose the second conviction in March 1972.

(2) What must be disclosed

The duty of disclosure is not restricted by the questions asked in the proposal form: where no questions are asked about a circumstance which is in fact material, the proposer must volunteer the necessary information (see *Schoolman* v. *Hall*, 11–85, above).

On the other hand, if the proposer does not answer all the questions in the proposal form and the insurer accepts the proposal without objecting to the omissions, the insurer will be barred from stating later that the omissions amounted to non-disclosure of material circumstances. Similarly, if the proposer gives an answer which ought to arouse the insurer's suspicions and the insurer makes no further investigations, the insurer will be unable to found on the non-disclosure.

11–110　　The duty of disclosure is not confined to circumstances which are within the *actual* knowledge of the insured: it extends to circumstances which are within his "imputed" (or presumed) knowledge, *i.e.* to circumstances which he *ought* to know. In marine insurance, as has been noticed, the assured is "deemed to know every circumstance which, in the ordinary course of business, ought to be known by him" (Marine Insurance Act 1906, s. 18(1)).

11–111　　Also in the Marine Insurance Act 1906, there is an express provision which has the effect of bringing the knowledge of the insured's agent within the range of circumstances which require to be disclosed. Section 19 of the Act provides that where insurance is being taken out by an agent for the insured, the agent must disclose to the insurer:

(a) every material circumstance which is known to himself (and an agent to insure is deemed to know every circumstance which in the ordinary course of business ought to be known by, or to have been communicated to, him); and

(b) every material circumstance which the insured is bound to disclose, unless it comes to his knowledge too late to communicate it to the agent.

11–112　　The insured has no duty to disclose facts which he did not know *and which he could not be reasonably expected to know.* An example is *Joel* v. *Law Union and Crown Insurance Co.* [1908] 2 K.B. 863 (C.A.):

Robina Morrison, when applying for life insurance, was asked by a doctor whether she had ever suffered from mental derangement, and gave an answer in the negative. In fact, she had, though she was not aware of the fact, been in confinement for acute mania. The question of the validity of the policy arose when she committed suicide.

Held that there was not sufficient evidence to prove that there had been such non-disclosure of material facts by the assured as to make the policy voidable.

Fletcher Moulton L.J. said (at p. 884): "The duty is a duty to disclose and you cannot disclose what you do not know. The obligation to disclose, therefore, necessarily depends on the knowledge you possess. I must not be misunderstood. Your opinion of the materiality of that knowledge is of no moment. If a reasonable man would have recognised that it was material to disclose the knowledge in question, it is no excuse that you did not recognise it to be so. But the question always is, Was the knowledge you possessed such that you ought to have disclosed it? Let me take an example. I will suppose that a man has, as is the case with most of us, occasionally had a headache. It may be that a particular one of these headaches would have told a brain specialist of hidden mischief. But to the man it was an ordinary headache undistinguishable from the rest. Now no reasonable man would deem it material to tell an insurance company of all the casual headaches he had had in his life, and, if he knew no more as to this particular headache, there would be no breach of his duty towards the insurance company in not disclosing it. He possessed no knowledge that it was incumbent on him to disclose, because he knew of nothing which a reasonable man would deem material or of a character to influence the insurers in their action. It was what he did not know which would have been of that character, but he cannot be held liable for non-disclosure in respect of facts which he did not know."

A Scottish illustration of the point is *Life Association of Scotland* v. *Foster* (1873) 11 M. 351:

F. in a proposal for life insurance did not disclose that she had a small swelling on the groin, which was a symptom of rupture, but which she did not know to be so. She died within six months as a direct result of the rupture.

Held that the insurance company was not entitled to reduce the policy, since F. did not know that she was suffering from rupture, and could not, without medical skill, have reasonably been expected to know that the small swelling was a symptom of a malady which was soon to prove fatal.

(The insurance company also failed to establish that there had been a breach of warranty (see 11–147, below).)

(3) What need not be disclosed

There are some matters which the proposer need not disclose unless the insurer specially inquires about them. The development of the law here is specially associated with the judgment of Lord Mansfield in *Carter* v. *Boehm* (1766) 1 Wm. Bl. 593; 96 E.R. 342, a case concerned with a policy of insurance on Fort Marlborough in the East Indies, which was taken by the French. The Governor, C., was successful in his claim because the condition of the fort ought only to have been such as to resist an Indian force and it was notorious that it could not resist a European attack.

Lord Mansfield identified many matters as to which the insured might be "innocently silent" (*i.e.* which he need not mention)—matters which the insurer knew, by whatever means, matters which he ought to have known, which he had taken upon himself the knowledge of or which he had waived being informed of, matters which lessened the risk, and "general topics of speculation" such as the difficulty of a voyage, the kind of seasons, the probability of lightning, hurricanes, earthquakes *etc.*, political perils and the consequences of war and peace.

The circumstances which need not be disclosed, as incorporated from the common law into the Marine Insurance Act 1906 (s. 18(3)), are:

(a) any circumstance which diminishes the risk. Examples given by Lord Mansfield were that an underwriter who insured for three years did not need to be told of any circumstance tending to show that the risk would be over in two years, and an underwriter who insured a voyage with liberty to deviate did not need to be told of any circumstance tending to show that there would be no deviation;

(b) any circumstance which is known or presumed to be known to the insurer. The insurer is presumed to know matters of common notoriety or knowledge, and matters which an insurer in the ordinary course of his business, as such, ought to know. The condition of the fort in *Carter* v. *Boehm* was a matter of "notoriety";

(c) any circumstances as to which information is waived by the insurer, *e.g.*:

Mann McNeal and Steeves Ltd. v. *General Marine Underwriters Ltd.* [1921] 2 K.B. 300 (C.A.): A wooden ship was insured for a voyage from the U.S.A. to France. Part of the cargo consisted of petrol, but that fact was not disclosed to the insurance company.

Held that the insurance company had waived disclosure of the fact, because the disclosure that the vessel was a wooden one with auxiliary motor engines and therefore dangerously liable to fire damage had been a sufficient disclosure to put the insurance company on inquiry;

11–120 (d) any circumstance which it is superfluous to disclose by reason of any express or implied warranty. *"Gunford" Ship Co. Ltd.* v. *Thames and Mersey Marine Insurance Co. Ltd.*, 1911 S.C. (H.L.) 84; 1910 S.C. 1072, provides a helpful example here:

In a voyage policy there is an implied warranty that at the commencement of the voyage the ship is seaworthy for the purpose of the particular adventure insured (Marine Insurance Act 1906, s. 39(1)).

A voyage policy was taken out by the owners of the "Gunford" without disclosing to the insurance company that the master appointed for the voyage had not been to sea for 22 years, had lost his last ship, and had had his certificate suspended for six months.

During the voyage the ship was stranded on a reef, and became a total loss. The insurance company repudiated liability on the ground of the failure to disclose the master's record.

Held that as the master's competency was covered by the owners' implied warranty of seaworthiness there was no duty on the owners to disclose the master's record.

(The master was, in the circumstances, held to have had the necessary qualifications of seamanship throughout the voyage, and so the owners were not in breach of their implied warranty of seaworthiness. However, as was noted above (11–45), the insurance company won its case in the House of Lords on the ground of the owners' failure to disclose the existence of the honour policies which over-insured the ship.)

(iii) *Representations*

11–121 The rule of the common law as to representations is stated thus in the Marine Insurance Act 1906: "Every material representation made by the assured or his agent to the insurer during the negotiations for the contract, and before the contract is concluded, must be true. If it be untrue the insurer may avoid the contract" (s. 20(1)).

11–122 The misrepresentation which makes the contract voidable may be fraudulent or innocent: there is no reference in this rule (as there is in the rule as to disclosure) to facts which are known or presumed to be known to the insured, and so there is no protection for an insured who has made a representation which is in fact untrue, however much he may have honestly believed that it was true. For example, in *Zurich General Accident and Liability Insurance Co. Ltd.* v. *Leven*, 1940 S.C. 406 (see 11–94, above), L. answered "No" to the question whether she, or any other person who to her knowledge would drive the car, had been convicted of any offence in connection with any other motor vehicle. That answer was honest, because L. did not know of her father's conviction for reckless driving about six years previously, but, as the answer was in fact untrue, it was a ground on which the insurance company was entitled to avoid the policy. Lord President Normand explained the distinction between non-disclosure and misrepresentation thus (at p. 415):

"In general, non-disclosure means that you have failed to disclose something which was not the subject of a question but which was known to you and which you ought to have considered for yourself would be material, whereas a representation is something directly said in answer to a specific question, and in the present case there can be no reasonable doubt that, if in answer to the question 'Has a person who is going to drive the car been convicted of an offence?' you answer 'No,' you are making a direct representation that such a person has not been convicted. Now, . . . if that representation is material, it is a ground for avoiding the contract, whether the party making it was aware of its truth or not."

As a guide to deciding whether a representation is true or not, the Marine Insurance Act 1906 provides that:

(1) A representation may be either a representation as to a matter of fact, or as to a matter of expectation or belief (s. 20(3)).

(2) A representation as to a matter of fact is true, if it be substantially correct, that is to say, if the difference between what is represented and what is actually correct would not be considered material by a prudent insurer (s. 20(4)).

(3) A representation as to a matter of expectation or belief is true if it be made in good faith (s. 20(5)).

The time for judging whether a representation is true or not is the stage of negotiation before the contract is formed. Up to the time when the contract is concluded by the insurer accepting the proposal made to him, a representation may be withdrawn or corrected (Marine Insurance Act 1906, s. 20(6)).

Cases, in addition to the *Zurich Insurance* case, which illustrate misrepresentation include *The "Spathari"* (11–77, above), in which the misrepresentation that the ship was sailing under the British flag and was therefore entitled to be registered as a British ship was held to be a material misrepresentation, and *Dawsons Ltd.* v. *Bonnin* (11–86, above), in which the untrue answer to the question as to the address at which the vehicle would usually be garaged was a non-material misrepresentation.

(iv) *Mitigation in Insurance Practice and Proposals for Reform*

The harshness of the present law relating to disclosure and representations has been strongly criticised by the courts and by academic writers. This has led to (1) the issue by the insurance industry of *Statements of Insurance Practice* and (2) proposals for reform of the law.

(1) Statements of Insurance Practice

Two *Statements of Insurance Practice* were issued in 1977, the *First Statement* restricted to non-life insurances of policyholders insured in their private capacity only, and the *Second Statement* relating to long-term insurance effected by individuals in a private capacity. The *Statements* have no legally binding force but represent the agreement reached by the vast majority of insurance companies as to the practices which they normally follow instead of taking full advantage of their legal rights.

11–128   Amongst the matters included in the *Statements* are the following:

(a) *Proposal Forms:* There should be a prominent statement on the proposal form drawing the attention of the proposer to the consequences of failure to disclose all material facts (explained as those facts which an insurer would regard as likely to influence the acceptance and assessment of the proposal), and warning that if the proposer is in any doubt about whether certain facts are material or not he should disclose them. Those matters which insurers have found generally to be material will be the subject of clear questions in proposal forms. So far as is practicable, insurers will avoid asking questions which would require expert knowledge beyond that which the proposer could reasonably be expected to possess or obtain. Unless the proposal form contains full details of the standard cover offered, the proposal form must include a statement that a copy of the policy form is available on request.

(b) *Claims:* Except where fraud, deception or negligence is involved, an insurer will not unreasonably repudiate liability to indemnify a policyholder on the ground of non-disclosure or misrepresentation of a material fact where knowledge of the fact would not materially have influenced the insurer's judgment in the acceptance or assessment of the insurance.

(c) *Renewals:* Renewal notices should contain a warning about the duty of disclosure including the necessity to advise changes affecting the policy which have occurred since the policy was first taken out or the previous renewal date, whichever was the later.

(2) Proposals for reform of the law

11–129   The most important of the proposals for reform are now those contained in the (English) Law Commission's *Report* of 1980—*Insurance Law: Non-disclosure and breach of warranty* (Cmnd. 8064; Law Com. No. 104).

11–130   Of the "four major mischiefs" in the present law the Commission identified two relating to disclosure (para. 9.3):

(a) "The duty of disclosure is far too stringent. It requires every insured to disclose any fact which a prudent insurer would consider to be material, and entitles the insurer to repudiate the policy and to reject any claim in the event of any breach of this duty. However, an honest and reasonable insured may be quite unaware of the existence and extent of this duty, and even if he is aware of it, he may have great difficulty in forming any view as to what facts a prudent insurer would consider to be material."

(b) "The duty of disclosure under the present law operates particularly harshly on the insured, and produces something of a trap for him, in relation to proposal forms and renewals of the cover. In relation to proposal forms even a reasonable insured is likely to be unaware that after answering a series of specific questions he remains under a residual duty to disclose any other material facts to which no question has been directed. In relation to renewals even a reasonable insured is likely to be unaware that in law these constitute fresh contracts of insurance and that the duty of disclosure arises afresh on the occasion of every renewal, with the result that the insured is successively under a duty to disclose any material facts which may have arisen in the interim. Moreover, since this duty will arise afresh on the occasion of every renewal, the insured will have even greater difficulty in complying with it if he does not have copies of any information previously supplied by him in a proposal form and on the occasion of prior renewals."

The Commission had no doubt that the *Statements of Insurance Practice* did not provide any adequate substitute for the reform of the law which was clearly needed, particularly since they left the insurer in the position of judge and jury as to whether or not the full rigour of the law should be applied in individual cases. The Commission had had before them a proposed E.E.C. Directive ("Directive on the co-ordination of laws, regulations and administrative provisions relating to insurance contracts"), but took the view that the Directive would provide an unsatisfactory and inadequate means of reforming the defects in the present law in comparison with the legislative reforms recommended by the Commission and incorporated in a draft Insurance Law Reform Bill in Appendix A to their Report. The effect of the reforms recommended would be, in the Commission's opinion, to eradicate the four defects identified by the Commission, including the two relating to disclosure (para. 9.7):

(a) "The stringency of the duty of disclosure under the present law will be cured by the reduction of the duty . . . to a duty to disclose any material facts which the proposer knows or can be assumed to know and which a reasonable man in the position of the proposer would disclose, having regard to the nature and extent of the cover which is sought and the circumstances in which it is sought."

(b) "The harshness of the present law, and the fact that it constitutes something of a trap for the insured, in the particular context of proposal forms and renewal notices, . . . will disappear with the introduction of our system of prominent warnings. These warnings on proposal forms and renewal notices will make clear to the insured the extent of his duty of disclosure, that he should keep copies of information supplied by him to the insurer and that his duty of disclosure arises not only when he first makes a contract of insurance, but also on renewal. The insured will be further protected by the requirement that he be supplied by the insurer with a copy of the proposal form which he has completed and of any information which he has given to the insurer on renewal."

(d) **Warranties**

An insurer seeking to avoid a policy is much more likely to rely on breach of a warranty by the insured than on either non-disclosure or mis-representation. If he relies on non-disclosure, it will be necessary for him to prove:

(i) that the fact not disclosed was material; and

(ii) that it was within the insured's actual or presumed knowledge.

If he relies on misrepresentation, it will be necessary for him to prove:

(i) that the representation was material; and

(ii) that it was in fact untrue.

Where, however, there is a warranty (and in practice there almost always is), the insurer is relieved of the difficulty of proving the point as to materiality, and also (provided the warranty is sufficiently strict in its wording) of the difficulty of proving what the insured's actual or presumed knowledge was. All that he need prove is that the insured has agreed, expressly or impliedly, to the warranty as part of the contract of insurance and that the insured has been in breach of the warranty.

11–133   Considered below are:

(i)   the nature of a warranty;
(ii)   examples of warranties, express and implied;
(iii)   questions of interpretation affecting warranties; and
(iv)   mitigation in insurance practice and proposals for reform.

(i)   *The Nature of a Warranty*

11–134   "Warranty" is defined in Bell's *Principles of the Law of Scotland* (§ 475) as "an absolute condition, express or implied, relative to the state of circumstances of the subject insured; which, if not true, or not complied with, defeats the insurance, whether material to the risk or not."

11–135   In Bell's *Commentaries on the Laws of Scotland* (Vol. I, p. 662) the definition of "warranty" is followed by an explanation of the distinction between a warranty and a representation:

"A warranty is an absolute condition, or, as the English lawyers call it, a condition precedent; and if not true, or not complied with, the insurance is ineffectual. It differs from a representation in this, that the breach of truth in a representation is fatal or otherwise to the insurance, as it happens to be material or immaterial to the risk undertaken. . . . A warranty is part of the contract; and if not true, whether material or not, there is no insurance."

11–136   This distinction between warranty and representation is supported by the speech of Lord Chancellor Eldon in the Scottish case of *Newcastle Fire Insurance Co.* v. *Macmorran and Co.* (1815) 3 Dow 255; 3 E.R. 1057:

A cotton mill in Lanarkshire was insured against fire with the N. Co., and was warranted as being of the first class, for which the rates were lower than for the second class. The mill was burnt.

Held that as the mill was truly of the second class, the N. Co. was not liable.

Lord Eldon said (at 3 Dow p. 262; 3 E.R. p. 1060): "It is a first principle in the law of insurance, on all occasions, that where a representation is material it must be complied with—if immaterial, that immateriality may be inquired into and shown; but that if there is a warranty, it is part of the contract that the matter is such as it is represented to be. Therefore the materiality or immateriality signifies nothing. The only question is as to the mere fact."

11–137   Warranties in marine insurance are governed by sections 33 to 41 of the Marine Insurance Act 1906. A "warranty" is defined as meaning "a promissory warranty, that is to say, a warranty by which the assured undertakes that some particular thing shall or shall not be done, or that some condition shall be fulfilled, or whereby he affirms or negatives the existence of a particular state of facts" (s. 33(1)). It is "a condition which must be exactly complied with, whether it be material to the risk or not. If it be not so complied with, then, subject to any express provision in the policy, the insurer is discharged from liability as from the date of the breach of warranty, but without prejudice to any liability incurred by him before that date" (s. 33(3)).

(ii) *Examples of Warranties, Express and Implied*

Like other terms of a contract, a warranty may be either express or implied. As regards marine insurance, this principle of the common law is stated in section 33(2) of the 1906 Act.

(1) Express warranties

Two examples of express warranties are:

(a) *Standard Life Assurance Co.* v. *Weems &c.* (1884) 11 R. (H.L.) 48: W., a businessman and provost of Johnstone, insured his life with the S. Co. for £1,500 in 1881. He died about nine months later, aged 45 years.

When applying for the policy, W. had filled up and signed a form including the statements: "7.(1) Are you temperate in your habits? (2) And have you always been strictly so? Answer—(1) Temperate. (2) Yes." The form also contained the declaration: "I, the said W. . . . , do hereby declare that . . . the foregoing statements of my age, health, and other particulars are true. . . . And I, the said W. . . . , do hereby agree that this declaration shall be the basis of the contract between me and the S. Co.; and that if any untrue averment has been made, or any information necessary to be made known to the company has been withheld, all sums which shall have been paid to the said company upon account of the assurance . . . shall be forfeited, and the assurance be absolutely null and void."

The policy itself referred to this declaration in stating that "if anything averred in the declaration . . . shall be untrue this policy shall be void, and all monies received by the said company . . . shall belong to the said company for their own benefit."

The S. Co. declined to pay the proceeds of the policy on the ground that the answers to question 7 were untrue since W. was at the time a person of intemperate habits and had been so for some time.

Held that because of the express warranty that W.'s answers were true and the fact that they were shown by the evidence to have been untrue the policy was void.

Lord Watson said (at p. 53): "I entertain no doubt that according to the law of Scotland the declaration of the assured, taken in connection with the policy itself, in his proposal to the company, constitutes an express warranty that the answer made by him to the seventh question was true. In other words, it is an express and essential condition of the contract that the policy shall be null and void in the event of the averment by the assured as to his habits, implied in his answer to that question, proving to be false. The doctrine of warranty as applied to such stipulations in a contract of assurance is the same in the law of Scotland as in that of England."

(b) *Dawsons Ltd.* v. *Bonnin*, 1922 S.C. (H.L.) 156: The proposal form for a comprehensive motor vehicle policy included the request: "State full address at which the vehicles will usually be garaged." The answer given was "above address," *i.e.* the proposers' ordinary place of business which was known to the insurers' agent to be a stone building in the centre of Glasgow. In fact the lorry in question was not garaged at that address but at a farm on the outskirts of Glasgow in a shed constructed mainly of wood and in which other motor vehicles and several barrels of oil or petrol were also accommodated.

The proposal form contained no declaration by the proposers as to the truth of the information supplied, but the policy stated that the proposal form "shall be the basis of this contract and be held as incorporated herein." The policy also stated that it was granted subject to certain conditions one of which was "4. Material misstatement or concealment of any circumstance by the insured material to assessing the premium herein, or in connection with any claim, shall render the policy void."

A fire occurred and the shed and lorry were destroyed.

Held that since the proposal form had been made by the parties the basis of the contract, the statements in the proposal form were fundamental to the contract, and that consequently the untrue statement as to the situation of the garage, although not "material" within the meaning of condition 4, made the policy void.

Lord Dunedin said (at p. 170): "'Basis' . . . must mean that the parties held that these statements are fundamental—*i.e.*, go to the root of the contract—and that consequently, if the statements are untrue, the contract is not binding."

(2) Implied warranties

11–142 The most notable implied warranty is that of seaworthiness in marine insurance. The provisions governing it are in sections 39 and 40 of the Marine Insurance Act 1906, and depend on whether the policy is a voyage policy or a time policy. By section 25(1) of the Act a policy is called a "voyage policy" where the contract is to insure the subject-matter at and from, or from one place to another or others, and a policy is called a "time policy" where the contract is to insure the subject-matter for a definite period of time.

11–143 The provisions in sections 39 and 40 are:

(a) In a voyage policy there is an implied warranty that at the commencement of the voyage the ship shall be seaworthy for the purpose of the particular adventure insured (s. 39(1)).

(b) Where the policy attaches while the ship is in port, there is also an implied warranty that she shall, at the commencement of the risk, be reasonably fit to encounter the ordinary perils of the port (s. 39(2)).

(c) Where the policy relates to a voyage which is performed in different stages, during which the ship requires different kinds of or further preparation or equipment, there is an implied warranty that at the commencement of each stage the ship is seaworthy in respect of such preparation or equipment for the purposes of that stage (s. 39(3)).

(d) A ship is deemed to be seaworthy when she is reasonably fit in all respects to encounter the ordinary perils of the seas of the adventure insured (s. 39(4)).

(e) In a time policy there is no implied warranty that the ship shall be seaworthy at any stage of the adventure, but where, with the privity of the assured, the ship is sent to sea in an unseaworthy state, the insurer is not liable for any loss attributable to unseaworthiness (s. 39(5)).

(f) In a policy on goods or other moveables there is no implied warranty that they are seaworthy, but in a voyage policy on goods or other moveables there is an implied warranty that at the commencement of the voyage the ship is not only seaworthy as a ship, but also that she is reasonably fit to carry the goods or other moveables to the destination contemplated by the policy (s. 40(1) and (2)).

(iii) *Questions of Interpretation affecting Warranties*

The law does not favour the extension of warranties: implied warranties are recognised only in marine insurance, and in the interpretation of express warranties the rule applied is that in a case of ambiguity the words used are construed *contra proferentem* ("against the person putting them forward"), *i.e.* against the interests of the insurer who has had the advantage of composing the detailed provisions of the contract; the effect is to restrict express warranties to situations where they have been clearly and unambiguously undertaken by the insured. The following illustrations may be given:

(1) The words used may be interpreted as merely describing or limiting the risk and not as amounting to a warranty:

Provincial Insurance Co. Ltd. v. *Morgan* [1933] A.C. 240; [1932] 2 K.B. 70 (C.A.): In taking out insurance for a lorry, M., who was a coal merchant, stated in the proposal form that the lorry was to be used to carry coal.

On one occasion the lorry was carrying a load of timber along with five bags of coal. All the timber and three bags of coal were delivered and when the lorry was on its way to deliver the remaining two bags of coal, a collision occurred which resulted in a claim being made under the policy.

Held by the Court of Appeal in interpreting the proposal form, and expressly not dissented from in the House of Lords, that it had not been the intention of either party to exact or give a warranty that the lorry should never be used for any purpose other than the carriage of coal, but that the questions had been intended merely to ascertain the intentions of the insured with regard to the use of the lorry, and that the effect of M.'s statement was only to limit the risk to the use of the lorry while carrying coal; the claim under the policy was therefore valid.

(2) The words used may be interpreted as a warranty of belief and not of fact:

Hutchison v. *National Loan Assurance Society* (1845) 7 D. 467: In a proposal for life insurance A. declared that she had no disease, or symptom of disease, and was then in good health and ordinarily enjoyed good health. A policy was issued on the basis of this proposal. A. died a few months later, and the insurance company refused to pay the claim made under the policy, on the ground that at the date of the proposal A. had had a disease of the liver which had resulted in dropsy of which she died.

Held that A. had merely warranted that, according to her own knowledge and reasonable belief, she was free from any disease or symptom of disease, and had given no warranty that she had no latent disease such as could only be discovered by *post mortem* examination.

11–147   Similarly, in *Life Association of Scotland* v. *Foster* (1873) 11 M. 351, F. had replied, in answer to a question put by a medical officer of the insurers, that she had never had rupture and had made a written statement that her answers were "faithful and true," and that if any of them were untrue the policy would be void. In fact she did have rupture at the time and died shortly afterwards as a result of it.

Held that the words used indicated that the object had been to get a faithful account of what F. knew about herself, and did not amount to a warranty that she did not have rupture.

11–148   (3) Warranties are interpreted as relating to an existing state of affairs and not as extending, unless the intention is clear, to a future state of affairs:

Kennedy v. *Smith*, 1975 S.C. 266: In a proposal form for motor insurance S. declared: "I am a Total Abstainer from alcoholic drinks and have been since birth."

Held that this abstinence declaration was to be interpreted as referring to the state of affairs existing when it was made and not as extending to cover S.'s future conduct.

Lord President Emslie said (at p. 277): "If insurers seek to limit their liability under a policy by relying upon an alleged undertaking as to the future, prepared by them and accepted by the insured, the language they use must be such that the terms of the alleged undertaking and its scope are clearly and unambiguously expressed or plainly implied and . . . any such alleged undertaking will be construed, *in dubio*,[4] *contra proferentem*.

". . . The statement does not require to be given a future promissory content to make it intelligible. . . . It would have been simple to include in the statement, if this had been intended, that the insured shall continue to be a Total Abstainer for the period of the insurance. No such statement was, however, included and in my opinion is not, without undue straining of the language used, to be implied."

(iv) *Mitigation in Insurance Practice and Proposals for Reform*

11–149   Several aspects of the law on warranties have been criticised by the courts and others. The "basis of the contract" clause, as seen in such cases as *Standard Life Assurance Co.* v. *Weems &c.* (11–140, above) and *Dawsons Ltd.* v. *Bonnin* (11–141, above), has been recognised as being particularly harsh to the insured. Also attracting criticism is the circumstance that an insurer may avail himself of a breach of warranty to avoid liability even where the warranty was not material to the risk and breach of it had no connection with the loss. However, as with disclosures and representations (see 11–126 *et seq.*, above), so also with warranties it is appropriate to take some note of (1) the mitigation permitted by the *Statements of Insurance Practice* and (2) proposals for reform of the law.

(1) Statements of Insurance Practice

11–150   The *First Statement of Insurance Practice* (see 11–127, above) includes the following:

---

[4] "if ambiguous."

(a) *Proposal Forms:* "The declaration at the foot of the proposal form should be restricted to completion according to the proposer's knowledge and belief."

(b) *Claims:* "Except where fraud, deception or negligence is involved, an insurer will not unreasonably repudiate liability to indemnify a policy-holder . . . on the grounds of a breach of warranty or condition where the circumstances of the loss are unconnected with breach."

In practice the "basis" clause is still used, but the warranty required of the insured is a warranty of opinion, not a warranty of fact, *i.e.* the insured will not be required to declare that his answers are "true," but merely that they are true to the best of his knowledge and belief. The significance of such a declaration in a proposal form was considered in *McPhee* v. *Royal Insurance Co. Ltd.,* 1979 S.C. 304:

McP., the owner of a Senior 31 cabin cruiser, "Don Juan," insured the vessel with R. Ltd. for £12,300. The proposal form stated that the overall length of the vessel was 36 feet and the extreme breadth 12 feet, and it included the declaration: "I declare that to the best of my know-ledge and belief the above answers are true. . . . I agree that this proposal . . . shall be the basis of the contract." The policy contained the condition: "the proposal and all declarations made by the insured are the basis of and form part of this contract."

McP. had obtained the measurements of 36 feet and 12 feet from the previous owner whom he did not know but whom he telephoned for that purpose. The vessel was in fact 31 feet long and had an extreme breadth of 10 feet.

The vessel sank and became a "constructive total loss" (see 11–225 *et seq.,* below).

R. Ltd. sought to avoid liability on the ground that the answers given in the proposal form were not true to the best of the proposer's knowledge and belief.

Held that McP. did not satisfy the test of having answered the questions truly to the best of his knowledge and belief, and so his action against R. Ltd. for £12,300 was unsuccessful.

Lord President Emslie said (at p. 322): "I ask myself what is to be understood by the words 'to the best of my knowledge and belief.' They certainly do not import a warranty of absolute truth or accuracy. So what is the measure of the proposer's obligation? It is common ground that these words require a proposer to answer the questions honestly and in this case we are obliged . . . to assume that the pursuer's honesty, in stating the dimensions as he did, is not in issue. Honesty, however, is not all that is expected of a proposer. . . . I hold that there must be a reasonable basis for any answer given and that a question which ought to receive careful consideration must not be answered lightly and recklessly. . . . I . . . consider . . . that in light of the evidence the pursuer, in stating the dimensions as he did, displayed a casualness and lack of care so gross as to demonstrate that the answers were not true to the best of his knowledge and belief."

(2) Proposals for reform of the law

The most important proposals for reform are those contained in the Law Commission's *Report* of 1980 (see 11–129, above).

11–154   Of the "four major mischiefs" identified by the Commission the two which relate to warranties are (para. 9.3):

(a) "The present law concerning warranties given by the insured (both as to past or present fact and promissory warranties) operates with great unfairness on the insured. It entitles the insurer to repudiate the policy and to reject any claim whether or not the warranty in question is material to the risk, and whether or not any breach of any particular warranty has had any connection with any particular claim which may have arisen. Further, unless an insured is supplied with a copy of any warranty to which his policy may be subject, he will have difficulty in remembering its terms and, in appropriate cases, complying with it."

(b) "The position under [(a)] above is greatly exacerbated by the device frequently used in proposal forms of transforming all statements, and all answers given by the insured to questions in proposal forms, *en bloc* into warranties by means of 'basis of the contract' clauses or similar provisions."

11–155   The Commission made recommendations for the reform of the law. The effect would be, in their opinion, the eradication of the present defects in the following way (para. 9.7):

(a) ". . . The only warranties which will be effective will be those material to the risk and the insurer will not be able to rely on even those unless he has provided the insured with a copy of the warranty. Furthermore, an insurer will only be able to reject a claim on the grounds of breach of warranty if there is a connection, a 'nexus,' between the breach of warranty and the event which gave rise to the claim."

(b) "The use of the device of 'basis of the contract' clauses which exacerbate the insured's difficulties under the present law of warranties by (for example) turning all the answers in proposal forms into warranties as to their correctness, will in future be ineffective in relation to warranties as to past or present facts."

III THE POLICY

11–156   The policy is the formal document in which a contract of insurance comes to be expressed. The normal practice is for a policy not to be issued until the premium, or the first premium, has been paid, and for the policy to acknowledge receipt of that premium. The Marine Insurance Act 1906, in accordance with that practice, provides that unless otherwise agreed, the duty of the assured to pay the premium and the duty of the insurer to issue the policy to the assured are concurrent conditions, and the insurer is not bound to issue the policy until payment or tender of the premium (s. 52).

11–157   Once a policy has been issued, the rights and obligations of the parties are normally governed solely by it and not by any other documents. However, some other document (*e.g.* a proposal form) may require to be read along with the policy where the policy incorporates that other document or to resolve an ambiguity in the policy.

Some consideration may be given here of:

(a) classifications of policies;
(b) form and contents of a policy; and
(c) assignation of a policy.

(a) Classifications of Policies

There are two recognised classifications of policies:

First, policies may be classified according to the description of the subject-matter insured.

Some policies contain a precise definition of the subject-matter insured, and the cover is then limited to that specific subject-matter (*e.g.* a policy covering the loss of a particular item of property, or the loss which might be caused by the faults of a specified employee or by the insolvency of a specified debtor).

Other policies define their subject-matter in general terms, and the cover then extends to any object falling within the general definition (*e.g.* a policy on property generally or a policy giving protection against public liability).

Secondly, policies may be classified according to the amount recoverable. They are then divisible into "unvalued" policies and "valued" policies.

In an "unvalued" policy the sum to be paid in the event of a loss is not fixed by the policy but is left to be ascertained after the loss has occurred. Most policies of insurance on property are "unvalued" policies. Any sum stated in the policy as the amount of the insurance is then taken to be the limit (or ceiling) on the insurer's liability and not as fixing the amount which the insurer will be bound to pay. In the Marine Insurance Act 1906, an "unvalued policy" is defined as "a policy which does not specify the value of the subject-matter insured, but, subject to the limit of the sum insured, leaves the insurable value to be subsequently ascertained, in the manner herein-before specified" (s. 28). The words "herein-before specified" are a reference to section 16 of the Act which sets out rules for ascertaining the insurable value of the ship, the freight, the goods or merchandise and any other subject-matter.

In a "valued" policy the sum to be paid is fixed by the policy. All personal accident policies fall into this category. A policy of insurance on property may be a valued policy: if so, the value of the property as fixed by agreement is inserted in the policy as the amount recoverable in the event of loss, and that valuation is binding. The Marine Insurance Act 1906 provides that a "valued policy" is a "policy which specifies the agreed value of the subject-matter insured" (s. 27(2)), and that "subject to the provisions of this Act, and in the absence of fraud, the value fixed by the policy is, as between the insurer and assured, conclusive of the insurable value of the subject intended to be insured, whether the loss be total or partial" (s. 27(3)).

(b) Form and Contents of a Policy

The form and contents of a policy are in practice always those chosen by the insurer. Usually the policy is a printed document with spaces available for the insertion, in manuscript or typescript, of information specially appropriate for each individual case.

11–167   The fact that the terms of the insurance contract are expressed in the manner chosen by the insurer gives rise to the application of the most important of the rules for the interpretation of insurance policies, namely, the rule that the words used are, if ambiguous, construed *contra proferentem* ("against the person putting them forward"), *i.e.* in the way which is less favourable to the insurer. Illustrations of this rule of construction in relation to warranties have been given above (see 11–144 *et seq.*). Two more recent instances in relation to other contents of a policy may be mentioned at this point:

11–168   (i) *Carrick Furniture House Ltd.* v. *General Accident Fire and Life Assurance Corporation Ltd.*, 1977 S.C. 308 (O.H.): C. Ltd. insured a furniture store at Ayr with G. Ltd. for £100,000. By the terms of the policy G. Ltd. agreed that if the property insured were destroyed by fire G. Ltd. would pay to C. Ltd. "the value of the property at the time of the happening of its destruction."

The furniture store was destroyed by fire. C. Ltd., maintaining that the value of the store at the date of destruction was at least £150,000, measured by the cost of reinstatement, claimed £100,000, but G. Ltd. averred that the market value of the store immediately before the fire was the true measure of the loss and that that was not more than £40,000.

Held that the word "value" did not necessarily connote only "market value," and that since the policy had to be construed *contra proferentem*, C. Ltd. was entitled to prove the real value of the store.

Lord Grieve (Ordinary) said (at p. 321): "The pursuers' claim is a claim for the value of the property at the time it was destroyed. . . . In my opinion, such a claim is within the terms of the policy which provides that if the property is destroyed by fire the insurers will pay to the insured 'the value of the property at the time of the happening of its destruction.' The policy does not refer to market value and to construe the word 'value' as 'market value' in the defenders' favour would violate the principle that documents such as this are to be construed *contra proferentem*."

11–169   (ii) *Davidson* v. *Guardian Royal Exchange Assurance*, 1981 S.L.T. 81: A car was damaged by fire in July 1976. Insurers with whom it was comprehensively insured opted, as they were entitled to do, to repair the car, and it was eventually returned to the owner in April 1977.

The owner raised an action of damages for loss of use of the car. He claimed that it was an implied term of the insurance policy that the car should be repaired in a reasonable time, such as eight weeks, and that 40 weeks was an unreasonable time.

The insurers sought to rely on an exceptions clause in the policy, but the court held that the exceptions clause limited the extent of the indemnity against the risks specified but did not cover breach of contract.

The case was therefore remitted to the sheriff court for further procedure on the question of damages.

The opinion of the Second Division of the Inner House includes the following statement of the familiar principle (at p. 85):

"This was a policy of insurance framed and printed by the defenders and, if there was any ambiguity, the construction had to be contra proferentem."

The Unfair Contract Terms Act 1977, despite its general aim of protecting the weaker party to a bargain from unduly harsh terms virtually imposed upon him by the other party, does not apply to contracts of insurance (1977 Act, s. 15(3)). In response to the exclusion of insurance contracts from the scope of that Act, the insurance industry adopted measures of self-regulation embodied in the *Statements of Insurance Practice* issued in the same year (see 11–127 and 11–150, above).

Apart from the provisions in sections 22 to 31 of the Marine Insurance Act 1906, the form and contents of a policy are fixed by the parties to the contract (and in practice by the insurer).

The form of the policy is always a matter of choice for the parties. The First Schedule to the Marine Insurance Act 1906 sets out a form of marine policy, known as "Lloyd's S.G. policy," but this is only a form which the parties *may* adopt if they so wish (s. 30(1)). The Schedule also gives rules for interpretation of terms used in the statutory form, and these rules will be applied, unless the context of a policy requires otherwise, in the interpretation of a policy in the statutory form or any other like form (s. 30(2)). Examples of these rules of construction are:

"1.—*Lost or not Lost.*—Where the subject-matter is insured 'lost or not lost,' and the loss has occurred before the contract is concluded, the risk attaches unless, at such time the assured was aware of the loss, and the insurer was not."

"7.—*Perils of the Seas.*—The term 'perils of the seas' refers only to fortuitous accidents or casualties of the seas. It does not include the ordinary action of the winds and waves."

"15.—*Ship.*—The term 'ship' includes the hull, materials and outfit, stores and provisions for the officers and crew, and, in the case of vessels engaged in a special trade, the ordinary fittings requisite for the trade, and also, in the case of a steamship, the machinery, boilers, and coals and engine stores, if owned by the assured."

"17.—*Goods.*—The term 'goods' means goods in the nature of merchandise, and does not include personal effects or provisions and stores for use on board.

"In the absence of any usage to the contrary, deck cargo and living animals must be insured specifically, and not under the general denomination of goods."

As regards the contents of a policy the Act of 1906 requires the policy to specify the name of the assured, or of some person who effects the insurance on his behalf (s. 23, as amended by the Finance Act 1959), but the nature and extent of the interest of the assured in the subject-matter insured need not be specified (s. 26(2)). Where the contract is to insure the subject-matter at and from, or from one place to another or others, the policy is called a "voyage policy," and where the contract is to insure the subject-matter for a definite period of time, the policy is called a "time policy." A contract for both voyage and time may be included in the same policy (s. 25).

It is, however, possible for a marine policy to be a "floating policy," *i.e.* a policy which describes the insurance in general terms, and leaves the name of the ship or ships and other particulars to be defined by subsequent declarations which may be made by indorsements on the policy or in other customary manner (s. 29(1) and (2)).

11–175   In the case of non-marine insurance the policy will always in practice state such obvious matters as the insurer and the insured, the subject-matter insured, the risk insured against and the sum insured.

11–176   In addition, a policy for any type of insurance is likely to include:

11–177   (1) a declaration that the proposal signed by the insured is to be the basis of the contract of insurance. For the significance of this, see the section on warranties, above, especially the case of *Dawsons Ltd.* v. *Bonnin* (11–141, above);

11–178   (2) provisions relating to the payment of future premiums;

11–179   (3) exceptions to the risk insured against. The insurer usually expressly provides that he will not be liable for a loss resulting from specified rare occurrences which would otherwise be likely to give rise to claims quite out of the ordinary course of business; *e.g.* common exceptions are losses caused by foreign enemies, riot, civil commotion, military or usurped power, insurrection and hostilities. Exceptions must always be clearly and unambiguously expressed; otherwise they will be held to be of no effect under the *contra proferentem* rule of construction (see 11–167, above); an instance is *Glenlight Shipping Ltd.* v. *Excess Insurance Co. Ltd.*, 1983 S.L.T. 241:

Grierson died by drowning as a result of driving his car off a ferryboat when it was in the mid-channel between Kyle of Lochalsh and Kyleakin. He had been under the mistaken belief that the vessel had already berthed at Kyleakin.

His employers, G. Ltd., made a claim under a policy of insurance by which the insurance company had agreed to pay a sum in respect of the death of certain of G. Ltd.'s employees if death resulted from "bodily injury caused by violent accidental external and visible means." The policy included an exception clause which excluded liability where the claim was the consequence of the deceased's "wilfully exposing himself to needless peril."

In defence the insurance company maintained that (i) Grierson's death was the result of a deliberate act and could not properly be described as "accidental"; and (ii) the exception clause applied because Grierson had been drinking before the incident and his consumption of alcohol amounted to "wilfully exposing himself to needless peril."

Held that (i) Grierson's death had been caused by accidental means and (ii) Grierson, despite his consumption of alcohol, had not wilfully exposed himself to needless peril.

G. Ltd.'s claim was therefore sustained.

Lord Hunter said (at p. 242): "In my opinion an exception clause of this nature should be read contra proferentem. . . . If, against that background, one asks the question: 'Did the deceased wilfully expose himself to needless peril?', the answer must in my opinion be 'no'. The peril or danger to which the deceased was in the circumstances exposed was in my opinion the existence, unknown to him, of a gap of sea between the end of the ramp and the pier. In the context of the exception clause under consideration in the present case the word 'wilfully' conveys, in my opinion, the meaning that the claim is the consequence of the insured deliberately or intentionally exposing himself to needless peril or danger, of the existence of which he is aware. . . . If the defenders . . . had wished to protect themselves against claims arising out of accidents occurring while the insured was under the influence of intoxicating liquor, they could no doubt have done so by means of an exception clause in appropriate terms."

(4) conditions to be fulfilled by the insured. For instance, in *Kennedy* v. *Smith* (11–148, above), the abstinence declaration was followed by the words: "I undertake to advise the company if the information given in this form ceases to apply." Breach of a condition may be waived by the insurer, *e.g.:*

Donnison v. *Employers' Accident and Live Stock Insurance Co. Ltd.* (1897) 22 R. 681: An accident policy taken out by D. stated: "This policy is subject to the conditions endorsed hereon, which are to be taken as part hereof, and are hereby agreed to be conditions precedent to the right of the insured to sue or recover hereunder." One of the conditions was that in the event of any accident, whether fatal or not, occurring to D., written notice had to be delivered to the insurance company within 14 days. Another condition was that in case of death, the legal representatives had to deliver a death certificate to the company and agree to a *post mortem* examination if the company so required.

On February 3, 1896, D. sustained an injury to a toe when a heavy travelling case accidentally fell on it. At first he did not regard the injury as serious, but ultimately gangrene set in, and he notified the company of a claim on March 2. D. died on March 5, and the insurance company required a *post mortem* examination, which took place on March 7.

The company then attempted to resist the claim made by D.'s widow on the ground that timeous notice had not been given of the accident.

Held that the insurance company, by requiring a *post mortem* examination, had waived the defence of want of timeous notice.

(c) Assignation of a Policy

Under the common law of Scotland any policy of insurance can be assigned by the holder of it unless it contains a provision to the contrary. For life insurance and for marine insurance there are also statutory provisions, namely, the Policies of Assurance Act 1867 and sections 50 and 51 of the Marine Insurance Act 1906 respectively. These statutory provisions are aimed at technicalities of English law; in Scotland they substantially declare the common law.

The main points which arise in connection with assignation are:

(i) A *transfer of the subject-matter* insured does not of itself amount to an assignation of the policy. The express provision of the Marine Insurance Act 1906 on this point is: "Where the assured assigns or otherwise parts with his interest in the subject-matter insured, he does not thereby transfer to the assignee his rights under the contract of insurance, unless there be an express or implied agreement with the assignee to that effect" (s. 15).

(ii) A *mere physical transfer of the policy* does not amount to an assignation of the policy: there must be a *written document* signed by the cedent (the person who is assigning the policy), and also *intimation to the insurance company*.

The writing which is necessary may take the form of an indorsement on the policy or be a separate document. The Act of 1867 gives a short statutory form in the Schedule to the Act, but does not require the form to be strictly followed (s. 5). Alternatives are the ordinary forms in the Schedules to the Transmission of Moveable Property (Scotland) Act 1862, and the case of *Brownlee* v. *Robb*, 1907 S.C. 1302 (see 11–187, below), gives an instance of less formal language: the words "I, J.R., hand over my life policy to my daughter E.S.R.," signed by J.R. in the presence of two witnesses, were in that case held to amount to a valid assignation. The Marine Insurance Act 1906 provides that a marine policy may be assigned "by indorsement thereon or in other customary manner" (s. 50(3)).

11–184 The effect of the written assignation is to give the assignee a personal right against the cedent (*i.e.* the insured who is granting the assignation). The effect of intimation to the insurance company is to convert that personal right into a real right: intimation regulates competing claims to the proceeds of the policy, and until intimation has been made, the company is entitled to pay the proceeds to the cedent. The Act of 1867 requires that every life policy must specify the principal place of business at which written notice of an assignation may appropriately be given (s. 4), and also places on the company an obligation to give a written acknowledgment of the notice, if this is requested, and this acknowledgment is declared to be conclusive evidence as against the company of its having duly received the written notice of the assignation (s. 6).

11–185 The following three cases illustrate these points:

11–186 (1) *Wylie's Executrix* v. *McJannet* (1901) 4 F. 195: In this case there was no written assignation:

W. insured his life for £500 with the Life Association of Scotland. In doing so he was acting on the suggestion of McJ., a solicitor and agent of the Association, who had advanced money to W.

The policy was left in the custody of McJ., who paid all the premiums.

On W.'s death, some 32 years later, the Association brought a multiplepoinding to decide the rival claims of McJ. and W.'s executrix.

Held that W.'s executrix had the preferable claim.

Lord Trayner (at p. 196) said that McJ.'s claim was based upon two grounds—"(1) that he is the actual custodier of the policy in question, and (2) has paid all the premiums due upon it on behalf of the assured. The first of these grounds will not sustain his claim, for the mere possession of the policy without any assignation to it confers no right to the policy or any claim arising in respect of it. The second ground also fails the appellant, for it amounts to no more than this, that he made certain cash advances on behalf of the assured. These constitute a debt against the assured, but give no preferential right over any other creditor to the fund produced by the policy."

11–187 (2) *Brownlee* v. *Robb*, 1907 S.C. 1302: In this case there was a written assignation, it had not been intimated to the insurance company, and the competing claims to the proceeds came from the assignee and the deceased insured's personal representatives:

J.R., by an assignation in an unusual form (see 11–183, above), assigned a life policy on his own life to his daughter E.S.R. who had married B.

J.R. died in 1905, and his daughter died the following year. The competition for the proceeds of the policy was between J.R.'s widow, who was executrix and beneficiary under his will, and B. in his capacity as executor of his deceased wife. An action of multiplepoinding was brought by the insurance company.

Held that B. had the preferable claim, because only a personal right was involved.

Lord McLaren said (at p. 1312): "Against the effect of the assignation it was argued that the transfer was incomplete because it was not intimated to the Assurance Company in Mr Robb's lifetime, but I think this argument is founded on a misapprehension. Intimation is necessary to give a real right to the subject assigned. All the authorities who speak to the importance of intimation limit its effect in this way, and I can see no reason for doubting that an assignment of a policy of assurance, like any other deed purporting to give a contract right, is binding on the granter and his heirs. The law is so stated in Bell's Principles, sec. 1462. . . . It follows that the executrix being under obligation to warrant the assignment cannot set up her title in opposition to that of the assignee."

(3) *Strachan* v. *McDougle* (1835) 13 S. 954: The question in this case was between the assignee and a creditor of the deceased insured; a real right, as distinct from a personal right, was involved:

A life policy had been intended to give a lender security, but, though the policy was physically transferred to the lender, no intimation was given to the insurance company until after the borrower's death, by which time the proceeds of the policy had already been arrested in the hands of the company by another creditor of the borrower.

In a multiplepoinding raised by the insurance company for the purpose of deciding between the competing claims of the assignee and the arrester, the court held that the arrester had the preferable claim. (For a fuller account of the facts, see 8–94, above.)

Lord Mackenzie said (at p. 959): "The question then remains, whether the right of the arrester was excluded by the prior right of the assignee? I think there is in substance a good assignation in her favour, but it was not intimated, and, by the law of Scotland, an unintimated assignation cannot compete with an arrestment. To obviate this it is pleaded that the delivery of the policy completes the assignee's right without intimation. This is a doctrine of a dangerous tendency. It is an important general principle of our law, and there is none more vital, that the delivery of the corpus of a deed or instrument will not carry the real right that is contained within such deed or instrument."

(iii) It is a general principle of the common law that *the assignee may sue the insurance company in his own name*, but that *the insurance company may put forward* in a claim made by the assignee *any defence* which it could have put forward if the claim had been made by the original insured. This general principle has been given statutory expression in the Policies of Assurance Act 1867 (ss. 1 and 2) and in the Marine Insurance Act 1906 (s. 50(2)).

11–190   The maxim applicable is: *assignatus utitur jure auctoris"* ("the assignee enjoys the right of his cedent"), *i.e.* the assignee stands in the shoes of his cedent, and has no stronger claim than the cedent would have had. An illustration is:

11–191   *Buist &c.* v. *Scottish Equitable Life Assurance Society* (1878) 5 R. (H.L.) 64; (1877) 4 R. 1076: Moir took out insurance on his own life with the S. Society, and in doing so declared that all his answers on the proposal form were true, and that he had made full disclosure and that he agreed to the proposal being the basis of the contract between himself and the Society. In fact, several of Moir's answers to questions relating to his health and habits and to proposals made to other insurance companies were deliberately false.

The policy was assigned to B. and others, who in good faith advanced certain sums of money to Moir on security of the policy and intimated the assignation to the Society.

Held that the Society was entitled to have the policy reduced (*i.e.* set aside) on the ground of Moir's false statements.

Lord President Inglis (at 4 R. p. 1081) made observations on the duty of an insurance company which came to know of a ground of invalidity after it had received intimation of an assignation:

"If after a policy has been assigned the insurance company become aware of objections to its validity, so clear and conclusive that the mere statement of them is enough, I do not say that there may not then be a duty of communication to those whom the company know to be interested in the policy. It would not be consistent with good faith that they should, in such circumstances, go on receiving the premiums on a policy that they intended to challenge in the end. But there is nothing approaching such a case here."

11–192   There is an important statutory modification of the general principle described above in motor vehicle insurance: the provision is now in section 149 of the consolidating Road Traffic Act 1972. It relates to the insurance for third-party risks, which is compulsory under section 143 of that Act. Section 149 provides that a third party who has succeeded in court in establishing liability which falls within the policy has a right to have his claim met by the insurance company, even although the company would be entitled to avoid the policy in a question with the insured (s. 149(1)). It is a condition of this right that the insurance company must have had notice of the bringing of the proceedings before or within seven days after their commencement (s. 149(2)). However, the insurance company can escape liability if, before or within three months after the commencement of the proceedings referred to, it applies to court for a declaration that it is entitled to avoid the policy on the ground of material non-disclosure or material misrepresentation (s. 149(3)). The case of *Zurich General Accident and Liability Insurance Co.* v. *Leven*, 1940 S.C. 406 (11–94, above), is an instance of a case in which the insurance company succeeded in obtaining a declaration entitling it to avoid the policy under the corresponding provision of the Road Traffic Act 1934 (s. 10(3)).

IV THE CLAIM

When an event insured against has occurred, the insured becomes entitled to enforce the policy by making a claim which the insurer is bound to pay. It is usual for the policy to impose various conditions as regards the making of a claim, *e.g.* the policy will stipulate the time within which and the manner in which notice of the event insured against must be given to the insurer. Failure to observe a condition may be waived by the insurer; see, *e.g., Donnison* v. *Employers' Accident and Live Stock Insurance Co. Ltd.* (1897) 22 R. 681 (11–180, above).

The amount which the insured can recover may be limited by an "excess" clause or by a "franchise" clause in the policy. Excess clauses, common in household and motor insurance, provide that the insured is to bear the first amount of any loss. The amount may be expressed as a fixed sum of money or as a fixed percentage of the loss. Franchise clauses, used especially in marine insurance, relieve the insurer from liability for a loss which is less than a specified amount or specified percentage, but, if the loss is greater, permit a claim to be made for the full amount of the loss without any deduction in respect of the first portion.

Another limitation on the amount which may be recovered applies where there is under-insurance and the policy is "subject to average." The possibility of under-insurance (*i.e.* where the sum insured is less than the value of the property insured) frequently arises in times of high inflation, and so it is at such times particularly important from the insurer's point of view that policies insuring property should include a "subject-to-average" clause. Such a clause does not come into operation where there is a total loss; *e.g.* if the property is truly worth £60,000, but has been insured for only £40,000, and is then totally destroyed, the insured is entitled to receive £40,000. The clause operates where there is a partial loss: its effect is that the insured can recover only that proportion of the partial loss which the sum insured bears to the value of the property; the insured is regarded as "being his own insurer," as it is usually expressed in policies, for the balance; *e.g.* if a property worth £60,000, insured for only £40,000, is partially destroyed, the insured is entitled to recover only two-thirds of the partial loss.

The onus of proof is on the insured: he must, if his claim is to succeed, prove that the loss was caused by a peril insured against under the policy, and is not an excepted peril. However, the proof need not be conclusive: the insured is required only to establish a *prima facie* ("apparent") case. If he does so, then the onus of proof will pass to the insurer to show that the loss falls within an exception. An illustration is *Macdonald* v. *Refuge Assurance Co. Ltd.* (1890) 17 R. 955:

B. insured his life with R. Ltd. for £50. The policy contained these conditions: "The full sum assured shall become payable if the assured shall die from accident happening at any time after the date of this policy, or shall die from any other cause after twelve calendar months from such date." "On the death of the assured the claimant under this policy shall transmit to the company's manager . . . a registrar's certificate of the death, and also such other evidence and information as the directors may require . . . , and, if the claim is made on the ground of death from accident, satisfactory evidence of the accident."

Within two months after the issue of the policy, B. was found drowned in the Clyde, and his daughter, as his executrix, claimed the sum insured on the ground that B. had died from accident. R. Ltd. refused payment, on the ground that she had not produced proof of accidental death.

Held that, since there was no evidence to the contrary, it was to be presumed that B. died from accident.

Lord Justice-Clerk J.H.A. Macdonald said (at p. 957): "Now, the evidence which the pursuer brings forward is that the deceased was a reputable man . . . and a man in no way likely to commit suicide, and that he disappeared and was subsequently found drowned in the Clyde.

"That on the face of it points to accident and to nothing else, and it is reasonable to say that in such a case the presumption is in favour of accident. . . . If the pursuer brings forward evidence of the death having happened in such a manner as naturally points to accident, she fulfils all that is incumbent on her, and I hold that she has done so here. To call upon the pursuer to disprove negatively other causes of death, would be to put upon her a burden which is not according to a fair reading of the contract."

11–197 An insured who makes a fraudulent claim forfeits all benefit under the policy.

11–198 A brief explanation is given below of the following terms in relation to the making and settlement of claims:

    (a) proximate cause;
    (b) subrogation;
    (c) contribution; and
    (d) reinstatement.

In addition, terms specially noteworthy in marine insurance are:

    (e) constructive total loss;
    (f) notice of abandonment;
    (g) average; and
    (h) suing and labouring clause,

while, in motor insurance, claims may be affected by:

    (i) a "knock-for-knock" agreement.

(a) Proximate Cause

11–199 When the question arises of whether a particular loss was caused by a peril insured against, the general rule applied is known as "the proximity rule" or "the doctrine of proximate cause." The maxim is *causa proxima non remota spectatur* ("it is the nearest cause, not the remote cause, which is looked at").

11–200 As expressed in the Marine Insurance Act 1906 the rule is: "Subject to the provisions of this Act, and unless the policy otherwise provides, the insurer is liable for any loss proximately caused by a peril insured against, but, subject as aforesaid, he is not liable for any loss which is not proximately caused by a peril insured against" (s. 55(1)).

11–201 "By 'proximate' cause is not meant the latest, but the direct, dominant, operative and efficient one. If this cause is within the risks covered, the insurers are liable in respect of the loss; if it is within the perils excepted, the insurers are not liable. A loss may be the combined effect of a whole number of causes, but, for the purposes of insurance law, one direct or dominant cause must in each case be singled out" (Raoul Colinvaux, *The Law of Insurance* (4th ed.), para. 4-32).

A question which frequently arises is whether there has been a *novus actus interveniens* ("new act intervening"), which breaks the chain of causation. If the chain is broken, the earlier act cannot be the proximate cause.

There are copious illustrations of the proximity rule both in marine and in non-marine insurance. For the purposes of this elementary account three illustrations may suffice:

(i) Where property is damaged by water used to extinguish a fire, the proximate cause of the damage is fire.

(ii) *Johnston* v. *West of Scotland Insurance Co.* (1828) 7 S. 52: Duncan's house was insured against fire. A fire broke out in a neighbouring house as a result of which a gable in front of Duncan's house was left standing unsupported, and, in the interests of public safety, the Dean of Guild ordered the gable to be taken down. While this operation was being carried out, the gable fell on to Duncan's house and caused damage.

Held that, although Duncan's house had not been on fire, and although the gable of the other house had stood for two days after the fire had been extinguished and only fell during operations deliberately undertaken on the orders of the Dean of Guild, Duncan's insurance company was liable under the fire policy for the damage to his house.

(iii) *Leyland Shipping Co. Ltd.* v. *Norwich Union Fire Insurance Society Ltd.* [1918] A.C. 350: A ship was insured under a marine policy which provided that the insurers were not to be liable for consequences of hostilities and warlike operations. The ship was torpedoed by a German submarine near Havre, and was brought into harbour there. Because the harbour authorities feared that the ship would sink, it was directed to an outer berth, and there it grounded with each fall of the tide and ultimately became a total wreck.

Held that the grounding was not a *novus actus interveniens* and that the torpedoing was the proximate cause of loss; as a result, the insurers were not liable since the proximate cause came within the exception in the policy.

Lord Dunedin said (at p. 363): "The question of what is *proxima*[5] is not solved by the mere point of order in time."

(b) Subrogation

The right of subrogation may be described in general terms as the right which enables the insurer who has indemnified the insured to stand in the shoes of the insured and himself exercise any right which the insured had to hold a third party liable for the loss which has occurred. The third party's liability to the insured may have been created by contract or by delict. From the more precise definitions of the right of subrogation given in statute and in decided cases it will be apparent that the right extends to other situations besides the typical situations mentioned: it may arise

---

[5] "nearest."

even where the insured has himself no enforceable claim against a third party.

11–208   Subrogation is one of the consequences of the principle of indemnity in the law of insurance: if the insured were entitled to claim under the policy and also retain his right to enforce a third party's liability for his own benefit, he would be in breach of the principle of indemnity which prevents an insured from making a profit out of a loss. The right of subrogation is co-extensive with the indemnification provided by the insurer in paying the insured's claim, and it is on this point that the precise definitions of subrogation turn. The best known of these definitions are in section 79 of the Marine Insurance Act 1906 and in the case of *Castellain* v. *Preston* (1883) 11 Q.B.D. 380, a decision of the Court of Appeal (see 11–37, above).

11–209   (i) Section 79 of the Marine Insurance Act 1906 provides that:

"(1) Where the insurer pays for a total loss, either of the whole, or in the case of goods of any apportionable part, of the subject-matter insured, he thereupon becomes entitled to take over the interest of the assured in whatever may remain of the subject-matter so paid for, and he is thereby subrogated to all the rights and remedies of the assured in and in respect of that subject-matter as from the time of the casualty causing the loss.

"(2) Subject to the foregoing provisions, where the insurer pays for a partial loss, he acquires no title to the subject-matter insured, or such part of it as may remain, but he is thereupon subrogated to all rights and remedies of the assured in and in respect of the subject-matter insured as from the time of the casualty causing the loss, in so far as the assured has been indemnified, according to this Act, by such payment for the loss."

11–210   (ii) In *Castellain* v. *Preston*, Brett L.J., having referred to indemnity as being the fundamental principle of insurance, said (at p. 387): "The doctrine of subrogation . . . is only another proposition which has been adopted for the purpose of carrying out the fundamental rule which I have mentioned, and it is a doctrine in favour of the underwriters or insurers in order to prevent the assured from recovering more than a full indemnity; it has been adopted solely for that reason. . . . The question is, whether that doctrine as applied in insurance law can be in any way limited. Is it to be limited to this, that the underwriter is subrogated into the place of the insured so far as to enable the underwriter to enforce a contract, or to enforce a right of action? Why is it to be limited to that, if when it is limited to that, it will, in certain cases, enable the assured to recover more than a full indemnity? . . . In order to apply the doctrine of subrogation, it seems to me that the full and absolute meaning of the word must be used, that is to say, the insurer must be placed in the position of the assured. Now it seems to me that in order to carry out the fundamental rule of insurance law, this doctrine of subrogation must be carried to the extent which I am now about to endeavour to express, namely, that as between the underwriter and the assured the underwriter is entitled to the advantage of every right of the assured, whether such right consists in contract, fulfilled or unfulfilled, or in remedy for tort[6] capable of being

---

[6] The term "tort" in English law corresponds to the term "delict" in Scots law.

insisted on or already insisted on, or in any other right, whether by way of condition or otherwise, legal or equitable, which can be, or has been exercised or has accrued, and whether such right could or could not be enforced by the insurer in the name of the assured by the exercise or acquiring of which right or condition the loss against which the assured is insured, can be, or has been diminished. That seems to me to put this doctrine of subrogation in the largest possible form. . . . It will be observed that I use the words 'of every right of the assured.' I think that the rule does require that limit. . . . Innumerable cases would be taken out of the doctrine if it were to be confined to existing rights of action."

The situation in *Castellain* v. *Preston* was that P., the insured, had recovered from the purchasers the very sum which he would have got if the loss had not happened.

Bowen L.J. said (at p. 401): "Then what is the principle which must be applied? It is a corollary of the great law of indemnity, and is to the following effect:— That a person who wishes to recover for and is paid by the insurers as for a total loss, cannot take with both hands. If he has a means of diminishing the loss, the result of the use of those means belongs to the underwriters. If he does diminish the loss, he must account for the diminution to the underwriters."

Further important points concerning subrogation are:

(i) The insurer is not entitled to refuse to pay a claim merely on the ground that a third party is liable for the loss. Thus, the Marine Insurance Act 1906 provides: "The owner of insurable property has an insurable interest in respect of the full value thereof, notwithstanding that some third person may have agreed, or be liable, to indemnify him in case of loss (s. 14(3)).

Conversely, the third party is not entitled to put forward the insurance as a defence when a claim is made against him by the insured:

Port-Glasgow and Newark Sailcloth Co. v. *Caledonian Railway Co.* (1892) 19 R. 608: The P. Co., owners of a flax store near a railway line, brought an action against the railway company for damages on the ground that through the company's negligence the store had been set on fire by a spark from one of the railway company's engines.

As well as denying negligence the railway company put forward the defence that the P. Co., since they were fully insured, had no interest to maintain the action. That defence was rejected by the court. (The railway company was, however, held not liable, because there was no proof that it had been negligent.)

(ii) If, after a claim has been paid by the insurer, the insured recovers anything from a third party in respect of the loss which has been made good, the insured must account to the insurer for the amount recovered. A striking illustration of this point in relation to a valued policy is *North of England Iron Steamship Insurance Association* v. *Armstrong* (1870) L.R. 5 Q.B. 244:

In a valued policy the ship "Hetton" was insured for £6,000. It was run down and sunk by another ship, and the underwriters paid the owners £6,000 as for a total loss. Later £5,000 was recovered in the Court of Admiralty against the owners of the other ship.

The real value of the ship had been £9,000, and there was no other insurance.

Held that, as between the underwriters and the insured, the value of the "Hetton" had to be taken to be £6,000 for all purposes, and that therefore the damages recovered, which were in the nature of salvage, belonged entirely to the underwriters.

Cockburn C.J. said (at p. 249): "It has always been considered as a settled rule in insurance law, . . . that where there is a total loss the underwriters, who pay upon a total loss, whether it is actual or whether it is constructive, are entitled to anything that remains of the vessel, and to anything which would otherwise have accrued to the owner of the vessel by reason of his ownership."

11–215   However, according to the decision in *Yorkshire Insurance Co. Ltd.* v. *Nisbet Shipping Co. Ltd.* [1962] 2 Q.B. 330, the insurer cannot recover from the insured more than he has paid to the insured:

A vessel insured for £72,000 under a valued policy became a total loss as a result of a collision with a Canadian Government ship.

The insurers paid £72,000 to the insured. The insured then successfully claimed damages from the Canadian Government. Owing to a devaluation. in the £, the damages, when converted into English currency, amounted to nearly £127,000. The insured then repaid £72,000 to the insurers, and retained the balance of about £55,000.

Held that the insurers were not entitled to recover any of that balance from the insured.

11–216   (iii) Subrogation probably developed out of the principle of abandonment in early marine insurance law, but there are significant differences between the two doctrines. In particular, the rule applied in *Yorkshire Insurance Co. Ltd.* v. *Nisbet Shipping Co. Ltd.* (11–215, above) does not apply to abandonment, because the insurer in the case of abandonment obtains a right to take over the insured's interest in whatever remains of the subject-matter and is not limited to retaining only the amount of the payment which he has made to the insured. For example, in the case of abandonment the insurer is entitled to any freight earned by a ship after the happening of the event which has resulted in the abandonment. This is provided for by section 63 of the Marine Insurance Act 1906, and is illustrated by *Stewart and Others* v. *Greenock Marine Insurance Co.* (1848) 1 Macq. 328:

S. and others insured their ship the "Laurel" of Greenock with G. Co., and insured the freight with the Scottish Marine Insurance Co. of Glasgow.

The "Laurel" sailed from Quebec for Liverpool on July 14, 1842. On July 27, she encountered and was seriously damaged by an iceberg, but, on August 11, reached the Mersey, where on the receding of the tide she took ground and sustained further injury. The following day, however, she was floated into dock and delivered her cargo of timber to the consignees, who duly paid the freight.

Some days later, the ship was surveyed and found not worth repairing. The owners gave notice of abandonment to the underwriters, but the underwriters refused to accept it. The owners then brought an action against G. Co., claiming as for a total loss.

Held that there had been a total loss and a proper notice of abandonment, and that the freight earned belonged to G. Co. and not to the owners.

Lord Chancellor Cottenham said (at p. 331): "The assured... claiming, as upon a total loss, must give up to the underwriters all the remains of the property recovered, together with all benefit and advantage belonging or incident to it, or rather such property vests in the underwriters. Now the freight which a ship is in the course of earning is a benefit or advantage belonging to it, and is as much to be given up to, or to become the property of the underwriters paying for a total loss of ship, as any other matter of value belonging to or incident to the subject insured."

(iv) The insured is not entitled to discharge his claims against a third party so as to defeat the insurer's right of subrogation. If he does so, he is liable to the insurer to the extent of the discharge. An instance is:

Phoenix Assurance Co. v. *Spooner* [1905] 2 K.B. 753: Mrs S. owned a house and two shops in Plymouth and insured them against fire with P. Co.

The Plymouth Corporation decided to acquire the property by compulsory purchase and served on Mrs S. a notice to treat. Before anything had been done under this notice, a fire occurred and the buildings were destroyed. P. Co. paid to Mrs S., as the agreed amount of her loss, £925.

After the fire, the amount to be paid by the Corporation was agreed between Mrs S. and the Corporation at a figure arrived at by taking into account the £925 paid by P. Co. to Mrs S.

Held that P. Co. could not be deprived of its right of subrogation by the agreement between Mrs S. and the Corporation.

(v) Subrogation does not give the insurer any higher right against a third party than the insured himself had, and so the third party may put forward against the insurer any defence which he could have put forward against the insured; this aspect of subrogation operated in *Simpson & Co. &c.* v. *Thomson &c.* (1877) 5 R. (H.L.) 40:

Burrell was the sole owner of two vessels, the "Dunluce Castle" and the "Fitzmaurice," which came into collision at sea owing to the negligence of those in charge of the "Fitzmaurice." The "Dunluce Castle" and her cargo were wholly lost, and T., the underwriter who had insured that vessel under a valued policy, paid £6,000 to Burrell as for a total loss.

Burrell, as owner of the ship at fault, availed himself of the provisions of the Merchant Shipping Acts which enabled him to limit his liability to a sum based on the ship's tonnage, and so paid into a bank under order of the court the sum of £3,590, to be distributed by the court among those entitled to it.

S., the owner of the cargo which had been on board the "Dunluce Castle," and also the master and seamen who had lost their belongings in the collision, made claims against the fund of £3,590. The question was whether T. was entitled to rank on the fund in respect of the £6,000 paid to Burrell.

Held that T. was not entitled to rank on the fund because T. could only claim to stand in the place of Burrell, and Burrell would have had no right of action against himself.

"It is clear that if the owner of the 'Dunluce Castle' had not been insured he could have had no claim against himself as the owner of the 'Fitzmaurice,' which caused the injury to the 'Dunluce Castle.' The injury to that ship was substantially caused by its own owner, and he could not be liable to himself for the damage so caused. And if he could not be liable to himself he could not assign any right, either expressly or by implication of law, to any third person, as he had none to convey. No doubt the rights of underwriters are well established, and it is one of these that on payment of the risk as for a total loss they are entitled to all the rights in the injured ship which belonged to its owner, but they are not entitled to more. And if the owner of the 'Dunluce Castle' had no right to sue the owner of the 'Fitzmaurice' neither can the underwriters on the 'Dunluce Castle,' whose rights were derived from the owner of that vessel" (*per* Lord Gordon at p. 50).

(c) Contribution

11–219　The question of contribution arises where there is more than one policy and a loss occurs which is less than the combined amount payable under the policies. It would be an infringement of the principle of indemnity if the insured were to be entitled to claim the full amount payable under several policies so as to make a profit out of his loss.

11–220　It is common for a policy to include a "rateable proportion clause," *i.e.* a clause providing that each insurer is to be liable to contribute only rateably when a loss occurs. Where there is no such clause preventing the insured from claiming the full amount of his loss from one insurer, the insured is entitled to hold that one insurer liable to himself, but that insurer will then have a right, implied by law, to recover a rateable contribution from any other insurer.

11–221　The right of contribution is explained thus in the Marine Insurance Act 1906 (s. 80):

"(1) Where the assured is over-insured by double insurance, each insurer is bound, as between himself and the other insurers, to contribute rateably to the loss in proportion to the amount for which he is liable under his contract.

"(2) If any insurer pays more than his proportion of the loss, he is entitled to maintain an action for contribution against the other insurers."

11–222　Contribution is required only where the several policies cover the same interest in the subject matter, and not where they cover separate interests. An illustration is *North British and Mercantile Insurance Co.* v. *London, Liverpool and Globe Insurance Co.* (1876) 5 Ch. D. 569:

A large amount of grain and seed belonging to merchants R. & Co. was destroyed in a fire when stored in the granaries of B. & Co., wharfingers. R. & Co. had "merchants' policies" and B. & Co. had "wharfingers' policies," and an action was brought to ascertain the liability of the different insurance companies.

Held that the grantors of the merchants' policies were not liable to contribute to the loss; B. & Co. were primarily liable, but, since they were indemnified by the grantors of the wharfingers' policies, the latter were ultimately liable.

However, the rule applied in that case is often ignored in practice; in particular, by one of the rules of the Fire Offices' Committee contribution operates by agreement between insurers where the same heritable property is insured by several persons with different interests.

(d) **Reinstatement**

The normal liability of an insurer is to pay a sum of money in satisfaction of a claim. Fire policies, however, always in practice include a reinstatement clause, the effect of which is to give the insurer an option to rebuild damaged premises or replace goods lost by fire instead of paying a sum of money. The clause is for the benefit of the insurer: the insured is not entitled to insist on reinstatement.

The insurer, once he has made his election between payment and reinstatement, is bound by his decision: he is not entitled to change his mind should he discover that he has made an unwise choice.

(e) **Constructive Total Loss**

The Marine Insurance Act 1906 includes the following provisions:

(i) A loss may be either total or partial (s. 56(1)).

(ii) A total loss may be either an actual total loss, or a constructive total loss (s. 56(2)).

(iii) Unless a different intention appears from the terms of the policy, an insurance against total loss includes a constructive, as well as an actual, total loss (s. 56(3)).

(iv) There is an actual total loss where the subject-matter insured is destroyed, or so damaged as to cease to be a thing of the kind insured, or where the assured is irretrievably deprived of it (s. 57(1)). In the case of an actual total loss no notice of abandonment need be given (s. 57(2)). An actual total loss may be presumed where the ship concerned in the adventure is missing and after the lapse of a reasonable time no news of her has been received (s. 58).

(v) Subject to any express provision in the policy, there is a constructive total loss where the subject-matter insured is reasonably abandoned on account of its actual total loss appearing to be unavoidable, or because it could not be preserved from actual total loss without an expenditure which would exceed its value when the expenditure had been incurred (s. 60(1)).

In particular, there is a constructive total loss—

(1) where the assured is deprived of the possession of his ship or goods by a peril insured against, and (a) it is unlikely that he can recover the ship or goods, as the case may be, or (b) the cost of recovering the ship or goods, as the case may be, would exceed their value when recovered; or

(2) in the case of damage to a ship, where she is so damaged by a peril insured against that the cost of repairing the damage would exceed the value of the ship when repaired; or

(3) in the case of damage to goods, where the cost of repairing the damage and forwarding the goods to their destination would exceed their value on arrival (s. 60(2)).

Where there is a constructive total loss the assured may either treat the loss as a partial loss, or abandon the subject-matter insured to the insurer and treat the loss as if it were an actual total loss (s. 61).

With some exceptions provided for in the Act, notice of abandonment must always be given to the insurer where a claim is being made on the basis of a constructive total loss: if no notice is given, the loss must, as a general rule, be treated as a partial loss (s. 62(1)).

11–226 An illustration of constructive total loss is *British and Foreign Marine Insurance Co. Ltd.* v. *Samuel Sanday & Co.* [1916] 1 A.C. 650:

Two British ships with merchandise belonging to British merchants for sale in Germany were on a voyage from the Argentine to Hamburg when war broke out between the United Kingdom and Germany, and further prosecution of the voyage became illegal. The vessels were directed to proceed to British ports.

The cargo owners warehoused their goods and gave notice of abandonment to their underwriters, claiming on a constructive total loss. The perils insured against included "restraints of princes."

Held that as there was a constructive total loss of the goods directly caused by a "restraint of princes" (the declaration of war), the cargo owners were entitled to recover from their underwriters.

(f) Notice of Abandonment

11–227 As regards the notice of abandonment which is required where the assured elects to abandon the subject-matter to the insurer, the Marine Insurance Act 1906 provides as follows:

(i) The notice may be in writing or by word of mouth, and may be in any terms which indicate the assured's intention to abandon his insured interest in the subject-matter unconditionally to the insurer (s. 62(2)).

(ii) The notice must be given with reasonable diligence after receipt of reliable information of the loss, but where the information is of a doubtful character the assured is entitled to a reasonable time to make inquiry (s. 62(3)).

(iii) The acceptance of an abandonment by the insurer may be express or implied from his conduct; mere silence on his part after notice is not an acceptance (s. 62(5)).

(iv) Where notice of abandonment is accepted, the abandonment is irrevocable; by accepting the notice the insurer conclusively admits that he is liable for the loss and that the notice of abandonment was sufficient (s. 62(6)).

(v) Notice of abandonment need not be given in the following circumstances:

(1) where, at the time when the assured receives information of the loss, there would be no possibility of benefit to the insurer if notice were given to him;

(2) where the insurer waives notice; or

(3) where the insurer has re-insured his risk (s. 62(7)-(9)).

(vi) The effect of abandonment is that the insurer is entitled to take over the assured's interest in whatever may remain of the subject-matter; the insurer is entitled, on the abandonment of a ship, to any freight earned by the ship after the event which caused the loss (s. 63).

11–228 In *Robertson* v. *Royal Exchange Assurance Corporation*, 1925 S.C. 1 (O.H.), the question was whether the insurers, who had declined to accept a notice of abandonment, had by their subsequent actings impliedly accepted the notice:

The steamship "Tarv," owned by R., sprang a leak on a voyage from Ayr to Portrush, then encountered heavy weather and was beached by her master on Rathlin Island.

The day after the stranding, R. gave notice of abandonment to the underwriters.

A clause in the policy provided that no acts of the insurer or insured in "recovering, saving, or preserving" the property insured was to be considered as a waiver or acceptance of abandonment.

The underwriters refused to accept R.'s notice of abandonment, and contracted with a salvage association for the salving of the vessel. Intimation of the making of the salvage contract was sent to R.

Salvage operations were begun, but were later suspended for several weeks, without R.'s knowledge, in order that the salvors might proceed with the salving of another ship. During the period of suspension the "Tarv" suffered further damage.

Held that the suspension was not an act done for "recovering, saving, or preserving" the "Tarv," that in permitting the suspension the underwriters had taken a course which was prejudicial to R. and consistent only with the ownership of the ship being in themselves, and that they had therefore either impliedly accepted the notice of abandonment or were in some other way barred from denying that they had accepted it.

The result was that R. was entitled to be indemnified on the basis that there had been a constructive total loss.

While the notice of abandonment described in the above paragraphs is required only in marine insurance, the doctrine of abandonment itself is of general application to contracts of indemnity. Brett L.J. said in *Kaltenbach* v. *Mackenzie* (1878) 3 C.P.D. 467 (C.A.) (a marine insurance case) (at p. 470):

"There is a distinction between abandonment and notice of abandonment, and . . . abandonment is not peculiar to policies of marine insurance; abandonment is part of every contract of indemnity. Whenever, therefore, there is a contract of indemnity and a claim under it for an absolute indemnity, there must be an abandonment on the part of the person claiming indemnity of all his right in respect of that for which he receives indemnity. The doctrine of abandonment in cases of marine insurance arises where the assured claims for a total loss. There are two kinds of total loss; one which is called an actual total loss, another which in legal language is called a constructive total loss; but in both the assured claims as for a total loss. Abandonment, however, is applicable to the claim, whether it be for an actual total loss or for a constructive total loss. If there is anything to abandon, abandonment must take place; as, for instance, when the loss is an actual total loss, and that which remains of a ship is what has been called a congeries of planks, there must be an abandonment of the wreck. Or where goods have been totally lost . . . , but something has been produced by the loss, which would not be the goods themselves, if it were of any value at all, it must be abandoned. But that abandonment takes place at the time of the settlement of the claim; it need not take place before.

"With regard to the notice of abandonment, I am not aware that in any contract of indemnity, except in the case of contracts of marine insurance, a notice of abandonment is required. In the case of marine insurance where the loss is an actual total loss, no notice of abandonment is necessary; but in the case of a constructive total loss it is necessary, unless it be excused."

(g) Average

11–230 The term "average" is of significance where the damage caused by a peril insured against is a partial loss, *i.e.* does not amount to an actual total loss and is not treated as a constructive total loss. The term is not confined to marine insurance: average clauses are common in non-marine property insurance (see 11–195, above).

11–231 The starting point in connection with average in marine insurance is the distinction between "particular average loss" and "general average loss."

11–232 "A particular average loss" is defined in the Marine Insurance Act 1906 as "a partial loss of the subject-matter insured, caused by a peril insured against, and which is not a general average loss" (s. 64(1)). An instance of a particular average loss is damage caused to a ship when it strikes a rock. Liability for a particular average loss lies with the person whose property is lost or damaged—the shipowner in the instance referred to. Where that person is insured against the loss or damage, ultimate liability will lie with his insurer. In the case of a particular average loss no question arises of making other persons whose property has not been harmed (*e.g.* the cargo-owners) liable to contribute towards the loss; nor can the insurers of such other persons be made liable.

11–233 "A general average loss" is defined in the Marine Insurance Act 1906 as "a loss caused by or directly consequential on a general average act" (s. 66(1)), and "there is a general average act where any extraordinary sacrifice or expenditure is voluntarily and reasonably made or incurred in time of peril for the purpose of preserving the property imperilled in the common adventure" (s. 66(2)).

11–234 Some instances of general average losses will clarify the statutory definition. There are three interests at risk during a voyage—the ship, the cargo and the freight. There is a general average loss to the ship when part of its equipment is jettisoned or is damaged by being used in an abnormal way (*e.g.* engines used to move a stranded ship). There is a general average loss to the cargo when it is jettisoned or landed at some place other than its proper destination, and these same circumstances give rise to a general average loss to the freight.

11–235 It is considered only just and fair that a general average loss should be shared by all persons whose interests have been saved by the deliberate sacrifice or expenditure. Hence the Marine Insurance Act 1906 provides that where there is a general average loss, the party on whom it falls is entitled to a rateable contribution from the other parties interested (called "a general average contribution") (s. 66(3)).

11–236 Liability to pay general average contributions will ultimately rest on each insurer of the separate interests. The Marine Insurance Act 1906 accordingly provides that, subject to any express provision in the policy, the assured who has incurred a general average expenditure or a general average sacrifice may recover his loss from his insurer without having himself enforced his right of contribution from the other parties liable to contribute (s. 66(4)), and that, subject again to any express provision in the policy, where the assured has paid, or is liable to pay, a general average contribution, he may recover it from his insurer (s. 66(5)).

The doctrine of general average is believed to have its origin in the *Lex Rhodia de Jactu* ("Law of Rhodes concerning Jettison"), a rule adopted in Roman law from the maritime law of the Mediterranean island of Rhodes.

In modern practice, questions of general average are often governed by the York-Antwerp Rules, which were drawn up, and later revised, by international conferences. The latest version is the York–Antwerp Rules 1974. The Rules do not have the force of law; their importance stems from the frequency with which they are in practice adopted by the parties (*e.g.* by incorporation into bills of lading).

Where the parties neither adopt the York-Antwerp Rules nor make other special provisions, any question of general average is decided in accordance with the law applicable at the port of destination (or, where the ship does not reach its destination, at the port at which the voyage is discontinued).

Provisions relating to average may be specified in a "Memorandum" at the end of the policy. The specimen form of policy given in the First Schedule to the Act of 1906 includes such a Memorandum:

"Corn, fish, salt, fruit, flour, and seed are warranted free from average, unless general, or the ship be stranded—sugar, tobacco, hemp, flax, hides and skins are warranted free from average, under five pounds per cent., and all other goods, also the ship and freight, are warranted free from average, under three pounds per cent. unless general, or the ship be stranded."

The Schedule explains that the term "average unless general" means a partial loss of the subject-matter insured other than a general average loss.

The effect of these provisions is that the insurer will not be liable for a partial loss of corn, fish, *etc.* unless:

    (i) the loss is a general average loss; or
    (ii) the ship is stranded,

and will not be liable for a partial loss of the other items mentioned unless:

    (i) the partial loss is five per cent or more (or three per cent or more, as the case may be) of the total value of the items; or
    (ii) the loss is a general average loss; or
    (iii) the ship is stranded.

(h) Suing and Labouring Clause

A marine policy may include a "suing and labouring clause," the effect of which is to enable a larger sum to be recovered than that fixed in the policy.

The form of policy set out in the First Schedule to the Marine Insurance Act 1906 includes such a clause:

"In case of any loss or misfortune it shall be lawful to the assured, their factors, servants and assigns, to sue, labour, and travel for, in and about the defence, safeguards, and recovery of the said goods and merchandises, and ship, &c., or any part thereof, without prejudice to this insurance; to the charges whereof we, the assurers, will contribute each one according to the rate and quantity of his sum herein assured."

11–243   The Act of 1906 provides that the undertaking in a suing and labouring clause is considered to be supplementary to the contract of insurance and entitles the assured to recover from the insurer any expenses properly incurred in accordance with the clause, even although the insurer may have paid for a total loss or the policy may declare that the insurance is free from particular average (either wholly or under a certain percentage) (s. 78(1)).

(i) "Knock-for-Knock" Agreement

11–244   In motor insurance a claim may be affected by a "knock-for-knock" agreement entered into between insurance companies. The effect of such an agreement is that each company undertakes to pay valid claims made by its own policyholders without enforcing the right of subrogation, where the effect of enforcing that right would be that ultimate liability would lie with the other insurance company.

11–245   The general nature of a "knock-for-knock" agreement was explained thus by Sir Boyd Merriman (President) in *Morley* v. *Moore* [1936] 2 K.B. 359 (C.A.), at p. 361:

"We are informed that the purpose of this agreement is that each insurance company pays its own assured, without question, that which the assured is entitled to receive under the particular policy and that both of them do their utmost to discourage either of their own assureds from making claims against the other, or, putting it in another way, the insurance companies amongst themselves do not insist upon their assured bringing such action as they may be entitled to bring against the party insured by the other insurance company."

11–246   It is clear from the language used in that passage that the existence of a "knock-for-knock" agreement between two insurance companies does not affect the right of an assured to sue the other party: the insurance companies can only "do their utmost to discourage" claims being made by their assureds one against another. A concise statement of this point is: "'Knock-for-knock' agreements between insurance companies not to exercise their rights of action against each other in the shoes of their respective assureds cannot in any way affect the assured's own right of action against a third party" (Raoul Colinvaux, *The Law of Insurance* (4th ed.), para. 19-17).

11–247   The Court of Appeal case *Morley* v. *Moore* (11–245, above) provides an illustration:

The plaintiff's car had been damaged in collision through the negligence of the defendant to the extent of £33 2s.8d. The plaintiff's insurance policy included a "£5 excess" clause, *i.e.* the insured himself was to be responsible for the first £5 of a claim. For the damage caused by the collision the plaintiff therefore recovered £28 2s.8d. from his insurance company. In paying him, the insurance company directed him that they did not want him to claim the sum of £28 2s.8d. from the defendant; this was because there was a "knock-for-knock" agreement between the plaintiff's insurance company and the defendant's insurance company.

The plaintiff did, however, bring an action against the defendant for £33 2s.8d., the whole of the damage sustained, and obtained judgment for that amount in the county court. The defendant appealed to the Court of Appeal.

Held that the plaintiff had been entitled to bring his action against the defendant for the full amount: he could not be deprived of his right to sue the defendant by arrangements made "behind the scenes between the insurance companies" (*per* Sir Boyd Merriman, P., at [1936] 2 K.B. p. 367).

Scott L.J. said (at p. 369): "My view is that there is no right whatever in an insurer to dictate to his assured whether he shall or shall not abstain from enforcing his remedies against a third party which go in diminution of the loss against which the policy is issued; they have an absolute right to require him to enforce his remedies, but, in my opinion, they have no right to prevent him enforcing them. Their right is a right purely consequential on the nature of the contract of indemnity, and it arises because of it being a contract of indemnity, and nothing more. If the assured by some process of recovery, whether by an action at law or by an ex gratia payment, obtains a payment in diminution of the loss, the underwriters or the insurers are entitled to the excess over[7] the amount paid by them to him by way of strict indemnity, and no more. To my mind that is the remedy of the insurers, and that is the only remedy they have in respect of the assured's rights of recovery at common law."

The judgment of the Court of Appeal in *Morley* v. *Moore* was approved by the House of Lords in *Hobbs* v. *Marlowe* [1978] A.C. 16:

H.'s car was involved in a collision with M.'s car. The sole cause of the collision was M.'s negligence.

Both vehicles were insured under comprehensive policies—H.'s car with the United Standard Insurance Co. Ltd. ("United Standard") under a policy containing a £10 excess clause and M.'s car with the Guardian Royal Exchange Assurance Ltd. ("G.R.E."). There was a "knock-for-knock" agreement between the two insurance companies.

The cost of repairing H.'s car was £237·59 and United Standard paid £227·59 to H. in accordance with the policy.

H. sought the assistance of the Automobile Association ("the A.A.") to recover his uninsured loss of £73·53 (made up of the £10 excess and £63·53, the expense of hiring another car while his own was being repaired).

The A.A. brought an action in H.'s name against M., claiming the full amount of £301·12.

Held that the "knock-for-knock" agreement did not preclude H. from enforcing his right of action against M. for the full amount of damages.

The underlying reason for the A.A.'s action in claiming the full amount was that G.R.E. refused, in this and other cases, to pay the A.A.

---

[7] The passage makes more obvious sense if the words "the excess over" are omitted or (as reported at (1936) 55 Ll.L.Rep. 14) are replaced by the words "be paid."

solicitors' costs in settling small claims because of a court rule introduced in 1973 disallowing solicitors' charges in claims under £75.

On this, the real practical, issue in the case the A.A. were unsuccessful: the inflation of H.'s claim for the sole purpose of obtaining costs which would not otherwise have been claimable and where H. had nothing to gain directly from that inflation was held to be a misuse of the process of the court, and so only the court fee of £7·50, appropriate to the actual amount at stake (the uninsured losses of £73·53), was awarded as costs.

Lord Diplock's speech includes the following explanation of the effect of a "knock-for-knock" agreement (at p. 36):

"The amount claimed in the summons dated June 28, 1974, was the liquidated sum of £313·62, made up of damages of £301·12, together with small amounts for court fees and solicitors' charges. The action was brought, as it had to be, in the name of Mr. Hobbs, and with his nominal consent. It was defended by G.R.E. in the name of Mr. Marlowe, whose negligence was admitted. On July 17, 1974, on his behalf they paid into court the sum of £73·53 in satisfaction of Mr. Hobbs' claim. This was all that Mr. Hobbs had any personal interest in recovering. He had nothing to gain by the proceedings continuing thereafter. . . . United Standard, his insurers, have at no time taken any part in the proceedings, nor given Mr. Hobbs any instructions about them. . . .

"As respects £227·59 of the total amount of the judgment, which Mr. Hobbs had already been paid by United Standard, this was paid to the registrar on Mr. Marlowe's behalf by G.R.E. as his insurers. On receipt of this sum Mr. Hobbs, if he ever in fact received it, would have held it on behalf of United Standard under their right of subrogation, and United Standard would have been under a contractual duty under the knock-for-knock agreement to pay it back to G.R.E. The sum would thus come round full circle back into the hands of G.R.E. from which it had originated."

V THE PRINCIPLE OF INDEMNITY

11–249 The principle of indemnity is commonly described, as Brett L.J. described it in the leading English case of *Castellain* v. *Preston* (1883) 11 Q.B.D. 380 (at p. 386), as the "fundamental principle of insurance." In simple terms insurance enables the insured to recover from the insurer the amount, but no more than the amount, which the insured has lost by the happening of the event insured against. The statutory definition of marine insurance in the Marine Insurance Act 1906 is centred on the principle of indemnity: "A contract of marine insurance is a contract whereby the insurer undertakes to indemnify the assured, in manner and to the extent thereby agreed, against marine losses, that is to say, the losses incident to marine adventure" (1906 Act, s. 1).

11–250 In any consideration of the principle of indemnity in insurance law, it is necessary to keep in mind:

(a) the exceptions to the principle of indemnity, before describing:
(b) the consequences of the principle of indemnity.

(a) Exceptions to the Principle of Indemnity

The principle of indemnity does not apply to contingency insurance or where the policy is a valued one, and its operation may be modified by express terms in a policy:

(i) *Contingency Insurance*

In contingency insurance the insurer undertakes to pay on the happening of the event insured against, even although no loss may be involved. The principal type of contingency insurance is life insurance; some accident insurance and some sickness insurance are also within this category. Contingency insurance is not founded on the principle of indemnity.

(ii) *Valued Policies*

The insurer and the insured may agree on the value of the subject-matter being insured, and specify this value in the policy. In the event of a loss the insurer will then be barred from maintaining that the agreed value was not the true value and that the insured is entitled to recover only the amount of his loss if that be less than the agreed value. Whether a policy is a valued policy or not is a question depending on the interpretation of the words used in the insurance contract. *Prima facie* ("until the contrary is proved"), an insurance contract is a contract of indemnity and not a valued policy.

Valued policies are common in marine insurance, but rare in other branches. See also 11–163 *et seq.*, above.

(iii) *Express Terms in Policies*

The parties may modify the operation of the principle of indemnity by express terms in the policy; *e.g.* the policy may include an "excess" clause (11–194, above) or an "average" clause (11–195, above).

(b) Consequences of the Principle of Indemnity

The best-known judicial account of these is to be found in the judgment of Brett L.J. in *Castellain* v. *Preston* (1883) 11 Q.B.D. 380 in the passage which begins thus (at p. 386):

"In order to give my opinion upon this case, I feel obliged to revert to the very foundation of every rule which has been promulgated and acted on by the Courts with regard to insurance law. The very foundation, in my opinion, of every rule which has been applied to insurance law is this, namely, that the contract of insurance contained in a marine or fire policy is a contract of indemnity, and of indemnity only, and that this contract means that the assured, in case of a loss against which the policy has been made, shall be fully indemnified, but shall never be more than fully indemnified. That is the fundamental principle of insurance."

The consequences of the principle are:

(i) *Limitation of the Claim*

The amount which the insured can recover is limited not only to the sum insured but also to the extent of the loss or damage and to the insured's interest in the subject-matter at the time of the loss or damage. The insurer will never be obliged to pay more than the sum insured, even where the value of the subject-matter exceeds the sum insured: the insured has taken the risk of under-insurance (probably so as to incur a lower premium), and he must shoulder the consequences. On the other hand, if the insured has over-insured, the insurer is protected by the principle of indemnity: he will not be obliged to pay the sum insured but he will be liable to pay only the value of the subject-matter so far as the insured has an interest in it at the time of the event insured against. Where the insured obtains more than an indemnity for loss sustained, the insurer is entitled to recover the excess: see the facts of *Castellain* v. *Preston* (11–37, above).

(ii) *Insurer's Right of Subrogation*

11–258 If the insurer has indemnified his insured, he is entitled to stand in the shoes of his insured and exercise any right which the insured had to hold a third party liable for the loss or damage in respect of which the indemnity has been paid. See 11–207 *et seq.*, above.

(iii) *Co-Insurer's Right of Contribution*

11–259 Where there is double insurance, the insurer who has indemnified the insured has the right to call on the other insurers to contribute their share of the loss. The effect is that the insured cannot by making claims under several policies obtain a total sum which would more than reimburse him for the loss sustained. See 11–219 *et seq.*, above.

(iv) *The Doctrine of Abandonment*

11–260 Where the subject-matter insured has not been totally destroyed, the insured cannot claim for a total loss unless he surrenders all that remains of the subject-matter to the insurer. This is sometimes referred to as "the salvage rule." For example, in fire insurance if the insurer agrees to make full payment of the sum insured or to reinstate, he is entitled to all the old materials left after the fire. See also 11–229, above.

11–261 In marine insurance the doctrine of abandonment is linked to the doctrine of constructive total loss (11–225 *et seq.*, above). How they operate together to enable the insured to obtain a full indemnity but no more than a full indemnity is explained by Brett L.J. in *Castellain* v. *Preston* (1883) 11 Q.B.D. 380 (at p. 386):

"To speak of marine insurance, the doctrine of a constructive total loss originated solely to carry out the fundamental rule which I have mentioned [*the principle of indemnity*]. It was a doctrine introduced for the benefit of the assured; for, as a matter of business, a constructive total loss is equivalent to an actual total loss; and if a constructive total loss could not be treated as an actual total loss, the assured would not recover a full indemnity. But grafted upon the doctrine of constructive total loss came the doctrine of abandonment, which is a doctrine in favour of the insurer or underwriter, in order that the assured may not recover more than a full indemnity. The doctrine of constructive total loss and the doctrine of notice of abandonment engrafted upon it were invented or promulgated for the purpose of making a policy of marine insurance a contract of indemnity in the fullest sense of the term."

VI STATUTORY PROVISIONS

Mention has already been made of some of the statutes relating to aspects of the law of insurance: the codifying Marine Insurance Act 1906 has been frequently referred to, and notice has been taken of the Life Assurance Act 1774 (11–13 *et seq.*, above), the Marine Insurance (Gambling Policies) Act 1909 (11–44, above), the Policies of Assurance Act 1867 (11–181 *et seq.*, above) and provisions of the Road Traffic Act 1972 as to third-party motor vehicle insurance (11–192, above).

No reference has so far been made to:

(a) the Third Parties (Rights against Insurers) Act 1930,

(b) the Policyholders Protection Act 1975, or

(c) the extensive statutory provisions contained in and made by regulations under the Insurance Companies Act 1982.

Future legislation may include measures for the reform of aspects of the law (*e.g.* to eradicate deficiencies in the present law on non-disclosure and breach of warranty, perhaps on the lines recommended by the Law Commission in its *Report* on these aspects ((1980) Cmnd. 8064; Law Com. No. 104) (see 11–129 *et seq.* and 11–153 *et seq.*, above)).

E.E.C. Directives have necessitated, and may in future necessitate further, changes in the law of the United Kingdom. Two Freedom of Establishment Directives (concerning the right of insurers from one E.E.C. member State to establish branches or agencies in other E.E.C. member States) have already been implemented. Further Directives, aimed at achieving freedom of services by harmonisation of certain aspects of insurance contract law, may require to be implemented in future.

(a) Third Parties (Rights against Insurers) Act 1930

This Act was passed to confer on third parties rights against insurers of third-party risks in the event of the insured becoming insolvent. At common law an injured third party had no right to the money paid by the insurer to the insolvent insured; he could only claim as an ordinary creditor in the insured's sequestration or liquidation.

Two circumstances are necessary to bring the Act into operation:

(i) A person (the insured) must incur liability to a third party against which he is insured under a contract of insurance.

(ii) The insured must (either before or after that event) become bankrupt, or make a composition or arrangement with his creditors, or, if the insured is a company, go into liquidation or receivership.

The insured's rights against the insurer are then transferred to and vest in the third party to whom the liability was incurred (s. 1(1)).

There can be no contracting out of the provisions of the Act (ss. 1(3), 3).

The insurer is under the same liability to the third party as he would have been under to the insured, but—

(a) if the liability of the insurer to the insured exceeds the liability of the insured to the third party, the Act does not affect the rights of the insured against the insurer in respect of the excess; and

(b) if the liability of the insurer to the insured is less than the liability of the insured to the third party, the Act does not affect the rights of the third party against the insured in respect of the balance (s. 1(4)).

11–270   In motor insurance the rights of third parties against insurers are now, under the Road Traffic Act 1972, much more extensive than the rights conferred by this Act of 1930.

(b) Policyholders Protection Act 1975

11–271 This Act made provision for the protection of policyholders whose insurance companies are unable to meet their liabilities. The Act established a body corporate called the Policyholders Protection Board (s. 1), which acts under the guidance of the Secretary of State for Trade (s. 2).

11–272   The Board has two main functions:

(i) to protect policyholders of companies in financial difficulties (*e.g.* by arranging for all or part of the insurance business of the company to be transferred to another insurance company) (ss. 16, 17); and

(ii) to protect policyholders of companies in liquidation: it has a duty to ensure that the liabilities of the company in respect of compulsory insurances (*e.g.* third-party motor insurance and employers' liability insurance) are fully met and that in respect of non-compulsory insurance the policyholders receive 90 per cent of the benefits due to them (ss. 5-12).

11–273   The performance of the Board's functions is financed by levies made by the Board on the insurance industry (ss. 18-22).

(c) Insurance Companies Act 1982

11–274 The Insurance Companies Act 1982, together with the regulations made under its authority, comprises the present statutory provisions by which the state exercises control over insurance companies. The Act consolidates the Insurance Companies Acts of 1974 and 1981. This body of legislation has a history going back to 1870, when the Life Assurance Companies Act of that year introduced the requirement that insurance companies deposit a sum of money with the court as security.

11–275   The Act of 1974 consolidated substantially the whole of the Insurance Companies Act 1958, Part II of the Companies Act 1967, and the Insurance Companies Amendment Act 1973. The Act of 1981 was an amending Act, its primary objective being to implement the E.E.C. Insurance Establishment Directives of 1973 and 1979 (which concern the right of insurers in life and non-life business respectively to establish branches or agencies in other E.E.C. States). The Directive of 1973 had already been implemented by regulations made under the European Communities Act 1972; these regulations were revoked and their provisions were consolidated in the Act of 1981.

11–276   The Act of 1982 has 100 sections and is divided into five Parts:

I. Restriction on Carrying on Insurance Business;
II. Regulation of Insurance Companies;
III. Conduct of Insurance Business;
IV. Special Classes of Insurers; and
V. Supplementary Provisions.

11–277   The following is a brief indication of the main provisions of the Act of 1982:

(i) *Restriction on Carrying on Insurance Business*

The central provision here is that no person can carry on insurance business in the United Kingdom unless he is authorised to do so by the Secretary of State for Trade (ss. 2-4).

Applications for authorisation must be in accordance with regulations made under the Act, and the Secretary of State must be satisfied on the basis of information received by him that the application ought to be granted (s. 5).

For the purposes of the Act insurance business is divided into "long term business" (*i.e.* life insurance and related sorts of insurance) and "general business" (s. 1), and the Secretary of State must not authorise new insurers to carry on both long term and general business (s. 6).

A United Kingdom applicant must normally be a registered company, and authorisation will not be given if any of the applicant's directors or controllers is in the Secretary of State's opinion not a fit and proper person to hold the position held by him (s. 7).

An applicant from another member State of the E.E.C. must, in order to obtain authorisation from the Secretary of State, have a "general representative" (a representative authorised to act generally, and to accept service of any document, on behalf of the applicant) resident in the United Kingdom, and must be a body corporate entitled under the law of its own State to carry on insurance business there. None of its executives operating in the United Kingdom must be a person whom the Secretary of State considers to be not a fit and proper person to hold the position held by him (ss. 8, 10).

An applicant from outside the E.E.C. has additional conditions to satisfy: the applicant must have assets of a prescribed amount in the United Kingdom and must make a deposit of a prescribed amount (s. 9).

Authorisation may be withdrawn by the Secretary of State, either at the request of the company or compulsorily on certain grounds by following a notification procedure (ss. 11-13).

(ii) *Regulation of Insurance Companies*

An insurance company must not carry on any activities, in the United Kingdom or elsewhere, except in connection with or for the purposes of its insurance business (s. 16).

There are detailed provisions as to accounts and statements: every company must prepare annual accounts and balance sheets in a form prescribed by regulations (s. 17); every company carrying on long term business must appoint an actuary (s. 19), and such a company must cause an actuarial investigation to be made every 12 months (s. 18); prescribed statements of separate classes of business must be prepared (s. 20); accounts must be audited in accordance with regulations (s. 21); the accounts, an abstract of the actuarial investigation and the statements of business must be deposited with the Secretary of State (s. 22); shareholders and policyholders are entitled to obtain from the company on application copies of the deposited documents (s. 23).

There are further detailed provisions designed to ensure that assets and liabilities attributable to long term business are kept separate from those attributable to general business if the company is carrying on both categories of business (ss. 28-31).

11–288   An important group of provisions deals with the concept of "margin of solvency," aimed at ensuring that insurance companies will never approach actual insolvency; the calculation of the margin is complex, and there are differing provisions applicable to United Kingdom companies, to other E.E.C. companies and to non-E.E.C. companies (ss. 32-35).

11–289   Wide powers of intervention are available to the Secretary of State under sections 37 to 48 of the Act. He may exercise these powers if he considers that desirable for protecting policyholders against the risk that the company may be unable to meet its liabilities, or if it appears to him that the company has failed to satisfy its obligations under the Act or has furnished misleading or inaccurate information to him or has a director or controller who is in his opinion not a fit and proper person, and on other specified grounds. The powers which the Secretary of State may exercise include requiring assets of the company to a certain value to be maintained in the United Kingdom, limiting premium income, accelerating the production of accounts and other documents, calling for the production of specified books, papers and information, and giving instructions as to the company's investments.

11–290   Transfers of general business from one insurance company to another are facilitated if the approval of the Secretary of State is first obtained (ss. 51, 52). Schemes for the transfer of long term business can be facilitated if sanctioned by the court (ss. 49, 50).

11–291   Special provisions relating to the winding up of insurance companies are contained in the Act (ss. 53-59). Amongst these is the provision that the Secretary of State may present a petition for the winding up of a company which has failed to satisfy its obligations under the Acts or has failed to keep or produce proper accounting records (s. 54).

11–292   Appointments of a new managing director, chief executive or controller must be notified in advance to and approved by the Secretary of State (ss. 60, 61).

(iii) *Conduct of Insurance Business*

11–293 The provisions in Part III of the Act include the provision that insurance advertisements must comply with regulations (s. 72), and the provision that there is a right to withdraw from a transaction in respect of a long term policy—of which right a statutory notice must be given (ss. 75, 76).

Further Reading

Gloag and Henderson, *Introduction to the Law of Scotland,* Chapter XXVII

David M. Walker, *Principles of Scottish Private Law,* Chapter 4.20

J. J. Gow, *The Mercantile and Industrial Law of Scotland,* Chapter 6

E.   John Birds, *Modern Insurance Law* (1982, Sweet & Maxwell)

MacGillivray & Parkington on Insurance Law relating to all risks other than marine, 7th ed. by Michael Parkington, Anthony O'Dowd, Nicholas Legh-Jones and Andrew Longmore (1981, Sweet & Maxwell)

Raoul Colinvaux, *The Law of Insurance* (4th ed., 1979, Sweet & Maxwell)

E.R. Hardy Ivamy, *General Principles of Insurance Law* (3rd ed., 1975, Butterworths)

Butterworths Insurance Law Handbook, edited by Lexis Editorial Staff, consultant editor E.R. Hardy Ivamy (1983, Butterworths)

Law Commission, *Report: Insurance Law: Non-disclosure and breach of warranty* (Cmnd. 8064, Law Com. No. 104) (1980, H.M.S.O.)

ARBITRATION

INTRODUCTION

12–01 IT is a general rule of the common law that parties to a dispute are entitled to have their dispute settled by litigation (*i.e.* by bringing or defending an action in the courts). In many situations, however, the parties prefer arbitration to litigation and so agree to refer their dispute instead to a person of their own choice (an "arbiter"), whose decision ("decree-arbitral" or "award") they will accept as binding. It is common for there to be two arbiters, one appointed by each party, with the further provision that if the two arbiters disagree the matter will "devolve on" (pass to the decision of) an "oversman" appointed by the parties or by the two arbiters. The agreement of the parties (referred to as the "contract of submission") has the general effect of "ousting" (*i.e.* excluding) the jurisdiction of the courts on the matter referred.[1] A central issue in many arbitration cases is whether the parties have used in their agreement words which, on the court's interpretation, effectively oust the court's jurisdiction in the particular dispute which has arisen.

This chapter deals with commercial arbitration and not with statutory arbitration. The latter is not based on the agreement of parties but is prescribed by various Acts of Parliament as the means of settling disputes arising out of the statutory provisions. Statutory arbitrations became common from the middle of the nineteenth century for the settlement of disputed claims for compensation where land was required for large undertakings such as railways (*e.g.* the arbitrations provided for by the Lands Clauses Consolidation (Scotland) Act 1845 and the Railways Clauses Consolidation (Scotland) Act 1845). Other instances of statutory arbitrations include those provided for by the Agricultural Holdings (Scotland) Act 1949 for the settlement of claims between landlord and tenant. The scope of and procedure in such arbitrations depend on the provisions of the particular Act in question.

The general Scots law of arbitration is almost wholly common law. Such statutory provisions as there are affect only specific aspects of the subject and are to be found in an odd assortment of legislation—the Articles of Regulation of 1695 (which are not an Act of Parliament but have legislative force), the Arbitration (Scotland) Act 1894, section 3 of the Administration of Justice (Scotland) Act 1972, and section 17 of the Law Reform (Miscellaneous Provisions) (Scotland) Act 1980.

The English law of arbitration has a distinct source: its main principles form Part I of the Arbitration Act 1950 (which consolidated earlier legislation applicable to England), as amended by the Arbitration Act 1979. The English courts have a supervisory role in relation to arbitrations such as does not exist in Scots law. The leading provision of Part I of the Act of 1950 (re-enacting a provision of the Arbitration Act 1889) is that if any party to an arbitration agreement commences any legal proceedings in any court against any other party to the agreement, in respect of any matter agreed to be referred, the court *may* make an order staying the proceedings (1950 Act, s. 4(1)). Of the differing approaches to arbitration in the two countries Lord Dunedin said in *Sanderson & Son* v. *Armour & Co. Ltd.,* 1922 S.C. (H.L.) 117, at p. 126:

"The English common law doctrine,—eventually swept away by the Arbitration Act of 1889—that a contract to oust the jurisdiction of the Courts was against public policy and invalid, never obtained in Scotland. In the same way, the right which in England pertains to the Court under that Act to apply or not to apply the arbitration clause in its discretion never was the right of the Court in Scotland. If the parties have contracted to arbitrate, to arbitration they must go."

---

[1] The jurisdiction of the courts is, however, not wholly ousted (see 12–157 *et seq.,* below).

12–05   In relation to international commercial arbitration, however, there is legislation applicable to both Scotland and England alike, namely, Part II of the Arbitration Act 1950 ("Enforcement of Certain Foreign Awards") and the Arbitration Act 1975 which enabled the New York Convention on the Recognition and Enforcement of Foreign Arbitral Awards of 1958 to be given effect in the United Kingdom. The leading provision of the Act of 1975 is to be contrasted with the leading provision of Part I of the Act of 1950 (see 12–04, above): it is to the effect that if any party to an international arbitration agreement commences any legal proceedings in any court against any other party to the agreement, in respect of a matter agreed to be referred, the court *must* make an order staying (or, in Scotland, "sisting") the proceedings, unless the court is satisfied that the arbitration agreement is null and void, inoperative or incapable of being performed or that there is not in fact any dispute between the parties with regard to the matter agreed to be referred (1975 Act, s. 1(1)).

12–06   The subject-matter of this chapter is confined to non-international arbitrations governed by the law of Scotland and is dealt with under the following headings:

    I. General nature of arbitration.
    II. Constitution of the contract of submission.
    III. Scope of the submission.
    IV. Arbiters and oversmen.
    V. Conduct of the arbitration.
    VI. Challenge of the award.

There is also a brief consideration of:

    VII. Judicial references.

I GENERAL NATURE OF ARBITRATION

12–07   It is appropriate to look first at the questions of:

    (a) what matters may be referred to arbitration; and
    (b) whether there is a distinction between arbitration and valuation;
before considering:
    (c) the inherent characteristics of arbitration; and
    (d) the possible advantages of arbitration over litigation.

(a) What Matters may be Referred to Arbitration

12–08   Criminal matters cannot be made the subject of an arbitration. It might be suggested on the authority of *Earl of Kintore* v. *Union Bank of Scotland* (1863) 1 M. (H.L.) 11; (1861) 24 D. 59 that a criminal matter such as fraud, if incidental to the main question in the submission, could be dealt with in arbitration proceedings. The case concerned a deed by which a truster and trustee, under a voluntary trust for creditors, and the creditors submitted to arbitration "all claims, debts, and demands" against the truster's estate. The Bank were creditors for substantial sums, for which they held documents of debt. The truster, trustee and other parties, alleging fraud, raised an action of reduction of these documents of debt and the court held that their action was excluded by the submission to arbitration. The case is thus restricted to the civil aspect of fraud and is not itself an exception to the proposition that criminal matters cannot be made the subject of an arbitration.

In general any matter involving civil rights and obligations, whether affecting heritable or moveable property and whether raising questions of fact or law, may be referred to arbitration, but, on grounds of public policy, questions of public rights and of status (*e.g.* as to whether a person is legitimate or is married) are exceptions to the general rule.

Two cases decided under the workmen's compensation legislation might be taken to suggest that where a question of status is incidental to the determination of another question, an arbiter has power to settle the question of status. However, it seems preferable to regard these cases as applications of particular statutory provisions and not as part of the common law. The Workmen's Compensation Acts of 1906 and 1925 provided that any question as to who was a "dependant" might be settled by arbitration under the Acts, *i.e.* by the sheriff as arbiter. In *Johnstone* v. *Spencer & Co.*, 1908 S.C. 1015, the question of whether a girl was the illegitimate child of a deceased workman was held to be a question which could competently be decided by the sheriff because it was incidental to deciding whether she was a "dependant." Similarly, in *Turnbull* v. *Wilsons and Clyde Coal Co. Ltd.*, 1935 S.C. 580, it was held competent for the sheriff, as arbiter, to allow proof of the claimant's marriage by habit and repute, this being incidental to determining whether she was a "dependant." Apart from the statutory provision with which these two cases were concerned, there may be no other instance of a question of status being competently referred to arbitration.

An arbiter's power to give a final decision on questions of law arising in an arbitration was to some extent modified by section 3 of the Administration of Justice (Scotland) Act 1972. That section provides that, unless there is an express provision to the contrary in the arbitration agreement, the arbiter or oversman *may*, on the application of a party to the arbitration, at any stage in the arbitration state a case for the opinion of the Court of Session on any question of law arising in the arbitration, and the arbiter or oversman *must* do so if the party applies to the Court of Session and that court directs a case to be stated. The application must be made at a "stage in the arbitration" (*e.g.* after the arbiter has issued proposed findings): it is no longer competent after the arbiter has issued his final award (*Fairlie Yacht Slip Ltd.* v. *Lumsden*, 1977 S.L.T. (Notes) 41). It would seem that the arbiter would be bound to accept as conclusive the opinion of the Court of Session on the question of law submitted to it: see *Mitchell-Gill* v. *Buchan*, 1921 S.C. 390 (12–160, below).

(b) Whether there is a Distinction between Arbitration and Valuation

A distinction has been drawn in English law between arbitration proper and valuation, and opinions in some Scottish cases suggest that a similar distinction, though with different effects, exists in Scots law. In this connection an "arbitration proper" has been defined as "the submission of a *lis*, [2] the purpose of which is the determination of an existing dispute," whereas a "valuation" has been defined as "the submission of a

---

[2] "dispute."

negotium,[3] the object of which is not the settlement of an existing dispute but the prevention of a dispute; as for instance where parties submit to an arbiter or valuer to assess a claim whose existence is admitted, but which there has been no attempt to adjust, so that the parties cannot in strict language be said to have differed" (Guild, *The Law of Arbitration in Scotland*, p. 3).

12–12   A valuation has been held to require less formality than an arbitration. Several cases relating to agricultural leases illustrate this point, *e.g.*:

12–13   (i) *Nivison* v. *Howat* (1883) 11 R. 182: At the expiry of a lease two neighbouring farmers were chosen by the outgoing and incoming tenant respectively to value the crop *etc.* They agreed on some points, but differed on others, and appointed a third farmer, as oversman, to decide between them.

The oversman issued an award, which the incoming tenant refused to implement on the ground that there had been irregularity in procedure.

Held that in such circumstances no formalities were necessary and that the award was therefore binding.

Lord Young said (at p. 191): "No formalities require to be observed by two farmers in valuing a crop, or by a third who is competently called in to decide where they differ. All the parties here desired or bargained for was the intelligent opinion of two skilled persons, and if they differed then the decision of another skilled man. That is what they have got."

12–14   (ii) *Robertson* v. *Boyd and Winans* (1885) 12 R. 419: An informal sublease of a portion of a farm provided that the rent was to be fixed by valuators.

The valuators were appointed by a probative deed, but their award was not in probative form.

Held that, in the circumstances of the case, the award had been homologated.

Lord Young expressed the opinion that neither the nomination of the valuators nor the award required to be in probative form. Lord Young's observation, however, may carry little weight in view of the fact that the other two judges (Lord Craighill and Lord Rutherfurd Clark) would apparently have held that the award, being improbative, would not have been binding, had it not been homologated.

12–15   (iii) *Gibson* v. *Fotheringham*, 1914 S.C. 987: In terms of a farm lease the landlord and the outgoing tenant referred certain questions of valuation to two arbiters mutually chosen and their oversman under the declaration that whatever the arbiters or their oversman should "determine . . . by decree or decrees arbitral, interim or final," should be binding on the parties.

Held that a formal devolution of the reference upon the oversman was not necessary, and that an award of the oversman would not be invalid merely because it included decisions which had already been arrived at by the arbiters.

Lord Justice-Clerk (John H.A. Macdonald) said (at p. 996): "This is a case of a very ordinary arbitration in which the questions relate to skilled valuation only. There was, therefore, no call for formality of procedure."

---

[3] "matter" (about which parties are negotiating).

(iv) *Cameron* v. *Nicol,* 1930 S.C. 1: The owner of a farm and the out-going tenant entered into a submission by which they referred the valuation of certain crops, stock and implements to two arbiters and to an oversman to be appointed by the arbiters to act in the event of their differing in opinion.

An award was issued, signed by the two arbiters and the oversman, which did not show on which, if any, of the items being valued the arbiters had differed in their estimate.

Held that the valuation belonged to a class of arbitrations where rigid conformity with formal procedure was not required, and that the award was therefore not invalid merely because it did not show the items on which the arbiters had differed.

Lord Sands said (at p. 15): "The first ground of challenge is that the award is signed by the two arbiters and the oversman indiscriminately, without any indication of how far it represents agreement arrived at by the two arbiters, or a decision by the oversman in regard to a matter about which the arbiters had differed. This objection would be fatal in the case of a formal arbitration to determine a dispute. But that was not the nature of the proceedings here in question. There is here no question of the resolution of matters in dispute, but there is simply a valuation to determine the amount payable in respect of certain things which it had been agreed were to be taken over at an agricultural waygoing. It is well settled that in such valuations the same strictness of form is not required as in an arbitration to determine a dispute, whether as regards heritable or moveable rights of property, or as regards claims of damages."

(v) *Stewart* v. *Williamson,* 1910 S.C. (H.L.) 47; 1909 S.C. 1254: The Agricultural Holdings (Scotland) Act 1908 provided that all questions which under a lease were referred to "arbitration" should (in spite of any agreement under the lease providing for a different method of arbitration) be determined by a single arbiter.

The lease in question provided that the tenant should, at the expiry of the lease, leave the sheep stock on the farm to the owners or incoming tenant according to the "valuation" of men mutually chosen, with power to name an oversman.

Held that the valuation of the sheep stock was referred to arbitration within the meaning of the statutory provision, and therefore fell to be determined by a single arbiter and not by two arbiters as stipulated in the lease.

A conclusion which may be drawn from such cases is that there is no distinct dividing line in Scots law between arbitration and valuation: rather there is a range of types of arbitration of varying degrees of formality.

(c) The Inherent Characteristics of Arbitration

The arbitration with which this chapter deals is based on contract and has the following inherent characteristics:

(i) "The evident and leading object of the contract is to exclude a court of law from the determination of some matter which is in dispute; and to take, in its place, the judgment or award of some private person or persons, selected by the parties to arbitrate between them" (Bell, *Treatise on the Law of Arbitration in Scotland,* p. 20).

12–21   (ii) The parties bind themselves to abide by the award and to implement it; they have no right to have the matter tried over again in a court of law or to appeal to a court against the award. "It would be a piece of idle curiosity, and nothing more, to ascertain an arbiter's opinion and take his judgment on a disputed matter, if either party could afterwards, at his pleasure, have that judgment reviewed on its merits in a court of law. The forum of the arbiter would then be converted into a mere ante-chamber to the Courts of Law, serving no other purpose except that of creating great extra expense and delay, without any rational or intelligible motive whatsoever" (*op. cit.,* p. 21). By resorting to arbitration the parties have accepted the risk that their arbiter may make a wrong decision.

12–22   (iii) Because the arbiter has a judicial role, he must be honest and impartial. "It clearly appears to be an *implied condition* under the contract, that [*the parties*] shall only be bound by [*the award*] if it be pronounced with *honesty* and *impartiality* by the arbiter" (*op. cit.,* p. 22). The element of honesty would seem to be satisfied "wherever the arbiter had conscientiously believed he was doing what was right and just, however much he might have erred in judgment" (*op. cit.,* p. 23). To satisfy the condition of impartiality, there must be "equal and even-handed procedure towards both parties alike; . . . no hearing of one side only (for example) and refusing to hear the other" (*op. cit.,* p. 26).

12–23   (iv) There is an implied condition in the contract of submission that the parties will observe fairness of procedure in their relations towards each other. They must "abstain from practising any fraudulent and deceitful devices on the arbiter, for the purpose of thereby impetrating from him an unjust award, pronounced under essential error, so induced" (*op. cit.,* p. 27).

12–24   (v) The arbiter must keep within the powers which have been conferred upon him: he must observe the conditions imposed on him by the contract of submission, and must not act *ultra fines compromissi* ("beyond the bounds of the submission") or fail to exhaust the submission by not deciding matters referred to him.

12–25   Where there is breach of the conditions mentioned in (iii), (iv), or (v), above, the award can be reduced (*i.e.* set aside by the court).

(d) **The Possible Advantages of Arbitration over Litigation**

12–26   The parties to an arbitration agreement may regard arbitration as having the following advantages over litigation:

(i) *Informality*

12–27   In an arbitration the parties are free to decide on the degree of formality or may leave that matter to the arbiter's discretion. Strict adherence to court procedures is not required unless the parties so specify.

12–28   The arbiter is, however, bound to do equal justice to both sides (see 12–22, above).

(ii) *Speed*

12–29   In an arbitration the timetable is arranged by the parties and the arbiter, whereas in litigation the case must await its turn in the court timetable. An arbiter's decision may therefore be more speedily obtained.

On the other hand, in some situations arbitration proceedings may be long drawn out: this is especially so in large-scale arbitrations where the arbiters are likely to be well-known professional persons whose services are much in demand and whose commitments prevent them from giving their uninterrupted attention to any one particular arbitration. The case of *Crudens Ltd.* v. *Tayside Health Board*, 1979 S.C. 142 may be referred to as an illustration:

C. Ltd. had entered into a building contract in 1963 with Tayside Health Board for the construction of a new teaching hospital and medical school at Ninewells, Dundee. Several disputes arose and were in 1969 submitted to David M. Doig, F.R.I.C.S., as sole arbiter, acting with the assistance of A.J. Mackenzie Stuart, Q.C., B.A., LL.B., as legal assessor. At the end of the arbitration C. Ltd. was awarded £2,313,497, and it is narrated that "the parties . . . spent about 100 days in a very long, expensive and involved arbitration" (*per* Lord Allanbridge (Ordinary) at p. 149).

(C. Ltd.'s subsequent action against the board for damages for loss of use of the money awarded was held to be competent on the ground that that matter had not been referred to the arbiter.)

(iii) *Cheapness*

Litigation is often costly, especially for the unsuccessful party, and an arbitration may prove less expensive.

However, a formal arbitration is not necessarily less expensive than litigation: litigants do not pay remuneration to the judge or the clerk of court or a hire-charge for the court room, whereas an arbiter's fee may be substantial and there may also be charges for a legal assessor, for a clerk's services and for suitable accommodation for the hearing.

(iv) *Privacy*

Most court proceedings take place in public, and may be reported in the press. Parties may wish to keep their disputes from the public gaze: they may, for instance, have been on intimate terms as partners or they may be business organisations wishing to avoid disclosure of financial details.

(v) *Expertise*

The arbiter chosen may be an expert in a particular line of business, perhaps capable of giving a decision as to the quality of goods by a simple "sniff and look," or well acquainted with the circumstances and terminology of the branch of commerce concerned. The parties may feel more satisfied with such an expert's findings than with a judge's decision.

II CONSTITUTION OF THE CONTRACT OF SUBMISSION

The general law of contract applies to contracts of submission, and only brief notice need be taken here of some points relating to:

(a) the capacity of the parties; and
(b) the form of the contract.

(a) The Capacity of the Parties

12–37   The parties must have contractual capacity; *e.g.* a pupil cannot enter into a contract of submission, and a minor's submission would require his curator's consent and be voidable until the end of the *quadriennium utile* ("useful four-year period") on the ground of lesion unless the minor were engaged in trade on his own account and the subject-matter were concerned with his trade.

12–38   A person who is acting in a representative capacity may or may not have authority to refer a matter to arbitration. In some situations there is a statutory provision which will apply: *e.g.* the Bankruptcy (Scotland) Act 1913 (s. 172) provides that the trustee in a sequestration may, with the consent of the commissioners, refer to arbitration any questions which may arise in the course of the sequestration regarding the estate, or any demand or claim made on it, and by the Trusts (Scotland) Act 1921 (s. 4) trustees have power to refer all claims connected with the trust estate unless that is at variance with the terms or purposes of the trust. An agent has, as a general rule, no authority to refer a matter to arbitration: he will normally require special authority to do so. Counsel are an exception to the general rule (*Gilfillan* v. *Brown* (1833) 11 S. 548), but solicitors are not (*Black* v. *Laidlaw* (1844) 6 D. 1254). Similarly, a partner cannot without the consent of his co-partners enter into an arbitration which will be binding on the firm (*Lumsden* v. *Gordon* (1728) Mor. 14567).

(b) The Form of the Contract

12–39   There are conflicting views as to how the rule relating to the constitution of contracts of submission should be stated:

12–40   On the one hand the rule may be stated as being that submissions are to be regarded as *obligationes literis* ("contracts requiring writing for their constitution") unless they fall into one of a number of categories of exceptions to that rule (Walker and Walker, *The Law of Evidence in Scotland* (2nd ed.), paras. 101-103; Scottish Law Commission, *Memorandum No. 39 ("Constitution and Proof of Voluntary Obligations: Formalities of Constitution and Restrictions on Proof")*, para. 4).

12–41   On the other hand the rule may be stated as being that a contract of submission is not, of itself, one of the *obligationes literis* (though it may be brought into that category by its subject-matter), but falls into the category of contracts which can be proved only by "writ or oath," with the results that writing is in practice required, not as a solemnity, but *in modum probationis* ("by way of proof") and that the writing may be informal (Guild, *The Law of Arbitration in Scotland*, pp. 18-20).

12–42   Whichever view is correct, account must be taken of the following points:

12–43   (i) If the arbitration is concerned with heritable property, an alternative to a formal probative deed is an informal writing followed by some form of personal bar such as *rei interventus* ("actings following on"), homologation or acquiescence.

12–44   (ii) There was a well-recognised exception to the rule that in an arbitration concerned with heritable property a formal probative deed or an informal writing followed by personal bar was required, namely, that where a dispute as to marches (boundaries) had been referred to arbitration and the arbiter had at the site caused the march-stones to be set along the boundary line as fixed by him, no writing was required either for the submission or for the award (*Laird of Livingston* v. *Feuars of Falhouse* (1662) Mor. 2200, 12409; *Procurator-Fiscal of Roxburgh* v. *Ker* (1672) Mor. 12410).

A modern equivalent may also be an exception: this is supported by the opinion of Lord Justice-Clerk Moncreiff in *Otto &c.* v. *Weir* (1871) 9 M. 660, at p. 661:

"If two village proprietors, having a dispute about their marches, agree verbally to build a march fence at mutual expense, in a line to be fixed by arbiters . . .; and if the fence is thereafter put up on the line so fixed, and the expense mutually paid, I think both parties are conclusively bound." In the case before the court the fence was held not to have been erected in the line fixed by the arbiters.

(iii) It may be that an arbitration on a matter of small importance does not require writing even for its proof: opinions on this point were reserved in *Ferrie* v. *Mitchell &c.* (1824) 3 S. 113, concerned with a promissory note for £414: the report states (at p. 114):

"The Judges considered it unnecessary to decide whether there might not possibly be cases of so simple and trifling a nature as to admit of parole evidence of a submission; but they were unanimously of opinion, that, in the present case, it was an incompetent mode of proof." The accepted limit for "small importance" is £100 Scots (*i.e.* £8·33 stg.); hence this possible exception is of little significance.

(iv) The form of the submission governs the form required for the award. If the parties have embodied their contract of submission in a formal deed, then the award also must be of that nature (*Percy* v. *Meikle*, 25 Nov. 1808, F.C.; *Mclaren* v. *Aikman*, 1939 S.C. 222 (12–148, below)), whereas if the parties have used informal writings (such as ordinary letters in a mercantile matter) to constitute their contract of submission, then the award also may be informal (*e.g.* a letter signed by the arbiter).

III SCOPE OF THE SUBMISSION

It is essential that the parties define the scope of the submission precisely. Otherwise it is likely that the arbitration will at some stage come before the courts—which is just the situation which the parties originally sought to avoid. If the scope of the arbiter's jurisdiction has not been clearly expressed, there may be litigation at the start of the arbitration proceedings: one party, thinking that the matter in dispute is not covered by the contract of submission, may raise an action in court and the other party may then apply for the action to be sisted to await the result of an arbitration; it is also possible that a party may apply to the court for an interdict against an arbiter who is about to deal with matters which have not been referred to him. At the conclusion of an arbitration an action of reduction may be brought to set aside the award if the arbiter has gone *ultra fines compromissi* ("beyond the bounds of the submission") or has failed to exhaust the submission (*i.e.* has failed to decide matters properly referred to him); each of these grounds of reduction is more likely to be open if the contract of submission itself has not been clearly expressed.

12–48   Some of the principal points which affect the scope of the submission may be considered under the following headings:

(a) the court's role in fixing the scope of the submission;
(b) the assumption that the arbiter will not exceed his jurisdiction;
(c) *ad hoc* submissions and ancillary arbitrations; and
(d) the duration of the submission.

(a) The Court's Role in Fixing the Scope of the Submission

12–49   The final decision as to the scope of the submission lies with the court.

12–50   The arbiter is bound in the first instance to "expiscate" his own jurisdiction, *i.e.* examine the terms of the submission and decide whether or not the particular matter is within his jurisdiction as stated by the parties. Since, however, the leading principle of the law of arbitration is that the court's jurisdiction is ousted only to the extent to which the parties have agreed that it should be ousted, the final decision as to the extent of the arbiter's jurisdiction depends on the interpretation placed by the court on the words used by the parties in their contract of submission. The leading authority Bell states (*op. cit.,* p. 58):

"If an arbiter's judgment as to the construction of the contract of submission itself were exempt from all review, he might exercise, without control, a usurped jurisdiction to any extent over subjects which the parties never intended to submit, and never had submitted to him."

12–51   It is, however, possible for the actings of the parties to extend the scope of a reference beyond the strict terms of the original contract of submission. The principle operating in such a situation is that of personal bar. The court does not readily infer that there has been such an extension; for example, the mere inclusion in the pleadings before the arbiter of questions beyond the scope of the original submission would not take effect as an extension; the consent of both parties is required (*per* Lord President Dunedin in *Miller & Son* v. *Oliver & Boyd* (1906) 8 F. 390, at pp. 401–402, a case in which the scope of the submission was held not to have been enlarged by the pleadings of the parties before the arbiter).

(b) The Assumption that the Arbiter will not Exceed his Jurisdiction

12–52   Until the arbiter has taken some irrevocable step to indicate that he is exceeding his jurisdiction, the court assumes that his final decision will be within his jurisdiction, and so decided cases reveal an unwillingness on the court's part to grant an interdict to prevent an arbitration from proceeding.

12–53   An instance is *Bennets* v. *Bennet* (1903) 5 F. 376: A contract of co-partnery contained an arbitration clause. In an arbitration under that clause, the parties on one side raised the preliminary objection that while some of the matters referred to the arbiter were admittedly within the reference, others were clearly outside his jurisdiction. The arbiter rejected that preliminary objection, and allowed the parties a proof.

The objectors then sought from the court an interdict to prohibit the arbiter from dealing with the matters objected to.

The court *refused* interdict, *holding* that the arbiter had only decided a question of procedure and had done nothing to indicate conclusively that in deciding the merits of the claim he would exceed his jurisdiction.

Lord President Kinross said (at p. 381): "We are bound to assume that he will keep within his powers."

A similar case in the same year was *Moore* v. *McCosh* (1903) 5 F. 946: In an arbitration under a mining lease the landlord claimed that the arbiter should order the tenant to perform certain works of restoration. The tenant presented to the court a note for interdict against the arbiter proceeding with the reference, on the ground that the order asked for was not within the scope of the arbitration clause in the lease.

The court *refused* to interdict the arbiter from proceeding with the reference, since the court could not assume that the arbiter would make an incompetent order.

On similar grounds the court refused in *Wemyss* v. *Ardrossan Harbour Co.* (1893) 20 R. 500 to reduce an arbiter's interim orders and note of proposed findings.

Lord McLaren said (at p. 505): "We can only interfere with the decrees of arbiters by way of reduction when we have a final decree, and can only restrain them from proceeding when the proceedings are outwith the reference.

"This case does not fall under either of these heads. We have here no final decree; everything is open."

(c) Ad Hoc Submissions and Ancillary Arbitrations

A contract of submission may be either an *ad hoc* submission or an ancillary arbitration.

(i) Ad Hoc *Submissions*

An *ad hoc* (literally, "for this purpose") submission is one entered into by parties who have no pre-existing arrangement for settling disputes. On the occasion of a particular dispute having arisen they agree that it be settled by arbitration, and make a contract of submission which relates only to that dispute.

The scope of the contract of submission is governed by the terms used by the parties, but since the dispute which it is intended to settle is already in existence, difficulties of interpretation as to the scope of the contract are comparatively unlikely to arise.

(ii) *Ancillary Arbitrations*

An ancillary arbitration is one founded on an arbitration clause in a contract the main purpose of which is to deal with some other matter; *e.g.* it is usual to have an arbitration clause in a building contract and in a contract of co-partnery.

Ancillary arbitrations have featured in many decided cases. The points which have been settled by these cases include the following:

(1) Restricted and ample clauses

Arbitration clauses are commonly divided into two varieties—the restricted or limited variety on the one hand and the ample or general or universal variety on the other. The former extends only to disputes which occur during the execution of the principal contract; it is often referred to as being "executorial" of the principal contract (but see the quotation from Lord Rutherfurd Clark's opinion in *Mackay* v. *Parochial Board of Barry* (1883) 10 R. 1046 (12–63, below)). The other variety of arbitration clause is of wider scope and covers disputes which, though they arise out of the principal contract, do not occur until after its execution. The distinction is described thus by Lord Dunedin in *Sanderson & Son* v. *Armour & Co. Ltd.,* 1922 S.C. (H.L.) 117, at p. 125:

"By the law of Scotland, it has always been possible for the parties in framing the original contract to insert a clause binding themselves to refer future possible disputes to arbitration. This clause may be of two characters. It may be of a limited character, generally known as executory arbitration, providing for the adjustment of disputes concerned with the working out of the contract. But it may also be of a universal character, submitting all disputes which may arise either in the carrying out of the contract or in respect of breach of the contract after the actual execution has been finished. Whether the clause is of the one sort or the other is a matter of construction."

(a) *Example of restricted clause*

12–62   An example of the restricted or limited variety of arbitration clause occurs in *Beattie* v. *Macgregor* (1883) 10 R. 1094:

A building contract contained the following clause: "Should any difference arise between the proprietor and any of the contractors in regard to the true meaning of the plans, drawings, or specifications, or the manner in which the work is to be executed, or any matter arising thereout or connected therewith, the same is hereby submitted to the determination of William Hamilton Beattie . . . , whose decision shall be final and binding upon all parties."

Held that this clause applied only to disputes arising during the execution of the contract and did not extend to a dispute concerning the accuracy of the measurements obtained by a contractor after the work had been completed.

The case was one of a series of cases on the interpretation of arbitration clauses in building contracts, and Lord President Inglis observed (at p. 1096):

"I really hope that there will be an end to cases of this class. A very little care in the choice of language would prevent all ambiguity. Let parties only distinctly express themselves so as to mean that the reference is to cover every kind of claim arising out of the contract, and the Court cannot interfere. On the other hand, if they will use language like that in the clause here, let them clearly understand that it is now settled law that such a clause covers only questions which arise during the execution of the contract."

(b) *Examples of ample clause*

12–63   One of the earliest cases giving effect to the ample, general or universal variety of arbitration clause was *Mackay* v. *Parochial Board of Barry* (1883) 10 R. 1046:

A contract for the introduction of a water supply to Carnoustie included the clause: "Arbiter.—Should any dispute arise as to the true nature, sufficiency, times, or extent of the work intended to be performed under the specification and drawings or as to the works having been duly and properly completed, or as to the construction of these presents, or as to any matter, claim, or obligation whatever arising out of or in connection with the works, the same shall be submitted and referred to the amicable decision, final sentence, and decreet-arbitral of Alexander McCulloch . . ."

McCulloch, who was the local authority's engineer, had power under the contract to alter, add to or modify the specified works during the course of the contract, and any alterations, additions or modifications were to be deemed to be a part of the contract.

Numerous and extensive alterations were made on the works as they proceeded, and McCulloch brought out as due to the contractor for the extra work involved a sum far below what the contractor claimed.

The contractor raised an action against the local authority for an additional payment.

Held that the contractor's claim fell within the arbitration clause.

Lord Rutherfurd Clark said (at p. 1050): "The contracting parties may create a tribunal for settling differences which may occur in the course of executing the works, and which has no other function. But of course they may do more, and extend it to the decision of any claim which may arise out of the contract. In this sense the reference is not less executorial of the contract than when it is confined to the settlement of questions which may arise during the execution of the works."

Another instance of a general clause—more briefly expressed—occurs in *North British Railway Co.* v. *Newburgh and North Fife Railway Co.*, 1911 S.C. 710:

An agreement between two railway companies concerning share capital and dividends contained the clause: "All questions which may arise between the parties hereto in relation to this agreement or to the import or meaning thereof or to the carrying out of the same shall be referred to arbitration . . ."

Held that questions which arose between the parties were questions of the construction of the agreement and therefore had to be determined by the arbiter, even although their determination depended upon the question of *ultra vires* ("beyond the powers" (conferred by Act of Parliament)) and even although it involved a point of law.

Lord President Dunedin said (at p. 718): "It has long ago, I think, been settled in the law of Scotland that arbitration clauses in contracts may be of two descriptions. They may be either in the form of what has been called an executory arbitration clause, which is limited to dealing with matters as they arise during the carrying out of the contract. Most of the clauses in the older cases in the books were of that character. But I think it is also perfectly well settled in the law of Scotland that there is nothing wrong in having a general arbitration clause, which may give to the determination of arbiters everything which can be decided either in respect of the carrying out of the contract or in respect of the breach thereof. . . . Now, I have no doubt that on a proper construction of Article

Fourteen here it is one of that class of clauses, that is to say, it is not a mere executory clause, but it is a general clause which refers to an arbiter all questions which may properly arise either upon the import and meaning or upon the carrying out of the contract."

(2) Assessing damages

12–65   An arbiter has no power under an arbitration clause to assess damages unless power to do so is conferred expressly. This point was established by the House of Lords in *Blaikies* v. *Aberdeen Railway Co.* (1852) 1 Paterson's App. 119; 15 D. (H.L.) 20, and was held to be settled law in later decisions of the Court of Session including *Mackay & Son* v. *Leven Police Commissioners* (1893) 20 R. 1093:

M. & Son entered into a contract for the execution of water-works for the town of Leven. The contract included an arbitration clause.

M. & Son claimed from the Police Commissioners (i) £1,470 17s.3d. as the balance due by the Commissioners for the work done under the contract and (ii) £3,255 4s. for loss and damage sustained by M. & Son.

M. & Son brought an action concluding for declarator that the Police Commissioners were bound to join in submitting both claims to the arbiter named in the arbitration clause.

Held that the second claim did not fall within the arbitration clause and that the Police Commissioners were therefore not bound to submit that claim to the arbiter.

It was admitted that the first claim fell within the arbitration clause and the court sisted the action in order that that claim might be submitted to the arbiter.

12–66   An arbitration clause may be so worded as to confer on the arbiter power to decide the question whether liability for damages has been incurred. Assessment of the damages would still remain a matter for the court unless express power to assess the damages were also conferred on the arbiter.

(3) Incorporation into subcontract

12–67   It is common to find, *e.g.* in building contracts, an arbitration clause incorporated, along with other clauses, from a main contract into a subcontract. The effect of a simple incorporation is to make the arbiter's decision on a dispute between the employer and the main contractor binding on the subcontractor but the clause will not extend to disputes between the main contractor and the subcontractor: special provision to that effect would be required.

12–68   An instance is *Goodwins, Jardine & Co. Ltd.* v. *Brand & Son* (1905) 7 F. 995:

B. & Son were the general contractors with the Caledonian Railway Company for the formation of portions of the Glasgow Central Railway. B. & Son, since they did not do bridge work themselves, entered into a subcontract with G. Ltd. for the bridge work.

The subcontract provided that the work was to be executed according to plans and specifications which formed part of the general contract between the Caledonian Railway Company and B. & Son. One of these specifications was an arbitration clause.

The bridge work was made and part of the price was paid, but there was a dispute as to the balance.

In an action by G. Ltd. against B. & Son for this balance, B. & Son pleaded that the claim should be submitted to arbitration and the action sisted until the arbiter had given his decision.

Held that the arbitration clause was not incorporated in the subcontract in relation to matters which concerned only the rights *inter se* ("between themselves") of B. & Son and G. Ltd.

Lord President Dunedin said (at p. 1000): "For some purposes there is no doubt that the arbitration clause is incorporated. It is, I think, quite clear that for anything in dispute between the Brands and the Caledonian Railway Company the arbitration clause has effect, and the result arrived at under that arbitration clause is binding on the pursuers. In that respect it is just like all the other clauses in the specification. But the point is not whether it is incorporated at all, but whether it is incorporated in regard to another matter altogether, namely, the dispute about prices between the pursuers and the defenders. That is a matter outside the relations of the defenders and the Caledonian Railway Company. What is binding on the one is not binding on the other. . . . I think the contract incorporated was the contract so far as it existed between the principal contractor and the employer—that is to say, the Brands and the Railway Company—but that you cannot over and above cut out of the provisions of that contract one clause and make it apply *mutatis mutandis*[4] to the rights *inter se* of the principal contractor and the subcontractor—that is, the pursuers and the defenders—in a matter in which the employer never had and never can have any concern."

(4) Termination of the main contract

Doubt can arise as to whether an arbitration clause is still operative where the question between the parties is whether the main contract itself of which the arbitration clause forms part has been terminated. Decided cases show that an arbitration clause may be sufficiently wide as to remain operative in such a situation:

(a) *Repudiation of the main contract*

The case of *Sanderson & Son* v. *Armour & Co. Ltd.*, 1922 S.C. (H.L.) 117, involved an alleged repudiation of the main contract:

S. & Son purchased from A. Ltd. a quantity of American eggs which were to be delivered in three instalments. On delivery of the first instalment S. & Son found half of the eggs to be unmerchantable and the remainder to be of inferior quality. On the arrival of the second instalment they proposed to make an examination of the eggs before taking delivery, but A. Ltd. refused to allow an examination. S & Son then rescinded the contract on the ground that it had been repudiated by A. Ltd., and brought an action of damages against A. Ltd.

In defence A. Ltd. pleaded that the dispute fell to be referred to arbitration under a clause in the contract which provided: "Any dispute on this contract to be settled by arbitration in the usual way."

---

[4] "with the necessary changes having been made," *i.e.* "in corresponding terms."

Held that the question of whether the contract had been repudiated was a question for the arbiter to decide, and the procedure was therefore sisted to enable the dispute to be referred to arbitration.

The Court of Session (1921 S.C. 18) had also held that the dispute fell to be referred to arbitration but on the ground that S. & Son's allegations, if proved, would not have amounted to a repudiation of the contract as a whole by A. Ltd.

(b) *Supervening impossibility of performance of the main contract*

12–71   *James Scott & Sons Ltd.* v. *Del Sel*, 1923 S.C. (H.L.) 37; 1922 S.C. 592, was concerned with contracts which became in part impossible to perform on account of the 1914-18 war:

By 27 contracts made in 1917 jute merchants in Dundee agreed to sell and to ship from Calcutta to Buenos Aires 2,800 bales of jute. Each contract contained provisions relating to late and short shipment attributable to war or "any other unforeseen circumstances," and also an arbitration clause in the following terms: "Any dispute that may arise under this contract to be settled by arbitration in Dundee."

Before all the bales had been shipped, the further export of jute from India to the Argentine was prohibited by an Order in Council of the Governor-General of India. The sellers then intimated to the purchasers that they held the contracts cancelled on the ground that further performance had become impossible.

A controversy arose between the parties, and the purchasers invoked the arbitration clause.

The sellers sought to prevent the arbitration from proceeding, on the ground that the question whether the contracts had been brought to an end was not a dispute arising under the contracts: they argued that the contracts, and with them the arbitration clauses, had been terminated by the Order in Council.

Held on an interpretation of the contracts that the question was a dispute arising under the contracts and that it therefore fell to be decided by arbitration.

Because of the express provisions in the contracts as to war and other unforeseen circumstances the case was not one which raised the general doctrine of frustration.

(c) *Frustration of the main contract*

12–72   A case which raised the general doctrine of frustration was *Charles Mauritzen Ltd.* v. *Baltic Shipping Co.*, 1948 S.C. 646 (O.H.):

British merchants chartered a Polish ship under a charterparty which provided that the ship should load a cargo of salt for the Faroe Islands at a Spanish port. The charterparty contained a provision that "any dispute arising under this charter" should be referred to arbitration.

On the ship's arrival at the Spanish port the port authorities would not allow loading without a certificate that the ship was running in British service.

The charterers' London agents intimated this to the shipowners' London agents, and also obtained from the Spanish authorities permission for the loading.

Meantime the shipowners' agents, treating the intimation as a claim that the charterparty had been frustrated, had accepted other employment for the ship.

The charterers brought an action of damages for breach of contract.

The shipowners averred that there had been frustration and pleaded the arbitration clause. The charterers contended that this defence was irrelevant since, if there had been frustration, the whole contract including the arbitration clause had been brought to an end.

Held that the question between the parties was a dispute arising under the charterparty and had therefore to be referred to arbitration; and action *sisted*.

The Lord Ordinary (Blades), relying on the English case *Heyman* v. *Darwins Ltd.* [1942] A.C. 356 and on *James Scott & Sons Ltd.* v. *Del Sel* as authorities, said (at p. 650):

"The clause in this charter-party is framed in wide and general terms. . . . The parties are at one in asserting that they entered into a binding contract, there was partial performance of the charter, and now differences have arisen between the parties as to whether the defenders are liable to the pursuers for breach of the charter-party or whether the defenders are discharged from further performance. In my opinion, these are differences which the parties have chosen to refer to arbitration, and, there being no good reason to the contrary, to arbitration they should go."

(5) Date of the arbitration agreement

The agreement to refer to arbitration dates from the main contract and not merely from the submission which is commonly entered into at the time when a dispute has arisen. This point arose in *Clydebank District Council* v. *Clink*, 1977 S.C. 147, in relation to the commencement of section 3 of the Administration of Justice (Scotland) Act 1972.

The section introduced a power enabling an arbiter to state a case for the opinion of the Court of Session on any question of law and imposed a duty on him to do so if so directed by the Court of Session (see 12–10, above). The statutory provision was declared not to be applicable to "an agreement to refer to arbitration made before the commencement" of the Act. The date of commencement fixed for section 3 of the Act was April 2, 1973 (S.I. 1973 No. 339).

A local authority had entered into two building contracts in 1966 and 1968 respectively for the erection of houses in a housing scheme. Each contract incorporated the customary arbitration clause.

Disputes arose, an arbiter was appointed, and in March 1974 the parties to the contracts entered into a probative deed of submission identifying their disputes. The arbiter issued a proposed award in June 1976.

The local authority then applied to the arbiter for a case to be stated by him for the opinion of the Court of Session on a question of law. The arbiter rejected that request, and the local authority applied to the Court of Session for an order to direct the arbiter to state a case.

Held that the "agreement to refer to arbitration" was contained in the contracts of 1966 and 1968, and was therefore not one to which the

statutory provision applied. The deed of submission was regarded a
"purely executorial of the agreement on which it proceeded" (*per* Lor
President Emslie at p. 153).

(d) The Duration of the Submission

12–74   The duration of the submission is a matter for the parties to decide.

12–75   Where the submission is a formal deed, it is usual for the arbiter to b
given power to decide the dispute "between this and the . . . day of . .
next to come." If the blanks are not filled up, the submission is regarde
as lasting (on the authority of Lord Bankton as applied in *Earl o
Dunmore* v. *McInturner* (1829) 7 S. 595) for a year and a day.

12–76   Where there is no reference to any time-limit the submission last
for the 20-year prescriptive period.

12–77   Where the submission expressly fixes a time-limit without conferrin
on the arbiter power to extend the time, the submission automaticall
falls on the expiry of the specified time, unless the parties by expres
agreement or by their actings extend its duration.

12–78   It is usual practice to confer on the arbiter a power of "prorogation
(*i.e.* a power to extend the duration of the submission). Such a powe
requires to be exercised before the fixed time has expired and before th
submission has devolved on the oversman. An arbiter has no implie
power of prorogation, except, possibly,[5] in ancillary submissions.

12–79   A case which illustrates several of these points is *Paul* v. *Henderso
(1867) 5 M. 613:

P. had raised against H. an action for count and reckoning for hi
intromissions, as P.'s factor, with the rents of certain houses i
Linlithgow. Instead of proceeding with the action, the parties agreed t
submit the matter to the Accountant of Court as sole arbiter. The sub
mission included a blank time-limit clause and conferred on the arbite
power to prorogate the submission. It bore the date June 29, 1857.

After a great deal of procedure the arbiter finally issued his decree
arbitral on June 27, 1863.

P. then contended that by that date the arbiter's jurisdiction had falle
as a result of his not having duly exercised the power of prorogatio
conferred on him.

The only prorogation was that dated June 29, 1859, by which the arbite
had extended the duration of the submission to June 29, 1860. Althoug
P. had had ample opportunity to ascertain that fact, he had gone on wit
his proof without objection.

Held that the submission, though it would otherwise have lapsed on th
expiry of a year and a day without prorogation by the arbiter, had bee
kept in force *rebus ipsis et factis* ("by the circumstances themselves an
the actings (of the parties)").

12–80   In the absence of agreement to the contrary a submission terminate
on the death of either of the parties. It also necessarily terminates on th
death of the arbiter.

12–81   A submission also falls if the particular form of arbitration contem
plated by the parties becomes impossible, as in *Graham* v. *Mill* (1904) 6 F

---

[5] Irons and Melville, *Law of Arbitration in Scotland*, p. 135.

886 where in a question between an outgoing tenant of a farm and the incoming tenant the phrase "arbitration in common form" was held to mean a valuation by skilled persons who had personally inspected the subjects, and this had become impossible on account of the subjects having been consumed and used.

IV ARBITERS AND OVERSMEN

The parties to a dispute may agree on the nomination of a sole arbiter (e.g. as in *Paul* v. *Henderson* (12–79, above)).

Since, however, it is quite possible that the parties, if they are already in disagreement or at least have opposing interests, may fail to agree on the choice of a sole arbiter, it is common for a dispute to be referred to two arbiters, one nominated by each party. In such a situation it is appropriate to have an oversman whose jurisdiction will come into operation only if the two arbiters disagree. The oversman may be nominated by the parties, but the more usual practice is for him to be nominated by the two arbiters.

In English law the terms corresponding to "arbiter" and "oversman" are respectively "arbitrator" and "umpire."

This fourth part of the chapter deals first with:

(a) the relationship between arbiters and oversman,

and then with matters which relate to both arbiters and oversmen:

(b) appointment;
(c) disqualification; and
(d) remuneration.

The powers and duties of arbiters and oversmen can be gathered from Part V, below ("Conduct of the Arbitration").

(a) The Relationship between Arbiters and Oversman

The jurisdiction of the oversman is described as an "ulterior" or "conditional" jurisdiction: the matter must first be considered by the arbiters, and it is only if the arbiters disagree that the jurisdiction of the oversman comes into operation.

"Devolution" is the term used to denote the step by which the submission passes from the arbiters to the oversman.

It is a common and prudent practice for arbiters who have power to appoint an oversman to do so at the commencement of the arbitration. This avoids the difficulty which may otherwise possibly arise at a later stage when the arbiters, having failed to agree on the subject-matter submitted to them, fail also to agree on the selection of the oversman. This initial appointment of the oversman does not amount to devolution:

Brysson v. *Mitchell* (1823) 2 S. 382: B. and M. entered into a building contract and agreed that all disputes should be settled by two arbiters who had power to appoint an oversman.

Before proceeding with an arbitration, the arbiters named an oversman.

The arbiters issued a decree-arbitral against B.

B. raised an action of reduction on the ground that since the arbiters had appointed an oversman they were no longer competent to give a decision.

Held that the oversman had been correctly named by the arbiters, but that as the arbiters had not differed in opinion it was their decision which prevailed, there having been no devolution on the oversman.

12–91   An advantage of an initial appointment of the oversman is that he may sit in at the proceedings before the arbiters and hear the evidence of the witnesses and the arguments of the parties and so be in a position to give a decision without delay should the arbiters disagree. An illustration is *Crawford* v. *Paterson* (1858) 20 D. 488:

12–92   C. was the tenant of a farm owned by P. Disputes about the repair of fences and water embankments were submitted to two farmers as arbiters or in the event of their disagreeing in opinion to an oversman to be appointed by them.

The arbiters nominated the oversman at an early stage in the proceedings. He inspected the farm along with the arbiters, was present at the subsequent proof, and then heard the arguments put to the arbiters by agents for the parties.

The arbiters differed in opinion and referred the matters in dispute to the oversman.

The oversman issued a draft decree-arbitral, and C. requested to be heard by him. The oversman refused this request, and pronounced his final decree-arbitral.

Held that the fact that the oversman had taken part in the proceedings throughout did not invalidate the arbitration or disqualify the oversman, and that the parties were not entitled to be reheard.

C.'s action of reduction was therefore unsuccessful.

12–93   In selecting the oversman, arbiters must exercise a judicial discretion: they must not make the selection by drawing lots unless they have first decided that all the persons from whom the choice is thus to be made are fit persons for the appointment:

12–94   *Smith* v. *Liverpool and London and Globe Insurance Co.* (1887) 14 R. 931: S., a shoemaker, incurred a loss of stock in a fire and made claims under an insurance policy.

The claims were referred by S. and the insurance company to two arbiters mutually chosen and in case they differed to an oversman to be chosen by the arbiters before the arbitration proceedings began.

One arbiter suggested Lyon as oversman, and the other arbiter suggested Dowell. Both arbiters stated that they had no objection to either Lyon or Dowell, but each preferred his own nominee. To resolve the difficulty the arbiters drew lots and Lyon was nominated.

The arbiters differed in opinion, and so the submission devolved on Lyon.

S. brought an action of reduction of the deed nominating Lyon and of his decree-arbitral on the grounds (i) that Lyon's nomination had been decided by chance and not by choice and that all that had followed it should be set aside and (ii) that Lyon was personally disqualified because he held shares in the insurance company.

Held that this was not a case in which there had been no choice made by the arbiters.

Lord President Inglis said (at p. 937): "It was represented to us by counsel for the pursuer that by the method thus pursued there was a substitution of chance for choice. . . . But I do not think it can be said there was no choice. There was in point of fact a *delectus*,[6] not of one person but of two. Both arbiters were agreed that both the persons suggested by them were equally eligible as oversmen. . . . The element of chance does come in, but to a very limited extent. What was submitted to chance was the choice between two persons acknowledged to be both equally suitable. That is not a good objection to a nomination."

(The court gave decree of reduction on ground (ii).)

Devolution usually takes the form of a minute of devolution signed by the arbiters. This minute need not be a formal deed, at least in farm valuations (*Gibson* v. *Fotheringham*, 1914 S.C. 987 (12–15, above)). In the same case it was taken as having been settled by earlier cases that no written devolution is necessary provided the oversman has been appointed in writing and there is evidence that the arbiters have applied their minds to the subject of reference and have differed in opinion.

Where arbiters have power to make part or interim awards, it is open to them to make a partial devolution on the oversman. Thus in *Gibson* v. *Fotheringham* where the arbiters had power to pronounce "decrees arbitral, interim or final," it was competent for them partially to devolve the subject-matter of the reference, while retaining in their own hands the decision of claims which they had not at that time considered and which required further inquiry (such as valuation at a later date).

Where there is a partial devolution care must be taken to avoid a failure to exhaust the submission, which would invalidate the award:

Runciman v. *Craigie* (1831) 9 S. 629: Arbiters issued notes of their opinions in a document which was entitled "joint report and interim decree" and which concluded with a clause devolving on the oversman the "determination of these points on which we have differed."

The oversman's award was confined to the points of difference.

Held that the arbiter's notes were not valid as a decree arbitral and that the oversman's decree arbitral, since it decided only part of the subject-matter, could not stand by itself; and reduction *granted*.

(b) Appointment

Statutory provisions to be noted here are:

(i) the Arbitration (Scotland) Act 1894; and
(ii) section 17 of the Law Reform (Miscellaneous Provisions) (Scotland) Act 1980.

(i) *The Arbitration (Scotland) Act 1894*

This Act was passed mainly to remedy two deficiencies which had become apparent in the common law.

---

[5] "choice."

(1) Deficiencies in the common law

(a) *Unnamed arbiter*

12–101   It was a principle of the common law that the appointment of an arbiter involved *delectus personae* ("choice of person"). As a result the parties had to make a deliberate selection of a named individual and not merely agree that the arbiter would be the holder of a particular office for the time being or would be named by another person. The courts would not, as a general rule, enforce an arbitration agreement in which the arbiter was not named. There were some exceptions to the general rule (*e.g.* the arbitration agreement would be enforceable if the arbitration was necessary for the purpose of giving effect to another contract).

12–102   The common law had the unsatisfactory effect of bringing before the courts matters which the parties had really intended should be settled by arbitration.

12–103   The defect was particularly noticeable in connection with ancillary arbitrations, as shown in *Tancred, Arrol & Co.* v. *Steel Co. of Scotland Ltd.* (1890) 17 R. (H.L.) 31; (1887) 15 R. 215:

12–104   An arbitration clause included in a contract for the building of the Forth Railway Bridge stated that any dispute that might arise as to the meaning of the contract was to be referred to "the engineer of the Forth Bridge Railway Company for the time being."

Held that the clause was ineffectual because of the absence of *delectus personae*.

Lord Watson said (at p. 36): "It has been settled by a uniform course of judicial decisions, extending over nearly a century, that according to the law of Scotland an agreement to refer future disputes, if and when they shall arise, to the person who shall then be the holder of a certain office is not binding."

(b) *No implied power to appoint oversman*

12–105   At common law where there was a reference to two arbiters, one appointed by each side, the two arbiters had no implied power to appoint an oversman: where the arbiters failed to agree, the result was deadlock (*Cochrane* v. *Guthrie* (1861) 23 D. 865 and *Merry and Cunninghame* v. *Brown* (1863) 1 M. (H.L.) 14; (1860) 22 D. 1148—both cases relating to an arbitration clause in a mineral lease referring matters in dispute to two persons mutually chosen).

(2) The provisions of the Act

12–106   An agreement to refer to arbitration is no longer invalid or ineffectual merely because the reference is to a person not named, or to a person to be named by another person, or to a person merely described as the holder for the time being of any office or appointment (s. 1).

12–107   Where there is an agreement to refer to a single arbiter and one of the parties refuses to concur in the nomination and there is no operative provision for carrying out the reference, then any party to the agreement may apply to the court for an arbiter to be appointed by the court. The arbiter so appointed has the same powers as if he had been duly nominated by all the parties (s. 2).

Where there is an agreement to refer to two arbiters and one of the parties refuses to name an arbiter and there is no operative provision for carrying out the reference, then the other party may apply to the court for an arbiter to be appointed by the court. The arbiter so appointed has the same powers as if he had been duly nominated by the party refusing (s. 3).

Unless the agreement to refer provides otherwise, arbiters have power to name an oversman on whom the reference is to be devolved in the event of their differing in opinion. If the arbiters fail to agree in the nomination of an oversman, any party to the agreement may apply to the court for an oversman to be appointed (s. 4).

The meaning of "the court" in these provisions is normally the sheriff court or the Outer House of the Court of Session, but if any arbiter appointed is a Court of Session judge or if by the terms of the agreement to refer to arbitration an arbiter or oversman to be appointed must be a Court of Session judge, "the court" means the Inner House of the Court of Session (s. 6, as amended by Law Reform (Miscellaneous Provisions) (Scotland) Act 1980, s. 17(4)).

(3) Applications under the Act

The procedure contemplated by the Act for the exercise of the court's powers of nomination of arbiters and oversmen is of a summary nature. It is suitable for the simple situation where an arbitration is being hindered by the refusal of one of the parties to concur in nominating or to nominate an arbiter.

It can, however, happen that other matters will require to be decided before the court can exercise a power under the Act. To some extent such other matters can appropriately be decided by the court in the course of an application under the Act of 1894. Where, on the other hand, complex questions are involved, the summary procedure is inappropriate and the questions must be decided in an ordinary action. The following are two illustrations:

(a) *Cooper & Co.* v. *Jessop Brothers* (1906) 8 F. 714: The case concerned sales of shoddy by J. in Yorkshire to C. in Glasgow. "Contract-notes" contained the condition: "Any dispute arising from this contract to be settled by arbitration here in the usual way."

Certain disputes arose concerning the quality of the shoddy supplied. C. nominated an arbiter, J. refused to do so, and C. applied to the court under section 3 of the Act of 1894 craving the court to appoint an arbiter on behalf of J.

C. averred that the contracts had been made in Glasgow and that the usual way of arbitration in the shoddy trade in Glasgow was for each party to nominate an arbiter and for these arbiters to appoint an oversman.

J. averred (i) that there had been no *consensus in idem* ("agreement"), (ii) that, if there was a contract, it was to be found in correspondence and not in the "contract-notes" containing the arbitration clause and it had been made in Yorkshire, and (iii) that there was no shoddy trade in Glasgow and no practice in the shoddy trade either in Glasgow or in Yorkshire with regard to arbitration.

Held that the questions raised in the case could not competently be dealt with in a petition under section 3 of the Act; and process *sisted* in order that they might be decided in an ordinary action.

Lord Low said (at p. 723): "The procedure authorised by the Act was intended to be of a summary nature, and . . . it was not contemplated that an application under the Act should be used for the determination of questions requiring investigation and procedure appropriate to an action in the ordinary Courts."

12–114   (b) *United Creameries Co. Ltd. v. Boyd & Co.,* 1912 S.C. 617: A contract for the sale of oil by B. & Co. to U. Ltd. contained the clause "Arbitration.—Disputes to be settled by arbitration in Glasgow."

A dispute arose. U. Ltd. nominated an arbiter, but B. & Co. refused to do so, and U. Ltd. presented a petition under the Act of 1894 craving the court to appoint an arbiter. U. Ltd. averred that, by a custom of the oil trade in Glasgow, where a contract provided for "arbitration in Glasgow," each party nominated one arbiter and the arbiters named an oversman.

Held that the summary procedure of the Act was inappropriate: an ordinary action was required for proof of the alleged custom.

(4) Shortcomings of the Act

12–115   (a) The court has no power to appoint an arbiter unless the parties have agreed to refer to a single arbiter or to two arbiters:

McMillan & Son Ltd. v. Rowan & Co. (1903) 5 F. 317: A contract relating to the construction by R. & Co. of machinery for M. Ltd. contained a clause referring all disputes "to arbitration."

M. Ltd. made a claim against R. & Co. for damages for delay. R. & Co. resisted the claim and declined arbitration. M. Ltd. presented a petition to the court under the Act of 1894.

Held that as there was neither an agreement to refer to a single arbiter nor an agreement to refer to two arbiters, neither section 2 nor section 3 of the Act applied, and that the court had therefore no power to appoint an arbiter.

12–116   (b) The Act has no provision corresponding to what is now section 6 of the Arbitration Act 1950, which is to the effect that in English arbitrations the reference is to be deemed to be to a single arbitrator if no other mode of reference is provided. The absence of such a provision in Scots law was regretted by Lord McLaren in *Douglas & Co. v. Stiven* (1900) 2 F. 575:

D. & Co. sold a quantity of wood goods to S. under a contract which provided that disputes were to be "referred to arbitration in the customary manner of the timber trade."

A dispute arose. D. & Co. raised an action for payment of the price. S. pleaded the arbitration clause and proved that the most usual mode of arbitration in the timber trade was by a reference to two arbiters, one chosen by each party, and by an oversman appointed by the two arbiters.

The court *found* that the parties had had that mode in view, that the reference was therefore equivalent to a reference to unnamed arbiters and was valid under section 1 of the Act of 1894.

With reference to the Arbitration Act 1889, Lord McLaren said (at p. 582): "This question could hardly have arisen if the contract had been made in England, because in the relative English Arbitration Act there is a section to the effect that where no particular mode of arbitration is provided, the reference shall be understood to be to a single arbitrator. Why this useful provision of the English Arbitration Act was not extended to Scotland I have difficulty in understanding."

(c) The Act does not provide a remedy for the situation where the clause of reference names an arbiter and he refuses to act:

British Westinghouse Electric and Manufacturing Co. Ltd. v. *Provost, &c., of Aberdeen* (1906) 14 S.L.T. 391 (O.H.): B. Ltd. entered into a contract with the Town Council of Aberdeen to supply an engine for the council's electricity works at Dee Village.

A clause in the contract provided that disputes were to be submitted to William Chamen, electrical engineer for the time being to the Town Council of Glasgow, whom failing to the electrical engineer for the time being.

A dispute arose, and B. Ltd. requested in the first instance William Chamen, and then W. W. Leckie, the electrical engineer for the time being, to accept the office of arbiter.

Both refused to act, and B. Ltd. applied for an appointment to be made by the court under section 2 of the Act of 1894.

Petition *refused* because it was not warranted by the section upon which it professed to be based.

Lord Dundas said (at p. 391): "It is to be remembered that the jurisdiction of the Court under the Act can only be exercised when the specific condition of matters prescribed in the Act exists. . . . It can not, in my judgment, be properly said that the parties had or have any 'agreement to refer to a single arbiter,' within the meaning of the section, which, as I think, plainly means an arbiter unnamed. What the parties agreed to was to refer to a single arbiter, whom they named, whom failing, to an arbiter whom they sufficiently indicated by description, looking to the remedial provision contained in section 1. In order to bring this petition within the scope of section 2, it would, I apprehend, be necessary to read into the submission clause some further words such as, 'Whom failing, to an arbiter to be named by the parties'—an insertion which would not be in accordance with recognised principles of construction."

(ii) *Section 17 of the Law Reform (Miscellaneous Provisions) (Scotland) Act 1980*

This section enables a Court of Session judge, if in all the circumstances he thinks fit, to accept appointment as arbiter or as oversman under an arbitration agreement where the dispute appears to him to be of a commercial character. It is a condition of his accepting appointment that the Lord President of the Court of Session has informed him that, having regard to the state of business in that court, he can be made available to do so.

The fees for the judge's services as arbiter or oversman are paid into public funds and are of an amount fixed by statutory instrument. The fees are at present £500 on appointment plus £500 for each additional day of the hearing (Appointment of Judges as Arbiters (Fees) (Scotland) Order 1980 (S.I. 1980 No. 1823)).

(c) Disqualification

12–120 The office of arbiter "is essentially of a judicial character, and requires complete impartiality as one of its inherent attributes. Wherever, therefore, an arbiter is affected by any circumstances having a plain practical tendency to bias him in favour of one of the parties, and so to destroy his impartiality, his acting as arbiter will be open to challenge" (Bell, *op. cit.*, p. 130). The same principle applies to the office of oversman.

12–121 An instance of a successful challenge of an award on the ground of an arbiter's interest is *Sellar* v. *Highland Railway Co.*, 1919 S.C. (H.L.) 19; 1918 S.C. 838:

In an arbitration between S., the owner of certain fishings, and a railway company, the arbiters disagreed, and the reference devolved upon the oversman.

After the oversman had issued proposed findings, S. discovered that the arbiter appointed by the railway company held a small quantity of ordinary stock in the company—a fact not known to the directors personally at the time of the appointment.

S. notified the company that he would not regard himself as bound by the award.

Later the oversman issued his final award, and S. brought an action for reduction of the award on the ground of the arbiter's disqualification.

Held that the arbiter's holding of stock was sufficient to disqualify him and that his disqualification vitiated the oversman's award, which therefore fell to be reduced.

12–122 A person who is originally qualified to act as arbiter may become disqualified during the course of a contract:

Magistrates of Edinburgh v. *Lownie* (1903) 5 F. 711: In 1897 the magistrates of Edinburgh entered into a contract with L., a builder, for the mason work of Colinton Mains Hospital. The contract provided that disputes were to be referred to Ormiston, an Edinburgh surveyor.

In May 1898 a question arose under the contract, and was disposed of by Ormiston as arbiter.

In November 1898 Ormiston was elected Dean of Guild and became *ex officio* ("by virtue of his office") a member of the town council.

Another question arose under the contract in July 1902, and L. called upon Ormiston to act as arbiter. The town council craved the court to interdict Ormiston from proceeding with the arbitration on the ground that he was disqualified by virtue of being Dean of Guild and so a member of one of the parties to the dispute.

In November 1902 Ormiston ceased to be Dean of Guild and consequently also ceased to be a member of the town council.

Held that (1) Ormiston's election to the office of Dean of Guild disqualified him from acting as arbiter, (2) this disqualification might be pleaded by the town council, and (3) the disqualification was not removed by Ormiston's ceasing to hold the office of Dean of Guild.

Lord President Kinross said (at p. 714): "It is not suggested . . . that Mr Ormiston would consciously allow his judgment in regard to the question submitted to be affected by his connection with the Town-Council, but what we have to do is to apply the general rule irrespective of the character of particular individuals. That rule is that a man cannot be judge in his own cause, or in the cause of a body of which he is a member. . . . A Dean of Guild might in that capacity or in his capacity of a member of the council acquire information or become imbued with views as to this contract and as to the buildings to which it relates—information or views from the inside—which it would not be desirable that he should have when he came to act as arbiter between parties who should be at arm's length. He might well form views as to this contract while acting as a unit of one of the parties to it which might unconsciously affect his judgment as arbiter. It would, in my view, be contrary to the fundamental rule to which I have referred to allow a party in such a position to act as arbiter."

The mere existence of a business relationship between the arbiter and one of the parties is not a disqualification:

Johnson v. *Lamb*, 1981 S.L.T. 300 (O.H.): J. had entered into a contract with Alexander Morrison (Builders) Ltd. ("M. Ltd.") for the erection of a bungalow. A dispute arose and was submitted to L., as arbiter.

After L. had issued his decree-arbitral, J. raised an action of reduction, averring that, unknown to him at the time when he had entered into the submission, L. was acting as architect for Ross and Cromarty District Council in a school building contract in which M. Ltd. were the main contractors.

Held that the "regular business contact" which J. averred to have resulted from this relationship between L. and M. Ltd. was not sufficient to disqualify L. from acting as arbiter in the dispute between J. and M. Ltd., because (i) the relationship had nothing to do with the subject-matter of the arbitration, (ii) it was not suggested that L. had any interest whatever in the outcome of the arbitration, and (iii) the relationship was not one in which L. and M. Ltd. had a common interest since L. was being employed by the district council in that relationship and not by M. Ltd.

Where the arbiter's interest is known, it may be waived by the agreement of both parties and it will then be no disqualification. Even a reference to one of the parties has been held valid:

Buchan v. *Melville* (1902) 4 F. 620: B. entered into a contract to execute the mason-work of two houses belonging to M., who was an architect. The contract included an arbitration clause providing that any dispute was to be referred to M., whose decision would be final and binding on the parties.

B. raised an action against M. for payment for the work, and M. stated the preliminary plea that the action was excluded by the arbitration clause.

Held that the arbitration clause was binding, and cause *sisted* to allow M. to issue his award.

Lord President Kinross said (at p. 623): "I think the conclusion to be deduced from the authorities is, that where an arbiter has an interest in the subject of the reference well known to the parties before they enter into the submission, the award is good notwithstanding this interest; in other words, that it is only a concealed or unknown interest which invalidates an award. If therefore a person chooses to make another with whom he is contracting the final judge of all questions which may arise between them under the contract, it is difficult to see any reason of public policy which should lead to effect being refused to such a contract."

12–126   In construction contracts it is common for the parties to agree that the arbiter should be the employer's engineer or architect. Though such a person has no immediate financial interest in the matter in dispute, he has an indirect interest and he may also be affected, perhaps unconsciously by the viewpoint of the employer. The parties' agreement, however removes the disqualification which would otherwise arise from his office The following are some instances:

12–127   (i) *Scott* v. *Carluke Local Authority* (1879) 6 R. 616: In a contrac for the execution of water-works for a local authority the engineer of the local authority was appointed arbiter.

During the progress of the work he made a report to the local authority complaining in strong terms of the manner in which the work was being executed by the contractor.

Held that the engineer was not disqualified from acting as arbiter.

12–128   (ii) *Mackay* v. *Parochial Board of Barry* (1883) 10 R. 1046: A contrac for the execution of water-works for a local authority named the loca authority's engineer as arbiter.

During the execution of the work he complained that some of the contractor's materials were disconform to contract. He also measured the work and brought out as due to the contractor for extra work a sum fa below what the contractor claimed.

Held that the engineer was not disqualified from acting as arbiter.

(On this case, see also 12–63, above.)

12–129   (iii) *Adams* v. *Great North of Scotland Railway Co.* (1889) 16 R. 84: (affirmed on other points (1890) 18 R. (H.L.) 1): A contract for the making of a railway included an arbitration clause providing that a named person should not be disqualified from acting as arbiter by being o becoming consulting engineer to the railway company.

As consulting engineer that person revised the specifications and schedules upon which the work in dispute was performed.

Held that he was not barred from acting as arbiter.

12–130   (iv) *Halliday* v. *Duke of Hamilton's Trustees* (1903) 5 F. 800: A contract for the construction of a pier named the employers' engineer a arbiter.

After the pier had been built a question arose as to whether a sum fo extra work was due to the contractor. The engineer, in answer to a request by the employers, wrote letters to them giving a detailed opinio to the effect that the greater part of the sum in question was not due to the contractor.

Held that the engineer had not disqualified himself from acting a arbiter.

Lord Justice-Clerk J.H.A. Macdonald said (at p. 808): "In a case where the engineer is named as arbiter, and the contractor comes forward with a claim for a sum of money as being due to him, it is the most natural thing possible for the employers to inquire of their engineer what view he takes of the work done by the contractor and the account rendered by him, because if the engineers are satisfied that the claim is proper, there will not be any need for arbitration, and an engineer who expresses a general opinion, not ultroneously but in answer to his employers, cannot I think be excluded on that account from acting as arbiter. If the employers proceed to arbitration, then the engineer, as arbiter, must receive all competent evidence which the contractor thinks proper to bring before him and give an honest opinion upon it. The fact that he has expressed an opinion as an engineer before receiving the evidence does not prevent him from afterwards applying his mind judicially to the questions at issue in the light of the evidence adduced."

(v) *Scott* v. *Gerrard*, 1916 S.C. 793: A contract for the execution of the joiner work in connection with the building of a church included an arbitration referring disputes to the architect.

After some work had been done the architect declared the contract at an end because of the contractors' delay.

The contractors brought an action against the building committee of the church for payment maintaining that the architect was disqualified from acting as arbiter because any delay in the execution of the work had been due, in part at least, to the fault of the architect and because he had exhibited hostility towards them. They averred that the architect had said that he would "make it hot for them" meaning that he would use his position as architect to their detriment.

Held that there were no averments relevant to infer disqualification of the architect from acting as arbiter.

Lord Salvesen said (at p. 806): "It is not, according to our law, considered against public policy to enforce a clause of reference, though the reference be to the servant or agent of the building owner. It is also alleged by the pursuers that, on one occasion, the architect said that he 'would make it hot for them'; but I should be slow to assume that a casual expression of this kind, possibly uttered in the heat of a discussion, would indicate such a bias as would prevent the architect from acting judicially (so far as his position permits of his doing so) when a reference fell to be made to him. What is to my mind of far more importance is that the cause of the disputes is alleged to have been the personal fault of the architect; but that, according to our decisions, is not sufficient to withdraw from him the jurisdiction which the parties have chosen to confer. I cannot help saying that I think that, in this respect, the law of England is very much more satisfactory than our own. . . . Unfortunately . . . we have no Arbitration Act in Scotland which vests us with any discretion. Unless the arbiter has actually disqualified himself, it is not relevant to consider whether a dispute arises from his own arbitrary or unreasonable conduct, and the Court has no power to extricate the contractor from the difficulties which he has brought upon himself by consenting to be bound by the decision of a person in whom he is presumed to have reposed implicit confidence; but who, in fact, is generally imposed upon him as a condition of his getting the work."

These cases show that the employer's engineer or architect, if agreed to in the arbitration clause, is unlikely to be held to be disqualified from acting as arbiter. If, however, he has placed himself in such a position as to be unable to act judicially in a dispute, he is disqualified from acting as arbiter; an illustration is *Dickson* v. *Grant and Others* (1870) 8 M. 566:

12–133   D., a joiner, contracted with the trustees of a church to execute certain alterations and repairs on the church. A clause of the contract provided that any dispute was to be referred to Coyne, the architect of the works, whose decision was to be final and binding on the parties.

Disputes arose and Coyne often expressed opinions adverse to D. in regard to them.

D. raised an action against the trustees for reduction of the contract or at least of the clause of reference and also for payment of sums which he alleged were due to him by the trustees for joiner work.

The Lord Ordinary allowed a proof and in the course of it Coyne was called as a witness by the trustees and gave evidence which was adverse to D.

Held that Coyne was thereby disqualified from acting as arbiter and that it was therefore for the court to decide the dispute.

Lord Cowan said (at p. 568): "Up to the date when this action was brought, although there had been some conduct on the part of the arbiter not quite so guarded as could have been wished, nothing had occurred to prevent the reference to Mr Coyne from being carried out. . . .

"But there now exists an objection to the carrying out of this reference, which has emerged since the raising of the action. The arbiter has been examined in the course of this case as a witness for the defenders, with reference to the very matters in dispute between the parties. That, I think, is utterly inconsistent with the subsistence of the reference to him. The two positions,—that of witness cited and examined by one of the parties, and that of judge with regard to the same matters between the parties,—are utterly inconsistent. By examining him as witness the party debars himself from resorting to him thereafter as arbiter. The defenders were not obliged to call Mr Coyne as a witness; but having done so, they have by their own act precluded themselves from insisting in the reference to him being gone on with, and from pleading the clause of reference as excluding the Court from dealing with the matters in dispute between them and the pursuer."

12–134   A view to the same general effect was expressed by Lord Kyllachy (Ordinary) in *Aviemore Station Hotel Co. Ltd.* v. *Scott* (1904) 12 S.L.T. 494 (O.H.):

This was an action by A. Ltd. against S., contractors and plasterers, for damages for loss caused by alleged defective execution of plaster-work in a hotel building. By the terms of the contract for the plaster-work the architect was to be sole arbiter.

Lord Kyllachy held that the clause of reference did not cover the matters in dispute.

Had his decision been otherwise the second question would have arisen of whether the architect had become disqualified from acting as arbiter. On that second question Lord Kyllachy's opinion was that the architect had become disqualified: the correspondence and the proceedings in an earlier action showed that the architect had committed himself to a particular view and had repeated and insisted upon that view; he had also intervened in the earlier action and placed himself in a position quite inconsistent with his afterwards taking up the office of arbiter.

In *Crawford Brothers* v. *Commissioners of Northern Lighthouses,* 1925 S.C. (H.L.) 22, which concerned certain operations at Cape Wrath lighthouse, the question arose of whether the commissioners' engineer, named as arbiter in the construction contract, could competently deal with matters which involved a conflict of evidence between himself as engineer and the contractors.

The question did not require to be decided because the Commissioners gave an undertaking in the House of Lords that if, in the course of the arbitration any question of evidence arose which put their engineer in a conflicting position as judge and witness, the matter would be referred to the court for settlement.

(d) Remuneration

The original rule of the common law was that an arbiter or oversman had no legal claim to be remunerated unless he had stipulated for remuneration before he accepted appointment.

The rule was modified with the passage of time, and by the nineteenth century a condition that the arbiter would be remunerated for his services could be readily implied in an arbitration agreement, especially if the arbiter were a professional man who would be paid in the exercise of his profession for duties similar to those which he was called on to perform as arbiter. An instance was *Henderson* v. *Paul* (1867) 5 M. 628:

P. raised an action of count and reckoning against H. The action was taken out of court and referred to Maitland, Accountant of the Court of Session, as arbiter.

Maitland pronounced a decree-arbitral in favour of H., who then raised an action against P. for payment of £31 10s., the amount of the arbiter's fee, which H. had paid.

Held that, though the deed of submission had made no mention of remuneration for the arbiter, the parties had understood that as a professional accountant he was to be remunerated, and that H. was therefore entitled to recover from P. half of the fee which he had paid, *viz.* £15 15s.

Lord Justice-Clerk Patton said (at p. 632): "I think, in point of fact, that the parties conceived that they were going to an accountant on the footing of payment. The presumption, no doubt, is, that an arbiter acts without any right to remuneration; but the presumption is capable of being redargued, and I find what satisfies me, in the facts of the case, that the presumed condition did not hold in this case. The pleadings seem to me strongly to confirm this view—namely, that it was the understanding of parties all along that the arbiter should be paid."

By the time *Macintyre Brothers* v. *Smith,* 1913 S.C. 129, came to be decided there was no longer even a presumption that an arbiter, if he were a professional man, was acting gratuitously:

A dispute arose out of a contract between M. Brothers and S. for the purchase of a quarry. The dispute was submitted to Cook, a Glasgow solicitor, by a deed of agreement which made no reference to the arbiter's remuneration.

Cook issued a decree-arbitral in which he found S. liable to M. Brothers in a sum which did not include any fee for the arbiter.

Later M. Brothers paid the arbiter a sum of £63, the fee fixed by the Auditor of the Faculty of Procurators in Glasgow as suitable remuneration for his services.

S. refused to pay his share of the arbiter's fee, and M. Brothers brought an action against him for £31 10s.

Held that the arbiter was entitled to remuneration and that S. as one of the parties to the arbitration was liable for half.

Lord Kinnear said (at p. 132): "I think that, in accordance with general practice, the rule must now be assumed that a professional man undertaking the duties of an arbiter is entitled, in the absence of any agreement to the contrary, to be remunerated for his services as arbiter in the same way as he is entitled to receive remuneration for his services in any other professional employment. The general rule is that a request for professional service implies a promise to pay for it; and I do not see why this rule should be the less applicable because the particular service is for the benefit of two parties who are at variance with one another."

12–140   Where the amount of the arbiter's remuneration is not expressly agreed on, he is entitled to charge a reasonable fee for professional work, and this may be based on a scale of fees fixed by the professional body of which he is a member. The case of *Wilkie* v. *Scottish Aviation Ltd.*, 1956 S.C. 198, involved a consideration of the schedule of professional charges of the Royal Institution of Chartered Surveyors:

12–141   W., a chartered surveyor, had been employed professionally as a valuer in arbitration proceedings concerned with the compulsory purchase of Prestwick Airport by the Ministry of Civil Aviation. There was no specific agreement as to his remuneration.

After he had performed his services, W. rendered an account for £3,009 10s.9d., the scale fee based, in accordance with the schedule of professional charges, on the amount awarded in the arbitration.

His employers refused to pay more than £1,000 and W. brought an action against them for the balance, averring that remuneration on the basis of the schedule was customary and therefore an implied condition of the contract for his services.

Held that W. was entitled to remuneration at the customary rate if he could prove the existence of a custom which was reasonable, certain and notorious, and that accordingly if the schedule were shown to be the basis upon which in practice the profession operated, the court could take the schedule into account but would not be bound rigidly to apply it unless satisfied that the resulting fee were reasonable; and a proof before answer *allowed*.

V CONDUCT OF THE ARBITRATION

12–142 In the conduct of the arbitration the arbiter is always bound to observe those implied conditions of arbitration which are designed for "securing the proper administration of justice" (see the quotation from Lord Watson's speech in *Holmes Oil Co. Ltd.* v. *Pumpherston Oil Co. Ltd.* at

12–183, below). The parties may in their agreement to resort to arbitration lay down additional conditions as to the way in which the arbitration is to be conducted; the arbiter is then bound to observe such conditions since his jurisdiction is derived solely from the agreement of the parties. More usually the parties do not expressly specify the procedure which is to be followed, and in that case the arbiter's powers and duties in the conduct of the proceedings depend on what is implied in the arbitration agreement and in other respects on the arbiter's own discretion.

Some description is given in the following paragraphs of:

(a) formal and informal procedure;

(b) the requirement of impartiality; and

(c) specific steps in the procedure.

(a) Formal and Informal Procedure

The degree of formality of the procedure varies greatly: at one extreme the procedure may be as formal as court procedure and counsel may be instructed to plead the case of each party; at the other extreme the procedure may be very informal, particularly in agricultural and mercantile circles where the arbiter's function often is rather to fix the value of crops, stock or other goods than to decide a dispute.

Where the submission is a formal one, the following are usual steps in the procedure. The arbiter fixes a time within which one party must lodge written claims. He then allows a specified time within which the other party must lodge written answers. A "record" (a document setting out both sides of the dispute) may then be made up, "adjusted" and "closed" in much the same way as in a court case. The arbiter then decides what "proof" (*i.e.* evidence) should be allowed. He may wrongly allow or exclude certain evidence, but such errors are part of the risk which the parties have taken in resorting to arbitration and will not be a ground on which the award could be challenged. Sometimes it will be necessary for the arbiter to inspect premises or other property in order to inform himself of the matters in dispute, but inadequacy of inspection is not a ground on which an award may be reduced by the court (*Johnston* v. *Lamb,* 1981 S.L.T. 300 (O.H.)). The arbiter will almost always allow a hearing to both parties at the conclusion of the proof, and will often issue "proposed findings" so that the parties may have an opportunity to make final "representations" criticising the proposed findings. A further hearing may be allowed for these representations.

In less formal submissions the question is often a practical one to be decided by an arbiter chosen for his knowledge and experience of such practical questions, and there may be no objection to the arbiter's dispensing with both a proof and a hearing and deciding the question on the basis of personal inspection only. For examples of informal arbitrations, see the "valuation" cases at 12–13 *et seq.*, above.

Where an arbitration is started by a formal probative submission, the award also must be formal and probative:

McLaren v. *Aikman,* 1939 S.C. 222: McL., the owner of certain heritable property in Melrose, let the property to A. under a lease which gave A. an option to purchase the property at a price to be fixed by arbitration.

A. desired to exercise this option, and the parties referred the price to Hall, an architect, as sole arbiter. The reference was embodied in a formal and probative minute of agreement.

After various procedure the arbiter issued an award in the form of a letter addressed to the firm of solicitors which was acting for both parties. In that document, which was signed by the arbiter but was neither holograph nor attested, the value of the property was put at £1,350.

McL. was satisfied with that figure, but A. made representations to the arbiter against it.

The arbiter later issued a formal and probative decree-arbitral in which he fixed the price at £950.

McL. brought an action against A. for £1,350.

Held that since the submission was a formal one not falling within the category of mercantile and agricultural arbitrations, the award had to be formal and probative, and that the arbiter's first informal valuation was therefore not binding on A.; and action *dismissed*.

(b) The Requirement of Impartiality

12–149 Although the arbiter usually has a wide discretion as to the procedure to be followed, he is in all circumstances subject to the overriding principle of impartiality: he must adhere to "equal and even-handed procedure towards both parties alike" (Bell, *op. cit.,* p. 23).

12–150 The arbiter must not allow to one party what he denies to the other. If, for instance, he is to be accompanied at an inspection of property by one of the parties, he ought to give the other party the opportunity of being present as well. Similarly, if he allows a hearing to one party and not to the other, his award will be open to challenge unless it is in favour of the party not heard. An illustrative case is:

12–151 *Earl of Dunmore* v. *McInturner* (1835) 13 S. 356: The Earl and McI. entered into a submission referring disputes as to the marches between their lands to arbitration.

The oversman inspected the marches in the presence of McI. without intimation of the inspection having been given to the Earl. After the inspection a minute of award was drawn up in McI.'s house in the absence of the Earl or any person representing him. The minute was intimated to the Earl's agent the next day, but the Earl was not warned that if he did not give in objections by a certain day, the decree-arbitral would be extended and executed.

Some two months later without further notice to the Earl the formal decree was made out embodying the words of the minute.

Held that the Earl was entitled to have the decree set aside on the ground that a decree pronounced in such circumstances, with the assistance of the other party and without an opportunity having been given to the Earl to be heard, was "contrary to the principles of fair justice between man and man" (*per* Lord Justice-Clerk Boyle at p. 360).

12–152 Similarly, in *Black* v. *John Williams & Co. (Wishaw) Ltd.*, 1924 S.C. (H.L.) 22; 1923 S.C. 510, there had been procedure which Lord President Clyde said (at p. 515) had been "deservedly criticised and might easily have been fatal to the award":

B., a plasterer, had contracted with W. Ltd. to do certain rough-casting work at their premises. Disputes arose as to whether the work had been properly executed, and McGhie was appointed arbiter.

During the arbitration proceedings the question arose of whether B. had had permission from W. Ltd. to use coke breeze instead of granite chips for part of the work.

McGhie requested B. to leave the room when certain witnesses (B.'s son and B.'s foreman) were giving evidence on this point. W., one of the directors of W. Ltd., was present during that examination.

The arbiter issued an award in which he found in favour of B. upon the question of the material used but held, upon other grounds, that the work had not been properly executed.

B. brought an action for reduction of the award on the ground that the arbiter had invalidated the proceedings by examining the two witnesses in the presence of one party only.

Held that the arbiter's procedure had been improper but that it did not in the circumstances of the case invalidate the award since B. had suffered no injustice as a result of being excluded during the examination of the witnesses.

Lord Dunedin said (at p. 27): "There are many cases . . . where it has been held that you must not examine witnesses on one side and not on the other, and that you must not examine witnesses without the parties being properly represented. But, after all, those cases, one and all of them, are only illustrations of the general principle that the procedure of the arbiter must not violate the principles of essential justice. How can it be said in this instance that the principles of essential justice have been violated? . . . As a matter of fact, upon this one question whether one material was substituted with the consent of the employers for another, the arbiter decided in favour of the person who is now challenging the award. I think, therefore, that on this matter he fails."

(c) Specific Steps in the Procedure
(i) *Appointment of Clerk*

Except in very informal proceedings, it is usual for the arbiter to appoint a clerk to take charge of the documents in the case and to act as a channel of communication between the parties and the arbiter.

If the arbiter is not himself a lawyer but a layman chosen for his technical knowledge and experience, the clerk is often a solicitor, and in practice takes a key role in the proceedings since the arbiter will to a great extent rely on his guidance when a point of law arises in the course of the arbitration.

(ii) *Proceedings* Ex Parte

In certain circumstances an arbiter is justified in proceeding *ex parte* ("without a party"). This could occur where one party refused to take any further part in the arbitration proceedings, although given full opportunity by the arbiter to do so.

(iii) *Prorogation of the Submission*

Where the submission is subject to a time-limit and the fixed duration is about to expire before the proceedings have been concluded, a prorogation is necessary to keep the submission operative. Prorogation may be an act of the parties, but normally it is an act of the arbiter, on whom the parties will have expressly conferred power to prorogate the submission. (See also 12–74 *et seq.*, above.)

(iv) *Applications to Court*

12–157   Although the parties to an arbitration agreement have the general aim of preventing the intervention of the court in the decision of their dispute, the jurisdiction of the court is not wholly ousted by the agreement. A well-known passage in the speech of Lord Watson in *Hamlyn & Co.* v. *Talisker Distillery* (1894) 21 R. (H.L.) 21, at p. 25, enlarges on this point:

"The jurisdiction of the Court is not wholly ousted by such a contract [*a contract to submit the matter in dispute to arbitration*]. It deprives the Court of jurisdiction to inquire into and decide the merits of the case, while it leaves the Court free to entertain the suit, and to pronounce a decree in conformity with the award of the arbiter. Should the arbitration from any cause prove abortive, the full jurisdiction of the Court will revive, to the effect of enabling it to hear and determine the action upon its merits. When a binding reference is pleaded *in limine*,[7] the proper course to take is either to refer the question in dispute to the arbiter named or to stay procedure until it has been settled by arbitration."

12–158   If there is disagreement as to the scope of the arbitration agreement, that is necessarily in the last resort a matter for the court to decide.

12–159   As is indicated in Lord Watson's speech, there are several occasions when application may be made to court for assistance to enable an arbitration to proceed effectively. Where one party raises an action in respect of a matter which ought to have been submitted to arbitration, the court will sist the action on the application of the other party. Where an arbiter's orders for witnesses to appear or documents to be produced are not complied with, the party desiring the attendance of the witnesses or the production of the documents may apply to court for a warrant for citation. The court may also be applied to for the purpose of enforcing the award by granting "decree conform to it."

12–160   The parties may expressly agree to be bound by the arbiter's decision on questions of law as well as on questions of fact, but if there is no such express agreement, then, by section 3 of the Administration of Justice (Scotland) Act 1972, a party may apply to the arbiter or to the Court of Session for a case to be stated for the opinion of the Court of Session. (See 12–10, above.) Before the date of that Act stated cases were in Scots law confined to statutory arbitrations, such as those under the Lands Clauses Consolidation (Scotland) Act 1845, the Workmen's Compensation Acts and the Agricultural Holdings (Scotland) Acts. In *Mitchell-Gill* v. *Buchan*, 1921 S.C. 390, the court held, in relation to a stated case under the Agricultural Holdings (Scotland) Act 1908, that an arbiter was not entitled to disregard the answer given by the court on the question of law.

(v) *Issue of Award*

12–161   The conduct of an arbitration comes to an end when the award is issued. The arbiter is then said to be "*functus*," an abbreviation of "*functus*

---

[7] "as a preliminary plea."

officio" ("having performed his role"). The effect is that he no longer has any jurisdiction in connection with the matter in question.

An arbiter may have power conferred on him to issue interim and part awards. An interim award is of a tentative nature: it may be altered or recalled. A part award, on the other hand, is a final decision on part of the subject-matter of the submission.

An arbiter has power to award expenses without any express power to that effect having been included in the deed of submission (*Ferrier* v. *Alison* (1845) 4 Bell's App. 161; (1843) 5 D. 456).

VI CHALLENGE OF THE AWARD

The parties to an arbitration have voluntarily agreed to take the arbiter's decision instead of a court's decision. In doing so they have taken the risk that the arbiter will err on questions of fact and (subject to the stated case provisions in section 3 of the Administration of Justice (Scotland) Act 1972) on questions of law, and the parties have no right to appeal to the court on the "merits" (substance) of their case.

The finality of the arbiter's decision is expressed in memorable, but perhaps unduly strong, terms by Lord Jeffrey in *Mitchell* v. *Cable* (1848) 10 D. 1297, a case in which an award was set aside because the arbiter had considered only proof taken in this country and not proof which ought to have been taken on commission at Bombay. Lord Jeffrey said (at p. 1309):

"On every matter touching the merits of the case, the judgment of the arbiter is beyond our control; and beyond question or cavil. He may believe what nobody else believes, and he may disbelieve what all the world believes. He may overlook or flagrantly misapply the most ordinary principles of law; and there is no appeal for those who have chosen to subject themselves to his despotic power."

Lord Jeffrey then proceeded to explain that, while an arbiter's errors of judgment could not be set right, his decree-arbitral could stand only where he had dealt "*fairly, that is equally*, with both parties."

The judicial nature of the arbiter's office which so much qualifies the arbiter's "despotic power" was concisely described by Lord President Clyde in *Mitchell-Gill* v. *Buchan*, 1921 S.C. 390 (at p. 395):

"When it is said that an arbiter in Scotland is the final judge both of fact and law, it is not implied that he is entitled either to make the facts as he would like them to be, or to make the law what he thinks it ought to be. Like any other judge, he must take the facts as they are presented to him, and the law as it is. Otherwise he would act, not as the parties' judge, but as their oracle; his function would be not judicial but arbitrary; and his award would be given, not according to the principles of justice, but according to the caprice of personal preferences. . . . If it could be proved that, in arriving at his award, an arbiter had invented the facts to suit some view of his own, or had fashioned the law to suit his own ideas, then, however innocent in itself might be the eccentricity which had seduced him into such a travesty of judicial conduct, his behaviour would naturally imply that justice had not been done; he would be guilty of that which

Lord Watson in *Adams* v. *Great North of Scotland Railway Co.* (18 R. (H.L.) 1, at p. 8) described as misconduct; and his award would be reduced."

12–167 The limited grounds on which an arbiter's decree-arbitral may be set aside—by an action of reduction brought in the Court of Session—are considered below under the following headings:

(a) corruption, bribery or falsehood;
(b) *ultra fines compromissi*;
(c) improper procedure; and
(d) defective award.

12–168 Partial reduction is competent but only where one part of the award is open to objection, the other part is valid and the two parts are clearly severable. An instance is *Cox Brothers* v. *Binning and Son* (1867) 6 M. 161, in which an arbiter superadded an incompetent finding to an award which was already exhaustive of the reference.

12–169 Where an award is partially reduced, but the arbiter had no power to make a part award, the partial reduction may cause the remainder of the award also to be open to reduction on the ground that the arbiter has failed to exhaust the submission.

12–170 In *Miller & Son* v. *Oliver & Boyd* (1906) 8 F. 390 the question arose of whether an arbiter was *functus* where his award had been reduced on the grounds that it was beyond the arbiter's powers and did not exhaust the reference. Lord Pearson (Ordinary) held that an arbiter in that position was not *functus* and so was not disqualified from again taking up the reference. In the Inner House, however, opinions were reserved on that point; Lord McLaren referred to English law as being undoubtedly to the contrary and was unwilling, unless compelled by principle or authority, to establish a different rule in Scotland from that which had been established and found to work conveniently in England.

(a) Corruption, Bribery or Falsehood

12–171 The authority for this ground of reduction is the twenty-fifth Act of the Articles of Regulation of 1695. These Articles were made by Commissioners under the special sanction of an Act of the Scottish Parliament of 1693 (c. 34), and the twenty-fifth of them dealt with the grounds on which an arbiter's award might be challenged. It was in these terms:

"That for the cutting off of groundless and expensive pleas and processes in time coming, the Lords of Session sustain no reduction of any decreet-arbitral, that shall be pronounced hereafter upon a subscribed submission, at the instance of either of the parties-submitters, upon any cause or reason whatsoever, unless that of corruption, bribery, or falsehood, to be alleged against the judges-arbitrators who pronounced the same."

12–172 The provision must be viewed in its historical context. Before 1695 the courts of law had come to allow an award to be challenged in court on the grounds of "iniquity" committed by an arbiter or of "enorm lesion" suffered by a party, *i.e.* on the grounds that an arbiter had made a mistake or that a party had suffered undue hardship. The result was that in practically every case an award could be reviewed upon its merits at the discretion of the court—a situation which defeated the main object of the parties in resorting to arbitration.

The aim of the twenty-fifth Article was to end the practice of review by the courts: arbiters' awards were to be final and binding on the parties and were no longer to be open to challenge merely because the arbiter had made a mistake or one party had suffered undue hardship. Corruption, bribery and falsehood on the part of the arbiter, however, were to remain grounds on which an award could be challenged in court.

If this statutory provision had been given a literal interpretation it would have prevented an award from being set aside on any ground other than corruption, bribery or falsehood. Decided cases, however, and particularly the speech of Lord Watson in *Adams* v. *Great North of Scotland Railway Co.* (1890) 18 R. (H.L.) 1; (1889) 16 R. 843, established that the object for which the provision was made had to be looked to: the provision had never been intended to go beyond the point of putting an end to the practice of review upon the merits; other common law grounds of challenge (see (b) to (d), below) remained available.

In some cases there were attempts to extend the word "corruption" so as to include "legal corruption" or "constructive corruption," *i.e.* conduct on the part of the arbiter which was mistaken but not strictly corrupt. Lord Watson in *Adams* v. *Great North of Scotland Railway Co.* protested against this extended meaning of "corruption"; actual corruption was necessary if an award was to be set aside on the ground of the Articles of Regulation: if the arbiter's mistake was innocent, it could not be brought within the term "corruption," though it might lead to reduction of the award on one of the other grounds (b) to (d), below.

Within a year another appeal to the House of Lords—*Holmes Oil Co. Ltd.* v. *Pumpherston Oil Co. Ltd.* (1891) 18 R. (H.L.) 52; (1890) 17 R. 624—provided an opportunity for further observations to the same effect. The decision in that case was that the question raised was one as to the interpretation of the contract—a matter which was within the jurisdiction of the arbiter—and that the arbiter had interpreted the contract in a way which made certain evidence which had been offered irrelevant; there was therefore no ground for reduction on account of the arbiter's refusal to allow the evidence. Lord Watson said (at p. 55):

"I think the only serious argument latterly insisted in by the appellants was founded upon the allegation, not that the arbiter had corruptly given a judgment upon the materials before him, but that there had been misconduct on his part in declining to receive evidence which was tendered to him before he proceeded to dispose of the question submitted.

"Now, I am of opinion that that ground of exception, which may be a good ground of exception to the validity of the award, does not rest at all upon the Regulations of 1695. I think that in so far as regards the conduct of the case, and in so far as regards the jurisdiction of the arbiter to dispose of the case, the Regulations of 1695 make no provision whatever. These rest upon the common law."

Reported cases give few illustrations of what may properly be classed as corruption, bribery or falsehood within the meaning of the Regulations. In *Morisons* v. *Thomson's Trustees* (1880) 8 R. 147 the court held that it was not corrupt for an arbiter to apply first to one party and then to the other party in the arbitration proceedings for a loan of £1,000 to assist him with his financial difficulties, which were caused by the failure of the City of Glasgow Bank. The arbiter was a mutual friend of both parties, and the court found that there was no ground for supposing that his mind had been influenced one way or the other by each party's refusal to give him the desired loan.

(b) Ultra Fines Compromissi

12–178 An award which is *ultra fines compromissi* ("beyond the bounds of the submission") may be set aside. This follows from the very nature of arbitration, since the parties have agreed to implement the decision of their private judge on certain questions only. Any question which is beyond the bounds of the submission continues to be within the court's jurisdiction, and any attempted decision of such a question by the arbiter has no authority behind it.

12–179 Where only a part of an award is *ultra fines compromissi,* it may be possible to enforce the award in so far as it is valid, but this will depend on whether the invalid part is severable from the rest of the award or not. This was one of the points which arose in *Miller & Son* v. *Oliver & Boyd* (1903) 6 F. 77:

M., a printer, entered into an agreement with O. & B. by which O. & B. purchased M.'s business. Under an article of the agreement M. was to become an employee of O. & B. at a salary of £150 a year. Other articles of the agreement dealt with the price of the goodwill and of the stock, plant, machinery and fittings. There was an arbitration clause naming Ritchie as arbiter.

Disputes arose and the parties referred to Ritchie claims by M. for (1) goodwill, (2) salary, (3) commission, (4) the price of plant and (5) damages for breach of contract and a counter-claim by O. & B. for damages for breach of contract.

Ritchie issued an award in which he found O. & B. liable to M. in a lump sum of £618 7s.11d., and on the parties implementing the award declared them freed of all claims one against the other and ordained each of them to execute and deliver a valid discharge to the other.

M. brought an action for reduction of the award on the ground that it was *ultra vires* ("beyond the powers" (of the arbiter)) and that it did not exhaust the reference. O. & B. admitted that the award was *ultra vires* in so far as it ordained the parties to execute mutual discharges but they contended that this order was separable from the rest of the award.

Held that the award fell to be reduced because (1) M.'s claims were not all *ejusdem generis* ("of the same kind") and it was impossible to discover from the face of the award how far the arbiter had considered all M.'s claims, (2) the award did not show how the arbiter had dealt with O. & B.'s counter-claim and (3) the order for mutual discharges, which was admittedly *ultra vires,* was not separable from the rest of the award.

(c) Improper Procedure

12–180 The parties may specify the procedure which the arbiter is to follow. If he then fails to comply, his award may be challenged.

More often the procedure is left to the arbiter's discretion, and if so, failure to observe strict court procedure will not be a ground for challenging the award.

There are, however, in every contract of submission implied conditions of honesty and impartiality, breach of which is a ground of reduction. See 12–22 and 12–149 *et seq.*, above.

It is under this heading that the supposed cases of "constructive corruption" properly fall, as was made clear by the two House of Lords cases *Adams* v. *Great North of Scotland Railway Co.* and *Holmes Oil Co. Ltd.* v. *Pumpherston Oil Co. Ltd.* In the latter case Lord Watson said (at 18 R. (H.L.) p. 55):

"The arbiter must confine himself to the jurisdiction which the parties have conferred upon him, and in the conduct of the arbitration before it comes to final judgment he is bound to observe any condition which the parties may have chosen to impose upon him by the deed of submission, and he must also conform to all those rules for securing the proper administration of justice which the law implies in the case of every proceeding before a Court of justice."

The parties themselves, as well as the arbiter, must refrain from fraudulent and unfair procedure. For example, an award would be set aside if a deliberately false case had been presented to the arbiter.

(d) Defective Award

In *Mackenzie* v. *Girvan* (1840) 3 D. 318 (affirmed (1843) 2 Bell's App. 43), a case relating to a judicial reference, Lord Moncreiff gave a well-known description of the requisites of a valid award. He said (at p. 328) that it was "the established rule and essential principle of the law of Scotland, that, when an award in a judicial reference is clear in its terms, correct in its form, embracing nothing which was not referred, and exhausting all that was referred, it is not competent for this Court to review such an award on its general merits, or to set it aside, or refuse effect to it, on any idea of mere error in judgment in the matters properly within the cognizance of the referee."

(i) The first requisite is that the award should be clear in its terms: if it is unintelligible, it will be set aside; if it is merely ambiguous or obscure, the court (but not the arbiter) has the right to interpret it.

(ii) Secondly, the award should be correct in its form. What is the proper form depends on circumstances; if, for instance, the arbitration proceedings were started by a formal deed of submission in probative form, the award also would require to be in that form (*McLaren* v. *Aikman*, at 12–148, above); on the other hand, an informal award would be quite sufficient where the reference to arbitration was itself informal.

(iii) The award must embrace nothing which was not referred. This point has been considered under the heading *"ultra fines compromissi"* (12–178 *et seq.*, above).

(iv) The award must exhaust the submission, *i.e.* it must give a complete decision. The parties have agreed that certain disputes be decided by arbitration, and it is not a proper fulfilment of their agreement if the arbiter decides one question but leaves another question undecided. See

Miller & Son v. *Oliver & Boyd* (12–179, above). Another instance of reduction on the ground of failure to exhaust the submission is:

12–190   *Donald* v. *Shiell's Executrix*, 1937 S.C. 52: In an arbitration between the outgoing and the incoming tenants of a farm the questions submitted for the arbiter's decision were (1) what sum should be paid by the incoming tenant to the outgoing tenant for corn crop and various other items, and (2) the sum, "if any," to be paid by the outgoing tenant to the incoming tenant in order to put the buildings on the farm into the condition provided for under the conditions of let in favour of the incoming tenant.

The award ordered the incoming tenant to pay certain sums under the first head, but made no mention of items under the second head.

The incoming tenant brought an action for reduction of the award, and was successful on the ground of the omission: it could not be assumed that the arbiter had considered items under the second head and had found nothing to be due for them.

12–191   The mere fact that an arbiter has made no finding as to expenses is not a ground for reducing an award:

Pollich v. *Heatley*, 1910 S.C. 469: A charterparty provided for claims for demurrage to be settled by arbitration.

After an arbitration in which arbiters found a certain sum due by the shipper to the shipowner as demurrage, the shipowner brought an action to reduce the award on the ground that the arbiters had not exhausted the submission in that they had not dealt with (1) interest and (2) expenses.

Held that (1) the question of interest was not one with which the arbiters had power to deal and (2) the question of expenses was not part of the submission but was merely incidental to the conduct of the arbitration and therefore the fact that the arbiters had made no finding as to expenses was not a ground for reducing their award.

Lord President Dunedin said (at p. 482):

"The matter of expenses is not part of the submission. There may be cases in which special power is given to an arbiter to dispose of expenses, but that really is pleonastic. The matter of expenses is incidental to the conduct of the case, and there is an inherent power in the tribunal to grant them. . . . I do not think it is a case of the submission not having been exhausted; it is merely that no expenses have been awarded."

12–192   According to the early case of *Lord Lovat* v. *Fraser of Phopachy* (1738) Mor. 625, where there is a submission of certain particulars and also a general submission of all other claims and the arbiter decides only the particulars, his decree-arbitral is not open to reduction on the ground of failure to exhaust the submission provided no claim under the general submission having a connection with any of the particulars decided is left undecided.

12–193   Reduction on the ground of failure to exhaust the submission was described by Lord Maxwell (Ordinary) in *Johnston* v. *Lamb*, 1981 S.L.T. 300 (at p. 306) as a "somewhat obscure and unsatisfactory" area of law. The following obstacles in the way of reduction on this ground are considered in Lord Maxwell's opinion in that case:

(1) The arbiter cannot be heard as a witness as to the matters on which he reached his decision.

(2) There is doubt as to whether reference may be made to the pleadings in the arbitration or to the arbiter's notes.

(3) Where the award expressly bears that the arbiter has heard counsel for the parties on the whole matters submitted to him and that he has reached a decision on the whole matters submitted, there is at least a very strong presumption that the arbiter has in fact considered and determined all matters put before him.

Lord Maxwell's decision in the case was that, even if it were competent to look at the pleadings in the arbitration and the arbiter's notes, the evidence which they provided was wholly unconvincing and insufficient to overcome the presumption described in (3), above.

VII JUDICIAL REFERENCES

By a judicial reference is meant the procedure by which parties to a court action agree to withdraw the decision of the whole or some of the questions raised in the action from the decision of the court and, while still formally leaving the action in court, refer these questions to an arbiter.

A judicial reference is started by the lodging with the court of a "minute" stating the agreement of the parties, and the court then, if it thinks fit, "interpones authority to the minute," *i.e.* authorises the judicial reference to proceed.

The selection of the judicial referee is a matter for the parties to decide. Like an ordinary arbiter, a judicial referee is not bound by strict court procedure.

The scope of the reference is limited to the subject-matter of the action as set out in the "record."

The decision of a judicial referee is set out in a report to the court (not an award). The report may be challenged on the same grounds as an award in an ordinary arbitration. The court will either approve of the report and grant "decree conform" (*i.e.* make a court order in conformity with the terms of the report) or set the report aside; the court has no power to amend the report.

Further Reading

Gloag and Henderson, *Introduction to the Law of Scotland*, Chapter II (part)

David M. Walker, *Principles of Scottish Private Law*, Chapter 1.6

J.J. Gow, *The Mercantile and Industrial Law of Scotland*, Chapter 13

David Alexander Guild, *The Law of Arbitration in Scotland* (1936, W. Green & Son Ltd.)

M.E.L. Weir, *A Synopsis of the Law and Practice of Arbitration in Scotland* (2nd ed., 1980, Department of Building, Heriot-Watt University)

Enid A. Marshall, "The Law of Arbitration—A Difference between Scots and English" [1970] J.R. 115

John Montgomerie Bell, *Treatise on the Law of Arbitration in Scotland* (2nd ed., 1877, T. & T. Clark)

James Campbell Irons and R.D. Melville, *Treatise on the Law of Arbitration in Scotland* (1903, William Green & Sons)

INDEX

A.P.R., 5–54

ABANDONMENT (INSURANCE), 11–216, 11–229, 11–260
notice of, 11–227 *et seq.*

"ABBREVIATE," 10–94

ACCEPTANCE, BUYER'S DUTY OF, 4–147, 4–177 *et seq.*
damages for failure in, 4–259 *et seq.*

ACCEPTANCE OF BILL OF EXCHANGE, 7–37 *et seq.*
for honour *supra* protest, 7–137 *et seq.*

ACCEPTOR OF BILL OF EXCHANGE,
becoming holder, 7–129
liability of, 7–105 *et seq.*

ACCOMMODATION BILL, 7–55, 7–127

"ACCOUNT PAYEE ONLY,"
on cheque, 7–193

ACCOUNTANT, 1–84, 1–134, 2–15, 8–142 *et seq.*

ACCOUNTANT OF COURT, 10–82, 10–197, 10–290, 10–327, 10–334 *et seq.*, 10–349
Notes for Guidance in Sequestrations, 10–186, 10–202

ACQUIRENDA, 10–223 *et seq.*, 10–235 *et seq.*

ACT AND WARRANT, TRUSTEE'S (SEQUESTRATION), 10–170 *et seq.*

ACTIO REDHIBITORIA, 4–276

ACTIO QUANTI MINORIS, 4–276

AD FACTUM PRAESTANDUM, 9–87

AD HOC SUBMISSIONS, 12–57 *et seq.*

ADVERTISING (CONSUMER CREDIT), 5–160 *et seq.*

AFFREIGHTMENT, CONTRACT OF, 6–161

AGENCY, 1–01 *et seq.*, 2–50 *et seq.*, 4–297
agent's authority, 1–67 *et seq.*
capacity, 1–13 *et seq.*
categories of agent, 1–31 *et seq.*
constitution, 1–15 *et seq.*
duties of agent to principal, 1–97 *et seq.*
rights of agent against principal, 1–124 *et seq.*
termination, 1–162 *et seq.*
third party's rights and liabilities, 1–35 *et seq.*

AIR CONSIGNMENT NOTE, 6–366

AIR WAYBILL, 6–366

AIRCRAFT,
mortgage of, 8–76

ALIMENTARY PROVISIONS,
in sequestration, 10–238 *et seq.*

ALLONGE ATTACHED TO BILL OF EXCHANGE, 7–62

ANCILLARY ARBITRATIONS, 12–59 *et seq.*, 12–78

ANCILLARY CREDIT BUSINESSES, 5–27, 5–323 *et seq.*

ANNULMENT OF SEQUESTRATION, 10–135

"ANTECEDENT NEGOTIATIONS,"
consumer credit, 5–189

APPARENT AUTHORITY, 1–72 *et seq.*, 1–85 *et seq.*, 2–71

APPROPRIATION OF PAYMENTS,
consumer credit, 5–227 *et seq.*

APPROVAL,
sale of goods on, 4–123 *et seq.*

"ARBITER," 12–84

ARBITERS, 12–01, 12–82 *et seq.*

ARBITRATION, 12–01 *et seq.*
ad hoc submissions, 12–57 *et seq.*
advantages over litigation, 12–26 *et seq.*
ancillary, 12–59 *et seq.*
arbiters and oversmen, 12–82
Articles of Regulation, 12–03, 12–171 *et seq.*
capacity of parties, 12–37 *et seq.*
challenge of award, 12–164 *et seq.*
characteristics of, 12–19 *et seq.*
conduct of, 12–142 *et seq.*
constitution of contract, 12–36 *et seq.*
distinguished from valuation, 12–11 *et seq.*
duration of submission, 12–74 *et seq.*
form of contract of submission, 12–39 *et seq.*
judicial reference, 12–194 *et seq.*
matters which may be referred, 12–08 *et seq.*
prorogation of submission, 12–156
scope of submission, 12–47 *et seq.*
stated case, 12–10, 12–160, 12–164
statutory, 12–02, 12–160

ARBITRATION CLAUSE, 2–140, 12–59 *et seq.*
ample, 12–61, 12–63 *et seq.*
executorial, 12–61
incorporation into subcontract, 12–67 *et seq.*
restricted or limited, 12–61 *et seq.*

"ARBITRATOR," 12–84

ARCHITECT, 1–82, 1–105

ARRESTMENT, 2–42

ARRESTMENT OR POINDING,
unpaid seller's right of, 4–239 *et seq.*

"ARRIVED SHIP" CASES, 6–234 *et seq.*

651

DLP

Return items to **any** Swindon Library by closing time on or before the date stamped. Only books and Audio Books can be renewed - phone your library or visit our website,
www.swindon.gov.uk/libraries

Deposits
Tel: 01793
465555

02/13

AS
B5
C2

CX
D2
B3
D6
A2

WITHDRAWN
Borough Swindon
Film Swindon
Libraries

D3
H1A
E1
F4
G3
A6

B4
C1
D1
E2
A
G4

A
G3
A8
B1
G1

SWINDON
BOROUGH COUNCIL

Playing Dead